THE COMPLETE DODGERS RECORD BOOK

THE COMPLETE DODGERS RECORD BOOK
Gene Schoor

Facts On File, Inc.
New York, New York • Bicester, England

THE COMPLETE DODGERS RECORD BOOK

Copyright © 1984 by Gene Schoor

All rights reserved. No part of this book may be reproduced or utilized in any form or by any means, electronic or mechanical, including photocopying, recording or by any information storage and retrieval systems, without permission in writing from the Publisher.

Library of Congress Cataloging in Publication Data

Schoor, Gene

   The complete Dodgers record book.

   Includes index.
   1. Los Angeles Dodgers (Baseball team)—Statistics.
2. Baseball—United States—Records.   I. Title.
GV875.L6S36   1984   796.357′64′0979494   82-15695
ISBN 0-87196-117-2
ISBN 0-87196-696-4 (pbk)

Printed in the United States of America

10 9 8 7 6 5 4 3 2 1

To my darling sister, Tess Palmer, for her
unwavering faith and love through the years,
and to Sondra Palmer, my number two gal.

ACKNOWLEDGMENTS

I wish to thank the following people for assisting me in the development of THE COMPLETE DODGERS RECORD BOOK:

Dr. Edwin Haislet, University of Minnesota
Mr. Toby Zwikel, press director, Los Angeles Dodgers
Danny Goodman, late vice president, Los Angeles Dodgers
Mr. Irving Rudd, publicity director, Brooklyn Dodgers
Mr. Paul Zimmerman, author of the fine book *Dodger Daze and Nights*

Information and inspiration were provided by Dr. Alex Schoenbrun, historian of the Los Angeles Dodgers; the late Tommy Holmes, author of *The Dodgers*; the late Frank Graham, author of *The Brooklyn Dodgers*; Mr. Ross Newhan, sportswriter for the Los Angeles *Times*; the editors of *The Sporting News*; former members of the New York *Post* sports desk: the writers Milt Gross, Jimmy Cannon, Jerry Mitchell and Larry Merchant and the sports editor Ike Gellis—and the compilers of those invaluable reference books, *The Official Baseball Encyclopedia* and *The Baseball Encyclopedia*.

My thanks go also to my great editor at Facts On File, Jamie Warren, who has the patience of Job, and to the best literary agent in New York, Julian Bach.

And a very special note of thanks to the entire public relations staff and front office of the Los Angeles Dodgers, who responded instantly to my every phone call; and my classmate at New York University, the former captain of N.Y.U.'s football and baseball clubs, now executive vice president of the Los Angeles Dodgers, Mr. Al Campanis.

CONTENTS

I	**INTRODUCTION**	**1**
II	**THE COMPLETE CATALOGUE OF PLAYERS**	**19**
	The Pitchers' Catalogue	155
III	**THE DODGERS YEAR-BY-YEAR RECORD AND ROSTER**	**247**
IV	**THE WORLD SERIES**	**319**
	World Series highlights, box scores, and pitching and batting summaries	
V	**DODGER BATTING LEADERS**	**403**
	Lifetime Batting Leaders	
	Batting Records, One Season	
	Batting Records, One Game	
	National League Leaders	
	Grand-Slam Home Runs, in Chronological Order	
VI	**DODGER PITCHING LEADERS**	**413**
	Lifetime Leaders	
	Pitching Records, One Season	
	Twenty-Game Winners	
	No-Hit Games	
	Los Angeles Dodgers One-Hitters	
	Most Strikeouts, One Game	
	National League Leaders	
VII	**AWARDS AND HIGHLIGHTS**	**423**
	Dodgers in Baseball's Hall of Fame	
	National League Most Valuable Player Award Winners	
	National League Rookies of the Year	
	All-Time Stolen-Base Leaders	
	National League Stolen-Base Leaders	
	Dodgers Selected for All-Star Game Teams	
VIII	**DODGERS ALL-TIME ROSTER AT A GLANCE**	**429**

1

INTRODUCTION

CHARLIE EBBETS didn't found the only professional baseball club to ever represent Brooklyn, but he was there when it started and he grew up with it. More properly speaking, it grew up with him, for it was he, who through years of terrific enterprise, made it a major league club; he built the park that bore his name for many years (until 1957) and paved the way for the MacPhails, the Rickeys, the Smiths, and the O'Malleys. He received financial help first from Henry Medicus and later from the McKeever brothers, Ed and Steve. But he alone bore the burden of work and worry, dreamed the dreams and made them come true.

George Taylor, city editor of the *New York Herald* in 1883, was the father of the Brooklyn Dodgers. The team that was created at his suggestion was not called by that name, nor was it part of the National League, which had been organized only seven years before. But it was the first professional team that claimed Brooklyn as its home and requested the support of the city's numerous potential fans. It was the embryo from which the Dodgers took form and, in the years that followed, begat their glory and their daffiness.

Yet this man has been completely overlooked by most of the game's historians. Anyone connected with baseball in Los Angeles today would be hard pressed to identify him, and there is nothing in the yellowing records to indicate that he received as much as a penny for an idea which, in the long run, would make some men rich and famous. His sole reward was probably the privilege of sitting in the modest wooden grandstand at the original Washington Park and heckling the ballplayers, for that was a Brooklyn custom undoubtedly as old as the ball club itself.

Baseball was played in Brooklyn long before 1883, of course. As far back as 1849, the Atlantic, Excelsior, Putnams, and Eckford clubs were among the best in the nation, and when the National Organization of Baseball Players, composed of amateurs, came into being in 1857, it included a strong Brooklyn representation. The Atlantics were recognized as national champions in 1864 and again in 1866, and to this same team fell, in 1870, the distinction of being the first to beat the famous Cincinnati Red Stockings.

The Red Stockings, the first professional team in baseball's history, began to play for pay in 1869 and were unbeaten in 65 games as they toured the East and the Middle West that year, meeting the best of the amateurs. They were unbeaten in 27 games in 1870 when they encountered the Atlantics on the Capitoline Grounds in Brooklyn on June 14. The score at the end of the ninth inning was 5–5, and the Red Stockings insisted that the game continue. The Atlantics pushed across three runs in the 10th inning to win the game, 8–7.

In 1883 George Taylor conveyed his desire for a professional baseball team in Brooklyn to three friends, who like himself, were baseball fans, and who unlike himself, were financially able to enter the baseball business, which was then an even more precarious means of making money than it is today. His friends were Charles Byrne and Joseph Doyle, New York businessmen, and Ferdinand Abell, described as the proprietor of a gambling house at Narragansett, Rhode Island. Byrne became the president of the new club, although Abell furnished most of the money.

Byrne first obtained a franchise in the Interstate League, an offshoot of the American Association, and got most of his players from the Merritts, of Camden, N.J., which had belonged to the league but had disbanded; then Byrne set about building a ball park. He purchased land between Fourth and Fifth Avenues, extending from Third to Fifth Streets. He called it Washington Park and, with Doyle managing the team, Byrne was ready to start operations in earnest. One of the men he hired to help in his organization was Charles Ebbets, who was to sell tickets and keep books for the new club. Ebbets was to become one of the great names in the story of baseball, certainly one of the brightest names in Brooklyn baseball.

The venture was successful from the very beginning. The first pro baseball team organized in 1883 in Brooklyn was lively, quickly attracted a large following and won the pennant. Byrne, his enthusiasm mounting, sold his franchise in the Interstate League and bought one in the American Association. Brooklyn remained in the association for six seasons, and it was during that period that the team was first called the Trolley Dodgers. The name had originated when horse-drawn trolley cars were the backbone of the transportation system that linked the Dutch villages of Brooklyn. The network seemed especially complicated to residents of Manhattan. "Trolley Dodgers" was one of the gibes they tossed at their neighbors across the East River. As time passed, the nickname came to be applied first to the common citizens of Brooklyn, and then to the town's baseball team and players. Rather swiftly, the name was shortened to plain "Dodgers," but long years passed before it won universal acceptance.

In 1889 Byrne hired Bill McGunnigle to manage the team and the Dodgers proceeded to win the pennant. In so doing, they practically destroyed their chief rival, the Brooklyn team in the Brotherhood League. As a matter of fact the Dodgers were so successful that the team folded at season's end. The big hero of the Dodgers that year was "original" Billy Terry, a handsome pitcher who was known as the "Adonis."

Henry Chadwick, who had played rounders as a young boy in England, was a reporter for the *Brooklyn Eagle* and it was Chadwick who became fascinated with the American version of the game and duly reported local results for the *Eagle*.

Chadwick fashioned the first box score and became author of the first baseball rule book. A colleague who frequently accompanied him to ball games was Walt Whitman. Another was the famous pacifist Joseph Howard.

In 1889 the Dodgers changed the name of the team, since six of the regular players were married during the season; they became "The Bridegrooms." Bill McGunnigle won the pennant and the six honeymoons apparently having ended, the team was again called the Dodgers. In 1890 Brooklyn entered the National League and won another championship. Right after that McGunnigle was fired. Another partner, George Chauncey, had been taken into the Dodger front office, and he persuaded the other officers to fire McGunnigle. His replacement was John Montgomery Ward.

A climax of sorts occurred in 1890, when the Players League was formed. Now there were three leagues pretending to be major—the National League, the American League, and the Players' League—and Brooklyn had teams in all of them.

The "Brotherhood War," as the interleague jumping and raiding was called, was a disaster. In one year, the Players' League not only ruined itself but the American Association as well. In the ensuing realignment John Montgomery Ward, who had managed the Brooklyn team in the Players' League, replaced Bill McGunnigle.

Events moved swiftly through the next several years. Chauncey, the first to recognize Ebbets's genius as a baseball man, sold him half his stock in the club, and when Byrne and Doyle died within a year of each other, Ebbets was elected president.

Meanwhile Ward had flopped as manager, and the team staggered under Dave Tout, Bill Barnie, and Mike Griffin. Business fell off and Ebbets moved the team to new grounds. He leased an area between First and Third Streets and Third and Fourth Avenues, built a new park and in 1898 called it Washington Park.

The 12-club National League was unwieldy at this time, and unprofitable, and so a sort of syndicate baseball developed. Players were freely assigned from one city to another, the club owners sharing in all the teams' proceeds. In one of these shuttle operations, Baltimore's Ned Hanlon, the dominant manager of baseball in the Nineties, skipped to Brooklyn with a number of his key players. Hanlon had developed the likes of John McGraw, Hughie Jennings, Willie Keeler, and Wilbert Robinson, but when Hanlon moved over to Brooklyn, Robinson and McGraw refused to go along.

Even without them Hanlon had a team he thought could win the championship, with pitchers Bill Kennedy, Jack Dunn, Doc McJames, and Jim Hughes. Duke Farrell and Jim McGuire were the catchers. Jennings at first base, Bill Dahlen at shortstop, Tom Daly at second, and Jim Casey at third comprised a crack infield. Willie Keeler, Joe Kelly, and Fielder Jones were in the outfield and when they won the championship that year, the team became known as the Superbas, after a celebrated vaudeville act of the time, called "Hanlon's Superbas."

The Superbas won again in 1900, with Iron Man Joe McGinnity added to their pitching staff and Jimmy Sheckard to the outfield, but in 1901 and again in 1902, their ranks were depleted by the "outlaw" American League. Although they were third in 1901 and second in 1902, attendance dropped and Ebbets bought out his other partners and became the principal owner of the club. Ebbets gave Henry Medicus, his financial backer, 750 shares of the stock in gratitude for his backing.

The Superbas wound up in fifth place in 1903, but picked up a hard-hitting first baseman named Tim Jordan, who was to become a great favorite in Brooklyn. The next year, Ebbets bought Doc Scanlon, a top-notch pitcher from Pittsburgh, and Billy Bergen, a catcher, and outfielder Harry Lumley, and still the team reeled and slipped. When the Superbas hit bottom in 1905, Hanlon was dismissed and Patsy Donovan, who had managed the Cardinals and Senators, was named to manage the team.

In 1906, the Superbas became the Dodgers once more and finished in fifth place. In 1907, Ebbets picked up a wild left-handed pitcher from the Sally League, Nap Rucker. Rucker would take his place among the all-time Dodger heroes. They were fifth again that year, and when they plunged to seventh in 1908, Ebbets released Donovan and appointed Harry Lumley to succeed him.

It was in 1908 that Ebbets dreamed up a site for a new ball park—and found it in Flatbush. It was on the edge of a disreputable section called Pigtown. Bounded on Bedford Avenue, Sullivan Street, Franklin Avenue, and Montgomery Street, it was a garbage dump surrounded by squatters' shanties. Friends told Ebbets he was crazy. Nobody would come to as squalid an area as Pigtown.

Crazy or not, Ebbets went ahead with his plans. But it took him four long years, during which he saved, scrimped, borrowed, and mortgaged everything he could lay his hands on; on March 4, 1912, ground was broken for the new ball park.

"What are you going to call the joint?" Abe Yeager, sports editor of the *Brooklyn Eagle*, asked.

"I don't know," Ebbets said. "Washington Park, maybe."

"That wouldn't mean anything out here," said Yeager. "Why don't you call it Ebbets Field?"

And so it was called, and little more than a year later, it became a reality. The first game was played there on April 5, 1913, with a turn-away crowd of 25,000 looking on, as Nap Rucker beat the hated New York Giants, 3–2.

In 1908 Ebbets hired a frustrated ball player, Larry Sutton, as a scout for the Dodgers and Sutton scoured the hinterlands for the kind of players that would in the years to come turn the Dodgers into contenders. He came up with Zach Wheat, a 21-year-old farmhand who became one of the greatest Dodgers. Another find was Casey Stengel, and others were to follow as the Dodgers continued to wallow in sixth and seventh place through most of 1908, 1909, 1910, and 1911.

In 1910 Bill Dahlen replaced Lumley as manager. By 1913 the Dodgers were packing the new ball park, but they were still unable to win. Finally in November Dahlen resigned as manager and Ebbets announced that Wilbert Robinson of the old Baltimore Orioles would be the new manager.

Brooklyn fans knew little about Robbie when he took command of the team, but they got to know him quickly and took him to their hearts. In practically no time, he was Uncle Robbie, his wife was called "Ma"—and the team was called the Robins.

It was a better team than Brooklyn had seen since Ned Hanlon's early days at Washington Park and it would get better; within two years a pennant would be won at Ebbets Field. Now in 1914, Robbie was building a contending team.

The player he was most pleased to discover was a moon-faced kid catcher named Otto Miller. Robbie believed that pitching was about 70 percent of a ball club, but he also believed that Miller could handle the temperamental pitchers on the club. Otto was patient, unruffled in a pinch and understanding, and in the years to come would prove Robbie was right in holding on to him.

The pitchers were Ed Pfeffer, Rucker, Ed Reulbach,

and Pat Ragan. Jake Daubert at first base was the best in the league; he had won the batting title in 1913 with a .350 average. George Cutshaw was at second base, Ollie O'Mara at shortstop, and Red Smith at third base. Gus Getz was the utility infielder and Zack Wheat, Caey Stengel, and Jack Dalton were in the outfield, with Hy Myers in reserve.

Mainly because his pitchers couldn't win consistently (with the exception of Pfeffer), it was evident that Brooklyn wouldn't finish high in the standings, but Ebbets was pleased with Uncle Robbie's handling of the team and in midseason handed him a new two-year contract that called for more money.

Daubert won the batting title once again with a lusty .329 average and Pfeffer won 23 games, but those were the positive factors as the Robins finished fifth.

In 1915 Robbie went all out for pitchers. He got Jack Coombs from the Athletics, Phil Douglas from Cincinnati, Larry Cheney from the Cubs, and Rube Marquard from the Giants. Rucker won nine games, Pfeffer 19, and Sherry Smith, a newcomer, came through with 14 wins as the Robins finished in third place in 1915.

In 1916 the Robins got off to a fast start and were in first place by the middle of May; the fans responded by coming to the ball park by the thousands. Hustling, laughing, fighting with their opponents and often among themselves, the Robins came on to win the pennant and all of Brooklyn celebrated. The *Brooklyn Eagle* paid tribute to Robins' utility infielder Gus Getz with this front-page headline after the Robins clinched the pennant: "GUS GETZ HAS GOT GUTS." It was Getz's base hit in the final game of the season that brought the pennant to Brooklyn.

The time of triumph, however, was brief. The Boston Red Sox hammered the Brooklyn pitchers, winning the Series in five games. Jack Coombs was the only Brooklyn hurler to win a game against a great Red Sox team. In the second game of the Series, a young twenty-one-year-old lefty named George Herman Ruth outpitched Brooklyn's Sherry Smith in a 14-inning, 2–1 overtime battle.

America entered World War I in 1917; the baseball was left hurting. In 1917 the Robins set an unenviable record: pennant winners in 1916, they fell all the way back to seventh place. No other team had ever slipped so far down in one season. In 1918 the Robins had a hodgepodge team as all the other clubs had, including the Cubs who won the pennant.

Robbie rebuilt his Robins in 1919 and didn't do too badly as the club finished in fifth place. The Pirates, Cubs, and Giants finished ahead of the Robins; Cincinnati won the pennant.

Once again in 1920 Robbie shuffled players around like a chess master and came up with an exciting team. Burleigh Grimes and Leon Cadore were added to a pitching staff that already had Sherry Smith and Rube Marquard. Pete Kilduff was at second base, Ed Konetchy was at first, Ivy Olson was the shortstop, Jimmy Johnston was at third base. Tommy Griffith, Hy Myers, and Zack Wheat were the outfielders and Otto Miller, Ernie Krueger, and Rowdy Elliot the catchers.

On Saturday, June 1, 1920, the sun had long since dropped behind the fence at Braves Field and the twilight was fading. Barry McCormick, the plate umpire, waited for a third Boston out, then waved his arms and called, "That's enough."

"No, no," protested Dodger shortstop Olson. "Just one more inning so we can say we played three games in one day."

"Nothing doing," ruled McCormick firmly. "My feet are killing me and I'm having trouble seeing the ball."

Thus ended a 26-inning, 1–1 tie, with Boston. The starting pitchers, Leon Cadore and Joe Oeschger, went the entire distance for the longest game in baseball history.

That night the Robins traveled home to Brooklyn to play a game with the Phillies. They left Cadore in a Boston bed, exhausted from pitching the entire game. When they returned to Boston on Monday morning to play off the 26-inning tie game, Cadore was still in bed. Unfortunately, Leon's great pitching feat took so much out of him that he never was an effective hurler again; nor was Oeschger.

The Robins won the pennant by 10½ games over the second-place Giants. Burleigh Grimes had one of his finest years, winning 23 games while losing 11. Cadore won 15 games, Pfeffer won 16, and Rube Marquard won 10.

But the Robins would have been luckier if the year had ended there, for they ran up against one of the finest teams to ever play in a Series. Tris Speaker's Cleveland Indians were outstanding in 1920 and they handed the Robins a crushing defeat in the five-out-of-nine-game series. Robbie started Marquard against Stan Coveleski in the first game and the Indians won 3–1 as first baseman George Burns slammed a hit to right field and circled the bases when Olson flubbed an accurate throw from Wheat. Grimes shut out the Indians in the second game, 2–0, and the Dodgers repeated in the third game, 2–1, as Smith bested Duster Mails in a fine pitching duel. But Coveleski won the fourth game, 5–1, and in the fifth game Jim Bagby of the Indians defeated Grimes, 8–1. Mails of the Indians shut out the Dodgers in the sixth game, 1–0, and then Coveleski came back in the finale, beating Burleigh Grimes, 3–0.

It was in this classic series that Bill Wambsganss of the Indians made the first unassisted triple play ever executed in a World Series game and his teammate Elmer Smith hit the first World Series grand slam home run. That was also the year that Rube Marquard was fined for speculating in World Series tickets. He was arrested by a detective, fined, and then was traded to the Reds at the end of the season.

Uncle Robbie never did regain the formula after winning his second pennant, although he gave the Giants a tremendous challenge right up to the last day of the 1924 season. The Robins finished in fifth place in 1921, slipped to sixth in 1922, stayed there in 1923, and closed to within two games of the hated Giants in 1924, as Dazzy Vance, a fastball pitcher won 28 games, lost six, and fanned 262 batters. The incredible Zack Wheat hit .375 that year; Jake Fournier hit 27 homers and hit for a .334 average. Grimes won 22 games and Dutch Ruether, a 20-game winner in 1922, slipped badly, winning only eight games. If Ruether hadn't slumped to an 8–13 record, the Robins might have won again.

Everything seemed to go wrong with the Robins after the 1924 season. Charlie Ebbets died on April 18, 1925, and then within one month, Ed McKeever, acting president of the team, caught a chill at Ebbets' funeral and within a week he too was dead.

Uncle Robbie was appointed president of the club and he in turn delegated his managerial duties to Zach Wheat. It soon became clear that Wheat was no manager and Robbie once again took over the reins as the club languished in sixth place; they were to remain mired there for five long, lean years.

Robbie, Steve McKeever, and sports editor Joe Vila of the *New York Sun* became embroiled in a bitter fight over a series of articles Vila had written blasting Robbie's handling of the team. Robbie became so angry he called the publisher of the paper and complained about Vila. The publisher, Keats Speed, in turn ordered Vila never again to mention Robbie's name in any story and then McKeever jumped into the fray and he and Robbie became bitter enemies.

But even the *Sun,* Robbie, and McKeever regained their enthusiasm that incredible summer of 1926 when Babe Herman joined the Robins. Herman was a tall, raw-boned, muscular farmboy from Buffalo, N.Y. The Babe played first base and the outfield with equal disregard for his own safety and the art of fielding. He ran the bases like a fire truck, often stealing second or third with men already on those bases. But all was forgiven whenever he hit the ball for distance and in his first year with the Robins in 1926, the Babe hit for a .319 average.

About this time, Westbrook Pegler, a poison-pen sports columnist, before he became a famous syndicated columnist, first called the Dodgers "the Daffiness Boys." The nickname was appropriate and popular because the team was quite often confusing and amusing, and sometimes both.

Players came and went by the dozen during the next several seasons. And nearly all of them were found wanting. Old stars such as Zack Wheat, Grimes, and Fournier were gone. In 1928 Dave Bancroft joined the team, but soon found such indifference and confusion that he resigned as assistant manager. In spite of the confusion, Dazzy Vance won 22 games and the incomparable Babe Herman hit for a .340 average—but the Robins still finished in sixth place.

Despite the fact that Robbie and McKeever feuded throughout the early 1930s and such stalwarts as Max Carey, Jess Petty, Rabbit Maranville, Dave Bancroft, Irish Meusel, Jack Quinn, Dolf Luque, and Rube Bressler came and went, the Dodgers still could not finish better than fourth. In 1930 Robbie put a team on the field that was in first place for 75 days, but wore itself out in the stretch and finally finished once again in fourth place.

The 1930 team was a bit saner than previous teams, but with Babe Herman in the lineup there were still times when Del Bissonette or Glenn Wright had homers cut down to singles because they passed the lingering Herman on the base paths. Anyone who could hit .393, as Babe did that year, could nullify a dozen homers while he clogged up the bases and still retain the affection of Brooklyn fans. But Robbie's precarious position, mostly due to his battles with the front office, was strengthened meanwhile by the showing of his club and a record attendance of 1.1 million for the season.

At the end of the 1931 season, the Dodgers' board of directors did not renew Robbie's contract and his 18-year reign came to an end. But it was a memorable period and one that most Brooklyn fans will never forget. The Dodgers were to have more exciting baseball dynasties in the years to come, but with the rotund Robbie's exit the very colorful era of the Daffiness Boys had come to an end. More than anyone else who had previously been connected with the Dodgers, Robbie caught the essential flavor of this baseball stronghold and found a way into its warm heart.

The next half-dozen seasons were a dark age at Ebbets Field. With Robbie gone, the color and brightness, the dizziness and daffiness that had made Ebbets Field the premier site for rollicking fun disappeared. The new manager, Max Carey, who had been an outstanding center fielder for the Pirates for 17 years, was a smart baseball man. The tall, lean Carey was more reserved and less boisterous than Robbie and a strict disciplinarian. This was a new approach to the game for the old Dodger hands and they did not warm to Max, though they did respect him and they were more careful in their conduct.

Carey made some quick moves. He bought Hack Wilson from the Cubs for $45,000, hired Casey Stengel as a coach, and when Babe Herman held out for more money, traded him to Cincinnati. Ernie Lombardi and Wally Gilbert also went to the Reds for Joe Stripp, Tony Cuccinello, and Clyde Sukeforth.

Under Carey the Dodgers played sound baseball and with Lefty O'Doul, Hack Wilson, and Joe Stripp slugging the ball and Watty Clark's 20–12 pitching the Dodgers finished a very respectable third in 1932, their best finish since 1924.

In 1933 a link with the Golden Age of the Dodgers was severed when Carey traded Dazzy Vance for a young pitcher, Ownie Carroll, who never lived up to his college reputation in the majors. When Carey appealed to the board of directors for some real players their response was to trade Lefty O'Doul, the best hitter on the club, for Sam Leslie and somebody named Joe Hutcheson. The aroused fans began to cry for Carey's scalp—and they got it.

In February 1934, the Dodgers' directors offered Casey Stengel Carey's job and Casey accepted. Casey didn't get much help for his club either. Linus Frey was acquired to play shortstop, and Emil Leonard, Tom Zachary, and Lefty Clark were added to the pitching staff. Al Lopez was the catcher, Tony Cuccinello was at second base, Sam Leslie on first, Joe Stripp was at third base and the outfielders were Danny Taylor, Hack Wilson, and Johnny Fredericks. The Dogers once again finished in sixth place, nearly 20 games behind the fifth-place Cardinals.

In the last two days of the dreary 1934 season Stengel rallied his players to beat the Giants twice and kill their pennant hopes. An overflow crowd of more than 50,000 fans packed the old Polo Grounds for each of the crucial games between the intercity rivals. Those two wins over the hated Giants solidified Stengel's position and, before going south with the team in 1935, Casey's two-year contract was extended to the end of the 1937 season.

Stengel's Dodgers were popular enough in 1935 when

they pulled themselves up and finished in fifth place, but attendance was falling off as the fans were beginning to lose interest. The 1936 season was a nightmare for Casey and it was only partly relieved by the birthday party his New York and Brooklyn sportswriter friends gave him in midseason, with the team languishing in last place. At season's end with the Dodgers in seventh place, Casey was released and paid off for the 1937 season.

Burleigh Grimes, the contentious spitball pitcher who had joined the Dodgers in 1918, won 19 games in his first season and then continued to be a big winner for them until 1926, took over as manager. He worked his team hard and completely revamped the club. He brought in Buddy Hassett at first base, Cookie Lavagetto to play second, Woody English at shortstop, Joe Stripp remained at third, and the outfield consisted of Heinie Manush, Johnny Cooney, and Tom Winsett. His catcher was Babe Phelps. Max Butcher, Luke Hamlin, Waite Hoyt (the former Yankee star), Van Mungo, and Freddy Fitzsimmons were his pitchers. The team played good ball at the beginning of the season, but tailed off and finished in sixth place, a favorite Dodger spot.

Grimes, in a desperate move, shook up his club and traded Stripp, Butcher, Cooney, and Roy Henshaw to the Cardinals for veteran shortstop Leo Durocher. Leo had been well-seasoned with the Yankees, Reds, and Cardinals and arrived in Brooklyn knowing all the answers—especially for umpires. He was past his peak as a player but had managerial ambitions, and he was welcomed to Brooklyn enthusiastically.

George McLaughlin, a stern, hard-jawed banker began to exert a powerful influence on the Dodger front office at about this time. McLaughlin was sometimes referred to as "George the Fifth." He was president of the Brooklyn Trust Co., and a civic leader who wished the ball club well. At the same time, he had his duty to the bank, to which the Dodgers' indebtedness had grown to more than $1.2 million.

McLaughlin let the Dodgers know that its future credit would be severely limited unless there was some new and vital leadership guiding the team. Ford Frick, then president of the league, proposed to the Dodgers' board of directors that Larry MacPhail, an explosive, innovative, and successful man, take the job. MacPhail had recently accomplished a miracle with the Cincinnati Reds. He had introduced night baseball to the major leagues in that city, had built a contending team and had completely rebuilt the Red's ball park within a few years. After a feud with Cincinnati owner Powell Crosley, he had left the organization.

MacPhail was then 49 years old. Behind him was a colorful career in several fields. He had been in the banking business in Michigan, had played minor-league ball, and had completed law school at the University of Michigan. He had practiced law for a short time, then become head of a department store in Nashville, Tenn. A captain during World War I, he and a group of officers headed by Colonel Luke Lea stole an automobile after the Armistice and invaded Holland with a scheme to kidnap the former Kaiser. The plan failed.

Back home, Larry went into the automobile business in Ohio and then operated the Columbus farm team for the Cardinals under Branch Rickey. Then it was on to Cincinnati, and finally Brooklyn. Larry took the job on January 19, 1938, only after being assured of unlimited financial backing and "full and complete authority over the operations of the ball club."

The Dodgers' new boss started right off by buying Dolf Camilli, a hard-hitting first baseman from the Phillies for $50,000, and then borrowed $200,000 for park improvements. The Brooklyn board of directors, accustomed to penny-pinching efficiency, didn't know what to make of the ball of fire to whom they had given a free reign in spending all that money, but MacPhail went fearlessly on his way as he set out to repair the run-down ball park and hire and outfit a new staff of ushers to replace the grafting hoodlum element who had been creating ill will for the club over the years.

MacPhail provided one of the landmark events in the history of baseball as an added attraction for the Dodgers: the first night game at Ebbets Field, on June 13, 1938. Johnny Vander Meer, the Cincinnati Reds star, had pitched a no-hit game against the Braves four days earlier. That night he held the Dodgers hitless, thus becoming the only pitcher in major-league history to hurl two successive no-hitters.

The following week MacPhail signed Babe Ruth as first base coach for the Dodgers for the last half of the season. Babe hadn't played ball for five years, but seeing him take those tremendous swings in practice was enough of a magnet for the Dodger fans and they turned out in record numbers.

The Dodgers were never in the race that year, but they nearly doubled their home attendance to almost 800,000 fans. "You haven't seen anything yet," MacPhail told reporters.

Immediately after the World Series, MacPhail announced that Leo Durocher, the Dodgers' shortstop for the past two seasons, would become player-manager for 1939, succeeding Grimes. During the winter, Larry completed plans to give New York City its first radio coverage of big-league baseball from Ebbets Field and lured Cincinnati sportscaster Red Barber to Brooklyn.

MacPhail also was an active trader, acquiring pitchers Hugh Casey and Whit Wyatt, who, along with Luke Hamlin and Fred Fitzsimmons, gave the Dodgers a sound pitching staff. In midseason Dixie Walker was claimed at the waiver price from the Tigers. Walker came into his own in Brooklyn, and his timely hitting brought him Dodger immortality.

With Walker, Lavagetto, and Camilli hitting the ball consistently, combined with tight pitching by Wyatt and Fitzsimmons, the Dodgers became the talk of the league. In addition, Red Barber's colorful broadcasting helped to popularize the club, so that by midseason the Dodgers were the favorites not only of Brooklyn but the entire nation as they battled for the championship. It was a colorful Dodger season as the fiery Durocher fought with umpires, opponents, and sometimes his own teammates. But both the Reds and Cardinals finished ahead of them, so the Dodgers had to settle for third place, with high hopes for 1940.

In 1940 MacPhail got the biggest Dodger bargain in history when he claimed Pete Reiser on waivers from the Cardinals' farm system for $100. Another Dodger great, Pee Wee Reese, was purchased from Louisville for

$50,000. Other newcomers included outfielder Joe Vosmik, Jim Wasdell, and pitcher Tex Carleton. In his very first start for the Dodgers Tex pitched a no-hitter against the Reds.

MacPhail negotiated his biggest deal when he landed Joe Medwick from the Cardinals. At the time Joe was 29 years old and had played in St. Louis for eight seasons. He brought a lifetime batting average of .338 to Brooklyn. In the Medwick deal the Cards also threw in pitcher Curt Davis. Medwick arrived in Brooklyn and every sportscaster, editor, and sports writer in the area covered his entry onto Ebbets Field. Six days later he was in a Brooklyn hospital after a beaning incident in a Dodger-Cardinal game. Former teammate Joe Bowman's very first pitch in the game hit Medwick in the head and Joe suffered a concussion.

Fortunately, it was only a mild concussion. But the head injury affected Medwick's play. He lost some of his cocky poise at the plate. Although he hit .301 for the season, he was never the power hitter he had been in the past.

After finishing second in 1940, the Dodgers won it all in 1941. The 1941 team was the first Brooklyn team that ever won 100 games and they came within an eyelash of beating the Yankees in the World Series.

The Yankees won the Series four games to one, which sounds decisive. It might have been a different story, though, if catcher Mickey Owen hadn't dropped Tommy Henrichs' third strike after Hugh Casey fanned him for the third out and what would have been a 4–3 win for Brooklyn. That would have tied the Series at two games each. Instead, Owen allowed the ball to get away from him, Henrich reached first base and the Yanks went on to a 7–4 win.

The previous day, Fitzsimmons had shut out the Yankees with only four hits, but was struck on the kneecap by a line drive and forced to leave the game. The Yanks immediately jumped on Hugh Casey and scored two runs to win the game. The Dodgers had won the second game, 3–2, behind the fine pitching of Whit Wyatt. But the fourth game was the turning point of the Series.

The Dodgers had drawn more than 1.2 million fans at home in 1941 with their incredible run for the championship. Two months after the World Series came Pearl Harbor, and long-range baseball plans were thrown into a state of confusion. Cookie Lavagetto was one of the first Dodgers to enlist and others would soon follow.

The Dodgers meanwhile had a war of their own going—with the Cubs, Braves, and Cardinals, as a beanball war broke out between the contending teams. The Dodgers, protesting their innocence, were accused of being the aggressors. If they were guilty of anything it was overconfidence—they were in first place by seven-and-a-half games with five weeks to go when they began to slide. The Cardinals took three out of four games in a torrid series and suddenly it was a red-hot pennant race.

Meanwhile as the race wound down, Larry MacPhail offered his services to the army and General Brehon Somerville gave him a commission and a job in charge of the Service of Supply office.

As the pennant race came down to the final day, the Dodgers had to beat the Phillies to tie the Cards for the league lead, while the Cardinals had to lose a doubleheader.

The Dodgers won their game, then sat in the ramshackle clubhouse at Shibe Park and listened to a broadcast of the opening Cardinal game. And when the Cards won that game, the Dodger players started their long, sad trip back to Brooklyn—in second place.

Once again Ford Frick came to the aid of the Dodgers, suggesting they hire Branch Rickey to take over Larry MacPhail's job as president. Rickey took over, but he could not untrack the Dodgers in 1943 as the Cardinals, behind the great Stan Musial, ran away from the Reds and Dodgers. Musial hit for a .357 average that led the Cards to the championship. The third-place Dodgers finished some thirty games behind them.

The 1944 season was a series of lost weekends for the Dodgers as they lost most of their stars to the military. They finished in seventh place, but Dixie Walker won the batting title with a .357 average in a close battle with Musial. In 1945 with such players as Ed Stanky, Luis Olmo, Tuck Stainback, Augie Galan, Goody Rosen, and Walker, the Dodgers climbed back into the third place behind the Cardinals as the Chicago Cubs won the pennant.

In the fall of 1945, Branch Rickey electrified the baseball world by announcing that he had signed Jackie Robinson, Negro infielder of the Kansas City Monarchs, and that Jackie would play for the Dodgers' Montreal farm team. Rickey's scouts had scoured the nation looking for outstanding black players and they touted Robinson as the "most likely" to succeed in the major leagues. Rickey promised Robinson that he would be given every opportunity to make the big team, if he played well in 1945 for Montreal. The rest is baseball history.

In 1946, with Pee Wee Reese out of action with a chipped vertebra and Pete Reiser in and out of the lineup with various injuries, the Dodgers fought gamely all season long and managed to stay even with St. Louis. The season ended with the Dodgers and Cardinals tied for first. In a best two-out-of-three playoff, the Cardinals won two straight to take the title.

In 1947 Larry MacPhail, who had left Brooklyn to join the armed forces in 1942, came out of retirement to take over the Yankees, along with Dan Topping and Del Webb. Dodger fans viewed this switch as unforgivable, since the Yanks were second only to the Giants on the Dodger enemy list. That spring the Dodgers and Yankees met in Havana for a series of exhibition games. Leo Durocher, who had been warned by Commissioner Happy Chandler to stay out of trouble, noticed a couple of well-known gamblers sitting in MacPhail's box. He turned to a group of reporters and said: "If I even talked to those guys, I'd be barred from baseball."

Previously Durocher had been accused of scandalous conduct prior to announcing his marriage to movie star Laraine Day. It seemed that Leo had been named as corespondent by Laraine's former husband. The story was front-paged for days on end. Then Leo and Laraine went to Mexico and Miss Day was granted a "quickie" divorce. The happy couple then crossed the border at El Paso, Texas where they were married.

At this point sportswriter Westbrook Pegler got into the act, raking up Leo's past associations with gamblers and linking him to movie star George Raft. Pegler then tied Raft to Las Vegas gambling kingpin, Bugsy Siegel.

Upon hearing about Durocher's comments during the Havana game, an angry MacPhail put in a formal complaint to Commissioner Chandler.

Chandler called for a hearing on March 24, and both Durocher and MacPhail were questioned. At the conclusion of the meeting Leo shook hands with Larry and it looked as if things had been settled between the warring parties. And then on April 9, Chandler suspended Durocher for a period of one year. The baseball world was shocked.

Branch Rickey made a Shakespearean production out of selecting an interim manager and finally called in former Yankee manager, Joe McCarthy, who had resigned a year earlier. But Joe turned the job down when he learned it was only an interim job. Rickey then appointed an old friend and assistant, Burt Shotton, as manager.

Shotton had been an infielder with the St. Louis Browns and went to the Cardinals when Rickey got the top job. He was Rickey's aide and assistant at St. Louis for several years, managed the Phillies for six years, then shuttled to the minor leagues to take over as manager at Rochester and then Columbus. He was tough and knowledgeable and knew the Dodger players.

The Brooklyn fans soon had something more sensational to think about, however. Jackie Robinson had made good with a vengeance in the International League, becoming its most valuable player, and was being brought up to the Dodgers, thus becoming the first black player to play in the major leagues.

What difference did Jack make? Ebbets Field drew a total of 1,807,526 customers, the largest seasonal attendance in Brooklyn history and at the time a National League record. On the road the Dodgers were equally popular, drawing 1,863,542, also a National League record.

Of course, much of the team's success was due to Robinson. In making his debut at first base, Jackie proved that a qualified black athlete could play baseball in any league. The rest of the Dodgers played alert, smart baseball and justified Rickey's hopes by winning the pennant handily, by five games over the second-place Cardinals.

Once more the old familiar World Series jinx reared its ugly head. The Yankees won the first two games. The Dodgers then rallied on their home field to top the Yanks in a slugfest, 9–8. But the Dodgers' greatest moment of glory lay ahead. In the fourth game Yankee pitcher Floyd Bevens was one out away from pitching the first no-hit World Series game. He had a 2–1 lead when he walked Carl Furillo and put Pete Reiser on base with an intentional pass. Cookie Lavagetto then hit Bevens' second pitch against the right-field wall for a two-bagger that scored two runs, robbing Bevens of his no-hitter and winning the game for the Dodgers, 3–2.

The Yankees took the lead again the next day with a 2–1 win. But the game Dodgers battled back to even the Series as the scene switched back to Yankee Stadium.

A great clutch team, the Yankees wrapped up the Series in the seventh game against the Dodgers' Hal Gregg as Spec Shea, Bevens, and Page pitched for the Yanks. Joe Page turned in one of his greatest relief efforts as he blanked the Dodgers in the last five innings, allowing only one hit. The final score was 5–2. And so for the fourth time in baseball history the Dodgers had failed in a World Series.

The following December, Rickey announced that Durocher would return as manager in 1948. When Commissioner Chandler heard the news, he commented: "I neither approve nor disapprove."

Leo's return to the managerial scene was not easy. There was considerable opposition to him from various church groups and early in July, with the Dodgers in sixth place, Rickey sent Leo a curt note requesting that he do something about the team's spirit.

On July 16 the baseball world was astounded by the news that Durocher would be replaced once again by Burt Shotton and that Leo would take over *as manager of the Giants.*

Under Shotton, the Dodgers moved up in the standings and were in first place for about 10 days during August. They slipped back during the final month, however, when they broke even in 30 games and finished the season in third place.

The Dodgers started off with a rush in 1949 and they were in and out of first place during May and early June. Luis Olmo and Mickey Owen returned to the fold in June after a couple of seasons in the Mexican League and then the Dodgers took over the lead until late in July, when the Cards beat them in three straight games at Ebbets Field. It looked as if the Dodgers were going to finish behind the Cardinals, but in the final week the Cards folded.

On the final day of the season, the Dodgers were one game up on the Cards. They had to defeat the Phillies in the seasons' final game to clinch the pennant and it looked safe for the Dodgers as they quickly ran up a 5–0 lead over the Phils. But the Phils rallied, scored seven runs off Dodger ace Don Newcombe to tie the score at 7–7 at the end of the sixth inning. The teams battled on even terms until the 10th inning, when the Dodgers broke through and scored twice to win the game, 9–7, and the pennant.

Once again the Dodgers faced the Yankees in the World Series, and once again they lost. The Yankees won the opener, 1–0, as Allie Reynolds allowed the Brooks only two hits. The Dodgers came right back to defeat their Bronx rivals, behind the six-hit pitching of Preacher Roe in another 1–0 game. Then the Yankees won three straight and it was "Wait 'til next year" once again.

On the opening day of 1950, the Dodgers played in Philadelphia against the Phillies. Don Newcombe pitched brilliantly against Robin Roberts but the Phillies won. One of the Dodger players casually remarked, "We might have to beat them in the last few days for the pennant." His words proved prophetic.

The Phils, in quest of their first pennant in 35 years, led the Dodgers by nine games as late as September 19. Then the Dodgers closed fast as the Phils began to fade. By September 30th, the Phils' margin had shrunk to two games. And then the Phils came to Ebbets Field for a two-game series that would close out the season.

The Dodgers won the first game—their ninth straight win. When the final Sunday dawned, the red-hot Dodgers needed just one more win to tie the Phils. But the season ended just as it began, with Robin Roberts beating Newcombe in a magnificent pitching duel. In the 10th inning, Dick Sisler hit a two-strike pitch for a home run and a 4–1 win for the Phillies, clinching the pennant.

Walter O'Malley took over the presidency of the Dodgers in the fall of 1950 when Branch Rickey went to the Pittsburgh Pirates. O'Malley announced that Charley Dressen would manage the Dodgers in 1951 and Dressen and the Dodgers took a commanding 13½ game lead by early August. Dressen was telling everyone that the rest of the season was a mere formality and then . . . the hated Giants, under Durocher, caught fire. They had brought up the spectacular Willie Mays from their Minneapolis farm team and started to win. They put together a sensational 16-game winning streak and suddenly there was a pennant race.

The Dodgers won only four of their last ten games while the Giants won all their remaining games, and suddenly the two teams were in a playoff. The Giants won the first game of the playoff, but the Dodgers took the second and when the Dodgers led in the third game by a 4–1 score in the last of the ninth, it looked as if the Giants were dead. There was one out and Ralph Branca came in to relieve Don Newcombe, who had tired badly.

The Giants electrified the jam-packed crowd by getting one run across and putting the tying runs on second and third. There was still only one out and in this heart-stopping moment, Durocher called his hitter Bobby Thomson aside, and said, "Bobby, we need a hit. I'm counting on you."

Bobby Thomson, Glasgow-born and living in Staten Island, gained instant immortality by slamming a Branca fastball into the stands for a three-run homer that won the pennant for the Giants. And so another heartbreak year ended for the Dodgers.

The tale of 1952 was so much like a postscript to the drama of the year before that it seemed to lack a separate identity. The Dodgers drove hard to restore their self-respect and there were many times when it seemed that the Giants would produce another "miracle," but this time it did not happen.

Chuck Dressen performed his own miracles, however. Though Don Newcombe had been called into the Army, Joe Black came up with 15 wins, while Preacher Roe won 11 games and Carl Erskine won 14 as the Dodgers coasted to a six-and-a-half game advantage over the second-place Giants.

The World Series against the Yankees and Casey Stengel found the Dodgers putting up a terrific battle before going down in seven games. Joe Black, aided by Duke Snider's homer, beat the Yankees in game 1 by a 4–2 score. The Yanks' Billy Martin homered in the second game as the Bronx Bombers went on to win, 7–1. Preacher Roe pitched the Brooks to a 5–3 victory in game 3 and Allie Reynolds shut out the Dodgers, 2–0, in game number 4. Carl Erskine retired the last 19 Yankees to beat them 6–5 in game number 5. The Yankees tied the Series at three games each as they won the sixth game by a 3–2 score, and finally Mickey Mantle's homer won the Series in the seventh game as the Yanks won, 4–2.

The 1953 season was much easier for the Dodgers; they finished in first place by 13 games over the emerging Milwaukee Braves. The pitching was better, with Erskine and Roe going well all season. Furillo led the league in hitting, as Snider, Robinson, Campanella, and Hodges provided the Dodgers' power.

But if the pennant race was easy, the World Series wasn't. The Yankees won again, this time in six games. A grand slam home run by Mickey Mantle off Dodger pitcher Russ Meyer in the fifth game was the blow that shattered the Dodgers' hopes.

During the winter Charley Dressen asked president Walter O'Malley for more than a one-year contract to manage the club, and O'Malley responded by firing Dressen and selecting Walter Alston as the teams' new manager for the 1954 season.

The Giants, with Willie Mays leading the league in hitting, won the pennant. The Dodgers, with much the same personnel as in 1953, won 13 fewer games and finished in second place.

Brooklyn came closest to heaven in 1955. In Walt Alston's second year as manager, the Dodgers ran away from the rest of the league to win another pennant. They jumped off to a great start by winning their first 10 games. Then, after losing a game, they won 11 of their next 12. At season's end they were 13½ games in front of the second-place Milwaukee Braves.

In the World Series, the Dodgers finally reached the heights with a stunning win in seven games over the heavy-hitting Yankees.

Heavy hitting marked the first five games of the Series. The Yankees had hammered Newcombe hard and won the opening game, 6–5. First baseman Joe Collins homered in the sixth inning with two mates aboard and that was the big difference. Jackie Robinson almost broke the game open with a ninth-inning steal of home, but Whitey Ford held the battling Dodgers. The next day the Yanks pounded Billy Loes for four runs in the fourth inning to again defeat the struggling Dodgers, 4–2. Yankee ace Tommy Byrne held the Dodgers to only five hits as he became the first left-handed pitcher to pitch and win a complete game over the 1955 Dodgers.

Game 3 was marked by the slugging of Dodger catcher Roy Campanella and the steady hurling of Johnny Podres. Campy slammed three hits, including a home run and three runs batted in as the Dodgers battered Bob Turley for 11 hits in an 8–3 victory. In the fourth game the Dodgers stroked 14 hits off five Yankee pitchers. Homers by Campanella and Hodges gave the Dodgers the lead, 4–3, in the fourth inning, and then Duke Snider's three-run drive into Bedford Avenue, in the fifth inning gave the Dodgers a lead they never relinquished, as they romped to an 8–5 win that evened the Series at two each.

The Dodgers jumped out in front in game 5, as they blasted three homers off Yankee pitcher Bob Grim in the first five innings. Sandy Amoros homered with a man on base, while Duke Snider blasted two homers in the 5–3 victory.

Manager Alston gambled with pitcher Karl Spooner in game 6, but the Yankees jumped on Karl and knocked him out of the box in the first inning with a barrage of base hits. The Yanks 5–1 victory evened the Series at three games apiece.

Casey Stengel selected Tommy Byrne to pitch the seventh game. Byrne did not pitch badly, but he was beaten by his nemesis, Gil Hodges. In the fourth inning, Campy doubled and Gil drove Roy in for the first run of the game. In the sixth inning Reese singled and Snider was safe on Skowron's error. Campy advanced both runners with a sacrifice, Furillo walked, filling the bases, and then Gil Hodges scored run number 2 for the Dodgers with a long sacrifice fly. The Dodgers were out in front, 2–0.

Billy Martin opened the sixth with a walk, Gil McDougald beat out a bunt and then it was up to Berra. Yogi drove a pitch deep to left field and Sandy Amoros, after a long run, made one of the great diving World Series catches. He quickly recovered, threw to Reese, and Pee Wee's throw to Hodges on first base doubled up McDougald. That play broke the back of the Yankee threat and the Dodgers, behind the five-hit pitching of Johnny Podres, wrapped up their first World Series triumph.

That was the night that delirious Dodger fans drove around the borough's streets screaming, yelling and honking their horns—and there were no traffic tickets issued on that October night in 1955 in Brooklyn.

The Milwaukee Braves fought the Dodgers tooth and nail in 1956 and it wasn't until the final game of the regular season that the Dodgers won out over the Braves by a game and a half, with the Cincinnati Reds in third place by three games. Duke Snider had one of his greatest years, blasting 43 home runs to lead the league, while Gil Hodges slugged 32 home runs. Newcombe was superb, winning 27 games while losing only 7.

But after winning the pennant once more, the Dodgers slipped into their old habits, losing the Series in seven games to the Yankees. The Series feature was Don Larsen's perfect game—a no-hit, no-run game in the 5th game of the Series. It was the first no-hit game in World Series history. In the seventh and final game, Johnny Kucks of the Yanks allowed the Dodgers only three hits as the Yankees overwhelmed the Dodgers, 9–0.

Walter O'Malley was 47 years old when he became president of the Dodgers, and from the very first day he took over, he exhibited a determination to make the Brooklyn franchise the richest one in the game. He improved and enlarged Ebbets Field, televised all of the home and away games, sold the ground rights underneath the ball park, but still felt that he had to make other moves for more dollars.

In 1956 O'Malley got the National League's permission to play 10 games in an old ball park in Jersey City. The signs were plain that O'Malley had other motives and other moves in mind. He purchased the ball park in Los Angeles that was the home of the Los Angeles team of the Pacific Coast League and then at a special meeting of the National League in May 1957, the League approved the relocation of the Dodgers to Los Angeles and the Giants to San Francisco.

Tragedy struck the Dodgers the first year they played in Los Angeles. Several weeks before the season began, Roy Campanella, the great and colorful Dodger catcher, was severely injured in an automobile accident near his home on Long Island and would never play another game. Don Newcombe pitched poorly in Los Angeles and didn't win a single game. He was traded in June of that year. There were a couple of bright spots, however: a hard-throwing youngster named Don Drysdale won 12 games and Sandy Koufax, who had won only nine games in three previous years with the Dodgers, came up with 11 wins. However Hodges, Reese, Snider, and Furillo had ordinary years and as a result the club finished in seventh place. It was a drab year, except for the excitement the Dodgers created among their new fans. Home attendance that first year was a sensational, 1,845,556, a gain of more than 800,000 over the final year in Brooklyn.

In 1959 the L.A. Dodgers really captured the old west as they finished just three games in front of the Milwaukee Braves to win the pennant. Don Drysdale won 17 games, Podres won 14, and Larry Sherry was outstanding in the bull pen. Maury Wills took over for Pee Wee Reese, who had retired, and Wally Moon was obtained in a trade with the Cardinals. Moon blasted 19 home runs and hit .302, while Hodges hit 25 homers and Snider drove out 23.

In the World Series the Dodgers faced the formidable White Sox and the Sox showed they would be tough, winning the first game, as they drove out an 11–0 victory. It was one of the most one-sided games in Series history as the Sox pounded five Dodger hurlers for 11 hits.

But after a good night's rest and a Walt Alston pep talk, the Dodgers bounced right back. Behind Johnny Podres, they defeated the Sox, 4–3.

In game 3 at the Coliseum in Los Angeles, Don Drysdale bore down in the pinches and although allowing the Sox 12 hits, he held them at bay when they threatened; the Dodgers won it, 3–1. In the fourth game, Gil Hodges's homer off Gerry Staley in the eighth inning was the big difference as the Dodgers again came from behind to win, 5–4. In the fifth game, the Sox got only five hits off Sandy Koufax but won, 1–0. The game was attended by the largest crowd in World Series history: 92,706 fans.

In the sixth game in Chicago, the Dodgers hit Early Wynn hard and knocked him out of the box in the fourth inning. They built up an 8–0 lead, and then went on to win easily as Larry Sherry relieved Podres in the fourth inning and held the Sox in check. The final score was 9–3. The hero of the Series was Larry Sherry, who relieved in all four games that the Dodgers won. He was credited with two wins and two saves. Overall, the 1959 World Series was the richest Series in baseball history. More than 92,000 fans attended each of the three games in Los Angeles.

Nineteen hundred and sixty marked the end of the trail for several of the older Dodgers who had journeyed to Los Angeles. An injured Carl Furillo refused to go to Spokane so that the Dodgers could bring in a replacement, and was released. Duke Snider had his poorest year, hitting a meager .243, while Gil Hodges slumped to .193. The Dodgers finished in fourth place, behind the Cardinals, the Braves, and the pennant-winning Pittsburgh Pirates.

Sandy Koufax came into his own in 1961, appearing in 42 games, winning 18 and losing 13. It was Sandy's best performance in his six years as a Dodger. He struck out 269 hitters for a new league record. Johnny Podres also won 18 games. Stan Williams and Drysdale each won 15, but the Dodgers were just edged out by the Cincinnati Reds, led by Frank Robinson, who hit 37 home runs.

In 1962 the new multimillion dollar Dodger Stadium opened to great acclaim and it proved to be one of the most beautiful ball parks in the country. Walter O'Malley's dream had truly come to pass. The Dodgers were in the thick of it all the way, behind the marvelous pitching of

Don Drysdale who won 25 games and the Cy Young award; the great hitting of young Tommy Davis who won the batting title with a .346 average; the daring of Maury Wills who broke Ty Cobb's stolen base record with 104 steals; and the slugging of big Frank Howard who hit 31 homers. But in the final game of the season, with the pennant riding on the game, the Giants scored four runs in the ninth inning to win the game, 6–4, and the pennant. It was a heartbreaking end to one of the finest Dodger seasons in history.

The key to the Dodgers' success in 1963 was the pitching of the magnificent twins, Sandy Koufax and Don Drysdale. Sandy won 25 games while losing only five; he pitched another no-hitter and struck out 308 for a new league record. Koufax wound up with both the Cy Young and the MVP awards. Ron Perranoski, currently a coach with the Dodgers, was another valuable asset, winning 16 games and losing only 3. Gone from the Dodger lineup was the once fabled Duke Snider, who was sold to the New York Mets.

The Dodgers took over first place in July and staved off a late threat by the Cardinals. They finished with a comfortable nine-game lead. Then the high-flying Dodgers met with their hated rivals, the New York Yankees, for the eighth time in World Series play.

This time the Dodgers surprised the baseball world with their confident, driving spirit. They swept the Yankees in four games, Sandy Koufax winning twice and Johnny Podres and Don Drysdale once each.

In game one, Koufax and Whitey Ford hooked up in a classic pitching duel. Sandy struck out 15 Yankees as he allowed only six hits and the Dodgers won, 6–2. Sandy was aided by John Roseboro's three-run homer in the second inning.

In the second game Podres shut the Yankees down with only seven hits as he beat them, 4–1. Outfielder Willie Davis of the Dodgers clubbed a two-out double in the first inning that scored two runs and the Dodgers were never headed.

In the third game at Dodger Stadium, Don Drysdale pitched air-tight ball, allowing the hard-hitting Yankees only three hits. It was a classic pitching duel against the Yankees' Jim Bouton. The final score was 1–0.

In the fourth game, Sandy Koufax pitched one of his finer games as the Dodgers won the finale, 2–1, and the Series. Frank Howard of the Dodgers clubbed a 450-foot homer, but he was matched by Mickey Mantle, who also drove one out of the park. It was a 1–1 game until Willie Davis sacrifice fly scored Junior Gilliam in the seventh inning for the 2–1 edge—and the World Championship.

In 1964 Sandy Koufax injured his left elbow in the middle of the season and wasn't able to pitch at all after August 16. Yet Koufax and Don Drysdale were able to win 19 and 18 games, respectively, but there was little else to console Dodger fans. The team was not hitting well and despite heroic efforts by Alston to juggle his lineup in trying to put together a winning combination, it just wasn't a Dodger year. They finished in sixth place, 19½ games behind the St. Louis Cardinals, who squeaked through to the pennant by a game-and-a-half over the Reds.

By 1965 Koufax was well again and able to pitch effectively throughout the season. Sandy had a remarkable year, winning 26 games while losing only eight. Don Drysdale combined with Sandy to give the Dodgers the best one-two pitching punch in the major leagues. Don won 23 games while losing 12, and Claude Osteen had a 15 and 15 record. Osteen excelled in the World Series against the Minnesota Twins, shutting them out 4–0 after the Twins had beaten Koufax and Drysdale and seemingly were on their way to an easy sweep of the Series.

The Twins had pounded Drysdale and Koufax in the first two games. They beat Drysdale 8–2, then clubbed Koufax for nine hits and a 5–1 win in the second game. Osteen turned it around in game 3 and then big Don Drysdale returned to form in game 4, striking out 11 Twins on the way to a 7–2 win. In game 5 Koufax struck out 10 and shut down the Twins with four hits as the Dodgers won, 7–0. The Twins' Mudcat Grant was the star of the sixth game as he homered with two men on and pitched a six-hitter, defeating the Dodgers, 5–1. With the Series tied at three games, Koufax pitched one of his finest games. He held the slugging Twins to three hits, striking out 10. Lou Johnson homered with a man on base to give the Dodgers a 2–0 triumph in the final game.

By 1966 a number of the Dodger regulars had become full-fledged stars. Wes Parker had developed into an outstanding first baseman; switch-hitting Jim Lefebvre became a standout at second base and was a fixture at that position until 1972; Willie Davis developed into one of the finest center fielders in baseball and was a constant threat on the base paths; at shortstop Maury Wills blossomed into one of the all-time Dodger stars over the next 14 years. And when Tommy Davis fractured an ankle in 1965, Lou Johnson came in to fill the gap and did so with a .270 plus batting average through 1966 and 1967.

In 1966 Sandy Koufax reached a new peak with 27 wins while losing 9, with an ERA of 1.73. Drysdale slipped, but managed to win 13 while losing 16. Claude Osteen won 17 games and Don Sutton had a 12 and 12 record as the Dodgers just managed to edge the San Francisco Giants by two-and-a-half games. It was Koufax who, with only two days' rest, pitched the pennant-winning clincher for the Dodgers, a 6–3 win over the Phillies in the second half of a doubleheader.

Walter Alston was worried about his pitching staff as the Dodgers prepared to battle the Baltimore Orioles in the World Series, with good reason. Sandy's arm hurt and became inflamed after every game he had pitched during the last half of the regular season and it still ached as the Series began. Don Drysdale was Alston's choice to pitch the opener and he was not up to it. Don lasted only two innings as the Orioles clubbed him for two home runs by the Robinsons—Brooks and Frank—and the Orioles won the game, 5–2.

The second game also went to the Orioles after Koufax was hit hard in the fifth inning. Three successive Willie Davis errors didn't help the Dodgers and they went down to their second straight loss by a 6–0 score. In game 3, the Orioles, behind superb pitching by Wally Bunker, won, by a 1–0 score, and then Frank Robinson slugged a fourth-inning homer in the final game to give the Orioles another 1–0 victory and a four-game sweep over the hapless Dodgers.

In 1967 the morale of the entire team was affected by Sandy Koufax's early retirement just a few days after he accepted the Cy Young award, his third award for pitching excellence. Sandy expressed fear that he might face amputation of his left arm if he continued to pitch. In addition Maury Wills was traded and it would be several years before the Dodgers would be able to fill his position. They finished eighth in 1967 and seventh in 1968; no regular player hit .300 in either year.

Manager Walt Alston came up with a couple of 20-game winners in pitchers Claude Osteen and Bill Singer in 1969, and Willie Davis clubbed the ball for a .311 average. With the help of pitcher Don Sutton who won 17 games, Manny Mota who hit .323 as a utility outfielder and Andy Kosco who hit 19 homers, the Dodgers moved up to fourth place in the Western Division. Don Drysdale, the last of the old Brooklyn Dodgers, retired after a 14-year career.

In 1970 the Dodgers rose to second place as the Cincinnati Reds simply ran away with the divisional title by 14½ games. Don Sutton with 15 wins and Claude Osteen with 16 victories were the leading pitchers. Wes Parker hit a gaudy .319, while Ted Sizemore, Manny Mota, and Willie Davis hit more than .300. Maury Wills rejoined the club and was the steadying influence that the infield had lacked since his departure in 1965.

The Cardinals traded Richie Allen to the Dodgers in 1971 and Richie hit 23 homers, while Al Downing, a Yankee pitching castoff, won 20 games as the Dodgers made a great run for the pennant. The Giants seemed to have it wrapped up, but the scrappy Dodgers won 13 out of 15 in late September and climbed to within one game of the Giants. But the Giants spurted and came back to win four of their last five games and hung in to take the pennant by a one-game margin.

After the season was over, Richie Allen was traded to the White Sox for pitcher Tommy John. The Dodgers also acquired slugger Frank Robinson from the Baltimore Orioles. Two new faces were in the Dodger lineup in 1972. They were shortstop Bill Russell and first baseman, Steve Garvey, two of the finest young players the Dodger farm system had ever developed. Garvey and Russell would be the nucleus of several championship teams over the next ten years.

The Dodgers finished third as Robinson had one of the least productive years in his long career. Claude Osteen won 20 games, Don Sutton had 19 wins and Tommy John won 11 games as the Dodgers finished behind Houston and the first-place Reds.

The year 1973 saw the Dodgers move into a commanding lead behind the fine pitching of newcomer Andy Messersmith. Don Sutton and Tommy John pitched very well, and by mid-July the Dodgers were in front of the Cincinnati Reds by eight full games. It looked like a romp for the Los Angeles club as catcher Joe Ferguson, Steve Garvey, Manny Mota, and Willie Davis hammered the ball. Suddenly the Reds started to move, caught fire, won 60 of their last 86 games and finished three games ahead of the Dodgers. It was one of the most exciting races in years and Dodger fans anticipated 1974 with strong hopes for victory.

In 1974, general manager Al Campanis of the Dodgers acquired relief pitcher Mike Marshall from the Montreal Expos in exchange for Willie Davis. A day later, after manager Alston complained about filling the center field slot, Campanis promptly dealt pitcher Claude Osteen to Houston for center fielder Jimmy Wynn. It proved to be one of Campanis' better deals, for Wynn slammed out 32 home runs and was a solid center fielder for the Dodgers in 1974. Pitchers Andy Messersmith and Don Sutton also had outstanding years. Messersmith won 20 and Sutton won 19 as the Dodgers won the divisional title and then went on to the World Series against the Oakland Athletics.

This was the third straight World Series for the Oakland team. They were poised, experienced, old hands in World Series' play, and that proved to be the big difference. The Dodgers failed to hit in the pinches and stranded 36 men on base. They were not outplayed, just outgamed by the Athletics, who defeated them in the Series, 4 games to 1. Four of the games were decided by scores of 3-2, including the single game the Dodgers won. The championship A's simply had too much going for them in 1974.

The 1975 season was to be the "Year of the Dodgers," but that slogan proved to be premature. There was the matter of the "Big Red Machine." The Cincinnati Reds with Pete Rose, Ken Griffey, Joe Morgan, Johnny Bench, and George Foster hitting consistently, combined with outstanding pitching by Fred Norman, Don Gullett, Pat Darcy, and Jack Billingham, simply ran roughshod over every team in the West. The Reds finished 29 games ahead of the second-place Dodgers.

The year 1976 was a repeat of 1975 as the Reds continued to play championship ball and beat out the Dodgers by 15 games to win the Western Division. But the Dodgers with their new young stars—Steve Garvey, Ron Cey, Davey Lopes, and Dusty Baker and pitchers Don Sutton, Doug Rau, and Burt Hooton—were on their way. They also had a new manager. Tommy LaSorda had replaced Walter Alston at the end of the 1976 season.

Tommy LaSorda began his pitching career as a third-string pitcher for the Norristown, Pa. High School team and showed so much promise that he was signed by the Philadelphia Phillies in 1945. But Tommy toiled almost exclusively in the minor leagues, eventually setting a team record of 125 wins in nine years with Montreal. His first chance to make the Dodgers came in 1945, when Walt Alston succeeded Charley Dressen as manager of the Dodgers. A cocky LaSorda announced, "I don't intend to let anyone push me off this club, regardless of the record he has." These were the Dodgers of Don Newcombe, Johnny Podres, Clem Labine, Carl Erskine, Preacher Roe, and Billy Loes, and somebody must have pushed Tommy because he did not make the team.

Toward the end of spring training there came a call for LaSorda to report to Buzzy Bavasi, the Dodgers' general manager. Such a call generally meant that the player was being shipped back to the minors, and LaSorda knew it.

"Tommy, I've got some bad news," Bavasi began.

"What's wrong, Buzz, someone in your family sick?" Tommy said quickly.

"You gotta go back to Montreal."

"Why, Buzz? I'm doing a good job for you, ain't I?"

"Yeah, but we have to cut the roster by one man."

"Gee whiz, Buzzie. Get rid of the wild kid, Koufax. He'll never be a pitcher. He can't hit the side of a barn door from 60 feet away. No control. And you're going to keep him?"

Sandy Koufax, of course, went on to become one of the Dodgers' all-time great pitchers and a member of Baseball's Hall of Fame.

In his freshman year as a major-league manager LaSorda handled his 1977 Dodger team masterfully. Utilizing practically the same lineup that Alston had in 1976 when the Dodgers had finished some 15 games behind Cincinnati, LaSorda moved the Dodgers into first place for most of the season. Steve Garvey slammed 33 home runs, Ron Cey hit 30, Reggie Smith smacked 32, and Dusty Baker had 30, giving the Dodgers the hardest hitting lineup in the major leagues. Tommy John won 20 games, Rick Rhoden had 16, Doug Rau won 14, Hooton had 12 and the Dodgers finished 15 games ahead of Cincinnati. In the playoffs, the Dodgers defeated the Philadelphia Phillies three games to one, to win the National League flag.

The World Series between the powerful Yankees and the scrappy Dodgers opened with a fine pitching duel between Don Gullett, a former Cincinnati Reds' star, and Don Sutton. It was a sensational opening game that went into the 12th inning with the score tied at 3–3. Willie Randolph, the Yankees' second baseman, opened the 12th inning with a slashing double. Paul Blair scored Randolph with the winning run, on a single off relief pitcher Rick Rhoden, and the Yankees took the series opener, 4–3.

In the second game the Dodgers blasted Catfish Hunter for four home runs. Burt Hooton allowed the Yankees only seven hits and the Dodgers evened the Series, 6–1.

Mickey Rivers cracked out two doubles and a single to lead the Yankee attack on pitcher Tommy John and the Yanks took game number 3, 5–3. In game number 4, it was Reggie Jackson who exploded with a homer and double and Ron Guidry pitched a four-hitter as the Yanks won, 4–2. The Dodgers fought back in game 5, as Steve Yeager homered and drove in four runs. Dusty Baker got three hits and Don Sutton pitched well enough to take the game, 10–4. Reggie Jackson turned the sixth game into a personal demonstration of power hitting. Reggie clouted three successive home runs and drove in five runs as the Yankees pounded Hooton, Doug Rau, Sosa, and Hough to win the final game, 8–4.

In 1978 with practically the same lineup that he used in 1977, LaSorda won his second straight National League pennant. The Dodgers broke fast, vaulted into first place and remained there behind the steady hitting of first baseman Steve Garvey, who hit .319 and slugged 21 home runs. Reggie Smith had 29 homers; Terry Forster was the pitching staff workhorse, appearing in 47 games, and saving 22; Tommy John won 19 games; and the Dodgers beat out hard-hitting Cincinnati. This time the margin over the Reds was four games. The Dodgers then defeated the Phillies three games to one for the pennant. In the playoffs, Garvey hit for a .389 average, including four home runs and once again the Dodgers faced the Yankees in the World Series.

In game 1 it appeared that the Dodgers would sweep the Yankees. They overpowered the Bronx Bombers with an 11-hit attack as Davey Lopes drove out two homers and knocked in five runs. Bill Russell and Dusty Baker got three hits each as the Dodgers knocked out four Yankee pitchers in an 11–5 rout.

In game 2 Ron Cey drove in all four of the Dodger runs with a single and a three-run home run off Catfish Hunter as the Dodgers again defeated the Yankees, 4–3. Bob Welch, a fireballing 22-year-old rookie in his first World Series appearance, was spectacular as he fanned Yankee slugger Reggie Jackson in the ninth inning to preserve Burt Hooton's victory.

But the Yankees came back in the third game to slug out 10 hits behind the outstanding pitching of Ron Guidry and went on to win, 5–1. The Yanks also took game 4 behind the fine pitching of Ed Figueroa, Dick Tidrow, and Goose Gossage. It was the timely hitting of Lou Piniella, who singled off Bob Welch in the 10th inning with two out, that enabled the Yankees to even the Series at two games each. The final score was 4–3.

In game 5, the Yankees savaged three Dodger pitchers with an 18-hit attack that included three hits each by Mickey Rivers, Bucky Dent, and Brian Doyle. Rookie pitcher Jim Beattie won his first World Series game, 12–2.

The Yankees took the Series finale with an 11-hit attack off Don Sutton, Welch, and Doug Rau as they defeated the Dodgers, 7–2. It was their 22nd series championship.

Tommy John, who won 17 games for the Dodgers in 1978, went to the New York Yankees, after the Dodgers could not meet his free-agency demands. That was the big difference in the 1979 race. The Dodgers finished third, 17 games behind the Reds and Astros in the West and LaSorda made extensive plans to shake up his team and improve their standing in 1980.

With Dusty Baker, Steve Garvey, and Ron Cey pounding out home runs, the Dodgers came within an eyelash of winning the divisional title in 1980. The Houston Astros just managed to win out over a spirited Dodger team by 1½ games. Jay Johnstone came over in a deal from the Yankees and hit for a .307 average, while Rick Monday and Pedro Guerrero provided additional power. Jerry Reuss, Bob Welch, Sutton, and Burt Hooton contributed some fine pitching, setting the stage for 1981.

"You gotta have heart . . . miles and miles and miles of heart," according to the hit song from the musical comedy, *Damn Yankees*. And the 1981 edition of the Dodgers had enough heart to extend through a dozen zip codes. It was a team with a porous, over-the-hill infield, a team constantly flirting with disaster, and in the end, a team with great courage.

Going strictly by the records, the Dodgers had no right to be in the World Series, let alone the playoffs. It has been said of the baseball strike of 1981 that nobody really benefited from the enforced layoff, but that wasn't quite true. The ensuing split season allowed Los Angeles to compete against Houston for the National League Western title. Actually, Houston shouldn't have been there either, because the team with the combined (both halves of the season) best record was Cincinnati.

In addition to courage, the 1981 Dodgers had added some charismatic mystique in the person of a roly-poly 20-year-old pitcher named Fernando Valenzuela who, in the course of a single season, had become an instant folk hero for Dodger fans. He had arrived in Los Angeles at the tail end of 1980, with two things going for him: a flamboyant personality and a controlled screwball that danced a cha-cha as it broke over the plate. The Dodgers tried him out as a relief pitcher. He worked a little more than 17 innings, struck out 16 batters, walked only five and gave up eight hits. His ERA was exactly 0.00. Tommy LaSorda decided that the kid might do well as a starting pitcher.

In 1981 it was pitching the Dodgers were counting on to get them all the way home. There was Valenzuela, to be sure, plus Jerry Reuss, Burt Hooton, and Bob Welch; this was as good a rotation as could be found. Once upon a time Los Angeles used the long ball to blow away the opposition, like the array of bats that powered the 1977 Dodgers. Those days were gone. As second baseman Davey Lopes put it, "This year we had to rely more on intangibles for success, the stolen base, the extra base on a single, the hit and run. But our desire to win was greater in 1981. This team had more character."

But it didn't seem that character would be enough as the playoffs got under way. According to baseball lore, in a short series pitching dominates hitting. But when both teams have good pitching, one timely hit can turn things around. The Astros had some very good pitching, and in the beginning they had the clutch hits as well.

Houston started Nolan Ryan in the first game, which gave the Astros a psychological advantage immediately. The million-dollar right-hander had tossed a no-hitter against Los Angeles on September 26th. LaSorda countered with Valenzuela, and it was a great pitching duel all the way. The game was tied at 1–1 in the bottom of the ninth when Houston's Alan Ashby socked a two-run homer off reliever Dave Stewart. Ryan limited the Dodgers to two hits.

The second game was even tighter. Neither team scored for 10 innings. Once again the Los Angeles relief corps took the loss. In the bottom of the 11th, with the bases loaded, pinch hitter Denny Walling lined a base hit off young Tom Niedenfuer to break the tie.

Before 1981, no team that had lost the first two games in a best three-out-of-five playoff had ever come back to win. Tommy LaSorda knew that, and it was his willingness to gamble that kept the Dodgers in contention.

The original plan was to pitch Bob Welch in the third game and come back with Burt Hooton, the man with the knuckle curve ball, in the fourth game. Hooton usually did well against Houston and the Dodger manager felt he had to go with his best.

The strategy worked. Los Angeles scored three runs in the first inning and coasted to a 6–1 decision. The Dodger bats woke up, perhaps because they were playing on their home field. The early damage was done by Dusty Baker's RBI double and Steve Garvey's two-run shot into the cheap seats. Both batters later conceded that their blows would have been loud outs in the vast Houston Astrodome.

The match-up for game 4 was Valenzuela, pitching with three days' rest, and Vern Ruhle for Houston. It was another pitching duel. Nobody got on base through four innings, but in the fifth, Pedro Guerrero hit his first home run since September 11th, more than a month earlier. Both Fernando and Ruhle gave up just four hits, but the Dodgers scored one more run and won it, 2–1, tying the series.

The showdown game pitted Reuss against Ryan, and now the Dodgers had the psychological edge. It wasn't merely momentum, because the Astros had a full head of steam up after winning the first two games. Ryan, who had humbled the Dodgers the last two times he faced them, had never won a game in Dodger Stadium (he was 0–5 lifetime). Reuss, on the other hand, had allowed Houston only two runs in 26 innings.

After both clubs had sputtered and left runners on base in the early innings, Los Angeles broke the game open in the sixth. A walk to Baker, followed by singles by Garvey, veteran outfielder Rick Monday, and catcher Mike Scioscia, plus a Houston error, meant three runs and eventually a 4–0 win, on a five-hitter by Reuss.

It had been a pitchers' series. The Astros team batting average for the five games was .179; the Dodgers hit a lusty .198.

With the divisional title tucked away, Los Angeles took on Montreal for the National League pennant, but a feeling of uneasiness hung over Los Angeles rooters. The Dodgers were accustomed to sunshine and the kind of weather that permits oranges and grapefruits to grow. Montreal at the end of October was really polar-bear country. Therefore, it behooved Los Angeles to win the first two games at home, and trust to fate for another victory north of the border.

Montreal never did have much luck at Chavez Ravine. Before game 1 of the playoffs, the Expos, in 20 attempts, had won one game and lost 19 in Dodger Stadium. The opener was played under ideal conditions, and Los Angeles fans were delirious in the home eighth when Pedro Guerrero and Mike Scioscia belted back-to-back round-trippers. One game up, the Dodgers were going to send wunderkind Fernando to the mound the following day, to face a journeyman named Ray Burris, who had previously labored for the Cubs, Yankees, and Mets, before coming to Montreal. The veteran Burris had pitched well for the Expos, especially in the second half of the split season.

Montreal scored some runs against Valenzuela. The Dodgers got five hits and no runs against Burris. "It is very nice," said Expo Warren Cromartie politely, "to come here and beat the mayor of Los Angeles."

So the Dodgers had to journey to Canada for games 3 and 4. At game time Expo Andre Dawson came bounding onto the field breathing deeply in the invigorating, 46-degree air and remarked, "This is one of our better nights."

Jerry Reuss, pitching his heart out, had a 1–0 lead going into the bottom of the seventh, but with two out everything fell apart. Dawson singled, Gary Carter walked, and Larry Parrish got a base hit. There goes the shutout, exulted the fans. Then the unheralded Jerry White hit one out, winning it for Steve Rogers. Rogers had been outstanding in the pressure-cooker games of October, allowing only two runs in 36 innings.

Once again the Dodgers were within one game of elimination. To stave off defeat, Tommy LaSorda handed the ball to Burt Hooton, as he had done against Houston. Hooton held the Expos while his teammates wasted several scoring opportunities. It was 1–1 in the top of the eighth when Steve Garvey drilled a Gullickson pitch into the stands with one on to give Hooton a two-run lead. In the ninth Los Angeles added four more, to ice the game at 7–1.

Steve Spielberg couldn't have created a more dramatic setting for the fifth encounter. Ray Burris, whose off-speed assortment had baffled the Dodgers in game 2, was rematched against Valenzuela. To add to the Dodger miseries, the game had been postponed by rain the previous day and the temperature was down to 41 degrees, hardly ideal baseball weather.

The Expos got a run in the first on a double by Tim Raines and a Rodney Scott bunt. Valenzuela fielded the ball but his throw to third was too late to catch Raines. The Dodgers had Scott caught off first but failed to run him down, and that proved costly. A moment later Andre Dawson hit a grounder to second, which was turned into a double play but it scored Raines.

Burris frustrated the Dodgers until the fifth. Then Rick Monday led off with a single and made it to third on Guerrero's single to right center. At this point Burris bounced a pitch into the dirt. Catcher Gary Carter alertly blocked the ball toward third base, holding Monday in check but allowing Guerrero to take second. Mike Scioscia lined out to second, the runners holding. Then Valenzuela bounced out to second base as Monday scored. Had Burris not delivered the wild pitch, Guerrero would have been doubled up on Valenzuela's grounder, ending the inning.

Burris departed for a pinch hitter in the bottom of the eighth after allowing only five hits, one walk, and a somewhat tainted run. He was replaced by Steve Rogers, the ace of the staff, not normally a relief pitcher. Rogers got Garvey on an infield pop and Ron Cey on a fly to deep left. Up stepped Rick Monday, a 35-year-old campaigner, who had seriously considered retiring before the 1981 season. The count went to 3-and-1. Rogers threw a sinker that failed to sink, and Monday drove it high and far over the wall in right center, giving the Dodgers the lead.

In the bottom of the ninth Valenzuela, who had yielded only three hits so far, got the first two batters in routine fashion. Then Gary Carter walked on a 3-and-2 pitch. Larry Parrish walked on a 3-and-2 pitch. A weary Valenzuela was replaced by Bob Welch.

Welch had first made a name for himself in the 1978 World Series by striking out Reggie Jackson in a clutch situation, and later successfully won his battle with alcoholism. The batter was Jerry White, who had hit that big home run to win the third game. Welch threw exactly one pitch. White hit a bouncer to second and the game was over.

Once again Los Angeles had pulled it out, and now they had to face the Yankees, who had defeated them in 1978 by taking four in a row after losing the opening pair. The Yanks had been idle for four days waiting for the National League pennant to be decided.

For LaSorda and those Dodgers who had been with the team in 1978, it was almost a case of déjà vu, starting with leadoff man Davey Lopes. He slammed a ball to the left side of the infield. Third baseman Graig Nettles made a diving stop and gunned him down at first on a disputed call.

In the bottom of the first the Yankees pummeled Jerry Reuss. Jerry Mumphrey singled, Lou Piniella hit a ground-rule double, and first baseman Bob Watson lifted one over the wall in right center, thus staking Yankee lefty Ron Guidry to a three-run lead.

By the bottom of the third Reuss was gone after Humphrey's second hit, a stolen base, and Piniella's RBI single. In the fourth inning Dodger reliever Bobby Castillo walked four batters to force in a run.

Steve Yeager got one run back in the fifth with a solo home run, and after seven innings the Yanks led, 5–1. Ron Davis, a tall, lean, bespectacled right-hander, came on to close things out, but Davis had control problems, walking the first two batters. Goose Gossage, New York's relief ace, replaced Davis, but the long layoff had taken the heat out of his blazer. Pinch hitter Jay Johnstone singled home a run and Dusty Baker's sacrifice fly got in another. Steve Garvey then blasted a murderous drive toward the left-field corner—but the ball never reached the outfield. Graig Nettles dove to his right and speared the shot in the webbing of his glove. That was the ball game: Yanks, 5, Dodgers, 3.

"Nettles is amazing," moaned LaSorda, as he watched Nettles's repeat performance of his 1978 spectacular fielding. "I get sick to my stomach seeing him make those plays all the time. He must go to bed hoping and praying he can kill us with his glove."

Added Gossage, "I don't care what the box score shows, that save belongs to Nettles."

Los Angeles faced former Dodger Tommy John in game 2, and the man with the "bionic" arm allowed just three hits in the seven innings he worked. Goose Gossage, anxious to get in more work, clamped the lid on the Dodgers in his two innings. Neither pitcher allowed a run. Burt Hooton also pitched a strong game. The Yanks scored an unearned run in the fifth on an error by Davey Lopes and a double by fill-in shortstop Larry Milbourne. New York got two more in the eighth against the Dodger relief corps.

Once again the Dodgers had their backs to the wall. And when a mild earthquake hit southern California on the morning of the third game, Los Angeles fans took it as an omen of disaster for the team. Even third baseman Ron Cey's three-run homer in the first inning didn't seem to be enough as the Yankees roughed up Valenzuela in the second with Watson's homer, Cerone's double, and Milbourne's single, which accounted for two runs, and then another pair in the third on Piniella's hit and Cerone's home run. The young screwball pitcher was wild, got behind the hitters, and when he came in with a pitch he was clobbered. The experts in the stands were already second-guessing Lasorda; why was he leaving Fernando in to take a pounding when he just didn't have it?

LaSorda was thinking of giving his rookie sensation the hook. In the fifth inning the score was tied at 4–4, and the Dodgers had the bases loaded with nobody out. Mike Scioscia was at bat and if he couldn't knock in the lead run, Lasorda had Reggie Smith in the on-deck circle to hit for the pitcher. Scioscia did get the run home, hitting into a double play. Valenzuela hit for himself and stayed in the game. But he wasn't out of the woods yet.

In the eighth Aurelio Rodriguez and Larry Milbourne led off with singles. Bobby Murcer batted for relief pitcher Rudy May, with orders to bunt for a base hit. On the first pitch Murcer did bunt, but the ball was hit harder than he intended. It was a kind of soft line drive foul. Ron Cey made a diving catch a-la-Nettles and doubled Milbourne off first, while Rodriguez got back to second base.

Then Randolph chopped one in Cey's direction. There was no way for Cey to get Randolph at first, but he didn't have to, because Rodriguez ran right into Cey's tag. Valenzuela was out of the inning.

"Terrible base running," fumed Yankee owner George Steinbrenner. And he was right. As Milbourne himself later admitted, "I broke with the bunt. First, I've got to make sure the ball is fair, and it looked fair from my angle. And I've got to make sure the ball is down. I was overly aggressive. I reacted too fast."

Rodriguez had a somewhat more valid excuse. With two out, representing the tying run, he had to go on any fair ball regardless of where it was hit. Overall, it was more a case of the Yankees losing the game than the Dodgers winning it.

The Dodgers continued their uphill struggle in game 4, and again it was Yankee ineptness that turned the tide in favor of Los Angeles. Bob Welch started for Los Angeles, and the only man he got out was himself as he gave up three hits and a walk. By the end of three innings the New Yorkers had a 4–2 lead, and going into the bottom of the sixth it was extended to 6–3. However, a walk to Scioscia and Jay Johnstone's pinch-hit homer got back two runs. Then came the turnaround play.

Davey Lopes looped a high, slicing fly to right. Reggie Jackson said later that he lost the ball in the sun. The ball went through his glove and bounced off his chest as Lopes hustled to second on the error. A dazed Ron Davis seemed to forget Lopes was on second, and the runner stole third as Davis was delivering a pitch. Russell singled to left and the score was tied, 6–6.

In the home seventh, center fielder Bobby Brown misplayed Rick Monday's routine fly into a double, which led to two more Dodger runs. Reggie Jackson's home run halved the Dodger lead, but that was how the game ended, 8–7, Dodgers. LaSorda and his troops had tied the series.

In game 5 Ron Guidry was clinging to a 1–0 lead into the seventh inning when Dodger coach Manny Mota offered a bit of sound advice to the hapless Dodger batters. He told them to crouch a bit, wait on the pitch a little and not swing so hard. Pedro Guerrero and Steve Yeager promptly slugged back-to-back home runs, Jerry Reuss limited the Yanks to five hits, and the Dodgers led in the Series. Not even the heart-stopping beaning of Ron Cey by a Gossage fastball could dampen the surging optimism that enveloped Los Angeles.

The sixth game was lopsided and anticlimactic. The Yankees got off to a 1–0 lead in the first inning. The Dodgers tied the score in the fourth and got all the runs they needed in the fifth. It was only poetic justice that the bad-hop single that delivered the game-winner should come off the bat of Ron Cey. The final score was 9–2, Dodgers.

To call the Dodgers comeback incredible would be an understatement. They had been down two games to none against Houston and had swept the next three. They had been behind, two games to one against Montreal and had taken the final two to win the National League pennant. Finally, trailing two games to none in the World Series, they had taken the Yanks in four straight, exactly as the Yanks had steamrollered them in 1978.

According to the running gag in and around Los Angeles, Tommy LaSorda has no red corpuscles in his veins, because when he cuts himself shaving he bleeds Dodger blue. He has always been a team man, a Dodger who gets emotional about his club for any reason or for no reason at all. He gave vent to his feelings after the 1981 victory:

"This is the greatest thing that ever happened to me in baseball. These guys have given me a lifetime of thrills in one season. . . . I've always wished that if the good Lord ever let us win the World Series, it would be against the club that beat us twice."

2

THE COMPLETE CATALOGUE OF PLAYERS

THE COMPLETE CATALOGUE OF PLAYERS contains an alphabetical listing of every player who ever played for the Dodger ball club, from 1890 through 1983. The first section of the Catalogue contains information on batters only; information on pitchers can be found in part II of the section. For every Dodger batter who has played 154 games or more for the team, complete year-by-year statistics are included, even for those years that the player was on the roster of another major league team. For players who have appeared in less than 154 Dodger games, statistics are found for the games that player appeared as a Dodger. These players' major league *lifetime* statistics are also included; they are found on the line where the word "total" appears.

The Players Catalogue contains the following data, if available:

Player's name	Peter Smither (fictional)
Date and place of birth	B. Dec. 14, 1937, Clifton, N.J.
Player's batting and throwing style	Bats L., Throws R.
Player's height and playing weight	6' 2", 195 lbs.
Player's position(s)	Shortstop
Date and place of death	D. Dec. 5, 1981, Sarasota, Fla.
Team affiliation and league	LOS ANGELES (N)
Years played	1958–1965

EXPLANATION OF COLUMN HEADINGS AND STATISTICAL ABBREVIATIONS

YEAR	Year played
CLUB	BROOKLYN
BA	Batting average
G	Games played
AB	Number of times at bat
R	Runs scored
H	Number of hits
2B	Doubles
3B	Triples
HR	Home runs
RBI	Runs batted in
B.L.	Bats left handed
T.R.	Throws right handed
B.B.	Switch-hitter

A number of players were active with various teams prior to 1890. An asterisk indicates the teams and years played prior to 1890, for which statistics are generally not available. Although only the initial year a player played with a team is listed ("1880 Buffalo (N), 1885 Louisville (AA)"), generally the period of time is inclusive, so that the reader can generally assume the player was with Buffalo from 1880 through 1885 and with Louisville from 1885 on.

THE BASEBALL LEAGUES, 1871–1982

DATE OF ORIGIN	NAME OF LEAGUE	ABBREVIATION
March 1871	National Association of Professional Baseball Players	NAP
February 1876	National League	N
January 1884	The Union Association	U
February 1885	Brotherhood of Professional Ball Players	P
February 1891	American Association	AA
January 1894	Western Association	W
February 1901	American League	A
January 1914	Federal League	F

CAL ABRAMS B. March 2, 1924, Philadelphia, Pa.
B.L., T.L. 5'11½" 195 lbs.
(OUTFIELD, 1ST BASE)

YEAR	CLUB	BA	G	AB	R	H	2B	3B	HR	RBI
1949	BROOKLYN (N)	.083	8	24	6	2	1	0	0	0
1950	BROOKLYN (N)	.205	38	44	4	9	1	0	0	4
1951	BROOKLYN (N)	.280	67	150	27	42	8	0	3	19
1952	BROOKLYN (N)	.200	10	10	1	2	0	0	0	0
1952	Cincinnati (N)									
	(year totals)	.274	71	168	24	46	9	2	2	24
1953	Pittsburgh (N)	.286	119	448	66	128	10	6	15	43
1954	Pittsburgh (N)									
1954	Baltimore (A)									
	(year totals)	.280	132	465	73	130	23	8	6	27
1955	Baltimore (A)	.243	118	309	56	75	12	3	6	32
1956	Chicago (A)	.333	4	3	0	1	0	0	0	0
	Eight years	.269	567	1611	257	433	64	19	32	138

MORRIE ADERHOLT B. Sept. 13, 1915, Mount Olive, N.C.
D. March 18, 1955
B.L., T.R. 6'1" 188 lbs.
(2ND BASE, OUTFIELD)

YEAR	CLUB	BA	G	AB	R	H	2B	3B	HR	RBI
1944	BROOKLYN (N)	.271	17	59	9	16	2	3	0	10
1945	BROOKLYN (N)	.217	39	60	4	13	1	0	0	6
1945	Boston (N)									
	(year totals)	.290	70	162	19	47	5	0	2	17
	Five years (total)	.267	106	262	36	70	7	3	3	32

EDDIE AINSMITH B. Feb. 4, 1890, Cambridge, Mass.
B.R., T.R. 5'11" 180 lbs.
(CATCHER, PITCHER, 1ST BASE)

YEAR	CLUB	BA	G	AB	R	H	2B	3B	HR	RBI
1923	BROOKLYN (N)	.200	2	5	0	1	0	0	0	0
	Fifteen years (total)	.232	1068	3048	299	707	108	54	22	317

LUIS ALCARAZ B. June 20, 1941, Humacao, Puerto Rico
B.R., T.R. 5'9" 165 lbs.
(2ND BASE, 3RD BASE, SHORTSTOP)

YEAR	CLUB	BA	G	AB	R	H	2B	3B	HR	RBI
1967	LOS ANGELES (N)	.233	17	60	1	14	1	0	0	3
1968	LOS ANGELES (N)	.151	41	106	4	16	1	0	2	5
	Four years (total)	.192	115	365	30	70	9	2	4	29

HORACE ALLEN B. June 11, 1899, DeLand, Fla.
B.B., T.R. 6' 187 lbs.
(OUTFIELD)

YEAR	CLUB	BA	G	AB	R	H	2B	3B	HR	RBI
1919	BROOKLYN (N)	.000	4	7	0	0	0	0	0	0

RICHIE ALLEN B. March 8, 1942, Wampum, Pa.
B.R., T.R. 5'8½" 185 lbs.
(OUTFIELD, 1ST BASE, 2ND BASE, SHORTSTOP)

YEAR	CLUB	BA	G	AB	R	H	2B	3B	HR	RBI
1963	Philadelphia (N)	.292	10	24	6	7	2	1	0	2
1964	Philadelphia (N)	.318	162	632	125	201	38	13	29	91
1965	Philadelphia (N)	.302	161	619	93	187	31	14	20	85
1966	Philadelphia (N)	.317	141	524	112	166	25	10	40	110
1967	Philadelphia (N)	.307	122	463	89	142	31	10	23	77
1968	Philadelphia (N)	.263	152	521	87	137	17	9	33	90
1969	Philadelphia (N)	.288	118	438	79	126	23	3	32	89
1970	St. Louis (N)	.279	122	459	88	128	17	5	34	101
1971	LOS ANGELES (N)	.295	155	549	82	162	24	1	23	90
1972	Chicago (A)	.308	148	506	90	156	28	5	37	113

YEAR	CLUB	BA	G	AB	R	H	2B	3B	HR	RBI
1973	Chicago (A)	.316	72	250	39	79	20	3	16	41
1974	Chicago (A)	.301	128	462	84	139	23	1	32	88
1975	Philadelphia (N)	.233	119	412	52	97	21	3	12	62
1976	Philadelphia (N)	.268	85	298	52	80	16	1	15	49
1977	Oakland (A)	.240	54	171	19	41	4	0	5	31
	Fifteen years	.292	1749	6332	1099	1848	320	79	351	1119

MEL ALMADA   B. Feb. 7, 1913, Hwatabampo, Mexico
B.L., T.L. 6' 170 lbs.
(OUTFIELD, 1ST BASE)

YEAR	CLUB	BA	G	AB	R	H	2B	3B	HR	RBI
1939	BROOKLYN (N)	.214	39	112	11	24	4	0	0	3
	Seven years (total)	.284	646	2483	363	706	107	27	15	197

WHITEY ALPERMAN   B. Nov. 11, 1879, Etna, Pa.
D. Dec. 25, 1942, Pittsburgh, Pa.
B.R., T.R. 5'10" 180 lbs.
(OUTFIELD, 2nd BASE, 3rd BASE, SHORTSTOP)

YEAR	CLUB	BA	G	AB	R	H	2B	3B	HR	RBI
1906	BROOKLYN (N)	.252	128	441	38	111	15	7	3	46
1907	BROOKLYN (N)	.233	141	558	44	130	23	16	2	39
1908	BROOKLYN (N)	.197	70	213	17	42	3	1	1	15
1909	BROOKLYN (N)	.248	111	420	35	104	19	12	1	41
	Four years	.237	450	1632	134	387	60	36	7	141

JESUS ALVAREZ   B. Feb. 28, 1953, Cinega Baja, Puerto Rico
B.R., T.R. 6' 165 lbs.
(OUTFIELD)

YEAR	CLUB	BA	G	AB	R	H	2B	3B	HR	RBI
1973	LOS ANGELES (N)	.250	4	4	0	1	1	0	0	0
1974	LOS ANGELES (N)	.000	2	1	0	0	0	0	0	0
1975	LOS ANGELES (N)	.000	4	4	0	0	0	0	0	0
	Four years (total)	.157	25	51	4	8	2	0	2	8

SANDY AMOROS   B. Jan. 30, 1930, Havana, Cuba
B.L., T.R. 5'8½" 165 lbs.
(OUTFIELD)

YEAR	CLUB	BA	G	AB	R	H	2B	3B	HR	RBI
1952	BROOKLYN (N)	.250	20	44	10	11	3	1	0	3
1954	BROOKLYN (N)	.274	79	263	44	72	18	6	9	34
1955	BROOKLYN (N)	.247	119	388	59	96	16	7	10	51
1956	BROOKLYN (N)	.260	114	292	53	76	11	8	16	58
1957	BROOKLYN (N)	.277	106	238	40	66	7	1	7	26
1959	LOS ANGELES (N)	.200	5	5	1	1	0	0	0	1
1960	LOS ANGELES (N)									
1960	Detroit (A)									
	(year totals)	.148	74	81	8	12	0	0	1	7
	Seven years	.255	517	1311	215	334	55	23	43	180
	World Series									
	Three years	.161	12	31	4	5	0	0	1	4

FERRELL ANDERSON   B. Jan. 9, 1918, Maple City, Kan.
D. March 12, 1978, Joplin, Mo.
B.R., T.R. 6'1" 200 lbs.
(CATCHER)

YEAR	CLUB	BA	G	AB	R	H	2B	3B	HR	RBI
1946	BROOKLYN (N)	.256	70	199	19	51	10	0	2	14
	Two years (total)	.261	88	234	20	61	12	0	2	15

GEORGE ANDERSON B. Sept. 26, 1889, Cleveland, Ohio
D. May 28, 1962, Warrensville Heights, Ohio
B.L., T.R. 5'8½" 160 lbs.
(OUTFIELD)

YEAR	CLUB	BA	G	AB	R	H	2B	3B	HR	RBI
1914	BROOKLYN (F)	.316	98	364	58	115	13	3	3	24
1915	BROOKLYN (F)	.264	136	511	70	135	23	9	2	39
1918	St. Louis (N)	.295	35	132	20	39	4	5	0	6
	Three years	.287	269	1007	148	289	40	17	5	69

JOHN ANDERSON B. Dec. 14, 1873, Sasbourg, Norway
D. July 23, 1949, Worcester, Mass.
B.B., T.R. 6'2" 180 lbs.
(OUTFIELD, 1st BASE)

YEAR	CLUB	BA	G	AB	R	H	2B	3B	HR	RBI
1894	BROOKLYN (N)	.302	17	63	14	19	1	3	1	19
1895	BROOKLYN (N)	.286	102	419	76	120	11	14	9	37
1896	BROOKLYN (N)	.314	108	430	70	135	23	17	1	55
1897	BROOKLYN (N)	.325	117	492	93	160	28	12	4	85
1898	BROOKLYN (N)	.243	25	70	15	17	6	4	1	15
1898	Washington (A)									
	(year totals)	.294	135	520	82	153	33	22	9	81
1899	BROOKLYN (N)	.269	117	439	65	118	18	7	3	92
1901	Milwaukee (A)	.330	138	576	90	190	46	7	8	99
1902	St. Louis (A)	.284	126	524	60	149	29	6	4	85
1903	St. Louis (A)	.284	138	550	65	156	34	8	2	78
1904	New York (A)	.278	143	558	62	155	27	12	3	82
1905	New York (A)									
1905	Washington (A)									
	(year totals)	.279	125	499	62	139	24	7	1	52
1906	Washington (A)	.271	151	583	62	158	25	4	3	70
1907	Washington (A)	.288	87	333	33	96	12	4	0	44
1908	Chicago (A)	.262	123	355	36	93	17	1	0	47
	Fourteen years	.290	1627	6341	870	1841	328	124	48	976

ED ANDREWS B. April 5, 1859, Painesville, Ohio
D. Aug. 12, 1934, West Palm Beach, Fla.
B.R., T.R. 5'8" 160 lbs.
(OUTFIELD, 2ND BASE)

YEAR	CLUB	BA	G	AB	R	H	2B	3B	HR	RBI
1890	BROOKLYN (P)	.253	94	395	84	100	14	2	3	38
	Eight years (total)	.257	774	3233	602	830	117	26	12	232

STAN ANDREWS B. April 17, 1917, Lynn, Mass.
B.R., T.R. 5'11" 178 lbs.
(CATCHER)

YEAR	CLUB	BA	G	AB	R	H	2B	3B	HR	RBI
1944	BROOKLYN (N)	.125	4	8	1	1	0	0	0	1
1945	BROOKLYN (N)	.163	21	49	5	8	0	1	0	2
	Four years (total)	.215	70	149	11	32	2	1	1	12

PAT ANKENMAN B. Dec. 23, 1912, Houston, Texas
B.R., T.R. 5'4" 125 lbs.
(2ND BASE, OUTFIELD)

YEAR	CLUB	BA	G	AB	R	H	2B	3B	HR	RBI
1943	BROOKLYN (N)	.500	1	2	1	1	0	0	0	0
1944	BROOKLYN (N)	.250	13	24	1	6	1	0	0	3
	Three years (total)	.241	15	29	2	7	1	0	0	3

BILL ANTONELLO B. May 19, 1927, Brooklyn, N.Y.
B.R., T.R. 5'9" 160 lbs.
(OUTFIELD)

YEAR	CLUB	BA	G	AB	R	H	2B	3B	HR	RBI
1953	BROOKLYN (N)	.163	40	43	9	7	1	1	1	4

JIMMY ARCHER   B. May 13, 1883, Dublin, Ireland
B.R., T.R. 5'10" 168 lbs.
(CATCHER, 1ST BASE, 2ND BASE, OUTFIELD, 3RD BASE)

YEAR	CLUB	BA	G	AB	R	H	2B	3B	HR	RBI
1918	BROOKLYN (N)	.273	9	22	3	6	0	0	1	0
	(year totals)	.208	42	106	10	22	2	3	0	5
	Twelve years (total)	.250	846	2645	247	660	106	34	16	296

BOB ASPROMONTE   B. June 19, 1938, Brooklyn, N.Y.
B.R., T.R. 6'2" 170 lbs.
(3RD BASE, SHORTSTOP, OUTFIELD)

YEAR	CLUB	BA	G	AB	R	H	2B	3B	HR	RBI
1956	BROOKLYN (N)	.000	1	1	0	0	0	0	0	0
1960	LOS ANGELES (N)	.182	21	55	1	10	1	0	1	6
1961	LOS ANGELES (N)	.241	47	58	7	14	3	0	0	2
	Thirteen years (total)	.252	1324	4369	386	1103	135	26	60	457

RICK AUERBACH   B. Feb. 15, 1950, Glendale, Calif.
B.R., T.R. 6' 165 lbs.
(SHORTSTOP, 2ND BASE, 3RD BASE)

YEAR	CLUB	BA	G	AB	R	H	2B	3B	HR	RBI
1971	Milwaukee (A)	.203	79	236	22	45	10	0	1	9
1972	Milwaukee (A)	.218	153	554	50	121	16	3	2	30
1973	Milwaukee (A)	.100	6	10	2	1	1	0	0	0
1974	LOS ANGELES (N)	.342	45	73	12	25	0	0	1	4
1975	LOS ANGELES (N)	.224	85	170	18	38	9	0	0	12
1976	LOS ANGELES (N)	.128	36	47	7	6	0	0	0	1
1977	Cincinnati (N)	.156	33	45	5	7	2	0	0	3
1978	Cincinnati (N)	.327	63	55	17	18	6	0	2	5
1979	Cincinnati (N)	.210	62	100	17	21	8	1	1	12
1980	Cincinnati (N)	.333	24	33	5	11	1	1	1	4
1981	Seattle (A)	.155	38	84	12	13	3	0	1	6
	Eleven years	.220	624	1407	167	309	56	5	9	86
League Championship										
	Two years	.333	3	3	0	1	1	0	0	0
World Series										
	One year		1	0	0	0	0	0	0	0

CHARLIE BABB   B. Feb. 20, 1873, Milwaukie, Ore.
D. March 20, 1954, Portland, Ore.
B.B., T.R. 5'10½" 165 lbs.
(SHORTSTOP, 1ST BASE, 2ND BASE, 3RD BASE)

YEAR	CLUB	BA	G	AB	R	H	2B	3B	HR	RBI
1903	New York (N)	.248	121	424	68	105	15	8	46	46
1904	BROOKLYN (N)	.265	151	521	49	138	18	3	53	53
1905	BROOKLYN (N)	.187	75	235	27	44	8	2	17	17
	Three years	.243	347	1180	144	287	41	13	0	116

BOB BAILEY   B. Oct. 13, 1942, Long Beach, Calif.
B.R., T.R. 6'1" 180 lbs.
(1ST BASE, 3RD BASE, SHORTSTOP, OUTFIELD)

YEAR	CLUB	BA	G	AB	R	H	2B	3B	HR	RBI
1962	Pittsburgh (N)	.167	14	42	6	7	2	1	0	6
1963	Pittsburgh (N)	.228	154	570	60	130	15	3	12	45
1964	Pittsburgh (N)	.281	143	530	73	149	26	3	11	51
1965	Pittsburgh (N)	.256	159	626	87	160	28	3	11	49
1966	Pittsburgh (N)	.279	126	380	51	106	19	3	13	46
1967	LOS ANGELES (N)	.227	116	322	21	73	8	2	4	28
1968	LOS ANGELES (N)	.227	105	322	24	73	9	3	8	39
1969	Montreal (N)	.265	111	358	46	95	16	6	9	53
1970	Montreal (N)	.287	131	352	77	101	19	3	28	84
1971	Montreal (N)	.251	157	545	65	137	21	4	14	83
1972	Montreal (N)	.233	143	489	55	114	10	4	16	57
1973	Montreal (N)	.273	151	513	77	140	25	4	26	86
1974	Montreal (N)	.280	152	507	69	142	20	2	20	73
1975	Montreal (N)	.273	106	227	23	62	5	0	5	30
1976	Cincinnati (N)	.298	69	124	17	37	6	1	6	23

YEAR	CLUB	BA	G	AB	R	H	2B	3B	HR	RBI
1977	Cincinnati (N)									
1977	Boston (A)									
	(year totals)	.247	51	81	9	20	2	1	2	11
1978	Boston (A)	.191	43	94	12	18	3	0	4	9
	Seventeen years	.257	1931	6082	772	1564	234	43	189	773

GENE BAILEY B. Nov. 25, 1893, Pearsall, Texas
D. Nov. 14, 1973, Houston, Texas
B.R., T.R. 5'8" 160 lbs.
(OUTFIELD, 1st BASE)

YEAR	CLUB	BA	G	AB	R	H	2B	3B	HR	RBI
1923	BROOKLYN (N)	.265	127	411	71	109	11	7	1	42
1924	BROOKLYN (N)	.239	18	46	7	11	3	0	1	4
	Five years (total)	.246	213	634	95	156	16	7	2	52

DOUG BAIRD B. Sept. 27, 1891, St. Charles, Mo.
D. June 13, 1967, Thomasville, Ga.
B.R., T.R. 5'9½" 148 lbs.
(OUTFIELD, SHORTSTOP, 2nd BASE, 3rd BASE)

YEAR	CLUB	BA	G	AB	R	H	2B	3B	HR	RBI
1919	BROOKLYN (N)	.183	20	60	6	11	0	1	0	8
	(year totals)	.236	102	335	43	79	13	5	2	42
1920	BROOKLYN (N)	.333	6	6	1	2	0	0	0	1
	Six years (total)	.234	617	2106	230	492	86	45	6	191

DUSTY BAKER B. June 15, 1949, Riverside, Calif.
B.R., T.R. 6'2" 183 lbs.
(OUTFIELD)

YEAR	CLUB	BA	G	AB	R	H	2B	3B	HR	RBI
1968	Atlanta (N)	.400	6	5	0	2	0	0	0	0
1969	Atlanta (N)	.000	3	7	0	0	0	0	0	0
1970	Atlanta (N)	.292	13	24	3	7	0	0	0	4
1971	Atlanta (N)	.226	29	62	2	14	2	0	0	4
1972	Atlanta (N)	.321	127	446	62	143	27	2	17	76
1973	Atlanta (N)	.288	159	604	101	174	29	4	21	99
1974	Atlanta (N)	.256	149	574	80	147	35	0	20	69
1975	Atlanta (N)	.261	142	494	63	129	18	2	19	72
1976	LOS ANGELES (N)	.242	112	384	36	93	13	0	4	39
1977	LOS ANGELES (N)	.291	153	533	86	155	26	1	30	86
1978	LOS ANGELES (N)	.262	149	522	62	137	24	1	11	66
1979	LOS ANGELES (N)	.274	151	554	86	152	29	1	23	88
1980	LOS ANGELES (N)	.294	153	579	80	170	26	4	29	97
1981	LOS ANGELES (N)	.320	103	400	48	128	17	3	9	49
1982	LOS ANGELES (N)	.300	147	570	80	171	19	1	23	88
1983	LOS ANGELES (N)	.260	149	531	71	138	25	1	15	73
	Sixteen years (total)	.280	1745	6289	860	1760	290	20	221	910
Division Playoff										
	One year	.167	5	18	2	3	1	0	0	1
League Championship										
	Three years	.375	13	48	8	18	4	0	2	12

World Series

YEAR	CLUB	BA	G	AB	R	H	2B	3B	HR	RBI
1977	LOS ANGELES (N)	.292	6	24	4	7	0	0	1	5
1978	LOS ANGELES (N)	.238	6	21	2	5	0	0	1	1
1981	LOS ANGELES (N)	.167	6	24	3	4	0	0	0	1
	Three years	.232	18	69	9	16	0	0	2	7

DAVE BANCROFT B. April 20, 1891, Sioux City, Iowa
B.B., T.R. 5'9½" 160 lbs.
(SHORTSTOP, 2ND BASE, 3RD BASE, OUTFIELD)

YEAR	CLUB	BA	G	AB	R	H	2B	3B	HR	RBI
1915	Philadelphia (N)	.254	153	563	85	143	18	2	7	30
1916	Philadelphia (N)	.212	142	477	53	101	10	0	3	33

YEAR	CLUB	BA	G	AB	R	H	2B	3B	HR	RBI
1917	Philadelphia (N)	.243	127	478	56	116	22	5	4	43
1918	Philadelphia (N)	.265	125	499	69	132	19	4	0	26
1919	Philadelphia (N)	.272	93	335	45	91	13	7	0	25
1920	Philadelphia (N)									
1920	New York (N)									
	(year totals)	.299	150	613	102	183	36	9	0	36
1921	New York (N)	.318	153	606	121	193	26	15	6	67
1922	New York (N)	.321	156	651	117	209	41	5	4	60
1923	New York (N)	.304	107	444	80	135	33	3	1	31
1924	Boston (N)	.279	79	319	49	89	11	1	2	21
1925	Boston (N)	.319	128	479	75	153	29	8	2	49
1926	Boston (N)	.311	127	453	70	141	18	6	1	44
1927	Boston (N)	.243	111	375	44	91	13	4	1	31
1928	BROOKLYN (N)	.247	149	515	47	127	19	5	0	51
1929	BROOKLYN (N)	.277	104	358	35	99	11	3	1	44
1930	New York (N)	.059	10	17	0	1	1	0	0	0
	Sixteen years	.279	1913	7182	1048	2004	320	77	32	591
World Series										
	Four years	.172	24	93	10	16	1	0	0	7

RED BARKLEY   B. March 12, 1936, Martinsburg, W. Va.
B.R., T.R. 5'11" 160 lbs.
(2ND BASE, SHORTSTOP, 3RD BASE)

YEAR	CLUB	BA	G	AB	R	H	2B	3B	HR	RBI
1943	BROOKLYN (N)	.314	20	51	6	16	3	0	0	7
	Three years (total)	.264	63	163	16	43	9	0	0	21

BOB BARRETT   B. Jan. 27, 1899, Atlanta, Ga.
B.R., T.R. 5'11" 175 lbs.
(3RD BASE, 2ND BASE, 1ST BASE, OUTFIELD)

YEAR	CLUB	BA	G	AB	R	H	2B	3B	HR	RBI
1925	BROOKLYN (N)	.000	1	1	0	0	0	0	0	1
	(year totals)	.303	15	33	1	10	1	0	0	8
1927	BROOKLYN (N)	.259	99	355	29	92	10	2	5	38
	Five years (total)	.260	239	650	57	169	23	5	10	86

BOYD BARTLEY   B. Feb. 11, 1920, Chicago, Ill.
B.R., T.R. 5'8½" 165 lbs.
(SHORTSTOP)

YEAR	CLUB	BA	G	AB	R	H	2B	3B	HR	RBI
1943	BROOKLYN (N)	.048	9	21	0	1	0	0	0	1

AL BASHANG   B. Aug. 22, 1888, Cincinnati, Ohio
B.B., T.R. 5'8" 150 lbs.
(OUTFIELD)

YEAR	CLUB	BA	G	AB	R	H	2B	3B	HR	RBI
1918	BROOKLYN (N)	.200	2	5	0	1	0	0	0	0
	Two years (total)	.118	7	17	3	2	0	0	0	0

EDDIE BASINSKI   B. Nov. 4, 1922, Buffalo, N.Y.
B.R., T.R. 6'1" 172 lbs.
(SHORTSTOP, 2ND BASE)

YEAR	CLUB	BA	G	AB	R	H	2B	3B	HR	RBI
1944	BROOKLYN (N)	.257	39	105	13	27	4	1	0	9
1945	BROOKLYN (N)	.262	108	336	30	88	9	4	0	33
	Three years (total)	.244	203	602	58	147	19	7	4	59

EMIL BATCH
B. Jan. 21, 1880, Brooklyn, N.Y.
B.R., T.R.
(3RD BASE, OUTFIELD, SHORTSTOP, 2ND BASE)

YEAR	CLUB	BA	G	AB	R	H	2B	3B	HR	RBI
1904	BROOKLYN (N)	.255	28	94	9	24	1	2	2	7
1905	BROOKLYN (N)	.252	145	568	64	143	20	11	5	49
1906	BROOKLYN (N)	.256	59	203	23	52	7	6	0	11
1907	BROOKLYN (N)	.247	116	388	38	96	10	3	0	31
	Four years	.251	348	1253	134	315	38	22	7	98

JIM BAXES
B. July 5, 1928, San Francisco, Calif.
B.R., T.R. 6'1" 190 lbs.
(2ND BASE, 3RD BASE)

YEAR	CLUB	BA	G	AB	R	H	2B	3B	HR	RBI
1959	LOS ANGELES (N)	.303	11	33	4	10	1	0	2	5
	One year (total)	.246	88	280	39	69	12	0	17	39

ERVE BECK
B. July 19, 1878, Toledo, Ohio
B.R., T.R. 5'10" 168 lbs.
(2ND BASE, 1ST BASE, OUTFIELD, SHORTSTOP)

YEAR	CLUB	BA	G	AB	R	H	2B	3B	HR	RBI
1899	BROOKLYN (N)	.167	8	24	2	4	2	0	0	2
	Three years (total)	.291	232	912	122	265	42	11	9	123

WAYNE BELARDI
B. Sept. 5, 1930, Calistoga, Calif.
B.L., T.L. 6'1" 185 lbs.
(1ST BASE, OUTFIELD)

YEAR	CLUB	BA	G	AB	R	H	2B	3B	HR	RBI
1950	BROOKLYN (N)	.000	10	10	0	0	0	0	0	0
1951	BROOKLYN (N)	.333	3	3	1	1	0	1	0	0
1953	BROOKLYN (N)	.239	69	163	19	39	3	2	11	34
1954	BROOKLYN (N)	.222	11	9	0	2	0	0	0	1
	Six years (total)	.242	263	592	71	143	13	5	28	74
World Series	One year	.000	2	2	0	0	0	0	0	0

MOE BERG
B. March 2, 1902, New York, N.Y.
D. May 29, 1972, Belleville, N.J.
B.R., T.R. 6'1" 185 lbs.
(CATCHER, SHORTSTOP, 2ND BASE, 3RD BASE, 1ST BASE)

YEAR	CLUB	BA	G	AB	R	H	2B	3B	HR	RBI
1923	BROOKLYN (N)	.186	49	129	9	24	3	2	0	6
	Fifteen years (total)	.243	662	1812	150	441	71	6	6	206

BILL BERGEN
B. June 13, 1873, North Brookfield, Mass.
B.R., T.R. 6' 184 lbs.
(CATCHER, 1ST BASE)

YEAR	CLUB	BA	G	AB	R	H	2B	3B	HR	RBI
1901	Cincinnati (N)	.179	87	308	15	55	6	4	1	17
1902	Cincinnati (N)	.180	89	322	19	58	8	3	0	19
1903	Cincinnati (N)	.227	58	207	21	47	4	2	0	21
1904	BROOKLYN (N)	.182	96	329	17	60	4	2	0	12
1905	BROOKLYN (N)	.190	79	247	12	47	3	2	0	22
1906	BROOKLYN (N)	.159	103	353	9	56	3	3	0	19
1907	BROOKLYN (N)	.159	51	138	2	22	3	0	0	14
1908	BROOKLYN (N)	.175	99	302	8	53	8	2	0	15
1909	BROOKLYN (N)	.139	112	346	16	48	1	1	1	15
1910	BROOKLYN (N)	.161	89	249	11	40	2	1	0	14
1911	BROOKLYN (N)	.132	84	227	8	30	3	1	0	10
	Eleven years	.170	947	3028	138	516	45	21	2	193

RAY BERRES

B. Aug. 21, 1908, Kenosha, Wis.
B.R., T.R. 5'9" 170 lbs.
(CATCHER)

YEAR	CLUB	BA	G	AB	R	H	2B	3B	HR	RBI
1934	BROOKLYN (N)	.215	39	79	7	17	4	0	0	3
1936	BROOKLYN (N)	.240	105	267	16	64	10	1	1	13
	Eleven years (total)	.216	561	1330	96	287	37	3	3	78

LOU BIERBAUER

B. Sept. 28, 1865, Erie, Pa.
B.R., T.R.
(2ND BASE, 3RD BASE, CATCHER, PITCHER, SHORTSTOP)

YEAR	CLUB	BA	G	AB	R	H	2B	3B	HR	RBI
*1890	BROOKLYN (P)	.306	133	589	128	180	31	11	7	99
	Thirteen years (total)	.267	1383	5706	819	1521	208	95	33	706

*1886 Philadelphia (AA)

DEL BISSONETTE

B. Sept. 6, 1899, Winthrop, Maine
B.L., T.L. 5'1" 180 lbs.
(1ST BASE)

YEAR	CLUB	BA	G	AB	R	H	2B	3B	HR	RBI
1928	BROOKLYN (N)	.320	155	587	90	188	30	13	25	106
1929	BROOKLYN (N)	.281	116	431	68	121	28	10	12	75
1930	BROOKLYN (N)	.336	146	572	102	192	33	13	16	113
1931	BROOKLYN (N)	.290	152	587	90	170	19	14	12	87
1933	BROOKLYN (N)	.246	35	114	9	28	7	0	0	10
	Five years	.305	604	2291	359	699	117	50	65	391

LU BLUE

B. March 5, 1897, Washington, D.C.
B.B., T.L. 5'10" 165 lbs.
(1ST BASE)

YEAR	CLUB	BA	G	AB	R	H	2B	3B	HR	RBI
1933	BROOKLYN (N)	.000	1	1	0	0	0	0	0	0
	Thirteen years (total)	.287	1615	5904	1151	1696	319	109	44	692

JOHN BOLLING

B. Feb. 20, 1917, Mobile, Ala.
B.L., T.L. 5'11" 168 lbs.
(1ST BASE)

YEAR	CLUB	BA	G	AB	R	H	2B	3B	HR	RBI
1944	BROOKLYN (N)	.351	56	131	21	46	14	1	1	25
	Two years (total)	.313	125	342	48	107	25	1	4	38

FRANK BONNER

B. Aug. 20, 1869, Lowell, Mass.
T.R.
(2ND BASE)

YEAR	CLUB	BA	G	AB	R	H	2B	3B	HR	RBI
1896	BROOKLYN (N)	.176	9	34	8	6	2	0	0	5
	Six years (total)	.257	246	949	115	244	44	8	4	115

IKE BOONE

B. Feb. 17, 1897, Samantha, Ala.
B.L., T.R. 6' 195 lbs.
(OUTFIELD)

YEAR	CLUB	BA	G	AB	R	H	2B	3B	HR	RBI
1930	BROOKLYN (N)	.297	40	101	13	30	9	1	3	13
1931	BROOKLYN (N)	.200	6	5	0	1	0	0	0	0
1932	BROOKLYN (N)	.143	13	21	2	3	1	0	0	2
	Eight years (total)	.319	356	1159	176	370	77	10	26	192

FRENCHY BORDAGARAY

B. Jan. 3, 1912, Coalinga, Calif.
B.R., T.R. 5'7½" 175 lbs.
(OUTFIELD, 3RD BASE)

YEAR	CLUB	BA	G	AB	R	H	2B	3B	HR	RBI
1934	Chicago (A)	.322	29	87	12	28	3	1	0	2
1935	BROOKLYN (N)	.282	120	422	69	119	19	6	1	39
1936	BROOKLYN (N)	.315	125	372	63	117	21	3	4	31
1937	St. Louis (N)	.293	96	300	43	88	11	4	1	37
1938	St. Louis (N)	.282	81	156	19	44	5	1	0	21
1939	Cincinnati (N)	.197	63	122	19	24	5	1	0	12
1941	New York (A)	.260	36	73	10	19	1	0	0	4
1942	BROOKLYN (N)	.241	48	58	11	14	2	0	0	5
1943	BROOKLYN (N)	.302	89	268	47	81	18	2	0	19
1944	BROOKLYN (N)	.281	130	501	85	141	26	4	6	51
1945	BROOKLYN (N)	.256	113	273	32	70	9	6	2	49
	Eleven years	.283	930	2632	410	745	120	28	14	270
World Series	Two years	—	3	0	0	0	0	0	0	0

BOB BORKOWSKI

B. Jan. 27, 1926, Dayton, Ohio
B.R., T.R. 6' 182 lbs.
(OUTFIELD)

YEAR	CLUB	BA	G	AB	R	H	2B	3B	HR	RBI
1955	BROOKLYN (N)	.105	9	19	2	2	0	0	0	0
	Six years (total)	.251	470	1170	126	294	43	10	16	112

BUZZ BOYLE

B. Feb. 9, 1908, Cincinnati, Ohio
B.L., T.L. 5'11½" 170 lbs.
(OUTFIELD)

YEAR	CLUB	BA	G	AB	R	H	2B	3B	HR	RBI
1929	Boston (N)	.263	17	57	8	15	2	1	1	2
1930	Boston (N)	.000	1	1	0	0	0	0	0	0
1933	BROOKLYN (N)	.299	93	338	38	101	13	4	0	31
1934	BROOKLYN (N)	.305	128	472	88	144	26	10	7	48
1935	BROOKLYN (N)	.272	127	475	51	129	17	9	4	44
	Five years	.290	366	1343	185	389	58	24	12	125

GIB BRACK

B. March 29, 1912, Chicago, Ill.
B.R., T.R. 5'9" 170 lbs.
(OUTFIELD)

YEAR	CLUB	BA	G	AB	R	H	2B	3B	HR	RBI
1937	BROOKLYN (N)	.274	112	372	60	102	27	9	5	38
1938	BROOKLYN (N)	.214	40	56	10	12	2	1	1	6
	Three years (total)	.279	315	980	150	273	70	18	16	113

BILL BRADLEY

B. Feb. 13, 1878, Cleveland, Ohio
B.R., T.R. 6' 185 lbs.
(3RD BASE)

YEAR	CLUB	BA	G	AB	R	H	2B	3B	HR	RBI
1914	BROOKLYN (F)	.500	7	6	1	3	1	0	0	3
	Fourteen years (total)	.271	1461	5433	756	1473	275	84	34	552

HUGH BRADLEY

B. May 23, 1885, Grafton, Mass.
B.R., T.R.
(1ST BASE)

YEAR	CLUB	BA	G	AB	R	H	2B	3B	HR	RBI
1915	Pittsburgh (F)									
1915	BROOKLYN (F)									
1915	Newark (F)									
	(year totals)	.240	75	225	10	54	7	3	0	26
	Five years (total)	.261	277	913	84	238	46	12	2	117

MARK BRADLEY B. Dec. 3, 1956, Elizabethtown, Ky.
B.R., T.R. 6'1" 180 lbs.
(OUTFIELD)

YEAR	CLUB	BA	G	AB	R	H	2B	3B	HR	RBI
1981	LOS ANGELES (N)	.167	9	6	2	1	1	0	0	0
1982	LOS ANGELES (N)	.333	8	3	1	1	0	0	0	0
	Two years	.118	17	9	3	2	1	0	0	0

BOBBY BRAGAN B. Oct. 30, 1917, Birmingham, Ala.
B.R., T.R. 5'10½" 175 lbs.
(SHORTSTOP, CATCHER)

YEAR	CLUB	BA	G	AB	R	H	2B	3B	HR	RBI
1940	Philadelphia (N)	.222	132	474	36	105	14	1	7	44
1941	Philadelphia (N)	.251	154	557	37	140	19	3	4	69
1942	Philadelphia (N)	.218	109	335	17	73	12	2	2	15
1943	BROOKLYN (N)	.264	74	220	17	58	7	2	2	24
1944	BROOKLYN (N)	.267	94	266	26	71	8	4	0	17
1947	BROOKLYN (N)	.194	25	36	3	7	2	0	0	3
1948	BROOKLYN (N)	.167	9	12	0	2	0	0	0	0
	Seven years	.240	597	1900	136	456	62	12	15	172
World Series										
	One year	1.000	1	1	0	1	1	0	0	1

RUBE BRESSLER B. Oct. 23, 1894, Coder, Pa.
B.R., T.L. 6' 187 lbs.
(OUTFIELD, 1ST BASE, PITCHER)

YEAR	CLUB	BA	G	AB	R	H	2B	3B	HR	RBI
1914	Philadelphia (A)	.216	29	51	6	11	1	1	0	4
1915	Philadelphia (A)	.145	33	55	9	8	0	1	1	4
1916	Philadelphia (A)	.200	4	5	1	1	0	1	0	1
1917	Cincinnati (N)	.200	3	5	0	1	0	0	0	0
1918	Cincinnati (N)	.274	23	62	10	17	5	0	0	6
1919	Cincinnati (N)	.206	61	165	22	34	3	4	2	17
1920	Cincinnati (N)	.267	21	30	4	8	1	0	0	3
1921	Cincinnati (N)	.307	109	323	41	99	18	6	1	54
1922	Cincinnati (N)	.264	52	53	7	14	0	2	0	8
1923	Cincinnati (N)	.277	54	119	25	33	3	1	0	18
1924	Cincinnati (N)	.347	115	383	41	133	14	13	4	49
1925	Cincinnati (N)	.348	97	319	43	111	17	6	4	61
1926	Cincinnati (N)	.357	86	297	58	106	15	9	1	51
1927	Cincinnati (N)	.291	124	467	43	136	14	8	3	77
1928	BROOKLYN (N)	.295	145	501	78	148	29	13	4	70
1929	BROOKLYN (N)	.318	136	456	72	145	22	8	9	77
1930	BROOKLYN (N)	.299	109	335	53	100	12	8	3	52
1931	BROOKLYN (N)	.281	67	153	22	43	4	5	0	26
1932	Philadelphia (N)									
1932	St. Louis (N)									
	(year totals)	.216	37	102	9	22	6	1	0	8
	Nineteen years	.301	1305	3881	544	1170	164	87	32	586

ROCKY BRIDGES B. Aug. 7, 1927, Refugio, Texas
B.R., T.R. 5'8" 170 lbs.
(SHORTSTOP, 2ND BASE, 3RD BASE)

YEAR	CLUB	BA	G	AB	R	H	2B	3B	HR	RBI
1951	BROOKLYN (N)	.254	63	134	13	34	7	0	1	15
1952	BROOKLYN (N)	.196	51	56	9	11	3	0	0	2
	Eleven years (total)	.247	919	2272	245	562	80	11	16	187

MATT BRODERICK B. Dec. 2, 1876, Lattimer Mines, Pa.
T.R. 5'6½" 135 lbs.
(2ND BASE)

YEAR	CLUB	BA	G	AB	R	H	2B	3B	HR	RBI
1903	BROOKLYN (N)	.000	2	2	0	0	0	0	0	0

DAN BROUTHERS B. May 8, 1858, Sylvan Lake, N.Y.
D. Aug. 2, 1932, East Orange, N.J.
B.L., T.L. 6'2" 207 lbs.
(1ST BASE)

YEAR	CLUB	BA	G	AB	R	H	2B	3B	HR	RBI
*1890	Boston (P)	.345	123	464	117	160	36	9	1	97
1891	Boston (AA)	.350	130	486	117	170	26	19	5	108
1892	BROOKLYN (N)	.335	152	588	121	197	30	20	5	124
1893	BROOKLYN (N)	.337	77	282	57	95	21	11	2	59
1894	Baltimore (N)	.347	123	525	137	182	39	23	9	128
1895	Baltimore (N)									
1895	Louisville (N)									
	(year totals)	.300	29	120	15	36	12	1	2	20
1896	Philadelphia (N)	.344	57	218	42	75	13	3	1	41
1904	New York (N)	.000	2	5	0	0	0	0	0	0
	Nineteen years (total)	.343	1673	6716	1523	2304	461	206	106	1056

*1879 Troy (N), 1881 Buffalo (N), 1886 Detroit (N)

EDDIE BROWN B. July 17, 1891, Milligan, Neb.
B.R., T.R. 6'3" 190 lbs.
(OUTFIELD)

YEAR	CLUB	BA	G	AB	R	H	2B	3B	HR	RBI
1920	New York (N)	.125	3	8	1	1	1	0	0	0
1921	New York (N)	.281	70	128	16	36	6	2	0	12
1924	BROOKLYN (N)	.308	114	455	56	140	30	4	5	78
1925	BROOKLYN (N)	.306	153	618	88	189	39	11	5	99
1926	Boston (N)	.328	153	612	71	201	31	8	2	84
1927	Boston (N)	.306	155	558	64	171	35	6	2	75
1928	Boston (N)	.268	142	523	45	140	28	2	2	59
	Seven years	.303	790	2902	341	878	170	33	16	407

LINDSAY BROWN B. July 22, 1911, Mason, Texas
B.R., T.R. 5'10" 160 lbs.
(SHORTSTOP)

YEAR	CLUB	BA	G	AB	R	H	2B	3B	HR	RBI
1937	BROOKLYN (N)	.270	48	115	16	31	3	1	0	6

TOMMY BROWN B. Dec. 6, 1927, Brooklyn, N.Y.
B.R., T.R. 6'1" 170 lbs.
(SHORTSTOP, OUTFIELD, 3RD BASE)

YEAR	CLUB	BA	G	AB	R	H	2B	3B	HR	RBI
1944	BROOKLYN (N)	.164	46	146	17	24	4	0	0	8
1945	BROOKLYN (N)	.245	57	196	13	48	3	4	2	19
1947	BROOKLYN (N)	.235	15	34	3	8	1	0	0	2
1948	BROOKLYN (N)	.241	54	145	18	35	4	0	2	20
1949	BROOKLYN (N)	.303	41	89	14	27	2	0	3	18
1950	BROOKLYN (N)	.291	48	86	15	25	2	1	8	20
1951	BROOKLYN (N)	.160	11	25	2	4	2	0	0	1
1951	Philadelphia (N)									
	(year totals)	.213	89	221	26	47	4	1	10	33
1952	Philadelphia (N)									
1952	Chicago (N)									
	(year totals)	.302	79	225	26	68	12	0	4	26
1953	Chicago (N)	.196	65	138	19	27	7	1	2	13
	Nine years	.241	494	1280	151	309	39	7	31	159
World Series										
	One year	.000	2	2	0	0	0	0	0	0

GEORGE BROWNE B. Jan. 12, 1876, Richmond, Va.
B.L., T.R. 5'10" 160 lbs.
(OUTFIELD)

YEAR	CLUB	BA	G	AB	R	H	2B	3B	HR	RBI
1911	BROOKLYN (N)	.333	8	12	1	4	0	0	0	2
	Twelve years (total)	.273	1102	4300	614	1176	119	55	18	303

PETE BROWNING B. July 17, 1858, Louisville, Ky.
B.R., T.R. 6' 180 lbs.
(OUTFIELD)

YEAR	CLUB	BA	G	AB	R	H	2B	3B	HR	RBI
1894	BROOKLYN (N)	1.000	1	0	1	0	0	0	0	0
	Thirteen years (total)	.343	1185	4829	956	1654	299	89	47	353

*1882 Louisville (AA)

JIM BUCHER B. March 11, 1911, Manassas, Va.
B.L., T.R. 5'11" 170 lbs.
(3RD BASE, 2ND BASE)

YEAR	CLUB	BA	G	AB	R	H	2B	3B	HR	RBI
1934	BROOKLYN (N)	.226	47	84	12	19	5	2	0	8
1935	BROOKLYN (N)	.302	123	473	72	143	22	1	7	58
1936	BROOKLYN (N)	.251	110	370	49	93	12	8	2	41
1937	BROOKLYN (N)	.253	125	380	44	96	11	2	4	37
1938	St. Louis (N)	.228	17	57	7	13	3	1	0	7
1944	Boston (A)	.274	80	277	39	76	9	2	4	31
1945	Boston (A)	.225	52	151	19	34	4	3	0	11
	Seven years	.265	554	1792	242	474	66	19	17	193

BILL BUCKNER B. Dec. 14, 1949, Vallejo, Calif.
B.L., T.L. 6' 185 lbs.
(1ST BASE, OUTFIELD)

YEAR	CLUB	BA	G	AB	R	H	2B	3B	HR	RBI
1969	LOS ANGELES (N)	.000	1	1	0	0	0	0	0	0
1970	LOS ANGELES (N)	.191	28	68	6	13	3	1	0	4
1971	LOS ANGELES (N)	.277	108	358	37	99	15	1	5	41
1972	LOS ANGELES (N)	.319	105	383	47	122	14	3	5	37
1973	LOS ANGELES (N)	.275	140	575	68	158	20	0	8	46
1974	LOS ANGELES (N)	.314	145	580	83	182	30	3	7	58
1975	LOS ANGELES (N)	.243	92	288	30	70	11	2	6	31
1976	LOS ANGELES (N)	.301	154	642	76	193	28	4	7	76
1977	Chicago (N)	.284	122	426	40	121	27	0	11	60
1978	Chicago (N)	.323	117	446	47	144	26	1	5	74
1979	Chicago (N)	.284	149	591	72	168	34	7	14	66
1980	Chicago (N)	.324	145	578	69	187	41	3	10	68
1981	Chicago (N)	.311	106	421	45	131	35	3	10	75
1982	Chicago (N)	.306	161	657	93	201	34	5	15	105
1983	Chicago (N)	.280	153	626	79	175	38	6	16	66
	Fifteen years (total)	.295	1726	6640	792	1964	356	39	119	791
League Championship										
	LOS ANGELES (N)									
	One Year	.167	4	18	0	3	1	0	0	0
World Series										
	(LOS ANGELES)									
	One Year	.250	5	20	1	5	1	0	1	1

AL BURCH B. Oct. 7, 1883, Albany, N.Y.
B.L., T.R. 5'8½" 160 lbs.
(OUTFIELD)

YEAR	CLUB	BA	G	AB	R	H	2B	3B	HR	RBI
1906	St. Louis (N)	.266	91	355	40	89	5	1	0	11
1907	St. Louis (N)									
1907	BROOKLYN (N)	.292	40	120	12	35	2	2	0	12
	(year totals)	.255	88	274	30	70	5	3	0	17
1908	BROOKLYN (N)	.243	123	456	45	111	8	4	2	18
1909	BROOKLYN (N)	.271	152	601	80	163	20	6	1	30
1910	BROOKLYN (N)	.236	103	352	41	83	8	3	1	20
1911	BROOKLYN (N)	.228	54	167	18	38	2	3	0	7
	Six years	.254	611	2185	254	554	48	20	4	103

JACK BURDOCK B. 1851, Brooklyn, N.Y.
B.R., T.R. 5'9½" 158 lbs.
(2ND BASE)

YEAR	CLUB	BA	G	AB	R	H	2B	3B	HR	RBI
1891	BROOKLYN (N)	.083	3	12	1	1	0	0	0	1
	Fourteen years (total)	.244	960	3873	578	944	131	40	15	341

*1876 Hartford (N), 1877 Brooklyn (N), 1878 Boston (N), 1888 Brooklyn (AA)

TOM BURGESS B. Sept. 1, 1927, London, Ontario, Canada
B.L., T.L. 6' 180 lbs.
(1ST BASE)

YEAR	CLUB	BA	G	AB	R	H	2B	3B	HR	RBI
1962	LOS ANGELES (N)	.196	87	143	17	28	7	1	2	13
	Two years (total)	.177	104	164	19	29	8	1	2	14

GLENN BURKE B. Nov. 16, 1952, Oakland, Calif.
B.R., T.R. 6' 195 lbs.
(OUTFIELD)

YEAR	CLUB	BA	G	AB	R	H	2B	3B	HR	RBI
1976	LOS ANGELES (N)	.239	25	46	9	11	2	0	0	5
1977	LOS ANGELES (N)	.254	83	169	16	43	8	0	1	13
1978	LOS ANGELES (N)	.211	16	19	2	4	0	0	0	2
	Four years (total)	.237	225	523	50	124	18	2	2	38
League Championship	One year	.000	3	7	0	0	0	0	0	0
World Series	One year	.200	3	5	0	1	0	0	0	0

TOM BURNS B. Sept. 6, 1862, Philadelphia, Pa.
B.R., T.R. 5'8" 183 lbs.
(OUTFIELD, SHORTSTOP)

YEAR	CLUB	BA	G	AB	R	H	2B	3B	HR	RBI
1890	BROOKLYN (N)	.284	119	472	102	134	22	13	13	128
1891	BROOKLYN (N)	.285	123	470	75	134	24	13	4	75
1892	BROOKLYN (N)	.315	141	542	91	171	27	18	4	96
1893	BROOKLYN (N)	.270	109	415	68	112	22	8	7	60
1894	BROOKLYN (N)	.361	126	513	107	185	32	14	5	109
1895	BROOKLYN (N)	.186	20	70	9	13	0	1	0	13
1895	New York (N)									
	(year totals)	.258	53	190	28	49	5	8	1	32
	Eleven years (total)	.301	1188	4644	874	1398	224	134	66	675

*1884 Baltimore (AA), Wilmington (U), 1885 Baltimore (AA), 1888 Brooklyn (AA), Brooklyn (AA)

LARRY BURRIGHT B. July 10, 1937, Roseville, Ill.
B.R., T.R. 5'11" 170 lbs.
(2ND BASE)

YEAR	CLUB	BA	G	AB	R	H	2B	3B	HR	RBI
1962	LOS ANGELES (N)	.205	115	249	35	51	6	5	4	30
	Three years (total)	.205	159	356	44	73	8	6	4	33

DOC BUSHONG B. Jan. 10, 1856, Philadelphia, Pa.
B.R., T.R. 5'11" 165 lbs.
(CATCHER)

YEAR	CLUB	BA	G	AB	R	H	2B	3B	HR	RBI
*1890	BROOKLYN (N)	.236	16	55	5	13	2	0	0	7
	Twelve years (total)	.214	671	2392	287	511	58	12	2	78

*1876 Philadelphia (N), 1880 Worcester (N), 1883 Cleveland (N), 1885 St. Louis (AA), 1888 Brooklyn (AA)

JOHNNY BUTLER
B. March 20, 1894, Eureka, Kan.
B.R., T.R. 6' 175 lbs.
(SHORTSTOP, 3RD BASE)

YEAR	CLUB	BA	G	AB	R	H	2B	3B	HR	RBI
1926	BROOKLYN (N)	.269	147	501	54	135	27	5	1	68
1927	BROOKLYN (N)	.238	149	521	39	124	13	6	2	57
1928	Chicago (N)	.270	62	174	17	47	7	0	0	16
1929	St. Louis (N)	.164	17	55	5	9	1	1	0	5
	Four years	.252	375	1251	115	315	48	12	3	146

LEO CALLAHAN
B. Aug. 9, 1890, Boston, Mass.
B.L., T.L. 5'6" 142 lbs.
(OUTFIELD)

YEAR	CLUB	BA	G	AB	R	H	2B	3B	HR	RBI
1913	BROOKLYN (N)	.171	33	41	6	7	3	1	0	3
	Two years (total)	.221	114	276	32	61	17	5	1	12

DOLF CAMILLI
B. April 23, 1907, San Francisco, Calif.
B.L., T.L. 5'10" 185 lbs.
(1ST BASE)

YEAR	CLUB	BA	G	AB	R	H	2B	3B	HR	RBI
1933	Chicago (N)	.224	16	58	8	13	2	1	2	7
1934	Chicago (N)									
1934	Philadelphia (N)									
	(year totals)	.267	134	498	69	133	28	3	16	87
1935	Philadelphia (N)	.261	156	602	88	157	23	5	25	83
1936	Philadelphia (N)	.315	151	530	106	167	29	13	28	102
1937	Philadelphia (N)	.339	131	475	101	161	23	7	27	80
1938	BROOKLYN (N)	.251	146	509	106	128	25	11	24	100
1939	BROOKLYN (N)	.290	157	565	105	164	30	12	26	105
1940	BROOKLYN (N)	.287	142	512	92	147	29	13	23	96
1941	BROOKLYN (N)	.285	149	529	92	151	29	6	34	120
1942	BROOKLYN (N)	.252	150	524	89	132	23	7	26	109
1943	BROOKLYN (N)	.246	95	353	56	87	15	6	6	43
1945	Boston (A)	.212	63	198	24	42	5	2	2	19
	Twelve years	.277	1490	5353	936	1482	261	86	239	950
World Series										
	One year	.167	5	18	1	3	1	0	0	1

DOUG CAMILLI
B. Sept. 22, 1936, Philadelphia, Pa.
B.R., T.R. 5'11" 195 lbs.
(CATCHER)

YEAR	CLUB	BA	G	AB	R	H	2B	3B	HR	RBI
1960	LOS ANGELES (N)	.333	6	24	4	8	2	0	1	3
1961	LOS ANGELES (N)	.133	13	30	3	4	0	0	3	4
1962	LOS ANGELES (N)	.284	45	88	16	25	5	2	4	22
1963	LOS ANGELES (N)	.162	49	117	9	19	1	1	3	10
1964	LOS ANGELES (N)	.179	50	123	1	22	3	0	0	10
1965	Washington (A)	.192	75	193	13	37	6	1	3	18
1966	Washington (A)	.206	44	107	5	22	4	0	2	8
1967	Washington (A)	.183	30	82	5	15	1	0	2	5
1969	Washington (A)	.333	1	3	0	1	0	0	0	0
	Nine years	.199	313	767	56	153	22	4	18	80

ROY CAMPANELLA
B. Nov. 19, 1921, Philadelphia, Pa.
B.R., T.R. 5'9½" 190 lbs.
(CATCHER)

YEAR	CLUB	BA	G	AB	R	H	2B	3B	HR	RBI
1948	BROOKLYN (N)	.258	83	279	32	72	11	3	9	45
1949	BROOKLYN (N)	.287	130	436	65	125	22	2	22	82
1950	BROOKLYN (N)	.281	126	437	70	123	19	3	31	89
1951	BROOKLYN (N)	.325	143	505	90	164	33	1	33	108
1952	BROOKLYN (N)	.269	128	468	73	126	18	1	22	97

YEAR	CLUB	BA	G	AB	R	H	2B	3B	HR	RBI
1953	BROOKLYN (N)	.312	144	519	103	162	26	3	41	142
1954	BROOKLYN (N)	.207	111	397	43	82	14	3	19	51
1955	BROOKLYN (N)	.318	123	446	81	142	20	1	32	107
1956	BROOKLYN (N)	.219	124	388	39	85	6	1	20	73
1957	BROOKLYN (N)	.242	103	330	31	80	9	0	13	62
	Ten years	.276	1215	4205	627	1161	178	18	242	856

World Series

YEAR	CLUB	BA	G	AB	R	H	2B	3B	HR	RBI
1949	BROOKLYN (N)	.267	5	15	2	4	1	0	1	2
1952	BROOKLYN (N)	.214	7	28	0	6	0	0	0	1
1953	BROOKLYN (N)	.273	6	22	6	6	0	0	1	2
1955	BROOKLYN (N)	.259	7	27	4	7	3	0	2	4
1956	BROOKLYN (N)	.182	7	22	2	4	1	0	0	3
	Five years	.237	32	114	14	27	5	0	4	12

ALEX CAMPANIS   B. Nov. 2, 1916, Kos, Greece
B.B., T.R. 6′ 185 lbs.
(2ND BASE)

YEAR	CLUB	BA	G	AB	R	H	2B	3B	HR	RBI
1943	BROOKLYN (N)	.100	7	20	3	2	0	0	0	0

JIM CAMPANIS   B. Feb. 9, 1944, New York, N.Y.
B.R., T.R. 6′ 195 lbs.
(CATCHER)

YEAR	CLUB	BA	G	AB	R	H	2B	3B	HR	RBI
1966	LOS ANGELES (N)	.000	1	1	0	0	0	0	0	0
1967	LOS ANGELES (N)	.161	41	62	3	10	1	0	2	2
1968	LOS ANGELES (N)	.091	4	11	0	1	0	0	0	0
	Six years (total)	.147	113	217	13	32	6	0	4	9

GILLY CAMPBELL   B. Feb. 13, 1907, Kansas City, Kan.
B.L., T.R. 5′7½″ 182 lbs.
(CATCHER)

YEAR	CLUB	BA	G	AB	R	H	2B	3B	HR	RBI
1938	BROOKLYN (N)	.246	54	126	10	31	5	0	0	11
	Five years (total)	.263	295	708	78	186	30	2	5	93

JIMMY CANAVAN   B. Nov. 26, 1866, New Bedford, Mass.
B.R., T.R. 5′8″ 160 lbs.
(OUTFIELD, 2ND BASE, SHORTSTOP)

YEAR	CLUB	BA	G	AB	R	H	2B	3B	HR	RBI
1897	BROOKLYN (N)	.217	63	240	25	52	9	3	2	24
	Five years (total)	.223	539	2064	322	461	63	48	30	287

MAX CAREY   B. Jan. 11, 1890, Terre Haute, Ind.
D. May 30, 1976, Miami Beach, Fla.
B.B., T.R. 5′11½″ 170 lbs.
(OUTFIELD)

YEAR	CLUB	BA	G	AB	R	H	2B	3B	HR	RBI
1910	Pittsburgh (N)	.500	2	6	2	3	0	1	0	2
1911	Pittsburgh (N)	.258	129	427	77	110	15	10	5	43
1912	Pittsburgh (N)	.302	150	587	114	177	23	8	5	66
1913	Pittsburgh (N)	.277	154	620	99	172	23	10	5	49
1914	Pittsburgh (N)	.243	156	593	76	144	25	17	1	31
1915	Pittsburgh (N)	.254	140	564	76	143	26	5	3	27
1916	Pittsburgh (N)	.264	154	599	90	158	23	11	7	42
1917	Pittsburgh (N)	.296	155	588	82	174	21	12	1	82
1918	Pittsburgh (N)	.274	126	468	70	128	14	6	3	48
1919	Pittsburgh (N)	.307	66	244	41	75	10	2	0	9
1920	Pittsburgh (N)	.289	130	485	74	140	18	4	1	35

YEAR	CLUB	BA	G	AB	R	H	2B	3B	HR	RBI
1921	Pittsburgh (N)	.309	140	521	85	161	34	4	7	56
1922	Pittsburgh (N)	.329	155	629	140	207	28	12	10	70
1923	Pittsburgh (N)	.308	153	610	120	188	32	19	6	63
1924	Pittsburgh (N)	.297	149	599	113	178	30	9	7	55
1925	Pittsburgh (N)	.343	133	542	109	186	39	13	5	44
1926	Pittsburgh (N)									
1926	BROOKLYN (N)	.260	27	100	18	26	3	1	0	7
	(year totals)	.231	113	424	64	98	17	6	0	35
1927	BROOKLYN (N)	.266	144	538	70	143	30	10	1	54
1928	BROOKLYN (N)	.247	108	296	41	73	11	0	2	19
1929	BROOKLYN (N)	.304	19	23	2	7	0	0	0	1
	Twenty years	.285	2476	9363	1545	2665	419	159	69	800
	World Series									
	One year	.458	7	24	6	11	4	0	0	2

BOB CARUTHERS B. Jan. 5, 1864, Memphis, Tenn.
B.L., T.R. 5'7" 138 lbs.
(OUTFIELD, PITCHER)

YEAR	CLUB	BA	G	AB	R	H	2B	3B	HR	RBI
1890	BROOKLYN (N)	.265	71	238	46	63	7	4	1	29
1891	BROOKLYN (N)	.281	56	171	24	48	5	3	2	23
	Ten years (total)	.282	705	2465	508	694	104	50	29	213

*1884 St. Louis (AA), 1888 Brooklyn (AA)   *1890

DOC CASEY B. March 15, 1871, Lawrence, Mass.
B.L., T.R.
(3RD BASE)

YEAR	CLUB	BA	G	AB	R	H	2B	3B	HR	RBI
1898	Washington (N)	.277	28	112	13	31	2	0	0	15
1899	Washington (N)									
1899	BROOKLYN (N)	.269	134	542	77	143	15	8	1	44
	(year totals)	.259	143	559	78	145	16	8	1	45
1900	BROOKLYN (N)	.333	1	3	0	1	0	0	0	1
1901	Detroit (A)	.283	128	540	105	153	16	9	2	46
1902	Detroit (A)	.273	132	520	69	142	18	7	3	55
1903	Chicago (N)	.290	112	435	56	126	8	3	1	40
1904	Chicago (N)	.268	136	548	71	147	20	4	1	43
1905	Chicago (N)	.232	144	526	66	122	21	10	1	56
1906	BROOKLYN (N)	.233	149	571	71	133	17	8	0	34
1907	BROOKLYN (N)	.231	141	527	55	122	19	3	0	19
	Ten years	.258	1114	4341	584	1122	137	52	9	354

TOM CATTERSON B. Aug. 25, 1884, Warwick, R.I.
B.L., T.L. 5'10" 170 lbs.
(OUTFIELD)

YEAR	CLUB	BA	G	AB	R	H	2B	3B	HR	RBI
1908	BROOKLYN (N)	.191	19	68	5	13	1	1	1	2
1909	BROOKLYN (N)	.222	9	18	0	4	0	0	0	1
	Two years	.198	28	86	5	17	1	1	1	3

RON CEY B. Feb. 15, 1948, Tacoma, Wash.
B.R., T.R. 5'10" 185 lbs.
(3RD BASE)

YEAR	CLUB	BA	G	AB	R	H	2B	3B	HR	RBI
1971	LOS ANGELES (N)	.000	2	2	0	0	0	0	0	0
1972	LOS ANGELES (N)	.270	11	37	3	10	1	0	1	3
1973	LOS ANGELES (N)	.245	152	507	60	124	18	4	15	80
1974	LOS ANGELES (N)	.262	159	577	88	151	20	2	18	88
1975	LOS ANGELES (N)	.283	158	566	72	160	29	2	25	101
1976	LOS ANGELES (N)	.277	145	502	69	139	18	3	23	80
1977	LOS ANGELES (N)	.241	153	564	77	136	22	3	30	110
1978	LOS ANGELES (N)	.270	159	555	84	150	32	0	23	84
1979	LOS ANGELES (N)	.281	150	487	77	137	20	1	28	81
1980	LOS ANGELES (N)	.254	157	551	81	140	25	0	28	77
1981	LOS ANGELES (N)	.288	85	312	42	90	15	2	13	50

38 • The Complete Dodgers Record Book

YEAR	CLUB	BA	G	AB	R	H	2B	3B	HR	RBI
1982	LOS ANGELES (N)	.254	150	556	62	141	23	1	24	79
1983	Chicago (N)	.275	159	581	73	160	33	1	24	90
	Thirteen years	.268	1640	5797	788	1538	256	19	252	932
League Championship										
	Four years	.302	17	11	11	19	6	0	3	11

World Series

YEAR	CLUB	BA	G	AB	R	H	2B	3B	HR	RBI
1974	LOS ANGELES (N)	.176	5	17	1	3	0	0	0	0
1977	LOS ANGELES (N)	.190	6	21	2	4	1	0	1	3
1978	LOS ANGELES (N)	.286	6	21	2	6	0	0	1	4
1981	LOS ANGELES (N)	.350	6	20	3	7	0	0	1	6
	Four years	.253	23	79	8	20	1	0	3	13

BEN CHAPMAN B. Dec. 25, 1908, Nashville, Tenn.
B.R., T.R. 6' 190 lbs.
(OUTFIELD)

YEAR	CLUB	BA	G	AB	R	H	2B	3B	HR	RBI
1944	BROOKLYN (N)	.368	20	38	11	14	4	0	0	11
1945	BROOKLYN (N)	.136	13							
1946	Philadelphia (N)	.000	1	1	1	0	0	0	0	0
	Fifteen years (total)	.302	1716	6478	1144	1958	407	107	90	977

GLENN CHAPMAN B. Jan. 21, 1906, Cambridge City, Ind.
B.R., T.R. 5'11½" 170 lbs.
(OUTFIELD, 2ND BASE)

YEAR	CLUB	BA	G	AB	R	H	2B	3B	HR	RBI
1934	BROOKLYN (N)	.280	67	93	19	26	5	1	1	10

PAUL CHERVINKO B. July 23, 1910, Trauger, Pa.
B.R., T.R. 5'8" 185 lbs.
(CATCHER)

YEAR	CLUB	BA	G	AB	R	H	2B	3B	HR	RBI
1937	BROOKLYN (N)	.146	30	48	1	7	0	1	0	2
1938	BROOKLYN (N)	.148	12	27	0	4	0	0	0	3
	Two years	.147	42	75	1	11	0	1	0	5

FELIX CHOUINARD B. 1888, Chicago, Ill.
B.B., T.R.
(OUTFIELD)

YEAR	CLUB	BA	G	AB	R	H	2B	3B	HR	RBI
1914	BROOKLYN (F)									
1915	BROOKLYN (F)	.500	4	4	1	2	0	0	0	2
	Four years	.244	88	221	22	54	5	4	1	23

GINO CIMOLI B. Dec. 18, 1929, San Francisco, Calif.
B.R., T.R. 6'1" 180 lbs.
(OUTFIELD)

YEAR	CLUB	BA	G	AB	R	H	2B	3B	HR	RBI
1956	BROOKLYN (N)	.111	73	36	3	4	1	0	0	4
1957	BROOKLYN (N)	.293	142	532	88	156	22	5	10	57
1958	LOS ANGELES (N)	.246	109	325	35	80	6	3	9	27
1959	St. Louis (N)	.279	143	519	61	145	40	7	8	72
1960	Pittsburgh (N)	.267	101	307	36	82	14	4	0	28
1961	Pittsburgh (N)									
1961	Milwaukee (N)									
	(year totals)	.234	58	184	16	43	8	1	3	10
1962	Kansas City (A)	.275	152	550	67	151	20	15	10	71
1963	Kansas City (A)	.263	145	529	56	139	19	11	4	48
1964	Kansas City (A)									
1964	Baltimore (A)									
	(year totals)	.119	42	67	7	8	3	2	0	3

YEAR	CLUB	BA	G	AB	R	H	2B	3B	HR	RBI
1965	California (A)	.000	4	5	1	0	0	0	0	1
	Ten years	.265	969	3054	370	808	133	48	44	321
World Series										
	Two years	.250	8	20	4	5	0	0	0	1

GEORGE CISAR
B. Aug. 25, 1912, Chicago, Ill.
B.R., T.R. 6' 175 lbs.
(OUTFIELD)

YEAR	CLUB	BA	G	AB	R	H	2B	3B	HR	RBI
1937	BROOKLYN (N)	.207	20	29	8	6	0	0	0	4

MOOSE CLABAUGH
B. Nov. 13, 1901, Albany, Mo.
B.L., T.R. 6' 185 lbs.
(OUTFIELD)

YEAR	CLUB	BA	G	AB	R	H	2B	3B	HR	RBI
1926	BROOKLYN (N)	.071	11	14	2	1	1	0	0	1

BUD CLANCY
B. Sept. 15, 1900, Odell, Ill.
B.L., T.L. 6' 170 lbs.
(1ST BASE)

YEAR	CLUB	BA	G	AB	R	H	2B	3B	HR	RBI
1932	BROOKLYN (N)	.306	53	196	14	60	4	2	0	14
	Nine years (total)	.281	522	1796	204	504	69	26	12	198

BOB CLARK
B. May 18, 1864, Covington, Ky.
B.R., T.R. 5'10" 175 lbs.
(CATCHER)

YEAR	CLUB	BA	G	AB	R	H	2B	3B	HR	RBI
1890	BROOKLYN (N)	.219	43	151	24	33	3	3	0	15
	Seven years (total)	.230	288	1011	145	233	25	11	1	63

*1886 Brooklyn (AA)   *1890

WALLY CLEMENT
B. July 21, 1881, Auburn Maine
T.R.
(OUTFIELD)

YEAR	CLUB	BA	G	AB	R	H	2B	3B	HR	RBI
1909	BROOKLYN (N)	.256	92	340	35	87	8	4	0	17
	Two years (total)	.251	111	379	35	95	11	4	0	18

ALTA COHEN
B. Dec. 25, 1908, New York, N.Y.
B.L., T.L. 5'10½" 170 lbs.
(OUTFIELD)

YEAR	CLUB	BA	G	AB	R	H	2B	3B	HR	RBI
1931	BROOKLYN (N)	.667	1	3	1	2	0	0	0	0
1932	BROOKLYN (N)	.156	9	32	1	5	1	0	0	1
	Three years (total)	.194	29	67	8	13	2	0	0	2

ROCKY COLAVITO
B. Aug. 10, 1933, New York, N.Y.
B.R., T.R. 6'3" 190 lbs.
(OUTFIELD)

YEAR	CLUB	BA	G	AB	R	H	2B	3B	HR	RBI
1968	LOS ANGELES (N)	.204	40	113	8	23	3	0	3	11
	Fourteen years (total)	.266	1841	6503	971	1730	283	21	374	1159

BILL COLLINS B. March 17, 1884, Chestertown, Ind.
B.R., T.R.
(OUTFIELD)

YEAR	CLUB	BA	G	AB	R	H	2B	3B	HR	RBI
1913	BROOKLYN (N)	.189	32	95	8	18	1	0	0	4
	Four years (total)	.223	228	775	91	173	11	10	3	54

HUB COLLINS B. April 15, 1864, Louisville, Ky.
B.R., T.R.
(2ND BASE, OUTFIELD)

YEAR	CLUB	BA	G	AB	R	H	2B	3B	HR	RBI
1890	BROOKLYN (N)	.278	129	510	148	142	32	7	3	69
1891	BROOKLYN (N)	.276	107	435	82	120	16	5	3	31
1892	BROOKLYN (N)	.299	21	87	17	26	5	1	0	17
	Seven years (total)	.284	680	2779	653	790	127	38	11	243

*1886 Louisville (AA), 1888 Brooklyn (AA), Louisville (AA), 1889 Brooklyn (AA) *1890

CHUCK CONNORS B. April 10, 1921, Brooklyn, N.Y.
B.L., T.L. 6'5" 190 lbs.
(1ST BASE)

YEAR	CLUB	BA	G	AB	R	H	2B	3B	HR	RBI
1949	BROOKLYN (N)	.000	1	1	0	0	0	0	0	0
	Two years (total)	.238	67	202	16	48	5	1	2	18

PAUL COOK B. May 5, 1863, Caledonia, N.Y.
B.R., T.R.
(CATCHER)

YEAR	CLUB	BA	G	AB	R	H	2B	3B	HR	RBI
1890	BROOKLYN (P)	.252	58	218	32	55	3	3	0	31
	Seven years (total)	.223	378	1364	172	304	27	9	0	83

*1884 Philadelphia (N), 1886 Louisville (AA) *1890

JOHNNY COONEY B. March 18, 1901, Cranston, R.I.
B.R., T.L. 5'10" 165 lbs.
(OUTFIELD, PITCHER)

YEAR	CLUB	BA	G	AB	R	H	2B	3B	HR	RBI
1921	Boston (N)	.200	8	5	0	1	0	0	0	0
1922	Boston (N)	.000	4	8	0	0	0	0	0	0
1923	Boston (N)	.379	42	66	7	25	1	0	0	3
1924	Boston (N)	.254	55	130	10	33	2	1	0	4
1925	Boston (N)	.320	54	103	17	33	7	0	0	13
1926	Boston (N)	.302	64	126	17	38	3	2	0	18
1927	Boston (N)	.000	10	1	3	0	0	0	0	0
1928	Boston (N)	.171	33	41	2	7	0	0	0	2
1929	Boston (N)	.319	41	72	10	23	4	1	0	6
1930	Boston (N)	.000	4	3	0	0	0	0	0	0
1935	BROOKLYN (N)	.310	10	29	3	9	0	1	0	1
1936	BROOKLYN (N)	.282	130	507	71	143	17	5	0	30
1937	BROOKLYN (N)	.293	120	430	61	126	18	5	0	37
1938	Boston (N)	.271	120	432	45	117	25	5	0	17
1939	Boston (N)	.274	118	368	39	101	8	1	2	27
1940	Boston (N)	.318	108	365	40	116	14	3	0	21
1941	Boston (N)	.319	123	442	52	141	25	2	0	29
1942	Boston (N)	.207	74	198	23	41	6	0	0	7
1943	BROOKLYN (N)	.206	37	34	7	7	0	0	0	2
1944	BROOKLYN (N)	.750	7	4	0	3	0	0	0	0
1944	New York (A)									
	(year totals)	.333	17	12	1	4	0	0	0	2
	Twenty years	.286	1172	3372	408	965	130	26	2	219

CLAUDE COOPER

B. April 1, 1893, Troupe, Texas
B.L., T.L. 5'9" 158 lbs.
(OUTFIELD)

YEAR	CLUB	BA	G	AB	R	H	2B	3B	HR	RBI
1913	New York (N)	.300	27	30	11	9	4	0	0	4
1914	BROOKLYN (F)	.241	113	399	56	96	14	11	2	25
1915	BROOKLYN (F)	.294	153	527	75	155	26	12	2	63
1916	Philadelphia (N)	.192	56	104	9	20	2	0	0	11
1917	Philadelphia (N)	.103	24	29	5	3	1	0	0	1
	Five years	.260	373	1089	156	283	47	23	4	104
World Series	One year	—	2	0	0	0	0	0	0	0

CLAUDE CORBITT

B. July 21, 1915, Sunbury, N.C.
B.R., T.R. 5'10" 170 lbs.
(SHORTSTOP, 2ND BASE)

YEAR	CLUB	BA	G	AB	R	H	2B	3B	HR	RBI
1945	BROOKLYN (N)	.500	2	4	1	2	0	0	0	0
	Four years (total)	.243	215	630	60	153	22	1	1	37

TOMMY CORCORAN

B. Jan. 4, 1869, New Haven, Conn.
B.R., T.R. 5'9" 164 lbs.
(SHORTSTOP)

YEAR	CLUB	BA	G	AB	R	H	2B	3B	HR	RBI
1890	Pittsburgh (P)	.240	123	505	80	121	14	13	1	61
1891	Philadelphia (AA)	.254	133	511	84	130	11	15	7	71
1892	BROOKLYN (N)	.237	151	615	77	146	12	6	1	74
1893	BROOKLYN (N)	.275	115	459	61	126	11	10	2	58
1894	BROOKLYN (N)	.300	129	576	123	173	21	20	5	92
1895	BROOKLYN (N)	.277	128	541	85	150	17	10	2	69
1896	BROOKLYN (N)	.289	132	532	63	154	15	7	3	73
1897	Cincinnati (N)	.288	109	445	76	128	30	5	3	57
1898	Cincinnati (N)	.250	153	619	80	155	28	15	2	87
1899	Cincinnati (N)	.277	137	537	91	149	11	8	0	81
1900	Cincinnati (N)	.245	127	523	64	128	21	9	1	54
1901	Cincinnati (N)	.209	31	115	14	24	3	3	0	15
1902	Cincinnati (N)	.253	138	538	54	136	18	4	0	54
1903	Cincinnati (N)	.246	115	459	61	113	18	7	2	73
1904	Cincinnati (N)	.230	150	578	55	133	17	9	2	74
1905	Cincinnati (N)	.248	151	605	70	150	21	11	2	85
1906	Cincinnati (N)	.207	117	430	29	89	13	1	1	33
1907	New York (N)	.265	62	226	21	60	9	2	0	24
	Eighteen years	.257	2201	8814	1188	2265	290	155	34	1135

CHUCK CORGAN

B. Dec. 3, 1903, Wagoner, Okla.
B.B., T.R. 5'11" 180 lbs.
(SHORTSTOP, 2ND BASE)

YEAR	CLUB	BA	G	AB	R	H	2B	3B	HR	RBI
1925	BROOKLYN (N)	.170	14	47	4	8	1	1	0	0
1927	BROOKLYN (N)	.263	19	57	3	15	1	0	0	1
	Two years	.221	33	104	7	23	2	1	0	1

POP CORKHILL

B. April 11, 1858, Parkesburg, Pa.
B.L., T.R. 5'10" 180 lbs.
(OUTFIELD)

YEAR	CLUB	BA	G	AB	R	H	2B	3B	HR	RBI
1890	BROOKLYN (N)	.225	51	204	23	46	4	2	1	21
	Ten years (total)	.254	1086	4404	650	1120	110	81	30	268

*1883 Cincinnati (AA), 1888 Brooklyn (AA), Cincinnati (AA)   *1890

JOHN CORRIDEN

B. Oct. 6, 1918, Logansport, Ind.
B.B., T.R. 5'6" 160 lbs.

YEAR	CLUB	BA	G	AB	R	H	2B	3B	HR	RBI
1946	BROOKLYN (N)	—	1	0	1	0	0	0	0	0

PETE COSCARART
B. June 16, 1913, Escondido, Calif.
B.R., T.R. 5'11½" 175 lbs.
(2ND BASE, SHORTSTOP)

YEAR	CLUB	BA	G	AB	R	H	2B	3B	HR	RBI
1938	BROOKLYN (N)	.152	32	79	10	12	3	0	0	6
1939	BROOKLYN (N)	.277	115	419	59	116	22	2	4	43
1940	BROOKLYN (N)	.237	143	506	55	120	24	4	9	58
1941	BROOKLYN (N)	.129	43	62	13	8	1	0	0	5
1942	Pittsburgh (N)	.228	133	487	57	111	12	4	3	29
1943	Pittsburgh (N)	.242	133	491	57	119	19	6	0	48
1944	Pittsburgh (N)	.264	139	554	89	146	30	4	4	42
1945	Pittsburgh (N)	.242	123	392	59	95	17	2	8	38
1946	Pittsburgh (N)	.500	2	2	0	1	1	0	0	0
	Nine years	.243	864	2992	399	728	129	22	28	269

World Series

	One year	.000	3	7	1	0	0	0	0	0

BOB COULSON
B. June 17, 1887, Donora, Pa.
B.R., T.R. 5'10½" 175 lbs.
(OUTFIELD)

YEAR	CLUB	BA	G	AB	R	H	2B	3B	HR	RBI
1908	Cincinnati (N)	.333	8	18	3	6	1	1	0	1
1910	BROOKLYN (N)	.247	25	89	14	22	3	4	1	13
1911	BROOKLYN (N)	.234	146	521	52	122	23	7	0	50
1914	Pittsburgh (F)	.203	18	64	7	13	1	0	0	3
	Four years	.236	197	692	76	163	28	12	1	67

WES COVINGTON
B. March 27, 1932, Laurinburg, N.C.
B.L., T.R. 6'1" 205 lbs.
(OUTFIELD)

YEAR	CLUB	BA	G	AB	R	H	2B	3B	HR	RBI
1966	LOS ANGELES (N)	.121	37	33	1	4	0	1	1	6
	(year totals)	.114	46	44	1	5	0	1	1	6
	Eleven years (total)	.279	1025	2978	355	832	128	17	131	499

World Series

	Three years	.235	15	51	3	12	1	0	0	5

BILLY COX
B. Aug. 29, 1919, Newport, Pa.
B.R., T.R. 5'10" 150 lbs.
(3RD BASE, SHORTSTOP)

YEAR	CLUB	BA	G	AB	R	H	2B	3B	HR	RBI
1941	Pittsburgh (N)	.270	10	37	4	10	3	1	0	2
1946	Pittsburgh (N)	.290	121	411	32	119	22	6	2	36
1947	Pittsburgh (N)	.274	132	529	75	145	30	7	15	54
1948	BROOKLYN (N)	.249	88	237	36	59	13	2	3	15
1949	BROOKLYN (N)	.233	100	390	48	91	18	2	8	40
1950	BROOKLYN (N)	.257	119	451	44	116	17	2	8	44
1951	BROOKLYN (N)	.279	142	455	62	127	25	4	9	51
1952	BROOKLYN (N)	.259	116	455	56	118	12	3	6	34
1953	BROOKLYN (N)	.291	100	327	44	95	18	1	10	44
1954	BROOKLYN (N)	.235	77	226	26	53	9	2	2	17
1955	Baltimore (A)	.211	53	194	25	41	7	2	3	14
	Eleven years	.262	1058	3712	470	974	174	32	66	351

World Series

YEAR	CLUB	BA	G	AB	R	H	2B	3B	HR	RBI
1949	BROOKLYN (N)	.333	2	3	0	1	0	0	0	0
1952	BROOKLYN (N)	.296	7	27	4	8	2	0	0	0
1953	BROOKLYN (N)	.304	6	23	3	7	3	0	1	6
	Three years	.302	15	53	7	16	5	0	1	6

DICK COX   B. Sept. 3, 1897, Pasadena, Calif.
B.R., T.R. 5'7½" 158 lbs.
(OUTFIELD)

YEAR	CLUB	BA	G	AB	R	H	2B	3B	HR	RBI
1925	BROOKLYN (N)	.329	122	434	68	143	23	10	7	64
1926	BROOKLYN (N)	.296	124	398	53	118	17	4	1	45
	Two years	.314	246	832	121	261	40	14	8	109

ED CRANE   B. May, 1862, Boston, Mass.
B.R., T.R. 5'10½" 204 lbs.
(PITCHER, OUTFIELD)

YEAR	CLUB	BA	G	AB	R	H	2B	3B	HR	RBI
1890	New York (P)	.315	43	146	27	46	5	4	0	16
1891	Cin.-Milw. (AA)									
1891	Cincinnati (N)									
	(year totals)	.141	49	156	16	22	0	0	1	9
1892	New York (N)	.245	48	163	20	40	1	1	0	14
1893	New York (N)									
1893	BROOKLYN (N)	.400	3							
	(year totals)	.452	15	31	9	14	2	0	0	3
	Nine years	.238	391	1409	199	335	45	15	18	85

*1884 Boston (U), 1885 Buffalo (N), Providence (N), 1886 Washington (N), 1888 New York (N)   *1890

SAM CRANE   B. Sept. 13, 1894, Harrisburg, Pa.
B.R., T.R. 5'11½" 154 lbs.
(SHORTSTOP)

YEAR	CLUB	BA	G	AB	R	H	2B	3B	HR	RBI
1922	BROOKLYN (N)	.250	3	8	1	2	1	0	0	0
	Seven years (total)	.208	174	495	51	103	19	2	0	30

WILLIE CRAWFORD   B. Sept. 7, 1946, Los Angeles, Calif.
B.L., T.L. 6'1" 197 lbs.
(OUTFIELD)

YEAR	CLUB	BA	G	AB	R	H	2B	3B	HR	RBI
1964	LOS ANGELES (N)	.313	10	16	3	5	1	0	0	0
1965	LOS ANGELES (N)	.148	52	27	10	4	0	0	0	0
1966	LOS ANGELES (N)	—	6	0	0	0	0	0	0	0
1967	LOS ANGELES (N)	.250	4	4	0	1	0	0	0	0
1968	LOS ANGELES (N)	.251	61	175	25	44	12	1	4	14
1969	LOS ANGELES (N)	.247	129	389	64	96	17	5	11	41
1970	LOS ANGELES (N)	.234	109	299	48	70	8	6	8	40
1971	LOS ANGELES (N)	.281	114	342	64	96	16	6	9	40
1972	LOS ANGELES (N)	.251	96	243	28	61	7	3	8	27
1973	LOS ANGELES (N)	.295	145	457	75	135	26	2	14	66
1974	LOS ANGELES (N)	.295	139	468	73	138	23	4	11	61
1975	LOS ANGELES (N)	.263	124	373	46	98	15	2	9	46
1976	St. Louis (N)	.304	120	392	49	119	17	5	9	50
1977	Houston (N)									
1977	Oakland (A)									
	(year totals)	.216	101	250	21	54	10	1	3	21
	Fourteen years	.268	1210	3435	507	921	152	35	86	419
League Championship										
	One Year	.250	2	4	1	1	0	0	0	1

World Series

YEAR	CLUB	BA	G	AB	R	H	2B	3B	HR	RBI
1965	LOS ANGELES (N)	.500	2	2	0	1	0	0	0	0
1974	LOS ANGELES (N)	.333	3	6	1	2	0	0	1	1
	Two years	.375	5	8	1	3	0	0	1	0

LAVE CROSS B. May 11, 1867, Milwaukee, Wis.
B.R., T.R. 5'8½" 155 lbs.
(3RD BASE)

YEAR	CLUB	BA	G	AB	R	H	2B	3B	HR	RBI
1900	BROOKLYN (N)	.293	117	312	47	91	9	4	3	43
Twenty-one years (total)		.292	2292	9068	1332	2644	411	135	47	1345
World Series										

*1887 Louisville (AA), 1889 Philadelphia (AA)

HENRY CRUZ B. Feb. 27, 1952, St. Croix, Virgin Islands
B.L., T.L. 6' 175 lbs.
(OUTFIELD)

YEAR	CLUB	BA	G	AB	R	H	2B	3B	HR	RBI
1975	LOS ANGELES (N)	.266	53	94	8	25	3	1	0	5
1976	LOS ANGELES (N)	.182	49	88	8	16	2	1	4	14
Four years (total)		.229	171	280	32	64	7	3	8	34

TONY CUCCINELLO B. Nov. 8, 1907, Long Island City, N.Y.
B.R., T.R. 5'7" 160 lbs.
(2ND BASE, 3RD BASE)

YEAR	CLUB	BA	G	AB	R	H	2B	3B	HR	RBI
1930	Cincinnati (N)	.312	125	443	64	138	22	5	10	78
1931	Cincinnati (N)	.315	154	575	67	181	39	11	2	93
1932	BROOKLYN (N)	.281	154	597	76	168	32	6	12	77
1933	BROOKLYN (N)	.252	134	485	58	122	31	4	9	65
1934	BROOKLYN (N)	.261	140	528	59	138	32	2	14	94
1935	BROOKLYN (N)	.292	102	360	49	105	20	3	8	53
1936	Boston (N)	.308	150	565	68	174	26	3	7	86
1937	Boston (N)	.271	152	575	77	156	36	4	11	80
1938	Boston (N)	.265	147	555	62	147	25	2	9	76
1939	Boston (N)	.306	81	310	42	95	17	1	2	40
1940	Boston (N)									
1940	New York (N)									
	(year totals)	.226	122	433	40	98	18	2	5	55
1942	Boston (N)	.202	40	104	8	21	3	0	1	8
1943	Boston (N)									
1943	Chicago (A)									
	(year totals)	.230	47	122	5	28	5	0	2	13
1944	Chicago (A)	.262	38	130	5	34	3	0	0	17
1945	Chicago (A)	.308	118	402	50	124	25	3	2	49
	Fifteen years	.280	1704	6184	730	1729	334	46	94	884

ROY CULLENBINE B. Oct. 18, 1914, Nashville, Tenn.
B.B., T.R. 6'1" 190 lbs.
(OUTFIELD, 1ST BASE)

YEAR	CLUB	BA	G	AB	R	H	2B	3B	HR	RBI
1940	BROOKLYN (N)	.180	22	61	8	11	1	0	1	9
Ten years (total)		.276	1181	3879	627	1072	209	32	110	599

NICK CULLOP B. Oct. 16, 1900, St. Louis, Mo.
B.R., T.R. 6' 200 lbs.
(OUTFIELD)

YEAR	CLUB	BA	G	AB	R	H	2B	3B	HR	RBI
1929	BROOKLYN (N)	.195	13	41	7	8	2	2	1	5
Five years (total)		.249	173	490	49	122	29	12	11	67

GEORGE CUTSHAW B. July 29, 1887, Wilmington, Ill.
D. Aug. 22, 1973, San Diego, Calif.
B.R., T.R. 5'9" 160 lbs.
(2ND BASE)

YEAR	CLUB	BA	G	AB	R	H	2B	3B	HR	RBI
1912	BROOKLYN (N)	.280	102	357	41	100	14	4	0	28
1913	BROOKLYN (N)	.267	147	592	72	158	23	13	7	80

The Complete Catalogue of Players • 45

YEAR	CLUB	BA	G	AB	R	H	2B	3B	HR	RBI
1914	BROOKLYN (N)	.257	153	583	69	150	22	12	2	78
1915	BROOKLYN (N)	.246	154	566	68	139	18	9	0	62
1916	BROOKLYN (N)	.260	154	581	58	151	21	4	2	63
1917	BROOKLYN (N)	.259	135	487	42	126	17	7	4	49
1918	Pittsburgh (N)	.285	126	463	56	132	16	10	5	68
1919	Pittsburgh (N)	.242	139	512	49	124	15	8	3	51
1920	Pittsburgh (N)	.252	131	488	56	123	16	8	0	47
1921	Pittsburgh (N)	.340	98	350	46	119	18	4	0	53
1922	Detroit (A)	.267	132	499	57	133	14	8	2	61
1923	Detroit (A)	.224	45	143	15	32	1	2	0	13
	Twelve years	.265	1516	5621	629	1487	195	89	25	653
World Series										
	One year	.105	5	19	2	2	1	0	0	2

KIKI CUYLER   B. Aug. 30, 1899, Harrisville, Mich.
B.R., T.R. 5'10½" 180 lbs.
(OUTFIELD)

YEAR	CLUB	BA	G	AB	R	H	2B	3B	HR	RBI
1938	BROOKLYN (N)	.273	82	253	45	69	10	8	2	23
	Eighteen years (total)	.321	1879	7161	1305	2299	394	157	127	1065

BILL DAHLEN   B. Jan. 5, 1870, Nelliston, N.Y.
D. Dec. 5, 1950, Brooklyn, N.Y.
B.R., T.R. 5'9" 180 lbs.
(SHORTSTOP)

YEAR	CLUB	BA	G	AB	R	H	2B	3B	HR	RBI
1891	Chicago (N)	.263	135	551	116	145	20	13	9	76
1892	Chicago (N)	.295	143	587	116	173	23	19	5	58
1893	Chicago (N)	.301	116	485	113	146	28	15	5	64
1894	Chicago (N)	.362	121	508	150	184	32	14	15	107
1895	Chicago (N)	.273	129	509	107	139	19	10	7	62
1896	Chicago (N)	.361	125	476	153	172	30	19	9	74
1897	Chicago (N)	.296	75	277	67	82	18	8	6	40
1898	Chicago (N)	.290	142	524	96	152	35	8	1	79
1899	BROOKLYN (N)	.283	121	428	87	121	22	7	4	76
1900	BROOKLYN (N)	.259	133	483	87	125	16	11	1	69
1901	BROOKLYN (N)	.266	131	511	69	136	17	9	4	82
1902	BROOKLYN (N)	.264	138	527	67	139	25	8	2	74
1903	BROOKLYN (N)	.262	138	474	71	124	17	9	1	64
1904	New York (N)	.268	145	523	70	140	26	2	2	80
1905	New York (N)	.242	148	520	67	126	20	4	7	81
1906	New York (N)	.240	143	471	63	113	18	3	1	49
1907	New York (N)	.207	143	464	40	96	20	1	0	34
1908	Boston (N)	.239	144	524	50	125	23	2	3	48
1909	Boston (N)	.234	69	197	22	46	6	1	2	16
1910	BROOKLYN (N)	.000	3	2	0	0	0	0	0	0
1911	BROOKLYN (N)	.000	1	3	0	0	0	0	0	0
	Twenty-one years	.275	2443	9044	1611	2484	415	163	84	1233
World Series										
	One year	.000	5	15	1	0	0	0	0	1

BABE DAHLGREN   B. June 15, 1912, San Francisco, Calif.
B.R., T.R. 6' 190 lbs.
(1ST BASE)

YEAR	CLUB	BA	G	AB	R	H	2B	3B	HR	RBI
1942	BROOKLYN (N)	.053	17	19	2	1	0	0	0	0
	Twelve years (total)	.261	1139	4045	470	1056	174	37	82	569

CON DAILY   B. Sept. 11, 1864, Blackstone, Mass.
(CATCHER)

YEAR	CLUB	BA	G	AB	R	H	2B	3B	HR	RBI
1890	BROOKLYN (P)	.250	46	168	20	42	6	3	0	35
1891	BROOKLYN (N)	.320	60	206	25	66	10	1	0	30
1892	BROOKLYN (N)	.234	80	278	38	65	10	1	0	28

46 • **The Complete Dodgers Record Book**

YEAR	CLUB	BA	G	AB	R	H	2B	3B	HR	RBI
1893	BROOKLYN (N)	.265	61	215	33	57	4	2	1	32
1894	BROOKLYN (N)	.256	67	234	40	60	14	7	0	32
1895	BROOKLYN (N)	.211	40	142	17	30	3	2	1	11
1896	Chicago (N)	.074	9	27	1	2	0	0	0	1
	Thirteen years	.243	630	2222	280	541	74	22	2	262

*1884 Philadelphia (U), 1885 Providence (N), 1886 Boston (N), 1888 Indianapolis (N)   *1890

JUD DALEY   B. March 14, 1884, South Coventry, Conn.
B.L., T.R. 5'8" 172 lbs.
(OUTFIELD)

YEAR	CLUB	BA	G	AB	R	H	2B	3B	HR	RBI
1911	BROOKLYN (N)	.292	19	65	8	15	2	1	0	7
1912	BROOKLYN (N)	.256	61	199	22	51	9	1	2	13
	Two years	.250	80	264	30	66	11	2	2	20

JACK DALTON   B. July 3, 1885, Henderson, Tenn.
B.R., T.R. 5'10½" 187 lbs.
(OUTFIELD)

YEAR	CLUB	BA	G	AB	R	H	2B	3B	HR	RBI
1910	BROOKLYN (N)	.227	77	273	33	62	9	4	1	21
1914	BROOKLYN (N)	.319	128	442	65	141	13	8	1	45
1915	Buffalo (F)	.293	132	437	68	128	17	3	2	46
1916	Detroit (A)	.182	8	11	1	2	0	0	0	0
	Four years	.286	345	1163	167	333	39	15	4	112

TOM DALY   B. Feb. 7, 1866, Philadelphia, Pa.
B.B., T.R. 5'7" 170 lbs.
(2ND BASE, CATCHER)

YEAR	CLUB	BA	G	AB	R	H	2B	3B	HR	RBI
1890	BROOKLYN (N)	.243	82	292	55	71	9	4	5	43
1891	BROOKLYN (N)	.250	58	200	29	50	11	5	2	27
1892	BROOKLYN (N)	.256	124	446	76	114	15	6	4	51
1893	BROOKLYN (N)	.289	126	470	94	136	21	14	8	70
1894	BROOKLYN (N)	.341	123	492	135	168	22	10	8	82
1895	BROOKLYN (N)	.281	120	455	89	128	17	8	2	68
1896	BROOKLYN (N)	.281	67	224	43	63	13	6	3	29
1898	BROOKLYN (N)	.329	23	73	11	24	3	1	0	11
1899	BROOKLYN (N)	.313	141	498	95	156	24	9	5	88
1900	BROOKLYN (N)	.312	97	343	72	107	17	3	4	55
1901	BROOKLYN (N)	.315	133	520	88	164	38	10	3	90
1902	Chicago (A)	.225	137	489	57	110	22	3	1	54
1903	Chicago (A)									
1903	Cincinnati (N)									
	(year totals)	.265	123	457	62	121	25	9	1	57
	Sixteen years	.278	1564	5684	1024	1582	262	103	49	811

*1887 Chicago (N), 1889 Washington (N)   *1890

JAKE DANIEL   B. April 22, 1912, Roanoke, Ala.
B.L., T.L. 5'11" 175 lbs.
(1ST BASE)

YEAR	CLUB	BA	G	AB	R	H	2B	3B	HR	RBI
1937	BROOKLYN (N)	.185	12	27	3	5	1	0	0	3

FATS DANTONIO   B. Dec. 31, 1919, New Orleans, La.
B.R., T.R. 5'8" 165 lbs.
(CATCHER)

YEAR	CLUB	BA	G	AB	R	H	2B	3B	HR	RBI
1944	BROOKLYN (N)	.143	3	7	0	1	0	0	0	0
1945	BROOKLYN (N)	.250	47	128	12	32	6	1	0	12
	Two years	.244	50	135	12	33	6	1	0	12

CLIFF DAPPER   B. Jan. 2, 1920, Los Angeles, Calif.
B.R., T.R. 6'2" 190 lbs.
(CATCHER)

YEAR	CLUB	BA	G	AB	R	H	2B	3B	HR	RBI
1942	BROOKLYN (N)	.471	8	17	2	8	1	0	1	9

JAKE DAUBERT   B. April 17, 1884, Shamokin, Pa.
D. Oct. 9, 1924, Cincinnati, Ohio
B.L., T.L. 5'10½" 160 lbs.
(1ST BASE)

YEAR	CLUB	BA	G	AB	R	H	2B	3B	HR	RBI
1910	BROOKLYN (N)	.264	144	552	67	146	15	15	8	50
1911	BROOKLYN (N)	.307	149	573	89	176	17	8	5	45
1912	BROOKLYN (N)	.308	145	559	81	172	19	16	3	66
1913	BROOKLYN (N)	.350	139	508	76	178	17	7	2	52
1914	BROOKLYN (N)	.329	126	474	89	156	17	7	6	45
1915	BROOKLYN (N)	.381	150	544	62	164	21	8	2	47
1916	BROOKLYN (N)	.316	127	478	75	151	16	7	3	33
1917	BROOKLYN (N)	.261	125	468	59	122	4	4	2	30
1918	BROOKLYN (N)	.308	108	396	50	122	12	15	2	47
1919	Cincinnati (N)	.276	140	537	79	148	10	12	2	44
1920	Cincinnati (N)	.304	142	553	97	168	28	13	4	48
1921	Cincinnati (N)	.306	136	516	69	158	18	12	2	64
1922	Cincinnati (N)	.336	156	610	114	205	15	22	12	66
1923	Cincinnati (N)	.292	125	500	63	146	27	10	2	54
1924	Cincinnati (N)	.281	102	405	47	114	14	9	1	31
	Fifteen years	.303	2014	7673	1117	2326	250	165	56	722
World Series										
	Two years	.217	12	46	5	10	0	2	0	1

VIC DAVALILLO   B. July 31, 1939, Cabimas, Venezuela
B.L., T.L. 5'7" 150 lbs.
(OUTFIELD)

YEAR	CLUB	BA	G	AB	R	H	2B	3B	HR	RBI
1977	LOS ANGELES (N)	.313	24	48	3	15	2	0	0	4
1978	LOS ANGELES (N)	.312	75	77	15	24	1	1	1	11
1979	LOS ANGELES (N)	.259	29	27	2	7	1	0	0	2
1980	LOS ANGELES (N)	.167	7	6	1	1	0	0	0	0
	Sixteen years	.279	1458	4017	509	1122	160	37	36	329
League Championship										
	Four years	.500	8	4	1	2	1	0	0	0
World Series										
	Four years	.200	14	20	1	4	0	0	0	1

BILL DAVIDSON   B. May 10, 1887, Lafayette, Ind.
B.R., T.R.
(OUTFIELD)

YEAR	CLUB	BA	G	AB	R	H	2B	3B	HR	RBI
1909	Chicago (N)	.143	2	7	2	1	0	0	0	0
1910	BROOKLYN (N)	.238	136	509	48	121	13	7	0	34
1911	BROOKLYN (N)	.233	87	292	33	68	3	4	1	26
	Three years	.235	225	808	83	190	16	11	1	60

LEFTY DAVIS   B. Feb. 4, 1875, Nashville, Tenn.
B.L., T.L.
(OUTFIELD)

YEAR	CLUB	BA	G	AB	R	H	2B	3B	HR	RBI
1901	BROOKLYN (N)	.209	25	91	11	19	2	0	0	7
	Four years (total)	.261	348	1296	232	338	32	19	3	110

48 • **The Complete Dodgers Record Book**

TOMMY DAVIS B. March 21, 1939, Brooklyn, N.Y.
B.R., T.R. 6'2" 195 lbs.
(OUTFIELD)

YEAR	CLUB	BA	G	AB	R	H	2B	3B	HR	RBI
1959	LOS ANGELES (N)	.000	1	1	0	0	0	0	0	0
1960	LOS ANGELES (N)	.276	110	352	43	97	18	1	11	44
1961	LOS ANGELES (N)	.278	132	460	60	128	13	2	15	58
1962	LOS ANGELES (N)	.346	163	665	120	230	27	9	27	153
1963	LOS ANGELES (N)	.326	146	556	69	181	19	3	16	88
1964	LOS ANGELES (N)	.275	152	592	70	163	20	5	14	86
1965	LOS ANGELES (N)	.250	17	60	3	15	1	1	0	9
1966	LOS ANGELES (N)	.313	100	313	27	98	11	1	3	27
1967	New York (N)	.302	154	577	72	174	32	0	16	73
1968	Chicago (A)	.268	132	456	30	122	5	3	8	50
1969	Seattle (A)									
1969	Houston (N)									
	(year totals)	.266	147	533	54	142	32	1	7	89
1970	Houston (N)									
1970	Oakland (A)									
1970	Chicago (N)									
	(year totals)	.284	134	455	45	129	23	3	6	65
1971	Oakland (A)	.324	79	219	26	71	8	1	3	42
1972	Chicago (N)									
1972	Baltimore (A)									
	(year totals)	.259	41	108	12	28	4	0	0	12
1973	Baltimore (A)	.306	137	552	52	169	21	3	7	89
1974	Baltimore (A)	.289	158	626	67	181	20	1	11	84
1975	Baltimore (A)	.283	116	460	43	130	14	1	6	57
1976	California (A)									
1976	Kansas City (A)									
	(year totals)	.265	80	238	17	63	5	0	3	26
	Eighteen years	.294	1999	7223	810	2121	273	35	153	1052
League Championship										
	Three years	.295	12	44	2	13	2	0	0	3

World Series

YEAR	CLUB	BA	G	AB	R	H	2B	3B	HR	RBI
1963	LOS ANGELES (N)	.400	4	15	0	6	0	2	0	3
1966	LOS ANGELES (N)	.250	4	8	0	2	0	0	0	0
	Two years	.348	8	23	0	8	0	2	0	3

WILLIE DAVIS B. April 15, 1940, Mineral Springs, Ark.
B.L., T.L. 5'11" 180 lbs.
(OUTFIELD)

YEAR	CLUB	BA	G	AB	R	H	2B	3B	HR	RBI
1960	LOS ANGELES (N)	.318	22	88	12	28	6	1	2	10
1961	LOS ANGELES (N)	.254	128	339	56	86	19	6	12	45
1962	LOS ANGELES (N)	.285	157	600	103	171	18	10	21	85
1963	LOS ANGELES (N)	.245	156	515	60	126	19	8	9	60
1964	LOS ANGELES (N)	.294	157	613	91	180	23	7	12	77
1965	LOS ANGELES (N)	.238	142	558	52	133	24	3	10	57
1966	LOS ANGELES (N)	.284	153	624	74	177	31	6	11	61
1967	LOS ANGELES (N)	.257	143	569	65	146	27	9	6	41
1968	LOS ANGELES (N)	.250	160	643	86	161	24	10	7	31
1969	LOS ANGELES (N)	.311	129	498	66	155	23	8	11	59
1970	LOS ANGELES (N)	.305	146	593	92	181	23	16	8	93
1971	LOS ANGELES (N)	.309	158	641	84	198	33	10	10	74
1972	LOS ANGELES (N)	.289	149	615	81	178	22	7	19	79
1973	LOS ANGELES (N)	.285	152	599	82	171	29	9	16	77
1974	Montreal (N)	.295	153	611	86	180	27	9	12	89
1975	Texas (A)									
1975	St. Louis (N)									
	(year totals)	.277	140	519	57	144	27	8	11	67
1976	San Diego (N)	.268	141	493	61	132	18	10	5	46
1979	California (A)	.250	43	56	9	14	2	1	0	2
	Eighteen years	.279	2429	9174	1217	2561	395	138	182	1053
League Championship										
	One year	.500	2	2	1	1	1	0	0	0

World Series

YEAR	CLUB	BA	G	AB	R	H	2B	3B	HR	RBI
1963	LOS ANGELES (N)	.167	4	12	2	2	2	0	0	3
1965	LOS ANGELES (N)	.231	7	26	3	6	0	0	0	0
1966	LOS ANGELES (N)	.063	4	16	0	1	0	0	0	0
	Three years	.167	15	54	5	9	2	0	0	3

LINDSAY DEAL B. Sept. 3, 1911, Lenoir, N.C.
B.L., T.R. 6' 175 lbs.
(OUTFIELD)

YEAR	CLUB	BA	G	AB	R	H	2B	3B	HR	RBI
1939	BROOKLYN (N)	.000	4	7	0	0	0	0	0	0

TOMMY DEAN B. Aug. 30, 1945, Iuka, Miss.
B.R., T.R. 6' 165 lbs.
(SHORTSTOP)

YEAR	CLUB	BA	G	AB	R	H	2B	3B	HR	RBI
1967	LOS ANGELES (N)	.143	12	28	1	4	1	0	0	2
	Four years (total)	.180	215	529	35	95	15	3	4	25

HANK DeBERRY B. Dec. 29, 1893, Savannah, Tenn.
B.R., T.R. 5'11" 195 lbs.
(CATCHER)

YEAR	CLUB	BA	G	AB	R	H	2B	3B	HR	RBI
1916	Cleveland (A)	.273	15	33	7	9	4	0	0	4
1917	Cleveland (A)	.273	25	33	3	9	2	0	0	1
1922	BROOKLYN (N)	.301	85	259	29	78	10	1	3	35
1923	BROOKLYN (N)	.285	78	235	21	67	11	6	1	48
1924	BROOKLYN (N)	.243	77	218	20	53	10	3	3	26
1925	BROOKLYN (N)	.259	67	193	26	50	8	1	2	24
1926	BROOKLYN (N)	.287	48	115	6	33	11	0	0	13
1927	BROOKLYN (N)	.234	68	201	15	47	3	2	1	21
1928	BROOKLYN (N)	.252	82	258	19	65	8	2	0	23
1929	BROOKLYN (N)	.262	68	210	13	55	11	1	1	25
1930	BROOKLYN (N)	.295	35	95	11	28	3	0	0	14
	Eleven years	.267	648	1850	170	494	81	16	11	234

ARTIE DEDE B. July 12, 1895, Brooklyn, N.Y.
B.R., T.R. 5'9" 155 lbs.
(CATCHER)

YEAR	CLUB	BA	G	AB	R	H	2B	3B	HR	RBI
1916	BROOKLYN (N)	.000	1	1	0	0	0	0	0	0

RAOUL DEDEAUX B. Feb. 17, 1915, New Orleans, La.
B.R., T.R. 5'11" 160 lbs.
(SHORTSTOP)

YEAR	CLUB	BA	G	AB	R	H	2B	3B	HR	RBI
1935	BROOKLYN (N)	.250	2	4	0	1	0	0	0	1

PAT DEISEL B. April 29, 1875, Ripley, Ohio
B.R., T.R. 5'5" 145 lbs.
(CATCHER)

YEAR	CLUB	BA	G	AB	R	H	2B	3B	HR	RBI
1902	BROOKLYN (N)	.667	1	3	0	2	0	0	0	1
	Two years (total)	.667	3	3	0	2	0	0	0	1

IVAN DeJESUS

B. Jan. 9, 1953, Santurce, Puerto Rico
B.R., T.R. 5'11" 175 lbs.
(SHORTSTOP)

YEAR	CLUB	BA	G	AB	R	H	2B	3B	HR	RBI
1974	LOS ANGELES (N)	.333	3	3	1	1	0	0	0	0
1975	LOS ANGELES (N)	.184	63	87	10	16	2	1	0	2
1976	LOS ANGELES (N)	.171	22	41	4	7	2	1	0	2
	Nine years (total)	.255	987	3567	482	908	140	38	17	236

BERT DELMAS

B. May 20, 1911, San Francisco, Calif.
B.L., T.R. 5'11" 165 lbs.
(2ND BASE)

YEAR	CLUB	BA	G	AB	R	H	2B	3B	HR	RBI
1933	BROOKLYN (N)	.250	12	28	4	7	0	0	0	0

DON DEMETER

B. June 25, 1935, Oklahoma City, Okla.
B.R., T.R. 6'4" 190 lbs.
(OUTFIELD)

YEAR	CLUB	BA	G	AB	R	H	2B	3B	HR	RBI
1956	BROOKLYN (N)	.333	3	3	1	1	0	0	1	1
1958	LOS ANGELES (N)	.189	43	106	11	20	2	0	5	8
1959	LOS ANGELES (N)	.256	139	371	55	95	11	1	18	70
1960	LOS ANGELES (N)	.274	64	168	23	46	7	1	9	29
1961	LOS ANGELES (N)	.172	15	29	3	5	0	0	1	2
1961	Philadelphia (N)									
	(year totals)	.251	121	411	57	103	18	4	21	70
1962	Philadelphia (N)	.307	153	550	85	169	24	3	29	107
1963	Philadelphia (N)	.258	154	515	63	133	20	2	22	83
1964	Detroit (A)	.256	134	441	57	113	22	1	22	80
1965	Detroit (A)	.278	122	389	50	108	16	4	16	58
1966	Detroit (A)									
1966	Boston (A)									
	(year totals)	.268	105	325	43	87	18	1	14	41
1967	Boston (A)									
1967	Cleveland (A)									
	(year totals)	.226	71	164	22	37	9	0	6	16
	Eleven years	.265	1109	3443	467	912	147	17	163	563
World Series										
	One year	.250	6	12	2	3	0	0	0	0

GENE DeMONTREVILLE

B. March 26, 1874, St. Paul, Minn.
B.R., T.R. 5'8" 165 lbs.
(2ND BASE, SHORTSTOP)

YEAR	CLUB	BA	G	AB	R	H	2B	3B	HR	RBI
1900	BROOKLYN (N)	.244	69	234	34	57	8	1	0	28
	Eleven years (total)	.305	922	3615	537	1104	130	35	17	497

DICK DIETZ

B. Sept. 18, 1941, Crawfordsville, Ind.
B.R., T.R. 6'1" 195 lbs.
(CATCHER)

YEAR	CLUB	BA	G	AB	R	H	2B	3B	HR	RBI
1972	LOS ANGELES (N)	.161	27	56	4	9	1	0	1	6
	Eight years (total)	.261	646	1829	226	478	89	6	66	301

POP DILLON

B. Oct. 17, 1873, Normal, Ill.
B.L., T.R.
(1ST BASE)

YEAR	CLUB	BA	G	AB	R	H	2B	3B	HR	RBI
1904	BROOKLYN (N)	.258	135	511	60	132	18	6	0	31
	Five years (total)	.252	312	1181	146	298	44	16	1	116

JOHN DOBBS

B. June 3, 1876, Chattanooga, Tenn.
B.L., T.R. 5'9½" 170 lbs.
(OUTFIELD)

YEAR	CLUB	BA	G	AB	R	H	2B	3B	HR	RBI
1901	Cincinnati (N)	.274	109	435	71	119	17	4	2	27
1902	Cincinnati (N)									
1902	Chicago (N)									
	(year totals)	.299	122	491	70	147	15	5	1	51
1903	Chicago (N)									
1903	BROOKLYN (N)	.237	111	460	59	117	21	4	2	36
	(year totals)	.236	127	475	69	112	16	8	2	63
1904	BROOKLYN (N)	.248	101	363	36	90	16	2	0	30
1905	BROOKLYN (N)	.254	123	460	59	117	21	4	2	36
	Five years	.263	582	2224	305	585	85	23	7	207

COZY DOLAN

B. Dec. 3, 1872, Cambridge, Mass.
B.L., T.L., 5'10" 160 lbs.
(OUTFIELD)

YEAR	CLUB	BA	G	AB	R	H	2B	3B	HR	RBI
1895	Boston (N)	.241	26	83	12	20	4	1	0	7
1896	Boston (N)	.143	6	14	4	2	0	0	0	0
1900	Chicago (N)	.271	13	48	5	13	1	0	0	2
1901	Chicago (N)									
1901	BROOKLYN (N)	.261	66	253	33	66	11	1	0	29
	(year totals)	.262	109	424	62	111	12	3	0	45
1902	BROOKLYN (N)	.280	141	592	72	166	16	7	1	54
1903	Chicago (A)									
1903	Cincinnati (N)									
	(year totals)	.282	120	489	80	138	25	4	0	65
1904	Cincinnati (N)	.284	129	465	88	132	8	10	6	51
1905	Cincinnati (N)									
1905	Boston (N)									
	(year totals)	.269	134	510	51	137	13	8	3	52
1906	Boston (N)	.248	152	549	54	136	20	4	0	39
	Nine years	.269	830	3174	428	855	99	37	10	315

PATSY DONOVAN

B. March 16, 1865, County Cork, Ireland
B.R., T.L. 5'11½" 175 lbs.
(OUTFIELD)

YEAR	CLUB	BA	G	AB	R	H	2B	3B	HR	RBI
1890	BROOKLYN (N)	.352	28	114	15	25	2	0	0	8
1906	BROOKLYN (N)	.238	7	21	1	5	0	0	0	0
1907	BROOKLYN (N)	.000	1	1	0	0	0	0	0	0
	Seventeen years (total)	.301	1821	7496	1318	2256	208	75	16	736

MICKEY DOOLAN

B. May 7, 1880, Ashland, Pa.
B.R., T.R. 5'10½" 170 lbs.
(SHORTSTOP)

YEAR	CLUB	BA	G	AB	R	H	2B	3B	HR	RBI
1918	BROOKLYN (N)	.179	92	308	14	55	8	2	0	18
	Thirteen years (total)	.230	1727	5976	513	1376	244	81	15	554

JOHN DOUGLAS

B. Sept. 14, 1917, Thayer, W.Va.
B.L., T.L. 6'2½" 195 lbs.
(1ST BASE)

YEAR	CLUB	BA	G	AB	R	H	2B	3B	HR	RBI
1945	BROOKLYN (N)	.000	5	9	0	0	0	0	0	0

SNOOKS DOWD

B. Dec. 29, 1897, Springfield, Mass.
B.R., T.R. 5'8" 163 lbs.
(2ND BASE, SHORTSTOP)

YEAR	CLUB	BA	G	AB	R	H	2B	3B	HR	RBI
1926	BROOKLYN (N)	.000	2	8	0	0	0	0	0	0
	Two years (total)	.115	16	26	4	3	0	0	0	6

RED DOWNEY
B. Feb. 6, 1889, Aurora, Ind.
B.L., T.L. 5'11" 174 lbs.
(OUTFIELD)

YEAR	CLUB	BA	G	AB	R	H	2B	3B	HR	RBI
1909	BROOKLYN	.256	19	78	7	20	1	0	0	8

RED DOWNS
B. Aug. 23, 1883, Neola, Iowa
B.R., T.R.
(2ND BASE)

YEAR	CLUB	BA	G	AB	R	H	2B	3B	HR	RBI
1912	BROOKLYN (N)	.250	9	32	2	8	3	0	0	3
	Three years (total)	.227	241	790	68	179	30	11	3	94

JACK DOYLE
B. Oct. 25, 1869, Killorgin, Ireland
B.R., T.R. 5'9" 155 lbs.
(1ST BASE)

YEAR	CLUB	BA	G	AB	R	H	2B	3B	HR	RBI
1903	BROOKLYN (N)	.313	139	524	84	164	27	6	0	91
1904	BROOKLYN (N)	.227	8	22	5	1	0	0	0	2
	Seventeen years (total)	.301	1564	6051	980	1822	315	64	25	924

SOLLY DRAKE
B. Oct. 23, 1930, Little Rock, Ark.
B.B., T.R. 6' 170 lbs.
(OUTFIELD)

YEAR	CLUB	BA	G	AB	R	H	2B	3B	HR	RBI
1959	LOS ANGELES (N)	.250	9	8	2	2	0	0	0	6
	Two years (total)	.232	141	285	41	66	10	1	2	18

JOE DUNN
B. March 11, 1885, Springfield, Ohio
B.R., T.R.
(CATCHER)

YEAR	CLUB	BA	G	AB	R	H	2B	3B	HR	RBI
1908	BROOKLYN (N)	.172	20	64	3	11	3	0	0	5
1909	BROOKLYN (N)	.160	10	25	1	4	1	0	0	2
	Two years	.169	30	89	4	15	4	0	0	7

LEO DUROCHER
B. July 27, 1905, West Springfield, Mass.
B.R., T.R. 5'10" 160 lbs.
(SHORTSTOP)

YEAR	CLUB	BA	G	AB	R	H	2B	3B	HR	RBI
1925	New York (A)	.000	2	1	1	0	0	0	0	0
1928	New York (A)	.270	102	296	46	80	8	6	0	31
1929	New York (A)	.246	106	341	53	84	4	5	0	32
1930	Cincinnati (N)	.243	119	354	31	86	15	3	3	32
1931	Cincinnati (N)	.227	121	361	26	82	11	5	1	29
1932	Cincinnati (N)	.217	143	457	43	99	22	5	1	33
1933	Cincinnati (N)									
1933	St. Louis (N)									
	(year totals)	.253	139	446	51	113	19	4	3	44
1934	St. Louis (N)	.260	146	500	62	130	26	5	3	70
1935	St. Louis (N)	.265	143	513	62	136	23	5	8	78
1936	St. Louis (N)	.286	136	510	57	146	22	3	1	58
1937	St. Louis (N)	.203	135	477	46	97	11	3	1	47
1938	BROOKLYN (N)	.219	141	479	41	105	18	5	1	56
1939	BROOKLYN (N)	.277	116	390	42	108	21	6	1	34
1940	BROOKLYN (N)	.231	62	160	10	37	9	1	1	14
1941	BROOKLYN (N)	.286	18	42	2	12	1	0	0	6
1943	BROOKLYN (N)	.222	6	18	1	4	0	0	0	1
1945	BROOKLYN (N)	.200	2	5	1	1	0	0	0	2
	Seventeen years	.247	1637	5350	575	1320	210	56	24	567
World Series										
	Two years	.241	11	29	4	7	1	1	0	0

The Complete Catalogue of Players • 53

RED DURRETT B. Feb. 3, 1921, Sherman, Texas
B.L., T.L. 5'10" 170 lbs.
(OUTFIELD)

YEAR	CLUB	BA	G	AB	R	H	2B	3B	HR	RBI
1944	BROOKLYN (N)	.156	11	32	3	5	1	0	1	1
1945	BROOKLYN (N)	.125	8	16	2	2	0	0	0	0
	Two years	.146	19	48	5	7	1	0	1	1

BILLY EARLE B. Nov. 10, 1867, Philadelphia, Pa.
B.R., T.R. 5'10½" 170 lbs.
(CATCHER)

YEAR	CLUB	BA	G	AB	R	H	2B	3B	HR	RBI
1894	BROOKLYN (N)	.340	14	53	9	18	3	0	0	5
	Five years (total)	.286	142	465	102	133	20	12	6	62

OX ECKHARDT B. Dec. 23, 1901, Yorktown, Texas
B.L., T.R. 6'1" 185 lbs.
(OUTFIELD)

YEAR	CLUB	BA	G	AB	R	H	2B	3B	HR	RBI
1936	BROOKLYN (N)	.182	16	44	5	8	1	0	1	6
	Two years (total)	.192	24	52	6	10	1	0	1	7

BRUCE EDWARDS B. July 15, 1923, Quincy, Ill.
B.R., T.R. 5'8" 180 lbs.
(CATCHER)

YEAR	CLUB	BA	G	AB	R	H	2B	3B	HR	RBI
1946	BROOKLYN (N)	.267	92	292	24	78	13	5	1	25
1947	BROOKLYN (N)	.295	130	471	53	139	15	8	9	80
1948	BROOKLYN (N)	.276	96	286	36	79	17	2	8	54
1949	BROOKLYN (N)	.209	64	148	24	31	3	0	8	25
1950	BROOKLYN (N)	.183	50	142	16	26	4	1	8	16
1951	BROOKLYN (N)	.250	17	36	6	9	2	0	1	8
1951	Chicago (N)									
	(year totals)	.237	68	177	25	42	11	2	4	25
1952	Chicago (N)	.245	50	94	7	23	2	2	1	12
1954	Chicago (N)	.000	4	3	1	0	0	0	0	1
1955	Washington (A)	.175	30	57	5	10	2	0	0	3
1956	Cincinnati (N)	.200	7	5	0	1	0	0	0	0
	Ten years	.256	591	1675	191	429	67	20	39	241

World Series

YEAR	CLUB	BA	G	AB	R	H	2B	3B	HR	RBI
1947	BROOKLYN (N)	.222	7	27	3	6	1	0	0	2
1949	BROOKLYN (N)	.500	2	2	0	1	0	0	0	0
	Two years	.241	9	29	3	7	1	0	0	2

HANK EDWARDS B. Jan. 29, 1919, Elmwood Place, Ohio
B.L., T.L. 6' 190 lbs.
(OUTFIELD)

YEAR	CLUB	BA	G	AB	R	H	2B	3B	HR	RBI
1951	BROOKLYN (N)	.226	35	31	1	7	3	0	0	3
	Eleven years (total)	.280	735	2191	285	613	116	41	51	276

DICK EGAN B. June 23, 1884, Portland, Ore.
B.R., T.R. 5'11" 162 lbs.
(2ND BASE)

YEAR	CLUB	BA	G	AB	R	H	2B	3B	HR	RBI
1914	BROOKLYN (N)	.226	106	337	30	76	10	3	1	21
1915	BROOKLYN (N)	.000	3	3	0	0	0	0	0	0
	Nine years (total)	.249	917	3080	374	767	87	29	4	292

54 • The Complete Dodgers Record Book

KID ELBERFELD B. April 13, 1875, Pomeroy, Ohio
B.R., T.R. 5'7" 158 lbs.
(SHORTSTOP, 3RD BASE)

YEAR	CLUB	BA	G	AB	R	H	2B	3B	HR	RBI
1914	BROOKLYN (N)	.226	30	62	7	14	1	0	0	1
	Fourteen years (total)	.271	1292	4561	647	1235	169	56	10	535

HAROLD ELLIOTT B. July 8, 1890, Bloomington, Ill.
B.R., T.R.
(CATCHER)

YEAR	CLUB	BA	G	AB	R	H	2B	3B	HR	RBI
1920	BROOKLYN (N)	.241	41	112	13	27	4	0	1	13
	Five years (total)	.241	157	402	36	97	15	5	1	44

BONES ELY B. June 7, 1863, Girard, Pa.
B.R., T.R. 6'1" 155 lbs.
(SHORTSTOP)

YEAR	CLUB	BA	G	AB	R	H	2B	3B	HR	RBI
1891	BROOKLYN (N)	.153	31	111	9	17	0	1	0	11
	Fifteen years (total)	.258	1342	5162	656	1331	149	68	24	586

*1884 Buffalo (N), 1886 Louisville (AA)

GIL ENGLISH B. July 2, 1909, Glenola, N.C.
B.R., T.R. 5'11" 180 lbs.
(3RD BASE)

YEAR	CLUB	BA	G	AB	R	H	2B	3B	HR	RBI
1944	BROOKLYN (N)	.152	27	79	4	12	3	0	1	7
	Six years (total)	.245	240	791	74	194	22	7	8	90

WOODY ENGLISH B. March 2, 1907, Fredonia, Ohio
B.R., T.R. 5'10" 155 lbs.
(SHORTSTOP, 3RD BASE)

YEAR	CLUB	BA	G	AB	R	H	2B	3B	HR	RBI
1927	Chicago (N)	.290	87	334	46	97	14	4	1	28
1928	Chicago (N)	.299	116	475	68	142	22	4	2	34
1929	Chicago (N)	.276	144	608	131	168	29	3	1	52
1930	Chicago (N)	.335	156	638	152	214	36	17	14	59
1931	Chicago (N)	.319	156	634	117	202	38	8	2	53
1932	Chicago (N)	.272	127	522	70	142	23	7	3	47
1933	Chicago (N)	.261	105	398	54	104	19	2	3	41
1934	Chicago (N)	.278	109	421	65	117	26	5	3	31
1935	Chicago (N)	.202	34	84	11	17	2	0	2	8
1936	Chicago (N)	.247	64	182	33	45	9	0	0	20
1937	BROOKLYN (N)	.238	129	378	45	90	16	2	1	42
1938	BROOKLYN (N)	.250	34	72	9	18	2	0	0	7
	Twelve years	.286	1261	4746	801	1356	236	52	32	422
World Series										
	Two years	.184	9	38	3	7	2	0	0	1

TEX ERWIN B. Dec. 22, 1885, Forney, Texas
B.L., T.R. 6' 185 lbs.
(CATCHER)

YEAR	CLUB	BA	G	AB	R	H	2B	3B	HR	RBI
1907	Detroit (A)	.200	4	5	0	1	0	0	0	1
1910	BROOKLYN (N)	.188	81	202	15	38	3	1	1	10
1911	BROOKLYN (N)	.271	91	218	30	59	13	2	7	34
1912	BROOKLYN (N)	.211	59	133	14	28	3	0	2	14
1913	BROOKLYN (N)	.258	20	31	6	8	1	0	0	3
1914	BROOKLYN (N)	.455	9	11	0	5	0	0	0	1
1914	Cincinnati (N)									
	(year totals)	.348	21	46	5	16	3	0	1	8
	Six years	.236	276	635	70	150	23	3	11	70

The Complete Catalogue of Players • 55

CHUCK ESSEGIAN B. Aug. 9, 1931, Boston, Mass.
B.R., T.R. 5'11" 200 lbs.
(OUTFIELD)

YEAR	CLUB	BA	G	AB	R	H	2B	3B	HR	RBI
1959	LOS ANGELES (N)	.304	24	46	6	14	6	0	1	5
1960	LOS ANGELES (N)	.215	52	79	8	17	3	0	3	11
	Six years (total)	.255	404	1018	139	260	45	4	47	150
World Series										
	One Year	.667	4	3	2	2	0	0	2	2

DUDE ESTERBROOK B. June 20, 1860, Staten Island, N.Y.
B.R., T.R. 5'11" 167 lbs.
(3RD BASE, 1ST BASE)

YEAR	CLUB	BA	G	AB	R	H	2B	3B	HR	RBI
1891	BROOKLYN (N)	.375	3	8	1	3	0	0	0	0
	Eleven years (total)	.261	701	2837	387	741	120	34	6	159

*1880 Buffalo (N), 1882 Cleveland (N), 1883 New York (AA), 1885 New York (N), 1887 New York (AA), 1888 Indianapolis (N), Louisville (AA)

STEVE EVANS B. Feb. 17, 1885, Cleveland, Ohio
B.L., T.L.
(OUTFIELD)

YEAR	CLUB	BA	G	AB	R	H	2B	3B	HR	RBI
1908	New York (N)	.500	2	2	0	1	0	0	0	0
1909	St. Louis (N)	.259	143	498	67	129	17	6	2	56
1910	St. Louis (N)	.241	151	506	73	122	21	8	2	73
1911	St. Louis (N)	.294	154	547	74	161	24	13	5	71
1912	St. Louis (N)	.283	135	491	59	139	23	9	6	72
1913	St. Louis (N)	.249	97	245	18	61	15	6	1	31
1914	BROOKLYN (N)	.348	145	514	93	179	41	15	12	96
1915	BROOKLYN (F)									
1915	Baltimore (F)									
	(year totals)	.308	151	556	94	171	34	10	4	67
	Eight years	.287	978	3359	478	963	175	67	32	466

BUNNY FABRIQUE B. Dec. 23, 1887, Clinton, Mich.
B.B., T.R. 5'8½" 150 lbs.
(SHORTSTOP)

YEAR	CLUB	BA	G	AB	R	H	2B	3B	HR	RBI
1916	BROOKLYN (N)	.000	2	2	0	0	0	0	0	0
1917	BROOKLYN (N)	.205	25	88	8	18	3	0	1	3
	Two years	.200	27	90	8	18	3	0	1	3

JIM FAIREY B. Sept. 22, 1944, Orangeburg, S.C.
B.L., T.L. 5'10" 190 lbs.
(OUTFIELD)

YEAR	CLUB	BA	G	AB	R	H	2B	3B	HR	RBI
1968	LOS ANGELES (N)	.199	99	156	17	31	3	3	1	10
1973	LOS ANGELES (N)	.222	10	9	0	2	0	0	0	0
	Six years (total)	.235	399	766	86	180	28	7	7	75

RON FAIRLY B. July 12, 1938, Macon, Ga.
B.L., T.L. 5'10" 175 lbs.
(1ST BASE, OUTFIELD)

YEAR	CLUB	BA	G	AB	R	H	2B	3B	HR	RBI
1958	LOS ANGELES (N)	.283	15	53	6	15	1	0	2	6
1959	LOS ANGELES (N)	.238	118	244	27	58	12	1	4	23
1960	LOS ANGELES (N)	.108	14	37	6	4	0	3	1	3
1961	LOS ANGELES (N)	.322	111	245	42	79	15	2	10	48
1962	LOS ANGELES (N)	.278	147	460	80	128	15	7	14	71
1963	LOS ANGELES (N)	.271	152	490	62	133	21	0	12	77
1964	LOS ANGELES (N)	.256	150	454	62	116	19	5	10	74
1965	LOS ANGELES (N)	.274	158	555	73	152	28	1	9	70
1966	LOS ANGELES (N)	.288	117	351	53	101	20	0	14	61

YEAR	CLUB	BA	G	AB	R	H	2B	3B	HR	RBI
1967	LOS ANGELES (N)	.220	153	486	45	107	19	0	10	55
1968	LOS ANGELES (N)	.234	141	441	41	103	15	1	4	43
1969	LOS ANGELES (N)	.219	30	64	3	14	3	2	0	8
1969	Montreal (N)									
	(year totals)	.274	100	317	38	87	16	6	12	47
1970	Montreal (N)	.288	119	385	54	111	19	0	15	61
1971	Montreal (N)	.257	146	447	58	115	23	0	13	71
1972	Montreal (N)	.278	140	446	51	124	15	1	17	68
1973	Montreal (N)	.298	142	413	70	123	13	1	17	49
1974	Montreal (N)	.245	101	282	35	69	9	1	12	43
1975	St. Louis (N)	.301	107	229	32	69	13	2	7	37
1976	St. Louis (N)									
1976	Oakland (A)									
	(year totals)	.256	88	156	22	40	5	0	3	31
1977	Toronto (A)	.279	132	458	60	128	24	2	19	64
1978	California (A)	.217	91	235	23	51	5	0	10	40
	Twenty-one years	.266	2442	7184	931	1913	307	33	215	1044

World Series

YEAR	CLUB	BA	G	AB	R	H	2B	3B	HR	RBI
1959	LOS ANGELES (N)	.000	6	3	0	0	0	0	0	0
1963	LOS ANGELES (N)	.000	4	1	0	0	0	0	0	0
1965	LOS ANGELES (N)	.379	7	29	7	11	3	0	2	6
1966	LOS ANGELES (N)	.143	3	7	0	1	0	0	0	0
	Four years	.300	20	40	7	12	3	0	2	6

GEORGE FALLON B. July 8, 1916, Jersey City, N.J.
B.R., T.R. 5'9" 155 lbs.
(2ND BASE, SHORTSTOP)

YEAR	CLUB	BA	G	AB	R	H	2B	3B	HR	RBI
1937	BROOKLYN (N)	.250	4	8	0	2	1	0	0	0
	Four years (total)	.216	133	282	26	61	10	1	1	21

ALEX FARMER B. May 9, 1880, New York, N.Y.
B.R., T.R. 6' 175 lbs.
(CATCHER)

YEAR	CLUB	BA	G	AB	R	H	2B	3B	HR	RBI
1908	BROOKLYN (N)	.167	12	30	1	5	1	0	0	2

DUKE FARRELL B. August 31, 1866, Oakdale, Mass.
B.B., T.R. 6'2" 180 lbs.
(CATCHER, 3RD BASE)

YEAR	CLUB	BA	G	AB	R	H	2B	3B	HR	RBI
*1890	Chicago (P)	.290	117	451	79	131	21	12	2	84
1891	Boston (AA)	.302	122	473	108	143	19	13	12	110
1892	Pittsburgh (N)	.215	152	605	96	130	10	13	8	77
1893	Washington (N)	.280	124	511	84	143	13	13	4	75
1894	New York (N)	.284	114	401	47	114	20	12	4	66
1895	New York (N)	.288	90	312	38	90	16	9	1	58
1896	New York (N)									
1896	Washington (N)									
	(year totals)	.290	95	321	41	93	14	6	2	67
1897	Washington (N)	.322	78	261	41	84	9	6	0	53
1898	Washington (N)	.314	99	338	53	106	12	6	1	53
1899	Washington (N)									
1899	BROOKLYN (N)	.299	80	157	15	47	6	2	0	20
	(year totals)	.301	85	266	42	80	11	7	2	56
1900	BROOKLYN (N)	.275	76	273	33	75	11	5	0	39
1901	BROOKLYN (N)	.296	80	284	38	84	10	6	1	31
1902	BROOKLYN (N)	.242	74	264	14	64	5	2	0	24
1903	Boston (A)	.404	17	52	5	21	5	1	0	8
1904	Boston (A)	.212	68	198	11	42	9	2	0	15
1905	Boston (A)	.286	7	21	2	6	1	0	0	2
	Eighteen years	.275	1563	5679	826	1563	211	123	51	912

World Series
| | One year | .000 | 2 | 2 | 0 | 0 | 0 | 0 | 0 | 1 |

*1888 Chicago (N)

GUS FELIX B. May 24, 1895, Cincinnati, Ohio
B.R., T.R. 6' 180 lbs.
(OUTFIELD)

YEAR	CLUB	BA	G	AB	R	H	2B	3B	HR	RBI
1923	Boston (N)	.273	139	506	64	138	17	2	6	44
1924	Boston (N)	.211	59	204	25	43	7	1	1	10
1925	Boston (N)	.307	121	459	60	141	25	7	2	66
1926	BROOKLYN (N)	.280	134	432	64	121	21	7	3	53
1927	BROOKLYN (N)	.265	130	445	43	118	21	8	0	57
	Five years	.274	583	2046	256	561	91	25	12	230

JOE FERGUSON B. Sept. 19, 1946, San Francisco, Calif.
B.R., T.R. 6'2" 200 lbs.
(CATCHER, OUTFIELD)

YEAR	CLUB	BA	G	AB	R	H	2B	3B	HR	RBI
1970	LOS ANGELES (N)	.250	5	4	0	1	0	0	0	1
1971	LOS ANGELES (N)	.216	36	102	13	22	3	0	2	7
1972	LOS ANGELES (N)	.292	8	24	2	7	3	0	1	5
1973	LOS ANGELES (N)	.263	136	487	84	128	26	0	25	88
1974	LOS ANGELES (N)	.252	111	349	54	88	14	1	16	57
1975	LOS ANGELES (N)	.208	66	202	15	42	2	1	5	23
1976	LOS ANGELES (N)	.222	54	185	24	41	7	7	6	18
1976	St. Louis (N)									
	(year totals)	.211	125	374	46	79	15	4	10	39
1977	Houston (N)	.257	132	421	59	108	21	3	16	61
1978	Houston (N)									
1978	LOS ANGELES (N)	.224	118	348	40	78	16	0	14	50
	(two clubs)	.224	118	348	40	78	16	0	14	50
1979	LOS ANGELES (N)	.262	122	363	54	95	14	0	20	69
1980	LOS ANGELES (N)	.238	77	172	20	41	3	2	9	29
1981	LOS ANGELES (N)	.143	17	14	0	2		1		
1981	California (A)									
	(year totals)	.205	29	44	7	9	2	0	1	6
	Twelve years	.242	965	2890	394	698	119	11	119	435

League Championship

| | Two years | .200 | 6 | 15 | 3 | 3 | 0 | 0 | 0 | 2 |

World Series

YEAR	CLUB	BA	G	AB	R	H	2B	3B	HR	RBI
1974	LOS ANGELES (N)	.125	5	16	2	2	0	0	1	2
1977	LOS ANGELES (N)	.500	2	4	1	2	2	0	0	0
	Two years	.200	7	20	3	4	2	0	1	2

CHICO FERNANDEZ B. March 2, 1932, Havana, Cuba
B.R., T.R. 6' 165 lbs.
(SHORTSTOP)

YEAR	CLUB	BA	G	AB	R	H	2B	3B	HR	RBI
1956	BROOKLYN (N)	.227	34	66	11	15	2	0	1	9
	Eight years (total)	.240	856	2778	270	666	91	19	40	270

AL FERRARA B. Dec. 22, 1939, Brooklyn, N.Y.
B.R., T.R. 6'1" 200 lbs.
(OUTFIELD)

YEAR	CLUB	BA	G	AB	R	H	2B	3B	HR	RBI
1963	LOS ANGELES (N)	.159	21	44	2	7	0	0	1	1
1965	LOS ANGELES (N	.210	41	81	5	17	2	1	1	10
1966	LOS ANGELES (N)	.270	63	115	15	31	4	0	5	23
1967	LOS ANGELES (N)	.277	122	347	41	96	16	1	16	50
1968	LOS ANGELES (N)	.143	2	7	0	1	0	0	0	0
1969	San Diego (N)	.260	138	366	39	95	22	1	14	56
1970	San Diego (N)	.277	138	372	44	103	15	4	13	51
1971	San Diego (N)									
1971	Cincinnati (N)									
	(year totals)	.160	49	50	2	8	1	0	1	7
	Eight years	.259	574	1382	148	358	60	7	51	198

World Series

| | One year | 1.000 | 1 | 1 | 0 | 1 | 0 | 0 | 0 | 0 |

CHICK FEWSTER
B. Nov. 10, 1895, Baltimore, Md.
B.R., T.R. 5'11" 160 lbs.
(2ND BASE, OUTFIELD)

YEAR	CLUB	BA	G	AB	R	H	2B	3B	HR	RBI
1926	BROOKLYN (N)	.243	105	337	53	82	16	3	2	24
1927	BROOKLYN (N)	.000	4	1	1	0	0	0	0	0
	Eleven years (total)	.258	644	1963	282	506	91	12	6	167

MICKEY FINN
B. Jan. 24, 1902, New York, N.Y.
B.R., T.R. 5'11" 168 lbs.
(2ND BASE)

YEAR	CLUB	BA	G	AB	R	H	2B	3B	HR	RBI
1930	BROOKLYN (N)	.278	87	273	42	76	13	0	3	30
1931	BROOKLYN (N)	.274	118	413	46	113	22	2	0	45
1932	BROOKLYN (N)	.238	65	189	22	45	5	2	0	14
1933	Philadelphia (N)	.237	51	169	15	40	4	1	0	13
	Four years	.262	321	1044	125	274	44	5	3	102

BILL FISCHER
B. March 2, 1891, New York, N.Y.
B.L., T.R. 6' 174 lbs.
(CATCHER)

YEAR	CLUB	BA	G	AB	R	H	2B	3B	HR	RBI
1913	BROOKLYN (N)	.267	62	165	16	44	9	4	1	12
1914	BROOKLYN (N)	.257	43	105	12	27	1	2	0	8
	Five years (total)	.274	412	1099	109	301	50	15	10	115

BOB FISHER
B. Nov. 3, 1887, Nashville, Tenn.
B.R., T.R. 5'9½" 170 lbs.
(SHORTSTOP)

YEAR	CLUB	BA	G	AB	R	H	2B	3B	HR	RBI
1912	BROOKLYN (N)	.233	82	257	27	60	10	3	0	26
1913	BROOKLYN (N)	.262	132	474	42	124	11	10	4	54
1914	Chicago (N)	.300	15	50	5	15	2	2	0	5
1915	Chicago (N)	.287	147	568	70	163	22	5	5	53
1916	Cincinnati (N)	.272	61	136	9	37	4	3	0	11
1918	St. Louis (N)	.317	63	246	36	78	11	3	2	20
1919	St. Louis (N)	.273	3	11	0	3	1	0	0	1
	Seven years	.276	503	1742	189	480	61	26	11	189

TOM FITZSIMMONS
B. April 6, 1890, Oakland, Calif.
B.R., T.R. 6'1" 190 lbs.
(3RD BASE)

YEAR	CLUB	BA	G	AB	R	H	2B	3B	HR	RBI
1919	BROOKLYN (N)	.000	4	4	1	0	0	0	0	0

TIM FLOOD
B. March 13, 1877, Montgomery City, Mo.
B.R., T.R.
(2ND BASE)

YEAR	CLUB	BA	G	AB	R	H	2B	3B	HR	RBI
1899	St. Louis (N)	.290	10	31	0	9	0	0	0	3
1902	BROOKLYN (N)	.218	132	476	43	104	11	5	2	50
1903	BROOKLYN (N)	.249	89	309	27	77	15	2	0	32
	Three years	.233	231	816	70	190	26	7	2	85

JAKE FLOWERS
B. March 16, 1902, Cambridge, Mass.
B.R., T.R. 5'11½" 170 lbs.
(2ND BASE, SHORTSTOP, 3RD BASE)

YEAR	CLUB	BA	G	AB	R	H	2B	3B	HR	RBI
1923	St. Louis (N)	.094	13	32	0	3	1	0	0	2
1926	St. Louis (N)	.270	40	74	13	20	1	0	3	9
1927	BROOKLYN (N)	.234	67	231	26	54	5	5	2	20
1928	BROOKLYN (N)	.274	103	339	51	93	11	6	2	44

The Complete Catalogue of Players • 59

YEAR	CLUB	BA	G	AB	R	H	2B	3B	HR	RBI
1929	BROOKLYN (N)	.200	46	130	16	26	6	0	1	16
1930	BROOKLYN (N)	.320	89	253	37	81	18	3	2	50
1931	BROOKLYN (N)	.226	22	31	3	7	0	0	0	1
1931	St. Louis (N)									
	(year totals)	.244	67	168	22	41	11	1	2	20
1932	St. Louis (N)	.255	67	247	35	63	11	1	2	18
1933	BROOKLYN (N)	.233	78	210	28	49	11	2	2	22
1934	Cincinnati (N)	.333	13	9	1	3	0	0	0	0
	Ten years	.256	583	1693	229	433	75	18	16	201
World Series										
	Two years	.143	8	14	1	1	1	0	0	0

HOD FORD B. July 23, 1897, New Haven, Conn.
B.R., T.R. 5'10" 165 lbs.
(SHORTSTOP, 2ND BASE)

YEAR	CLUB	BA	G	AB	R	H	2B	3B	HR	RBI
1925	BROOKLYN (N)	.273	66	216	32	59	11	0	1	15
	Fifteen years (total)	.263	1446	4833	484	1269	200	55	16	494

JACK FOURNIER B. Sept. 28, 1892, Au Sable, Mich.
D. Sept. 5, 1973, Tacoma, Wash.
B.L., T.R. 6' 195 lbs.
(1ST BASE)

YEAR	CLUB	BA	G	AB	R	H	2B	3B	HR	RBI
1912	Chicago (A)	.192	35	73	5	14	5	2	0	2
1913	Chicago (A)	.233	68	172	20	40	8	5	1	23
1914	Chicago (A)	.311	109	379	44	118	14	9	6	44
1915	Chicago (A)	.322	126	422	86	136	20	18	5	77
1916	Chicago (A)	.240	105	313	36	75	13	9	3	44
1917	Chicago (A)	.000	1	1	0	0	0	0	0	0
1918	New York (A)	.350	27	100	9	35	6	1	0	12
1920	St. Louis (N)	.306	141	530	77	162	33	14	3	61
1921	St. Louis (N)	.343	149	574	103	197	27	9	16	86
1922	St. Louis (N)	.295	128	404	64	119	23	9	10	61
1923	BROOKLYN (N)	.351	133	515	91	181	30	13	22	102
1924	BROOKLYN (N)	.334	154	563	93	188	25	4	27	116
1925	BROOKLYN (N)	.350	145	545	99	191	21	16	22	130
1926	BROOKLYN (N)	.284	87	243	39	69	9	2	11	48
1927	Boston (N)	.283	122	374	55	106	18	2	10	53
	Fifteen years	.313	1530	5208	821	1631	252	113	136	859

DAVE FOUTZ B. Sept. 7, 1856, Carroll County, Md.
B.R., T.R. 6'2" 161 lbs.
(1ST BASE, OUTFIELD, PITCHER)

YEAR	CLUB	BA	G	AB	R	H	2B	3B	HR	RBI
*1890	BROOKLYN (N)	.303	129	509	106	154	25	13	5	98
1891	BROOKLYN (N)	.257	130	521	87	134	26	8	2	73
1892	BROOKLYN (N)	.186	61	220	33	41	5	3	1	26
1893	BROOKLYN (N)	.246	130	557	91	137	20	10	7	67
1894	BROOKLYN (N)	.307	72	293	40	90	12	9	0	51
1895	BROOKLYN (N)	.296	31	115	14	34	4	1	0	21
1896	BROOKLYN (N)	.250	2	8	0	2	1	0	0	0
	Thirteen years (total)	.277	1135	4533	784	1254	186	91	32	548

*1884 St. Louis (AA), 1888 Brooklyn (AA)

HERMAN FRANKS B. Jan. 4, 1914, Price, Utah
B.L., T.R. 5'10½" 187 lbs.
(CATCHER)

YEAR	CLUB	BA	G	AB	R	H	2B	3B	HR	RBI
1940	BROOKLYN (N)	.183	65	131	11	24	4	0	1	14
1941	BROOKLYN (N)	.201	59	139	10	28	7	0	1	11
	Six years (total)	.199	190	403	35	80	18	2	3	43
World Series										
	One year	.000	1	1	0	0	0	0	0	0

JOHNNY FREDERICK B. Jan. 26, 1901, Denver, Colo.
D. June 16, 1977, Tigard, Ore.
B.L., T.L. 5'11" 165 lbs.
(OUTFIELD)

YEAR	CLUB	BA	G	AB	R	H	2B	3B	HR	RBI
1929	BROOKLYN (N)	.328	148	628	127	206	52	6	24	75
1930	BROOKLYN (N)	.334	142	616	120	206	44	11	17	76
1931	BROOKLYN (N)	.270	146	611	81	165	34	8	17	71
1932	BROOKLYN (N)	.299	118	384	54	115	28	2	16	56
1933	BROOKLYN (N)	.308	147	556	65	171	22	7	7	64
1934	BROOKLYN (N)	.296	104	307	51	91	20	1	4	35
	Six years	.308	805	3102	498	954	200	35	85	377

HOWARD FREIGAU B. Aug. 1, 1902, Dayton, Ohio
B.R., T.R. 5'10½" 160 lbs.
(3RD BASE, SHORTSTOP)

YEAR	CLUB	BA	G	AB	R	H	2B	3B	HR	RBI
1928	BROOKLYN (N)	.206	17	34	6	7	2	0	0	3
	Seven years (total)	.272	579	1974	224	537	99	25	15	226

RAY FRENCH B. Jan. 9, 1897, Alameda, Calif.
B.R., T.R. 5'9½" 158 lbs.
(SHORTSTOP)

YEAR	CLUB	BA	G	AB	R	H	2B	3B	HR	RBI
1923	BROOKLYN (N)	.219	43	73	14	16	2	1	0	7
	Three years (total)	.193	82	187	29	36	6	1	0	19

LONNY FREY B. Aug. 23, 1910, St. Louis, Mo.
B.L. (B.B., 1933–38), T.R. 5'10" 160 lbs.
(2ND BASE, SHORTSTOP)

YEAR	CLUB	BA	G	AB	R	H	2B	3B	HR	RBI
1933	BROOKLYN (N)	.319	34	135	25	43	5	3	0	12
1934	BROOKLYN (N)	.284	125	490	77	139	24	5	8	57
1935	BROOKLYN (N)	.262	131	515	88	135	35	11	11	77
1936	BROOKLYN (N)	.279	148	524	63	146	29	4	4	60
1937	Chicago (N)	.278	78	198	33	55	9	3	1	22
1938	Cincinnati (N)	.265	124	501	76	133	26	6	4	36
1939	Cincinnati (N)	.291	125	484	95	141	27	9	11	55
1940	Cincinnati (N)	.266	150	563	102	150	23	6	8	54
1941	Cincinnati (N)	.254	146	543	78	139	29	5	6	59
1942	Cincinnati (N)	.266	141	523	66	139	23	6	2	39
1943	Cincinnati (N)	.263	144	586	78	154	20	8	2	43
1946	Cincinnati (N)	.246	111	333	46	82	10	3	3	24
1947	Chicago (N)									
1947	New York (A)									
	(year totals)	.197	48	71	14	14	2	0	0	5
1948	New York (A)									
1948	New York (N)									
	(year totals)	.255	30	51	7	13	1	0	1	6
	Fourteen years	.269	1535	5517	848	1482	263	69	61	549
World Series										
	Three years	.000	8	20	0	0	0	0	0	1

PEPE FRIAS B. July 15, 1948, San Piedro De Macoris, Dominican Republic
B.R., T.R. 5'10" 159 lbs.
(SHORTSTOP, 2ND BASE)

YEAR	CLUB	BA	G	AB	R	H	2B	3B	HR	RBI
1980	LOS ANGELES (N)	.200	14	10	1	2	1	0	0	0
1981	LOS ANGELES (N)	.250	25	36	6	9	1	0	0	3
	Nine years (total)	.240	723	1346	132	323	49	8	1	108

The Complete Catalogue of Players • 61

NIG FULLER B. Unknown
B.R., T.R.
(CATCHER)

YEAR	CLUB	BA	G	AB	R	H	2B	3B	HR	RBI
1902	BROOKLYN (N)	.000	3	9	0	0	0	0	0	1

CARL FURILLO B. March 8, 1922, Stony Creek Mills, Pa.
B.R., T.R. 6' 190 lbs.
(OUTFIELD)

YEAR	CLUB	BA	G	AB	R	H	2B	3B	HR	RBI
1946	BROOKLYN (N)	.284	117	335	29	95	18	6	3	35
1947	BROOKLYN (N)	.295	124	437	61	129	24	7	8	88
1948	BROOKLYN (N)	.297	108	364	55	108	20	4	4	44
1949	BROOKLYN (N)	.322	142	549	95	177	27	10	18	106
1950	BROOKLYN (N)	.305	153	620	99	189	30	6	18	106
1951	BROOKLYN (N)	.295	158	667	93	197	32	4	16	91
1952	BROOKLYN (N)	.247	134	425	52	105	18	1	8	59
1953	BROOKLYN (N)	.344	132	479	82	165	38	6	21	92
1954	BROOKLYN (N)	.294	150	547	56	161	23	1	19	96
1955	BROOKLYN (N)	.314	140	523	83	164	24	3	26	95
1956	BROOKLYN (N)	.289	149	523	66	151	30	0	21	83
1957	BROOKLYN (N)	.306	119	395	61	121	17	4	12	66
1958	LOS ANGELES (N)	.290	122	411	54	119	19	3	18	83
1959	LOS ANGELES (N)	.290	50	93	8	27	4	0	0	13
1960	LOS ANGELES (N)	.200	8	10	1	2	0	1	0	1
	Fifteen years	.299	1806	6378	895	1910	324	56	192	1058

World Series

YEAR	CLUB	BA	G	AB	R	H	2B	3B	HR	RBI
1947	BROOKLYN (N)	.353	6	17	2	6	2	0	0	3
1949	BROOKLYN (N)	.125	3	8	0	1	0	0	0	0
1952	BROOKLYN (N)	.174	7	23	1	4	2	0	0	0
1953	BROOKLYN (N)	.333	6	24	4	8	2	0	1	4
1955	BROOKLYN (N)	.296	7	27	4	8	1	0	1	3
1956	BROOKLYN (N)	.240	7	25	2	6	2	0	0	1
1959	LOS ANGELES (N)	.250	4	4	0	1	0	0	0	2
	Seven years	.266	40	128	13	34	9	0	2	13

LEN GABRIELSON B. Feb. 14, 1940, Oakland, Calif.
B.L., T.R. 6'4" 210 lbs.
(OUTFIELD)

YEAR	CLUB	BA	G	AB	R	H	2B	3B	HR	RBI
1960	Milwaukee (N)	.000	4	3	1	0	0	0	0	0
1963	Milwaukee (N)	.217	46	120	14	26	5	0	3	15
1964	Milwaukee (N)									
1964	Chicago (N)									
	(year totals)	.239	113	310	22	74	13	2	5	24
1965	Chicago (N)									
1965	San Francisco (N)									
	(year totals)	.293	116	317	40	93	6	5	7	31
1966	San Francisco (N)	.217	94	240	27	52	7	0	4	16
1967	California (A)									
1967	LOS ANGELES (N)	.261	90	238	20	62	10	3		29
	(year totals)	.252	101	250	22	63	10	3	7	31
1968	LOS ANGELES (N)	.270	108	304	38	82	16	1	10	35
1969	LOS ANGELES (N)	.270	83	178	13	48	5	1	1	18
1970	LOS ANGELES (N)	.190	43	42	1	8	2	0	0	6
	Nine years	.253	708	1764	178	446	64	12	37	176

AUGIE GALAN B. May 25, 1912, Berkeley, Calif.
B.B., T.R. 6' 175 lbs.
(OUTFIELD)

YEAR	CLUB	BA	G	AB	R	H	2B	3B	HR	RBI
1934	Chicago (N)	.260	66	192	31	50	6	2	5	22
1935	Chicago (N)	.214	154	646	133	203	41	11	12	79
1936	Chicago (N)	.264	145	575	74	152	26	4	8	81
1937	Chicago (N)	.252	147	611	104	154	24	10	18	78

YEAR	CLUB	BA	G	AB	R	H	2B	3B	HR	RBI
1938	Chicago (N)	.286	110	395	52	113	16	9	6	69
1939	Chicago (N)	.304	148	549	104	167	36	8	6	71
1940	Chicago (N)	.230	68	209	33	48	14	2	3	22
1941	Chicago (N)									
1941	BROOKLYN (N)	.259	17	27	3	7	3	0	0	4
	(year totals)	.218	82	147	21	32	6	0	1	17
1942	BROOKLYN (N)	.263	69	209	24	55	16	0	0	22
1943	BROOKLYN (N)	.287	139	495	83	142	26	3	9	67
1944	BROOKLYN (N)	.318	151	547	96	174	43	9	12	93
1945	BROOKLYN (N)	.307	152	576	114	177	36	7	9	92
1946	BROOKLYN (N)	.310	99	274	53	85	22	5	3	38
1947	Cincinnati (N)	.314	124	392	60	123	18	2	6	61
1948	Cincinnati (N)	.286	54	77	18	22	3	2	2	26
1949	New York (N)									
1949	Philadelphia (A)									
	(year totals)	.209	34	43	4	9	3	0	0	2
	Sixteen years	.287	1742	5937	1004	1706	336	74	100	830
World Series										
	Three years	.138	10	29	2	4	1	0	0	2

JOE GALLAGHER B. March 7, 1914, Buffalo, N.Y.
B.R., T.R. 6'2" 210 lbs.
(OUTFIELD)

YEAR	CLUB	BA	G	AB	R	H	2B	3B	HR	RBI
1940	BROOKLYN (N)	.264	57	110	10	29	6	1	3	16
	Four years (total)	.273	165	487	73	133	26	5	16	73

STEVE GARVEY B. Dec. 22, 1948, Tampa, Fla.
B.R., T.R. 5'10" 192 lbs.
(1ST BASE)

YEAR	CLUB	BA	G	AB	R	H	2B	3B	HR	RBI
1969	LOS ANGELES (N)	.333	3	3	0	1	0	0	0	0
1970	LOS ANGELES (N)	.269	34	93	8	25	5	0	1	6
1971	LOS ANGELES (N)	.227	81	225	27	51	12	1	7	26
1972	LOS ANGELES (N)	.269	96	294	36	79	14	2	9	36
1973	LOS ANGELES (N)	.304	114	349	37	106	17	3	8	50
1974	LOS ANGELES (N)	.312	156	642	95	200	32	3	21	111
1975	LOS ANGELES (N)	.319	160	659	85	210	38	6	18	95
1976	LOS ANGELES (N)	.317	162	631	85	200	37	4	13	80
1977	LOS ANGELES (N)	.297	162	646	91	192	25	3	33	115
1978	LOS ANGELES (N)	.316	162	639	89	202	36	9	21	113
1979	LOS ANGELES (N)	.315	162	648	92	204	32	1	28	110
1980	LOS ANGELES (N)	.304	163	658	78	200	27	1	26	106
1981	LOS ANGELES (N)	.283	110	431	63	122	23	1	10	64
1982	LOS ANGELES (N)	.282	162	625	66	176	35	1	16	86
1983	San Diego (N)	.284	100	388	76	114	22	0	14	59
	Fifteen years	.305	1827	6931	928	2082	355	36	225	1051
Divisional Playoff										
	One year	.368	5	19	4	7	0	1	2	4
League Championship										
	Four years	.343	17	70	14	24	2	1	7	14

World Series

YEAR	CLUB	BA	G	AB	R	H	2B	3B	HR	RBI
1974	LOS ANGELES (N)	.381	5	21	2	8	0	0	0	1
1977	LOS ANGELES (N)	.375	6	24	5	9	1	1	1	3
1978	LOS ANGELES (N)	.208	6	24	1	5	1	0	0	0
1981	LOS ANGELES (N)	.417	6	24	3	10	1	0	0	0
	Four years	.344	23	93	11	32	3	1	1	4

FRANK GATINS B. March 6, 1871, Johnstown, Pa.
(3RD BASE, SHORTSTOP)

YEAR	CLUB	BA	G	AB	R	H	2B	3B	HR	RBI
1901	BROOKLYN (N)	.228	50	197	21	45	7	2	1	21
	Two years (totals)	.227	67	255	27	58	9	2	1	26

SID GAUTREAUX
B. May 4, 1912, Schriever, La.
B.R., T.R. 5'8" 190 lbs.
(CATCHER)

YEAR	CLUB	BA	G	AB	R	H	2B	3B	HR	RBI
1936	BROOKLYN (N)	.268	75	71	8	19	3	0	0	16
1937	BROOKLYN (N)	.100	11	10	0	1	1	0	0	2
	Two years	.247	86	81	8	20	4	0	0	18

JIM GENTILE
B. June 3, 1934, San Francisco, Calif.
B.L., T.L. 6'3½" 210 lbs.
(1ST BASE)

YEAR	CLUB	BA	G	AB	R	H	2B	3B	HR	RBI
1957	BROOKLYN (N)	.167	4	6	1	1	0	0	1	1
1958	LOS ANGELES (N)	.133	12	30	0	4	1	0	0	4
	Nine years (total)	.260	936	2922	434	759	113	6	179	549

GREEK GEORGE
B. Dec. 25, 1912, Waycross, Ga.
B.R., T.R. 6'2" 200 lbs.
(CATCHER)

YEAR	CLUB	BA	G	AB	R	H	2B	3B	HR	RBI
1938	BROOKLYN (N)	.200	7	20	0	4	0	1	0	2
	Five years (total)	.177	118	299	15	53	9	2	0	24

BEN GERAGHTY
B. July 19, 1914, Jersey City, N.J.
B.R., T.R. 5'11" 175 lbs.
(SHORTSTOP, 2ND BASE, 3RD BASE)

YEAR	CLUB	BA	G	AB	R	H	2B	3B	HR	RBI
1936	BROOKLYN (N)	.194	51	129	11	25	4	0	0	0
	Three years (total)	.199	70	146	16	29	4	0	0	9

DOC GESSLER
B. Dec. 23, 1980, Indiana, Pa.
B.L., T.R.
(OUTFIELD, 1ST BASE)

YEAR	CLUB	BA	G	AB	R	H	2B	3B	HR	RBI
1903	Detroit (A)	.238	—	—	—	—	—	—	—	—
1903	BROOKLYN (N)	.247	49	154	20	38	8	3	0	18
	(year totals)	.243	78	259	29	63	13	7	0	30
1904	BROOKLYN (N)	.290	104	341	41	99	18	4	2	28
1905	BROOKLYN (N)	.290	126	431	44	125	17	4	3	46
1906	BROOKLYN (N)	.242	9	33	3	8	1	2	0	4
1906	Chicago (N)									
	(year totals)	.250	43	116	11	29	4	2	0	14
1908	Boston (A)	.308	128	435	55	134	13	14	3	63
1909	Boston (A)									
1909	Washington (A)									
	(year totals)	.291	128	440	66	128	26	2	0	54
1910	Washington (A)	.259	145	487	58	126	17	11	2	50
1911	Washington (A)	.282	128	450	65	127	19	5	4	78
	Eight years	.281	880	2959	369	831	127	49	14	363
World Series										
	One year	.000	2	1	0	0	0	0	0	0

GUS GETZ
B. Aug. 3, 1889, Pittsburgh, Pa.
D. May 28, 1969, Keansburg, N.J.
B.R., T.R. 5'11" 165 lbs.
(3RD BASE)

YEAR	CLUB	BA	G	AB	R	H	2B	3B	HR	RBI
1909	Boston (N)	.223	40	148	6	33	2	0	0	9
1910	Boston (N)	.194	54	144	14	28	0	1	0	7
1914	BROOKLYN (N)	.248	55	210	13	52	8	1	0	20
1915	BROOKLYN (N)	.258	130	477	39	123	10	5	2	46
1916	BROOKLYN (N)	.219	40	96	9	21	1	2	0	8
1917	Cincinnati (N)	.286	7	14	2	4	0	0	0	3

YEAR	CLUB	BA	G	AB	R	H	2B	3B	HR	RBI
1918	Cleveland (A)	.222	132	474	36	105	14	1	7	44
1918	Pittsburgh (N)									
	(year totals)	.160	13	25	2	4	1	0	0	0
	Seven years	.238	339	1114	85	265	0	0	0	0
World Series										
	One year	.000	1	1	0	0	0	0	0	0

CHARLIE GILBERT B. July 8, 1919, New Orleans, La.
B.L., T.L. 5'9" 165 lbs.
(OUTFIELD)

YEAR	CLUB	BA	G	AB	R	H	2B	3B	HR	RBI
1940	BROOKLYN (N)	.246	57	142	23	35	9	1	2	8
	Six years (total)	.229	364	852	109	195	27	9	5	55

PETE GILBERT B. Sept. 6, 1867, Baltic, Conn.
T.R.
(3RD BASE)

YEAR	CLUB	BA	G	AB	R	H	2B	3B	HR	RBI
1894	BROOKLYN (N)	.080	6	25	0	2	0	0	0	0
	Four years (total)	.242	206	761	120	184	20	9	5	87

WALLY GILBERT B. Dec. 19, 1901, Oscoda, Mich.
B.R., T.R. 6' 180 lbs.
(3RD BASE)

YEAR	CLUB	BA	G	AB	R	H	2B	3B	HR	RBI
1928	BROOKLYN (N)	.203	39	153	26	31	4	0	0	3
1929	BROOKLYN (N)	.304	143	569	88	173	31	4	3	58
1930	BROOKLYN (N)	.294	150	623	92	183	34	5	3	67
1931	BROOKLYN (N)	.266	145	552	60	147	25	6	0	46
1932	Cincinnati (N)	.214	114	420	35	90	18	2	1	40
	Five years	.269	591	2317	301	624	112	17	7	214

CARDEN GILLENWATER B. May 13, 1918, Riceville, Tenn.
B.R., T.R. 6'1" 175 lbs.
(OUTFIELD)

YEAR	CLUB	BA	G	AB	R	H	2B	3B	HR	RBI
1943	BROOKLYN (N)	.176	8	17	1	3	0	0	0	2
	Five years (total)	.260	335	1004	129	261	41	7	11	114

JIM GILLIAM B. Oct. 17, 1928, Nashville, Tenn.
D. Oct. 8, 1978, Los Angeles, Calif.
B.B., T.R. 5'10½" 175 lbs.
(2ND BASE, 3RD BASE, OUTFIELD)

YEAR	CLUB	BA	G	AB	R	H	2B	3B	HR	RBI
1953	BROOKLYN (N)	.278	151	605	125	168	31	16	6	63
1954	BROOKLYN (N)	.282	146	607	107	171	28	8	13	52
1955	BROOKLYN (N)	.249	147	538	110	134	20	8	7	40
1956	BROOKLYN (N)	.300	153	594	102	178	23	8	6	43
1957	BROOKLYN (N)	.250	149	617	89	154	26	4	2	37
1958	LOS ANGELES (N)	.261	147	555	81	145	25	5	2	43
1959	LOS ANGELES (N)	.282	145	553	91	156	18	4	3	34
1960	LOS ANGELES (N)	.248	151	557	96	138	20	2	5	40
1961	LOS ANGELES (N)	.244	144	439	74	107	26	3	4	32
1962	LOS ANGELES (N)	.270	160	588	83	159	24	1	4	43
1963	LOS ANGELES (N)	.282	148	525	77	148	27	4	6	49
1964	LOS ANGELES (N)	.228	116	334	44	76	8	3	2	27
1965	LOS ANGELES (N)	.280	111	372	54	104	19	4	4	39
1966	LOS ANGELES (N)	.217	88	235	30	51	9	0	1	16
	Fourteen years	.265	1956	7119	1163	1889	304	71	65	558

World Series

YEAR	CLUB	BA	G	AB	R	H	2B	3B	HR	RBI
1953	BROOKLYN (N)	.296	6	27	4	8	3	0	2	4
1955	BROOKLYN (N)	.292	7	24	2	7	1	0	0	3
1956	BROOKLYN (N)	.083	7	24	2	2	0	0	0	2
1959	LOS ANGELES (N)	.240	6	25	2	6	0	0	0	0
1963	LOS ANGELES (N)	.154	4	13	3	2	0	0	0	0
1965	LOS ANGELES (N)	.214	7	28	2	6	1	0	0	2
1966	LOS ANGELES (N)	.000	2	6	0	0	0	0	0	1
	Seven years	.211	39	147	15	31	5	0	2	12

AL GIONFRIDDO B. March 8, 1922, Dysart, Pa.
B.L., T.L. 5'6" 165 lbs.
(OUTFIELD)

YEAR	CLUB	BA	G	AB	R	H	2B	3B	HR	RBI
1947	BROOKLYN (N)	.177	35	62	10	11	2	1	0	6
	Four years (total)	.266	228	580	95	154	22	12	2	58

World Series

	One year	.000	4	3	2	0	0	0	0	0

TONY GIULIANI B. Nov. 24, 1912, St. Paul, Minn.
B.R., T.R. 5'11" 175 lbs.
(CATCHER)

YEAR	CLUB	BA	G	AB	R	H	2B	3B	HR	RBI
1940	BROOKLYN (N)	.000	1	1	0	0	0	0	0	0
1941	BROOKLYN (N)	.000	3	2	0	0	0	0	0	0
	Seven years (total)	.233	243	674	58	157	18	3	0	69

ROY GLEASON B. April 9, 1943, Melrose Park, Ill.
B.B., T.R. 6'5½" 220 lbs.

YEAR	CLUB	BA	G	AB	R	H	2B	3B	HR	RBI
1963	LOS ANGELES (N)	1.000	8	1	3	1	1	0	0	0

AL GLOSSOP B. July 23, 1912, Christopher, Ill.
B.B., T.R. 6' 170 lbs.
(2ND BASE)

YEAR	CLUB	BA	G	AB	R	H	2B	3B	HR	RBI
1943	BROOKLYN (N)	.171	87	217	28	37	9	0	3	21
	Five years (total)	.209	309	952	99	199	29	2	15	86

JOHN GOCHNAUR B. Sept. 12, 1875, Altoona, Pa.
B.R., T.R.
(SHORTSTOP)

YEAR	CLUB	BA	G	AB	R	H	2B	3B	HR	RBI
1901	BROOKLYN (N)	.364	3	11	1	4	0	0	0	2
	Three years (total)	.187	264	908	94	170	32	8	0	87

JOHNNY GOOCH B. Nov. 9, 1897, Smyrna, Tenn.
B.B., T.R. 5'11" 175 lbs.
(CATCHER)

YEAR	CLUB	BA	G	AB	R	H	2B	3B	HR	RBI
1928	BROOKLYN (N)	.317	42	101	9	32	1	2	0	12
1929	BROOKLYN (N)	.000	1	1	0	0	0	0	0	0
	Eleven years (total)	.280	815	2363	227	662	98	29	7	293

ED GOODSON
B. Jan. 25, 1948, Pulaski, Va.
B.L., T.R. 6'3" 180 lbs.
(1ST BASE, 3RD BASE)

YEAR	CLUB	BA	G	AB	R	H	2B	3B	HR	RBI
1976	LOS ANGELES (N)	.229	83	118	8	27	4	0	3	17
1977	LOS ANGELES (N)	.167	61	66	3	11	1	0	1	5
	Eight years (total)	.260	515	1266	108	329	51	2	30	170
League Championship										
	One year	.000	1	1	0	0	0	0	0	0
World Series										
	One year	.000	1	1	0	0	0	0	0	0

BILLY GRABARKEWITZ
B. Jan. 18, 1946, Lockhart, Texas
B.R., T.R. 5'10" 165 lbs.
(3RD BASE, 2ND BASE, SHORTSTOP)

YEAR	CLUB	BA	G	AB	R	H	2B	3B	HR	RBI
1969	LOS ANGELES (N)	.092	34	65	4	6	1	1	0	5
1970	LOS ANGELES (N)	.289	156	529	92	153	20	8	17	84
1971	LOS ANGELES (N)	.225	44	71	9	16	5	0	0	6
1972	LOS ANGELES (N)	.167	53	144	17	24	4	0	4	16
1973	California (A)									
1973	Philadelphia (N)									
	(year totals)	.205	86	195	39	40	8	1	5	16
1974	Philadelphia (N)									
1974	Chicago (N)									
	(year totals)	.226	87	155	28	35	3	2	2	14
1975	Oakland (A)	.000	6	2	0	0	0	0	0	0
	Seven years	.236	466	1161	189	274	41	12	28	141

JACK GRAHAM
B. Dec. 24, 1916, Minneapolis, Minn.
B.L., T.L. 6'2" 200 lbs.
(1ST BASE, OUTFIELD)

YEAR	CLUB	BA	G	AB	R	H	2B	3B	HR	RBI
1946	BROOKLYN (N)	.200	2	5	0	1	0	0	0	0
	Two years (total)	.231	239	775	105	179	28	5	38	126

DICK GRAY
B. July 11, 1931, Jefferson, Pa.
B.R., T.R. 5'11" 165 lbs.
(3RD BASE)

YEAR	CLUB	BA	G	AB	R	H	2B	3B	HR	RBI
1958	LOS ANGELES (N)	.249	58	197	25	49	5	6	9	30
1959	LOS ANGELES (N)	.154	21	52	8	8	1	0	2	4
	Three years (total)	.239	124	305	43	73	7	6	12	41

MIKE GRIFFIN
B. March 20, 1865
D. April 10, 1908, Utica, N.Y.
B.L., T.R. 5'7" 160 lbs.
(OUTFIELD)

YEAR	CLUB	BA	G	AB	R	H	2B	3B	HR	RBI
1890	Philadelphia (P)	.291	115	492	127	143	29	6	6	54
1891	BROOKLYN (N)	.271	134	521	106	141	36	9	3	65
1892	BROOKLYN (N)	.277	129	459	103	127	18	11	3	66
1893	BROOKLYN (N)	.293	95	362	85	106	22	8	5	59
1894	BROOKLYN (N)	.365	107	405	123	148	29	5	5	75
1895	BROOKLYN (N)	.335	131	522	140	175	38	7	4	65
1896	BROOKLYN (N)	.314	122	493	101	155	28	9	4	51
1897	BROOKLYN (N)	.318	134	534	136	170	25	11	2	56
1898	BROOKLYN (N)	.296	134	544	88	161	18	6	2	40
	Twelve years	.299	1511	5939	1406	1776	317	110	41	625

BERT GRIFFITH   B. March 3, 1897, St. Louis, Mo.
B.R., T.R. 5'11" 185 lbs.
(OUTFIELD)

YEAR	CLUB	BA	G	AB	R	H	2B	3B	HR	RBI
1922	BROOKLYN (N)	.308	106	325	45	100	22	8	2	35
1923	BROOKLYN (N)	.294	79	248	23	73	8	4	2	37
1924	Washington (A)	.125	6	8	1	1	0	0	0	0
	Three years	.299	191	581	69	174	30	12	4	72

DERRELL GRIFFITH   B. Dec. 12, 1943, Anadarko, Okla.
B.L., T.R. 6' 168 lbs.
(OUTFIELD, 3RD BASE)

YEAR	CLUB	BA	G	AB	R	H	2B	3B	HR	RBI
1963	LOS ANGELES (N)	.000	1	2	0	0	0	0	0	0
1964	LOS ANGELES (N)	.290	78	238	27	69	16	2	4	23
1965	LOS ANGELES (N)	.171	22	41	3	7	0	0	1	2
1966	LOS ANGELES (N)	.067	23	15	3	1	0	0	0	2
	Four years	.260	124	296	33	77	16	2	5	27

TOMMY GRIFFITH   B. Oct. 26, 1889, Prospect, Ohio
B.L., T.R. 5'10" 175 lbs.
(OUTFIELD)

YEAR	CLUB	BA	G	AB	R	H	2B	3B	HR	RBI
1913	Boston (N)	.252	37	127	16	32	4	1	1	12
1914	Boston (N)	.104	16	48	3	5	0	0	0	1
1915	Cincinnati (N)	.307	160	583	59	179	31	16	4	85
1916	Cincinnati (N)	.266	155	595	50	158	28	7	2	61
1917	Cincinnati (N)	.270	115	363	45	98	18	7	1	45
1918	Cincinnati (N)	.265	118	427	47	113	10	4	2	48
1919	BROOKLYN (N)	.281	125	484	65	136	18	4	6	57
1920	BROOKLYN (N)	.260	93	334	41	87	9	4	2	30
1921	BROOKLYN (N)	.312	129	455	66	142	21	6	12	71
1922	BROOKLYN (N)	.316	99	329	44	104	17	8	4	49
1923	BROOKLYN (N)	.293	131	481	70	141	21	9	8	66
1924	BROOKLYN (N)	.251	140	482	43	121	19	5	3	67
1925	BROOKLYN (N)	.000	7	4	2	0	0	0	0	0
1925	Chicago (N)									
	(year totals)	.280	83	239	40	67	12	1	7	27
	Thirteen years	.280	1401	4947	589	1383	208	72	52	619
World Series										
	One year	.190	7	21	1	4	2	0	0	3

ART GRIGGS   B. Dec. 10, 1883, Topeka, Kan.
B.R., T.R. 5'11" 185 lbs.
(1ST BASE, OUTFIELD, 2ND BASE)

YEAR	CLUB	BA	G	AB	R	H	2B	3B	HR	RBI
1914	BROOKLYN (F)	.286	40	112	10	32	6	1	1	15
1915	BROOKLYN (F)	.289	27	38	4	11	1	0	1	2
	Seven years (total)	.277	442	1370	127	379	73	20	5	152

JOHN GRIM   B. Aug. 9, 1867, Lebanon, Ky.
B.R., T.R. 6'2" 175 lbs.
(CATCHER)

YEAR	CLUB	BA	G	AB	R	H	2B	3B	HR	RBI
1890	Rochester (AA)	.266	50	192	30	51	6	9	2	
1891	Cin.-Milw. (AA)	.235	29	119	14	28	5	1	1	14
1892	Louisville (N)	.243	97	370	40	90	16	4	1	36
1893	Louisville (N)	.267	99	415	68	111	19	8	3	54
1894	Louisville (N)	.298	108	410	66	122	27	7	7	70
1895	BROOKLYN (N)	.280	93	329	54	92	17	5	0	44
1896	BROOKLYN (N)	.267	81	281	32	75	13	1	2	35
1897	BROOKLYN (N)	.248	80	290	26	72	10	1	0	25
1898	BROOKLYN (N)	.281	52	178	17	50	5	1	0	11
1899	BROOKLYN (N)	.277	15	47	3	13	1	0	0	7
	Eleven years	.267	706	2638	350	705	119	37	16	296

JERRY GROTE   B. Oct. 6, 1942, San Antonio, Texas
B.R., T.R. 5'10" 185 lbs.
(CATCHER)

YEAR	CLUB	BA	G	AB	R	H	2B	3B	HR	RBI
1977	LOS ANGELES (N)	.259	18	27	3	7	0	0	0	4
1978	LOS ANGELES (N)	.271	41	70	5	19	5	0	0	9
1981	LOS ANGELES (N)									
	(year totals)	.293	24	58	4	17	3	1	1	9
	Sixteen years (total)	.252	1421	4339	352	1092	160	22	39	404
League Championship										
	Four years	.194	11	31	5	6	1	0	0	3
World Series										
	Four years	.240	15	50	3	12	2	0	0	1

PEDRO GUERRERO   B. June 2, 1956, San Pedro, Dominican Republic
B.R., T.R. 5'11" 176 lbs.
(OUTFIELD, 3RD BASE)

YEAR	CLUB	BA	G	AB	R	H	2B	3B	HR	RBI
1978	LOS ANGELES (N)	.625	5	8	3	5	0	1	0	1
1979	LOS ANGELES (N)	.242	25	62	7	15	2	0	2	9
1980	LOS ANGELES (N)	.322	75	183	27	59	9	1	7	31
1981	LOS ANGELES (N)	.300	98	347	46	104	17	2	12	48
1982	LOS ANGELES (N)	.304	150	575	87	175	27	5	37	100
1983	LOS ANGELES (N)	.298	160	584	87	174	28	6	32	103
	Six years	.303	513	1759	257	532	83	15	90	292
Divisional Playoff										
	One year	.176	5	17	2	3	1	0	1	1
League Championship										
	One year	.105	5	19	1	2	0	0	1	2
World Series										
	One year	.333	6	21	2	7	1	1	2	7

BRAD GULDEN   B. June 10, 1956, New Ulm, N.M.
B.L., T.R. 5'10" 175 lbs.
(CATCHER)

YEAR	CLUB	BA	G	AB	R	H	2B	3B	HR	RBI
1978	LOS ANGELES (N)	.000	3	4	0	0	0	0	0	0
	Four years (total)	.165	53	115	11	19	6	0	1	9

BERT HAAS   B. Feb. 8, 1914, Naperville, Ill.
B.R., T.R. 5'11" 178 lbs.
(1ST BASE, 3RD BASE, OUTFIELD)

YEAR	CLUB	BA	G	AB	R	H	2B	3B	HR	RBI
1937	BROOKLYN (N)	.400	16	25	2	10	3	0	0	2
1938	BROOKLYN (N)	—	1	0	0	0	0	0	0	0
	Nine years (total)	.264	723	2440	263	644	93	32	22	263

JOHN HALE   B. Aug. 5, 1953, Fresno, Calif.
B.L., T.R. 6'2" 195 lbs.
(OUTFIELD)

YEAR	CLUB	BA	G	AB	R	H	2B	3B	HR	RBI
1974	LOS ANGELES (N)	1.000	4	4	2	4	1	0	0	2
1975	LOS ANGELES (N)	.211	71	204	20	43	7	0	6	22
1976	LOS ANGELES (N)	.154	44	91	4	14	2	1	0	8
1977	LOS ANGELES (N)	.241	79	108	10	26	4	1	2	11
1978	Seattle (A)	.171	107	211	24	36	8	0	4	22
1979	Seattle (A)	.222	54	63	6	14	3	0	2	7
	Six years	.201	359	681	66	137	25	2	14	72

BOB HALL

B. Dec. 20, 1878, Baltimore, Md.
T.R. 5'10" 158 lbs.
(OUTFIELD, 3RD BASE, SHORTSTOP, 1ST BASE)

YEAR	CLUB	BA	G	AB	R	H	2B	3B	HR	RBI
1905	BROOKLYN (N)	.236	56	203	21	48	4	1	2	15
	Two years (total)	.203	103	369	33	75	8	1	2	32

TOM HALLER

B. June 23, 1937, Lockport, Ill.
B.L., T.R. 6'4" 195 lbs.
(CATCHER)

YEAR	CLUB	BA	G	AB	R	H	2B	3B	HR	RBI
1961	San Francisco (N)	.145	30	62	5	9	1	0	2	8
1962	San Francisco (N)	.261	99	272	53	71	13	1	18	55
1963	San Francisco (N)	.255	98	298	32	76	8	1	14	44
1964	San Francisco (N)	.253	117	388	43	98	14	3	16	48
1965	San Francisco (N)	.251	134	422	40	106	4	3	16	49
1966	San Francisco (N)	.240	142	471	74	113	19	2	27	67
1967	San Francisco (N)	.251	141	455	54	114	23	5	14	49
1968	LOS ANGELES (N)	.285	144	474	37	135	27	5	4	53
1969	LOS ANGELES (N)	.263	134	445	46	117	18	3	6	39
1970	LOS ANGELES (N)	.286	112	325	47	93	16	6	10	47
1971	LOS ANGELES (N)	.267	84	202	23	54	5	0	5	32
1972	Detroit (A)	.207	59	121	7	25	5	2	2	13
	Twelve years	.257	1294	3935	461	1011	153	31	134	504
League Championship										
	One year	.000	1	1	0	0	0	0	0	0
World Series										
	One year	.286	4	14	1	4	1	0	1	3

BILL HALLMAN

B. March 30, 1867, Pittsburgh, Pa.
B.R., T.R.
(2ND BASE)

YEAR	CLUB	BA	G	AB	R	H	2B	3B	HR	RBI
1898	BROOKLYN (N)	.244	134	509	57	124	10	7	2	63
	Fourteen years (total)	.272	1503	6012	937	1634	234	81	20	769

AL HALT

B. Nov. 23, 1890, Sandusky, Ohio
B.L., T.R. 6' 180 lbs.
(3RD BASE, SHORTSTOP)

YEAR	CLUB	BA	G	AB	R	H	2B	3B	HR	RBI
1914	BROOKLYN (F)	.234	80	261	26	61	6	2	3	25
1915	BROOKLYN (F)	.250	151	524	41	131	22	7	3	64
1918	Cleveland (A)	.174	26	69	9	12	2	0	0	1
	Three years	.239	257	854	76	204	30	9	6	90

BERT HAMRIC

B. March 1, 1928, Clarksburg, W. Va.
B.L., T.R. 6' 165 lbs.

YEAR	CLUB	BA	G	AB	R	H	2B	3B	HR	RBI
1955	BROOKLYN (N)	.000	2	1	0	0	0	0	0	0
	Two years (total)	.111	10	9	0	1	0	0	0	0

PAT HANIFIN

B. 1873, Nova Scotia, Canada
(OUTFIELD, 2ND BASE)

YEAR	CLUB	BA	G	AB	R	H	2B	3B	HR	RBI
1897	BROOKLYN (N)	.250	10	20	4	5	0	0	0	2

CHARLIE HARGREAVES

B. Dec. 14, 1896, Trenton, N.J.
B.R., T.R. 6' 170 lbs.
(CATCHER)

YEAR	CLUB	BA	G	AB	R	H	2B	3B	HR	RBI
1923	BROOKLYN (N)	.281	20	57	5	16	0	0	0	4
1924	BROOKLYN (N)	.407	15	27	4	11	2	0	0	5

YEAR	CLUB	BA	G	AB	R	H	2B	3B	HR	RBI
1925	BROOKLYN (N)	.277	45	83	9	23	3	1	0	13
1926	BROOKLYN (N)	.250	85	208	14	52	13	2	2	23
1927	BROOKLYN (N)	.286	44	133	9	38	3	1	0	11
1928	BROOKLYN (N)	.197	20	61	3	12	2	0	0	5
1928	Pittsburgh (N)									
	(year totals)	.268	99	321	18	86	10	1	0	37
1929	Pittsburgh (N)	.268	102	328	33	88	12	5	1	44
1930	Pittsburgh (N)	.226	11	31	4	7	1	0	0	2
	Eight years	.270	421	1188	96	321	44	11	4	139

TIM HARKNESS   B. Dec. 23, 1937, Lachine, Quebec, Canada
B.L., T.L. 6'2" 182 lbs.
(1ST BASE)

YEAR	CLUB	BA	G	AB	R	H	2B	3B	HR	RBI
1961	LOS ANGELES (N)	.500	5	8	4	4	2	0	0	0
1962	LOS ANGELES (N)	.258	92	62	9	16	2	0	2	7
	Four years (total)	.235	259	562	59	132	18	4	14	61

JOE HARRIS   B. May 20, 1891, Coulters, Pa.
B.R., T.R. 5'9" 170 lbs.
(1ST BASE, OUTFIELD)

YEAR	CLUB	BA	G	AB	R	H	2B	3B	HR	RBI
1928	BROOKLYN (N)	.236	55	89	8	21	6	1	1	8
	Ten years (totals)	.317	971	3035	461	963	201	64	47	517

BILL HART   B. March 4, 1913, Wiconisco, Pa.
B.R., T.R. 6' 175 lbs.
(3RD BASE, SHORTSTOP)

YEAR	CLUB	BA	G	AB	R	H	2B	3B	HR	RBI
1943	BROOKLYN (N)	.158	8	19	0	3	0	0	0	1
1944	BROOKLYN (N)	.178	29	90	8	16	4	2	0	4
1945	BROOKLYN (N)	.230	58	161	27	37	6	2	3	27
	Three years	.207	95	270	35	56	10	4	3	32

CHRIS HARTJE   B. March 25, 1914, San Francisco, Calif.
B.R., T.R. 5'10½" 165 lbs.
(CATCHER)

YEAR	CLUB	BA	G	AB	R	H	2B	3B	HR	RBI
1939	BROOKLYN (N)	.313	9	16	2	5	1	0	0	5

BUDDY HASSETT   B. Sept. 5, 1911, New York, N.Y.
B.L., T.L. 5'11" 180 lbs.
(1ST BASE, OUTFIELD)

YEAR	CLUB	BA	G	AB	R	H	2B	3B	HR	RBI
1936	BROOKLYN (N)	.310	156	635	79	197	29	11	3	82
1937	BROOKLYN (N)	.304	137	556	71	169	31	6	1	53
1938	BROOKLYN (N)	.293	115	335	49	98	11	6	0	40
1939	Boston (N)	.308	147	590	72	182	15	3	2	60
1940	Boston (N)	.234	124	458	59	107	19	4	0	27
1941	Boston (N)	.296	118	405	59	120	9	4	1	33
1942	New York (A)	.284	132	538	80	153	16	6	5	48
	Seven years	.292	929	3517	469	1026	130	40	12	343
World Series										
	One year	.333	3	9	1	3	1	0	0	2

JACKIE HAYES   B. June 27, 1861, Brooklyn, N.Y.
T.R.
(CATCHER, OUTFIELD)

YEAR	CLUB	BA	G	AB	R	H	2B	3B	HR	RBI
*1890	BROOKLYN (P)	.190	12	42	3	8	0	0	0	5
	Seven years	.233	300	1148	106	267	63	10	10	68

*1882 Worcester (N), 1883 Pittsburgh (AA), 1884 Brooklyn (AA), 1886 Washington (N), 1887 Baltimore (AA)

MICKEY HATCHER

B. March 15, 1955, Cleveland, Ohio
B.R., T.R. 6'2" 200 lbs.
(OUTFIELD)

YEAR	CLUB	BA	G	AB	R	H	2B	3B	HR	RBI
1979	LOS ANGELES (N)	.269	33	93	9	25	4	1	1	5
1980	LOS ANGELES (N)	.226	57	84	4	19	2	0	1	5
	Four years (total)	.252	273	831	72	209	42	5	8	73

GIL HATFIELD

B. Jan. 27, 1855, Hoboken, N.J.
T.R.
(SHORTSTOP, 3RD BASE)

YEAR	CLUB	BA	G	AB	R	H	2B	3B	HR	RBI
1893	BROOKLYN (N)	.292	34	120	24	35	3	3	2	19
	Eight years (total)	.248	317	1190	173	295	31	18	5	129

RAY HAYWORTH

B. Jan. 29, 1904, Highpoint, N.C.
B.R., T.R. 6' 180 lbs.
(CATCHER)

YEAR	CLUB	BA	G	AB	R	H	2B	3B	HR	RBI
1938	BROOKLYN (N)	.000	5	4	0	0	0	0	0	0
1939	BROOKLYN (N)	.154	21	26	4	2	0	0	1	4
1944	BROOKLYN (N)	.000	7	10	1	0	0	0	0	0
1945	BROOKLYN (N)	.000	2	2	0	0	0	0	0	0
	Fifteen years (total)	.265	698	2062	221	546	92	16	5	238

HUGH HEARNE

B. April 18, 1874, Troy, N.Y.
B.R., T.R. 5'8" 182 lbs.
(CATCHER)

YEAR	CLUB	BA	G	AB	R	H	2B	3B	HR	RBI
1901	BROOKLYN (N)	.400	2	5	1	2	0	0	0	3
1902	BROOKLYN (N)	.281	66	231	22	65	10	0	0	28
1903	BROOKLYN (N)	.281	26	57	8	16	3	2	0	4
	Three years	.283	94	293	31	83	13	2	0	35

MIKE HECHINGER

B. Feb. 14, 1890, Chicago, Ill.
B.R., T.R. 6' 175 lbs.
(CATCHER)

YEAR	CLUB	BA	G	AB	R	H	2B	3B	HR	RBI
1913	BROOKLYN (N)	.182	9	11	1	2	1	0	0	0
	Two years (total)	.125	13	16	1	2	1	0	0	0

HARVEY HENDRICK

B. Nov. 9, 1897, Mason, Tenn.
B.L., T.R. 6'2" 190 lbs.
(1ST BASE, OUTFIELD, 3RD BASE)

YEAR	CLUB	BA	G	AB	R	H	2B	3B	HR	RBI
1923	New York (A)	.273	37	66	9	18	3	1	3	12
1924	New York (A)	.263	40	76	7	20	0	0	1	11
1925	Cleveland (A)	.286	25	28	2	8	1	2	0	9
1927	BROOKLYN (N)	.310	128	458	55	142	18	11	4	50
1928	BROOKLYN (N)	.318	126	425	83	135	15	10	11	59
1929	BROOKLYN (N)	.354	110	384	69	136	25	6	14	82
1930	BROOKLYN (N)	.257	68	167	29	43	10	1	5	28
1931	BROOKLYN (N)	.000	1	1	0	0	0	0	0	0
1931	Cincinnati (N)									
	(year totals)	.315	138	531	74	167	32	9	1	75
1932	St. Louis (N)									
1932	Cincinnati (N)									
	(year totals)	.294	122	470	64	138	32	3	5	45
1933	Chicago (N)	.291	69	189	30	55	13	3	4	23
1934	Philadelphia (N)	.293	59	116	12	34	8	0	0	19
	Eleven years	.308	922	2910	434	896	157	46	48	413
World Series										
	One year	.000	1	1	0	0	0	0	0	0

BUTCH HENLINE

B. Dec. 20, 1894, Fort Wayne, Ind.
B.R., T.R. 5'10" 175 lbs.
(CATCHER)

YEAR	CLUB	BA	G	AB	R	H	2B	3B	HR	RBI
1927	BROOKLYN (N)	.266	67	177	12	47	10	3	1	18
1928	BROOKLYN (N)	.212	55	132	12	28	3	1	2	8
1929	BROOKLYN (N)	.242	27	62	5	15	2	0	1	7
	Eleven years (total)	.291	740	2101	258	611	96	21	40	268

BABE HERMAN

B. June 26, 1903, Buffalo, N.Y.
B.L., T.L. 6'4" 190 lbs.
(OUTFIELD, 1ST BASE)

YEAR	CLUB	BA	G	AB	R	H	2B	3B	HR	RBI
1926	BROOKLYN (N)	.319	137	496	64	158	35	11	11	81
1927	BROOKLYN (N)	.272	130	412	65	112	26	9	14	73
1928	BROOKLYN (N)	.340	134	486	64	165	37	6	12	91
1929	BROOKLYN (N)	.381	146	569	105	217	42	13	21	113
1930	BROOKLYN (N)	.393	153	614	143	241	48	11	35	130
1931	BROOKLYN (N)	.313	151	610	93	191	43	16	18	97
1932	Cincinnati (N)	.326	148	577	87	188	38	19	16	87
1933	Chicago (N)	.289	137	508	77	147	36	12	16	93
1934	Chicago (N)	.304	125	467	65	142	34	5	14	84
1935	Pittsburgh (N)									
1935	Cincinnati (N)									
	(year totals)	.316	118	430	52	136	31	6	10	65
1936	Cincinnati (N)	.279	119	380	59	106	25	2	13	71
1937	Detroit (A)	.300	17	20	2	6	3	0	0	3
1945	BROOKLYN (N)	.265	37	34	6	9	1	0	1	9
	Thirteen years	.324	1552	5603	882	1818	399	110	181	997

BILLY HERMAN

B. July 7, 1909, New Albany, Ind.
B.R., T.R. 5'11" 180 lbs.
(2ND BASE)

YEAR	CLUB	BA	G	AB	R	H	2B	3B	HR	RBI
1931	Chicago (N)	.327	25	98	14	32	7	0	0	16
1932	Chicago (N)	.314	154	656	102	206	42	7	1	51
1933	Chicago (N)	.279	153	619	82	173	35	2	0	44
1934	Chicago (N)	.303	113	456	79	138	21	6	3	42
1935	Chicago (N)	.341	154	666	113	227	57	6	7	83
1936	Chciago (N)	.334	153	632	101	211	57	7	5	93
1937	Chicago (N)	.335	138	564	106	189	35	11	8	65
1938	Chicago (N)	.277	152	624	86	173	34	7	1	56
1939	Chicago (N)	.307	156	623	111	191	34	18	7	70
1940	Chicago (N)	.292	135	558	77	163	24	4	5	57
1941	Chicago (N)									
1941	BROOKLYN (N)	.291	133	536	77	156	30	4	3	41
	(year totals)	.285	144	572	81	163	30	5	3	41
1942	BROOKLYN (N)	.256	155	571	76	146	34	2	2	65
1943	BROOKLYN (N)	.330	153	585	76	193	41	2	2	100
1946	BROOKLYN (N)	.288	47	188	24	53	8	4	0	28
1946	Boston (N)									
	(year totals)	.298	122	436	56	130	31	5	3	50
1947	Pittsburgh (N)	.213	15	47	3	10	4	0	0	6
	Fifteen years	.304	1922	7707	1163	2345	486	82	47	839
World Series										
	Four years	.242	18	66	9	16	3	1	1	7

GENE HERMANSKI

B. May 11, 1920, Pittsfield, Mass.
B.L., T.R. 5'11½" 185 lbs.
(OUTFIELD)

YEAR	CLUB	BA	G	AB	R	H	2B	3B	HR	RBI
1943	BROOKLYN (N)	.300	18	60	6	18	2	1	0	12
1946	BROOKLYN (N)	.200	64	110	15	22	2	2	0	8
1947	BROOKLYN (N)	.275	79	189	36	52	7	1	7	39
1948	BROOKLYN (N)	.290	133	400	63	116	22	7	15	60
1949	BROOKLYN (N)	.299	87	224	48	67	12	3	8	42
1950	BROOKLYN (N)	.298	94	289	36	86	17	3	7	34

The Complete Catalogue of Players • 73

YEAR	CLUB	BA	G	AB	R	H	2B	3B	HR	RBI
1951	BROOKLYN (N)	.250	31	80	8	20	4	0	1	5
1951	Chicago (N)									
	(year totals)	.273	106	311	36	85	16	1	4	25
1952	Chicago (N)	.255	99	275	28	70	6	0	4	34
1953	Chicago (N)									
1953	Pittsburgh (N)									
	(year totals)	.167	59	102	8	17	1	0	1	5
	Nine years	.272	739	1960	276	533	85	18	46	259

World Series

YEAR	CLUB	BA	G	AB	R	H	2B	3B	HR	RBI
1947	BROOKLYN (N)	.158	7	19	4	3	0	1	0	1
1949	BROOKLYN (N)	.308	4	13	1	4	0	1	0	2
	Two years	.219	11	32	5	7	0	2	0	3

ENZO HERNANDEZ B. Feb. 12, 1949, Valle De Guanape, Puerto Rico
B.R., T.R. 5'8" 155 lbs.
(SHORTSTOP)

YEAR	CLUB	BA	G	AB	R	H	2B	3B	HR	RBI
1978	LOS ANGELES (N)	.000	4	3	0	0	0	0	0	0
	Eight years (total)	.224	714	2327	241	522	66	13	2	113

DAVE HICKMAN B. May 19, 1894, Union City, Tenn.
B.B., T.R. 5'7½" 170 lbs.
(OUTFIELDER)

YEAR	CLUB	BA	G	AB	R	H	2B	3B	HR	RBI
1915	Baltimore (F)	.210	20	81	7	17	4	1	1	7
1916	BROOKLYN (N)	.200	9	5	3	1	0	0	0	0
1917	BROOKLYN (N)	.219	114	370	46	81	15	4	6	36
1918	BROOKLYN (N)	.234	53	167	14	39	4	7	1	16
1919	BROOKLYN (N)	.192	57	104	14	20	3	1	0	11
	Five years	.217	253	727	84	158	26	13	8	70

JIM HICKMAN B. May 10, 1937, Henning, Tenn.
B.R., T.R. 6'3" 192 lbs.
(OUTFIELD, 1ST BASE)

YEAR	CLUB	BA	G	AB	R	H	2B	3B	HR	RBI
1967	LOS ANGELES (N)	.163	65	98	7	16	6	1	0	10
	Thirteen years (total)	.252	1421	3974	518	1002	163	25	159	560

BOB HIGGENS B. Sept. 23, 1886, Fayetteville, Tenn.
B.R., T.R. 5'8" 176 lbs.
(CATCHER)

YEAR	CLUB	BA	G	AB	R	H	2B	3B	HR	RBI
1911	BROOKLYN (N)	.300	4	10	1	3	0	0	0	2
1912	BROOKLYN (N)	.000	1	2	0	0	0	0	0	0
	Three years (total)	.143	13	35	1	5	0	0	0	2

ANDY HIGH B. Nov. 21, 1897, Ava, Ill.
B.L., T.R. 5'6" 155 lbs.
(3RD BASE, 2ND BASE)

YEAR	CLUB	BA	G	AB	R	H	2B	3B	HR	RBI
1922	BROOKLYN (N)	.283	153	579	82	164	27	10	6	65
1923	BROOKLYN (N)	.270	123	426	51	115	23	9	3	37
1924	BROOKLYN (N)	.328	144	582	98	191	26	13	6	61
1925	BROOKLYN (N)	.200	44	115	11	23	4	1	0	6
1925	Boston (N)									
	(year totals)	.257	104	334	42	86	15	2	4	34
1926	Boston (N)	.296	130	476	55	141	17	10	2	66
1927	Boston (N)	.302	113	384	59	116	15	9	4	46
1928	St. Louis (N)	.285	111	368	58	105	14	3	6	37
1929	St. Louis (N)	.295	146	603	95	178	32	4	10	63

YEAR	CLUB	BA	G	AB	R	H	2B	3B	HR	RBI
1930	St. Louis (N)	.279	72	215	34	60	12	2	2	29
1931	St. Louis (N)	.267	63	131	20	35	6	1	0	19
1932	Cincinnati (N)	.188	84	191	16	36	4	2	0	12
1933	Cincinnati (N)	.209	24	43	4	9	2	0	1	6
1934	Philadelphia (N)	.206	47	68	4	14	2	0	0	7
	Thirteen years	.284	1314	4400	618	1250	195	65	44	482
World Series										
	Three years	.294	9	34	5	10	2	0	0	1

GEORGE HILDEBRAND B. Sept. 6, 1878, San Francisco, Calif.
B.R., T.R. 5'8" 170 lbs.
(OUTFIELD)

YEAR	CLUB	BA	G	AB	R	H	2B	3B	HR	RBI
1902	BROOKLYN (N)	.220	11	41	3	9	1	0	0	5

HUNKEY HINES B. Sept. 29, 1870, Elgin, Ill.
(OUTFIELD)

YEAR	CLUB	BA	G	AB	R	H	2B	3B	HR	RBI
1895	BROOKLYN (N)	.000	2	8	3	2	0	0	0	1

DON HOAK B. Feb. 5, 1928, Roulette, Pa.
B.R., T.R. 6'1" 170 lbs.
(3RD BASE)

YEAR	CLUB	BA	G	AB	R	H	2B	3B	HR	RBI
1954	BROOKLYN (N)	.245	88	261	41	64	9	5	7	26
1955	BROOKLYN (N)	.240	94	279	50	67	13	3	5	19
1956	Chicago (N)	.215	121	424	51	91	18	4	5	37
1957	Cincinnati (N)	.293	149	529	78	155	39	2	19	89
1958	Cincinnati (N)	.261	114	417	51	109	30	0	6	50
1959	Pittsburgh (N)	.294	155	564	60	166	29	3	8	65
1960	Pittsburgh (N)	.282	155	553	97	156	24	9	16	79
1961	Pittsburgh (N)	.298	145	503	72	150	27	7	12	61
1962	Pittsburgh (N)	.241	121	411	63	99	14	8	5	48
1963	Philadelphia (N)	.231	115	377	35	87	11	3	6	24
1964	Philadelphia (N)	.000	6	4	0	0	0	0	0	0
	Eleven years	.265	1263	4322	598	1144	214	44	89	498
World Series										
	Two years	.231	10	26	3	6	2	0	0	3

ORIS HOCKETT B. Sept. 29, 1909, Bluffton, Ind.
B.L., T.R. 5'9" 182 lbs.
(OUTFIELD)

YEAR	CLUB	BA	G	AB	R	H	2B	3B	HR	RBI
1938	BROOKLYN (N)	.329	21	70	8	23	5	1	1	8
1939	BROOKLYN (N)	.231	9	13	3	3	0	0	0	1
	Seven years (total)	.276	551	2165	259	598	112	21	13	214

GIL HODGES B. April 4, 1924, Princeton, Ind.
D. April 2, 1972, West Palm Beach, Fla.
B.R., T.R. 6'1½" 200 lbs.
(1ST BASE)

YEAR	CLUB	BA	G	AB	R	H	2B	3B	HR	RBI
1943	BROOKLYN (N)	.000	1	2	0	0	0	0	0	0
1947	BROOKLYN (N)	.156	28	77	9	12	3	1	1	7
1948	BROOKLYN (N)	.249	134	481	48	120	18	5	11	70
1949	BROOKLYN (N)	.285	156	596	94	170	23	4	23	115
1950	BROOKLYN (N)	.283	153	561	98	159	26	2	32	113
1951	BROOKLYN (N)	.268	158	582	118	156	25	3	40	103
1952	BROOKLYN (N)	.254	153	508	87	129	27	1	32	102
1953	BROOKLYN (N)	.302	141	520	101	157	22	7	31	122
1954	BROOKLYN (N)	.304	154	579	106	176	23	5	42	130
1955	BROOKLYN (N)	.289	150	546	75	158	24	5	27	102
1956	BROOKLYN (N)	.265	153	550	86	146	29	4	32	87
1957	BROOKLYN (N)	.299	150	579	94	173	28	7	27	98

YEAR	CLUB	BA	G	AB	R	H	2B	3B	HR	RBI
1958	LOS ANGELES (N)	.259	141	475	68	123	15	1	22	64
1959	LOS ANGELES (N)	.276	124	413	57	114	19	2	25	80
1960	LOS ANGELES (N)	.198	101	197	22	39	8	1	8	30
1961	LOS ANGELES (N)	.242	109	215	25	52	4	0	8	31
1962	New York (N)	.252	54	127	15	32	1	0	9	17
1963	New York (N)	.227	11	22	2	5	0	0	0	3
	Eighteen years	.273	2071	7030	1105	1921	295	48	370	1274

World Series

YEAR	CLUB	BA	G	AB	R	H	2B	3B	HR	RBI
1947	BROOKLYN (N)	.000	1	1	0	0	0	0	0	0
1949	BROOKLYN (N)	.235	5	17	2	4	0	0	1	4
1952	BROOKLYN (N)	.000	7	21	1	0	0	0	0	1
1953	BROOKLYN (N)	.364	6	22	3	8	0	0	1	1
1955	BROOKLYN (N)	.292	7	24	2	7	0	0	1	5
1956	BROOKLYN (N)	.304	7	23	5	7	2	0	1	8
1959	LOS ANGELES (N)	.391	5	23	2	9	0	1	1	2
	Seven years	.267	39	131	15	35	2	1	5	21

SOLLY HOFMAN B. Oct. 29, 1882, St. Louis, Mo.
D. March 10, 1956, St. Louis, Mo.
B.R., T.R. 6' 160 lbs.
(OUTFIELD, 2ND BASE, 1ST BASE)

YEAR	CLUB	BA	G	AB	R	H	2B	3B	HR	RBI
1914	BROOKLYN (F)	.287	147	515	65	148	25	12	5	83
	Fourteen years	.269	1193	4070	554	1094	162	60	19	495

BERT HOGG B. April 21, 1913, Detroit, Mich.
B.R., T.R. 5'11½" 162 lbs.
(3RD BASE)

YEAR	CLUB	BA	G	AB	R	H	2B	3B	HR	RBI
1934	BROOKLYN (N)	.000	2	1	0	0	0	0	0	0

TOMMY HOLMES B. March 29, 1917, Brooklyn, N.Y.
B.L., T.L. 5'10" 180 lbs.
(OUTFIELD)

YEAR	CLUB	BA	G	AB	R	H	2B	3B	HR	RBI
1952	BROOKLYN (N)	.111	31	36	4	4	1	0	0	1
	Eleven years (total)	.302	1320	4992	698	1507	292	47	88	581

World Series

	Two years	.185	9	27	3	5	0	0	0	1

WALLY HOOD B. Feb. 9, 1895, Whittier, Calif.
D. May 2, 1965, Hollywood, Calif.
B.R., T.R. 5'11½" 160 lbs.
(OUTFIELD)

YEAR	CLUB	BA	G	AB	R	H	2B	3B	HR	RBI
1920	BROOKLYN (N)	.143	7	14	4	2	1	0	0	1
1921	BROOKLYN (N)	.262	56	65	16	17	1	2	1	4
1922	BROOKLYN (N)	—	2	0	2	0	0	0	0	0
	Three years (total)	.238	67	80	23	19	2	2	1	5

GAIL HOPKINS B. Feb. 19, 1943, Tulsa, Okla.
B.L., T.R. 5'10" 198 lbs.
(1ST BASE)

YEAR	CLUB	BA	G	AB	R	H	2B	3B	HR	RBI
1974	LOS ANGELES (N)	.222	15	18	1	4	0	0	0	0
	Seven years (total)	.266	514	1219	142	324	47	6	25	145

JOHNNY HOPP
B. July 18, 1916, Hastings, Neb.
B.L., T.L. 5'10" 170 lbs.
(OUTFIELD, 1ST BASE)

YEAR	CLUB	BA	G	AB	R	H	2B	3B	HR	RBI
1949	BROOKLYN (N)	.000	8	14	0	0	0	0	0	0
	Fourteen years (total)	.296	1393	4260	698	1262	216	74	46	458

ED HOUSEHOLDER
B. Oct. 12, 1869, Pittsburgh, Pa.
D. July 3, 1924, Los Angeles, Calif.
(OUTFIELD)

YEAR	CLUB	BA	G	AB	R	H	2B	3B	HR	RBI
1903	BROOKLYN (N)	.209	12	43	5	9	0	0	0	9

DAVE HOWARD
B. May 1, 1889, Washington, D.C.
D. Jan. 26, 1956, Dallas, Texas
B.R., T.R. 5'11" 165 lbs.
(2ND BASE)

YEAR	CLUB	BA	G	AB	R	H	2B	3B	HR	RBI
1915	BROOKLYN (F)	.222	24	36	5	8	1	0	0	1
	Two years (total)	.222	25	36	6	8	1	0	0	1

FRANK HOWARD
B. Aug. 8, 1936, Columbus, Ohio
B.R., T.R. 6'7" 255 lbs.
(OUTFIELD, 1ST BASE)

YEAR	CLUB	BA	G	AB	R	H	2B	3B	HR	RBI
1958	LOS ANGELES (N)	.241	8	29	3	7	1	0	1	2
1959	LOS ANGELES (N)	.143	9	21	2	3	0	1	1	6
1960	LOS ANGELES (N)	.268	117	448	54	120	15	2	23	77
1961	LOS ANGELES (N)	.296	99	267	36	79	10	2	15	45
1962	LOS ANGELES (N)	.296	141	493	80	146	25	6	31	119
1963	LOS ANGELES (N)	.273	123	417	58	114	16	1	28	64
1964	LOS ANGELES (N)	.226	134	433	60	98	13	2	24	69
1965	Washington (A)	.289	149	516	53	149	22	6	21	84
1966	Washington (A)	.278	146	493	52	137	19	4	18	71
1967	Washington (A)	.256	149	519	71	133	20	2	36	89
1968	Washington (A)	.274	158	598	79	164	28	3	44	106
1969	Washington (A)	.296	161	592	111	175	17	2	48	111
1970	Washington (A)	.283	161	566	90	160	15	1	44	126
1971	Washington (A)	.279	153	549	60	153	25	2	26	83
1972	Texas (A)									
1972	Detroit (A)									
	(year totals)	.244	109	320	29	78	10	0	10	38
1973	Detroit (A)	.256	85	227	26	58	9	1	12	29
	Sixteen years	.273	1902	6488	864	1774	245	35	382	1119
World Series										
	One year	.300	3	10	2	3	1	0	1	1

DIXIE HOWELL
B. April 24, 1919, Louisville, Ky.
B.R., T.R. 5'11½" 190 lbs.
(CATCHER)

YEAR	CLUB	BA	G	AB	R	H	2B	3B	HR	RBI
1953	BROOKLYN (N)	.000	1	1	0	0	0	0	0	0
1955	BROOKLYN (N)	.262	16	42	2	11	4	0	0	5
1956	BROOKLYN (N)	.231	7	13	0	3	2	0	0	1
	Eight years (total)	.246	340	910	98	224	39	4	12	93

JOHNNY HUDSON
B. June 30, 1912, Bryan, Texas
B.R., T.R. 5'10" 160 lbs.
(2ND BASE, SHORTSTOP)

YEAR	CLUB	BA	G	AB	R	H	2B	3B	HR	RBI
1936	BROOKLYN (N)	.167	6	12	1	2	0	0	0	2
1937	BROOKLYN (N)	.185	13	27	3	5	4	0	0	2
1938	BROOKLYN (N)	.261	135	498	39	130	21	5	2	37
1939	BROOKLYN (N)	.254	109	343	46	87	17	3	2	32
1940	BROOKLYN (N)	.218	85	179	13	39	4	3	0	19

YEAR	CLUB	BA	G	AB	R	H	2B	3B	HR	RBI
1941	Chicago (N)	.202	50	99	8	20	4	0	0	6
1945	New York (N)	.000	28	11	8	0	0	0	0	0
	Seven years	.242	426	1169	138	283	50	11	4	96

ED HUG B. July 14, 1880, Fayetteville, Ohio
D. May 11, 1953, Cincinnati, Ohio
B.R., T.R.
(CATCHER)

YEAR	CLUB	BA	G	AB	R	H	2B	3B	HR	RBI
1903	BROOKLYN (N)	—	1	0	0	0	0	0	0	0

JOHN HUMMEL B. April 4, 1883, Bloomsburg, Pa.
D. May 18, 1959, Springfield, Mass.
B.R., T.R. 5'11" 160 lbs.
(2ND BASE, OUTFIELD, SHORTSTOP, 1ST BASE)

YEAR	CLUB	BA	G	AB	R	H	2B	3B	HR	RBI
1905	BROOKLYN (N)	.266	30	109	19	29	3	4	0	7
1906	BROOKLYN (N)	.199	97	286	20	57	6	4	1	21
1907	BROOKLYN (N)	.234	107	342	41	80	12	3	3	31
1908	BROOKLYN (N)	.241	154	594	51	143	11	12	4	41
1909	BROOKLYN (N)	.280	146	542	54	152	15	9	4	52
1910	BROOKLYN (N)	.244	153	578	67	141	21	13	5	74
1911	BROOKLYN (N)	.270	137	477	54	129	21	11	5	58
1912	BROOKLYN (N)	.282	122	411	55	116	21	7	5	54
1913	BROOKLYN (N)	.242	67	198	20	48	7	7	2	24
1914	BROOKLYN (N)	.264	73	208	25	55	8	9	0	20
1915	BROOKLYN (N)	.230	53	100	6	23	2	3	0	8
1918	New York (A)	.295	22	61	9	18	1	2	0	4
	Twelve years	.254	1161	3906	421	991	128	84	29	394

AL HUMPHREY B. Feb. 28, 1886, Ashtabula, Ohio
D. May 13, 1961, Ashtabula, Ohio
B.L., T.R. 5'11" 180 lbs.
(OUTFIELD)

YEAR	CLUB	BA	G	AB	R	H	2B	3B	HR	RBI
1911	BROOKLYN (N)	.185	8	27	4	5	0	0	0	0

BERNIE HUNGLING B. March 5, 1896, Dayton, Ohio
D. March 30, 1968, Dayton, Ohio
B.R., T.R. 6'2" 180 lbs.
(CATCHER)

YEAR	CLUB	BA	G	AB	R	H	2B	3B	HR	RBI
1922	BROOKLYN (N)	.225	39	102	9	23	1	2	1	13
1923	BROOKLYN (N)	.000	2	4	0	0	0	0	0	0
	Three years (total)	.241	51	137	13	33	3	2	1	15

RON HUNT B. Feb. 23, 1941, St. Louis, Mo.
B.R., T.R. 6' 186 lbs.
(2ND BASE)

YEAR	CLUB	BA	G	AB	R	H	2B	3B	HR	RBI
1967	LOS ANGELES (N)	.263	110	388	44	102	17	3	3	33
	Twelve years (total)	.273	1483	5235	745	1429	223	23	39	370

GEORGE HUNTER B. July 8, 1886, Buffalo, N.Y.
D. Jan. 11, 1968, Harrisburg, Pa.
B.B., T.L. 5'8½" 165 lbs.
(OUTFIELD, PITCHER)

YEAR	CLUB	BA	G	AB	R	H	2B	3B	HR	RBI
1909	BROOKLYN (N)	.228	44	123	8	28	7	0	0	8
1910	BROOKLYN (N)	—	1	0	0	0	0	0	0	0
	Two years	.228	45	123	8	28	7	0	0	8

PAT HURLEY
B. Unknown
B.R., T.R.
(CATCHER)

YEAR	CLUB	BA	G	AB	R	H	2B	3B	HR	RBI
1907	BROOKLYN (N)	.000	1	2	0	0	0	0	0	0
	Two years (total)	.043	10	23	1	1	0	0	0	0

JOE HUTCHESON
B. Feb. 5, 1905, Springtown, Texas
B.L., T.R. 6'2" 200 lbs.
(OUTFIELD)

YEAR	CLUB	BA	G	AB	R	H	2B	3B	HR	RBI
1933	BROOKLYN (N)	.234	55	184	19	43	4	1	6	21

ROY HUTSON
B. Feb. 27, 1902, Luray, Mo.
D. May 20, 1957, La Mesa, Calif.
B.L., T.R. 5'9" 165 lbs.
(OUTFIELD)

YEAR	CLUB	BA	G	AB	R	H	2B	3B	HR	RBI
1925	BROOKLYN (N)	.500	7	8	1	4	0	0	0	1

TOM HUTTON
B. April 20, 1946, Los Angeles, Calif.
B.L., T.L. 5'11" 180 lbs.
(1ST BASE, OUTFIELD)

YEAR	CLUB	BA	G	AB	R	H	2B	3B	HR	RBI
1966	LOS ANGELES (N)	.000	3	2	0	0	0	0	0	0
1969	LOS ANGELES (N)	.271	16	48	2	13	0	0	0	4
	Twelve years (total)	.248	952	1655	196	410	63	7	22	186

CHARLIE IRWIN
B. Feb. 15, 1869, Sheffield, Ill.
D. Sept. 21, 1925, Chicago, Ill.
B.R., T.R. 5'10" 160 lbs.
(3RD BASE, SHORTSTOP)

YEAR	CLUB	BA	G	AB	R	H	2B	3B	HR	RBI
1893	Chicago (N)	.305	21	82	14	25	6	2	0	13
1894	Chicago (N)	.289	128	498	84	144	24	9	8	95
1895	Chicago (N)	.200	3	10	4	2	0	0	0	0
1896	Cincinnati (N)	.296	127	476	77	141	16	6	1	67
1897	Cincinnati (N)	.289	134	505	89	146	26	6	0	74
1898	Cincinnati (N)	.240	136	501	77	120	14	5	3	55
1899	Cincinnati (N)	.232	90	314	42	73	4	8	1	52
1900	Cincinnati (N)	.273	87	333	59	91	15	6	1	44
1901	Cincinnati (N)									
1901	BROOKLYN (N)	.215	65	242	25	52	13	2	0	20
	(year totals)	.227	132	502	50	114	25	4	0	45
1902	BROOKLYN (N)	.273	131	458	59	125	14	0	2	43
	Ten years	.267	989	3679	555	981	144	46	16	488

FRED JACKLITSCH
B. May 24, 1876, Brooklyn, N.Y.
D. July 18, 1937, Brooklyn, N.Y.
B.R., T.R.
(CATCHER)

YEAR	CLUB	BA	G	AB	R	H	2B	3B	HR	RBI
1903	BROOKLYN (N)	.267	60	176	31	47	8	3	1	21
1904	BROOKLYN (N)	.234	26	77	8	18	3	1	0	8
	Thirteen years (total)	.243	490	1344	160	327	64	12	5	153

RANDY JACKSON
B. Feb. 10, 1926, Little Rock, Ark.
B.R., T.R. 6'1½" 180 lbs.
(3RD BASE)

YEAR	CLUB	BA	G	AB	R	H	2B	3B	HR	RBI
1950	Chicago (N)	.225	34	111	13	25	4	3	3	6
1951	Chicago (N)	.275	145	557	78	153	24	6	16	76

The Complete Catalogue of Players • 79

YEAR	CLUB	BA	G	AB	R	H	2B	3B	HR	RBI
1952	Chicago (N)	.232	116	379	44	88	8	5	9	34
1953	Chicago (N)	.285	139	498	61	142	22	8	19	66
1954	Chicago (N)	.273	126	484	77	132	17	6	19	67
1955	Chicago (N)	.265	138	499	73	132	13	7	21	70
1956	BROOKLYN (N)	.274	101	307	37	84	15	7	8	53
1957	BROOKLYN (N)	.198	48	131	7	26	1	0	2	16
1958	LOS ANGELES (N)	.185	35	65	8	12	3	0	1	4
1958	Cleveland (A) (two clubs)	.218	64	156	15	34	6	1	5	17
1959	Cleveland (A)									
1959	Chicago (N) (year totals)	.235	44	81	7	19	5	1	1	10
	Ten years	.261	955	3203	412	835	115	44	103	415
World Series	One year	.000	3	3	0	0	0	0	0	0

MERWIN JACOBSON B. March 7, 1894, New Britain, Conn.
D. Jan. 13, 1978, Baltimore, Md.
B.L., T.L. 5'11½" 165 lbs.
(OUTFIELD)

YEAR	CLUB	BA	G	AB	R	H	2B	3B	HR	RBI
1926	BROOKLYN (N)	.247	110	288	41	71	9	2	0	23
1927	BROOKLYN (N)	.000	11	6	4	0	0	0	0	1
	Four years (total)	.230	133	331	47	76	9	2	0	24

CLEO JAMES B. Aug. 31, 1940, Clarksdale, Mich.
B.R., T.R. 5'10" 176 lbs.
(OUTFIELD)

YEAR	CLUB	BA	G	AB	R	H	2B	3B	HR	RBI
1968	LOS ANGELES (N)	.200	10	10	2	2	1	0	0	0
	Four years (total)	.228	208	381	69	87	15	2	5	27

HAL JANVRIN B. Aug. 27, 1892, Haverhill, Mass.
D. March 2, 1962, Boston, Mass.
B.R., T.R. 5'11½" 168 lbs.
(SHORTSTOP, 2ND BASE, 1ST BASE)

YEAR	CLUB	BA	G	AB	R	H	2B	3B	HR	RBI
1921	BROOKLYN (N)	.196	44	92	8	18	4	0	0	14
1922	BROOKLYN (N)	.298	30	57	7	17	3	1	0	1
	Ten years total	.232	756	2221	250	515	68	18	6	210
World Series	Two years	.208	6	24	2	5	3	0	0	1

ROY JARVIS B. June 7, 1926, Shawnee, Okla.
B.R., T.R. 5'9" 160 lbs.
(CATCHER)

YEAR	CLUB	BA	G	AB	R	H	2B	3B	HR	RBI
1944	BROOKLYN (N)	.000	1	1	0	0	0	0	0	0
	Three years (total)	.160	21	50	4	8	1	0	1	4

HUGHIE JENNINGS B. April 2, 1869, Pittston, Pa.
D. Feb. 1, 1928, Scranton, Pa.
B.R., T.R. 5'8½" 165 lbs.
(SHORTSTOP, 1ST BASE)

YEAR	CLUB	BA	G	AB	R	H	2B	3B	HR	RBI
1891	Louisville (AA)	.292	90	360	53	105	10	8	1	58
1892	Louisville (N)	.222	152	594	65	132	16	4	2	61
1893	Louisville (N)									
1893	Baltimore (N) (year totals)	.182	39	143	12	26	3	0	1	15
1894	Baltimore (N)	.335	128	501	134	168	28	16	4	109
1895	Baltimore (N)	.386	131	529	159	204	41	7	4	125
1896	Baltimore (N)	.398	130	523	125	208	27	9	0	121
1897	Baltimore (N)	.355	117	439	133	156	26	9	2	79

YEAR	CLUB	BA	G	AB	R	H	2B	3B	HR	RBI
1898	Baltimore (N)	.328	143	534	135	175	25	11	1	87
1899	Baltimore (N)									
1899	BROOKLYN (N)	.296	67	—	—	—	—	—	—	—
	(year totals)	.299	69	224	44	67	3	12	0	42
1900	BROOKLYN (N)	.272	115	441	61	120	18	6	1	69
1901	Philadelphia (N)	.262	82	320	38	79	21	2	1	39
1901	Philadelphia (N)	.272	78	290	32	79	13	4	1	32
1903	BROOKLYN (N)	.235	6	17	2	4	0	0	0	1
1907	Detroit (A)	.250	1	4	0	1	1	0	0	0
1909	Detroit (A)	.500	2	4	1	2	0	0	0	2
1912	Detroit (A)	.000	1	1	0	0	0	0	0	0
1918	Detroit (A)	—	1	0	0	0	0	0	0	0
	Seventeen years	.311	1285	4906	994	1526	232	88	18	840

LOU JOHNSON B. Sept. 22, 1934, Lexington, Ky.
B.R., T.R. 5'11" 170 lbs.
(OUTFIELD)

YEAR	CLUB	BA	G	AB	R	H	2B	3B	HR	RBI
1960	Chicago (N)	.206	34	68	6	14	2	1	0	1
1961	Los Angeles (A)	—	1	0	0	0	0	0	0	0
1962	Milwaukee (N)	.282	61	117	22	33	4	5	2	13
1965	LOS ANGELES (N)	.259	131	468	57	121	24	1	12	58
1966	LOS ANGELES (N)	.272	152	526	71	143	20	2	17	73
1967	LOS ANGELES (N)	.270	104	330	39	89	14	1	11	41
1968	Chicago (N)									
1968	Cleveland (A)									
	(year totals)	.251	127	407	39	102	25	4	6	37
1969	California (A)	.203	67	133	10	27	8	0	0	9
	Eight years	.258	677	2049	244	529	97	14	48	232

World Series

YEAR	CLUB	BA	G	AB	R	H	2B	3B	HR	RBI
1965	LOS ANGELES (N)	.296	7	27	3	8	2	0	2	4
1966	LOS ANGELES (N)	.267	4	15	1	4	1	0	0	0
	Two years	.286	11	42	4	12	3	0	2	4

JIMMY JOHNSTON B. Dec. 10, 1889, Cleveland, Tenn.
D. Feb. 14, 1967, Chattanooga, Tenn.
B.R., T.R. 5'10" 160 lbs.
(3RD BASE, OUTFIELD, 2ND BASE, SHORTSTOP)

YEAR	CLUB	BA	G	AB	R	H	2B	3B	HR	RBI
1911	Chicago (A)	.000	1	2	0	0	0	0	0	2
1914	Chicago (N)	.228	50	101	9	23	3	2	1	8
1916	BROOKLYN (N)	.252	118	425	58	107	13	8	1	26
1917	BROOKLYN (N)	.270	103	330	33	89	10	4	0	25
1918	BROOKLYN (N)	.281	123	484	54	136	16	8	0	27
1919	BROOKLYN (N)	.281	117	405	56	114	11	4	1	23
1920	BROOKLYN (N)	.291	155	635	87	185	17	12	1	52
1921	BROOKLYN (N)	.325	152	624	104	203	41	14	5	56
1922	BROOKLYN (N)	.319	138	567	110	181	20	7	4	49
1923	BROOKLYN (N)	.325	151	625	111	203	29	11	4	60
1924	BROOKLYN (N)	.298	86	315	51	94	11	2	2	29
1925	BROOKLYN (N)	.297	123	431	63	128	13	3	2	43
1926	Boston (N)									
1926	New York (N)									
	(year totals)	.238	60	126	18	30	1	0	1	10
	Thirteen years	.294	1377	5070	754	1493	185	75	22	410

World Series

YEAR	CLUB	BA	G	AB	R	H	2B	3B	HR	RBI
1916	BROOKLYN (N)	.300	3	10	1	3	0	1	0	3
1920	BROOKLYN (N)	.214	4	14	2	3	0	0	0	0
	Two years	.250	7	24	3	6	0	1	0	3

JAY JOHNSTONE

B. Nov. 20, 1945, Manchester, Conn.
B.L., T.R. 6'1" 175 lbs.
(OUTFIELD)

YEAR	CLUB	BA	G	AB	R	H	2B	3B	HR	RBI
1966	California (A)	.264	61	254	35	67	12	4	3	17
1967	California (A)	.209	79	230	18	48	7	1	2	10
1968	California (A)	.261	41	115	11	30	4	1	0	3
1969	California (A)	.270	148	540	64	146	20	5	10	59
1970	California (A)	.238	119	320	34	76	10	5	11	39
1971	Chicago (A)	.260	124	388	53	101	14	1	16	40
1972	Chicago (A)	.188	113	261	27	49	9	0	4	17
1973	Oakland (A)	.107	23	28	1	3	1	0	0	3
1974	Philadelphia (N)	.295	64	200	30	59	10	4	6	30
1975	Philadelphia (N)	.329	122	350	50	115	19	2	7	54
1976	Philadelphia (N)	.318	129	440	62	140	38	4	5	53
1977	Philadelphia (N)	.284	112	363	64	103	18	4	15	59
1978	Philadelphia (N)									
1978	New York (A)									
	(year totals)	.223	71	121	9	27	2	0	1	10
1979	New York (A)									
1979	San Diego (N)									
	(year totals)	.277	98	249	17	69	9	2	1	39
1980	LOS ANGELES (N)	.307	109	251	31	77	15	2	2	20
1981	LOS ANGELES (N)	.205	61	83	8	17	3	0	3	6
1982	LOS ANGELES (N)	.077	21	13	1	1	1	0	0	2
1982	Chicago (N)									
	(two clubs)	.241	119	282	40	68	14	1	10	45
1983	Chicago (N)	.257	86	140	16	36	7	0	6	22
	Eighteen years	.262	1700	4628	825	1232	213	36	102	528
Divisional Playoff										
	One year	.000	1	1	0	0	0	0	0	0
League Championship										
	Three years	.500	7	16	1	8	1	1	0	2
World Series										
	Two years	.667	5	3	1	2	0	0	1	3

BINKY JONES

B. July 11, 1899, St. Louis, Mo.
D. May 13, 1961, St. Louis, Mo.
B.R., T.R. 5'9" 154 lbs.
(SHORTSTOP)

YEAR	CLUB	BA	G	AB	R	H	2B	3B	HR	RBI
1924	BROOKLYN (N)	.108	10	37	0	4	1	0	0	2

FIELDER JONES

B. Aug. 13, 1874, Shinglehouse, Pa.
D. March 13, 1934, Portland, Ore.
B.L., T.R. 5'11" 180 lbs.
(OUTFIELD)

YEAR	CLUB	BA	G	AB	R	H	2B	3B	HR	RBI
1896	BROOKLYN (N)	.353	104	399	82	141	10	8	3	46
1897	BROOKLYN (N)	.322	135	553	134	178	14	10	2	49
1898	BROOKLYN (N)	.302	147	599	89	181	15	9	1	69
1899	BROOKLYN (N)	.285	102	365	75	104	8	2	2	38
1900	BROOKLYN (N)	.309	136	556	108	172	26	4	4	54
1901	Chicago (A)	.340	133	521	120	177	16	3	2	65
1902	Chicago (A)	.321	135	532	98	171	16	5	0	54
1903	Chicago (A)	.287	136	530	71	152	18	5	0	45
1904	Chicago (A)	.243	154	564	74	137	14	6	3	43
1905	Chicago (A)	.245	153	568	91	139	17	12	2	38
1906	Chicago (A)	.230	144	496	77	114	22	4	2	34
1907	Chicago (A)	.261	154	559	72	146	18	1	0	47
1908	Chicago (A)	.253	149	529	92	134	11	7	1	50
1914	St. Louis (F)	.333	5	3	0	1	0	0	0	0
1915	St. Louis (F)	.000	7	6	1	0	0	0	0	0
	Fifteen years	.287	1794	6780	1184	1947	205	76	22	632
World Series										
	One year	.095	6	21	4	2	0	0	0	0

DUTCH JORDAN B. Jan. 5, 1880, Pittsburgh, Pa.
D. Dec. 23, 1972, Allegheny, Pa.
B.R., T.R.
(2ND BASE)

YEAR	CLUB	BA	G	AB	R	H	2B	3B	HR	RBI
1903	BROOKLYN (N)	.236	78	267	27	63	11	1	0	21
1904	BROOKLYN (N)	.179	87	252	21	45	10	2	0	19
	Two years	.208	165	519	48	108	21	3	0	40

JIMMY JORDAN B. Jan. 13, 1908, Tucapau, S.C.
D. Dec. 4, 1957, Charlotte, N.C.
B.R., T.R. 5'9" 157 lbs.
(2ND BASE, SHORTSTOP)

YEAR	CLUB	BA	G	AB	R	H	2B	3B	HR	RBI
1933	BROOKLYN (N)	.256	70	211	16	54	12	1	0	17
1934	BROOKLYN (N)	.266	97	369	34	98	17	2	0	43
1935	BROOKLYN (N)	.278	94	295	26	82	7	0	0	30
1936	BROOKLYN (N)	.234	115	398	26	93	15	1	2	28
	Four years	.257	376	1273	102	327	51	4	2	118

TIM JORDAN B. Feb. 14, 1879, New York, N.Y.
D. Sept. 13, 1949, Bronx, N.Y.
B.L., T.R. 6'1" 170 lbs.
(1ST BASE)

YEAR	CLUB	BA	G	AB	R	H	2B	3B	HR	RBI
1901	Washington (A)									
1901	Baltimore (A)									
	(year totals)	.174	7	23	2	4	1	0	0	2
1902	Baltimore (A)	.000	1	4	0	0	0	0	0	0
1903	New York (A)	.125	2	8	2	1	0	0	0	0
1906	BROOKLYN (N)	.262	129	450	67	118	20	8	12	78
1907	BROOKLYN (N)	.274	147	485	43	133	15	8	4	53
1908	BROOKLYN (N)	.247	148	515	58	127	18	5	12	60
1909	BROOKLYN (N)	.273	103	330	47	90	20	3	3	36
1910	BROOKLYN (N)	.200	5	5	1	1	0	0	1	3
	Eight years	.260	542	1820	220	474	74	24	32	232

SPIDER JORGENSEN B. Nov. 3, 1919, Folsom, Calif.
B.L., T.R. 5'9" 155 lbs.
(3RD BASE)

YEAR	CLUB	BA	G	AB	R	H	2B	3B	HR	RBI
1947	BROOKLYN (N)	.274	129	441	57	121	29	8	5	67
1948	BROOKLYN (N)	.300	31	90	15	27	6	2	1	13
1949	BROOKLYN (N)	.269	53	134	15	36	5	1	1	14
1950	BROOKLYN (N)	.000	2	2	0	0	0	0	0	0
1950	New York (N)									
	(year totals)	.128	26	39	5	5	0	0	0	5
1951	New York (N)	.235	28	51	5	12	0	0	2	8
	Five years	.266	267	755	97	201	40	11	9	107

World Series

YEAR	CLUB	BA	G	AB	R	H	2B	3B	HR	RBI
1947	BROOKLYN (N)	.200	7	20	1	4	2	0	0	3
1949	BROOKLYN (N)	.182	4	11	1	2	2	0	0	0
	Two years	.194	11	31	2	6	4	0	0	3

VON JOSHUA B. May 1, 1948, Oakland, Calif.
B.L., T.L. 5'10" 170 lbs.
(OUTFIELD)

YEAR	CLUB	BA	G	AB	R	H	2B	3B	HR	RBI
1969	LOS ANGELES (N)	.250	14	8	2	2	0	0	0	0
1970	LOS ANGELES (N)	.266	72	109	23	29	1	3	1	8
1971	LOS ANGELES (N)	.000	11	7	2	0	0	0	0	0
1973	LOS ANGELES (N)	.252	75	159	19	40	4	1	2	17
1974	LOS ANGELES (N)	.234	81	124	11	29	5	1	1	16

YEAR	CLUB	BA	G	AB	R	H	2B	3B	HR	RBI
1975	San Francisco (N)	.318	129	507	75	161	25	10	7	43
1976	San Francisco (N)									
1976	Milwaukee (A)									
	(year totals)	.266	149	579	57	154	18	7	5	30
1977	Milwaukee (A)	.261	144	536	58	140	25	7	9	49
1979	LOS ANGELES (N)	.282	94	142	22	40	7	1	3	14
1980	San Diego (N)	.238	53	63	8	15	2	1	2	7
	Ten years	.273	822	2234	277	610	87	31	30	184
League Championship										
	One year	—	1	0	0	0	0	0	0	0
World Series										
	One year	.000	4	4	0	0	0	0	0	0

BILL JOYCE B. Sept. 21, 1865, St. Louis, Mo.
D. May 8, 1941, St. Louis, Mo.
B.L., T.R. 5'11" 185 lbs.
(3RD BASE, 1ST BASE)

YEAR	CLUB	BA	G	AB	R	H	2B	3B	HR	RBI
1890	BROOKLYN (P)	.252	133	489	121	123	18	18	1	78
1891	Boston (AA)	.309	65	243	76	75	9	15	3	51
1892	BROOKLYN (N)	.245	97	372	89	91	15	12	6	45
1894	Washington (N)	.355	99	355	103	126	25	14	17	89
1895	Washington (N)	.312	126	474	110	148	25	13	17	95
1896	Washington (N)									
1896	New York (N)									
	(year totals)	.333	130	475	121	158	25	12	14	94
1897	New York (N)	.306	110	396	110	121	15	13	3	64
1898	New York (N)	.258	145	508	91	131	20	9	10	91
	Eight years	.294	905	3312	821	973	152	106	71	607

JOE JUDGE B. May 25, 1894, Brooklyn, N.Y.
D. March 11, 1963, Washington, D.C.
B.L., T.L. 5'8½" 155 lbs.
(1ST BASE)

YEAR	CLUB	BA	G	AB	R	H	2B	3B	HR	RBI
1933	BROOKLYN (N)	.214	42	112	7	24	2	1	0	9
	Twenty years (total)	.297	2170	7901	1184	2350	433	159	71	1039

ALEX KAMPOURIS B. Nov. 13, 1912, Sacramento, Calif.
B.R., T.R. 5'8" 155 lbs.
(2ND BASE)

YEAR	CLUB	BA	G	AB	R	H	2B	3B	HR	RBI
1941	BROOKLYN (N)	.314	16	51	8	16	4	2	2	9
1942	BROOKLYN (N)	.238	10	21	3	5	2	1	0	3
1943	BROOKLYN (N)	.227	19	44	9	10	1	0	4	17
	Nine years (total)	.243	708	2182	272	531	94	20	45	284

FRANK KANE B. March 9, 1895, Whitman, Mass.
D. Dec. 2, 1962, Brockton, Mass.
B.L., T.R. 5'11½" 175 lbs.
(OUTFIELD)

YEAR	CLUB	BA	G	AB	R	H	2B	3B	HR	RBI
1915	BROOKLYN (F)	.200	3	10	2	2	0	1	0	2
	Two years (total)	.182	4	11	2	2	0	1	0	2

JOHN KARST B. Oct. 15, 1893, Philadelphia, Pa.
B.L., T.R. 5'11½" 175 lbs.
(3RD BASE)

YEAR	CLUB	BA	G	AB	R	H	2B	3B	HR	RBI
1915	BROOKLYN (N)	—	1	0	0	0	0	0	0	0

BENNY KAUFF B. Jan. 5, 1890, Pomeroy, Ohio
D. Nov. 17, 1961, Columbus, Ohio
B.L., T.L. 5'8" 157 lbs.
(OUTFIELD)

YEAR	CLUB	BA	G	AB	R	H	2B	3B	HR	RBI
1915	BROOKLYN (F)	.342	136	483	92	165	23	11	12	83
	Eight years (total)	.311	859	3094	521	961	169	57	49	454

WILLIE KEELER B. March 3, 1872, Brooklyn, N.Y.
D. Jan. 1, 1923, Brooklyn, N.Y.
B.L., T.L. 5'4½" 140 lbs.
(OUTFIELD)

YEAR	CLUB	BA	G	AB	R	H	2B	3B	HR	RBI
1892	New York (N)	.321	14	53	7	17	3	0	0	6
1893	New York (N)									
1893	BROOKLYN (N)	.313	20	80	14	26	2	2	1	13
	(year totals)	.317	27	104	19	33	3	2	2	16
1894	Baltimore (N)	.371	129	590	165	219	27	22	5	94
1895	Baltimore (N)	.391	131	565	162	221	24	15	4	78
1896	Baltimore (N)	.392	127	546	154	214	22	13	4	82
1897	Baltimore (N)	.432	128	562	147	243	27	19	1	74
1898	Baltimore (N)	.379	128	564	126	214	10	2	1	44
1899	BROOKLYN (N)	.377	143	571	140	215	13	14	1	61
1900	BROOKLYN (N)	.368	137	565	106	208	11	14	4	68
1901	BROOKLYN (N)	.355	136	589	123	209	16	15	2	43
1902	BROOKLYN (N)	.336	132	559	86	188	18	7	0	38
1903	New York (A)	.318	132	515	95	164	14	7	0	32
1904	New York (A)	.343	143	543	78	186	14	8	2	40
1905	New York (A)	.302	149	560	81	169	14	4	4	38
1906	New York (A)	.304	152	592	96	180	8	3	2	33
1907	New York (A)	.234	107	423	50	99	5	2	0	17
1908	New York (A)	.263	91	323	38	85	3	1	1	14
1909	New York (A)	.264	99	360	44	95	7	5	1	32
1910	New York (N)	.300	19	10	5	3	0	0	0	0
	Nineteen years	.345	2124	8594	1722	2962	239	153	34	810

JOHN KELLEHER B. Sept. 13, 1893, Brookline, Mass.
D. August 21, 1960
B.R., T.R. 5'11" 150 lbs.
(3RD BASE, 1ST BASE, SHORTSTOP, 2ND BASE)

YEAR	CLUB	BA	G	AB	R	H	2B	3B	HR	RBI
1916	BROOKLYN (N)	.000	2	3	0	0	0	0	0	0
	Six years (total)	.293	235	703	81	206	29	8	10	89

FRANK KELLERT B. July 6, 1924, Oklahoma City, Okla.
D. Nov. 19, 1976, Oklahoma City, Okla.
B.R., T.R. 6'2½" 185 lbs.
(1ST BASE)

YEAR	CLUB	BA	G	AB	R	H	2B	3B	HR	RBI
1955	BROOKLYN (N)	.325	39	80	12	26	4	2	4	19
	Four years	.231	122	247	25	57	9	3	8	37
World Series										
	One year	.333	3	3	0	1	0	0	0	0

JOE KELLEY B. Dec. 9, 1871, Cambridge, Mass.
D. Aug. 14, 1943, Baltimore, Md.
B.R., T.R. 5'11" 190 lbs.
(OUTFIELD)

YEAR	CLUB	BA	G	AB	R	H	2B	3B	HR	RBI
1891	Boston (N)									
1891	Pittsburgh (N)									
	(year totals)	.231	14	52	8	12	1	1	0	2
1892	Pittsburgh (N)									
1892	Baltimore (N)									
	(year totals)	.235	66	238	29	56	7	7	0	32
1893	Baltimore (N)	.305	125	502	120	153	27	16	9	76
1894	Baltimore (N)	.393	129	597	167	199	48	20	6	111

The Complete Catalogue of Players • 85

YEAR	CLUB	BA	G	AB	R	H	2B	3B	HR	RBI
1895	Baltimore (N)	.365	131	518	148	189	26	19	10	134
1896	Baltimore (N)	.364	131	519	148	189	31	19	8	100
1897	Baltimore (N)	.388	131	505	113	196	31	9	5	118
1898	Baltimore (N)	.328	124	467	71	153	18	15	2	110
1899	BROOKLYN (N)	.330	144	540	108	178	21	14	6	93
1900	BROOKLYN (N)	.319	121	454	92	145	23	17	6	91
1901	BROOKLYN (N)	.309	120	492	77	152	22	12	4	65
1902	Baltimore (A)									
1902	Cincinnati (N)									
	(year totals)	.315	100	378	74	119	26	9	2	46
1903	Cincinnati (N)	.316	105	383	85	121	22	4	3	45
1904	Cincinnati (N)	.281	123	449	75	126	21	13	0	63
1905	Cincinnati (N)	.277	90	321	43	89	7	6	1	37
1906	Cincinnati (N)	.228	129	465	43	106	19	11	1	53
1908	Boston (N)	.259	62	228	25	59	8	2	2	17
	Seventeen years	.319	1845	7018	1426	2242	358	194	65	1193

GEORGE KELLY B. Sept. 10, 1895, San Francisco, Calif.
B.R., T.R. 6'4" 190 lbs.
(1ST BASE)

YEAR	CLUB	BA	G	AB	R	H	2B	3B	HR	RBI
1932	BROOKLYN (N)	.243	64	202	23	49	9	1	4	22
	Sixteen years (total)	.297	1622	5993	819	1778	337	76	148	1020

BOB KENNEDY B. Aug. 18, 1920, Chicago, Ill.
B.R., T.R. 6'2" 193 lbs.
(OUTFIELD, 3RD BASE)

YEAR	CLUB	BA	G	AB	R	H	2B	3B	HR	RBI
1957	BROOKLYN (N)	.129	19	31	5	4	1	0	1	4
	Sixteen years (total)	.254	1483	4624	514	1176	196	41	63	514

JOHN KENNEDY B. May 29, 1941, Chicago, Ill.
B.R., T.R. 6' 185 lbs.
(3RD BASE, SHORTSTOP, 2ND BASE)

YEAR	CLUB	BA	G	AB	R	H	2B	3B	HR	RBI
1962	Washington (A)	.262	14	42	6	11	0	1	1	2
1963	Washington (A)	.177	36	62	3	11	1	1	0	4
1964	Washington (A)	.230	148	482	55	111	16	4	7	35
1965	LOS ANGELES (N)	.171	104	105	12	18	3	0	1	5
1966	LOS ANGELES (N)	.201	125	274	15	55	9	2	3	24
1967	New York (A)	.196	78	179	22	35	4	0	1	17
1969	Seattle (A)	.234	61	128	18	30	3	1	4	14
1970	Milwaukee (A)									
1970	Boston (A)									
	(year totals)	.255	68	184	23	47	9	1	6	23
1971	Boston (A)	.276	74	272	41	75	12	5	5	22
1972	Boston (A)	.245	71	212	22	52	11	1	2	22
1973	Boston (A)	.181	67	155	17	28	9	1	1	16
1974	Boston (A)	.133	10	15	3	2	0	0	1	1
	Twelve years (total)	.225	856	2110	237	475	77	17	32	185

World Series

YEAR	CLUB	BA	G	AB	R	H	2B	3B	HR	RBI
1965	LOS ANGELES (N)	.000	4	1	0	0	0	0	0	0
1966	LOS ANGELES (N)	.200	2	5	0	1	0	0	0	0
	Two years (total)	.167	6	6	0	1	0	0	0	0

PETE KILDUFF B. April 4, 1893, Weir City, Kan.
D. Feb. 14, 1930, Pittsburgh, Kan.
B.R., T.R. 5'7" 155 lbs.
(2ND BASE)

YEAR	CLUB	BA	G	AB	R	H	2B	3B	HR	RBI
1917	New York (N)									
1917	Chicago (N)									
	(year totals)	.257	87	280	35	72	12	5	1	27

YEAR	CLUB	BA	G	AB	R	H	2B	3B	HR	RBI
1918	Chicago (N)	.204	30	93	7	19	2	2	0	13
1919	Chicago (N)									
1919	BROOKLYN (N)	.301	32	73	9	22	3	1	0	8
	(year totals)	.286	63	161	14	46	7	3	0	16
1920	BROOKLYN (N)	.272	141	478	62	130	26	8	0	58
1921	BROOKLYN (N)	.288	107	372	45	107	15	10	3	45
	Five years	.270	428	1384	163	374	62	28	4	159
World Series										
	One year	.095	7	21	0	2	0	0	0	0

TOM KINSLOW
B. Jan. 12, 1866, Washington, D.C.
D. Feb. 22, 1901, Washington, D.C.
T.R.
(CATCHER)

YEAR	CLUB	BA	G	AB	R	H	2B	3B	HR	RBI
*1890	BROOKLYN (P)	.264	64	242	30	64	11	6	4	46
1891	BROOKLYN (N)	.237	61	228	22	54	6	0	0	33
1892	BROOKLYN (N)	.305	66	246	37	75	6	11	2	40
1893	BROOKLYN (N)	.244	78	312	38	76	8	4	4	45
1894	BROOKLYN (N)	.305	62	223	39	68	5	6	2	41
1895	Pittsburgh (N)	.226	19	62	10	14	2	0	0	5
1896	Louisville (N)	.280	8	25	4	7	0	1	0	7
1898	Washington (N)									
1898	St. Louis (N)									
	(year totals)	.258	17	62	5	16	2	1	0	4
	Ten years	.266	380	1414	186	376	40	29	12	222

*1886 Washington (N), 1887 New York (AA)

ENOS KIRKPATRICK
B. Dec. 9, 1889, Pittsburgh, Pa.
D. April 14, 1964, Pittsburgh, Pa.
B.R., T.R. 5'10" 175 lbs.
(3RD BASE)

YEAR	CLUB	BA	G	AB	R	H	2B	3B	HR	RBI
1912	BROOKLYN (N)	.191	32	94	13	18	1	1	0	6
1913	BROOKLYN (N)	.247	48	89	13	22	4	1	1	5
	Four years (total)	.237	203	528	70	125	20	6	3	46

JOE KLUGMAN
B. March 26, 1895, St. Louis, Mo.
D. July 18, 1951, Moberly, Mo.
B.R., T.R. 5'11" 175 lbs.
(2ND BASE)

YEAR	CLUB	BA	G	AB	R	H	2B	3B	HR	RBI
1924	BROOKLYN (N)	.165	31	79	7	13	2	1	0	3
	Four years (total)	.251	77	187	22	47	11	3	0	17

ELMER KLUMPP
B. Aug. 26, 1906, St. Louis, Mo.
B.R., T.R. 6' 184 lbs.
(CATCHER)

YEAR	CLUB	BA	G	AB	R	H	2B	3B	HR	RBI
1937	BROOKLYN (N)	.091	5	11	0	1	0	0	0	2
	Two years (total)	.115	17	26	2	3	0	0	0	2

BARNEY KOCH
B. March 23, 1923, Campbell, Neb.
B.R., T.R. 5'8" 140 lbs.
(2ND BASE)

YEAR	CLUB	BA	G	AB	R	H	2B	3B	HR	RBI
1944	BROOKLYN (N)	.219	33	96	11	21	2	0	0	1

LEN KOENECKE

B. Jan. 18, 1906, Baraboo, Wis.
B.L., T.R. 5'11" 180 lbs.
(OUTFIELD)

YEAR	CLUB	BA	G	AB	R	H	2B	3B	HR	RBI
1932	New York (N)	.255	42	137	33	35	5	0	4	14
1934	BROOKLYN (N)	.320	123	460	79	147	31	7	14	73
1935	BROOKLYN (N)	.283	100	325	43	92	13	2	4	27
	Three years	.297	265	922	155	274	49	9	22	114

ED KONETCHY

B. Sept. 3, 1885, LaCrosse, Wis.
D. May 27, 1947, Fort Worth, Texas
B.R., T.R. 6'2½" 195 lbs.
(1ST BASE)

YEAR	CLUB	BA	G	AB	R	H	2B	3B	HR	RBI
1907	St. Louis (N)	.252	90	330	34	83	11	8	3	30
1908	St. Louis (N)	.248	154	545	46	135	19	12	5	50
1909	St. Louis (N)	.286	152	576	88	165	23	14	4	80
1910	St. Louis (N)	.302	144	520	87	157	23	16	3	78
1911	St. Louis (N)	.289	158	571	90	165	38	13	6	88
1912	St. Louis (N)	.314	143	538	81	169	26	13	8	82
1913	St. Louis (N)	.273	139	502	74	137	18	17	7	68
1914	Pittsburgh (N)	.249	154	563	56	140	23	9	4	51
1915	Pittsburgh (F)	.314	152	576	79	181	31	18	10	93
1916	Boston (N)	.260	158	566	76	147	29	13	3	70
1917	Boston (N)	.272	130	474	56	129	19	13	2	54
1918	Boston (N)	.236	119	437	33	103	15	5	2	56
1919	BROOKLYN (N)	.298	132	486	46	145	24	9	1	47
1920	BROOKLYN (N)	.308	131	497	62	153	22	12	5	63
1921	BROOKLYN (N)	.269	55	197	25	53	6	5	3	23
1921	Philadelphia (N)									
	(year totals)	.299	127	465	63	139	23	9	11	82
	Fifteen years	.281	2083	7646	971	2148	344	181	74	992
World Series										
	One year	.174	7	23	0	4	0	1	0	2

ANDY KOSCO

B. Oct. 5, 1941, Youngstown, Ohio
B.R., T.R. 6'3" 205 lbs.
(OUTFIELD)

YEAR	CLUB	BA	G	AB	R	H	2B	3B	HR	RBI
1965	Minnesota (A)	.236	23	55	3	13	4	0	1	6
1966	Minnesota (A)	.222	57	158	11	35	5	0	2	13
1967	Minnesota (A)	.143	9	28	4	4	1	0	0	4
1968	New York (A)	.240	131	466	47	112	19	1	15	59
1969	LOS ANGELES (N)	.248	120	424	51	105	13	2	19	74
1970	LOS ANGELES (N)	.228	74	224	21	51	12	0	8	27
1971	Milwaukee (A)	.227	98	264	27	60	6	2	10	39
1972	California (A)									
1972	Boston (A)									
	(year totals)	.233	66	189	20	44	6	3	9	19
1973	Cincinnati (N)	.280	47	118	17	33	7	0	9	21
1974	Cincinnati (N)	.189	33	37	3	7	2	0	0	5
	Ten years	.236	658	1963	204	464	75	8	73	267
League Championship										
	One year	.300	3	10	0	3	0	0	0	0

ERNIE KOY

B. Sept. 17, 1909, Sealy, Texas
B.R., T.R. 6' 200 lbs.
(OUTFIELD)

YEAR	CLUB	BA	G	AB	R	H	2B	3B	HR	RBI
1938	BROOKLYN (N)	.299	142	521	78	156	29	13	11	76
1939	BROOKLYN (N)	.278	123	425	57	118	37	5	8	67
1940	BROOKLYN (N)	.229	24	48	9	11	2	1	1	8
1940	St. Louis (N)									
	(year totals)	.301	117	396	53	119	21	6	9	60
1941	St. Louis (N)									

YEAR	CLUB	BA	G	AB	R	H	2B	3B	HR	RBI
1941	Cincinnati (N)									
	(year totals)	.242	80	244	29	59	12	2	4	31
1942	Cincinnati (N)									
1942	Philadelphia (N)									
	(year totals)	.242	94	260	21	63	9	3	4	26
	Five years	.279	556	1846	238	515	108	29	36	260

CHARLIE KRESS
B. Dec. 9, 1921, Philadelphia, Pa.
B.L., T.L. 6' 190 lbs.
(1ST BASE)

YEAR	CLUB	BA	G	AB	R	H	2B	3B	HR	RBI
1954	BROOKLYN (N)	.083	13	12	1	1	0	0	0	2
	Four years (total)	.249	175	466	57	116	20	7	1	52

ERNIE KRUEGER
B. Dec. 27, 1890, Chicago, Ill.
D. April 22, 1976, Waukegan, Ill.
B.R., T.R. 5'10½" 185 lbs.
(CATCHER)

YEAR	CLUB	BA	G	AB	R	H	2B	3B	HR	RBI
1913	Cleveland (A)	.000	5	6	0	0	0	0	0	0
1915	New York (A)	.172	10	29	3	5	1	0	0	0
1917	New York (N)									
1917	BROOKLYN (N)	.272	31	81	10	22	2	2	1	6
	(year totals)	.242	39	91	10	22	2	2	1	6
1918	BROOKLYN (N)	.287	30	87	4	25	4	2	0	7
1919	BROOKLYN (N)	.248	80	226	24	56	7	4	5	36
1920	BROOKLYN (N)	.288	52	146	21	42	4	2	1	17
1921	BROOKLYN (N)	.264	65	163	18	43	11	4	3	20
1925	Cincinnati (N)	.307	37	88	7	27	4	0	1	7
	Eight years	.263	318	836	87	220	33	14	11	93
World Series										
	One year	.167	4	6	0	1	0	0	0	0

JOE KUSTUS
B. Detroit, Mich.
D. April 27, 1916, Eldis, Mich.
B.R., T.R.

YEAR	CLUB	BA	G	AB	R	H	2B	3B	HR	RBI
1909	BROOKLYN (N)	.145	53	173	12	25	5	0	1	11

CANDY LACHANCE
B. Feb. 15, 1870, Waterbury, Conn.
D. Aug. 18, 1932, Watertown, Vt.
B.B., T.R.
(1ST BASE)

YEAR	CLUB	BA	G	AB	R	H	2B	3B	HR	RBI
1893	BROOKLYN (N)	.171	11	35	1	6	1	0	0	6
1894	BROOKLYN (N)	.323	68	257	48	83	13	8	5	52
1895	BROOKLYN (N)	.312	127	536	99	167	22	8	8	108
1896	BROOKLYN (N)	.284	89	348	60	99	10	13	7	58
1897	BROOKLYN (N)	.308	126	520	86	160	28	16	4	90
1898	BROOKLYN (N)	.247	136	526	62	130	23	7	5	65
1899	Baltimore (N)	.307	125	472	65	145	23	10	1	75
1901	Cleveland (A)	.303	133	548	81	166	22	9	1	75
1902	Boston (A)	.279	138	541	60	151	13	4	6	56
1903	Boston (A)	.257	141	522	60	134	22	6	1	53
1904	Boston (A)	.227	157	573	55	130	19	5	1	47
1905	Boston (N)	.146	12	41	1	6	1	0	0	5
	Twelve years	.280	1263	4919	678	1377	197	86	39	690
World Series										
	One year	.222	8	27	5	6	2	1	0	4

LEE LACY

B. April 10, 1948, Longview, Texas
B.R., T.R. 6'1" 175 lbs.
(OUTFIELD, 2ND BASE)

YEAR	CLUB	BA	G	AB	R	H	2B	3B	HR	RBI
1972	LOS ANGELES (N)	.259	60	243	34	63	7	3	0	12
1973	LOS ANGELES (N)	.207	57	135	14	28	2	0	0	8
1974	LOS ANGELES (N)	.282	48	78	13	22	6	0	0	8
1975	LOS ANGELES (N)	.314	101	306	44	96	11	5	7	40
1976	Atlanta (N)									
1976	LOS ANGELES (N)	.266	53	158	17	42	7	1	0	14
	(year totals)	.269	103	338	42	91	11	3	3	34
1977	LOS ANGELES (N)	.266	75	169	28	45	7	0	6	21
1978	LOS ANGELES (N)	.261	103	245	29	64	16	4	13	40
1979	Pittsburgh (N)	.247	84	182	17	45	9	3	5	15
1980	Pittsburgh (N)	.335	109	278	45	93	20	4	7	33
1981	Pittsburgh (N)	.268	78	213	31	57	11	4	2	10
1982	Pittsburgh (N)	.312	121	359	66	112	16	3	5	31
1983	Pittsburgh (N)	.302	108	288	40	87	12	3	4	13
	Twelve years	.280	1047	2834	403	803	128	32	52	265
League Championship										
	Three years	.333	3	3	1	1	0	0	0	0
World Series										
	Four years	.231	13	26	1	6	0	0	0	3

BILL LAMAR

B. March 21, 1897, Rockville, Md.
D. May 24, 1970, Lockport, Mass.
B.L., T.R. 6'1" 185 lbs.
(OUTFIELD)

YEAR	CLUB	BA	G	AB	R	H	2B	3B	HR	RBI
1920	BROOKLYN (N)	.273	24	44	5	12	4	0	0	4
1921	BROOKLYN (N)	.333	3	3	2	1	0	0	0	0
	Nine years (total)	.310	550	2040	303	633	114	23	19	245

RAFAEL LANDESTOY

B. May 28, 1953, Bani, Dominican Republic
B.R., T.R. 5'10" 165 lbs.
(2ND BASE, SHORTSTOP)

YEAR	CLUB	BA	G	AB	R	H	2B	3B	HR	RBI
1977	LOS ANGELES (N)	.278	15	18	6	5	0	0	0	0
1982	Cincinnati (N)	.189	73	111	11	21	3	0	1	9
	Six years	.244	472	1107	118	270	31	16	2	80
League Championship										
	One year	.222	5	9	3	2	0	0	0	2
World Series										
	One year	—	1	0	0	0	0	0	0	0

KEN LANDREAUX

B. Dec. 22, 1954, Los Angeles, Calif.
B.R., T.R. 5'10" 165 lbs.
(OUTFIELD)

YEAR	CLUB	BA	G	AB	R	H	2B	3B	HR	RBI
1977	California (A)	.250	23	76	6	19	5	1	0	5
1978	California (A)	.223	93	260	37	58	7	5	5	23
1979	Minnesota (A)	.305	151	564	81	172	27	5	15	83
1980	Minnesota (A)	.281	129	484	56	136	23	11	7	62
1981	LOS ANGELES (N)	.251	99	390	48	98	16	4	7	41
1982	LOS ANGELES (N)	.284	129	461	71	131	23	7	7	50
1983	LOS ANGELES (N)	.281	141	481	63	135	25	3	17	66
	Seven years	.276	765	2716	362	749	126	36	58	336
Divisional Playoff										
	One year	.200	5	20	1	4	1	0	0	1
League Championship										
	One year	.100	5	10	0	1	1	0	0	0
World Series										
	One year	.167	5	6	1	1	1	0	0	0

NORM LARKER
B. Dec. 27, 1930, Beaver Meadows, Pa.
B.L., T.L. 6' 185 lbs.
(1ST BASE)

YEAR	CLUB	BA	G	AB	R	H	2B	3B	HR	RBI
1958	LOS ANGELES (N)	.277	99	253	32	70	16	5	4	29
1959	LOS ANGELES (N)	.289	108	311	37	90	14	1	8	49
1960	LOS ANGELES (N)	.323	133	440	56	142	26	3	5	78
1961	LOS ANGELES (N)	.270	97	282	29	76	16	1	5	38
1962	Houston (N)	.263	147	506	58	133	19	5	9	63
1963	Milwaukee (N)									
1963	San Francisco (N)									
	(year totals)	.168	83	161	15	27	6	0	1	14
	Six years	.275	667	1953	227	538	97	15	32	271

World Series

		BA	G	AB	R	H	2B	3B	HR	RBI
	One year	.188	6	16	2	3	0	0	0	0

LYN LARY
B. Jan. 28, 1906, Armona, Calif.
D. Jan. 9, 1973, Downey, Calif.
B.R., T.R. 6' 165 lbs.
(SHORTSTOP)

YEAR	CLUB	BA	G	AB	R	H	2B	3B	HR	RBI
1939	BROOKLYN (N)	.161	29	31	7	5	1	1	0	1
	Twelve years (total)	.269	1302	4604	805	1239	247	56	38	526

TACKS LATIMER
B. Nov. 30, 1875, Loveland, Ohio
D. April 24, 1936, Cincinnati, Ohio
T.R.
(CATCHER)

YEAR	CLUB	BA	G	AB	R	H	2B	3B	HR	RBI
1902	BROOKLYN (N)	.042	8	24	0	1	0	0	0	0
	Five years (total)	.221	27	86	5	19	3	0	0	7

COOKIE LAVAGETTO
B. Dec. 1, 1912, Oakland, Calif.
B.R., T.R. 6' 170 lbs.
(3RD BASE, 2ND BASE)

YEAR	CLUB	BA	G	AB	R	H	2B	3B	HR	RBI
1934	Pittsburgh (N)	.220	87	304	41	67	16	3	3	46
1935	Pittsburgh (N)	.290	78	231	27	67	9	4	0	19
1936	Pittsburgh (N)	.244	60	197	21	48	15	2	2	26
1937	BROOKLYN (N)	.282	149	503	64	142	26	6	8	70
1938	BROOKLYN (N)	.273	137	487	68	133	34	6	6	79
1939	BROOKLYN (N)	.300	153	587	93	176	28	5	10	87
1940	BROOKLYN (N)	.257	118	448	56	115	21	3	4	43
1941	BROOKLYN (N)	.277	132	441	75	122	24	7	1	78
1946	BROOKLYN (N)	.236	88	242	36	57	9	1	3	27
1947	BROOKLYN (N)	.261	41	69	6	18	1	0	3	11
	Ten years	.269	1043	3509	487	945	183	37	40	486

World Series

YEAR	CLUB	BA	G	AB	R	H	2B	3B	HR	RBI
1941	BROOKLYN (N)	.100	3	10	1	1	0	0	0	0
1947	BROOKLYN (N)	.143	5	7	0	1	1	0	0	3
	Two years	.118	8	17	1	2	1	0	0	3

RUDY LAW
B. Oct. 7, 1956, Boise, Idaho
B.L., T.L. 6'1" 165 lbs.
(OUTFIELD)

YEAR	CLUB	BA	G	AB	R	H	2B	3B	HR	RBI
1978	LOS ANGELES (N)	.250	11	12	2	3	0	0	0	1
1980	LOS ANGELES (N)	.260	128	388	55	101	5	4	1	23
	Two years	.260	139	400	57	104	5	4	1	24

TONY LAZZERI

B. Dec. 6, 1903, San Francisco, Calif.
D. Aug. 6, 1946, San Francisco, Calif.
B.R., T.R. 5'11½" 170 lbs.
(2ND BASE)

YEAR	CLUB	BA	G	AB	R	H	2B	3B	HR	RBI
1939	BROOKLYN (N)	.282	14	39	6	11	2	0	3	6
	Fourteen years (total)	.292	1739	6297	986	1840	334	115	178	1191

BILL LEARD

B. Oct. 14, 1885, Oneida, N.Y.
D. Jan. 15, 1970, San Francisco, Calif.
B.R., T.R. 5'10" 155 lbs.
(2ND BASE)

YEAR	CLUB	BA	G	AB	R	H	2B	3B	HR	RBI
1917	BROOKLYN (N)	.000	3	3	0	0	0	0	0	0

HAL LEE

B. Feb. 15, 1905, Ludlow, Miss.
B.R., T.R. 5'11" 180 lbs.
(OUTFIELD)

YEAR	CLUB	BA	G	AB	R	H	2B	3B	HR	RBI
1930	BROOKLYN (N)	.162	22	37	5	6	0	0	1	4
	Seven years (total)	.275	752	2750	316	755	144	40	33	323

LERON LEE

B. March 4, 1948, Bakersfield, Calif.
B.L., T.R. 6' 196 lbs.
(OUTFIELD)

YEAR	CLUB	BA	G	AB	R	H	2B	3B	HR	RBI
1975	LOS ANGELES (N)	.256	48	43	2	11	4	0	0	2
1976	LOS ANGELES (N)	.133	23	45	1	6	0	1	0	2
	Eight years (total)	.250	614	1617	173	404	83	13	31	152

JIM LEFEBVRE

B. Jan. 7, 1943, Hawthorne, Calif.
B.B., T.R. 6' 180 lbs.
(2ND BASE, 3RD BASE)

YEAR	CLUB	BA	G	AB	R	H	2B	3B	HR	RBI
1965	LOS ANGELES (N)	.250	157	544	57	136	21	4	12	69
1966	LOS ANGELES (N)	.274	152	544	69	149	23	3	24	74
1967	LOS ANGELES (N)	.261	136	494	51	129	18	5	8	50
1968	LOS ANGELES (N)	.241	84	286	23	69	12	1	5	31
1969	LOS ANGELES (N)	.236	95	275	29	65	15	2	4	44
1970	LOS ANGELES (N)	.252	109	314	33	79	15	1	4	44
1971	LOS ANGELES (N)	.245	119	388	40	95	14	2	12	68
1972	LOS ANGELES (N)	.201	70	169	11	34	8	0	5	24
	Eight years	.251	922	3014	313	756	126	18	74	404

World Series

YEAR	CLUB	BA	G	AB	R	H	2B	3B	HR	RBI
1965	LOS ANGELES (N)	.400	3	10	2	4	0	0	0	0
1966	LOS ANGELES (N)	.167	4	12	1	2	0	0	1	1
	Two years	.273	7	22	3	6	0	0	1	1

LARRY LeJEUNE

B. July 22, 1885, Chicago, Ill.
D. April 21, 1952, Eloise, Mich.
B.R., T.R.
(OUTFIELD)

YEAR	CLUB	BA	G	AB	R	H	2B	3B	HR	RBI
1911	BROOKLYN (N)	.158	6	19	2	3	0	0	0	2
	Two years (total)	.167	24	84	6	14	0	1	0	4

DON LeJOHN B. May 13, 1934, Daisytown, Pa.
B.R., T.R. 5'10" 175 lbs.
(3RD BASE)

YEAR	CLUB	BA	G	AB	R	H	2B	3B	HR	RBI
1965	LOS ANGELES (N)	.256	34	78	2	20	2	0	0	7
World Series										
	One year	.000	1	1	0	0	0	0	0	0

STEVE LEMBO B. Nov. 13, 1926, Brooklyn, N.Y.
B.R., T.R. 6'1" 185 lbs.
(CATCHER)

YEAR	CLUB	BA	G	AB	R	H	2B	3B	HR	RBI
1950	BROOKLYN (N)	.167	5	6	0	1	0	0	0	0
1952	BROOKLYN (N)	.200	2	5	0	1	0	0	0	1
	Two years	.182	7	11	0	2	0	0	0	1

ED LENNOX B. Nov. 3, 1885, Camden, N.J.
D. Oct. 26, 1939, Camden, N.J.
B.R., T.R. 5'10" 174 lbs.
(3RD BASE)

YEAR	CLUB	BA	G	AB	R	H	2B	3B	HR	RBI
1906	Philadelphia (A)	.059	6	17	1	1	1	0	0	0
1909	BROOKLYN (N)	.262	126	435	33	114	18	9	2	44
1910	BROOKLYN (N)	.259	110	367	19	95	19	4	3	32
1912	Chicago (N)	.235	27	81	13	19	4	1	1	16
1914	Pittsburgh (F)	.312	124	430	71	134	25	10	11	84
1915	Pittsburgh (F)	.302	55	53	1	16	3	1	1	9
	Six years	.274	448	1383	138	379	70	25	18	185

JEFF LEONARD B. Sept. 22, 1955, Philadelphia, Pa.
B.R., T.R. 6'2" 200 lbs.
(OUTFIELD)

YEAR	CLUB	BA	G	AB	R	H	2B	3B	HR	RBI
1977	LOS ANGELES (N)	.300	11	10	2	3	0	1	0	0
	Six years (total)	.269	365	1086	132	292	52	16	16	151

SAM LESLIE B. July 26, 1905, Moss Point, Miss.
D. Jan. 21, 1979, Pascagula, Fla.
B.L., T.L. 6' 192 lbs.
(1ST BASE)

YEAR	CLUB	BA	G	AB	R	H	2B	3B	HR	RBI
1929	New York (N)	.000	1	1	0	0	0	0	0	1
1930	New York (N)	.500	2	2	0	1	0	0	0	0
1931	New York (N)	.302	53	53	11	16	4	0	3	5
1932	New York (N)	.293	77	75	5	22	4	0	1	15
1933	New York (N)									
1933	BROOKLYN (N)	.286	96	364	41	104	11	4	5	46
	(year totals)	.295	136	501	62	148	23	7	8	73
1934	BROOKLYN (N)	.332	146	546	75	181	29	6	9	102
1935	BROOKLYN (N)	.308	142	502	72	160	30	7	5	93
1936	New York (N)	.295	117	417	49	123	19	5	6	54
1937	New York (N)	.309	72	191	25	59	7	2	3	30
1938	New York (N)	.253	76	154	12	39	7	1	1	16
	Ten years	.304	822	2460	311	749	123	28	36	389
World Series										
	Two years	.500	5	4	0	2	0	0	0	0

PHIL LEWIS B. Oct. 7, 1883, Pittsburgh, Pa.
D. Aug. 8, 1959, Port Wentworth, Ga.
B.R., T.R. 6' 195 lbs.
(SHORTSTOP)

YEAR	CLUB	BA	G	AB	R	H	2B	3B	HR	RBI
1905	BROOKLYN (N)	.254	118	433	32	110	9	2	3	33
1906	BROOKLYN (N)	.243	136	452	40	110	8	4	0	37

The Complete Catalogue of Players • 93

YEAR	CLUB	BA	G	AB	R	H	2B	3B	HR	RBI
1907	BROOKLYN (N)	.248	136	475	52	118	11	1	0	30
1908	BROOKLYN (N)	.219	118	415	22	91	5	6	1	30
	Four years	.242	508	1775	146	429	33	13	4	130

BOB LILLIS B. June 2, 1930, Altadena, Calif.
B.R., T.R. 5'11" 160 lbs.
(SHORTSTOP, 2ND BASE, 3RD BASE)

YEAR	CLUB	BA	G	AB	R	H	2B	3B	HR	RBI
1958	LOS ANGELES (N)	.391	20	69	10	27	3	1	1	5
1959	LOS ANGELES (N)	.229	30	48	7	11	2	0	0	2
1960	LOS ANGELES (N)	.267	48	60	6	16	4	0	0	6
1961	LOS ANGELES (N)	.111	9	0	1	0	0	0	0	0
1961	St. Louis (N)									
	(year totals)	.213	105	239	24	51	4	0	0	22
1962	Houston (N)	.249	129	457	38	114	12	4	1	30
1963	Houston (N)	.198	147	469	31	93	13	1	1	19
1964	Houston (N)	.268	109	322	31	89	11	2	0	17
1965	Houston (N)	.221	124	408	34	90	12	1	0	20
1966	Houston (N)	.232	68	164	14	38	6	0	0	11
1967	Houston (N)	.244	37	82	3	20	1	0	0	5
	Ten years	.236	817	2328	198	549	68	9	3	137

FREDDIE LINDSTROM B. Nov. 21, 1905, Chicago, Ill.
D. Oct. 4, 1981, Chicago, Ill.
B.R., T.R. 5'11" 170 lbs.
(3RD BASE, OUTFIELD)

YEAR	CLUB	BA	G	AB	R	H	2B	3B	HR	RBI
1936	BROOKLYN (N)	.264	26	106	12	28	4	0	0	10
	Thirteen years (total)	.311	1438	5611	895	1747	301	81	103	779

MICKEY LIVINGSTON B. Nov. 15, 1914, Newberry, S.C.
B.R., T.R. 6'1½" 185 lbs.
(CATCHER)

YEAR	CLUB	BA	G	AB	R	H	2B	3B	HR	RBI
1951	BROOKLYN (N)	.400	2	5	0	2	0	0	0	2
	Ten years (total)	.238	561	1490	128	354	56	9	19	153
World Series										
	One year	.364	6	22	3	8	3	0	0	4

DICK LOFTUS B. March 7, 1901, Concord, Mass.
B.L., T.R. 6' 155 lbs.
(OUTFIELD)

YEAR	CLUB	BA	G	AB	R	H	2B	3B	HR	RBI
1924	BROOKLYN (N)	.272	46	81	18	22	6	0	0	8
1925	BROOKLYN (N)	.237	51	131	16	31	6	0	0	13
	Two years	.250	97	212	34	53	12	0	0	21

ERNIE LOMBARDI B. April 6, 1908, Oakland, Calif.
D. Sept. 26, 1977, Santa Cruz, Calif.
B.R., T.R. 6'3" 230 lbs.
(CATCHER)

YEAR	CLUB	BA	G	AB	R	H	2B	3B	HR	RBI
1931	BROOKLYN (N)	.297	73	182	20	54	7	1	4	23
	Seventeen years (total)	.306	1853	5855	601	1792	277	27	190	990

DAVEY LOPES B. May 3, 1946, Providence, R.I.
B.R., T.R. 5'9" 170 lbs.
(2ND BASE)

YEAR	CLUB	BA	G	AB	R	H	2B	3B	HR	RBI
1972	LOS ANGELES (N)	.214	11	42	6	9	4	0	0	1
1973	LOS ANGELES (N)	.275	142	535	77	147	13	5	6	37

YEAR	CLUB	BA	G	AB	R	H	2B	3B	HR	RBI
1974	LOS ANGELES (N)	.266	145	530	95	141	26	3	10	35
1975	LOS ANGELES (N)	.262	155	618	108	162	24	6	8	41
1976	LOS ANGELES (N)	.241	117	427	72	103	17	7	4	20
1977	LOS ANGELES (N)	.283	134	502	85	142	19	5	11	53
1978	LOS ANGELES (N)	.278	151	587	93	163	25	4	17	58
1979	LOS ANGELES (N)	.265	153	582	109	154	20	6	28	73
1980	LOS ANGELES (N)	.251	141	553	79	139	15	3	10	49
1981	LOS ANGELES (N)	.206	58	214	35	44	2	0	5	17
1982	Oakland (A)	.242	128	450	58	109	19	3	11	42
1983	Oakland (A)	.277	147	494	64	137	13	4	17	67
	Twelve years	.270	1482	5534	881	1450	197	46	127	493
Divisional Playoff										
	One year	.200	5	20	1	4	1	0	0	0
League Championship										
	Four years	.294	17	68	9	20	1	2	2	11

World Series

YEAR	CLUB	BA	G	AB	R	H	2B	3B	HR	RBI
1974	LOS ANGELES (N)	.267	4	15	4	4	0	1	0	3
1977	LOS ANGELES (N)	.235	4	17	2	4	0	0	0	3
1978	LOS ANGELES (N)	.389	4	18	3	7	1	1	2	5
1981	LOS ANGELES (N)	.278	5	18	0	5	0	0	0	0
	Four years	.211	23	90	18	19	1	1	4	11

AL LOPEZ B. Aug. 20, 1908, Tampa, Fla.
B.R., T.R. 5'11" 165 lbs.
(CATCHER)

YEAR	CLUB	BA	G	AB	R	H	2B	3B	HR	RBI
1928	BROOKLYN (N)	.000	3	12	0	0	0	0	0	0
1930	BROOKLYN (N)	.309	128	421	60	130	20	4	6	57
1931	BROOKLYN (N)	.269	111	360	38	97	13	4	0	40
1932	BROOKLYN (N)	.275	126	404	44	111	18	6	1	43
1933	BROOKLYN (N)	.301	126	372	39	112	11	4	3	41
1934	BROOKLYN (N)	.273	140	439	58	120	23	2	7	54
1935	BROOKLYN (N)	.251	128	379	50	95	12	4	3	39
1936	Boston (N)	.242	128	426	46	103	12	4	8	50
1937	Boston (N)	.204	105	334	31	68	11	1	3	38
1938	Boston (N)	.267	71	236	19	63	6	1	1	14
1939	Boston (N)	.252	131	412	32	104	22	1	8	49
1940	Boston (N)									
1940	Pittsburgh (N)									
	(year totals)	.273	95	293	35	80	9	3	3	41
1941	Pittsburgh (N)	.265	114	317	33	84	9	1	5	43
1942	Pittsburgh (N)	.256	103	289	17	74	8	2	1	26
1943	Pittsburgh (N)	.263	118	372	40	98	9	4	1	39
1944	Pittsburgh (N)	.230	115	331	27	76	12	1	1	34
1945	Pittsburgh (N)	.218	91	243	22	53	8	0	0	18
1946	Pittsburgh (N)	.307	56	150	13	46	2	0	1	12
1947	Cleveland (A)	.262	61	126	9	33	1	0	0	14
	Nineteen years	.261	1950	5916	613	1547	206	42	52	652

CHARLIE LOUDENSLAGER B. Baltimore, Md.
D. Oct. 31, 1931, Baltimore, Md.
T.R. 5'9" 186 lbs.
(2ND BASE)

YEAR	CLUB	BA	G	AB	R	H	2B	3B	HR	RBI
1904	BROOKLYN (N)	.000	1	2	0	0	0	0	0	0

HARRY LUMLEY B. Sept. 29, 1880, Forest City, Pa.
D. May 22, 1938, Binghamton, N.Y.
B.L., T.R.
(OUTFIELD)

YEAR	CLUB	BA	G	AB	R	H	2B	3B	HR	RBI
1904	BROOKLYN (N)	.279	150	577	79	161	23	18	9	78
1905	BROOKLYN (N)	.293	130	505	50	148	19	10	7	47
1906	BROOKLYN (N)	.324	133	484	72	157	23	12	9	61

YEAR	CLUB	BA	G	AB	R	H	2B	3B	HR	RBI
1907	BROOKLYN (N)	.267	127	454	47	121	23	11	9	66
1908	BROOKLYN (N)	.216	127	440	36	95	13	12	4	39
1909	BROOKLYN (N)	.250	55	172	13	43	8	3	0	14
1910	BROOKLYN (N)	.143	8	21	3	3	0	0	0	0
	Seven years	.274	730	2653	300	728	109	66	38	305

DON LUND B. May 18, 1923, Detroit, Mich.
B.R., T.R. 6' 200 lbs.
(OUTFIELD)

YEAR	CLUB	BA	G	AB	R	H	2B	3B	HR	RBI
1945	BROOKLYN (N)	.000	4	3	0	0	0	0	0	0
1947	BROOKLYN (N)	.300	11	20	5	6	2	0	2	5
1948	BROOKLYN (N)	.188	27							
1948	St. Louis (A)									
	(year totals)	.230	90	230	30	53	11	4	4	30
1949	Detroit (A)	.000	2	2	0	0	0	0	0	0
1952	Detroit (A)	.304	8	23	1	7	0	0	0	1
1953	Detroit (A)	.257	131	421	51	108	21	4	9	47
1954	Detroit (A)	.130	35	54	4	7	2	0	0	3
	Seven years	.240	281	753	91	181	36	8	15	86

JIM LYTTLE B. May 20, 1946, Hamilton, Ohio
B.L., T.R. 6' 180 lbs.
(OUTFIELD)

YEAR	CLUB	BA	G	AB	R	H	2B	3B	HR	RBI
1976	LOS ANGELES (N)	.221	23	68	3	15	3	0	0	5
	Eight years (total)	.248	391	710	71	176	37	5	9	70

LEE MAGEE B. June 4, 1889, Cincinnati, Ohio
D. March 14, 1966, Columbus, Ohio
B.B., T.R. 5'11" 165 lbs.
(OUTFIELD, 2ND BASE)

YEAR	CLUB	BA	G	AB	R	H	2B	3B	HR	RBI
1911	St. Louis (N)	.261	26	69	9	18	1	1	0	8
1912	St. Louis (N)	.290	128	458	60	133	13	8	0	40
1913	St. Louis (N)	.265	136	529	53	140	13	7	2	31
1914	St. Louis (N)	.284	162	529	59	150	23	4	2	40
1915	BROOKLYN (F)	.323	121	452	87	146	19	10	4	49
1916	New York (A)	.257	131	510	57	131	18	4	3	45
1917	New York (A)									
1917	St. Louis (A)									
	(year totals)	.200	87	285	28	57	5	1	0	12
1918	Cincinnati (N)	.290	119	459	62	133	22	13	0	28
1919	BROOKLYN (N)	.238	45	181	16	43	7	2	0	7
1919	Chicago (N)									
	(year totals)	.270	124	448	52	121	19	6	1	24
	Nine years	.275	1034	3739	467	1029	103	54	12	277

GEORGE MAGOON B. May 27, 1875, St. Albans, Maine
D. Dec. 6, 1943, Rochester, N.H.
B.R., T.R. 5'10" 160 lbs.
(SHORTSTOP, 2ND BASE)

YEAR	CLUB	BA	G	AB	R	H	2B	3B	HR	RBI
1898	BROOKLYN (N)	.224	93	343	35	77	7	0	1	39
	Five years (total)	.239	522	1834	199	439	62	16	2	201

CHARLIE MALAY B. June 13, 1879, Brooklyn, N.Y.
D. Sept. 18, 1949
B.B., T.R. 5'11½" 175 lbs.
(2ND BASE, OUTFIELD)

YEAR	CLUB	BA	G	AB	R	H	2B	3B	HR	RBI
1905	BROOKLYN (N)	.252	102	349	33	88	7	2	1	31

CANDY MALDONADO
B. Sept. 5, 1960, Humacao, Puerto Rico
B.R., T.R. 6' 185 lbs.
(OUTFIELD)

YEAR	CLUB	BA	G	AB	R	H	2B	3B	HR	RBI
1981	LOS ANGELES (N)	.083	11	12	0	1	0	0	0	0
1982	LOS ANGELES (N)	.000	6	4	0	0	0	0	0	0
1983	LOS ANGELES (N)	.194	42	62	5	12	1	1	1	6
	Three years	.167	59	78	5	13	1	1	1	6

TONY MALINOSKY
B. Oct. 5, 1909, Collinsville, Ill.
B.R., T.R. 5'10½" 165 lbs.
(3RD BASE, SHORTSTOP)

YEAR	CLUB	BA	G	AB	R	H	2B	3B	HR	RBI
1937	BROOKLYN (N)	.228	35	79	7	18	2	0	0	3

LEW MALONE
B. March 13, 1897, Baltimore, Md.
D. Feb. 17, 1973, Brooklyn, N.Y.
B.R. T.R. 5'11" 175 lbs.
(3RD BASE, 2ND BASE)

YEAR	CLUB	BA	G	AB	R	H	2B	3B	HR	RBI
1917	BROOKLYN (N)	—	1	0	1	0	0	0	0	0
1919	BROOKLYN (N)	.204	51	162	9	33	7	3	0	11
	Four years (total)	.202	133	367	28	74	11	7	1	28

BILLY MALONEY
B. June 5, 1878, Lewiston, Maine
D. Sept. 2, 1960, Breckenridge, Texas
B.L., T.R. 5'10" 177 lbs.
(OUTFIELD, CATCHER)

YEAR	CLUB	BA	G	AB	R	H	2B	3B	HR	RBI
1901	Milwaukee (A)	.293	86	290	42	85	3	4	0	22
1902	St. Louis (A)									
1902	Cincinnati (N)									
	(year totals)	.224	57	201	21	45	7	0	1	18
1905	Chicago (N)	.260	145	558	78	145	17	14	2	56
1906	BROOKLYN (N)	.221	151	566	71	125	15	7	0	32
1907	BROOKLYN (N)	.229	144	502	51	115	7	10	0	32
1908	BROOKLYN (N)	.195	113	359	31	70	5	7	3	17
	Six years	.236	696	2476	294	585	54	42	6	177

GUS MANCUSO
B. Dec. 5, 1905, Galveston, Texas
B.R., T.R. 5'10" 185 lbs.
(CATCHER)

YEAR	CLUB	BA	G	AB	R	H	2B	3B	HR	RBI
1940	BROOKLYN (N)	.229	60	144	16	33	8	0	0	16
	Seventeen years (total)	.265	1460	4505	386	1194	197	16	53	543

CHUCK MANUEL
B. Jan. 4, 1944, North Fork, W. Va.
B.L., T.R. 6'4" 195 lbs.
(OUTFIELD)

YEAR	CLUB	BA	G	AB	R	H	2B	3B	HR	RBI
1974	LOS ANGELES (N)	.333	4	3	0	1	0	0	0	1
1975	LOS ANGELES (N)	.133	15	15	0	2	0	0	0	2
	Six years (total)	.198	242	384	25	76	12	0	4	43

HEINIE MANUSH
B. July 20, 1901, Tuscumbia, Ala.
D. May 12, 1971, Sarasota, Fla.
B.L., T.L. 6'1" 200 lbs.
(OUTFIELD)

YEAR	CLUB	BA	G	AB	R	H	2B	3B	HR	RBI
1937	BROOKLYN (N)	.333	132	466	57	155	25	7	4	73
1938	BROOKLYN (N)	.235	17	51	8	12	3	1	0	7
	Seventeen years (total)	.330	2009	7653	1287	2524	491	160	110	1173

RABBIT MARANVILLE

B. Nov. 11, 1891, Springfield, Mass.
D. Jan. 5, 1954, New York, N.Y.
B.R., T.R. 5'5" 155 lbs.
(SHORTSTOP, 2ND BASE)

YEAR	CLUB	BA	G	AB	R	H	2B	3B	HR	RBI
1926	BROOKLYN (N)	.235	78	234	32	55	8	5	0	24
	Twenty-three years (total)	.258	2670	10,078	1255	2605	380	177	28	884

BILL MARRIOTT

B. April 18, 1893, Pratt, Kan.
D. Aug. 11, 1961, Berkeley, Calif.
B.L., T.R. 6' 170 lbs.
(3RD BASE)

YEAR	CLUB	BA	G	AB	R	H	2B	3B	HR	RBI
1926	BROOKLYN (N)	.267	109	360	39	96	13	9	3	42
1927	BROOKLYN (N)	.111	6	9	0	1	0	1	0	1
	Six years (total)	.266	264	826	86	220	27	14	4	95

DOC MARSHALL

B. Sept. 22, 1875, Butler, Pa.
D. Dec. 11, 1959, Clinton, Ill.
B.R., T.R. 6'1" 185 lbs.
(CATCHER)

YEAR	CLUB	BA	G	AB	R	H	2B	3B	HR	RBI
1909	BROOKLYN (N)	.201	50	149	7	30	7	1	0	10
	Five years (total)	.210	261	756	51	159	23	8	2	54

MIKE MARSHALL

B. Jan. 12, 1960, Libertyville, Ill.
B.R., T.R. 6'5" 215 lbs.
(3RD BASE, 1ST BASE, OUTFIELD)

YEAR	CLUB	BA	G	AB	R	H	2B	3B	HR	RBI
1981	LOS ANGELES	.200	14	25	2	5	3	0	0	1
1982	LOS ANGELES	.242	49	95	10	23	3	0	5	9
1983	LOS ANGELES (N)	.284	140	465	47	132	17	1	17	65
	Three years	.274	203	585	59	160	23	1	22	75
Divisional Playoff										
	One year	.000	1	1	0	0	0	0	0	0

TEDDY MARTINEZ

B. Dec. 10, 1947, Central Barahona, Dominican Republic
B.R., T.R. 6' 165 lbs.
(SHORTSTOP, 2ND BASE, 3RD BASE, OUTFIELD)

YEAR	CLUB	BA	G	AB	R	H	2B	3B	HR	RBI
1970	New York (N)	.063	4	16	0	1	0	0	0	0
1971	New York (N)	.288	38	125	16	36	5	2	1	10
1972	New York (N)	.224	103	330	22	74	5	5	1	19
1973	New York (N)	.255	92	263	34	67	11	0	1	14
1974	New York (N)	.219	116	334	32	73	15	7	2	43
1975	St. Louis (N)									
1975	Oakland (A)									
	(year totals)	.176	102	108	8	19	2	0	0	5
1977	LOS ANGELES (N)	.299	67	137	21	41	6	1	1	10
1978	LOS ANGELES (N)	.255	54	55	13	14	1	0	1	5
1979	LOS ANGELES (N)	.268	81	112	19	30	5	1	0	2
	Nine years	.240	657	1480	165	355	50	16	7	108
League Championship										
	One year	—	3	0	0	0	0	0	0	0
World Series										
	One year	—	2	0	0	0	0	0	0	0

GENE MAUCH

B. Nov. 18, 1925, Salina, Kan.
B.R., T.R. 5'10" 165 lbs.
(2ND BASE, SHORTSTOP)

YEAR	CLUB	BA	G	AB	R	H	2B	3B	HR	RBI
1944	BROOKLYN (N)	.133	5	15	2	2	1	0	0	2
1948	BROOKLYN (N)	.154	12	13	1	2	0	0	0	0
	Nine years (total)	.239	304	737	93	176	25	7	5	62

AL MAUL
B. Oct. 9, 1865, Philadelphia, Pa.
D. May 3, 1958, Philadelphia, Pa.
B.R., T.R. 6' 175 lbs.
(PITCHER, OUTFIELD, 1ST BASE)

YEAR	CLUB	BA	G	AB	R	H	2B	3B	HR	RBI
1899	BROOKLYN (N)	.273	4	11	2	3	0	0	0	0
	Fifteen years (total)	.241	410	1376	193	331	45	30	7	179

CARMEN MAURO
B. Nov. 10, 1926, St. Paul, Minn.
B.L., T.R. 6' 167 lbs.
(OUTFIELD)

YEAR	CLUB	BA	G	AB	R	H	2B	3B	HR	RBI
1953	BROOKLYN (N)	.000	8	9	1	0	0	0	0	0
	Four years (total)	.231	167	416	40	96	9	8	2	33

BILL McCABE
B. Oct. 28, 1894, Chicago, Ill.
D. Sept. 2, 1966, Chicago, Ill.
B.B., T.R. 5'9½" 180 lbs.
(OUTFIELD, SHORTSTOP, 2ND BASE)

YEAR	CLUB	BA	G	AB	R	H	2B	3B	HR	RBI
1920	BROOKLYN (N)	.147	41	68	10	10	0	0	0	3
	Three years (total)	.161	106	199	28	32	3	2	0	13
World Series	Two years	.000	4	1	1	0	0	0	0	0

BILL McCARREN
B. Nov. 4, 1895, Honesdale, Pa.
B.R., T.R. 5'11½" 170 lbs.
(3RD BASE)

YEAR	CLUB	BA	G	AB	R	H	2B	3B	HR	RBI
1923	BROOKLYN (N)	.245	69	216	28	53	10	1	3	27

JACK McCARTHY
B. March 26, 1869, Gilbertville, Mass.
D. Sept. 11, 1931
B.L., T.L. 5'9" 155 lbs.
(OUTFIELD)

YEAR	CLUB	BA	G	AB	R	H	2B	3B	HR	RBI
1906	BROOKLYN (N)	.304	91	322	23	98	13	1	0	35
1907	BROOKLYN (N)	.220	25	91	4	20	2	0	0	8
	Twelve years (total)	.287	1091	4195	550	1203	171	66	7	474

JOHNNY McCARTHY
B. Jan. 7, 1910, Chicago, Ill.
B.L., T.L. 6'1½" 185 lbs.
(1ST BASE)

YEAR	CLUB	BA	G	AB	R	H	2B	3B	HR	RBI
1934	BROOKLYN (N)	.179	17	39	7	7	2	0	1	5
1935	BROOKLYN (N)	.250	22	48	9	12	1	1	0	4
	Eleven years (total)	.277	542	1557	182	432	72	16	25	209

TOMMY McCARTHY
B. July 24, 1864, Boston, Mass.
D. Aug. 5, 1922, Boston, Mass.
B.R., T.R. 5'7" 170 lbs.
(OUTFIELD)

YEAR	CLUB	BA	G	AB	R	H	2B	3B	HR	RBI
1896	BROOKLYN (N)	.249	104	377	62	94	8	6	3	47
	Thirteen years (total)	.292	1275	5128	1069	1496	192	58	44	666

LEW McCARTY

B. Nov. 17, 1888, Milton, Pa.
D. June 9, 1930, Reading, Pa.
B.R., T.R. 5'11½" 192 lbs.
(CATCHER)

YEAR	CLUB	BA	G	AB	R	H	2B	3B	HR	RBI
1913	BROOKLYN (N)	.231	9	26	1	6	0	0	0	2
1914	BROOKLYN (N)	.254	90	284	20	72	14	2	1	30
1915	BROOKLYN (N)	.239	84	276	19	66	9	4	0	19
1916	BROOKLYN (N)	.313	55	150	17	47	6	1	0	13
1916	New York (N)									
	(year totals)	.339	80	218	23	74	9	5	0	22
1917	New York (N)	.247	56	162	15	40	3	2	2	19
1918	New York (N)	.268	86	257	16	69	7	3	0	24
1919	New York (N)	.281	85	210	17	59	5	4	2	21
1920	New York (N)									
1920	St. Louis (N)									
	(year totals)	.156	41	45	2	7	0	0	0	0
1921	St. Louis (N)	.000	1	1	0	0	0	0	0	0
	Nine years	.266	532	1479	113	393	47	20	5	137
World Series										
	One year	.400	3	5	1	2	0	1	0	1

MIKE McCORMICK

B. 1883, Jersey City, N.J.
D. Nov. 19, 1953, Jersey City, N.J.
B.R., T.R.
(3RD BASE)

YEAR	CLUB	BA	G	AB	R	H	2B	3B	HR	RBI
1904	BROOKLYN (N)	.184	105	347	28	64	5	4	0	27

MIKE McCORMICK

B. May 6, 1917, Angels Camp, Calif.
D. April 14, 1976, Los Angeles, Calif.
B.R., T.R. 6' 195 lbs.
(OUTFIELD)

YEAR	CLUB	BA	G	AB	R	H	2B	3B	HR	RBI
*1949	BROOKLYN (N)	.209	55	139	17	29	5	1	2	14
	Ten years (total)	.275	748	2325	302	640	100	29	14	215
World Series										
	Three years (total)	.288	14	52	2	15	3	0	0	4

JUDGE McCREEDIE

B. Nov. 29, 1876, Manchester, Iowa
D. July 29, 1934, Portland, Ore.
(OUTFIELD)

YEAR	CLUB	BA	G	AB	R	H	2B	3B	HR	RBI
1903	BROOKLYN (N)	.324	56	213	40	69	5	0	0	20

TOM McCREERY

B. Oct. 19, 1874, Beaver, Pa.
D. July 3, 1941, Beaver, Pa.
B.B., T.R. 5'11" 180 lbs.
(OUTFIELD, 1ST BASE)

YEAR	CLUB	BA	G	AB	R	H	2B	3B	HR	RBI
1895	Louisville (N)	.324	31	108	18	35	3	1	0	10
1896	Louisville (N)	.351	115	441	87	155	23	21	7	65
1897	Louisville (N)									
1897	New York (N)									
	(year totals)	.289	138	515	91	149	13	11	5	68
1898	New York (N)									
1898	Pittsburgh (N)									
	(year totals)	.267	88	311	48	83	9	10	3	37
1899	Pittsburgh (N)	.323	118	455	76	147	21	9	2	64
1900	Pittsburgh (N)	.220	43	132	20	29	4	3	1	13
1901	BROOKLYN (N)	.290	91	335	47	97	11	14	3	53
1902	BROOKLYN (N)	.244	112	430	49	105	8	4	4	57
1903	BROOKLYN (N)	.262	40	141	13	37	5	2	0	10
1903	Boston (N)									
	(year totals)	.246	63	224	28	55	7	3	1	20
	Nine years	.290	799	2951	464	855	99	76	26	387

TERRY McDERMOTT B. March 20, 1951, Rockville Centre, N.Y.
B.R., T.R. 6'3" 205 lbs.
(1ST BASE)

YEAR	CLUB	BA	G	AB	R	H	2B	3B	HR	RBI
1972	LOS ANGELES (N)	.130	9	23	2	3	0	0	0	0

PRYOR McELVEEN B. Nov. 5, 1880, Atlanta, Ga.
D. Oct. 27, 1951, Pleasant Hill, Tenn.
T.R. 5'10" 168 lbs.
(3RD BASE)

YEAR	CLUB	BA	G	AB	R	H	2B	3B	HR	RBI
1909	BROOKLYN (N)	.198	81	258	22	51	8	1	3	25
1910	BROOKLYN (N)	.225	74	213	19	48	8	3	1	26
1911	BROOKLYN (N)	.194	16	31	1	6	0	0	0	5
	Three years	.209	171	502	42	105	16	4	4	56

ED McGAMWELL B. Jan. 10, 1878, Buffalo, N.Y.
D. Nov. 1, 1950, Buffalo, N.Y.
(1ST BASE)

YEAR	CLUB	BA	G	AB	R	H	2B	3B	HR	RBI
1905	BROOKLYN (N)	.250	4	16	0	4	0	0	0	0

DAN McGANN B. July 15, 1872, Shelbyville, Ky.
D. Dec. 13, 1910, Louisville, Ky.
B.B., T.R. 6' 190 lbs.
(1ST BASE)

YEAR	CLUB	BA	G	AB	R	H	2B	3B	HR	RBI
1899	BROOKLYN (N)	.243	63	233	41	57	9	5	3	41
	Thirteen years (total)	.286	1459	5304	851	1515	189	103	42	736

JACK McGEACHY B. Jan. 23, 1861, Clinton, Mass.
D. April 5, 1930
B.R., T.R.
(OUTFIELD)

YEAR	CLUB	BA	G	AB	R	H	2B	3B	HR	RBI
1890	BROOKLYN (N)	.244	104	443	84	108	24	4	1	65
	Six years (total)	.245	608	2464	345	604	106	18	9	276

DEACON McGUIRE B. Nov. 18, 1863, Youngstown, Ohio
D. Oct. 31, 1936, Albion, Mich.
B.R., T.R.
(CATCHER)

YEAR	CLUB	BA	G	AB	R	H	2B	3B	HR	RBI
1890	Rochester (AA)	.299	87	331	46	99	16	4	4	
1891	Washington (AA)	.303	114	413	55	125	22	10	3	66
1892	Washington (N)	.232	97	315	46	73	14	4	4	43
1893	Washington (N)	.262	63	237	29	62	14	3	1	26
1894	Washington (N)	.306	104	425	67	130	18	6	6	78
1895	Washington (N)	.336	132	533	89	179	30	8	10	97
1896	Washington (N)	.321	108	389	60	125	25	3	2	70
1897	Washington (N)	.343	93	327	51	112	17	7	4	53
1898	Washington (N)	.268	131	489	59	131	18	3	1	57
1899	Washington (N)									
1899	BROOKLYN (N)	.318	46	154	23	49	7	2	0	17
	(year totals)	.292	105	356	47	104	15	5	1	35
1900	BROOKLYN (N)	.286	71	241	20	69	15	2	0	34
1901	BROOKLYN (N)	.296	85	301	28	89	16	4	0	40
1902	Detroit (A)	.227	73	229	27	52	14	1	2	23
1903	Detroit (A)	.250	72	248	15	62	12	1	0	21
1904	New York (A)	.208	101	322	17	67	12	2	0	20
1905	New York (A)	.219	72	228	9	50	7	2	0	33
1906	New York (A)	.299	51	144	11	43	5	0	0	14

YEAR	CLUB	BA	G	AB	R	H	2B	3B	HR	RBI
1907	New York (A)									
1907	Boston (A)									
	(year totals)	.600	7	5	1	3	0	0	1	1
1908	Boston (A)									
1908	Cleveland (A)									
	(year totals)	.200	2	5	0	1	1	0	0	2
1910	Cleveland (A)	.333	1	3	0	1	0	0	0	0
1912	Detroit (A)	.500	1	2	1	1	0	0	0	0
	Twenty-six years	.278	1781	6290	770	1749	300	79	45	787

ED McLANE   B. Aug. 20, 1881, Weston, Mass.
(OUTFIELD)

YEAR	CLUB	BA	G	AB	R	H	2B	3B	HR	RBI
1907	BROOKLYN (N)	.000	1	2	0	0	0	0	0	0

FRANK McMANUS   B. Sept. 21, 1875, Lawrence, Mass.
D. Sept. 1, 1923, Syracuse, N.Y.
T.R.
(CATCHER)

YEAR	CLUB	BA	G	AB	R	H	2B	3B	HR	RBI
1903	BROOKLYN (N)	.000	2	7	0	0	0	0	0	0
	Three years (total)	.229	14	35	3	8	1	0	0	2

TOMMY McMILLAN   B. April 17, 1888, Pittston, Pa.
D. July 15, 1966, Orlando, Fla.
B.R., T.R. 5'5" 130 lbs.
(SHORTSTOP)

YEAR	CLUB	BA	G	AB	R	H	2B	3B	HR	RBI
1908	BROOKLYN (N)	.238	43	147	9	35	3	0	0	3
1909	BROOKLYN (N)	.212	108	373	18	79	15	1	0	24
1910	BROOKLYN (N)	.176	23	74	2	13	1	0	0	2
1910	Cincinnati (N)									
	(year totals)	.183	105	322	22	59	1	3	0	15
1912	New York (A)	.228	41	149	24	34	2	0	0	12
	Four years	.209	297	991	73	207	21	4	0	54

KEN McMULLEN   B. June 1, 1942, Oxnard, Calif.
B.R., T.R. 6'3" 190 lbs.
(3RD BASE)

YEAR	CLUB	BA	G	AB	R	H	2B	3B	HR	RBI
1962	LOS ANGELES (N)	.273	6	11	0	3	0	0	0	0
1963	LOS ANGELES (N)	.236	49	233	16	55	9	0	5	28
1964	LOS ANGELES (N)	.209	24	67	3	14	0	0	1	2
1965	Washington (A)	.263	150	555	75	146	18	6	18	54
1966	Washington (A)	.233	147	524	48	122	19	4	13	54
1967	Washington (A)	.245	146	563	73	138	22	2	16	67
1968	Washington (A)	.248	151	557	66	138	11	2	20	62
1969	Washington (A)	.272	158	562	83	153	25	2	19	87
1970	Washington (A)									
1970	California (A)									
	(year totals)	.229	139	481	55	110	11	3	14	64
1971	California (A)	.250	160	593	63	148	19	2	21	68
1972	California (A)	.269	137	472	36	127	18	1	9	34
1973	LOS ANGELES (N)	.247	42	85	6	21	5	0	5	18
1974	LOS ANGELES (N)	.250	44	60	5	15	1	0	3	12
1975	LOS ANGELES (N)	.239	39	46	4	11	1	1	2	14
1976	Oakland (A)	.220	98	186	20	41	6	2	5	23
1977	Milwaukee (A)	.228	63	136	15	31	7	1	5	19
	Sixteen years	.248	1553	5131	568	1273	172	26	156	606
League Championship										
	One year	.000	1	1	0	0	0	0	0	0

JOE MEDWICK   B. Nov. 24, 1911, Carteret, N.J.
D. March 21, 1975, Petersburg, Fla.
B.R., T.R. 5'10" 187 lbs.
(OUTFIELD)

YEAR	CLUB	BA	G	AB	R	H	2B	3B	HR	RBI
1932	St. Louis (N)	.349	26	106	13	37	12	1	2	12
1933	St. Louis (N)	.306	148	595	92	182	40	10	18	98
1934	St. Louis (N)	.319	149	620	110	198	40	18	18	106
1935	St. Louis (N)	.353	154	634	132	224	46	13	23	126
1936	St. Louis (N)	.351	155	636	115	223	64	13	18	138
1937	St. Louis (N)	.374	156	633	111	237	56	10	31	154
1938	St. Louis (N)	.322	146	590	100	190	47	8	21	122
1939	St. Louis (N)	.332	150	606	98	201	48	8	14	117
1940	St. Louis (N)									
1940	BROOKLYN (N)	.300	106	423	62	127	18	12	14	88
	(year totals)	.301	143	581	83	175	30	12	17	86
1941	BROOKLYN (N)	.318	133	538	100	171	33	10	18	88
1942	BROOKLYN (N)	.300	142	553	69	166	37	4	4	96
1943	BROOKLYN (N)	.272	41	77	7	24	4	0	2	18
1943	New York (N)									
	(year totals)	.278	126	497	54	138	30	3	5	70
1944	New York (N)	.337	128	490	64	165	24	3	7	85
1945	New York (N)									
1945	Boston (N)									
	(year totals)	.290	92	310	31	90	17	0	3	37
1946	BROOKLYN (N)	.312	41	77	7	24	4	0	2	18
1947	St. Louis (N)	.307	75	150	19	46	12	0	4	28
1948	St. Louis (N)	.211	20	19	0	4	0	0	0	2
	Seventeen years	.324	1984	7635	1198	2471	540	113	205	1383
World Series										
	Two years	.326	12	46	5	15	1	1	1	5

FRED MERKLE   B. Dec. 20, 1888, Watertown, Wis.
D. March 2, 1956, Daytona Beach, Fla.
B.R., T.R. 6'1" 190 lbs.
(1ST BASE)

YEAR	CLUB	BA	G	AB	R	H	2B	3B	HR	RBI
1916	BROOKLYN (N)	.232	23	69	6	16	1	0	0	2
1917	BROOKLYN (N)	.125	2	8	0	1	0	0	0	0
	Sixteen years (total)	.273	1637	5781	720	1579	289	83	59	733
World Series										
	Five years (total)	.239	27	88	10	21	3	1	1	8

BENNY MEYER   B. Jan. 1, 1888, Hematite, Mo.
D. Feb. 6, 1974, Festus, Mo.
B.R., T.R. 5'9" 170 lbs.
(OUTFIELD)

YEAR	CLUB	BA	G	AB	R	H	2B	3B	HR	RBI
1913	BROOKLYN (N)	.195	38	87	12	17	0	1	1	10
	Four years (total)	.265	310	1041	146	276	29	17	7	84

LEE MEYER   T.R.
(SHORTSTOP)

YEAR	CLUB	BA	G	AB	R	H	2B	3B	HR	RBI
1909	BROOKLYN (N)	.130	7	23	1	3	0	0	0	0

CHIEF MEYERS   B. July 29, 1880, Riverside, Calif.
D. July 25, 1971, San Bernardino, Calif.
B.R., T.R. 5'11" 194 lbs.
(CATCHER)

YEAR	CLUB	BA	G	AB	R	H	2B	3B	HR	RBI
1916	BROOKLYN (N)	.247	80	239	21	59	10	3	0	21
1917	BROOKLYN (N)	.212	47	132	8	28	3	0	0	3
	Nine years (total)	.291	992	2834	276	826	120	41	14	363
World Series										
	Four years (total)	.290	18	62	4	18	2	2	0	6

GENE MICHAEL
B. June 2, 1938, Kent, Ohio
B.B., T.R. 6'2" 183 lbs.
(SHORTSTOP)

YEAR	CLUB	BA	G	AB	R	H	2B	3B	HR	RBI
1967	LOS ANGELES (N)	.202	98	223	20	45	3	1	0	7
	Ten years (total)	.229	973	2806	249	642	86	12	15	226

EDDIE MIKSIS
B. Sept. 11, 1926, Burlington, N.J.
B.R., T.R. 6'1½" 185 lbs.
(2ND BASE, OUTFIELD, 3RD BASE, SHORTSTOP)

YEAR	CLUB	BA	G	AB	R	H	2B	3B	HR	RBI
1944	BROOKLYN (N)	.220	26	91	12	20	2	0	0	11
1946	BROOKLYN (N)	.146	23	48	3	7	0	0	0	5
1947	BROOKLYN (N)	.267	45	86	18	23	1	0	4	10
1948	BROOKLYN (N)	.213	86	221	28	47	7	1	2	16
1949	BROOKLYN (N)	.221	50	113	17	25	5	0	1	6
1950	BROOKLYN (N)	.250	51	76	13	19	2	1	2	10
1951	BROOKLYN (N)	.200	19	10	6	2	1	0	0	0
1951	Chicago (N)									
	(year totals)	.265	121	431	54	114	14	3	4	35
1952	Chicago (N)	.232	93	383	44	89	20	1	2	19
1953	Chicago (N)	.251	142	577	61	145	17	6	8	39
1954	Chicago (N)	.202	38	99	9	20	3	0	2	3
1955	Chicago (N)	.235	131	481	52	113	14	2	9	41
1956	Chicago (N)	.239	114	356	54	85	10	3	9	27
1957	St. Louis (N)									
1957	Baltimore (A)									
	(year totals)	.205	50	39	3	8	0	0	1	2
1958	Baltimore (A)									
1958	Cincinnati (N)									
	(year totals)	.135	72	52	15	7	0	0	0	4
	Fourteen years	.236	1042	3053	383	722	95	17	44	228

World Series

YEAR	CLUB	BA	G	AB	R	H	2B	3B	HR	RBI
1947	BROOKLYN (N)	.250	5	4	1	1	0	0	0	0
1949	BROOKLYN (N)	.286	3	7	0	2	1	0	0	0
	Two years	.273	8	11	1	3	1	0	0	0

DON MILES
B. March 13, 1936, Indianapolis, Ind.
B.L., T.L. 6'1" 210 lbs.
(OUTFIELD)

YEAR	CLUB	BA	G	AB	R	H	2B	3B	HR	RBI
1958	LOS ANGELES (N)	.182	8	22	2	4	0	0	0	0

HACK MILLER
B. Jan. 1, 1894, Chicago, Ill.
D. Sept. 17, 1971, Oakland, Calif.
B.R., T.R. 5'9" 195 lbs.
(OUTFIELD)

YEAR	CLUB	BA	G	AB	R	H	2B	3B	HR	RBI
1916	BROOKLYN (N)	.333	3	3	0	1	0	1	0	1
	Six years (total)	.323	349	1200	164	387	65	11	38	205

JOHN MILLER
B. March 14, 1944, Alhambra, Calif.
B.R., T.R. 5'11" 195 lbs.
(OUTFIELD, 1ST BASE)

YEAR	CLUB	BA	G	AB	R	H	2B	3B	HR	RBI
1969	LOS ANGELES (N)	.211	26	38	3	8	1	0	1	1
	Two years (total)	.164	32	61	4	10	1	0	2	3

OTTO MILLER B. June 1, 1889, Minden, Neb.
D. March 29, 1962, Brooklyn, N.Y.
B.R., T.R. 6' 196 lbs.
(CATCHER)

YEAR	CLUB	BA	G	AB	R	H	2B	3B	HR	RBI
1910	BROOKLYN (N)	.167	31	66	5	11	3	0	0	2
1911	BROOKLYN (N)	.210	25	62	7	13	2	2	0	8
1912	BROOKLYN (N)	.278	98	316	35	88	18	1	1	31
1913	BROOKLYN (N)	.272	104	320	26	87	11	7	0	26
1914	BROOKLYN (N)	.231	54	169	17	39	6	1	0	9
1915	BROOKLYN (N)	.224	84	254	20	57	4	6	0	25
1916	BROOKLYN (N)	.255	73	216	16	55	9	2	1	17
1917	BROOKLYN (N)	.230	92	274	19	63	5	4	1	17
1918	BROOKLYN (N)	.193	75	228	8	44	6	1	0	8
1919	BROOKLYN (N)	.226	51	164	18	37	5	0	0	5
1920	BROOKLYN (N)	.289	90	301	16	87	9	2	0	33
1921	BROOKLYN (N)	.234	91	286	22	67	8	6	1	27
1922	BROOKLYN (N)	.261	59	180	20	47	11	1	1	23
	Thirteen years	.245	927	2836	229	695	97	33	5	231

World Series

YEAR	CLUB	BA	G	AB	R	H	2B	3B	HR	RBI
1916	BROOKLYN (N)	.125	2	8	0	1	1	0	0	0
1920	BROOKLYN (N)	.143	6	14	0	2	0	0	0	0
	Two years	.136	8	22	0	3	1	0	0	0

ROD MILLER B. Jan. 16, 1940, Portland, Ore.
B.L., T.R. 5'9½" 150 lbs.

YEAR	CLUB	BA	G	AB	R	H	2B	3B	HR	RBI
1957	BROOKLYN (N)	.000	1	1	0	0	0	0	0	0

WALLY MILLIES B. Oct. 18, 1906, Chicago, Ill.
B.R., T.R. 5'10½" 170 lbs.
(CATCHER)

YEAR	CLUB	BA	G	AB	R	H	2B	3B	HR	RBI
1934	BROOKLYN (N)	.000	2	7	0	0	0	0	0	0
	Six years (total)	.243	246	651	60	158	20	3	0	65

BUSTER MILLS B. Sept. 16, 1908, Ranger, Texas
B.R., T.R. 5'11½" 195 lbs.
(OUTFIELD)

YEAR	CLUB	BA	G	AB	R	H	2B	3B	HR	RBI
1935	BROOKLYN (N)	.214	17	56	12	12	2	1	1	7
	Seven years (total)	.287	415	1379	200	396	62	19	14	163

BOBBY MITCHELL B. April 7, 1955, Salt Lake City, Utah
B.L., T.L. 5'10" 170 lbs.
(OUTFIELD)

YEAR	CLUB	BA	G	AB	R	H	2B	3B	HR	RBI
1980	LOS ANGELES (N)	.333	9	3	1	1	0	0	0	0
1981	LOS ANGELES (N)	.125	10	8	0	1	0	0	0	0
	Two years	.182	19	11	1	2	0	0	0	0

JOHNNY MITCHELL B. Aug. 9, 1894, Detroit, Mich.
D. Nov. 4, 1965, Birmingham, Mich.
B.B., T.R. 5'8" 155 lbs.
(SHORTSTOP)

YEAR	CLUB	BA	G	AB	R	H	2B	3B	HR	RBI
1921	New York (A)	.262	13	42	4	11	1	0	0	2
1922	New York (A)									
1922	Boston (A)									
	(year totals)	.246	63	207	21	51	4	1	1	8

The Complete Catalogue of Players • 105

YEAR	CLUB	BA	G	AB	R	H	2B	3B	HR	RBI
1923	Boston (A)	.225	92	347	40	78	15	4	0	19
1924	BROOKLYN (N)	.263	64	243	42	64	10	0	1	16
1925	BROOKLYN (N)	.250	97	336	45	84	8	3	0	18
	Five years	.245	329	1175	152	288	38	8	2	63

RICK MONDAY   B. Nov. 20, 1945, Batesville, Ark.
B.L., T.L. 6'3" 195 lbs.
(OUTFIELD)

YEAR	CLUB	BA	G	AB	R	H	2B	3B	HR	RBI
1966	Kansas City (A)	.098	17	41	4	4	1	1	0	2
1967	Kansas City (A)	.251	124	406	52	102	14	6	14	58
1968	Oakland (A)	.274	148	482	56	132	24	7	8	49
1969	Oakland (A)	.271	122	399	57	108	17	4	12	54
1970	Oakland (A)	.290	112	376	63	109	19	7	10	37
1971	Oakland (A)	.245	116	355	53	87	9	3	18	56
1972	Chicago (N)	.249	138	434	68	108	22	5	11	42
1973	Chicago (N)	.267	149	554	93	148	24	5	26	56
1974	Chicago (N)	.294	142	538	84	158	19	7	20	58
1975	Chicago (N)	.267	136	491	89	131	29	4	17	60
1976	Chicago (N)	.272	137	534	107	145	20	5	32	77
1977	LOS ANGELES (N)	.230	118	392	47	90	13	1	15	48
1978	LOS ANGELES (N)	.254	119	342	54	87	14	1	19	57
1979	LOS ANGELES (N)	.303	12	33	2	10	0	0	0	2
1980	LOS ANGELES (N)	.268	96	194	35	52	7	1	10	25
1981	LOS ANGELES (N)	.315	66	130	24	41	1	2	11	25
1982	LOS ANGELES (N)	.257	104	210	37	54	6	4	11	42
1983	LOS ANGELES (N)	.274	99	178	21	132	17	1	17	65
	Eighteen years	.264	1955	6089	946	1698	256	64	251	813
Divisional Playoff										
	One year	.214	5	14	1	3	0	0	0	1
League Championship										
	Four years	.241	10	29	5	7	1	1	1	1

World Series

YEAR	CLUB	BA	G	AB	R	H	2B	3B	HR	RBI
1977	LOS ANGELES (N)	.167	4	12	0	2	0	0	0	0
1978	LOS ANGELES (N)	.154	5	13	2	2	1	0	0	0
1981	LOS ANGELES (N)	.231	5	13	1	3	1	0	0	0
	Three years	.184	14	38	3	7	2	0	0	0

WALLY MOON   B. April 3, 1930, Bay, Ark.
B.L., T.R. 6' 169 lbs.
(OUTFIELD)

YEAR	CLUB	BA	G	AB	R	H	2B	3B	HR	RBI
1954	St. Louis (N)	.304	151	635	106	193	29	9	12	76
1955	St. Louis (N)	.295	152	593	86	175	24	8	19	76
1956	St. Louis (N)	.298	149	540	86	161	22	11	16	68
1957	St. Louis (N)	.295	142	516	86	152	28	5	24	73
1958	St. Louis (N)	.238	108	290	36	69	10	3	7	38
1959	LOS ANGELES (N)	.302	145	543	93	164	26	11	19	74
1960	LOS ANGELES (N)	.299	138	469	74	140	21	6	13	69
1961	LOS ANGELES (N)	.328	134	463	79	152	25	3	17	88
1962	LOS ANGELES (N)	.242	95	244	36	59	9	1	4	31
1963	LOS ANGELES (N)	.262	122	343	41	90	13	2	8	48
1964	LOS ANGELES (N)	.220	68	118	8	26	2	1	2	9
1965	LOS ANGELES (N)	.202	53	89	6	18	3	0	1	11
	Twelve years	.289	1457	4843	737	1399	212	60	142	661

World Series

YEAR	CLUB	BA	G	AB	R	H	2B	3B	HR	RBI
1959	LOS ANGELES (N)	.261	6	23	3	6	0	0	1	2
1965	LOS ANGELES (N)	.000	2	2	0	0	0	0	0	0
	Two years	.240	8	25	3	6	0	0	1	2

DEE MOORE B. April 6, 1914, Amarillo, Texas
B.R., T.R. 5'11" 190 lbs.
(CATCHER, 3RD BASE)

YEAR	CLUB	BA	G	AB	R	H	2B	3B	HR	RBI
1943	BROOKLYN (N)	.253	37	79	8	20	3	0	0	12
	Four years (total)	.232	98	228	29	53	9	2	1	22

EDDIE MOORE B. Jan. 18, 1899, Barlow, Ky.
D. Feb. 10, 1976, Fort Myers, Fla.
B.R., T.R. 5'7" 165 lbs.
(2ND BASE, OUTFIELD, SHORTSTOP, 3RD BASE)

YEAR	CLUB	BA	G	AB	R	H	2B	3B	HR	RBI
1923	Pittsburgh (N)	.269	6	26	6	7	1	0	0	1
1924	Pittsburgh (N)	.359	72	209	47	75	8	4	2	13
1925	Pittsburgh (N)	.298	142	547	106	163	29	8	6	77
1926	Pittsburgh (N)									
1926	Boston (N)									
	(year totals)	.250	97	316	36	79	11	3	0	34
1927	Boston (N)	.302	112	411	53	124	14	4	1	32
1928	Boston (N)	.237	68	215	27	51	9	0	2	18
1929	BROOKLYN (N)	.296	111	402	48	119	18	6	0	48
1930	BROOKLYN (N)	.281	76	196	24	55	13	1	1	20
1932	New York (N)	.264	37	87	9	23	3	0	1	6
1934	Cleveland (A)	.154	27	65	4	10	2	0	0	8
	Ten years	.285	748	2474	360	706	108	26	13	257
World Series										
	One year	.231	7	26	7	6	1	0	1	2

GENE MOORE B. Aug. 26, 1909, Lancaster, Texas
B.L., T.L. 5'11" 175 lbs
(OUTFIELD)

YEAR	CLUB	BA	G	AB	R	H	2B	3B	HR	RBI
1939	BROOKLYN (N)	.225	107	306	45	69	13	6	3	39
1940	BROOKLYN (N)	.269	10	26	3	7	2	0	0	2
	Fourteen years (total)	.270	1042	3543	497	958	179	53	58	436

RANDY MOORE B. June 21, 1905, Naples, Texas
B.L., T.R. 6' 185 lbs.
(OUTFIELD)

YEAR	CLUB	BA	G	AB	R	H	2B	3B	HR	RBI
1936	BROOKLYN (N)	.239	42	88	4	21	3	0	0	14
1937	BROOKLYN (N)	.136	13	22	3	3	1	0	0	2
	Ten years (total)	.278	749	2253	258	627	110	17	27	308

HERBIE MORAN B. Feb. 16, 1886, Costello, Pa.
D. Sept. 21, 1954, Brockport, N.Y.
B.L., T.R. 5'5"
(OUTFIELD)

YEAR	CLUB	BA	G	AB	R	H	2B	3B	HR	RBI
1908	Philadelphia (A)									
1908	Boston (N)									
	(year totals)	.193	27	88	7	17	0	0	0	6
1909	Boston (N)	.226	8	31	8	7	1	0	0	0
1910	Boston (N)	.119	20	67	11	8	0	0	0	3
1912	BROOKLYN (N)	.276	130	508	77	140	18	10	1	40
1913	BROOKLYN (N)	.266	132	515	71	137	15	5	0	26
1914	Cincinnati (N)									
1914	Boston (N)									
	(year totals)	.244	148	549	67	134	13	6	1	39
1915	Boston (N)	.200	130	419	59	84	13	5	0	21
	Seven years	.242	595	2177	300	527	60	26	2	135
World Series										
	One year	.077	3	13	2	1	1	0	0	0

BOBBY MORGAN B. June 29, 1926, Oklahoma City, Okla.
B.R., T.R. 5'9" 175 lbs.
(2ND BASE, SHORTSTOP, 3RD BASE)

YEAR	CLUB	BA	G	AB	R	H	2B	3B	HR	RBI
1950	BROOKLYN (N)	.226	67	199	38	45	10	3	7	21
1952	BROOKLYN (N)	.236	67	191	36	45	8	0	7	16
1953	BROOKLYN (N)	.260	69	196	35	51	6	2	7	33
1954	Philadelphia (N)	.262	135	455	58	119	25	2	14	50
1955	Philadelphia (N)	.232	136	483	61	112	20	2	10	49
1956	Philadelphia (N)									
1956	St. Louis (N)									
	(year totals)	.196	69	138	15	27	7	0	3	21
1957	Philadelphia (N)									
1957	Chicago (N)									
	(year totals)	.207	127	425	43	88	20	2	5	27
1958	Chicago (N)	.000	1	1	0	0	0	0	0	0
	Eight years	.233	671	2088	286	487	96	11	53	217

World Series

YEAR	CLUB	BA	G	AB	R	H	2B	3B	HR	RBI
1952	BROOKLYN (N)	.000	2	1	0	0	0	0	0	0
1953	BROOKLYN (N)	.000	1	1	0	0	0	0	0	0
	Two years	.000	3	2	0	0	0	0	0	0

EDDIE MORGAN B. Nov. 19, 1914, Brady Lake, Ohio
B.L., T.L. 5'10" 160 lbs.
(OUTFIELD, 1ST BASE)

YEAR	CLUB	BA	G	AB	R	H	2B	3B	HR	RBI
1937	BROOKLYN (N)	.188	31	48	4	9	3	0	0	5
	Two years (total)	.212	39	66	8	14	3	0	1	8

WALT MORYN B. April 12, 1926, St. Paul, Minn.
B.L., T.R. 6'2" 205 lbs.
(OUTFIELD)

YEAR	CLUB	BA	G	AB	R	H	2B	3B	HR	RBI
1954	BROOKLYN (N)	.275	48	91	16	25	4	2	2	14
1955	BROOKLYN (N)	.263	11	19	3	5	1	0	1	3
	Eight years (total)	.266	785	2506	324	667	116	16	101	354

MANNY MOTA B. Feb. 18, 1938, Santo Domingo, Dominican Republic
B.R., T.R. 5'10" 160 lbs.
(OUTFIELD)

YEAR	CLUB	BA	G	AB	R	H	2B	3B	HR	RBI
1962	San Francisco (N)	.176	47	74	9	13	1	0	0	9
1963	Pittsburgh (N)	.270	59	126	20	34	2	3	0	7
1964	Pittsburgh (N)	.277	115	271	43	75	8	3	5	32
1965	Pittsburgh (N)	.279	121	294	47	82	7	6	4	29
1966	Pittsburgh (N)	.332	116	322	54	107	16	7	5	46
1967	Pittsburgh (N)	.321	120	349	53	112	14	8	4	56
1968	Pittsburgh (N)	.281	111	331	35	93	10	2	1	33
1969	Montreal (N)									
1969	LOS ANGELES (N)	.323	85	294	35	95	6	4	3	30
	(year totals)	.321	116	383	41	123	7	5	3	30
1970	LOS ANGELES (N)	.305	124	417	63	127	12	6	3	37
1971	LOS ANGELES (N)	.312	91	269	24	84	13	5	0	34
1972	LOS ANGELES (N)	.323	118	371	57	120	16	5	5	48
1973	LOS ANGELES (N)	.314	89	293	33	92	11	2	0	23
1974	LOS ANGELES (N)	.281	66	57	5	16	2	0	0	16
1975	LOS ANGELES (N)	.265	52	49	3	13	1	0	0	10
1976	LOS ANGELES (N)	.288	50	52	1	15	3	0	0	13
1977	LOS ANGELES (N)	.395	49	38	5	15	1	0	1	4
1978	LOS ANGELES (N)	.303	37	33	2	10	1	0	0	6
1979	LOS ANGELES (N)	.357	47	42	1	15	0	0	0	3
1980	LOS ANGELES (N)	.429	7	7	0	3	0	0	0	2

YEAR	CLUB	BA	G	AB	R	H	2B	3B	HR	RBI
1982	LOS ANGELES (N)	.000	1	1	0	0	0	0	0	0
	Twenty years	.304	1536	3779	496	1149	125	52	31	438
League Championship										
	Three years	.600	6	5	1	3	2	0	0	1

World Series

YEAR	CLUB	BA	G	AB	R	H	2B	3B	HR	RBI
1977	LOS ANGELES (N)	.000	3	3	0	0	0	0	0	0
1978	LOS ANGELES (N)	—	1	0	0	0	0	0	0	0
	Two years	.000	4	3	0	0	0	0	0	0

RAY MOWE   B. July 12, 1889, Rochester, Ind.
D. Aug. 14, 1968, Sarasota, Fla.
B.L., T.R. 5'7½" 160 lbs.
(SHORTSTOP)

YEAR	CLUB	BA	G	AB	R	H	2B	3B	HR	RBI
1913	BROOKLYN (N)	.111	5	9	0	1	0	0	0	0

MIKE MOWREY   B. March 24, 1884, Brown's Mill, Pa.
D. March 20, 1947, Chambersburg, Pa.
B.R., T.R. 5'10" 180 lbs.
(3RD BASE)

YEAR	CLUB	BA	G	AB	R	H	2B	3B	HR	RBI
1905	Cincinnati (N)	.267	7	30	4	8	1	0	0	6
1906	Cincinnati (N)	.321	21	53	3	17	3	0	0	6
1907	Cincinnati (N)	.252	138	448	43	113	16	6	1	44
1908	Cincinnati (N)	.220	77	227	17	50	9	1	0	23
1909	Cincinnati (N)									
1909	St. Louis (N)									
	(year totals)	.201	50	144	13	29	6	0	0	9
1910	St. Louis (N)	.282	143	489	69	138	24	6	2	70
1911	St. Louis (N)	.268	137	471	59	126	29	7	0	61
1912	St. Louis (N)	.255	114	408	59	104	13	8	2	50
1913	St. Louis (N)	.258	131	449	61	116	18	4	0	33
1914	Pittsburgh (N)	.254	79	284	24	72	7	5	1	25
1915	Pittsburgh (F)	.280	151	521	56	146	26	6	1	49
1916	BROOKLYN (N)	.244	144	495	57	121	22	6	0	60
1917	BROOKLYN (N)	.214	83	271	20	58	9	5	0	25
	Thirteen years	.256	1275	4290	485	1098	183	54	7	461
World Series										
	One year	.176	5	17	2	3	0	0	0	1

BILLY MULLEN   B. Jan. 23, 1896, St. Louis, Mo.
D. May 4, 1971, St. Louis, Mo.
B.R., T.R. 5'8" 160 lbs.
(3RD BASE)

YEAR	CLUB	BA	G	AB	R	H	2B	3B	HR	RBI
1923	BROOKLYN (N)	.273	4	11	1	3	0	0	0	0
	Five years (total)	.234	35	47	5	11	1	0	0	2

JOE MULVEY   B. Oct. 27, 1858, Providence, R.I.
D. Aug. 21, 1928, Philadelphia, Pa.
B.R., T.R.
(3RD BASE)

YEAR	CLUB	BA	G	AB	R	H	2B	3B	HR	RBI
1895	BROOKLYN (N)	.306	13	49	8	15	4	1	0	8
	Twelve years (total)	.261	987	4063	598	1059	157	70	29	431

SIMMY MURCH B. Nov. 21, 1880, Castine, Maine
D. June 6, 1939, Exeter, N.H.
T.R. 6'4" 220 lbs.
(2ND BASE, 3RD BASE)

YEAR	CLUB	BA	G	AB	R	H	2B	3B	HR	RBI
1908	BROOKLYN (N)	.182	6	11	1	2	1	0	0	0
	Three years (total)	.141	22	71	4	10	2	0	0	1

DANNY MURPHY B. Aug. 11, 1876, Philadelphia, Pa.
D. Nov. 22, 1955, Jersey City, N.J.
B.R., T.R. 5'9" 175 lbs.
(2ND BASE, OUTFIELD)

YEAR	CLUB	BA	G	AB	R	H	2B	3B	HR	RBI
1914	BROOKLYN (F)	.304	52	161	16	49	9	0	4	32
1915	BROOKLYN (F)	.167	5	6	0	1	0	0	0	0
	Sixteen years (total)	.288	1518	5477	711	1577	292	101	44	708

HY MYERS B. April 27, 1889, East Liverpool, Ohio
D. May 1, 1965, Minerva, Ohio
B.R., T.R. 5'9½" 175 lbs.
(OUTFIELD)

YEAR	CLUB	BA	G	AB	R	H	2B	3B	HR	RBI
1909	BROOKLYN (N)	.227	6	22	1	5	1	0	0	6
1911	BROOKLYN (N)	.163	13	43	2	7	1	0	0	0
1914	BROOKLYN (N)	.286	70	227	35	65	3	9	0	17
1915	BROOKLYN (N)	.248	153	605	69	150	21	7	2	46
1916	BROOKLYN (N)	.262	113	412	54	108	12	14	3	36
1917	BROOKLYN (N)	.268	120	471	37	126	15	10	1	41
1918	BROOKLYN (N)	.256	107	407	36	104	9	8	4	40
1919	BROOKLYN (N)	.307	133	512	62	157	23	14	5	73
1920	BROOKLYN (N)	.304	154	582	83	177	36	22	4	80
1921	BROOKLYN (N)	.288	144	549	51	158	14	4	4	68
1922	BROOKLYN (N)	.317	153	618	82	196	20	9	6	89
1923	St. Louis (N)	.300	96	330	29	99	18	2	2	48
1924	St. Louis (N)	.210	43	124	12	26	5	1	1	15
1925	St. Louis (N)									
1925	Cincinnati (N)									
1925	St. Louis (N)									
	(year totals)	.250	5	8	2	2	1	0	0	0
	Fourteen years	.281	1310	4910	555	1380	179	100	32	559

World Series

YEAR	CLUB	BA	G	AB	R	H	2B	3B	HR	RBI
1916	BROOKLYN (N)	.182	5	22	2	4	0	0	1	3
1920	BROOKLYN (N)	.231	7	26	0	6	0	0	0	1
	Two years	.208	12	48	2	10	0	0	1	4

EARL NAYLOR B. May 19, 1919, Kansas City, Mo.
B.R., T.R. 6' 190 lbs.
(OUTFIELD, PITCHER)

YEAR	CLUB	BA	G	AB	R	H	2B	3B	HR	RBI
1946	BROOKLYN (N)	.000	3	2	1	0	0	0	0	0
	Three years (total)	.186	112	290	22	54	6	1	3	28

CHARLIE NEAL B. Jan. 30, 1931, Longview, Texas
B.R., T.R. 5'10" 165 lbs.
(2ND BASE, SHORTSTOP, 3RD BASE)

YEAR	CLUB	BA	G	AB	R	H	2B	3B	HR	RBI
1956	BROOKLYN (N)	.287	62	136	22	39	5	1	2	14
1957	BROOKLYN (N)	.270	128	448	62	121	13	7	12	62
1958	LOS ANGELES (N)	.254	140	473	87	120	9	6	22	65
1959	LOS ANGELES (N)	.287	151	616	103	177	30	11	19	83

110 • The Complete Dodgers Record Book

YEAR	CLUB	BA	G	AB	R	H	2B	3B	HR	RBI
1960	LOS ANGELES (N)	.256	139	477	60	122	23	2	8	40
1961	LOS ANGELES (N)	.235	108	341	40	80	6	1	10	48
1962	New York (N)	.260	136	508	59	132	14	9	11	58
1963	New York (N)									
1963	Cincinnati (N)									
	(year totals)	.211	106	317	28	67	13	1	3	21
	Eight years	.259	970	3316	461	858	113	38	87	391

World Series

YEAR	CLUB	BA	G	AB	R	H	2B	3B	HR	RBI
1956	BROOKLYN (N)	.000	1	4	0	0	0	0	0	0
1959	LOS ANGELES (N)	.370	6	27	4	10	2	0	2	6
	Two years	.323	7	31	4	10	2	0	2	6

BERNIE NEIS B. Sept. 26, 1895, Bloomington, Ill.
D. Nov. 29, 1972, Inverness, Fla.
B.B., T.R. 5'7" 160 lbs.
(OUTFIELD)

YEAR	CLUB	BA	G	AB	R	H	2B	3B	HR	RBI
1920	BROOKLYN (N)	.253	95	249	38	63	11	2	2	22
1921	BROOKLYN (N)	.257	102	230	34	59	5	4	4	34
1922	BROOKLYN (N)	.229	61	70	15	16	4	1	1	9
1923	BROOKLYN (N)	.274	126	445	78	122	17	4	5	37
1924	BROOKLYN (N)	.303	80	211	43	64	8	3	4	26
1925	Boston (N)	.285	106	355	47	101	20	2	5	45
1926	Boston (N)	.215	30	93	16	20	5	2	0	8
1927	Cleveland (A)									
1927	Chicago (A)									
	(year totals)	.297	77	172	26	51	14	0	4	29
	Eight years	.272	677	1825	297	496	84	18	25	210

World Series

	One year	.000	4	5	0	0	0	0	0	0

ROCKY NELSON B. Nov. 18, 1924, Portsmouth, Ohio
B.L., T.L. 5'10½" 175 lbs.
(1ST BASE)

YEAR	CLUB	BA	G	AB	R	H	2B	3B	HR	RBI
1952	BROOKLYN (N)	.256	37	39	6	10	1	0	0	3
1956	BROOKLYN (N)	.208	31	96	7	2	2	0	4	15
	Nine years (total)	.249	620	1394	186	347	61	14	31	173

World Series

	Two years	.250	8	12	2	3	0	0	1	2

DICK NEN B. Sept. 24, 1939, South Gate, Calif.
B.L., T.L. 6'2" 200 lbs.
(1ST BASE)

YEAR	CLUB	BA	G	AB	R	H	2B	3B	HR	RBI
1963	LOS ANGELES (N)	.125	7	8	2	1	0	0	1	1
	Six years (total)	.224	367	826	70	185	23	3	21	107

AL NIXON B. April 11, 1886, Atlantic City, N.J.
D. Nov. 9, 1960, Opelousas, La.
B.R., T.L. 5'7½" 164 lbs.
(OUTFIELD)

YEAR	CLUB	BA	G	AB	R	H	2B	3B	HR	RBI
1915	BROOKLYN (N)	.231	14	39	3	9	1	0	0	2
1916	BROOKLYN (N)	1.000	1	2	0	2	0	0	0	0
1918	BROOKLYN (N)	.455	6	11	1	5	0	0	0	0
	Nine years (total)	.276	422	1358	180	375	60	13	7	118

IRV NOREN
B. Nov. 29, 1924, Jamestown, N.Y.
B.L., T.L. 6' 190 lbs.
(OUTFIELD)

YEAR	CLUB	BA	G	AB	R	H	2B	3B	HR	RBI
1960	LOS ANGELES (N)	.200	26	25	1	5	0	0	1	1
	Eleven years (total)	.275	1093	3119	443	857	157	35	65	453

HUB NORTHEN
B. Aug. 16, 1885, Atlanta, Texas
D. Oct. 1, 1947, Shreveport, La.
B.L., T.L. 5'8" 175 lbs.
(OUTFIELD)

YEAR	CLUB	BA	G	AB	R	H	2B	3B	HR	RBI
1911	BROOKLYN (N)	.316	19	76	16	24	2	2	0	1
1912	BROOKLYN (N)	.282	118	412	54	116	26	6	2	46
	Three years (total)	.272	164	584	76	159	29	8	2	63

JOHNNY OATES
B. Jan. 21, 1946, Sylva, N.C.
B.L., T.R. 5'11" 188 lbs.
(CATCHER)

YEAR	CLUB	BA	G	AB	R	H	2B	3B	HR	RBI
1977	LOS ANGELES (N)	.269	60	156	18	42	4	0	3	11
1978	LOS ANGELES (N)	.307	40	75	5	23	1	0	0	6
1979	LOS ANGELES (N)	.130	26	46	4	6	2	0	0	2
	Eleven years	.250	593	1637	146	410	56	2	14	126

League Championship

| | One year | .000 | 1 | 1 | 0 | 0 | 0 | 0 | 0 | 0 |

World Series

YEAR	CLUB	BA	G	AB	R	H	2B	3B	HR	RBI
1977	LOS ANGELES (N)	.000	1	1	0	0	0	0	0	0
1978	LOS ANGELES (N)	1.000	1	1	0	1	0	0	0	0
	Two years	.500	2	2	0	1	0	0	0	0

DARBY O'BRIEN
B. Sept. 1, 1863, Peoria, Ill.
D. June 15, 1893, Peoria, Ill.
B.R., T.R.
(OUTFIELD)

YEAR	CLUB	BA	G	AB	R	H	2B	3B	HR	RBI
*1890	BROOKLYN (N)	.314	85	350	78	110	28	6	2	63
1891	BROOKLYN (N)	.253	103	395	79	100	18	6	5	57
1892	BROOKLYN (N)	.243	122	490	72	119	14	5	1	56
	Six years	.282	709	2856	577	805	147	47	20	321

*1887 New York (AA), 1888 Brooklyn (AA)

JOHN O'BRIEN
B. July 14, 1870, St. John, New Brunswick, Canada
D. May 13, 1913, Lewiston, Maine
B.L., T.R.
(2ND BASE)

YEAR	CLUB	BA	G	AB	R	H	2B	3B	HR	RBI
1891	BROOKLYN (N)	.246	43	167	22	41	4	2	0	26
	Six years (total)	.254	501	1910	246	486	47	17	12	229

LEFTY O'DOUL
B. March 4, 1897, San Francisco, Calif.
D. Dec. 7, 1969, San Francisco, Calif.
B. L., T. L. 6' 180 lbs.
(OUTFIELD)

YEAR	CLUB	BA	G	AB	R	H	2B	3B	HR	RBI
1919	New York (A)	.250	19	16	2	4	0	0	0	1
1920	New York (A)	.167	13	12	2	2	1	0	0	1
1922	New York (A)	.333	8	9	0	3	1	0	0	4
1923	Boston (A)	.143	36	35	2	5	0	0	0	4

YEAR	CLUB	BA	G	AB	R	H	2B	3B	HR	RBI
1928	New York (N)	.319	114	354	67	113	19	4	8	46
1929	Philadelphia (N)	.398	154	638	152	254	35	6	32	122
1930	Philadelphia (N)	.383	140	528	122	202	37	7	22	97
1931	BROOKLYN (N)	.336	134	512	85	172	32	11	7	75
1932	BROOKLYN (N)	.368	148	595	120	219	32	8	21	90
1933	BROOKLYN (N)	.252	43	159	14	40	5	1	5	21
1933	New York (N)									
	(year totals)	.284	121	388	45	110	14	2	14	56
1934	New York (N)	.316	83	177	27	56	4	3	9	46
	Eleven years	.349	970	3264	624	1140	175	41	113	542
World Series										
	One year	1.000	1	1	1	1	0	0	0	2

NATE OLIVER B. Dec. 13, 1940, St. Petersburg, Fla.
B.R., T.R. 5′10″ 160 lbs.
(2ND BASE)

YEAR	CLUB	BA	G	AB	R	H	2B	3B	HR	RBI
1963	LOS ANGELES (N)	.239	65	163	23	39	2	3	1	9
1964	LOS ANGELES (N)	.243	99	321	28	78	9	0	0	21
1965	LOS ANGELES (N)	1.000	8	1	3	1	0	0	0	0
1966	LOS ANGELES (N)	.193	80	119	17	23	2	0	0	3
1967	LOS ANGELES (N)	.237	77	232	18	55	6	2	0	7
1968	San Francisco (N)	.178	36	73	3	13	2	0	0	1
1969	New York (A)									
1969	Chicago (N)									
	(year totals)	.156	45	45	15	7	3	0	1	4
	Seven years	.226	410	954	107	216	24	5	2	45
World Series										
	One year	—	1	0	0	0	0	0	0	0

LUIS OLMO B. Aug. 11, 1919, Arecibo, Puerto Rico
B.R., T.R. 5′11½″ 185 lbs.
(OUTFIELD)

YEAR	CLUB	BA	G	AB	R	H	2B	3B	HR	RBI
1943	BROOKLYN (N)	.303	57	238	39	72	6	4	4	37
1944	BROOKLYN (N)	.258	136	520	65	134	20	5	9	85
1945	BROOKLYN (N)	.313	141	556	62	174	27	13	10	110
1949	BROOKLYN (N)	.305	38	105	15	32	4	1	0	14
1950	Boston (N)	.227	69	154	23	35	7	1	5	22
1951	Boston (N)	.196	21	56	4	11	1	1	0	4
	Six years	.281	462	1629	208	458	65	25	29	272
World Series										
	One year	.273	4	11	2	3	0	0	1	2

IVY OLSON B. Oct. 14, 1885, Kansas City, Mo.
D. Sept. 1, 1965, Inglewood, Calif.
B.R., T.R. 5′10½″ 175 lbs.
(SHORTSTOP, 2ND BASE, 3RD BASE)

YEAR	CLUB	BA	G	AB	R	H	2B	3B	HR	RBI
1911	Cleveland (A)	.261	140	545	89	142	20	8	1	50
1912	Cleveland (A)	.253	123	467	68	118	13	1	0	33
1913	Cleveland (A)	.249	104	370	47	92	13	3	0	32
1914	Cleveland (A)	.242	89	310	22	75	6	2	1	20
1915	Cincinnati (N)									
1915	BROOKLYN (N)	.077	18	26	2	2	0	1	0	3
	(year totals)	.215	81	233	20	50	5	5	0	17
1916	BROOKLYN (N)	.254	108	351	29	89	13	4	1	38
1917	BROOKLYN (N)	.269	139	580	64	156	18	5	2	38
1918	BROOKLYN (N)	.239	126	506	63	121	16	4	1	17
1919	BROOKLYN (N)	.278	140	590	73	164	14	9	1	38
1920	BROOKLYN (N)	.254	143	637	71	162	13	11	1	46
1921	BROOKLYN (N)	.267	151	652	88	174	22	10	3	35
1922	BROOKLYN (N)	.272	136	551	63	150	26	6	1	47
1923	BROOKLYN (N)	.260	82	292	33	76	11	1	1	35
1924	BROOKLYN (N)	.222	10	27	0	6	1	0	0	0
	Fourteen years	.258	1572	6111	730	1575	191	69	13	446

World Series

YEAR	CLUB	BA	G	AB	R	H	2B	3B	HR	RBI
1916	BROOKLYN (N)	.250	5	16	1	4	0	1	0	2
1920	BROOKLYN (N)	.320	7	25	2	8	1	0	0	0
	Two years	.293	12	41	3	12	1	1	0	2

OLLIE O'MARA B. March 8, 1891, St. Louis, Mo.
B.R., T.R. 5'9" 155 lbs.
(SHORTSTOP, 3RD BASE)

YEAR	CLUB	BA	G	AB	R	H	2B	3B	HR	RBI
1912	Detroit (A)	.000	1	4	0	0	0	0	0	0
1914	BROOKLYN (N)	.263	67	247	41	65	10	2	1	7
1915	BROOKLYN (N)	.244	149	577	77	141	26	3	0	31
1916	BROOKLYN (N)	.202	72	193	18	39	5	2	0	15
1918	BROOKLYN (N)	.213	121	450	29	96	8	1	1	24
1919	BROOKLYN (N)	.000	2	7	1	0	0	0	0	0
	Six years	.231	412	1478	166	341	49	8	2	77

World Series

	One year	.000	1	1	0	0	0	0	0	0

MICKEY O'NEIL B. April 12, 1898, St. Louis, Mo.
D. April 8, 1964, St. Louis, Mo.
B.R., T.R. 5'10" 185 lbs.
(CATCHER)

YEAR	CLUB	BA	G	AB	R	H	2B	3B	HR	RBI
1926	BROOKLYN (N)	.209	75	201	19	42	5	3	0	20
	Nine years (total)	.238	672	1995	177	475	41	23	4	179

CURLY ONIS B. Oct. 24, 1908, Tampa, Fla.
B.R., T.R. 5'9" 180 lbs.
(CATCHER)

YEAR	CLUB	BA	G	AB	R	H	2B	3B	HR	RBI
1935	BROOKLYN (N)	1.000	1	1	0	1	0	0	0	0

JOE ORENGO B. Nov. 29, 1914, San Francisco, Calif.
B.R., T.R. 6' 185 lbs.
(3RD BASE, 1ST BASE, 2ND BASE, SHORTSTOP)

YEAR	CLUB	BA	G	AB	R	H	2B	3B	HR	RBI
1943	BROOKLYN (N)	.200	7	15	1	3	0	0	0	0
	Six years (total)	.238	366	1120	129	266	54	8	17	122

FRANK O'ROURKE B. Nov. 28, 1891, Hamilton, Ontario, Canada
B.R., T.R. 5'10½" 165 lbs.
(3RD BASE, SHORTSTOP, 2ND BASE)

YEAR	CLUB	BA	G	AB	R	H	2B	3B	HR	RBI
1917	BROOKLYN (N)	.237	64	198	18	47	7	1	0	15
1918	BROOKLYN (N)	.167	4	12	0	2	0	0	0	2
	Fourteen years (total)	.254	1131	4069	547	1032	196	42	15	430

DAVE ORR B. Sept. 29, 1859, New York, N.Y.
D. June 3, 1915, Brooklyn, N.Y.
B.R., T.R.
(1ST BASE)

YEAR	CLUB	BA	G	AB	R	H	2B	3B	HR	RBI
*1890	BROOKLYN (P)	.373	107	464	89	173	32	13	6	124
	Eight years (total)	.342	791	3289	536	1126	198	108	37	270

*1883 New York (AA) and New York (N), 1884 New York (AA), 1888 Brooklyn (AA), 1889 Columbus (AA)

CHICK OUTEN   B. June 17, 1905, Mt. Holly, N.C.
D. Sept. 11, 1961, Durham, N.C.
B.L., T.R. 6' 200 lbs.
(CATCHER)

YEAR	CLUB	BA	G	AB	R	H	2B	3B	HR	RBI
1933	BROOKLYN (N)	.248	93	153	20	38	10	0	4	17

MICKEY OWEN   B. April 4, 1916, Nixa, Mo.
B.R., T.R. 5'10" 190 lbs.
(CATCHER)

YEAR	CLUB	BA	G	AB	R	H	2B	3B	HR	RBI
1937	St. Louis (N)	.231	80	234	17	54	4	2	0	20
1938	St. Louis (N)	.267	122	397	45	106	25	2	4	36
1939	St. Louis (N)	.259	131	344	32	89	18	2	3	35
1940	St. Louis (N)	.264	117	307	27	81	16	2	0	27
1941	BROOKLYN (N)	.231	128	386	32	89	15	2	1	44
1942	BROOKLYN (N)	.259	133	421	53	109	16	3	0	44
1943	BROOKLYN (N)	.260	106	365	31	95	11	2	0	54
1944	BROOKLYN (N)	.273	130	461	43	126	20	3	1	42
1945	BROOKLYN (N)	.286	24	84	5	24	9	0	0	11
1949	Chicago (N)	.273	62	198	15	54	9	3	2	18
1950	Chicago (N)	.243	86	259	22	63	11	0	2	21
1951	Chicago (N)	.184	58	125	10	23	6	0	0	15
1954	Boston (A)	.235	32	68	6	16	3	0	1	11
	Thirteen years	.255	1209	3649	338	929	163	21	14	378
World Series	One year	.167	5	12	1	2	0	1	0	2

FRANK OWENS   B. Jan. 25, 1884, Toronto, Ontario, Canada
D. July 2, 1958, Minneapolis, Minn.
B.R., T.R.
(CATCHER)

YEAR	CLUB	BA	G	AB	R	H	2B	3B	HR	RBI
1914	BROOKLYN (F)	.277	58	184	15	51	7	3	2	20
	Four years (total)	.245	222	694	59	170	25	11	5	65

RED OWENS   B. Nov. 1, 1874, Pottsville, Pa.
D. Aug. 21, 1952, Harrisburg, Pa.
B.R., T.R.
(2ND BASE)

YEAR	CLUB	BA	G	AB	R	H	2B	3B	HR	RBI
1905	BROOKLYN (N)	.214	43	168	14	36	6	2	1	20
	Two years (total)	.196	51	189	14	37	6	2	1	21

TOM PACIOREK   B. Nov. 2, 1946, Detroit, Mich.
B.R., T.R. 6'4" 215 lbs.
(OUTFIELD, 1ST BASE)

YEAR	CLUB	BA	G	AB	R	H	2B	3B	HR	RBI
1970	LOS ANGELES (N)	.222	8	9	2	2	1	0	0	0
1971	LOS ANGELES (N)	.500	2	2	0	1	0	0	0	1
1972	LOS ANGELES (N)	.255	11	47	4	12	4	0	1	6
1973	LOS ANGELES (N)	.262	96	195	26	51	8	0	5	18
1974	LOS ANGELES (N)	.240	85	175	23	42	8	6	1	24
1975	LOS ANGELES (N)	.193	62	145	14	28	8	0	1	5
1976	Atlanta (N)	.290	111	324	39	94	10	4	4	36
1977	Atlanta (N)	.239	72	155	20	37	8	0	3	15
1978	Atlanta (N)									
1978	Seattle (A)									
	(year totals)	.300	75	260	34	78	20	3	4	30
1979	Seattle (A)	.287	103	310	38	89	23	4	6	42
1980	Seattle (A)	.273	126	418	44	114	19	1	15	59
1981	Seattle (A)	.326	104	405	50	132	28	2	14	66
1982	Chicago (A)	.312	104	382	49	119	27	4	11	55

YEAR	CLUB	BA	G	AB	R	H	2B	3B	HR	RBI
1983	Chicago (A)	.307	115	420	65	129	32	3	9	63
	Fourteen years	.282	1074	3247	408	928	196	27	74	420
League Championship										
	One year	1.000	1	1	0	1	0	0	0	0
World Series										
	One year	.500	3	2	1	1	1	0	0	0

DON PADGETT

B. Dec. 5, 1911, Caroleen, N.C.
D. Dec. 9, 1980, High Point, N.C.
B.L., T.R. 6' 190 lbs.
(CATCHER, OUTFIELD)

YEAR	CLUB	BA	G	AB	R	H	2B	3B	HR	RBI
1946	BROOKLYN (N)	.167	19	30	2	5	1	0	1	9
	Eight years (total)	.288	699	1991	247	573	111	16	37	338

ANDY PAFKO

B. Feb. 25, 1921, Boyceville, Wis.
B.R., T.R. 6' 190 lbs.
(OUTFIELD, 3RD BASE)

YEAR	CLUB	BA	G	AB	R	H	2B	3B	HR	RBI
1943	Chicago (N)	.379	13	58	7	22	3	0	0	10
1944	Chicago (N)	.269	128	469	47	126	16	2	6	62
1945	Chicago (N)	.298	144	534	64	159	24	12	12	110
1946	Chicago (N)	.282	65	234	18	66	6	4	3	39
1947	Chicago (N)	.302	129	513	68	155	25	7	13	66
1948	Chicago (N)	.312	142	548	82	171	30	2	26	101
1949	Chicago (N)	.281	144	519	79	146	29	2	18	69
1950	Chicago (N)	.304	146	514	95	156	24	8	36	92
1951	Chicago (N)									
1951	BROOKLYN (N)	.249	84	277	42	69	11	0	18	58
	(year totals)	.255	133	455	68	116	16	3	30	93
1952	BROOKLYN (N)	.287	150	551	76	158	17	5	19	85
1953	Milwaukee (N)	.297	140	516	70	153	23	4	17	72
1954	Milwaukee (N)	.286	138	510	61	146	22	4	14	69
1955	Milwaukee (N)	.266	86	252	29	67	3	5	5	34
1956	Milwaukee (N)	.258	45	93	15	24	5	0	2	9
1957	Milwaukee (N)	.277	83	220	31	61	6	1	8	27
1958	Milwaukee (N)	.238	95	164	17	39	7	1	3	23
1959	Milwaukee (N)	.218	71	142	17	31	8	2	1	15
	Seventeen years	.285	1852	6292	844	1796	264	62	213	976
World Series										
	Four years	.222	24	72	6	16	3	1	0	5

WES PARKER

B. Nov. 13, 1939, Evanston, Ill.
B.B., T.L. 6'1" 180 lbs.
(1ST BASE, OUTFIELD)

YEAR	CLUB	BA	G	AB	R	H	2B	3B	HR	RBI
1964	LOS ANGELES (N)	.257	124	214	29	55	7	1	3	10
1965	LOS ANGELES (N)	.238	154	542	80	129	24	7	8	51
1966	LOS ANGELES (N)	.253	156	475	67	120	17	5	12	51
1967	LOS ANGELES (N)	.247	139	413	56	102	16	5	5	31
1968	LOS ANGELES (N)	.239	135	468	42	112	22	2	3	27
1969	LOS ANGELES (N)	.278	132	471	76	131	23	4	13	68
1970	LOS ANGELES (N)	.319	161	614	84	196	47	4	10	111
1971	LOS ANGELES (N)	.274	157	533	69	146	24	1	6	62
1972	LOS ANGELES (N)	.279	130	427	45	119	14	3	4	59
	Nine years	.267	1288	4157	548	1110	194	32	64	470

World Series

YEAR	CLUB	BA	G	AB	R	H	2B	3B	HR	RBI
1965	LOS ANGELES (N)	.304	7	23	3	7	0	1	1	2
1966	LOS ANGELES (N)	.231	4	13	0	3	2	0	0	0
	Two years	.278	11	36	3	10	2	1	1	2

ART PARKS
B. Nov. 1, 1911, Paris, Ark.
B.L., T.R. 5'9" 170 lbs.
(OUTFIELD)

YEAR	CLUB	BA	G	AB	R	H	2B	3B	HR	RBI
1937	BROOKLYN (N)	.313	7	16	2	5	2	0	0	0
1939	BROOKLYN (N)	.272	71	239	27	65	13	2	1	19
	Two years	.275	78	255	29	70	15	2	1	19

JAY PARTRIDGE
B. Nov. 15, 1902, Mountville, Ga.
D. Jan. 4, 1974, Nashville, Tenn.
B.L., T.R. 5'11" 160 lbs.
(2ND BASE)

YEAR	CLUB	BA	G	AB	R	H	2B	3B	HR	RBI
1927	BROOKLYN (N)	.260	146	572	72	149	17	6	7	40
1928	BROOKLYN (N)	.247	37	73	18	18	0	1	0	12
	Two years	.259	183	645	90	167	17	7	7	52

KEVIN PASLEY
B. July 22, 1953, New York, N.Y.
B.R., T.R. 6' 185 lbs.
(CATCHER)

YEAR	CLUB	BA	G	AB	R	H	2B	3B	HR	RBI
1974	LOS ANGELES (N)	—	1	0	0	0	0	0	0	0
1976	LOS ANGELES (N)	.231	23	52	4	12	2	0	0	2
1977	LOS ANGELES (N)	.333	2							
1977	Seattle (A)									
	(year totals)	.375	6	16	1	6	0	0	0	2
	Four years (total)	.254	55	122	8	31	7	0	1	9

HARRY PATTEE
B. Jan. 17, 1882, Charlestown, Mass.
D. July 17, 1971, Lynchburg, Va.
B.L., T.R. 5'8" 149 lbs.
(2ND BASE)

YEAR	CLUB	BA	G	AB	R	H	2B	3B	HR	RBI
1908	BROOKLYN (N)	.216	80	264	19	57	5	2	0	9

JOHNNY PEACOCK
B. Jan. 10, 1910, Fremont, N.C.
D. Nov. 1981, Fremont, N.C.
B.L., T.R. 5'11" 165 lbs.
(CATCHER)

YEAR	CLUB	BA	G	AB	R	H	2B	3B	HR	RBI
1945	BROOKLYN (N)	.255	48	110	11	28	5	1	0	14
	Nine years (total)	.262	619	1734	175	455	74	16	1	194

HAL PECK
B. April 20, 1917, Big Bend, Wis.
B.L., T.L. 5'11" 175 lbs.
(OUTFIELD)

YEAR	CLUB	BA	G	AB	R	H	2B	3B	HR	RBI
1943	BROOKLYN (N)	.000	1	1	0	0	0	0	0	0
	Seven years (total)	.279	355	1092	136	305	52	13	15	112

JOHN PERCONTE
B. Aug. 31, 1954, Joliet, Ill.
B.L., T.R. 5'10" 160 lbs.
(2ND BASE)

YEAR	CLUB	BA	G	AB	R	H	2B	3B	HR	RBI
1980	LOS ANGELES (N)	.235	14	17	2	4	0	0	0	2
1981	LOS ANGELES (N)	.222	8	9	2	2	0	1	0	1
1982	Cleveland (A)	.237	93	219	27	52	4	4	0	15
	Three years	.237	115	245	31	58	4	5	0	18

The Complete Catalogue of Players • 117

BABE PHELPS B. April 19, 1908, Odenton, Md.
B.L., T.R. 6'2" 225 lbs.
(CATCHER)

YEAR	CLUB	BA	G	AB	R	H	2B	3B	HR	RBI
1931	Washington (A)	.333	3	3	0	1	0	0	0	0
1933	Chicago (N)	.286	3	7	0	2	0	0	0	2
1934	Chicago (N)	.286	44	70	7	20	5	2	2	12
1935	BROOKLYN (N)	.364	47	121	17	44	7	2	5	22
1936	BROOKLYN (N)	.367	115	319	36	117	23	2	5	57
1937	BROOKLYN (N)	.313	121	409	42	128	37	3	7	58
1938	BROOKLYN (N)	.308	66	208	33	64	12	2	5	46
1939	BROOKLYN (N)	.285	98	323	33	92	21	2	6	42
1940	BROOKLYN (N)	.295	118	370	47	109	24	5	13	61
1941	BROOKLYN (N)	.233	16	30	3	7	3	0	2	4
1942	Pittsburgh (N)	.284	95	257	21	73	11	1	9	41
	Eleven years	.310	726	2117	239	657	143	19	54	345

ED PHELPS B. March 3, 1879, Albany, N.Y.
D. Jan. 31, 1942, Albany, N.Y.
B.R., T.R. 5'11" 185 lbs.
(CATCHER)

YEAR	CLUB	BA	G	AB	R	H	2B	3B	HR	RBI
1912	BROOKLYN (N)	.288	52	111	8	32	4	3	0	23
1913	BROOKLYN (N)	.222	15	18	0	4	0	0	0	0
	Eleven years (total)	.251	629	1832	186	460	45	20	3	205

VAL PICINICH B. Sept. 8, 1896, New York, N.Y.
D. Dec. 5, 1942, Nobleboro, Maine
B.R., T.R. 5'9" 165 lbs.
(CATCHER)

YEAR	CLUB	BA	G	AB	R	H	2B	3B	HR	RBI
1916	Philadelphia (A)	.195	40	118	8	23	3	1	0	5
1917	Philadelphia (A)	.333	2	6	0	2	0	0	0	0
1918	Washington (A)	.230	47	148	13	34	3	2	1	12
1919	Washington (A)	.274	80	212	18	58	12	3	3	22
1920	Washington (A)	.203	48	133	14	27	6	2	3	14
1921	Washington (A)	.277	45	141	10	39	9	0	0	12
1922	Washington (A)	.229	76	210	16	48	12	2	0	19
1923	Boston (A)	.276	87	268	33	74	21	1	2	31
1924	Boston (A)	.266	68	158	24	42	5	3	1	24
1925	Boston (A)	.255	90	251	31	64	21	0	1	25
1926	Cincinnati (N)	.263	89	240	33	63	16	1	2	31
1927	Cincinnati (N)	.254	65	173	16	44	8	3	0	12
1928	Cincinnati (N)	.302	96	324	29	98	15	1	7	35
1929	BROOKLYN (N)	.260	93	273	28	71	16	6	4	31
1930	BROOKLYN (N)	.217	35	46	4	10	3	0	0	3
1931	BROOKLYN (N)	.267	24	45	5	12	4	0	1	4
1932	BROOKLYN (N)	.257	41	70	8	18	6	0	1	11
1933	BROOKLYN (N)	.167	6	6	1	1	1	1	0	0
1933	Pittsburgh (N)									
	(year totals)	.241	22	58	7	14	5	0	1	7
	Eighteen years	.258	1048	2874	297	741	165	25	27	298

JOE PIGNATANO B. Aug. 4, 1929, Brooklyn, N.Y.
B.R., T.R. 5'10" 180 lbs.
(CATCHER)

YEAR	CLUB	BA	G	AB	R	H	2B	3B	HR	RBI
1957	BROOKLYN (N)	.214	8	14	0	3	1	0	0	1
1958	LOS ANGELES (N)	.218	63	142	18	31	4	0	9	17
1959	LOS ANGELES (N)	.237	52	139	17	33	4	1	1	11
1960	LOS ANGELES (N)	.233	58	90	11	21	4	0	2	9
1961	Kansas City (A)	.243	92	243	31	59	10	3	4	22
1962	San Francisco (N)									
1962	New York (N)									
	(year totals)	.230	34	61	4	14	2	0	0	2
	Six years	.234	307	689	81	161	25	4	16	62
World Series										
	One year	—	1	0	0	0	0	0	0	0

GEORGE PINCKNEY
B. Jan. 11, 1862, Peoria, Ill.
D. Nov. 9, 1926, Peoria, Ill.
B.R., T.R.
(3RD BASE)

YEAR	CLUB	BA	G	AB	R	H	2B	3B	HR	RBI
*1890	BROOKLYN (N)	.309	126	485	115	150	20	9	7	83
1891	BROOKLYN (N)	.273	135	501	80	137	19	6	2	71
1892	St. Louis (N)	.172	78	290	31	50	3	2	0	25
1893	Louisville (N)	.235	118	446	64	105	12	6	1	62
	Ten years	.263	1163	4610	874	1212	170	56	21	391

*1884 Cleveland (N), 1885 Brooklyn (AA)

NICK POLLY
B. April 18, 1917, Chicago, Ill.
B.R., T.R. 5'11" 190 lbs.
(3RD BASE)

YEAR	CLUB	BA	G	AB	R	H	2B	3B	HR	RBI
1937	BROOKLYN (N)	.222	10	18	2	4	0	0	0	2
1945	Boston (A)	.143	4	7	0	1	0	0	0	1
	Two years	.200	14	25	2	5	0	0	0	3

PAUL POPOVICH
B. Aug. 18, 1940, Flemington, W. Va.
B.R., T.R. 6' 175 lbs.
(2ND BASE, SHORTSTOP)

YEAR	CLUB	BA	G	AB	R	H	2B	3B	HR	RBI
1964	Chicago (N)	1.000	1	1	0	1	0	0	0	0
1966	Chicago (N)	.000	2	6	0	0	0	0	0	0
1967	Chicago (N)	.214	49	159	18	34	4	0	0	2
1968	LOS ANGELES (N)	.232	134	418	35	97	8	1	2	25
1969	LOS ANGELES (N)	.200	28	50	5	10	0	0	0	4
1969	Chicago (N)									
	(year totals)	.284	88	204	31	58	6	0	1	18
1970	Chicago (N)	.253	78	186	22	47	5	1	4	20
1971	Chicago (N)	.217	89	226	24	49	7	1	4	28
1972	Chicago (N)	.194	58	129	8	25	3	2	1	11
1973	Chicago (N)	.236	99	280	24	66	6	3	2	24
1974	Pittsburgh (N)	.217	59	83	9	18	2	1	0	5
1975	Pittsburgh (N)	.200	25	40	5	8	1	0	0	1
	Eleven years	.233	682	1732	176	403	42	9	14	134
League Championship										
	One year	.600	3	5	1	3	0	0	0	0

SAM POST
B. Nov. 17, 1896, Richmond, Va.
D. March 31, 1971, Portsmouth, Va.
B.L., T.L. 6'1½" 170 lbs.
(2ND BASE)

YEAR	CLUB	BA	G	AB	R	H	2B	3B	HR	RBI
1922	BROOKLYN (N)	.280	9	25	3	7	0	0	0	4

BOOG POWELL
B. Aug. 17, 1941, Lakeland, Fla.
B.L., T.R. 6'4½" 230 lbs.
(1ST BASE)

YEAR	CLUB	BA	G	AB	R	H	2B	3B	HR	RBI
1977	LOS ANGELES (N)	.244	50	41	0	10	0	0	0	5
Seventeen years (total)		.266	2042	6681	889	1776	270	11	339	1187

LARRY PRATT
B. Oct. 8, 1887, Gibson City, Ill.
D. Jan. 8, 1969, Peoria, Ill.
B.R., T.R. 6' 183 lbs.
(CATCHER)

YEAR	CLUB	BA	G	AB	R	H	2B	3B	HR	RBI
1915	BROOKLYN (F)									
Two years (total)		.193	30	57	7	11	3	0	1	2

MARV RACKLEY   B. July 25, 1921, Seneca, S.C.
B.L., T.L. 5'10" 170 lbs.
(OUTFIELD)

YEAR	CLUB	BA	G	AB	R	H	2B	3B	HR	RBI
1947	BROOKLYN (N)	.222	18	9	2	2	0	0	0	2
1948	BROOKLYN (N)	.327	88	281	55	92	13	5	0	15
1949	BROOKLYN (N)	.300	9							
1949	Pittsburgh (N)	.314	11							
1949	BROOKLYN (N)	.291	54							
	(year totals)	.303	74	185	30	56	7	1	1	17
1950	Cincinnati (N)	.500	5	2	0	1	0	0	0	1
	Four years	.317	185	477	87	151	20	6	1	35
World Series										
	One year	.000	2	5	0	0	0	0	0	0

JACK RADTKE   B. April 14, 1913, Denver, Colo.
B.B., T.R. 5'7" 160 lbs.
(2ND BASE)

YEAR	CLUB	BA	G	AB	R	H	2B	3B	HR	RBI
1936	BROOKLYN (N)	.097	33	31	8	3	0	0	0	2

BOB RAMAZZOTTI   B. Jan. 16, 1917, Elanora, Pa.
B.R., T.R. 5'8½" 175 lbs.
(2ND BASE, 3RD BASE, SHORTSTOP)

YEAR	CLUB	BA	G	AB	R	H	2B	3B	HR	RBI
1946	BROOKLYN (N)	.208	62	120	10	25	4	0	0	7
1948	BROOKLYN (N)	.000	4	3	0	0	0	0	0	0
1949	BROOKLYN (N)	.154	5	13	0	2	0	0	0	0
1949	Chicago (N)									
	(year totals)	.177	70	203	15	36	3	1	1	9
1950	Chicago (N)	.262	61	145	19	38	3	3	1	6
1951	Chicago (N)	.247	73	158	13	39	5	2	1	15
1952	Chicago (N)	.284	50	183	26	52	5	3	1	12
1953	Chicago (N)	.154	26	39	3	6	2	0	0	4
	Seven years	.230	346	851	86	196	22	9	4	53

PHIL REARDON   B. Oct. 3, 1883, Brooklyn, N.Y.
D. Sept. 28, 1920, Brooklyn, N.Y.
B.R., T.R.
(OUTFIELD)

YEAR	CLUB	BA	G	AB	R	H	2B	3B	HR	RBI
1906	BROOKLYN (N)	.071	5	14	0	1	0	0	0	0

HARRY REDMOND   B. Sept. 13, 1887, Cleveland, Ohio
D. July 10, 1960, Cleveland, Ohio
T.R.
(2ND BASE)

YEAR	CLUB	BA	G	AB	R	H	2B	3B	HR	RBI
1909	BROOKLYN (N)	.000	6	19	3	0	0	0	0	1

MILT REED   B. July 4, 1890, Atlanta, Ga.
D. July 27, 1938, Atlanta, Ga.
B.L., T.R. 5'9½" 150 lbs.
(SHORTSTOP, 2ND BASE)

YEAR	CLUB	BA	G	AB	R	H	2B	3B	HR	RBI
1915	BROOKLYN (F)	.290	10	31	2	9	1	1	0	8
	Four years (total)	.227	68	163	16	37	4	2	0	10

PEE WEE REESE B. July 23, 1918, Ekron, Ky.
B.R., T.R. 5'10" 160 lbs.
(SHORTSTOP)

YEAR	CLUB	BA	G	AB	R	H	2B	3B	HR	RBI
1940	BROOKLYN (N)	.272	84	312	58	85	8	4	5	28
1941	BROOKLYN (N)	.229	152	595	76	136	23	5	2	46
1942	BROOKLYN (N)	.255	151	564	87	144	24	5	3	53
1946	BROOKLYN (N)	.284	152	542	79	154	16	10	5	60
1947	BROOKLYN (N)	.284	142	476	81	135	24	4	12	73
1948	BROOKLYN (N)	.274	151	566	96	155	31	4	9	75
1949	BROOKLYN (N)	.279	155	617	132	172	27	3	16	73
1950	BROOKLYN (N)	.260	141	531	97	138	21	5	11	52
1951	BROOKLYN (N)	.286	154	616	94	176	20	8	10	84
1952	BROOKLYN (N)	.272	149	559	94	152	18	8	6	58
1953	BROOKLYN (N)	.271	140	524	108	142	25	7	13	61
1954	BROOKLYN (N)	.309	141	554	98	171	35	8	10	69
1955	BROOKLYN (N)	.282	145	553	99	156	29	4	10	61
1956	BROOKLYN (N)	.257	147	572	85	147	19	2	9	46
1957	BROOKLYN (N)	.224	103	330	33	74	3	1	1	29
1958	BROOKLYN (N)	.224	59	147	21	33	7	2	4	17
	Sixteen years	.269	2166	8058	1338	2170	330	80	126	885

World Series

YEAR	CLUB	BA	G	AB	R	H	2B	3B	HR	RBI
1941	BROOKLYN (N)	.200	5	20	1	4	0	0	0	2
1947	BROOKLYN (N)	.304	7	23	5	7	1	0	0	4
1949	BROOKLYN (N)	.316	5	19	2	6	1	0	1	2
1952	BROOKLYN (N)	.345	7	29	4	10	0	0	1	4
1953	BROOKLYN (N)	.208	6	24	0	5	0	1	0	0
1955	BROOKLYN (N)	.296	7	27	5	8	1	0	0	0
1956	BROOKLYN (N)	.222	7	27	3	6	0	1	0	2
	Seven years	.272	44	169	20	46	3	2	2	16

PETE REISER B. March 17, 1919, St. Louis, Mo.
D. Oct. 25, 1981, Palm Springs, Calif.
B.L. (B.B. 1948–51), T.R. 5'11" 185 lbs.
(OUTFIELD)

YEAR	CLUB	BA	G	AB	R	H	2B	3B	HR	RBI
1940	BROOKLYN (N)	.293	58	225	34	66	11	4	3	20
1941	BROOKLYN (N)	.343	137	536	117	184	39	17	14	76
1942	BROOKLYN (N)	.310	125	480	89	149	33	5	10	64
1946	BROOKLYN (N)	.277	122	423	75	117	21	5	11	73
1947	BROOKLYN (N)	.309	110	388	68	120	23	2	5	46
1948	BROOKLYN (N)	.236	64	127	17	30	8	2	1	19
1949	Boston (N)	.271	84	221	32	60	8	3	8	40
1950	Boston (N)	.205	53	78	12	16	2	0	1	10
1951	Pittsburgh (N)	.271	74	140	22	38	9	3	2	13
1952	Cleveland (A)	.136	34	44	7	6	1	0	3	7
	Ten years	.295	861	2662	473	786	155	41	58	368

World Series

YEAR	CLUB	BA	G	AB	R	H	2B	3B	HR	RBI
1941	BROOKLYN (N)	.200	5	20	1	4	1	1	1	3
1947	BROOKLYN (N)	.250	5	8	1	2	0	0	0	0
	Two years	.214	10	28	2	6	1	1	1	3

RIP REPULSKI B. Oct. 4, 1927, Sauk Rapids, Minn.
B.R., T.R. 6' 195 lbs.
(OUTFIELD)

YEAR	CLUB	BA	G	AB	R	H	2B	3B	HR	RBI
1959	LOS ANGELES (N)	.255	53	94	11	24	4	0	2	14
1960	LOS ANGELES (N)	.200	4	5	0	1	0	0	0	0
	Nine years (total)	.269	928	3088	407	830	153	23	106	416

BILLY RHIEL
B. Aug. 16, 1900, Youngstown, Ohio
D. Aug. 16, 1946, Youngstown, Ohio
B.R., T.R. 5'11" 175 lbs.
(3RD BASE, 2ND BASE)

YEAR	CLUB	BA	G	AB	R	H	2B	3B	HR	RBI
1929	BROOKLYN (N)	.278	76	205	27	57	9	4	4	25
	Four years (total)	.266	199	519	61	138	26	8	7	68

PAUL RICHARDS
B. Nov. 21, 1908, Waxahachie, Texas
B.R., T.R. 6'1½" 180 lbs.
(CATCHER)

YEAR	CLUB	BA	G	AB	R	H	2B	3B	HR	RBI
1932	BROOKLYN (N)	.000	3	8	0	0	0	0	0	0
	Eight years (total)	.227	523	1417	140	321	51	5	15	155

DANNY RICHARDSON
B. Jan. 25, 1863, Elmira, N.Y.
D. Sept. 12, 1926, New York, N.Y.
B.R., T.R. 5'8" 165 lbs.
(2ND BASE, SHORTSTOP, OUTFIELD)

YEAR	CLUB	BA	G	AB	R	H	2B	3B	HR	RBI
1893	BROOKLYN (N)	.223	54	206	36	46	6	2	0	27
	Eleven years (total)	.254	1131	4451	676	1129	149	52	33	506

HARRY RICONDA
B. March 17, 1897, New York, N.Y.
D. Nov. 15, 1958, Mahopac, N.Y.
B.R., T.R. 5'10" 175 lbs.
(3RD BASE, 2ND BASE)

YEAR	CLUB	BA	G	AB	R	H	2B	3B	HR	RBI
1928	BROOKLYN (N)	.224	92	281	22	63	15	4	3	35
	Six years (total)	.247	243	765	83	189	44	11	4	70

JOE RIGGERT
B. Dec. 11, 1886, Janesville, Wis.
D. Dec. 10, 1973, Kansas City, Mo.
B.R., T.R. 5'9½" 170 lbs.
(OUTFIELD)

YEAR	CLUB	BA	G	AB	R	H	2B	3B	HR	RBI
1914	BROOKLYN (N)	.193	27	83	6	16	1	3	2	6
	Three years (total)	.240	174	558	68	134	18	14	8	44

LEW RIGGS
B. April 22, 1910, Mebane, N.C.
B.L., T.R. 6' 175 lbs.
(3RD BASE)

YEAR	CLUB	BA	G	AB	R	H	2B	3B	HR	RBI
1941	BROOKLYN (N)	.305	77	197	27	60	13	4	5	36
1942	BROOKLYN (N)	.278	70	180	20	50	5	0	3	22
1946	BROOKLYN (N)	.000	1	4	0	0	0	0	0	0
	Ten years (total)	.262	760	2477	298	650	110	43	28	271
World Series	Two years	.182	6	11	1	2	0	0	0	1

JIMMY RIPPLE
B. Oct. 14, 1909, Export, Pa.
D. July 16, 1959, Greensburg, Pa.
B.L., T.R. 5'10" 170 lbs.
(OUTFIELD)

YEAR	CLUB	BA	G	AB	R	H	2B	3B	HR	RBI
1939	BROOKLYN (N)	.330	28	106	18	35	8	4	0	28
1940	BROOKLYN (N)	.231	7	13	0	3	0	0	0	0
	Seven years (total)	.282	554	1809	241	510	92	14	28	257

LOU RITTER
B. Sept. 7, 1875, Liverpool, Pa.
D. May 27, 1952, Harrisburg, Pa.
T.R.
(CATCHER)

YEAR	CLUB	BA	G	AB	R	H	2B	3B	HR	RBI
1902	BROOKLYN (N)	.211	16	57	5	12	1	0	0	2
1903	BROOKLYN (N)	.236	78	259	26	61	9	6	0	37
1904	BROOKLYN (N)	.248	72	214	23	53	4	1	0	19
1905	BROOKLYN (N)	.219	92	311	32	68	10	5	1	28
1906	BROOKLYN (N)	.208	73	226	22	47	1	3	0	15
1907	BROOKLYN (N)	.203	93	271	15	55	6	1	0	17
1908	BROOKLYN (N)	.192	38	99	6	19	2	1	0	7
	Seven years	.219	462	1437	129	315	33	17	1	120

JOHNNY RIZZO
B. July 30, 1912, Houston, Texas
D. Dec. 4, 1977, Houston, Texas
B.R., T.R. 6' 190 lbs.
(OUTFIELD)

YEAR	CLUB	BA	G	AB	R	H	2B	3B	HR	RBI
1942	BROOKLYN (N)	.230	78	217	31	50	8	0	4	27
	Five years (total)	.270	557	1842	268	497	90	16	61	289

EARL ROBINSON
B. Nov. 3, 1936, New Orleans, La.
B.R., T.R. 6'1" 190 lbs.
(OUTFIELD)

YEAR	CLUB	BA	G	AB	R	H	2B	3B	HR	RBI
1958	LOS ANGELES (N)	.200	8	15	3	3	0	0	0	0
	Four years (total)	.268	170	421	63	113	20	5	12	44

FRANK ROBINSON
B. Aug. 31, 1935, Beaumont, Texas
B.R., T.R. 6'1" 183 lbs.
(OUTFIELD)

YEAR	CLUB	BA	G	AB	R	H	2B	3B	HR	RBI
1972	LOS ANGELES (N)	.251	103	342	41	86	6	1	19	59
	Twenty-one years (total)	.294	2808	10006	1829	2943	528	72	586	1812

JACKIE ROBINSON
B. Jan. 31, 1919, Cairo, Ga.
D. Oct. 24, 1972, Stamford, Conn.
B.R., T.R. 5'11½" 195 lbs.
(2ND BASE, 3RD BASE, 1ST BASE, OUTFIELD)

YEAR	CLUB	BA	G	AB	R	H	2B	3B	HR	RBI
1947	BROOKLYN (N)	.297	151	590	125	175	31	5	12	48
1948	BROOKLYN (N)	.296	147	574	108	170	38	8	12	85
1949	BROOKLYN (N)	.342	156	593	122	203	38	12	16	124
1950	BROOKLYN (N)	.328	144	518	99	170	39	4	14	81
1951	BROOKLYN (N)	.338	153	548	106	185	33	7	19	88
1952	BROOKLYN (N)	.308	149	510	104	157	17	3	19	75
1953	BROOKLYN (N)	.329	136	484	109	159	34	7	12	95
1954	BROOKLYN (N)	.311	124	386	62	120	22	4	15	59
1955	BROOKLYN (N)	.256	105	317	51	81	6	2	8	36
1956	BROOKLYN (N)	.275	117	357	61	98	15	2	10	43
	Ten years	.311	1382	4877	947	1518	273	54	137	734
World Series										
1947	BROOKLYN (N)	.259	7	27	3	7	2	0	0	3
1949	BROOKLYN (N)	.188	5	16	2	3	1	0	0	2
1952	BROOKLYN (N)	.174	7	23	4	4	0	0	1	2
1953	BROOKLYN (N)	.320	6	25	3	8	2	0	0	2
1955	BROOKLYN (N)	.182	6	22	5	4	1	1	0	1
1956	BROOKLYN (N)	.250	7	24	5	6	1	0	1	2
	Six years	.234	38	137	22	32	7	1	2	12

SERGIO ROBLES B. April 16, 1946, Magdalena, Mexico
B.R., T.R. 6'2" 190 lbs.
(CATCHER)

YEAR	CLUB	BA	G	AB	R	H	2B	3B	HR	RBI
1976	LOS ANGELES (N)	.000	6	3	0	0	0	0	0	0
	Three years (total)	.095	16	21	0	2	0	0	0	0

LOU ROCHELLI B. Jan. 11, 1919, Williamson, Ill.
B.R., T.R. 6'1" 175 lbs.
(SHORTSTOP)

YEAR	CLUB	BA	G	AB	R	H	2B	3B	HR	RBI
1944	BROOKLYN (N)	.176	5	17	0	3	0	1	0	2

BUCK RODGERS B. Aug. 16, 1938, Delaware, Ohio
B.B., T.R. 6'2" 190 lbs.
(CATCHER)

YEAR	CLUB	BA	G	AB	R	H	2B	3B	HR	RBI
1961	LOS ANGELES (N)	.321	16	56	8	18	2	0	2	13
1962	LOS ANGELES (N)	.258	155	565	65	146	34	6	6	61
1963	LOS ANGELES (N)	.233	100	300	24	70	6	0	4	23
1964	LOS ANGELES (N)	.243	148	514	38	125	18	3	4	54
1965	California (A)	.209	132	411	33	86	14	3	1	32
1966	California (A)	.236	133	454	45	107	20	3	7	48
1967	California (A)	.219	139	429	29	94	13	3	6	41
1968	California (A)	.190	91	258	13	49	6	0	1	14
1969	California (A)	.196	18	46	4	9	1	0	0	2
	Nine years	.232	932	3033	259	704	114	18	31	288

ELLY RODRIGUEZ B. May 24, 1946, Fajardo, Puerto Rico
B.R., T.R. 5'11" 185 lbs.
(CATCHER)

YEAR	CLUB	BA	G	AB	R	H	2B	3B	HR	RBI
1976	LOS ANGELES (N)	.212	36	66	10	14	0	0	0	9
	Nine years (total)	.245	775	2173	220	533	76	6	16	203

RON ROENICKE B. Aug. 19, 1956, Covina, Calif.
B.B., T.L. 6' 180 lbs.
(OUTFIELD)

YEAR	CLUB	BA	G	AB	R	H	2B	3B	HR	RBI
1981	LOS ANGELES (N)	.234	22	47	6	11	0	0	0	0
1982	LOS ANGELES (N)	.259	109	143	18	37	8	0	1	12
1983	LOS ANGELES (N)	.221	81	145	12	32	4	0	2	12
	Three years	.247	212	335	36	80	12	0	3	24

OSCAR ROETTGER B. Feb. 19, 1900, St. Louis, Mo.
B.R., T.R. 6' 170 lbs.
(1ST BASE, PITCHER)

YEAR	CLUB	BA	G	AB	R	H	2B	3B	HR	RBI
1927	BROOKLYN (N)	.000	5	4	0	0	0	0	0	0
	Four years (total)	.212	37	66	7	14	1	0	0	6

PACKY ROGERS B. April 26, 1913, Swoyersville, Pa.
B.R., T.R. 5'8" 175 lbs.
(SHORTSTOP, 3RD BASE)

YEAR	CLUB	BA	G	AB	R	H	2B	3B	HR	RBI
1938	BROOKLYN (N)	.189	23	37	3	7	1	1	0	5

STAN ROJEK B. April 21, 1919, North Tonawanda, N.Y.
B.R., T.R. 5'10" 170 lbs.
(SHORTSTOP)

YEAR	CLUB	BA	G	AB	R	H	2B	3B	HR	RBI
1942	BROOKLYN (N)	—	1	0	1	0	0	0	0	0
1946	BROOKLYN (N)	.277	45	47	11	13	2	1	0	2
1947	BROOKLYN (N)	.263	32	80	7	21	0	1	0	7
	Eight years (total)	.266	522	1764	225	470	67	13	4	122

JOHNNY ROSEBORO B. May 13, 1933, Ashland, Ohio
B.L., T.R. 5'11½" 190 lbs.
(CATCHER)

YEAR	CLUB	BA	G	AB	R	H	2B	3B	HR	RBI
1957	BROOKLYN (N)	.145	35	69	6	10	2	0	2	6
1958	LOS ANGELES (N)	.271	114	384	52	104	11	9	14	43
1959	LOS ANGELES (N)	.232	118	397	39	92	14	7	10	38
1960	LOS ANGELES (N)	.213	103	287	22	61	15	3	8	42
1961	LOS ANGELES (N)	.251	128	394	59	99	16	6	18	59
1962	LOS ANGELES (N)	.249	128	389	45	97	16	7	7	55
1963	LOS ANGELES (N)	.236	135	470	50	111	13	7	9	49
1964	LOS ANGELES (N)	.287	134	414	42	119	24	1	3	45
1965	LOS ANGELES (N)	.233	136	437	42	102	10	0	8	57
1966	LOS ANGELES (N)	.276	142	445	47	123	23	2	9	53
1967	LOS ANGELES (N)	.272	116	334	37	91	18	2	4	24
1968	Minnesota (A)	.216	135	380	31	82	12	0	8	39
1969	Minnesota (A)	.263	115	361	33	95	12	0	3	32
1970	Washington (A)	.233	46	86	7	20	4	0	1	6
	Fourteen years	.249	1585	4847	512	1206	190	44	104	548
League Championship										
	One year	.200	2	5	0	1	0	0	0	0

World Series

YEAR	CLUB	BA	G	AB	R	H	2B	3B	HR	RBI
1959	LOS ANGELES (N)	.095	6	21	0	2	0	0	0	1
1963	LOS ANGELES (N)	.143	4	14	1	2	0	0	1	3
1965	LOS ANGELES (N)	.286	7	21	1	6	1	0	0	3
1966	LOS ANGELES (N)	.071	4	14	0	1	0	0	0	0
	Four years	.157	21	70	2	11	1	0	1	7

GOODY ROSEN B. Aug. 28, 1912, Toronto, Ontario, Canada
B.L., T.R. 5'10" 155 lbs.
(OUTFIELD)

YEAR	CLUB	BA	G	AB	R	H	2B	3B	HR	RBI
1937	BROOKLYN (N)	.312	22	77	10	24	5	1	0	6
1938	BROOKLYN (N)	.281	138	473	75	133	17	11	4	51
1939	BROOKLYN (N)	.251	54	183	22	46	6	4	1	12
1944	BROOKLYN (N)	.261	89	264	38	69	8	3	0	23
1945	BROOKLYN (N)	.325	145	606	126	197	24	11	12	75
1946	BROOKLYN (N)	.333	3	3	0	1	0	0	0	0
1946	New York (N)									
	(year totals)	.281	103	313	39	88	11	4	5	30
	Six years	.291	551	1916	310	557	71	34	22	197

MAX ROSENFELD B. Dec. 23, 1902, New York, N.Y.
D. March 10, 1969, Miami, Fla.
B.R., T.R. 5'8" 175 lbs.
(OUTFIELD)

YEAR	CLUB	BA	G	AB	R	H	2B	3B	HR	RBI
1931	BROOKLYN (N)	.222	3	9	0	2	1	0	0	0
1932	BROOKLYN (N)	.359	34	39	8	14	3	0	2	7
1933	BROOKLYN (N)	.111	5	9	0	1	0	0	0	0
	Three years	.298	42	57	8	17	4	0	2	7

JERRY ROYSTER

B. Oct. 18, 1952, Sacramento, Calif.
B.R., T.R. 6' 165 lbs.
(3RD BASE, 2ND BASE, SHORTSTOP)

YEAR	CLUB	BA	G	AB	R	H	2B	3B	HR	RBI
1973	LOS ANGELES (N)	.211	10	19	1	4	0	0	0	2
1974	LOS ANGELES (N)	—	6	0	2	0	0	0	0	0
1975	LOS ANGELES (N)	.250	13	36	2	9	2	1	0	1
	Ten years (total)	.252	907	2909	402	733	101	26	19	216

BILL RUSSELL

B. Oct. 21, 1948, Pittsburg, Kan.
B.R., T.R. 6' 175 lbs.
(SHORTSTOP)

YEAR	CLUB	BA	G	AB	R	H	2B	3B	HR	RBI
1969	LOS ANGELES (N)	.226	98	212	35	48	6	2	5	15
1970	LOS ANGELES (N)	.259	81	278	30	72	11	9	0	28
1971	LOS ANGELES (N)	.227	91	211	29	48	7	4	2	15
1972	LOS ANGELES (N)	.272	129	434	47	118	19	5	4	34
1973	LOS ANGELES (N)	.265	162	615	55	163	26	3	4	56
1974	LOS ANGELES (N)	.269	160	553	61	149	18	6	5	65
1975	LOS ANGELES (N)	.206	84	252	24	52	9	2	0	14
1976	LOS ANGELES (N)	.274	149	554	53	152	17	3	5	65
1977	LOS ANGELES (N)	.278	153	634	84	176	28	6	4	51
1978	LOS ANGELES (N)	.286	155	625	72	179	32	4	3	46
1979	LOS ANGELES (N)	.271	153	627	72	170	26	4	7	56
1980	LOS ANGELES (N)	.264	130	466	38	123	23	2	3	34
1981	LOS ANGELES (N)	.233	82	262	20	61	9	2	0	22
1982	LOS ANGELES (N)	.274	153	497	64	136	20	2	3	46
1983	LOS ANGELES (N)	.246	131	451	47	111	13	1	1	30
	Fourteen years	.264	1911	6671	731	1758	264	55	46	577

Divisional Playoff
| | One year | .250 | 5 | 16 | 1 | 4 | 1 | 0 | 0 | 2 |

League Championship
| | Four years | .348 | 17 | 69 | 7 | 24 | 2 | 1 | 0 | 8 |

World Series

YEAR	CLUB	BA	G	AB	R	H	2B	3B	HR	RBI
1974	LOS ANGELES (N)	.222	5	18	0	4	0	1	0	2
1977	LOS ANGELES (N)	.154	6	26	3	4	0	1	0	2
1978	LOS ANGELES (N)	.423	6	26	1	11	2	0	0	2
1981	LOS ANGELES (N)	.240	6	25	1	6	0	0	0	2
	Four years	.263	23	95	5	25	2	2	0	8

JIM RUSSELL

B. Oct. 1, 1918, Fayette City, Pa.
B.B., T.R. 6'1" 181 lbs.
(OUTFIELD)

YEAR	CLUB	BA	G	AB	R	H	2B	3B	HR	RBI
1950	BROOKLYN (N)	.229	78	214	37	49	8	2	10	32
1951	BROOKLYN (N)	.000	16	13	2	0	0	0	0	0
	Ten years (total)	.267	1034	3595	554	959	175	51	67	428

JOHN RYAN

B. Nov. 12, 1868, Haverhill, Mass.
Deceased
B.R., T.R. 5'10½" 165 lbs.
(CATCHER)

YEAR	CLUB	BA	G	AB	R	H	2B	3B	HR	RBI
1898	BROOKLYN (N)	.189	87	301	39	57	11	4	0	24
	Thirteen years (total)	.217	616	2192	245	476	69	29	4	154

MIKE SANDLOCK

B. Oct. 17, 1915, Old Greenwich, Conn.
B.B., T.R. 6'1" 180 lbs.
(CATCHER)

YEAR	CLUB	BA	G	AB	R	H	2B	3B	HR	RBI
1945	BROOKLYN (N)	.282	80	195	21	55	14	2	2	17
1946	BROOKLYN (N)	.147	19	34	1	5	0	0	0	0
	Five years (total)	.240	195	446	34	107	19	2	2	31

TED SAVAGE

B. Feb. 21, 1937, Venice, Ill.
B.R., T.R. 6'1" 185 lbs.
(OUTFIELD)

YEAR	CLUB	BA	G	AB	R	H	2B	3B	HR	RBI
1968	LOS ANGELES (N)	.206	61	126	7	26	6	1	2	7
	Nine years (total)	.233	642	1375	202	321	51	11	34	163

STEVE SAX

B. Jan. 20, 1960, Sacramento, Calif.
B.R., T.R. 5'11" 185 lbs.
(2ND BASE)

YEAR	CLUB	BA	G	AB	R	H	2B	3B	HR	RBI
1981	LOS ANGELES (N)	.277	31	119	15	33	2	0	2	9
1982	LOS ANGELES (N)	.282	150	638	88	180	23	7	4	47
1983	LOS ANGELES (N)	.281	155	623	94	175	18	5	5	41
	Three years	.281	336	1380	197	388	43	12	11	97
Divisional Playoff										
	One year	—	1	0	0	0	0	0	0	0
League Championship										
	One year	—	1	0	0	0	0	0	0	0
World Series										
	One year	.000	2	1	0	0	0	0	0	0

AL SCHEER

B. Oct. 27, 1889, Groveport, Ohio
D. May 6, 1959, Logansport, Ind.
B.L., T.R. 5'9" 165 lbs.
(OUTFIELD)

YEAR	CLUB	BA	G	AB	R	H	2B	3B	HR	RBI
1913	BROOKLYN (N)	.227	6	22	3	5	0	0	0	0
	Three years (total)	.281	281	931	141	262	48	20	5	105

DUTCH SCHLIEBNER

B. May 19, 1894, Berlin, Germany
D. April 15, 1975, Toledo, Ohio
B.R., T.R. 5'10" 180 lbs.
(1ST BASE)

YEAR	CLUB	BA	G	AB	R	H	2B	3B	HR	RBI
1923	BROOKLYN (N)	.250	19	76	11	19	4	0	0	4

RAY SCHMANDT

B. Jan. 25, 1896, St. Louis, Mo.
D. Feb. 1, 1969, St. Louis, Mo.
B.R., T.R. 6'1" 175 lbs.
(1ST BASE)

YEAR	CLUB	BA	G	AB	R	H	2B	3B	HR	RBI
1915	St. Louis (A)	.000	3	4	0	0	0	0	0	0
1918	BROOKLYN (N)	.307	34	114	11	35	5	4	0	18
1919	BROOKLYN (N)	.165	47	127	8	21	4	0	0	10
1920	BROOKLYN (N)	.238	28	63	7	15	2	1	0	7
1921	BROOKLYN (N)	.306	95	350	42	107	8	5	1	43
1922	BROOKLYN (N)	.268	110	396	54	106	17	3	2	44
	Six years	.269	317	1054	122	284	36	13	3	122
World Series										
	One year	.000	1	1	0	0	0	0	0	0

DICK SCHOFIELD

B. Jan. 7, 1935, Springfield, Ill.
B.B., T.R. 5'9" 163 lbs.
(SHORTSTOP, 2ND BASE, 3RD BASE)

YEAR	CLUB	BA	G	AB	R	H	2B	3B	HR	RBI
1966	LOS ANGELES (N)	.257	20	70	10	18	0	0	0	4
1967	LOS ANGELES (N)	.216	84	232	23	50	10	1	2	15
	Nineteen years (total)	.227	1321	3083	394	699	113	20	21	211

HOWIE SCHULTZ

B. July 3, 1922, St. Paul, Minn.
B.R., T.R. 6'6" 200 lbs.
(1ST BASE)

YEAR	CLUB	BA	G	AB	R	H	2B	3B	HR	RBI
1943	BROOKLYN (N)	.269	45	182	20	49	12	0	1	34
1944	BROOKLYN (N)	.255	138	526	59	134	32	3	11	83
1945	BROOKLYN (N)	.239	39	142	18	34	8	2	1	19
1946	BROOKLYN (N)	.253	90	249	27	63	14	1	3	27
1947	BROOKLYN (N)	.000	2	1	0	0	0	0	0	0
1947	Philadelphia (N)									
	(year totals)	.223	116	404	30	90	19	1	6	35
1948	Philadelphia (N)									
1948	Cincinnati (N)									
	(year totals)	.153	42	85	9	13	0	0	2	10
	Six years	.241	470	1588	163	383	85	7	24	208

JOE SCHULTZ

B. July 24, 1893, Pittsburgh, Pa.
D. April 13, 1941, Columbia, S.C.
B.R., T.R. 5'11½" 172 lbs.
(OUTFIELD)

YEAR	CLUB	BA	G	AB	R	H	2B	3B	HR	RBI
1915	BROOKLYN (N)	.292	56	120	13	35	3	2	0	4
	Eleven years (total)	.285	703	1959	235	558	83	19	15	249

MIKE SCIOSCIA

B. Nov. 27, 1958, Darby, Pa.
B.L., T.R. 6'2" 200 lbs.
(CATCHER)

YEAR	CLUB	BA	G	AB	R	H	2B	3B	HR	RBI
1980	LOS ANGELES (N)	.254	54	134	8	34	5	1	1	8
1981	LOS ANGELES (N)	.276	93	290	27	80	10	0	2	29
1982	LOS ANGELES (N)	.219	129	365	31	80	11	1	5	38
1983	LOS ANGELES (N)	.314	12	35	3	11	3	0	1	7
	Four years	.249	288	824	69	205	29	2	9	82
Divisional Playoff										
	One year	.154	4	13	0	2	0	0	0	1
League Championship										
	One year	.133	5	15	1	2	0	0	1	1
World Series										
	One year	.250	3	4	1	1	0	0	0	0

EMMETT SEERY

B. Feb. 13, 1861, Princeville, Ill.
Deceased
B.L., T.R.
(OUTFIELD)

YEAR	CLUB	BA	G	AB	R	H	2B	3B	HR	RBI
1890	BROOKLYN (P)	.223	104	394	78	88	12	7	1	50
	Nine years (total)	.252	916	3547	695	893	152	68	27	300

AL SHAW

B. March 1, 1881, Toledo, Ill.
D. Dec. 30, 1974, Danville, Ill.
B.L., T.R. 5'8½" 165 lbs.
(OUTFIELD)

YEAR	CLUB	BA	G	AB	R	H	2B	3B	HR	RBI
1914	BROOKLYN (F)	.324	112	376	81	122	27	7	5	49
	Five years (total)	.281	473	1545	235	434	74	28	14	170

MERV SHEA

B. Sept. 5, 1900, San Francisco, Calif.
D. Jan. 27, 1953, Sacramento, Calif.
B.R., T.R. 5'11" 175 lbs.
(CATCHER)

YEAR	CLUB	BA	G	AB	R	H	2B	3B	HR	RBI
1938	BROOKLYN (N)	.183	48	120	14	22	5	0	0	12
	Eleven years (total)	.220	439	1197	105	263	39	7	5	115

JIMMY SHECKARD B. Nov. 23, 1878, Upper Chanceford, Pa.
D. Jan. 15, 1947, Lancaster, Pa.
B.L., T.R. 5'9" 175 lbs.
(OUTFIELD)

YEAR	CLUB	BA	G	AB	R	H	2B	3B	HR	RBI
1897	BROOKLYN (N)	.327	13	49	12	16	3	2	3	14
1898	BROOKLYN (N)	.291	105	409	51	119	17	9	4	64
1889	Baltimore (N)	.295	147	536	104	158	18	10	3	75
1900	BROOKLYN (N)	.300	85	273	74	82	19	10	1	39
1901	BROOKLYN (N)	.353	133	558	116	197	30	21	11	104
1902	Baltimore (A)									
1902	BROOKLYN (N)	.273	122							
	(year totals)	.265	127	501	89	133	21	10	4	37
1903	BROOKLYN (N)	.332	139	515	99	171	29	9	9	75
1904	BROOKLYN (N)	.239	143	507	70	121	23	6	1	46
1905	BROOKLYN (N)	.292	130	480	58	140	20	11	3	41
1906	Chicago (N)	.262	149	549	90	144	27	10	1	45
1907	Chicago (N)	.263	142	482	75	127	22	1	1	36
1908	Chicago (N)	.231	115	403	54	93	18	3	2	22
1909	Chicago (N)	.255	148	525	81	134	29	5	1	43
1910	Chicago (N)	.256	144	507	82	130	27	6	5	51
1911	Chicago (N)	.276	156	539	121	149	26	11	4	50
1912	Chicago (N)	.245	146	523	85	128	22	10	3	47
1913	St. Louis (N)									
1913	Cincinnati (N)									
	(year totals)	.194	99	252	34	49	3	4	0	24
	Seventeen years	.275	2121	7608	1295	2091	354	138	56	813
World Series										
	Four years	.182	21	77	7	14	6	0	0	5

JACK SHEEHAN B. April 15, 1893, Chicago, Ill.
B.L., T.R. 5'8½" 165 lbs.
(SHORTSTOP, 3RD BASE, 2ND BASE)

YEAR	CLUB	BA	G	AB	R	H	2B	3B	HR	RBI
1920	BROOKLYN (N)	.400	3	5	0	2	1	0	0	0
1921	BROOKLYN (N)	.000	5	12	2	0	0	0	0	0
	Two years	.118	8	17	2	2	1	0	0	0
World Series										
	One year	.182	3	11	0	2	0	0	0	0

TOMMY SHEEHAN B. Nov. 6, 1877, Sacramento, Calif.
D. May 22, 1959, Canal Zone, Panama
T.R.

YEAR	CLUB	BA	G	AB	R	H	2B	3B	HR	RBI
1908	BROOKLYN (N)	.214	146	468	45	100	18	2	0	29
	Three years (total)	.236	316	1009	96	238	26	8	1	88

RED SHERIDAN B. Nov. 14, 1896, Brooklyn, N.Y.
D. Nov. 25, 1975, Queens, N.Y.
B.R., T.R. 5'10½" 160 lbs.
(SHORTSTOP, 3RD BASE)

YEAR	CLUB	BA	G	AB	R	H	2B	3B	HR	RBI
1918	BROOKLYN (N)	.250	2	4	0	1	0	0	0	0
1920	BROOKLYN (N)	.000	3	2	0	0	0	0	0	0
	Two years	.167	5	6	0	1	0	0	0	0

VINCE SHERLOCK B. March 27, 1909, Buffalo, N.Y.
B.R., T.R. 6' 180 lbs.
(2ND BASE)

YEAR	CLUB	BA	G	AB	R	H	2B	3B	HR	RBI
1935	BROOKLYN (N)	.462	9	26	4	12	1	0	0	6

NORM SHERRY   B. July 16, 1931, New York, N.Y.
B.R., T.R. 5'11" 180 lbs.
(CATCHER)

YEAR	CLUB	BA	G	AB	R	H	2B	3B	HR	RBI
1959	LOS ANGELES (N)	.333	2	3	0	1	0	0	0	2
1960	LOS ANGELES (N)	.283	47	138	22	39	4	1	8	19
1961	LOS ANGELES (N)	.256	47	121	10	31	2	0	5	21
1962	LOS ANGELES (N)	.182	35	88	7	16	2	0	3	16
1963	New York (N)	.136	63	147	6	20	1	0	2	11
	Five years	.215	194	497	45	107	9	1	18	69

BILL SHINDLE   B. Dec. 5, 1863, Gloucester City, N.J.
D. 1920, Gloucester City, N.J.
B.R., T.R. 5'8½" 155 lbs.
(3RD BASE)

YEAR	CLUB	BA	G	AB	R	H	2B	3B	HR	RBI
*1890	Philadelphia (P)	.322	132	584	127	188	21	21	10	90
1891	Philadelphia (N)	.210	103	415	68	87	13	1	0	38
1892	Baltimore (N)	.252	143	619	100	156	20	18	3	50
1893	Baltimore (N)	.261	125	521	100	136	22	11	1	75
1894	BROOKLYN (N)	.296	116	476	94	141	22	9	4	96
1895	BROOKLYN (N)	.278	118	486	92	135	22	3	3	69
1896	BROOKLYN (N)	.279	131	516	75	144	24	9	1	61
1897	BROOKLYN (N)	.284	134	542	83	154	32	6	3	105
1898	BROOKLYN (N)	.225	120	466	50	105	10	3	1	41
	Thirteen years	.269	1424	5816	993	1562	227	98	30	758

*1886 Detroit (N), 1888 Baltimore (AA)

BART SHIRLEY   B. Jan. 4, 1940, Corpus Christi, Texas
B.R., T.R. 5'10" 183 lbs.
(SHORTSTOP, 3RD BASE, 2ND BASE)

YEAR	CLUB	BA	G	AB	R	H	2B	3B	HR	RBI
1964	LOS ANGELES (N)	.274	18	62	6	17	1	1	0	7
1966	LOS ANGELES (N)	.200	12	5	2	1	0	0	0	0
1968	LOS ANGELES (N)	.181	39	83	6	15	3	0	0	4
	Four years (total)	.204	75	162	15	33	4	1	0	11

GEORGE SHOCH   B. Jan. 6, 1859, Philadelphia, Pa.
D. Sept. 30, 1937, Philadelphia, Pa.
B.R., T.R.
(OUTFIELD, SHORTSTOP, 2ND BASE, 3RD BASE)

YEAR	CLUB	BA	G	AB	R	H	2B	3B	HR	RBI
*1891	Cin. - Milw. (AA)	.315	34	127	29	40	7	1	1	16
1892	Baltimore (N)	.276	76	308	42	85	15	3	1	50
1893	BROOKLYN (N)	.263	94	327	53	86	17	1	2	54
1894	BROOKLYN (N)	.322	64	239	47	77	6	5	1	37
1895	BROOKLYN (N)	.259	61	216	49	56	9	7	0	29
1896	BROOKLYN (N)	.292	76	250	36	73	7	4	1	28
1897	BROOKLYN (N)	.278	85	284	42	79	9	2	0	38
	Eleven years	.265	706	2536	414	671	89	28	10	323

*1886 Washington (N)

GEORGE SHUBA   B. Dec. 13, 1924, Youngstown, Ohio
B.L., T.R. 5'11" 180 lbs.
(OUTFIELD)

YEAR	CLUB	BA	G	AB	R	H	2B	3B	HR	RBI
1948	BROOKLYN (N)	.267	63	161	21	43	6	0	4	32
1949	BROOKLYN (N)	.000	1	1	0	0	0	0	0	0
1950	BROOKLYN (N)	.207	34	111	15	23	8	2	3	12
1952	BROOKLYN (N)	.305	94	256	40	78	12	1	9	40
1953	BROOKLYN (N)	.254	74	169	19	43	12	1	5	23
1954	BROOKLYN (N)	.154	45	65	3	10	5	0	2	10
1955	BROOKLYN (N)	.275	44	51	8	14	2	0	1	8
	Seven years	.259	355	814	106	211	45	4	24	125

World Series

YEAR	CLUB	BA	G	AB	R	H	2B	3B	HR	RBI
1952	BROOKLYN (N)	.300	4	10	0	3	1	0	0	0
1953	BROOKLYN (N)	1.000	2	1	1	1	0	0	1	2
1955	BROOKLYN (N)	.000	1	1	0	0	0	0	0	0
	Three years	.333	7	12	1	4	1	0	1	2

DICK SIEBERT B. Feb. 19, 1912, Fall River, Mass.
D. Nov. 9, 1978, Minneapolis, Minn.
B.L., T.L. 6' 170 lbs.
(1ST BASE)

YEAR	CLUB	BA	G	AB	R	H	2B	3B	HR	RBI
1932	BROOKLYN (N)	.286	6	7	1	2	0	0	0	0
1936	BROOKLYN (N)	.000	2	2	0	0	0	0	0	0
	Eleven years	.282	1035	3917	439	1104	204	40	32	482

MIKE SIMON B. April 13, 1883, Hayden, Ind.
D. June 10, 1963
B.R., T.R. 5'11" 188 lbs.
(CATCHER)

YEAR	CLUB	BA	G	AB	R	H	2B	3B	HR	RBI
1915	BROOKLYN (F)	.176	47	142	7	25	5	1	0	12
	Seven years (total)	.225	378	1069	85	241	28	10	1	90

JOE SIMPSON B. Dec. 31, 1951, Purcell, Okla.
B.L., T.L. 6'3" 175 lbs.
(OUTFIELD)

YEAR	CLUB	BA	G	AB	R	H	2B	3B	HR	RBI
1975	LOS ANGELES (N)	.333	9	6	3	2	0	0	0	0
1976	LOS ANGELES (N)	.133	23	30	2	4	1	0	0	0
1977	LOS ANGELES (N)	.174	29	23	2	4	0	0	0	1
1978	LOS ANGELES (N)	.400	10	5	1	2	0	0	0	1
	Eight years (total)	.249	516	1278	150	318	52	10	9	116

DUKE SIMS B. June 5, 1941, Salt Lake City, Utah
B.L., T.R. 6'2" 197 lbs.
(CATCHER)

YEAR	CLUB	BA	G	AB	R	H	2B	3B	HR	RBI
1971	LOS ANGELES (N)	.274	90	230	23	63	7	2	6	25
1972	LOS ANGELES (N)	.192	51	151	7	29	7	0	29	11
	Eleven years (total)	.239	843	2422	263	580	80	6	100	310

FRED SINGTON B. Feb. 24, 1910, Birmingham, Ala.
B.R., T.R. 6'2" 215 lbs.
(OUTFIELD)

YEAR	CLUB	BA	G	AB	R	H	2B	3B	HR	RBI
1938	BROOKLYN (N)	.358	17	53	10	19	6	1	2	5
1939	BROOKLYN (N)	.274	32	84	13	23	5	0	1	7
	Six years (total)	.271	181	516	66	140	36	5	7	85

TED SIZEMORE B. April 15, 1946, Gadsden, Ala.
B.R., T.R. 5'10" 165 lbs.
(2ND BASE)

YEAR	CLUB	BA	G	AB	R	H	2B	3B	HR	RBI
1969	LOS ANGELES (N)	.271	159	590	69	160	20	5	4	46
1970	LOS ANGELES (N)	.306	96	340	40	104	10	1	1	34
1971	St. Louis (N)	.264	135	478	53	126	14	5	3	42
1972	St. Louis (N)	.264	120	439	53	116	17	4	2	38
1973	St. Louis (N)	.282	142	521	69	147	22	1	1	54
1974	St. Louis (N)	.250	129	504	68	126	17	0	2	47
1975	St. Louis (N)	.240	153	562	56	135	23	1	3	49
1976	LOS ANGELES (N)	.241	84	266	18	64	8	1	0	18

YEAR	CLUB	BA	G	AB	R	H	2B	3B	HR	RBI
1977	Philadelphia (N)	.281	152	519	64	146	20	3	4	47
1978	Philadelphia (N)	.219	108	351	38	77	12	0	0	25
1979	Chicago (N)									
1979	Boston (A)									
	(year totals)	.251	124	418	48	105	24	0	3	30
1980	Boston (A)	.217	9	23	1	5	1	0	0	0
	Twelve years	.262	1411	5011	577	1311	188	21	23	430
League Championship										
	Two years	.308	8	26	4	8	0	1	0	1

FRANK SKAFF

B. Sept. 30, 1913, LaCrosse, Wis.
B.R., T.R. 5'10" 185 lbs.
(1ST BASE)

YEAR	CLUB	BA	G	AB	R	H	2B	3B	HR	RBI
1935	BROOKLYN (N)	.545	6	11	4	6	1	1	0	3
	Two years (total)	.320	38	75	12	24	3	2	1	11

BILL SKOWRON

B. Dec. 18, 1930, Chicago, Ill.
B.R., T.R. 5'11" 195 lbs.
(1ST BASE)

YEAR	CLUB	BA	G	AB	R	H	2B	3B	HR	RBI
1963	LOS ANGELES (N)	.203	89	237	19	48	8	0	4	19
	Fourteen years (total)	.282	1658	5547	681	1566	243	53	211	888
World Series										
	Eight years (total)	.293	39	133	19	39	4	1	8	29

GORDON SLADE

B. Oct. 9, 1904, Salt Lake City, Utah
D. Jan. 2, 1974, Long Beach, Calif.
B.R., T.R. 5'10½" 160 lbs.
(SHORTSTOP)

YEAR	CLUB	BA	G	AB	R	H	2B	3B	HR	RBI
1930	BROOKLYN (N)	.216	25	37	8	8	2	0	1	2
1931	BROOKLYN (N)	.239	85	272	27	65	13	2	1	29
1932	BROOKLYN (N)	.240	79	250	23	60	15	1	1	23
1933	St. Louis (N)	.113	39	62	6	7	1	0	0	3
1934	Cincinnati (N)	.285	138	555	61	158	18	8	4	52
1935	Cincinnati (N)	.281	71	196	22	55	10	0	1	14
	Six years	.257	437	1372	147	353	60	11	8	123

BROADWAY ALECK SMITH

B. 1871, New York, N.Y.
D. July 9, 1919, New York, N.Y.
T.R.
(CATCHER, OUTFIELD)

YEAR	CLUB	BA	G	AB	R	H	2B	3B	HR	RBI
1897	BROOKLYN (N)	.300	66	237	36	71	13	1	1	39
1898	BROOKLYN (N)	.261	52	199	25	52	6	5	0	23
1899	BROOKLYN (N)	.180	17	61	5	11	2	1	0	8
1900	BROOKLYN (N)	.240	7	25	2	6	0	0	0	3
	Nine years (total)	.263	290	984	107	259	31	12	1	130

CHARLEY SMITH

B. Sept. 15, 1937, Charleston, S.C.
B.R., T.R. 6'1" 170 lbs.
(3RD BASE)

YEAR	CLUB	BA	G	AB	R	H	2B	3B	HR	RBI
1960	LOS ANGELES (N)	.167	18	60	2	10	1	1	0	5
1961	LOS ANGELES (N)	.250	9	24	4	6	0	0	0	3
	Ten years (total)	.239	771	2484	228	594	83	18	69	281

DICK SMITH   B. May 17, 1939, Lebanon, Ore.
B.R., T.R. 6'2" 205 lbs.
(OUTFIELD, 1ST BASE)

YEAR	CLUB	BA	G	AB	R	H	2B	3B	HR	RBI
1965	LOS ANGELES (N)	.000	10	6	0	0	0	0	0	1
	Three years (total)	.218	76	142	18	31	6	2	0	7

FRED SMITH   B. July 29, 1891, Cleveland, Ohio
D. May 28, 1961, Cleveland, Ohio
B.R., T.R. 5'11½" 185 lbs.
(3RD BASE, SHORTSTOP)

YEAR	CLUB	BA	G	AB	R	H	2B	3B	HR	RBI
1915	BROOKLYN (F)									
	(year totals)	.244	145	499	49	122	18	10	5	69
1917	St. Louis (N)	.182	56	165	11	30	0	2	1	17
	Four years (total)	.226	438	1422	143	321	39	25	8	158

GERMANY SMITH   B. April 21, 1863, Pittsburgh, Pa.
D. Dec. 1, 1927, Altoona, Pa.
B.R., T.R. 6' 175 lbs.
(SHORTSTOP)

YEAR	CLUB	BA	G	AB	R	H	2B	3B	HR	RBI
*1890	BROOKLYN (N)	.191	129	481	76	92	6	5	1	47
1891	Cincinnati (N)	.201	138	512	50	103	11	5	3	53
1892	Cincinnati (N)	.239	139	506	58	121	13	6	8	63
1893	Cincinnatti (N)	.236	130	500	63	118	18	6	3	56
1894	Cincinnati (N)	.263	127	482	73	127	33	5	3	76
1895	Cincinnati (N)	.300	127	503	75	151	23	6	4	74
1896	Cincinnati (N)	.287	120	456	65	131	22	9	2	71
1897	BROOKLYN (N)	.201	112	428	47	86	17	3	0	29
1898	St. Louis (N)	.159	51	157	16	25	2	1	1	9
	Fifteen years	.243	1710	6552	907	1592	252	94	45	618

*1884 Altoona (U) and Cleveland (N), 1885 Brooklyn (AA)

HAP SMITH   B. July 14, 1883, Coquille, Oreg.
D. Feb. 26, 1961, San Jose, Calif.
B.L., T.R. 6' 185 lbs.
(OUTFIELD)

YEAR	CLUB	BA	G	AB	R	H	2B	3B	HR	RBI
1910	BROOKLYN (N)	.237	35	76	6	18	2	0	0	5

HARRY SMITH   B. May 15, 1890, Baltimore, Md.
D. April 1, 1922, Charlotte, N.C.
B.R., T.R. 5'10" 180 lbs.
(CATCHER)

YEAR	CLUB	BA	G	AB	R	H	2B	3B	HR	RBI
1915	BROOKLYN (F)									
	Four years (total)	.182	75	148	10	27	1	3	1	14

RED SMITH   B. April 6, 1890, Greenville, S.C.
D. Oct. 10, 1966, Atlanta, Ga.
B.R., T.R. 5'11" 165 lbs.
(3RD BASE)

YEAR	CLUB	BA	G	AB	R	H	2B	3B	HR	RBI
1911	BROOKLYN (N)	.261	28	111	10	29	6	1	0	19
1912	BROOKLYN (N)	.286	128	486	75	139	28	6	4	57
1913	BROOKLYN (N)	.296	151	540	70	160	40	10	6	76
1914	BROOKLYN (N)	.245	90	330	39	81	10	8	4	48
1914	Boston (N)									
	(year totals)	.272	150	537	69	146	27	9	7	85
1915	Boston (N)	.264	157	549	66	145	34	4	2	65

YEAR	CLUB	BA	G	AB	R	H	2B	3B	HR	RBI
1916	Boston (N)	.259	150	509	48	132	16	10	3	60
1917	Boston (N)	.295	147	505	60	149	31	6	2	62
1918	Boston (N)	.298	119	429	55	128	20	3	2	65
1919	Boston (N)	.245	87	241	24	59	6	0	1	25
	Nine years	.278	1117	3907	477	1087	208	49	27	514

REGGIE SMITH   B. April 2, 1945, Shreveport, La.
B.B., T.R. 6' 180 lbs.
(OUTFIELD, 1ST BASE)

YEAR	CLUB	BA	G	AB	R	H	2B	3B	HR	RBI
1966	Boston (A)	.154	6	26	1	4	1	0	0	0
1967	Boston (A)	.246	158	565	78	139	24	6	15	61
1968	Boston (A)	.265	155	558	78	148	37	5	15	69
1969	Boston (A)	.309	143	543	87	168	29	7	25	93
1970	Boston (A)	.303	147	580	109	176	32	7	22	74
1971	Boston (A)	.283	159	618	85	175	33	2	30	96
1972	Boston (A)	.270	131	467	75	126	25	4	21	74
1973	Boston (A)	.303	115	423	79	128	23	2	21	69
1974	St. Louis (N)	.309	143	517	79	160	26	9	23	100
1975	St. Louis (N)	.302	135	477	67	144	26	3	19	76
1976	St. Louis (N)									
1976	LOS ANGELES (N)	.280	65	225	85	63	8	4	10	26
	(year totals)	.253	112	395	55	100	15	5	18	49
1977	LOS ANGELES (N)	.307	148	488	104	150	27	4	32	87
1978	LOS ANGELES (N)	.295	128	447	82	132	27	2	29	93
1979	LOS ANGELES (N)	.274	68	234	41	64	13	1	10	32
1980	LOS ANGELES (N)	.322	92	311	47	100	13	0	15	55
1981	LOS ANGELES (N)	.200	41	35	5	7	1	0	1	8
1982	San Francisco (N)	.284	106	349	51	99	11	0	18	56
1983	San Francisco (N)	.328	22	67	13	22	6	1	1	11
	Eighteen years	.301	2009	7100	1136	2042	369	58	315	1103
Divisional Playoff										
	One year	.000	2	1	0	0	0	0	0	1
League Championship										
	Three years	.212	9	33	4	7	1	1	0	3
World Series										
	Four years	.247	21	73	13	18	2	0	6	13

TONY SMITH   B. 1884, Chicago, Ill.
D. Feb. 27, 1964, Galveston, Texas
T.R.
(SHORTSTOP)

YEAR	CLUB	BA	G	AB	R	H	2B	3B	HR	RBI
1910	BROOKLYN (N)	.181	106	321	31	58	10	1	1	16
1911	BROOKLYN (N)	.150	13	40	3	6	1	0	0	2
	Three years (total)	.180	170	500	46	90	12	2	1	26

CLANCY SMYRES   B. May 24, 1922, Culver City, Calif.
B.B., T.L. 5'11½" 175 lbs.

YEAR	CLUB	BA	G	AB	R	H	2B	3B	HR	RBI
1944	BROOKLYN (N)	.000	5	2	1	0	0	0	0	0

RED SMYTH   B. Jan. 30, 1893, Holly Springs, Miss.
D. April 14, 1958, Inglewood, Calif.
B.L., T.R. 5'9" 152 lbs.
(OUTFIELD)

YEAR	CLUB	BA	G	AB	R	H	2B	3B	HR	RBI
1915	BROOKLYN (N)	.136	19	22	3	3	1	0	0	3
1916	BROOKLYN (N)	.000	2	5	0	0	0	0	0	0
1917	BROOKLYN (N)	.125	29	24	5	3	0	0	0	1
	Four years (total)	.191	118	236	32	45	2	4	0	12

DUKE SNIDER   B. Sept. 19, 1926, Los Angeles, Calif.
B.L., T.R. 6' 179 lbs.
(OUTFIELD)

YEAR	CLUB	BA	G	AB	R	H	2B	3B	HR	RBI
1947	BROOKLYN (N)	.241	40	83	6	20	3	1	0	5
1948	BROOKLYN (N)	.244	53	160	22	39	6	6	5	21
1949	BROOKLYN (N)	.292	146	552	100	161	28	7	23	92
1950	BROOKLYN (N)	.321	152	620	109	199	31	10	31	107
1951	BROOKLYN (N)	.277	150	606	96	168	26	9	29	101
1952	BROOKLYN (N)	.303	144	534	80	162	25	7	21	92
1953	BROOKLYN (N)	.336	153	590	132	198	38	4	42	126
1954	BROOKLYN (N)	.341	149	584	120	199	39	10	40	130
1955	BROOKLYN (N)	.309	148	538	126	166	34	6	42	136
1956	BROOKLYN (N)	.292	151	542	112	158	33	2	43	101
1957	BROOKLYN (N)	.274	139	508	91	139	25	7	40	92
1958	LOS ANGELES (N)	.312	106	327	45	102	12	3	15	58
1959	LOS ANGELES (N)	.308	126	370	59	114	11	2	23	88
1960	LOS ANGELES (N)	.243	101	235	38	57	13	5	14	36
1961	LOS ANGELES (N)	.296	85	233	35	69	8	3	16	56
1962	LOS ANGELES (N)	.278	80	158	28	44	11	3	5	30
1963	New York (N)	.243	129	354	44	86	8	3	14	45
1964	San Francisco (N)	.210	91	167	16	35	7	0	4	17
	Eighteen years	.295	2143	7161	1259	2116	358	85	407	1333

World Series

YEAR	CLUB	BA	G	AB	R	H	2B	3B	HR	RBI
1949	BROOKLYN (N)	.143	5	21	2	3	1	0	0	0
1952	BROOKLYN (N)	.345	7	29	5	10	2	0	4	8
1953	BROOKLYN (N)	.320	6	25	3	8	3	0	1	5
1955	BROOKLYN (N)	.320	7	25	5	8	1	0	4	7
1956	BROOKLYN (N)	.304	7	23	5	7	1	0	1	4
1959	LOS ANGELES (N)	.200	4	10	1	2	0	0	1	2
	Six years	.286	36	133	21	38	8	0	11	26

JACK SNYDER   B. 1892, Allegheny County, Pa.
B.R., T.R. 5'9" 170 lbs.
(CATCHER)

YEAR	CLUB	BA	G	AB	R	H	2B	3B	HR	RBI
1917	BROOKLYN (N)	.273	7	11	1	3	0	0	0	1
	Two years (total)	.273	8	11	1	3	0	0	0	1

DENNY SOTHERN   B. Jan. 20, 1904, Washington, D.C.
B.R., T.R. 5'11" 175 lbs.
(OUTFIELD)

YEAR	CLUB	BA	G	AB	R	H	2B	3B	HR	RBI
1931	BROOKLYN (N)	.161	19	31	10	5	1	0	0	0
	Five years (total)	.280	357	1355	219	379	80	9	19	115

DARYL SPENCER   B. July 13, 1929, Wichita, Kan.
B.R., T.R. 6'2½" 185 lbs.
(SHORTSTOP, 2ND BASE, 3RD BASE)

YEAR	CLUB	BA	G	AB	R	H	2B	3B	HR	RBI
1952	New York (N)	.294	7	17	0	5	0	1	0	3
1953	New York (N)	.208	118	408	55	85	18	5	20	56
1956	New York (N)	.221	146	489	46	108	13	2	14	42
1957	New York (N)	.249	148	534	65	133	31	2	11	50
1958	San Francisco (N)	.256	148	539	71	138	20	5	17	74
1959	San Francisco (N)	.265	152	555	59	147	20	1	12	62
1960	St. Louis (N)	.258	148	507	70	131	20	3	16	58
1961	St. Louis (N)									
1961	LOS ANGELES (N)	.243	60	189	27	46	7	0	8	27
	(year totals)	.248	97	319	46	79	11	0	12	48
1962	LOS ANGELES (N)	.236	77	157	24	37	5	1	2	12
1963	LOS ANGELES (N)	.111	7	9	0	1	0	0	0	0
1963	Cincinnati (N)									
	(year totals)	.232	57	164	21	38	7	0	1	23
	Ten years	.244	1098	3689	457	901	145	20	105	428

ROY SPENCER

B. Feb. 22, 1900, Scranton, N.C.
D. Feb. 8, 1973, Port Charlotte, Fla.
B.R., T.R. 5'10" 168 lbs.
(CATCHER)

YEAR	CLUB	BA	G	AB	R	H	2B	3B	HR	RBI
1937	BROOKLYN (N)	.205	51	117	5	24	2	2	0	4
1938	BROOKLYN (N)	.267	16	45	2	12	1	1	0	6
	Twelve years (total)	.247	636	1814	177	448	57	13	3	203

TUCK STAINBACK

B. Aug. 4, 1910, Los Angeles, Calif.
B.R., T.R. 5'11½" 175 lbs.
(OUTFIELD)

YEAR	CLUB	BA	G	AB	R	H	2B	3B	HR	RBI
1934	Chicago (N)	.306	104	359	47	110	14	3	2	46
1935	Chicago (N)	.255	47	94	16	24	4	0	3	11
1936	Chicago (N)	.173	44	75	13	13	3	0	1	5
1937	Chicago (N)	.231	72	160	18	37	7	1	0	14
1938	St. Louis (N)									
1938	Philadelphia (N)									
1938	BROOKLYN (N)	.327	35	104	15	34	6		0	20
	(year totals)	.282	71	195	26	55	9	3	1	31
1939	BROOKLYN (N)	.269	168	201	22	54	7	0	3	19
1940	Detroit (A)	.225	15	40	4	9	2	0	0	1
1941	Detroit (A)	.245	94	200	19	49	8	1	2	10
1942	New York (A)	.200	15	10	0	2	0	0	0	0
1943	New York (A)	.260	71	231	31	60	11	2	0	10
1944	New York (A)	.218	30	78	13	17	3	0	0	5
1945	New York (A)	.257	95	327	40	84	12	2	5	32
1946	Philadelphia (A)	.244	91	291	35	71	10	2	0	20
	Thirteen years	.259	917	2261	284	585	90	14	17	204

GEORGE STALLINGS

B. Nov. 17, 1867, Augusta, Ga.
D. May 13, 1929, Haddock, Ga.
B.R., T.R.
(CATCHER)

YEAR	CLUB	BA	G	AB	R	H	2B	3B	HR	RBI
1890	BROOKLYN (N)	.000	4	11	1	0	0	0	0	0
	Three years (total)	.100	7	20	3	2	1	0	0	0

EDDIE STANKY

B. Sept. 3, 1916, Philadelphia, Pa.
B.R., T.R. 5'8" 170 lbs.
(2ND BASE)

YEAR	CLUB	BA	G	AB	R	H	2B	3B	HR	RBI
1943	Chicago (N)	.245	142	510	92	125	15	1	0	47
1944	Chicago (N)									
1944	BROOKLYN (N)	.276	89	261	32	72	9	2	0	16
	(year totals)	.273	102	286	36	78	9	3	0	16
1945	BROOKLYN (N)	.258	153	555	128	143	29	5	1	39
1946	BROOKLYN (N)	.273	144	483	98	132	24	7	0	36
1947	BROOKLYN (N)	.252	146	559	97	141	24	5	3	53
1948	Boston (N)	.320	67	247	49	79	14	2	2	29
1949	Boston (N)	.285	138	506	90	144	24	5	1	42
1950	New York (N)	.300	152	527	115	158	25	5	8	51
1951	New York (N)	.247	145	515	88	127	17	2	14	43
1952	St. Louis (N)	.229	53	83	13	19	4	0	0	7
1953	St. Louis (N)	.267	17	30	5	8	0	0	0	1
	Eleven years	.268	1259	4301	811	1154	185	35	29	364

DOLLY STARK

B. Jan. 19, 1885, Ripley, Miss.
D. Dec. 1, 1924, Memphis, Tenn.
B.R., T.R.
(SHORTSTOP)

YEAR	CLUB	BA	G	AB	R	H	2B	3B	HR	RBI
1910	BROOKLYN (N)	.165	30	103	7	17	3	0	0	8
1911	BROOKLYN (N)	.295	70	193	25	57	4	1	0	19
1912	BROOKLYN (N)	.182	8	22	2	4	0	0	0	2
	Four years (total)	.238	127	378	38	90	7	1	0	30

JIGGER STATZ B. Oct. 20, 1897, Waukegan, Ill.
B.R., T.R., 5'7½" 150 lbs.
(OUTFIELD)

YEAR	CLUB	BA	G	AB	R	H	2B	3B	HR	RBI
1919	New York (N)	.300	21	60	7	18	2	1	0	6
1920	New York (N)									
1920	Boston (A)									
	(year totals)	.121	18	33	0	4	0	1	0	5
1922	Chicago (N)	.297	110	462	77	137	19	5	1	34
1923	Chicago (N)	.319	154	655	110	209	33	8	10	70
1924	Chicago (N)	.277	135	549	69	152	22	5	3	49
1925	Chicago (N)	.257	38	148	21	38	6	3	2	14
1927	BROOKLYN (N)	.274	130	507	64	139	24	7	1	21
1928	BROOKLYN (N)	.234	77	171	28	40	8	1	0	16
	Eight years	.285	683	2585	376	737	114	31	17	215

FARMER STEELMAN B. June 29, 1875, Millville, N.J.
D. Sept. 16, 1944, Merchantville, N.J.
T.R.
(CATCHER, OUTFIELD)

YEAR	CLUB	BA	G	AB	R	H	2B	3B	HR	RBI
1900	BROOKLYN (N)	.000	1	4	0	0	0	0	0	0
1901	BROOKLYN (N)	.000	1	3	0	1	0	0	0	0
	Four years (total)	.218	43	142	8	31	3	1	0	15

CASEY STENGEL B. July 30, 1890, Kansas City, Mo.
D. Sept. 29, 1975, Glendale, Calif.
B.L., T.L. 5'11" 175 lbs.
(OUTFIELD)

YEAR	CLUB	BA	G	AB	R	H	2B	3B	HR	RBI
1912	BROOKLYN (N)	.316	17	57	9	18	1	0	1	13
1913	BROOKLYN (N)	.272	124	438	60	119	16	8	7	43
1914	BROOKLYN (N)	.316	126	412	55	130	13	10	4	60
1915	BROOKLYN (N)	.237	132	459	52	109	20	12	3	50
1916	BROOKLYN (N)	.279	127	462	66	129	27	8	8	53
1917	BROOKLYN (N)	.257	150	549	69	141	23	12	6	73
1918	Pittsburgh (N)	.246	39	122	18	30	4	1	1	12
1919	Pittsburgh (N)	.293	89	321	38	94	10	10	4	43
1920	Philadelphia (N)	.292	129	445	53	130	25	6	9	50
1921	Philadelphia (N)									
1921	New York (N)									
	(year totals)	.284	42	81	11	23	4	1	0	6
1922	New York (N)	.368	84	250	48	92	8	10	7	48
1923	New York (N)	.339	75	218	39	74	11	5	5	43
1924	Boston (N)	.280	131	461	57	129	20	6	5	39
1925	Boston (N)	.077	12	13	0	1	0	0	0	2
	Fourteen years	.284	1277	4288	575	1219	182	89	60	535
World Series										
	Three years	.393	12	28	5	11	0	0	2	4

ED STEVENS B. Jan. 12, 1925, Galveston, Texas
B.L., T.L. 6'1" 190 lbs.
(1ST BASE)

YEAR	CLUB	BA	G	AB	R	H	2B	3B	HR	RBI
1945	BROOKLYN (N)	.274	55	201	29	55	14	3	4	29
1946	BROOKLYN (N)	.242	103	310	34	75	13	7	10	60
1947	BROOKLYN (N)	.154	5	13	0	2	1	0	0	0
1948	Pittsburgh (N)	.254	128	429	47	109	19	6	10	69
1949	Pittsburgh (N)	.262	67	221	22	58	10	1	4	32
1950	Pittsburgh (N)	.196	17	46	2	9	2	0	0	3
	Six years	.252	375	1220	134	308	59	17	28	193

STUFFY STEWART

B. Jan. 31, 1894, Jasper, Fla.
D. Sept. 30, 1930, Lake City, Fla.
B.R., T.R. 5'9½" 160 lbs.
(2ND BASE)

YEAR	CLUB	BA	G	AB	R	H	2B	3B	HR	RBI
1923	BROOKLYN (N)	.364	4	11	3	4	1	0	1	1
	Eight years (total)	.238	176	265	74	63	14	3	1	18

BOB STINSON

B. Oct. 11, 1945, Elkin, N.C.
B.B., T.R. 5'11" 180 lbs.
(CATCHER)

YEAR	CLUB	BA	G	AB	R	H	2B	3B	HR	RBI
1969	LOS ANGELES (N)	.375	4	8	1	3	0	0	0	2
1970	LOS ANGELES (N)	.000	4	3	1	0	0	0	0	0
	Twelve years (total)	.250	652	1634	166	408	61	7	33	180

MILT STOCK

B. July 11, 1893, Chicago, Ill.
D. July 16, 1977, Montrose, Ala.
B.R., T.R. 5'8" 154 lbs.
(3RD BASE)

YEAR	CLUB	BA	G	AB	R	H	2B	3B	HR	RBI
1913	New York (N)	.176	7	17	2	3	1	0	0	1
1914	New York (N)	.263	115	365	52	96	17	1	3	41
1915	Philadelphia (N)	.260	69	227	37	59	7	3	1	15
1916	Philadelphia (N)	.281	132	509	61	143	25	6	1	43
1917	Philadelphia (N)	.264	150	564	76	149	27	6	3	53
1918	Philadelphia (N)	.274	123	481	62	132	14	1	1	42
1919	St. Louis (N)	.307	135	492	56	151	16	4	0	52
1920	St. Louis (N)	.319	155	639	85	204	28	6	0	76
1921	St. Louis (N)	.307	149	587	96	180	27	6	3	84
1922	St. Louis (N)	.305	151	581	85	177	33	9	5	79
1923	St. Louis (N)	.289	151	603	63	174	33	3	2	96
1924	BROOKLYN (N)	.242	142	561	66	136	14	4	2	52
1925	BROOKLYN (N)	.328	146	615	98	202	28	9	1	62
1926	BROOKLYN (N)	.000	3	8	0	0	0	0	0	0
	Fourteen years	.289	1628	6249	839	1806	270	58	22	696
World Series										
	One year	.118	5	17	1	2	1	0	0	0

SAMMY STRANG

B. Dec. 16, 1876, Chattanooga, Tenn.
D. March 13, 1932, Chattanooga, Tenn.
B.B., T.R.
(3RD BASE, 2ND BASE, OUTFIELD)

YEAR	CLUB	BA	G	AB	R	H	2B	3B	HR	RBI
1896	Louisville (N)	.261	14	46	6	12	0	0	0	7
1900	Chicago (N)	.284	27	102	15	29	3	0	0	9
1901	New York (N)	.282	135	493	55	139	14	6	1	34
1902	Chicago (A)									
1902	Chicago (N)									
	(year totals)	.296	140	547	109	162	18	5	3	46
1903	BROOKLYN (N)	.272	135	508	101	138	21	5	0	38
1904	BROOKLYN (N)	.192	77	271	28	52	11	0	1	9
1905	New York (N)	.259	111	294	51	76	9	4	3	29
1906	New York (N)	.319	113	313	50	100	16	4	4	49
1907	New York (N)	.252	123	306	56	77	20	4	4	30
1908	New York (N)	.094	28	53	8	5	0	0	0	2
	Ten years	.269	903	2933	479	790	112	28	16	253
World Series										
	One year	.000	1	1	0	0	0	0	0	0

JOE STRIPP

B. Feb. 3, 1903, Harrison, N.J.
B.R., T.R. 5'11½" 175 lbs.
(3RD BASE)

YEAR	CLUB	BA	G	AB	R	H	2B	3B	HR	RBI
1928	Cincinnati (N)	.288	42	139	18	40	7	3	1	17
1929	Cincinnati (N)	.214	64	187	24	40	3	2	3	20

YEAR	CLUB	BA	G	AB	R	H	2B	3B	HR	RBI
1930	Cincinnati (N)	.306	130	464	74	142	37	6	3	64
1931	Cincinnati (N)	.324	105	426	71	138	26	2	3	42
1932	BROOKLYN (N)	.303	138	534	94	162	36	9	6	64
1933	BROOKLYN (N)	.277	141	537	69	149	20	7	1	51
1934	BROOKLYN (N)	.315	104	384	50	121	19	6	1	40
1935	BROOKLYN (N)	.306	109	373	44	114	13	5	3	43
1936	BROOKLYN (N)	.317	110	439	51	139	31	1	1	60
1937	BROOKLYN (N)	.243	90	300	37	73	10	2	1	26
1938	St. Louis (N)									
1938	Boston (N)									
	(year totals)	.280	113	428	43	120	17	0	1	37
	Eleven years	.294	1146	4211	575	1238	219	43	24	464

DICK STUART   B. Nov. 7, 1932, San Francisco, Calif.
B.R., T.R. 6'4" 212 lbs.
(1ST BASE)

YEAR	CLUB	BA	G	AB	R	H	2B	3B	HR	RBI
1966	LOS ANGELES (N)	.264	38	91	4	24	1	0	3	9
	Ten years (total)	.264	1112	3997	506	1055	157	30	228	743

BILL SUDAKIS   B. March 27, 1946, Joliet, Ill.
B.B., T.R. 6'1" 190 lbs.
(3RD BASE)

YEAR	CLUB	BA	G	AB	R	H	2B	3B	HR	RBI
1968	LOS ANGELES (N)	.276	24	87	11	24	4	2	3	12
1969	LOS ANGELES (N)	.234	132	462	50	108	17	5	14	53
1970	LOS ANGELES (N)	.264	94	269	37	71	11	0	14	44
1971	LOS ANGELES (N)	.193	41	83	10	16	3	0	3	7
1972	New York (N)	.143	18	49	3	7	0	0	1	7
1973	Texas (A)	.255	82	235	32	60	11	0	15	43
1974	New York (A)	.232	89	259	26	60	8	0	7	39
1975	California (A)									
1975	Cleveland (A)									
	(year totals)	.154	50	104	8	16	2	0	2	9
	Eight years	.234	530	1548	177	362	56	7	59	214

CLYDE SUKEFORTH   B. Nov. 30, 1901, Washington, Maine
B.L., T.R. 5'10" 155 lbs.
(CATCHER)

YEAR	CLUB	BA	G	AB	R	H	2B	3B	HR	RBI
1932	BROOKLYN (N)	.234	59	111	14	26	4	4	0	12
1933	BROOKLYN (N)	.056	20	36	1	2	0	0	0	0
1934	BROOKLYN (N)	.163	27	43	5	7	1	0	0	1
1945	BROOKLYN (N)	.294	18	51	2	15	1	0	0	1
	Ten years (total)	.264	486	1237	122	326	50	14	2	96

BILLY SULLIVAN   B. Oct. 23, 1910, Chicago, Ill.
B.L., T.R. 6' 170 lbs.
(CATCHER, 1ST BASE, 3RD BASE, OUTFIELD)

YEAR	CLUB	BA	G	AB	R	H	2B	3B	HR	RBI
1942	BROOKLYN (N)	.267	43	101	11	27	2	1	1	14
	Twelve years (total)	.289	962	2840	347	820	152	32	29	388

ART SUNDAY   B. Jan. 21, 1862, Springfield, Ohio
Deceased
(OUTFIELD)

YEAR	CLUB	BA	G	AB	R	H	2B	3B	HR	RBI
1890	BROOKLYN (P)	.265	24	83	26	22	5	1	0	13

TOMMY TATUM B. July 16, 1919, Boyd, Texas
B.R., T.R. 6' 185 lbs.
(OUTFIELD)

YEAR	CLUB	BA	G	AB	R	H	2B	3B	HR	RBI
1941	BROOKLYN (N)	.167	8	12	1	2	1	0	0	1
1947	BROOKLYN (N)	.000	4							
	Two years (total)	.258	81	194	20	50	6	2	1	17

DANNY TAYLOR B. Dec. 23, 1900, Lash, Pa.
D. Oct. 13, 1972, Latrobe, Pa.
B.R., T.R. 5'10" 190 lbs.
(OUTFIELD)

YEAR	CLUB	BA	G	AB	R	H	2B	3B	HR	RBI
1926	Washington (A)	.300	21	50	10	15	0	1	1	5
1929	Chicago (N)	.000	2	3	0	0	0	0	0	0
1930	Chicago (N)	.283	74	219	43	62	14	3	2	37
1931	Chicago (N)	.300	88	270	48	81	13	6	5	41
1932	Chicago (N)									
1932	BROOKLYN (N)	.324	105	395	84	128	22	7	11	48
	(year totals)	.319	111	417	87	133	24	7	11	51
1933	BROOKLYN (N)	.285	103	358	75	102	21	9	9	40
1934	BROOKLYN (N)	.299	120	405	62	121	24	6	7	57
1935	BROOKLYN (N)	.290	112	352	51	102	19	5	7	59
1936	BROOKLYN (N)	.293	43	116	12	34	6	0	2	15
	Nine years	.297	674	2190	388	650	121	37	44	305

ZACK TAYLOR B. July 27, 1898, Yulee, Fla.
D. July 6, 1974, Orlando, Fla.
B.R., T.R. 5'11½" 180 lbs.
(CATCHER)

YEAR	CLUB	BA	G	AB	R	H	2B	3B	HR	RBI
1920	BROOKLYN (N)	.385	9	13	3	5	2	0	0	5
1921	BROOKLYN (N)	.196	30	102	6	20	0	2	0	8
1922	BROOKLYN (N)	.214	7	14	0	3	0	0	0	2
1923	BROOKLYN (N)	.288	96	337	29	97	11	6	0	46
1924	BROOKLYN (N)	.290	99	345	36	100	9	4	1	39
1925	BROOKLYN (N)	.310	109	352	33	109	16	4	3	44
1926	Boston (N)	.255	125	432	36	110	22	3	0	42
1927	Boston (N)									
1927	New York (N)									
	(year totals)	.234	113	354	26	83	9	4	1	35
1928	Boston (N)	.251	125	399	36	100	15	1	2	30
1929	Boston (N)									
1929	Chicago (N)									
	(year totals)	.266	98	316	37	84	23	3	1	41
1930	Chicago (N)	.232	32	95	12	22	2	1	1	11
1931	Chicago (N)	.250	8	4	0	1	0	0	0	0
1932	Chicago (N)	.200	21	30	2	6	1	0	0	3
1933	Chicago (N)	.000	16	11	0	0	0	0	0	0
1934	New York (A)	.143	4	7	0	1	0	0	0	0
1935	BROOKLYN (N)	.130	26	54	2	7	3	0	0	5
	Sixteen years	.261	918	2865	258	748	113	28	9	311
World Series	One year	.176	5	17	0	3	0	0	0	3

DICK TEED B. March 8, 1926, Springfield, Mass.
B.B., T.R. 5'11" 180 lbs.

YEAR	CLUB	BA	G	AB	R	H	2B	3B	HR	RBI
1953	BROOKLYN (N)	.000	1	1	0	0	0	0	0	0

JOE TEPSIC B. Sept. 18, 1923, Slovan, Pa.
B.R., T.R. 5'9" 170 lbs.
(OUTFIELD)

YEAR	CLUB	BA	G	AB	R	H	2B	3B	HR	RBI
1946	BROOKLYN (N)	.000	15	5	2	0	0	0	0	0

WAYNE TERWILLIGER
B. June 27, 1925, Clare, Mich.
B.R., T.R. 5'11" 165 lbs.
(2ND BASE)

YEAR	CLUB	BA	G	AB	R	H	2B	3B	HR	RBI
1951	BROOKLYN (N)	.280	37	50	11	14	1	0	0	4
	Nine years (total)	.240	666	2091	271	501	93	10	22	162

AL TESCH
B. Jan. 27, 1891, Jersey City, N.J.
D. Aug. 3, 1947, Jersey City, N.J.
B.B., T.R. 5'10" 155 lbs.
(2ND BASE)

YEAR	CLUB	BA	G	AB	R	H	2B	3B	HR	RBI
1915	BROOKLYN (F)	.286	8	7	2	2	1	0	0	2

DERREL THOMAS
B. Jan. 14, 1951, Los Angeles, Calif.
B.B., T.R. 6' 160 lbs.
(2ND BASE, OUTFIELD, SHORTSTOP)

YEAR	CLUB	BA	G	AB	R	H	2B	3B	HR	RBI
1971	Houston (N)	.000	5	5	0	0	0	0	0	0
1972	San Diego (N)	.230	130	500	48	115	15	5	5	36
1973	San Diego (N)	.238	113	404	41	96	7	1	0	22
1974	San Diego (N)	.247	141	523	48	129	24	6	3	41
1975	San Francisco (N)	.276	144	540	99	149	21	9	6	48
1976	San Francisco (N)	.232	81	272	38	63	5	4	2	19
1977	San Francisco (N)	.267	148	506	75	135	13	10	8	44
1978	San Diego (N)	.227	128	352	36	80	10	2	3	26
1979	LOS ANGELES (N)	.256	141	406	47	104	15	4	5	44
1980	LOS ANGELES (N)	.266	117	297	32	79	18	3	1	22
1981	LOS ANGELES (N)	.248	80	218	25	54	4	0	4	24
1982	LOS ANGELES (N)	.265	66	98	13	26	2	1	0	2
1983	LOS ANGELES (N)	.250	118	192	38	48	6	6	2	8
	Thirteen years	.250	1412	4313	540	1078	140	51	39	436
Divisional Playoff	One year	.000	4	2	1	0	0	0	0	0
League Championship	One year	1.000	2	1	2	1	0	0	0	0
World Series	One year	.000	5	7	2	0	0	0	0	1

RAY THOMAS
B. July 8, 1912, Dover, N.H.
B.R., T.R. 5'10½" 175 lbs.
(CATCHER)

YEAR	CLUB	BA	G	AB	R	H	2B	3B	HR	RBI
1938	BROOKLYN (N)	.333	1	3	1	1	0	0	0	0

GARY THOMASSON
B. July 29, 1951, San Diego, Calif.
B.L., T.L. 6'1" 180 lbs.
(OUTFIELD, 1ST BASE)

YEAR	CLUB	BA	G	AB	R	H	2B	3B	HR	RBI
1972	San Francisco (N)	.333	10	27	5	9	1	1	0	1
1973	San Francisco (N)	.285	112	235	35	67	10	4	4	30
1974	San Francisco (N)	.244	120	315	41	77	14	3	2	29
1975	San Francisco (N)	.227	114	326	44	74	12	3	7	32
1976	San Francisco (N)	.259	103	328	45	85	20	5	8	38
1977	San Francisco (N)	.256	145	446	63	114	24	6	17	71
1978	Oakland (A)									
1978	New York (A)									
	(year totals)	.233	102	270	37	63	8	2	8	36
1979	LOS ANGELES (N)	.248	115	315	39	78	11	1	14	45
1980	LOS ANGELES (N)	.216	80	111	6	24	3	0	1	12
	Nine years	.249	901	2373	315	591	103	25	61	294
League Championship	One year	.000	3	1	0	0	0	0	0	0
World Series	One year	.250	3	4	0	1	0	0	0	0

DON THOMPSON

B. Dec. 28, 1923, Swepsonville, N.C.
B.L., T.L. 6' 185 lbs.
(OUTFIELD)

YEAR	CLUB	BA	G	AB	R	H	2B	3B	HR	RBI
1949	Boston (N)	.182	7	11	0	2	0	0	0	0
1951	BROOKLYN (N)	.229	80	118	25	27	3	0	0	6
1953	BROOKLYN (N)	.242	96	153	25	37	5	0	1	12
1954	BROOKLYN (N)	.040	34	25	2	1	0	0	0	1
	Four years	.218	217	307	52	67	8	0	1	19
World Series										
	One year	—	2	0	0	0	0	0	0	0

FRESCO THOMPSON

B. June 6, 1902, Centreville, Ala.
D. Nov. 20, 1968, Fullerton, Calif.
B.R., T.R. 5'8" 150 lbs.
(2ND BASE)

YEAR	CLUB	BA	G	AB	R	H	2B	3B	HR	RBI
1931	BROOKLYN (N)	.265	74	181	26	48	6	1	1	21
1932	BROOKLYN (N)	.000	3	1	0	0	0	0	0	0
	Nine years (total)	.298	669	2560	400	762	149	34	13	249

TIM THOMPSON

B. March 1, 1924, Coalport, Pa.
B.L., T.R. 5'11" 190 lbs.
(CATCHER)

YEAR	CLUB	BA	G	AB	R	H	2B	3B	HR	RBI
1954	BROOKLYN (N)	.154	10	13	2	2	1	0	0	1
	Four years (total)	.238	187	517	49	123	24	2	8	47

COTTON TIERNEY

B. Feb. 10, 1894, Kansas City, Kan.
D. April 18, 1953, Kansas City, Mo.
B.R., T.R. 5'8" 175 lbs.
(2ND BASE, 3RD BASE)

YEAR	CLUB	BA	G	AB	R	H	2B	3B	HR	RBI
1925	BROOKLYN (N)	.257	92	265	27	68	14	4	2	39
	Six years (total)	.296	630	2299	266	681	119	30	31	331

AL TODD

B. Jan. 7, 1904, Troy, N.Y.
B.R., T.R. 6'1" 198 lbs.
(CATCHER)

YEAR	CLUB	BA	G	AB	R	H	2B	3B	HR	RBI
1939	BROOKLYN (N)	.278	86	245	28	68	10	0	5	32
	Eleven years (total)	.276	863	2785	286	768	119	29	35	366

BERT TOOLEY

B. Aug. 30, 1886, Howell, Mich.
D. Aug. 17, 1976, Marshall, Mich.
B.R., T.R. 5'10" 155 lbs.
(SHORTSTOP)

YEAR	CLUB	BA	G	AB	R	H	2B	3B	HR	RBI
1911	BROOKLYN (N)	.206	119	433	55	89	11	3	1	29
1912	BROOKLYN (N)	.234	77	265	34	62	6	5	2	37
	Two years	.216	196	698	89	151	17	8	3	66

JEFF TORBORG

B. Nov. 26, 1941, Plainfield, N.J.
B.R., T.R. 6'½" 195 lbs.
(CATCHER)

YEAR	CLUB	BA	G	AB	R	H	2B	3B	HR	RBI
1964	LOS ANGELES (N)	.233	28	43	4	10	1	1	0	4
1965	LOS ANGELES (N)	.240	56	150	8	36	5	1	3	13
1966	LOS ANGELES (N)	.225	46	120	4	27	3	0	1	13
1967	LOS ANGELES (N)	.214	76	196	11	42	4	1	2	12
1968	LOS ANGELES (N)	.161	37	93	2	15	2	0	0	4
1969	LOS ANGELES (N)	.185	51	124	7	23	4	0	0	7

YEAR	CLUB	BA	G	AB	R	H	2B	3B	HR	RBI
1970	LOS ANGELES (N)	.231	64	134	11	31	8	0	1	17
1971	California (A)	.203	55	123	6	25	5	0	0	5
1972	California (A)	.209	59	153	5	32	3	0	0	8
1973	California (A)	.220	102	255	20	56	7	0	1	18
	Ten years	.214	574	1391	78	297	42	3	8	101

DICK TRACEWSKI B. Feb. 3, 1935, Eynon, Pa.
B.R., T.R. 5'11" 160 lbs.
(SHORTSTOP, 2ND BASE, 3RD BASE)

YEAR	CLUB	BA	G	AB	R	H	2B	3B	HR	RBI
1962	LOS ANGELES (N)	.000	15	2	3	0	0	0	0	0
1963	LOS ANGELES (N)	.226	104	217	23	49	2	1	1	10
1964	LOS ANGELES (N)	.247	106	304	31	75	13	4	1	26
1965	LOS ANGELES (N)	.215	78	186	17	40	6	0	1	20
1966	Detroit (A)	.194	81	124	15	24	1	1	0	7
1967	Detroit (A)	.280	74	107	19	30	4	2	1	9
1968	Detroit (A)	.156	90	212	30	33	3	1	4	15
1969	Detroit (A)	.139	66	79	10	11	2	0	0	4
	Eight years	.213	614	1231	148	262	31	9	8	91
World Series	Three years	.133	12	30	2	4	0	0	0	0

GEORGE TREADWAY B. Nov. 11, 1866, Greenup County, Ky.
D. Nov. 17, 1928, Riverside, Calif.
B.L.
(OUTFIELD)

YEAR	CLUB	BA	G	AB	R	H	2B	3B	HR	RBI
1893	Baltimore (N)	.260	115	458	78	119	16	17	1	67
1894	BROOKLYN (N)	.328	123	479	124	157	27	26	4	102
1895	BROOKLYN (N)	.257	86	339	54	87	14	3	7	54
1896	Louisville (N)	.143	2	7	0	1	0	0	0	1
	Four years	.284	326	1283	256	364	57	46	12	224

NICK TREMARK B. Oct. 15, 1912, Yonkers, N.Y.
B.L., T.L. 5'5" 150 lbs.
(OUTFIELD)

YEAR	CLUB	BA	G	AB	R	H	2B	3B	HR	RBI
1934	BROOKLYN (N)	.250	17	28	3	7	1	0	0	6
1935	BROOKLYN (N)	.231	10	13	1	3	1	0	0	3
1936	BROOKLYN (N)	.250	8	32	6	8	2	0	0	1
	Three years	.247	35	73	10	18	4	0	0	10

OVERTON TREMPER B. March 22, 1906, Brooklyn, N.Y.
B.R., T.R. 5'10" 163 lbs.
(OUTFIELD)

YEAR	CLUB	BA	G	AB	R	H	2B	3B	HR	RBI
1927	BROOKLYN (N)	.233	36	60	4	14	0	0	0	4
1928	BROOKLYN (N)	.194	10	31	1	6	2	1	0	1
	Two years	.220	46	91	5	20	2	1	0	5

TOMMY TUCKER B. Oct. 28, 1863, Holyoke, Mass.
D. Oct. 22, 1935, Montague, Mass.
B.B., T.R. 5'11" 165 lbs.
(1ST BASE)

YEAR	CLUB	BA	G	AB	R	H	2B	3B	HR	RBI
1898	BROOKLYN (N)	.279	73							
	Thirteen years (total)	.290	1687	6479	1084	1882	240	85	42	848

TY TYSON
B. June 1, 1892, Wilkes-Barre, Pa.
D. Aug. 16, 1953, Buffalo, N.Y.
B.R., T.R. 5'11" 169 lbs.
(OUTFIELD)

YEAR	CLUB	BA	G	AB	R	H	2B	3B	HR	RBI
1928	BROOKLYN (N)	.271	59	210	25	57	11	1	1	21
	Three years (total)	.280	199	704	89	197	34	4	5	73

BOBBY VALENTINE
B. May 13, 1950, Stamford, Conn.
B.R., T.R. 5'10" 189 lbs.
(SHORTSTOP, OUTFIELD, 2ND BASE, 3RD BASE)

YEAR	CLUB	BA	G	AB	R	H	2B	3B	HR	RBI
1969	LOS ANGELES (N)	—	5	0	3	0	0	0	0	0
1971	LOS ANGELES (N)	.249	101	281	32	70	10	2	1	25
1972	LOS ANGELES (N)	.274	119	391	42	107	11	2	3	32
1973	California (A)	.302	32	126	12	38	5	2	1	13
1974	California (A)	.261	117	371	39	97	10	3	3	39
1975	California (A)									
1975	San Diego (N)									
	(year totals)	.250	33	72	6	18	2	0	1	6
1976	San Diego (N)	.367	15	49	3	18	4	0	0	4
1977	San Diego (N)									
1977	New York (N)									
	(year totals)	.153	86	150	13	23	4	0	2	13
1978	New York (N)	.269	69	160	17	43	7	0	1	18
1979	Seattle (A)	.276	62	98	9	27	6	0	0	7
	Ten years	.260	639	1698	176	441	59	9	12	157

ELMER VALO
B. March 5, 1921, Ribnik, Czechoslovakia
B.L., T.R. 5'11" 190 lbs.
(OUTFIELD)

YEAR	CLUB	BA	G	AB	R	H	2B	3B	HR	RBI
1957	BROOKLYN (N)	.273	81	161	14	44	10	1	4	26
1958	LOS ANGELES (N)	.248	65	101	9	25	2	1	1	14
	Twenty years (total)	.282	1806	5029	768	1420	228	73	58	601

DEACON VAN BUREN
B. Dec. 14, 1870, La Salle County, Ill.
D. June 29, 1957, Portland, Ore.
(OUTFIELD)

YEAR	CLUB	BA	G	AB	R	H	2B	3B	HR	RBI
1904	BROOKLYN (N)	1.000	1	1	0	1	0	0	0	0

GEORGE VAN HALTREN
B. March 30, 1866, St. Louis, Mo.
D. Sept. 29, 1945, Oakland, Calif.
B.L., T.L. 5'11" 170 lbs.
(OUTFIELD)

YEAR	CLUB	BA	G	AB	R	H	2B	3B	HR	RBI
*1890	BROOKLYN (P)	.335	92	376	84	126	8	9	5	54
	Seventeen years (total)	.316	1984	8021	1639	2532	289	161	69	1014

ARKY VAUGHAN
B. March 9, 1912, Clifty, Ark.
D. Aug. 30, 1952, Eagleville, Calif.
B.L., T.R. 5'10½" 175 lbs.
(SHORTSTOP)

YEAR	CLUB	BA	G	AB	R	H	2B	3B	HR	RBI
1932	Pittsburgh (N)	.318	129	497	71	158	15	10	4	61
1933	Pittsburgh (N)	.314	152	573	85	180	29	19	9	97
1934	Pittsburgh (N)	.333	149	558	115	186	41	11	12	94
1935	Pittsburgh (N)	.385	137	499	108	192	34	10	19	99
1936	Pittsburgh (N)	.335	156	568	122	190	30	11	9	78
1937	Pittsburgh (N)	.322	126	469	71	151	17	17	5	72
1938	Pittsburgh (N)	.322	148	541	88	174	35	5	7	68
1939	Pittsburgh (N)	.306	152	595	94	182	30	11	6	62
1940	Pittsburgh (N)	.300	156	594	113	178	40	15	7	95

YEAR	CLUB	BA	G	AB	R	H	2B	3B	HR	RBI
1941	Pittsburgh (N)	.316	106	374	69	118	20	7	6	38
1942	BROOKLYN (N)	.277	128	495	82	137	18	4	2	49
1943	BROOKLYN (N)	.305	149	610	112	186	39	6	5	66
1947	BROOKLYN (N)	.325	64	126	24	41	5	2	2	25
1948	BROOKLYN (N)	.244	65	123	19	30	3	0	3	22
	Fourteen years	.318	1817	6622	1173	2103	356	128	96	926

ZOILO VERSALLES B. Dec. 18, 1939, Vedado, Cuba
B.R., T.R. 5'10" 146 lbs.
(SHORTSTOP)

YEAR	CLUB	BA	G	AB	R	H	2B	3B	HR	RBI
1968	LOS ANGELES (N)	.196	122	403	29	79	16	3	2	24
	Twelve years (total)	.242	1400	5141	650	1246	230	63	95	471

JOE VOSMIK B. April 4, 1910, Cleveland, Ohio
D. Jan. 27, 1962, Cleveland, Ohio
B.R., T.R. 6' 185 lbs.
(OUTFIELD)

YEAR	CLUB	BA	G	AB	R	H	2B	3B	HR	RBI
1940	BROOKLYN (N)	.282	116	404	45	114	14	6	1	42
1941	BROOKLYN (N)	.196	25	56	0	11	0	0	0	4
	Thirteen years (total)	.307	1414	5472	818	1682	335	92	65	874

DIXIE WALKER B. Sept. 24, 1910, Villa Rica, Ga.
B.L., T.R. 6'1" 175 lbs.
(OUTFIELD)

YEAR	CLUB	BA	G	AB	R	H	2B	3B	HR	RBI
1931	New York (A)	.300	2	10	1	3	2	0	0	1
1933	New York (A)	.274	98	328	68	90	15	7	15	51
1934	New York (A)	.118	17	17	2	2	0	0	0	0
1935	New York (A)	.154	8	13	1	2	1	0	0	1
1936	New York (A)									
1936	Chicago (A)									
	(year totals)	.289	32	90	15	26	2	2	1	16
1937	Chicago (A)	.302	154	593	105	179	28	16	9	95
1938	Detroit (A)	.308	127	454	84	140	27	6	6	43
1939	Detroit (A)									
1939	BROOKLYN (N)	.280	61	225	27	63	6	4	2	38
	(year totals)	.290	104	379	57	110	10	9	6	57
1940	BROOKLYN (N)	.308	143	556	75	171	37	8	6	66
1941	BROOKLYN (N)	.311	148	531	88	165	32	8	9	71
1942	BROOKLYN (N)	.290	118	393	57	114	28	1	6	54
1943	BROOKLYN (N)	.302	138	540	83	163	32	6	5	71
1944	BROOKLYN (N)	.357	147	535	77	191	37	8	13	91
1945	BROOKLYN (N)	.300	154	607	102	182	42	9	8	124
1946	BROOKLYN (N)	.319	150	576	80	184	29	9	9	116
1947	BROOKLYN (N)	.306	148	529	77	162	31	3	9	94
1948	Pittsburgh (N)	.316	129	408	39	129	19	3	2	54
1949	Pittsburgh (N)	.282	88	181	26	51	4	1	1	18
	Eighteen years	.306	1905	6740	1037	2064	376	96	105	1023
World Series										
	Two years	.222	12	45	4	10	3	0	1	4

RUBE WALKER B. May 16, 1926, Lenoir, N.C.
B.L., T.R. 6' 175 lbs.
(CATCHER)

YEAR	CLUB	BA	G	AB	R	H	2B	3B	HR	RBI
1948	Chicago (N)	.275	79	171	17	47	8	0	5	26
1949	Chicago (N)	.244	56	172	11	42	4	1	3	22
1950	Chicago (N)	.230	74	213	19	49	7	1	6	16
1951	Chicago (N)									
1951	BROOKLYN (N)	.243	36	74	6	18	4	0	2	9
	(year totals)	.238	73	181	15	43	8	0	4	14
1952	BROOKLYN (N)	.259	46	139	9	36	8	0	1	19
1953	BROOKLYN (N)	.242	43	95	5	23	6	0	3	9
1954	BROOKLYN (N)	.181	50	155	12	28	7	0	5	23

YEAR	CLUB	BA	G	AB	R	H	2B	3B	HR	RBI
1955	BROOKLYN (N)	.252	48	103	6	26	5	0	2	13
1956	BROOKLYN (N)	.212	54	146	5	31	6	1	3	20
1957	BROOKLYN (N)	.181	60	166	12	30	8	0	2	23
1958	LOS ANGELES (N)	.114	25	44	3	5	2	0	1	7
	Eleven years	.227	608	1585	114	360	69	3	35	192
World Series										
	One Year	.000	2	2	0	0	0	0	0	0

JOE WALL   B. July 24, 1873, Brooklyn, N.Y.
D. July 17, 1936, Brooklyn, N.Y.
B.L., T.L.
(CATCHER, OUTFIELD)

YEAR	CLUB	BA	G	AB	R	H	2B	3B	HR	RBI
1902	BROOKLYN (N)	.167	5	18	0	3	0	0	0	0
	Two years (total)	.300	15	40	2	12	2	0	0	1

LEE WALLS   B. Jan. 6, 1933, San Diego, Calif.
B.R., T.R. 6'3" 205 lbs.
(OUTFIELD)

YEAR	CLUB	BA	G	AB	R	H	2B	3B	HR	RBI
1952	Pittsburgh (N)	.188	32	80	6	15	0	1	2	5
1956	Pittsburgh (N)	.274	143	474	72	130	20	11	11	54
1957	Pittsburgh (N)									
1957	Chicago (N)									
	(year totals)	.237	125	388	45	92	11	5	6	33
1958	Chicago (N)	.304	136	513	80	156	19	3	24	72
1959	Chicago (N)	.257	120	354	43	91	18	3	8	33
1960	Cincinnati (N)									
1960	Philadelphia (N)									
	(year totals)	.223	94	265	31	59	9	3	4	26
1961	Philadelphia (N)	.280	91	261	32	73	6	4	8	30
1962	LOS ANGELES (N)	.266	60	109	9	29	3	1	0	17
1963	LOS ANGELES (N)	.233	64	86	12	20	1	0	3	11
1964	LOS ANGELES (N)	.179	37	28	1	5	1	0	0	3
	Ten years	.262	902	2558	331	670	88	31	66	284

LLOYD WANER   B. March 16, 1906, Harrah, Okla.
B.L., T.R. 5'9" 150 lbs.
(OUTFIELD)

YEAR	CLUB	BA	G	AB	R	H	2B	3B	HR	RBI
1944	BROOKLYN (N)	.286	15	14	3	4	0	0	0	1
	Eighteen years (total)	.316	1992	7772	1201	2459	281	118	28	598

PAUL WANER   B. April 16, 1903, Harrah, Okla.
D. Aug. 29, 1965, Sarasota, Fla.
B.L., T.L. 5'8½" 153 lbs.
(OUTFIELD)

YEAR	CLUB	BA	G	AB	R	H	2B	3B	HR	RBI
1926	Pittsburgh (N)	.336	144	536	101	180	35	22	8	79
1927	Pittsburgh (N)	.380	155	623	113	237	40	17	9	131
1928	Pittsburgh (N)	.370	152	602	142	223	50	19	6	86
1929	Pittsburgh (N)	.336	151	596	131	200	43	15	15	100
1930	Pittsburgh (N)	.368	145	589	117	217	32	18	8	77
1931	Pittsburgh (N)	.322	150	559	88	180	35	10	6	70
1932	Pittsburgh (N)	.341	154	630	107	215	62	10	7	82
1933	Pittsburgh (N)	.309	154	618	101	191	38	16	7	70
1934	Pittsburgh (N)	.362	146	599	122	217	32	16	14	90
1935	Pittsburgh (N)	.321	139	549	98	176	29	12	11	78
1936	Pittsburgh (N)	.373	148	585	107	218	53	9	5	94
1937	Pittsburgh (N)	.354	154	619	94	219	30	9	2	74
1938	Pittsburgh (N)	.280	148	625	77	175	31	6	6	69
1939	Pittsburgh (N)	.328	125	461	62	151	30	6	3	45
1940	Pittsburgh (N)	.290	89	238	32	69	16	1	1	32
1941	BROOKLYN (N)	.171	11	35	5	6	0	0	0	4
1941	Boston (N)									
	(year totals)	.267	106	329	45	88	10	2	2	50

YEAR	CLUB	BA	G	AB	R	H	2B	3B	HR	RBI
1942	Boston (N)	.258	114	333	43	86	17	1	1	39
1943	BROOKLYN (N)	.311	82	225	29	70	16	0	1	26
1944	BROOKLYN (N)	.287	83	136	16	39	4	1	0	16
1944	New York (A)									
	(year totals)	.280	92	143	17	40	4	1	0	17
1945	New York (A)	—	1	0	0	0	0	0	0	0
	Twenty years	.333	2549	9459	1626	3152	603	190	112	1309
World Series										
	One year	.333	4	15	0	5	1	0	0	3

CHUCK WARD B. July 31, 1893, St. Louis, Mo.
D. April 4, 1969, St. Petersburg, Fla.
B.R., T.R. 5'11½" 170 lbs.
(SHORTSTOP)

YEAR	CLUB	BA	G	AB	R	H	2B	3B	HR	RBI
1917	Pittsburgh (N)	.236	125	423	25	100	12	3	0	43
1918	BROOKLYN (N)	.333	2	6	0	2	0	0	0	3
1919	BROOKLYN (N)	.233	45	150	7	35	1	2	0	8
1920	BROOKLYN (N)	.155	19	71	7	11	1	0	0	4
1921	BROOKLYN (N)	.071	12	28	1	2	1	0	0	0
1922	BROOKLYN (N)	.275	33	91	12	25	5	1	0	14
	Six years	.228	236	769	52	175	20	6	0	72

MONTE WARD B. March 3, 1860, Bellefonte, Pa.
D. March 4, 1925, Augusta, Ga.
B.L., T.R. 5'9" 165 lbs.
(SHORTSTOP, 2ND BASE, PITCHER, OUTFIELD)

YEAR	CLUB	BA	G	AB	R	H	2B	3B	HR	RBI
*1890	BROOKLYN (P)	.369	128	561	134	207	15	12	4	60
1891	BROOKLYN (N)	.277	105	441	85	122	13	5	0	39
1892	BROOKLYN (N)	.265	148	614	109	163	13	3	2	47
1893	New York (N)	.328	135	588	129	193	27	9	2	77
1894	New York (N)	.265	136	540	100	143	12	5	0	77
	Seventeen years (total)	.278	1825	7647	1408	2123	232	97	26	686

*1878 Providence (N), 1883 New York (N)

PRESTON WARD B. July 24, 1927, Columbia, Mo.
B.L., T.R. 6'4" 190 lbs.
(1ST BASE)

YEAR	CLUB	BA	G	AB	R	H	2B	3B	HR	RBI
1948	BROOKLYN (N)	.260	42	146	9	38	9	2	1	21
	Nine years (total)	.253	744	2067	219	522	83	15	50	262

RUBE WARD B. Washington Court House, Ohio
D. Jan. 17, 1945, Akron, Ohio
(OUTFIELD)

YEAR	CLUB	BA	G	AB	R	H	2B	3B	HR	RBI
1902	BROOKLYN (N)	.290	13	31	4	9	1	0	0	2

JACK WARNER B. Aug. 29, 1903, Evansville, Ind.
B.R., T.R. 5'9½" 165 lbs.
(3RD BASE)

YEAR	CLUB	BA	G	AB	R	H	2B	3B	HR	RBI
1929	BROOKLYN (N)	.274	17	62	3	17	2	0	0	4
1930	BROOKLYN (N)	.320	21	25	4	8	1	0	0	0
1931	BROOKLYN (N)	.500	9	4	2	2	0	0	0	0
	Eight years (total)	.250	478	1546	199	387	52	20	1	120

JIMMY WASDELL B. May 15, 1914, Cleveland, Ohio
B.L., T.L. 5'11" 185 lbs.
(OUTFIELD, 1ST BASE)

YEAR	CLUB	BA	G	AB	R	H	2B	3B	HR	RBI
1937	Washington (A)	.255	32	110	13	28	4	4	2	12
1938	Washington (A)	.236	53	140	19	33	2	1	2	16
1939	Washington (A)	.303	29	109	12	33	5	1	0	13
1940	Washington (A)									
1940	BROOKLYN (N)	.278	77	230	35	64	14	4	3	37
	(year totals)	.253	87	265	38	67	15	4	3	37
1941	BROOKLYN (N)	.298	94	265	39	79	14	3	4	48
1942	Pittsburgh (N)	.259	122	409	44	106	11	2	3	38
1943	Pittsburgh (N)									
1943	Philadelphia (N)									
	(year totals)	.261	145	524	54	137	19	6	4	68
1944	Philadelphia (N)	.277	133	451	47	125	20	3	3	40
1945	Philadelphia (N)	.300	134	500	65	150	19	8	7	60
1946	Philadelphia (N)									
1946	Cleveland (A)									
	(year totals)	.261	58	92	8	24	0	2	1	9
1947	Cleveland (A)	.000	1	1	0	0	0	0	0	0
	Eleven years	.273	888	2866	339	782	109	34	29	341
World Series										
	One year	.200	3	5	0	1	1	0	0	2

RON WASHINGTON B. April 29, 1952, New Orleans, La.
B.R., T.R. 5'11" 155 lbs.
(SHORTSTOP)

YEAR	CLUB	BA	G	AB	R	H	2B	3B	HR	RBI
1977	LOS ANGELES (N)	.368	10	19	4	7	0	0	0	1
	Two years (total)	.252	38	103	12	26	3	1	0	6

GEORGE WATKINS B. June 4, 1902, Palestine, Texas
D. June 1, 1970, Houston, Texas
B.L., T.R. 6' 175 lbs.
(OUTFIELD)

YEAR	CLUB	BA	G	AB	R	H	2B	3B	HR	RBI
1936	BROOKLYN (N)	.255	105	364	54	93	24	6	4	43
	Seven years (total)	.288	904	3207	490	925	192	42	73	420

ART WATSON B. Jan. 11, 1884, Jeffersonville, Ky.
D. May 9, 1950, Buffalo, N.Y.
B.L., T.R. 5'10" 175 lbs.
(CATCHER)

YEAR	CLUB	BA	G	AB	R	H	2B	3B	HR	RBI
1914	BROOKLYN (F)	.283	22	46	7	13	4	1	1	3
1915	BROOKLYN (F)									
1915	Buffalo (F)									
	(year totals)	.388	31	49	10	19	1	3	1	14
	Two years	.337	53	95	17	32	5	4	2	17

GARY WEISS B. Dec. 27, 1955, Brenham, Texas
B.L., T.R. 5'10" 170 lbs.
(SHORTSTOP)

YEAR	CLUB	BA	G	AB	R	H	2B	3B	HR	RBI
1980	LOS ANGELES (N)	—	8	0	2	0	0	0	0	0
1981	LOS ANGELES (N)	.105	14	19	2	2	0	0	0	1
	Two years	.105	22	19	2	2	0	0	0	1

148 • **The Complete Dodgers Record Book**

JOHNNY WERHAS B. Feb. 7, 1938, Highland Park, Mich.
B.R., T.R. 6'2" 200 lbs.
(3RD BASE)

YEAR	CLUB	BA	G	AB	R	H	2B	3B	HR	RBI
1964	LOS ANGELES (N)	.193	29	83	6	16	2	1	0	8
1965	LOS ANGELES (N)	.000	4	3	1	0	0	0	0	0
1967	LOS ANGELES (N)	.143	7	7	0	1	0	0	0	0
1967	California (A)									
	(year totals)	.159	56	82	8	13	1	1	2	6
	Three years	.173	89	168	15	29	3	2	2	14

MAX WEST B. July 14, 1904, Sunset, Texas
D. April 25, 1971, Houston, Texas
B.R., T.R. 5'11" 165 lbs.
(OUTFIELD)

YEAR	CLUB	BA	G	AB	R	H	2B	3B	HR	RBI
1928	BROOKLYN (N)	.286	7	21	4	6	1	1	0	1
1929	BROOKLYN (N)	.250	5	8	1	2	1	0	0	1
	Two years	.276	12	29	5	8	2	1	0	2

TEX WESTERZIL B. March 7, 1891, Detroit, Mich.
D. June 27, 1964, San Antonio, Texas
B.R., T.R. 5'9½" 150 lbs.
(3RD BASE)

YEAR	CLUB	BA	G	AB	R	H	2B	3B	HR	RBI
1914	BROOKLYN (F)	.257	149	534	54	137	18	10	0	66
1915	BROOKLYN (F)									
	Two years (total)	.260	242	828	83	215	26	14	0	105

MACK WHEAT B. June 9, 1893, Polo, Mo.
D. Aug. 14, 1979, Los Banos, Calif.
B.R., T.R. 5'11½" 167 lbs.
(CATCHER)

YEAR	CLUB	BA	G	AB	R	H	2B	3B	HR	RBI
1915	BROOKLYN (N)	.071	8	14	0	1	0	0	0	0
1916	BROOKLYN (N)	.000	2	2	0	0	0	0	0	0
1917	BROOKLYN (N)	.133	29	60	2	8	1	0	0	0
1918	BROOKLYN (N)	.217	57	157	11	34	7	1	1	3
1919	BROOKLYN (N)	.205	47	112	5	23	3	0	0	8
	Seven years (total)	.204	231	602	34	123	23	5	4	35

ZACK WHEAT B. May 23, 1888, Hamilton, Mo.
D. March 11, 1972, Sedalia, Mo.
B.L., T.R. 5'10" 170 lbs.
(OUTFIELD)

YEAR	CLUB	BA	G	AB	R	H	2B	3B	HR	RBI
1909	BROOKLYN (N)	.304	26	102	15	31	7	3	0	4
1910	BROOKLYN (N)	.284	156	606	78	172	36	15	2	55
1911	BROOKLYN (N)	.287	140	534	55	153	26	13	5	76
1912	BROOKLYN (N)	.305	123	453	70	138	28	7	8	65
1913	BROOKLYN (N)	.301	138	535	64	161	28	10	7	71
1914	BROOKLYN (N)	.319	145	533	66	170	26	9	9	89
1915	BROOKLYN (N)	.258	146	528	64	136	15	12	5	66
1916	BROOKLYN (N)	.312	149	568	76	177	32	13	9	73
1917	BROOKLYN (N)	.312	109	362	38	113	15	11	1	41
1918	BROOKLYN (N)	.335	105	409	39	137	15	3	0	51
1919	BROOKLYN (N)	.297	137	536	70	159	23	11	5	62
1920	BROOKLYN (N)	.328	148	583	89	191	26	13	9	73
1921	BROOKLYN (N)	.320	148	568	91	182	31	10	14	85
1922	BROOKLYN (N)	.335	152	600	92	201	29	12	16	112
1923	BROOKLYN (N)	.375	98	349	63	131	13	5	8	65
1924	BROOKLYN (N)	.375	141	566	92	212	41	8	14	97
1925	BROOKLYN (N)	.359	150	616	125	221	42	14	14	103
1926	BROOKLYN (N)	.290	111	411	68	119	31	2	5	35
1927	Philadelphia (A)	.324	88	247	34	80	12	1	1	38
	Nineteen years	.317	2410	9106	1289	2884	476	172	132	1261

World Series

YEAR	CLUB	BA	G	AB	R	H	2B	3B	HR	RBI
1916	BROOKLYN (N)	.211	5	19	2	4	0	1	0	1
1920	BROOKLYN (N)	.333	7	27	2	9	2	0	0	2
	Two years	.283	12	46	4	13	2	1	0	3

ED WHEELER B. June 15, 1879, Sherman, Mich.
T.R.
(3RD BASE, 2ND BASE)

YEAR	CLUB	BA	G	AB	R	H	2B	3B	HR	RBI
1902	BROOKLYN (N)	.125	30	96	4	12	0	0	0	5

MYRON WHITE B. Aug. 1, 1957, Long Beach, Calif.
B.L., T.L. 5'11" 180 lbs.
(OUTFIELD)

YEAR	CLUB	BA	G	AB	R	H	2B	3B	HR	RBI
1978	LOS ANGELES (N)	.500	7	4	1	2	0	0	0	1

DICK WHITMAN B. Nov. 9, 1920, Woodburn, Ore.
B.L., T.R. 5'11" 170 lbs.
(OUTFIELD)

YEAR	CLUB	BA	G	AB	R	H	2B	3B	HR	RBI
1946	BROOKLYN (N)	.260	104	265	39	69	15	3	2	31
1947	BROOKLYN (N)	.400	4	10	1	4	0	0	0	2
1948	BROOKLYN (N)	.291	60	165	24	48	13	0	0	20
1949	BROOKLYN (N)	.184	23	49	8	9	2	0	0	2
1950	Philadelphia (N)	.250	75	132	21	33	7	0	0	12
1951	Philadelphia (N)	.118	19	17	0	2	0	0	0	0
	Six years	.259	285	638	93	165	37	3	2	67
World Series										
	Two years	.000	4	3	0	0	0	0	0	0

DICK WILLIAMS B. May 7, 1928, St. Louis, Mo.
B.R., T.R. 6' 190 lbs.
(OUTFIELD, 3RD BASE, 1ST BASE)

YEAR	CLUB	BA	G	AB	R	H	2B	3B	HR	RBI
1951	BROOKLYN (N)	.200	23	60	5	12	3	1	1	5
1952	BROOKLYN (N)	.309	36	68	13	21	4	1	0	11
1953	BROOKLYN (N)	.218	30	55	4	12	2	0	2	5
1954	BROOKLYN (N)	.147	16	34	5	5	0	0	1	2
1956	BROOKLYN (N)									
1956	Baltimore (A)									
	(year totals)	.286	94	360	45	103	18	4	11	37
1957	Baltimore (A)									
1957	Cleveland (A)									
	(year totals)	.261	114	372	49	97	17	2	7	34
1958	Baltimore (A)	.276	128	409	36	113	17	0	4	32
1959	Kansas City (A)	.266	130	488	72	130	33	1	16	75
1960	Kansas City (A)	.288	127	420	47	121	31	0	12	65
1961	Baltimore (A)	.206	103	310	37	64	15	2	8	24
1962	Baltimore (A)	.247	82	178	20	44	7	1	1	18
1963	Boston (A)	.257	79	136	15	35	8	0	2	12
1964	Boston (A)	.159	61	69	10	11	2	0	5	11
	Thirteen years	.260	1023	2959	358	768	157	12	70	331
World Series										
	One year	.500	3	2	0	1	0	0	0	0

RINALDO WILLIAMS B. Dec. 18, 1893, Santa Cruz, Calif.
D. April 24, 1966, Cottonwood, Ariz.
B.L., T.R.
(3RD BASE)

YEAR	CLUB	BA	G	AB	R	H	2B	3B	HR	RBI
1914	BROOKLYN (F)	.267	4	15	1	4	2	0	0	0

WOODY WILLIAMS B. Aug. 22, 1912, Pamplin, Va.
B.R., T.R. 5'11" 175 lbs.
(2ND BASE)

YEAR	CLUB	BA	G	AB	R	H	2B	3B	HR	RBI
1938	BROOKLYN (N)	.333	20	51	6	17	1	1	0	6
	Four years (total)	.250	338	1255	133	314	40	5	1	79

MAURY WILLS B. Oct. 2, 1932, Washington, D.C.
B.B., T.R. 5'11" 170 lbs.
(SHORTSTOP)

YEAR	CLUB	BA	G	AB	R	H	2B	3B	HR	RBI
1959	LOS ANGELES (N)	.260	83	242	27	63	5	2	0	7
1960	LOS ANGELES (N)	.295	148	516	75	152	15	2	0	27
1961	LOS ANGELES (N)	.282	148	613	105	173	12	10	1	31
1962	LOS ANGELES (N)	.299	165	695	130	208	13	10	6	48
1963	LOS ANGELES (N)	.302	134	527	83	159	19	3	0	34
1964	LOS ANGELES (N)	.275	158	630	81	173	15	5	2	34
1965	LOS ANGELES (N)	.286	158	650	92	186	14	7	0	33
1966	LOS ANGELES (N)	.273	143	594	60	162	14	2	1	39
1967	Pittsburgh (N)	.302	149	616	92	186	12	9	3	45
1968	Pittsburgh (N)	.278	153	627	76	174	12	6	0	31
1969	Montreal (N)									
1969	LOS ANGELES (N)	.297	104	434	57	129	7	8	4	39
	(year totals)	.274	151	623	80	171	10	8	4	47
1970	LOS ANGELES (N)	.270	132	522	77	141	19	3	0	34
1971	LOS ANGELES (N)	.281	149	601	73	169	14	3	3	44
1972	LOS ANGELES (N)	.129	71	132	16	17	3	1	0	4
	Fourteen years	.281	1942	7588	1067	2134	177	71	20	458

World Series

YEAR	CLUB	BA	G	AB	R	H	2B	3B	HR	RBI
1959	LOS ANGELES (N)	.250	6	20	2	5	0	0	0	1
1963	LOS ANGELES (N)	.133	4	15	1	2	0	0	0	0
1965	LOS ANGELES (N)	.367	7	30	3	11	3	0	0	3
1966	LOS ANGELES (N)	.077	4	13	0	1	0	0	0	0
	Four years	.244	21	78	6	19	3	0	0	4

BOB WILSON B. Feb. 22, 1928, Dallas, Texas
B.R., T.R. 5'11" 197 lbs.
(OUTFIELD)

YEAR	CLUB	BA	G	AB	R	H	2B	3B	HR	RBI
1958	LOS ANGELES (N)	.200	3	5	0	1	0	0	0	0

EDDIE WILSON B. Sept. 7, 1910, New Haven, Conn.
D. April 11, 1979, Hamden, Conn.
B.L., T.L. 5'11" 165 lbs.
(OUTFIELD)

YEAR	CLUB	BA	G	AB	R	H	2B	3B	HR	RBI
1936	BROOKLYN (N)	.347	52	173	28	60	8	1	3	25
1937	BROOKLYN (N)	.222	36	54	11	12	4	1	1	8
	Two years	.317	88	227	39	72	12	2	4	33

HACK WILSON B. April 26, 1900, Elwood City, Pa.
D. Nov. 23, 1948, Baltimore, Md.
B.R., T.R. 5'6" 190 lbs.
(OUTFIELD)

YEAR	CLUB	BA	G	AB	R	H	2B	3B	HR	RBI
1923	New York (N)	.200	3	10	0	2	0	0	0	0
1924	New York (N)	.295	107	383	62	113	19	12	10	57
1925	New York (N)	.239	62	180	28	43	7	4	6	30
1926	Chciago (N)	.321	142	529	97	170	36	8	21	109
1927	Chicago (N)	.318	146	551	119	175	30	12	30	129
1928	Chicago (N)	.313	145	520	89	163	32	9	31	120
1929	Chicago (N)	.345	150	574	135	198	30	5	39	159
1930	Chicago (N)	.356	155	585	146	208	35	6	56	190

YEAR	CLUB	BA	G	AB	R	H	2B	3B	HR	RBI
1931	Chicago (N)	.261	112	395	66	103	22	4	13	61
1932	BROOKLYN (N)	.297	135	481	77	143	37	5	23	123
1933	BROOKLYN (N)	.267	117	360	41	96	13	2	9	54
1934	BROOKLYN (N)									
1934	Philadelphia (N)									
	(year totals)	.245	74	192	24	47	5	0	6	30
	Twelve years	.307	1348	4760	884	1461	266	67	244	1062
World Series										
	Two years	.319	12	47	3	15	1	1	0	3

GORDIE WINDHORN
B. Dec. 19, 1933, Watseka, Ill.
B.R., T.R. 6'1" 185 lbs.
(OUTFIELD)

YEAR	CLUB	BA	G	AB	R	H	2B	3B	HR	RBI
1961	LOS ANGELES (N)	.242	34	33	10	8	2	1	2	6
	Three years (total)	.176	95	108	20	19	9	1	2	8

TOM WINSETT
B. Nov. 24, 1909, McKenzie, Tenn.
B.L., T.R. 6'2" 190 lbs.
(OUTFIELD)

YEAR	CLUB	BA	G	AB	R	H	2B	3B	HR	RBI
1936	BROOKLYN (N)	.235	22	85	13	20	7	0	1	18
1937	BROOKLYN (N)	.237	118	350	32	83	15	5	5	42
1938	BROOKLYN (N)	.300	12	30	6	9	1	0	1	7
	Seven years (total)	.237	230	566	60	134	25	5	8	76

WHITEY WITT
B. Sept. 28, 1895, Orange, Mass.
B.L., T.R. 5'7" 150 lbs.
(OUTFIELD, SHORTSTOP)

YEAR	CLUB	BA	G	AB	R	H	2B	3B	HR	RBI
1926	BROOKLYN (N)	.259	63	85	13	22	1	1	0	3
	Ten years (total)	.287	1139	4171	632	1195	144	62	18	302

GLENN WRIGHT
B. Feb. 6, 1901, Archie, Mo.
B.R., T.R. 5'11" 170 lbs.
(SHORTSTOP)

YEAR	CLUB	BA	G	AB	R	H	2B	3B	HR	RBI
1924	Pittsburgh (N)	.287	153	616	80	177	28	18	7	111
1925	Pittsburgh (N)	.308	153	614	97	189	32	10	18	121
1926	Pittsburgh (N)	.308	119	458	73	141	15	15	8	77
1927	Pittsburgh (N)	.281	143	570	78	160	26	4	9	105
1928	Pittsburgh (N)	.310	108	407	63	126	20	8	8	66
1929	BROOKLYN (N)	.200	24	25	4	5	0	0	1	6
1930	BROOKLYN (N)	.321	135	532	83	171	28	12	22	126
1931	BROOKLYN (N)	.284	77	268	36	76	9	4	9	32
1932	BROOKLYN (N)	.274	127	446	50	122	31	5	10	60
1933	BROOKLYN (N)	.255	71	192	19	49	13	0	1	18
1935	Chicago (A)	.120	9	25	1	3	1	0	0	1
	Eleven years	.294	1119	4153	584	1219	203	76	93	723
World Series										
	Two years	.175	11	40	4	7	1	0	1	5

ZEKE WRIGLEY
B. Jan. 18, 1873, Philadelphia, Pa.
D. Sept. 28, 1952, Philadelphia, Pa.
(SHORTSTOP)

YEAR	CLUB	BA	G	AB	R	H	2B	3B	HR	RBI
1899	BROOKLYN (N)	.204	15	54	4	11	2	2	0	9
	Four years (total)	.258	239	861	121	222	25	20	5	117

JIMMY WYNN
B. March 12, 1942, Cincinnati, Ohio
B.R., T.R. 5'10" 160 lbs.
(OUTFIELD)

YEAR	CLUB	BA	G	AB	R	H	2B	3B	HR	RBI
1963	Houston (N)	.244	70	250	31	61	10	5	4	27
1964	Houston (N)	.224	67	219	19	49	7	0	5	18
1965	Houston (N)	.275	157	564	90	155	30	7	22	73
1966	Houston (N)	.256	105	418	62	107	21	1	18	62
1967	Houston (N)	.249	158	594	102	148	29	3	37	107
1968	Houston (N)	.269	156	542	85	146	23	5	26	67
1969	Houston (N)	.269	149	495	113	133	17	1	33	87
1970	Houston (N)	.282	157	554	82	156	32	2	27	88
1971	Houston (N)	.203	123	404	38	82	16	0	7	45
1972	Houston (N)	.273	145	542	117	148	29	3	24	90
1973	Houston (N)	.220	139	481	90	106	14	5	20	55
1974	LOS ANGELES (N)	.271	150	535	104	145	17	4	32	108
1975	LOS ANGELES (N)	.248	130	412	80	102	16	0	18	58
1976	Atlanta (N)	.207	148	449	75	93	19	1	17	66
1977	New York (A)									
1977	Milwaukee (A)									
	(year totals)	.175	66	194	17	34	5	2	1	13
	Fifteen years	.250	1920	6653	1105	1665	285	39	291	964
League Championship										
	One year	.200	4	10	4	2	2	0	0	2
World Series										
	One year	.188	5	16	1	3	1	0	1	2

AD YALE
B. April 17, 1870, Bristol, Conn.
D. April 27, 1948, Bridgeport, Conn.
(1ST BASE)

YEAR	CLUB	BA	G	AB	R	H	2B	3B	HR	RBI
1905	BROOKLYN (N)	.077	4	13	1	1	0	0	0	1

STEVE YEAGER
B. Nov. 24, 1948, Huntington, W. Va.
B.R., T.R. 6' 190 lbs.
(CATCHER)

YEAR	CLUB	BA	G	AB	R	H	2B	3B	HR	RBI
1972	LOS ANGELES (N)	.274	35	106	18	29	0	1	4	15
1973	LOS ANGELES (N)	.254	54	134	18	34	5	0	2	10
1974	LOS ANGELES (N)	.266	94	316	41	84	16	1	12	41
1975	LOS ANGELES (N)	.228	135	452	34	103	16	1	12	54
1976	LOS ANGELES (N)	.214	117	359	42	77	11	3	11	35
1977	LOS ANGELES (N)	.256	125	387	53	99	21	2	16	55
1978	LOS ANGELES (N)	.193	94	228	19	44	7	0	4	23
1979	LOS ANGELES (N)	.216	105	310	33	67	9	2	13	41
1980	LOS ANGELES (N)	.211	96	227	20	48	8	0	2	20
1981	LOS ANGELES (N)	.209	42	86	5	18	2	0	3	7
1982	LOS ANGELES (N)	.245	82	196	13	48	5	2	2	18
1983	LOS ANGELES	.203	113	335	31	68	8	3	15	41
	Twelve years	.229	1092	3236	327	719	108	15	96	360
Divisional Playoff										
	One year	.400	2	5	1	2	1	0	0	0
League Championship										
	Four years	.189	11	37	5	7	0	0	1	4

World Series

YEAR	CLUB	BA	G	AB	R	H	2B	3B	HR	RBI
1974	LOS ANGELES (N)	.364	4	11	0	4	1	0	0	1
1977	LOS ANGELES (N)	.316	6	19	2	6	1	0	2	5
1978	LOS ANGELES (N)	.231	5	13	2	3	1	0	0	0
1981	LOS ANGELES (N)	.286	6	14	2	4	1	0	2	4
	Four years	.298	21	57	6	17	4	0	4	10

DON ZIMMER B. Jan. 17, 1931, Cincinnati, Ohio
B.R., T.R. 5'9" 165 lbs.
(3RD BASE, 2ND BASE, SHORTSTOP)

YEAR	CLUB	BA	G	AB	R	H	2B	3B	HR	RBI
1954	BROOKLYN (N)	.182	24	33	3	6	0	1	0	0
1955	BROOKLYN (N)	.239	88	280	38	67	10	1	15	50
1956	BROOKLYN (N)	.300	17	20	4	6	1	0	0	2
1957	BROOKLYN (N)	.219	84	269	23	59	9	1	6	19
1958	LOS ANGELES (N)	.262	127	455	52	119	15	2	17	60
1959	LOS ANGELES (N)	.165	97	249	21	41	7	1	4	28
1960	Chicago (N)	.258	132	368	37	95	16	7	6	35
1961	Chicago (N)	.252	128	477	57	120	25	4	13	40
1962	New York (N)									
1962	Cincinnati (N)									
	(year totals)	.213	77	244	19	52	12	2	2	17
1963	LOS ANGELES (N)	.217	22	23	4	5	1	0	1	2
1963	Washington (A)									
	(year totals)	.246	105	321	41	79	13	1	14	46
1964	Washington (A)	.246	121	341	38	84	16	2	12	38
1965	Washington (A)	.199	95	226	20	45	6	0	2	17
	Twelve years	.235	1095	3283	353	773	130	22	91	352

World Series

YEAR	CLUB	BA	G	AB	R	H	2B	3B	HR	RBI
1955	BROOKLYN (N)	.222	4	9	0	2	0	0	0	2
1959	LOS ANGELES (N)	.000	1	1	0	0	0	0	0	0
	Two years	.200	5	10	0	2	0	0	0	2

BILL ZIMMERMAN B. Jan. 20, 1889, Kengen, Germany
D. Oct. 4, 1952, Newark, N.J.
B.R., T.R. 5'8½" 172 lbs.
(OUTFIELD)

YEAR	CLUB	BA	G	AB	R	H	2B	3B	HR	RBI
1915	BROOKLYN (N)	.281	22	57	3	16	2	0	0	7

EDDIE ZIMMERMAN B. Jan. 4, 1883, Oceanic, N.J.
D. May 6, 1945, Emmaus, Pa.
B.R., T.R.
(3RD BASE)

YEAR	CLUB	BA	G	AB	R	H	2B	3B	HR	RBI
1906	St. Louis (N)	.214	5	14	0	3	0	0	0	1
1911	BROOKLYN (N)	.185	122	417	31	77	10	7	3	36
	Two years	.186	127	431	31	80	10	7	3	37

THE PITCHERS' CATALOGUE

The Pitchers' Catalogue is an alphabetical list of every player who ever pitched for the Dodgers. For every pitcher with 25 or more decisions for the Dodgers, a complete year-by-year statistical record is included, even for those years that the player did *not* play for Brooklyn or Los Angeles. For pitchers with less than 25 decisions, statistics are included for the years that player pitched for the Dodgers along with the player's lifetime major league statistics. To avoid confusion, the word "totals" has been placed in the left-hand column of the line listing these pitchers' lifetime statistics.

The Pitchers' Catalogue information includes (where available):

Pitcher's name	Walter Baum (fictional)
Pitcher's birthdate and hometown	B. Dec. 4, 1904, Clifton, N.Y.
Pitcher's throwing form	Left handed
Batting form	B. R.
Height, weight	6'2", 210 lbs.
Date, place of death	D. Jan. 4, 1970, Santa Rosa, Calif.
Years played	1927–1938

EXPLANATION OF COLUMN HEADINGS AND ABBREVIATIONS USED

YEAR	1936	ERA	Earned Run Average for that season
CLUB	BROOKLYN	G	Games pitched in that season
LEAGUE	(N) NATIONAL LEAGUE	IP	Innings pitched in that season
W	Number of games won in a season	H	Hits allowed in that season
L	Number of games lost in a season	BB	Bases on Balls issued that season
PCT	Winning Percentage for that season	SO	Strikeouts in that season

RALEIGH AITCHISON B. Dec. 5, 1887, Tyndall, S.D.
D. Sept. 26, 1958, Columbus, Kan.
Left handed, B.R.
5'11½" 175 lbs.

YEAR	CLUB	W	L	PCT	ERA	G	IP	H	BB	SO
1911	BROOKLYN (N)	0	1	.000	0.00	1	1.1	1	1	0
1914	BROOKLYN (N)	12	7	.632	2.66	26	172.1	156	60	87
1915	BROOKLYN (N)	0	4	.000	4.96	7	32.2	36	6	14
	Three years	12	12	.500	3.01	34	206.1	193	67	101

ED ALBOSTA B. Oct. 27, 1918, Saginaw, Mich.
Right handed, B.R.
6'1" 175 lbs.

YEAR	CLUB	W	L	PCT	ERA	G	IP	H	BB	SO
1941	BROOKLYN (N)	0	2	.000	6.23	2	13	11	8	5
	Two years	0	8	.000	6.15	19	52.2	52	43	24

DOYLE ALEXANDER B. Sept. 4, 1950, Cordova, Ala.
Right handed, B.R.
6'3" 190 lbs.

YEAR	CLUB	W	L	PCT	ERA	G	IP	H	BB	SO
1971	LOS ANGELES (N)	6	6	.500	3.82	17	92	105	18	30
League Championship										
	One year	0	1	.000	4.91	1	3.2	5	0	1
World Series										
	One year	0	1	.000	7.50	1	6	9	2	1

FRANK ALLEN B. Aug. 26, 1888, Newbern, Ala.
D. July 30, 1933, Gainesville, Ala.
Left handed, B.R.
5'9" 175 lbs.

YEAR	CLUB	W	L	PCT	ERA	G	IP	H	BB	SO
1912	BROOKLYN (N)	3	9	.250	3.63	20	109	119	57	58
1913	BROOKLYN (N)	4	18	.182	2.83	34	174.2	144	81	82
1914	BROOKLYN (N)	8	14	.364	3.11	36	171		57	68
1914	Pittsburgh (F)									
	(year totals)	9	14	.391	3.18	37	178.1	174	57	71
1915	Pittsburgh (F)	23	12	.657	2.51	41	283.1	230	100	127
1916	Boston (N)	8	2	.800	2.07	19	113	102	31	63
1917	Boston (N)	3	11	.214	3.94	29	112	124	47	56
	Six years	50	66	.431	2.93	180	970.1	893	373	457

JOHNNY ALLEN B. Sept. 30, 1904, Lenoir, N.C.
D. March 29, 1959, St. Petersburg, Fla.
Right handed, B.R.
6' 180 lbs.

YEAR	CLUB	W	L	PCT	ERA	G	IP	H	BB	SO
1932	New York (A)	17	4	.810	3.70	33	192	162	76	109
1933	New York (A)	15	7	.682	4.39	25	184.2	171	87	119
1934	New York (A)	5	2	.714	2.89	13	71.2	62	32	54
1935	New York (A)	13	6	.684	3.61	23	167	149	58	113
1936	Cleveland (A)	20	10	.667	3.44	36	243	234	97	165
1937	Cleveland (A)	15	1	.938	2.55	24	173	157	60	87
1938	Cleveland (A)	14	8	.636	4.19	30	200	189	81	112
1939	Cleveland (A)	9	7	.563	4.58	28	175	199	56	79
1940	Cleveland (A)	9	8	.529	3.44	32	138.2	126	48	62
1941	St. Louis (A)									
1941	BROOKLYN (N)	3	0	1.000	2.53	11	57	—	12	21
	(year totals)	5	5	.500	4.71	31	124.1	127	41	48
1942	BROOKLYN (N)	10	6	.625	3.20	27	118	106	39	50
1943	BROOKLYN (N)	5	1	.833	4.26	17	38	—	25	15
1943	New York (N)									
	(year totals)	6	4	.600	3.65	32	79	79	39	39
1944	New York (N)	4	7	.364	4.07	18	84	88	24	33
	Thirteen years	142	75	.654	3.75	352	1950.1	1849	738	1070
World Series	Two years	0	0	—	6.23	4	4.1	6	3	0

ED APPLETON B. Feb. 29, 1892, Arlington, Texas
D. Jan. 27, 1932, Arlington, Texas
Right handed, B.R.
6'½" 173 lbs.

YEAR	CLUB	W	L	PCT	ERA	G	IP	H	BB	SO
1915	BROOKLYN (N)	4	10	.286	3.32	34	138.1	133	66	50
1916	BROOKLYN (N)	1	2	.333	3.06	14	47	49	18	14
	Two years	5	12	.294	3.25	48	185.1	182	84	64

JOHNNY BABICH B. May 14, 1913, Albion, Calif.
Right handed, B.R.
6'1½" 185 lbs.

YEAR	CLUB	W	L	PCT	ERA	G	IP	H	BB	SO
1934	BROOKLYN (N)	7	11	.389	4.20	25	135	148	51	62
1935	BROOKLYN (N)	7	14	.333	6.66	37	143.1	191	52	55
1936	Boston (N)	0	0	—	10.50	3	6	11	6	1
1940	Philadelphia (A)	14	13	.519	3.73	31	229.1	222	80	94
1941	Philadelphia (A)	2	7	.222	6.09	16	78.1	85	31	19
	Five years	30	45	.400	4.93	112	592	657	220	231

SWEETBREADS BAILEY

B. Feb. 12, 1895, Joliet, Ill.
D. Sept. 27, 1939, Joliet, Ill.
Right handed, B.R.
6' 184 lbs.

YEAR	CLUB	W	L	PCT	ERA	G	IP	H	BB	SO
1921	BROOKLYN (N)	0	0	000	5.25	7	24		7	6
	Three years (totals)	4	7	.364	4.59	52	137.1	154	40	35

TOM BAKER

B. June 11, 1915, Victoria, Texas
Right handed, B.R.
6'1½" 180 lbs.

YEAR	CLUB	W	L	PCT	ERA	G	IP	H	BB	SO
1935	BROOKLYN (N)	1	0	1.000	4.29	11	42	48	20	10
1936	BROOKLYN (N)	1	8	.111	4.72	35	87.2	98	48	35
1937	BROOKLYN (N)	0	1	.000		7	8		5	2
1937	New York (N)									
	(year totals)	1	1	.500	5.03	20	39.1	44	21	13
1938	New York (N)	0	0	—	6.75	2	4	5	3	0
	Four years	3	9	.250	4.73	68	173	195	92	58

LADY BALDWIN

B. April 10, 1859, Ormel, N.Y.
D. March 7, 1937, Hastings, Mich.
Left handed, B.L.

YEAR	CLUB	W	L	PCT	ERA	G	IP	H	BB	SO
1890	BROOKLYN (N)	1	0	1.000	3.00	2	11		8	4
	Six years (totals)	73	41	.640	2.85	118	1017	921	233	582

WIN BALLOU

B. Nov. 30, 1897, Mount Morgan, Ky.
D. Jan. 30, 1963, San Francisco, Calif.
Right handed, B.R.
5'10½" 170 lbs.

YEAR	CLUB	W	L	PCT	ERA	G	IP	H	BB	SO
1929	BROOKLYN (N)	2	3	.400	6.71	25	57.2	69	38	20
	Four years (totals)	19	20	.487	5.11	99	329.2	398	168	109

DAN BANKHEAD

B. May 3, 1920, Empire, Ala.
D. May 2, 1976, Houston, Texas
Right handed, B.R.
6'1" 184 lbs.

YEAR	CLUB	W	L	PCT	ERA	G	IP	H	BB	SO
1947	BROOKLYN (N)	0	0	—	7.20	4	10	15	8	6
1950	BROOKLYN (N)	9	4	.692	5.50	41	129.1	119	88	96
1951	BROOKLYN (N)	0	1	.000	15.43	7	14	14	27	14
	Three years	9	5	.643	6.52	52	153.1	161	110	111

JACK BANTA

B. June 24, 1925, Hutchinson, Kan.
Right handed, B.L.
6'2½" 175 lbs.

YEAR	CLUB	W	L	PCT	ERA	G	IP	H	BB	SO
1947	BROOKLYN (N)	0	1	.000	7.04	3	7.2	7	4	3
1948	BROOKLYN (N)	0	1	.000	8.10	2	3.1	5	5	1
1949	BROOKLYN (N)	10	6	.625	3.37	48	152.1	125	68	97
1950	BROOKLYN (N)	4	4	.500	4.35	16	41.1	39	36	15
	Four years	14	12	.538	3.78	69	204.2	176	113	116
World Series										
	One year	0	0	—	3.18	3	5.2	5	1	4

CY BARGER

B. May 18, 1885, Jamestown, Ky.
D. Sept. 23, 1964, Columbia, Ky.
Right handed, B.L.
160 lbs.

YEAR	CLUB	W	L	PCT	ERA	G	IP	H	BB	SO
1906	New York (A)	1	0	1.000	10.13	2	5.1	7	3	3
1907	New York (A)	0	0	—	3.00	1	6	10	1	0
1910	BROOKLYN (N)	15	15	.500	2.88	35	271.2	267	107	87
1911	BROOKLYN (N)	11	15	.423	3.52	30	217.1	224	71	60
1912	BROOKLYN (N)	1	9	.100	5.46	16	94	120	42	30
1914	Pittsburgh (F)	10	16	.385	4.34	33	228.1	252	63	70
1915	Pittsburgh (F)	10	7	.588	2.29	34	153	130	47	47
	Seven years	48	62	.436	3.56	151	975.2	1010	334	297

JESSE BARNES

B. Aug. 26, 1892, Perkins, Okla.
D. Sept. 9, 1961, Santa Rosa, N.M.
Right handed, B.L.
6' 170 lbs.

YEAR	CLUB	W	L	PCT	ERA	G	IP	H	BB	SO
1915	Boston (N)	4	0	1.000	1.39	9	45.1	41	10	16
1916	Boston (N)	6	14	.300	2.37	33	163	154	37	55
1917	Boston (N)	13	21	.382	2.68	50	295	261	50	107
1918	New York (N)	6	1	.857	1.81	9	54.2	53	13	12
1919	New York (N)	25	9	.735	2.40	38	295.2	263	35	92
1920	New York (N)	20	15	.571	2.64	43	292.2	271	56	63
1921	New York (N)	15	9	.625	3.10	42	258.2	298	44	56
1922	New York (N)	13	8	.619	3.51	37	212.2	236	38	52
1923	New York (N)									
1923	Boston (N)									
	(year totals)	13	15	.464	3.31	43	231.1	252	56	53
1924	Boston (N)	15	20	.429	3.23	37	267.2	292	53	49
1925	Boston (N)	11	16	.407	4.53	32	216.1	255	63	55
1926	BROOKLYN (N)	10	11	.476	5.24	31	158	204	35	29
1927	BROOKLYN (N)	2	10	.167	5.72	18	78.2	106	25	14
	Thirteen years	153	149	.507	3.22	422	2569.2	2686	515	653

World Series

| | Two years | 2 | 0 | 1.000 | 1.71 | 4 | 26.1 | 14 | 8 | 24 |

REX BARNEY

B. Dec. 19, 1924, Omaha, Neb.
Right handed, B.R.
6'3" 185 lbs.

YEAR	CLUB	W	L	PCT	ERA	G	IP	H	BB	SO
1943	BROOKLYN (N)	2	2	.500	6.35	9	45.1	36	41	23
1946	BROOKLYN (N)	2	5	.286	5.87	16	53.2	46	51	36
1947	BROOKLYN (N)	5	2	.714	4.98	28	77.2	66	59	36
1948	BROOKLYN (N)	15	13	.536	3.10	44	246.2	193	122	138
1949	BROOKLYN (N)	9	8	.529	4.41	38	140.2	108	89	80
1950	BROOKLYN (N)	2	1	.667	6.42	20	33.2	25	48	23
	Six years	35	31	.530	4.34	155	597.2	474	410	336

World Series

YEAR	CLUB	W	L	PCT	ERA	G	IP	H	BB	SO
1947	BROOKLYN (N)	0	1	.000	2.71	3	6.2		10	3
1949	BROOKLYN (N)	0	1	.000	16.88	1	2.2		6	2
	Two years	0	1	.000	6.75	4	9.1	7	16	5

BOB BARR

B. March 12, 1908, Newton, Mass.
Right handed, B.R.
6' 175 lbs.

YEAR	CLUB	W	L	PCT	ERA	G	IP	H	BB	SO
1935	BROOKLYN (N)	0	0	—	3.86	2	2.1	5	2	0

The Pitchers' Catalogue • 159

WALTER BOOM-BOOM BECK   B. Oct. 16, 1904, Decatur, Ill.
Right handed, B.R.
6'2" 200 lbs.

YEAR	CLUB	W	L	PCT	ERA	G	IP	H	BB	SO
1924	St. Louis (A)	0	0	—	0.00	1	1	2	1	0
1927	St. Louis (A)	1	0	1.000	5.56	3	11.1	15	5	6
1928	St. Louis (A)	2	3	.400	4.41	16	49	52	20	17
1933	BROOKLYN (N)	12	20	.375	3.54	43	257	270	69	89
1934	BROOKLYN (N)	2	6	.250	7.42	22	57	72	32	24
1939	Philadelphia (N)	7	14	.333	4.73	34	182.2	203	64	77
1940	Philadelphia (N)	4	9	.308	4.31	29	129.1	147	41	38
1941	Philadelphia (N)	1	9	.100	4.63	34	95.1	104	35	34
1942	Philadelphia (N)	0	1	.000	4.75	26	53	69	17	10
1943	Philadelphia (N)	0	0	—	9.88	4	13.2	24	5	3
1944	Detroit (A)	1	2	.333	3.89	28	74	67	27	25
1945	Cincinnati (N)									
1945	Pittsburgh (N)									
	(year totals)	8	5	.615	2.68	25	110.2	96	26	29
	Twelve years	38	69	.355	4.30	265	1034	1121	342	352

JOE BECKWITH   B. Jan. 28, 1955, Auburn, Ala.
Right handed, B.L.
6'3" 180 lbs.

YEAR	CLUB	W	L	PCT	ERA	G	IP	H	BB	SO
1979	LOS ANGELES (N)	1	2	.333	4.38	17	37	42	15	28
1980	LOS ANGELES (N)	3	3	.500	1.95	38	60	60	23	40
1982	LOS ANGELES (N)	2	1	.667	2.70	19	40	38	14	33
	Three years	6	6	.500	2.82	74	137	140	52	101

HANK BEHRMAN   B. June 27, 1921, Brooklyn, N.Y.
Right handed, B.R.
5'11" 174 lbs.

YEAR	CLUB	W	L	PCT	ERA	G	IP	H	BB	SO
1946	BROOKLYN (N)	11	5	.688	2.93	47	150.2	138	69	78
1947	Pittsburgh (N)									
1947	BROOKLYN (N)	5	3	.625	5.48	40	92		48	33
	(year totals)	5	5	.500	6.25	50	116.2	130	65	44
1948	BROOKLYN (N)	5	4	.556	4.05	34	91	95	42	42
1949	New York (N)	3	3	.500	4.92	43	71.1	64	52	25
	Four years	24	17	.585	4.40	174	429.2	427	228	189
World Series										
	One year	0	0	—	7.11	5	6.1	9	5	3

GEORGE BELL   B. Nov. 2, 1874, Greenwood, N.Y.
D. Dec. 25, 1941, New York, N.Y.
Right handed, B.R.
6' 195 lbs.

YEAR	CLUB	W	L	PCT	ERA	G	IP	H	BB	SO
1907	BROOKLYN (N)	8	16	.333	2.25	35	263.2	222	77	88
1908	BROOKLYN (N)	4	16	.200	3.59	29	155.1	162	45	63
1909	BROOKLYN (N)	16	15	.516	2.71	33	256	236	73	95
1910	BROOKLYN (N)	10	27	.270	2.64	44	310	267	82	102
1911	BROOKLYN (N)	5	6	.455	4.28	19	101	123	28	28
	Five years	43	80	.350	2.85	160	1086	1010	305	376

RAY BENGE   B. April 22, 1902, Jacksonville, Texas
Right handed, B.R.
5'9½" 160 lbs.

YEAR	CLUB	W	L	PCT	ERA	G	IP	H	BB	SO
1925	Cleveland (A)	1	0	1.000	1.54	2	11.2	9	3	3
1926	Cleveland (A)	1	0	1.000	3.86	8	11.2	15	4	3
1928	Philadelphia (N)	8	18	.308	4.55	40	201.2	219	88	68
1929	Philadelphia (N)	11	15	.423	6.29	38	199	255	77	78
1930	Philadelphia (N)	11	15	.423	5.70	38	225.2	305	81	70
1931	Philadelphia (N)	14	18	.438	3.17	38	247	251	61	117
1932	Philadelphia (N)	13	12	.520	4.05	41	222.1	247	58	89

160 • **The Complete Dodgers Record Book**

YEAR	CLUB	W	L	PCT	ERA	G	IP	H	BB	SO
1933	BROOKLYN (N)	10	17	.370	3.42	37	228.2	238	55	74
1934	BROOKLYN (N)	14	12	.538	4.32	36	227	252	61	64
1935	BROOKLYN (N)	9	9	.500	4.48	23	124.2	142	47	39
1936	Boston (N)									
1936	Philadelphia (N)									
	(year totals)	8	13	.381	5.49	36	160.2	231	57	45
1938	Cincinnati (N)	1	1	.500	4.11	9	15.1	13	6	5
	Twelve years	101	130	.437	4.52	346	1875.1	2177	598	655

DON BESSENT
B. March 13, 1931, Jacksonville, Fla.
Right handed, B.R.
6' 175 lbs.

YEAR	CLUB	W	L	PCT	ERA	G	IP	H	BB	SO
1955	BROOKLYN (N)	8	1	.889	2.70	24	63.1	51	21	29
1956	BROOKLYN (N)	4	3	.571	2.50	38	79.1	63	31	52
1957	BROOKLYN (N)	1	3	.250	5.73	27	44	58	19	24
1958	LOS ANGELES (N)	1	0	1.000	3.33	19	24.1	24	17	13
	Four years	14	7	.667	3.33	108	211	196	88	118

World Series

YEAR	CLUB	W	L	PCT	ERA	G	IP	H	BB	SO
1955	BROOKLYN (N)	0	0	—	0.00	3	3.1		1	1
1956	BROOKLYN (N)	1	0	1.000	1.80	2	10		3	5
	Two years	1	0	1.000	1.35	5	13.1	11	4	6

JACK BILLINGHAM
B. Feb. 21, 1943, Orlando, Fla.
Right handed, B.R.
6'4" 195 lbs.

YEAR	CLUB	W	L	PCT	ERA	G	IP	H	BB	SO
1968	LOS ANGELES (N)	3	0	1.000	2.14	50	71.1	54	30	46
	Thirteen years (totals)	145	113	.562	3.83	476	2231	2272	750	1141

RALPH BIRKOFER
B. Nov. 5, 1908, Cincinnati, Ohio
D. March 16, 1971, Cincinnati, Ohio
Left handed, B.L.
5'11" 213 lbs.

YEAR	CLUB	W	L	PCT	ERA	G	IP	H	BB	SO
1937	BROOKLYN (N)	0	2	.000	6.67	11	29.2	45	9	9
	Five years (totals)	31	28	.525	4.19	132	544	618	175	224

BABE BIRRER
B. July 4, 1928, Buffalo, N.Y.
Right handed, B.R.
6' 195 lbs.

YEAR	CLUB	W	L	PCT	ERA	G	IP	H	BB	SO
1958	LOS ANGELES (N)	0	0	—	4.50	16	34	43	7	16
	Three years (totals)	4	3	.571	4.36	56	119.2	129	37	45

JOE BLACK
B. Feb. 8, 1924, Plainfield, N.J.
Right handed, B.R.
6'2" 220 lbs.

YEAR	CLUB	W	L	PCT	ERA	G	IP	H	BB	SO
1952	BROOKLYN (N)	15	4	.789	2.15	56	142.1	102	41	85
1953	BROOKLYN (N)	6	3	.667	5.33	34	72.2	74	27	42
1954	BROOKLYN (N)	0	0	—	11.57	5	7	11	5	3
1955	BROOKLYN (N)	1	0	1.000	3.81	6				
1955	Cincinnati (N)									
	(year totals)	6	2	.750	4.05	38	117.2	121	30	63
1956	Cincinnati (N)	3	2	.600	4.52	32	61.2	61	25	27
1957	Washington (A)	0	1	.000	7.11	7	12.2	22	1	2
	Six years	30	12	.714	3.91	172	414	391	129	222

World Series

YEAR	CLUB	W	L	PCT	ERA	G	IP	H	BB	SO
1952	BROOKLYN (N)	1	2	.333	2.53	3	21.1		8	9
1953	BROOKLYN (N)	0	0	—	9.00	1	1		0	2
	Two years	1	2	.333	2.82	4	22.1	16	8	11

CLARENCE BLETHEN

B. July 11, 1893, Dover-Foxcroft, Maine
D. April 11, 1973, Frederick, Md.
Right handed, B.L.
5'11" 165 lbs.

YEAR	CLUB	W	L	PCT	ERA	G	IP	H	BB	SO
1929	BROOKLYN (N)	0	0	—	9.00	2	2	4	3	0
	Two years (totals)	0	0	—	7.32	7	19.2	33	10	2

JIM BLUEJACKET

B. July 8, 1887, Adair, Okla.
D. March 26, 1947, Pekin, Ill.
Right handed, B.R.
6'2½" 200 lbs.

YEAR	CLUB	W	L	PCT	ERA	G	IP	H	BB	SO
1914	BROOKLYN (F)	4	5	.444	3.76	17	67	77	19	29
1915	BROOKLYN (F)	9	11	.450	3.15	24	162.2	155	75	48
1916	Cincinnati (N)	0	1	.000	7.71	3	7	12	3	1
	Three years	13	17	.433	3.46	44	236.2	244	97	78

GEORGE BOEHLER

B. Jan. 2, 1892, Lawrenceburg, Ind.
D. June 23, 1958, Lawrenceburg, Ind.
Right handed, B.R.
6'2" 180 lbs.

YEAR	CLUB	W	L	PCT	ERA	G	IP	H	BB	SO
1926	BROOKLYN (N)	1	0	1.000	4.41	10	34.2	42	23	10
	Nine years (totals)	7	12	.368	4.74	60	201.1	231	134	91

JOE BRADSHAW

B. Aug. 17, 1897, Dyersburg, Tenn.
Right handed, B.R.
6'2½" 200 lbs.

YEAR	CLUB	W	L	PCT	ERA	G	IP	H	BB	SO
1929	BROOKLYN (N)	0	0	—	4.50	2	4	3	4	1

RALPH BRANCA

B. Jan. 6, 1926, Mt. Vernon, N.Y.
Right handed, B.R.
6'3" 220 lbs.

YEAR	CLUB	W	L	PCT	ERA	G	IP	H	BB	SO
1944	BROOKLYN (N)	0	2	.000	7.05	21	44.2	46	32	16
1945	BROOKLYN (N)	5	6	.455	3.04	16	109.2	73	79	69
1946	BROOKLYN (N)	3	1	.750	3.88	24	67.1	62	41	42
1947	BROOKLYN (N)	21	12	.636	2.67	43	280	251	98	148
1948	BROOKLYN (N)	14	9	.609	3.51	36	215.2	189	80	122
1949	BROOKLYN (N)	13	5	.722	4.39	34	186.2	181	91	109
1950	BROOKLYN (N)	7	9	.438	4.69	43	142	152	55	100
1951	BROOKLYN (N)	13	12	.520	3.26	42	204	180	85	118
1952	BROOKLYN (N)	4	2	.667	3.84	16	61	52	21	26
1953	BROOKLYN (N)	0	0	.000	9.82	7	11	—	5	5
1953	Detroit (A)									
	(year totals)	4	7	.364	4.70	24	113	113	36	55
1954	Detroit (A)									
1954	New York (A)									
	(year totals)	4	3	.571	5.12	22	58	72	43	22
1956	BROOKLYN (N)	0	0	—	0.00	1	2	1	2	2
	Twelve years	88	68	.564	3.79	322	1484	1372	663	829

World Series

YEAR	CLUB	W	L	PCT	ERA	G	IP	H	BB	SO
1947	BROOKLYN (N)	1	1	.500	8.67	3	8.1	—	5	8
1949	BROOKLYN (N)	0	1	.000	4.15	1	8.2	—	4	6
	Two years	1	2	.333	6.35	4	17	16	9	14

ED BRANDT
B. Feb. 17, 1905, Spokane, Wash.
D. Nov. 1, 1944, Spokane, Wash.
Left handed, B.L.
6'1" 190 lbs.

YEAR	CLUB	W	L	PCT	ERA	G	IP	H	BB	SO
1936	BROOKLYN (N)	11	13	.458	3.50	38	234	246	65	104
	Eleven years (totals)	121	146	.453	3.86	378	2268.1	2342	778	877

KEN BRETT
B. Sept. 18, 1948, Brooklyn, N.Y.
Left handed, B.L.
6' 190 lbs.

YEAR	CLUB	W	L	PCT	ERA	G	IP	H	BB	SO
1979	LOS ANGELES (N)	4	3	.571	3.75	39	60	68	18	16
	Fourteen years (totals)	83	85	.494	3.93	349	1526	1490	562	807

JIM BREWER
B. Nov. 14, 1937, Merced, Calif.
Left handed, B.L.
6'1" 186 lbs.

YEAR	CLUB	W	L	PCT	ERA	G	IP	H	BB	SO
1960	Chicago (N)	0	3	.000	5.82	5	21.2	25	6	7
1961	Chicago (N)	1	7	.125	5.82	36	86.2	116	21	57
1962	Chicago (N)	0	1	.000	9.53	6	5.2	10	3	1
1963	Chicago (N)	3	2	.600	4.89	29	49.2	59	15	35
1964	LOS ANGELES (N)	4	3	.571	3.00	34	93	79	25	63
1965	LOS ANGELES (N)	3	2	.600	1.82	19	49.1	33	28	31
1966	LOS ANGELES (N)	0	2	.000	3.68	13	22	17	11	8
1967	LOS ANGELES (N)	5	4	.556	2.68	30	100.2	78	31	74
1968	LOS ANGELES (N)	8	3	.727	2.49	54	76	59	33	75
1969	LOS ANGELES (N)	7	6	.538	2.56	59	88	71	41	92
1970	LOS ANGELES (N)	7	6	.538	3.13	58	89	66	33	91
1971	LOS ANGELES (N)	6	5	.545	1.89	55	81	55	24	66
1972	LOS ANGELES (N)	8	7	.533	1.26	51	78.1	41	25	69
1973	LOS ANGELES (N)	6	8	.429	3.01	56	71.2	58	25	56
1974	LOS ANGELES (N)	4	4	.500	2.54	24	39	29	10	26
1975	LOS ANGELES (N)	3	1	.750	2.54	21	33		12	21
1975	California (A)									
	(year totals)	4	1	.800	3.46	42	67.2	82	23	43
1976	California (A)	3	1	.750	2.70	13	20	20	6	16
	Seventeen years	69	65	.515	3.07	584	1039.1	898	360	810

World Series

YEAR	CLUB	W	L	PCT	ERA	G	IP	H	BB	SO
1965	LOS ANGELES (N)	0	0	—	4.50	1	2		0	1
1966	LOS ANGELES (N)	0	0	—	0.00	1	1		0	1
1974	LOS ANGELES (N)	0	0	—	0.00	1	.1		0	1
	Three years	0	0	—	2.70	3	3.1	3	0	3

ELMER BROWN
B. April 25, 1883, Southport, Ind.
D. Jan. 23, 1955, Indianapolis, Ind.
Right handed, B.L.
5'11½" 172 lbs.

YEAR	CLUB	W	L	PCT	ERA	G	IP	H	BB	SO
1913	BROOKLYN (N)	0	0	—	2.08	3	13	6	10	6
1914	BROOKLYN (N)	2	2	.500	3.93	11	36.2	33	23	22
1915	BROOKLYN (N)	0	0	—	9.00	1	2	4	3	1
	Five years (totals)	8	11	.421	3.49	43	188.1	181	92	79

JOHN BROWN
B. Trenton, N.J.
Deceased

YEAR	CLUB	W	L	PCT	ERA	G	IP	H	BB	SO
1897	BROOKLYN (N)	0	1	.000	7.20	1	5	7	4	0

LLOYD BROWN
B. Dec. 25, 1904, Beeville, Texas
Left handed, B.L.
5'9" 170 lbs.

YEAR	CLUB	W	L	PCT	ERA	G	IP	H	BB	SO
1925	BROOKLYN (N)	0	3	.000	4.12	17	63.1	79	25	23
	Twelve years (totals)	91	105	.464	4.20	404	1693	1899	590	510

MACE BROWN
B. May 21, 1909, North English, Iowa
Right handed, B.R.
6'1" 190 lbs.

YEAR	CLUB	W	L	PCT	ERA	G	IP	H	BB	SO
1941	BROOKLYN (N)	3	2	.600	3.07	24	43		26	22
	Ten years (totals)	76	57	.571	3.47	387	1075	1125	388	435

THREE FINGER BROWN
B. Oct. 19, 1876, Nyesville, Ind.
D. Feb. 14, 1948, Terre Haute, Ind.
Right handed, B.B.
5'10" 175 lbs.

YEAR	CLUB	W	L	PCT	ERA	G	IP	H	BB	SO
1914	BROOKLYN (F)									
	(year totals)	14	11	.560	3.52	35	232.2	235	61	113
	Fourteen years (totals)	239	130	.648	2.06	481	3172.1	2708	673	1375

BRUCE BRUBAKER
B. Dec. 29, 1941, Harrisburg, Pa.
Right handed, B.R.
6'1" 198 lbs.

YEAR	CLUB	W	L	PCT	ERA	G	IP	H	BB	SO
1967	Los Angeles (N)	0	0	—	20.25	1	1.1	3	0	2
	Two years (totals)	0	0	—	13.50	2	3.1	5	1	2

CY BUKER
B. Feb. 5, 1919, Greenwood, Wis.
Right handed, B.L.
5'11" 190 lbs.

YEAR	CLUB	W	L	PCT	ERA	G	IP	H	BB	SO
1945	BROOKLYN (N)	7	2	.778	3.30	42	87.1	90	45	48

JIM BUNNING
B. Oct. 23, 1931, Southgate, Ky.
Right handed, B.R.
6'3" 190 lbs.

YEAR	CLUB	W	L	PCT	ERA	G	IP	H	BB	SO
1969	LOS ANGELES (N)	3	1			9				
	(year totals)	13	10	.565	3.69	34	212.1	212	59	157
	Seventeen years (totals)	224	184	.549	3.27	591	3760.1	3433	1000	2855

SANDY BURK
B. April 22, 1887, Columbus, Ohio
D. Oct. 11, 1934, Brooklyn, N.Y.
Right handed, B.R.

YEAR	CLUB	W	L	PCT	ERA	G	IP	H	BB	SO
1910	BROOKLYN (N)	0	3	.000	6.05	4	19.1	17	27	14
1911	BROOKLYN (N)	1	3	.250	5.12	13	58	54	47	15
1912	BROOKLYN (N)	0	0	.000	3.38	2	8		3	2
	Five years (totals)	5	11	.313	4.25	52	218.1	206	133	86

MAX BUTCHER

B. Sept. 21, 1910, Holden, W. Va.
D. Sept. 15, 1957, Man, W. Va.
Right handed, B.R.
6'2" 220 lbs.

YEAR	CLUB	W	L	PCT	ERA	G	IP	H	BB	SO
1936	BROOKLYN (N)	6	6	.500	3.96	38	147.2	154	59	55
1937	BROOKLYN (N)	11	15	.423	4.27	39	191.2	203	75	57
1938	BROOKLYN (N)	5	4	.556	6.53	24	73		39	21
1938	Philadelphia (N)									
	(year totals)	9	12	.429	4.47	36	171	198	70	50
1939	Philadelphia (N)									
1939	Pittsburgh (N)									
	(year totals)	6	17	.261	4.62	33	191	235	74	48
1940	Pittsburgh (N)	8	9	.471	6.01	35	136.1	161	46	40
1941	Pittsburgh (N)	17	12	.586	3.05	33	236	249	66	61
1942	Pittsburgh (N)	5	8	.385	2.93	24	150.2	144	44	49
1943	Pittsburgh (N)	10	8	.556	2.60	33	193.2	191	57	45
1944	Pittsburgh (N)	13	11	.542	3.12	35	199	216	46	43
1945	Pittsburgh (N)	10	8	.556	3.03	28	169.1	184	46	37
	Ten years	95	106	.473	3.73	334	1786.1	1935	583	485

LEON CADORE

B. Nov. 20, 1891, Chicago, Ill.
D. March 16, 1958, Spokane, Wash.
Right handed, B.R.
6'1" 190 lbs.

YEAR	CLUB	W	L	PCT	ERA	G	IP	H	BB	SO
1915	BROOKLYN (N)	0	2	.000	5.57	7	21	28	8	12
1916	BROOKLYN (N)	0	0	—	4.50	1	6	10	0	2
1917	BROOKLYN (N)	13	13	.500	2.45	37	264	231	63	115
1918	BROOKLYN (N)	1	0	1.000	0.53	2	17	6	2	5
1919	BROOKLYN (N)	14	12	.538	2.37	35	250.2	228	39	94
1920	BROOKLYN (N)	15	14	.517	2.62	35	254.1	256	56	79
1921	BROOKLYN (N)	13	14	.481	4.17	35	211.2	243	46	79
1922	BROOKLYN (N)	8	15	.348	4.35	29	190.1	224	57	49
1923	BROOKLYN (N)	4	1	.800	3.25	8	36		13	5
1923	Chicago (A)									
	(year totals)	4	2	.667	4.46	9	38.1	45	15	8
1924	New York (N)	0	0	—	0.00	2	4	2	3	2
	Ten years	68	72	.486	3.14	192	1257.1	1273	289	445
World Series										
	One year	0	1	.000	9.00	2	2	4	1	1

DICK CALMUS

B. Jan. 7, 1944, Los Angeles, Calif.
Right handed, B.R.
6'4" 187 lbs.

YEAR	CLUB	W	L	PCT	ERA	G	IP	H	BB	SO
1963	LOS ANGELES (N)	3	1	.750	2.66	21	44	32	16	25
1967	Chicago (N)	0	0	—	8.31	1	4.1	5	0	1
	Two years	3	1	.750	3.17	22	48.1	37	16	26

GUY CANTRELL

B. April 9, 1904, Clarita, Okla.
D. Jan. 31, 1961, McAlester, Okla.
Right handed, B.R.
6' 190 lbs.

YEAR	CLUB	W	L	PCT	ERA	G	IP	H	BB	SO
1925	BROOKLYN (N)	1	0	1.000	3.00	14	36	42	14	13
1927	BROOKLYN (N)	0	0	.000	2.70	6	10		6	5
1927	Philadelphia (A)									
	(year totals)	0	2	.000	4.18	8	28	35	13	12
1930	Detroit (A)	1	5	.167	5.66	16	35	38	20	20
	Three years	2	7	.222	4.27	38	99	115	47	45

BEN CANTWELL B. April 13, 1902, Milan, Tenn.
D. Dec. 4, 1962, Salem, Mo.
Right handed, B.R.
6'1" 168 lbs.

YEAR	CLUB	W	L	PCT	ERA	G	IP	H	BB	SO
1927	New York (N)	1	1	.500	4.12	5	19.2	26	2	6
1928	New York (N)									
1928	Boston (N)									
	(year totals)	4	3	.571	4.98	29	108.1	132	40	18
1929	Boston (N)	4	13	.235	4.47	27	157	171	52	25
1930	Boston (N)	9	15	.375	4.88	31	173.1	213	45	43
1931	Boston (N)	7	9	.438	3.63	33	156.1	160	34	32
1932	Boston (N)	13	11	.542	2.96	37	146	133	33	33
1933	Boston (N)	20	10	.667	2.62	40	254.2	242	54	57
1934	Boston (N)	5	11	.313	4.33	27	143.1	163	34	45
1935	Boston (N)	4	25	.138	4.61	39	210.2	235	44	34
1936	Boston (N)	9	9	.500	3.04	34	133.1	127	35	42
1937	New York (N)									
1937	BROOKLYN (N)	0	0	.000	4.67	13			27	32
	(year totals)	0	1	.000	5.17	14	31.1	38	9	13
	Eleven years	76	108	.413	3.91	316	1534	1640	382	348

TEX CARLETON B. Aug. 19, 1906, Comanche, Texas
D. Jan. 11, 1977, Forth Worth, Texas
Right handed, B.B.
6'1½" 180 lbs.

YEAR	CLUB	W	L	PCT	ERA	G	IP	H	BB	SO
1932	St. Louis (N)	10	13	.435	4.08	44	196.1	198	70	113
1933	St. Louis (N)	17	11	.607	3.38	44	277	263	97	147
1934	St. Louis (N)	16	11	.593	4.26	40	240.2	260	52	103
1935	Chicago (N)	11	8	.579	3.89	31	171	169	60	84
1936	Chicago (N)	14	10	.583	3.65	35	197.1	204	67	88
1937	Chicago (N)	16	8	.667	3.15	32	208.1	183	94	105
1938	Chicago (N)	10	9	.526	5.42	33	167.2	213	74	80
1940	BROOKLYN (N)	6	6	.500	3.81	34	149	140	47	88
	Eight years	100	76	.568	3.91	293	1607.1	1630	561	808
World Series										
	Three years	0	1	.000	5.06	4	10.2	12	11	6

OWNIE CARROLL B. Nov. 11, 1902, Kearny, N.J.
D. June 18, 1975, Orange, N.J.
Right handed, B.R.
5'10½" 165 lbs.

YEAR	CLUB	W	L	PCT	ERA	G	IP	H	BB	SO
1925	Detroit (A)	3	1	.750	3.76	10	40.2	46	28	12
1927	Detroit (A)	10	6	.625	3.98	31	172	186	73	41
1928	Detroit (A)	16	12	.571	3.27	34	231	219	87	51
1929	Detroit (A)	9	17	.346	4.63	34	202	249	86	54
1930	Detroit (A)									
1930	New York (A)									
1930	Cincinnati (N)									
	(year totals)	0	7	.000	7.39	19	67	96	30	12
1931	Cincinnati (N)	3	9	.250	5.53	29	107.1	135	51	24
1932	Cincinnati (N)	10	19	.345	4.50	32	210	245	44	55
1933	BROOKLYN (N)	13	15	.464	3.78	33	226.1	248	54	45
1934	BROOKLYN (N)	1	3	.250	6.42	26	74.1	108	33	17
	Nine years	65	89	.422	4.43	248	1330.2	1532	486	311

KID CARSEY B. Oct. 22, 1870, New York, N.Y.
Deceased
Right handed, B.R.
5'7" 168 lbs.

YEAR	CLUB	W	L	PCT	ERA	G	IP	H	BB	SO
1891	Washington (AA)	14	37	.275	4.99	54	415	513	161	174
1892	Philadelphia (N)	19	16	.543	3.12	43	317.2	320	104	76
1893	Philadelphia (N)	20	15	.571	4.81	39	318.1	375	124	50
1894	Philadelphia (N	18	12	.600	5.56	35	277	349	102	41
1895	Philadelphia (N)	24	16	.600	4.92	44	342.1	460	118	64
1896	Philadelphia (N)	11	11	.500	5.62	27	187.1	273	72	36

YEAR	CLUB	W	L	PCT	ERA	G	IP	H	BB	SO
1897	Philadelphia (N)									
1897	St. Louis (N)									
	(year totals)	5	9	.357	5.81	16	127	168	47	15
1898	St. Louis (N)	2	12	.143	6.33	20	123.2	177	37	10
1899	Cleveland (N)									
1899	Washington (N)									
	(year totals)	2	10	.167	5.15	14	106.2	136	28	14
1901	BROOKLYN (N)	1	0	1.000	10.29	2	7	9	3	4
	Ten years	116	138	.457	4.95	294	2222	2780	796	484

BOB CARUTHERS B. Jan. 5, 1864, Memphis, Tenn.
D. Aug. 5, 1911, Peoria, Ill.
Right handed, B.L.
5'7" 138 lbs.

YEAR	CLUB	W	L	PCT	ERA	G	IP	H	BB	SO
*1890	BROOKLYN (N)	23	11	.676	3.09	37	300	292	87	64
1891	BROOKLYN (N)	18	14	.563	3.12	38	297	323	107	69
1892	St. Louis (N)	2	10	.167	5.84	16	101.2	131	27	21
	Nine years	218	99	.688	2.83	340	2828.2	2678	597	900

*1884 St. Louis (AA), 1888 Brooklyn (AA)

HUGH CASEY B. Oct. 14, 1913, Atlanta, Ga.
D. July 3, 1951, Atlanta, Ga.
Right handed, B.R.
6'1" 207 lbs.

YEAR	CLUB	W	L	PCT	ERA	G	IP	H	BB	SO
1935	Chicago (N)	0	0	—	3.86	13	25.2	29	14	10
1939	BROOKLYN (N)	15	10	.600	2.93	40	227.1	228	54	79
1940	BROOKLYN (N)	11	8	.579	3.62	44	154	136	51	53
1941	BROOKLYN (N)	14	11	.560	3.89	45	162	155	57	61
1942	BROOKLYN (N)	6	3	.667	2.25	50	112	91	44	54
1946	BROOKLYN (N)	11	5	.688	1.99	46	99.2	101	33	31
1947	BROOKLYN (N)	10	4	.714	3.99	46	76.2	75	29	40
1948	BROOKLYN (N)	3	0	1.000	8.00	22	36	59	17	7
1949	Pittsburgh (N)									
1949	New York (A)									
	(year totals)	5	1	.833	5.24	37	46.1	61	22	14
	Nine years	75	42	.641	3.45	343	939.2	935	321	349

World Series

YEAR	CLUB	W	L	PCT	ERA	G	IP	H	BB	SO
1941	BROOKLYN (N)	0	2	0.00	3.40	3	5.1		2	1
1947	BROOKLYN (N)	2	0	1.000	0.87	6	10.1		1	3
	Two years	2	2	.500	1.72	9	15.2	14	3	4

BOB CASTILLO B. April 18, 1955, Los Angeles, Calif.
Right handed, B.R.
5'10" 170 lbs.

YEAR	CLUB	W	L	PCT	ERA	G	IP	H	BB	SO
1977	LOS ANGELES (N)	1	0	1.000	4.09	6	11	12	2	7
1978	LOS ANGELES (N)	0	4	.000	3.97	18	34	28	33	30
1979	LOS ANGELES (N)	2	0	1.000	1.13	19	24	26	13	25
1980	LOS ANGELES (N)	8	6	.571	2.76	61	98	70	45	60
1981	LOS ANGELES (N)	2	4	.333	5.29	34	51	50	24	35
1982	Minnesota (A)	13	11	.542	3.66	40	218⅔	194	85	123
1983	Minnesota (A)	8	12	.400	4.77	27	158.1	170	65	90
	Seven years	34	37	.427	4.70	205	595	550	267	370

League Championship
| 1981 | (LOS ANGELES) | | | | | | | | | |
| | One year | 0 | 0 | — | 0.00 | 1 | 1 | 0 | 0 | 1 |

World Series
| 1981 | (LOS ANGELES) | | | | | | | | | |
| | One year | 0 | 0 | — | 9.00 | 1 | 1 | 0 | 5 | 0 |

ED CHANDLER
B. Feb. 17, 1922, Pinson, Ala.
Right handed, B.R.
6'2" 190 lbs.

YEAR	CLUB	W	L	PCT	ERA	G	IP	H	BB	SO
1947	BROOKLYN (N)	0	1	.000	6.37	15	29.2	31	12	8

ESTEY CHANEY
B. Jan. 29, 1891, Hadley, Pa.
D. Feb. 5, 1952, Cleveland, Ohio
Right handed, B.R.
5'11" 170 lbs.

YEAR	CLUB	W	L	PCT	ERA	G	IP	H	BB	SO
1913	Boston (A)	0	0	—	9.00	1	1	1	2	0
1914	BROOKLYN (F)	0	0	—	6.75	1	4	7	2	1
	Two years	0	0	—	7.20	2	5	8	4	1

BEN CHAPMAN
B. Dec. 25, 1908, Nashville, Tenn.
Right handed, B.R.
6' 190 lbs.

YEAR	CLUB	W	L	PCT	ERA	G	IP	H	BB	SO
1944	BROOKLYN (N)	5	3	.625	3.40	11	79.1	75	33	37
1945	BROOKLYN (N)	3	3	.500	5.50	10	54		32	23
	Three years (totals)	8	6	.571	4.39	25	141.1	147	71	65

BILL CHAPPELLE
B. March 22, 1884, Waterloo, N.Y.
D. Dec. 31, 1944, Mineola, N.Y.
Right handed, B.R.
6'2" 206 lbs.

YEAR	CLUB	W	L	PCT	ERA	G	IP	H	BB	SO
1914	BROOKLYN (F)	4	2	.667	3.15	16	74.1	71	29	31
	Three years (totals)	7	7	.500	2.38	35	177.2	167	59	62

LARRY CHENEY
B. May 2, 1886, Belleville, Kan.
D. Jan. 6, 1969, Daytona Beach, Fla.
Right handed, B.R.
6'1½" 185 lbs.

YEAR	CLUB	W	L	PCT	ERA	G	IP	H	BB	SO
1911	Chicago (N)	1	0	1.000	0.00	3	10	8	3	11
1912	Chicago (N)	26	10	.722	2.85	42	303.1	262	111	140
1913	Chicago (N)	20	14	.588	2.57	54	305	271	98	136
1914	Chicago (N)	20	18	.526	2.54	50	311.1	239	140	157
1915	Chicago (N)									
1915	BROOKLYN (N)	0	2	.000	1.67	5	27		17	11
	(year totals)	7	11	.389	3.24	30	158.1	136	72	79
1916	BROOKLYN (N)	18	12	.600	1.92	41	253	178	105	166
1917	BROOKLYN (N)	8	12	.400	2.35	35	210.1	185	73	102
1918	BROOKLYN (N)	11	13	.458	3.00	32	200.2	177	74	83
1919	BROOKLYN (N)	1	3	.250	4.15	9	39		14	14
1919	Boston (N)									
1919	Philadelphia (N)									
	(year totals)	3	10	.231	4.18	26	129.1	149	57	52
	Nine years	114	100	.533	2.70	313	1881.1	1605	733	926
World Series										
	One year	0	0	—	3.00	1	3	4	1	5

BOB CHIPMAN
B. Oct. 11, 1918, Brooklyn, N.Y.
D. Nov. 8, 1973, Huntington, N.Y.
Left handed, B.L.
6'2" 190 lbs.

YEAR	CLUB	W	L	PCT	ERA	G	IP	H	BB	SO
1941	BROOKLYN (N)	1	0	1.000	0.00	1	5	3	1	3
1942	BROOKLYN (N)	0	0	—	0.00	2	1.1	1	2	1
1943	BROOKLYN (N)	0	0	—	0.00	1	1.2	2	2	0
1944	BROOKLYN (N)	3	1	.750	4.25	11	36		24	20

YEAR	CLUB	W	L	PCT	ERA	G	IP	H	BB	SO
1944	Chicago (N)									
	(year totals)	12	10	.545	3.65	37	165.1	185	64	61
1945	Chicago (N)	4	5	.444	3.50	25	72	63	34	29
1946	Chicago (N)	6	5	.545	3.13	34	109.1	103	54	42
1947	Chicago (N)	7	6	.538	3.68	32	134.2	135	66	51
1948	Chicago (N)	2	1	.667	3.58	34	60.1	73	24	16
1949	Chicago (N)	7	8	.467	3.97	38	113.1	110	63	46
1950	Boston (N)	7	7	.500	4.43	27	124	127	37	40
1951	Boston (N)	4	3	.571	4.85	33	52	59	19	17
1952	Boston (N)	1	1	.500	2.81	29	41.2	28	20	16
	Twelve years	51	46	.526	3.72	293	880.2	889	386	322
World Series										
	One year	0	0	—	0.00	1	1	0	1	0

CHUCK CHURN

B. Feb. 1, 1930, Bridgetown, Va.
Right handed, B.R.
6'3" 205 lbs.

YEAR	CLUB	W	L	PCT	ERA	G	IP	H	BB	SO
1957	Pittsburgh (N)	0	0	—	4.32	5	8.1	9	4	4
1958	Cleveland (A)	0	0	—	6.23	6	8.2	12	5	4
1959	LOS ANGELES (N)	3	2	.600	4.99	14	30.2	28	10	24
	Three years	3	2	.600	5.10	25	47.2	49	19	32
World Series										
	One year	0	0	—	27.00	1	.2	5	0	0

WATTY CLARK

B. May 16, 1902, St. Joseph, La.
D. March 4, 1972, Clearwater, Fla.
Left handed, B.L.
6'½" 175 lbs.

YEAR	CLUB	W	L	PCT	ERA	G	IP	H	BB	SO
1924	Cleveland (A)	1	3	.250	7.01	12	25.2	38	14	6
1927	BROOKLYN (N)	7	2	.778	2.32	27	73.2	74	19	32
1928	BROOKLYN (N)	12	9	.571	2.68	40	194.2	193	50	85
1929	BROOKLYN (N)	16	19	.457	3.74	41	279	295	71	140
1930	BROOKLYN (N)	13	13	.500	4.19	44	200	209	38	81
1931	BROOKLYN (N)	14	10	.583	3.20	34	233.1	243	52	96
1932	BROOKLYN (N)	20	12	.625	3.49	40	273	282	49	99
1933	BROOKLYN (N)	2	4	.333	4.76	11	51		6	14
1933	New York (N)									
	(year totals)	5	8	.385	4.75	27	94.2	119	17	25
1934	New York (N)									
1934	BROOKLYN (N)	2	0	1.000	5.40	17	25		9	10
	(year totals)	3	2	.600	5.93	22	44	63	14	16
1935	BROOKLYN (N)	13	8	.619	3.30	33	207	215	28	35
1936	BROOKLYN (N)	7	11	.389	4.43	33	120	162	28	28
1937	BROOKLYN (N)	0	0	—	7.71	2	2.1	4	3	0
	Twelve years	111	97	.534	3.66	355	1747.1	1897	383	643

JACKIE COLLUM

B. June 21, 1927, Victor, Iowa
Left handed, B.L.
5'7½" 160 lbs.

YEAR	CLUB	W	L	PCT	ERA	G	IP	H	BB	SO
1957	BROOKLYN (N)	0	0	.000	9.00	3	4	—	4	7
1958	LOS ANGELES (N)	0	0	—	8.10	2	3.1	4	2	0
	Nine years (totals)	32	28	.533	4.15	171	464.1	480	173	171

JACK COOMBS

B. Nov. 18, 1882, LeGrande, Iowa
D. April 15, 1957, Palestine, Texas
Right handed, B.B.
6' 185 lbs.

YEAR	CLUB	W	L	PCT	ERA	G	IP	H	BB	SO
1906	Philadelphia (A)	11	10	.524	2.50	23	173	144	68	90
1907	Philadelphia (A)	6	9	.400	3.12	23	132.2	109	64	73
1908	Philadelphia (A)	8	5	.615	2.00	26	153	130	64	80
1909	Philadelphia (A)	12	12	.500	2.32	31	205.2	156	73	97
1910	Philadelphia (A)	31	9	.775	1.30	45	353	248	115	224

YEAR	CLUB	W	L	PCT	ERA	G	IP	H	BB	SO
1911	Philadelphia (A)	28	12	.700	3.53	47	336.2	360	119	185
1912	Philadelphia (A)	20	10	.667	3.29	40	262.1	227	94	120
1913	Philadelphia (A)	1	0	1.000	10.13	2	5.1	5	6	0
1914	Philadelphia (A)	0	1	.000	4.50	2	8	8	3	1
1915	BROOKLYN (N)	14	10	.583	2.58	29	195.2	166	91	56
1916	BROOKLYN (N)	12	8	.600	2.66	27	159	136	44	47
1917	BROOKLYN (N)	7	11	.389	3.96	31	141	147	49	34
1918	BROOKLYN (N)	8	14	.364	3.81	27	189	191	49	44
1920	Detroit (A)	0	0	—	3.18	2	5.2	7	2	1
	Fourteen years	158	111	.587	2.78	355	2320	2034	841	1052
World Series										
	Three years	5	0	1.000	2.70	6	53.1	41	21	34

GEORGE CRABLE B. 1886, Brooklyn, N.Y.
Left handed, B.L.
6'1" 190 lbs.

YEAR	CLUB	W	L	PCT	ERA	G	IP	H	BB	SO
1910	BROOKLYN (N)	1	0	1.000	4.91	2	7.1	5	5	3

ROGER CRAIG B. Feb. 17, 1931, Durham, N.C.
Right handed, B.R.
6'4" 185 lbs.

YEAR	CLUB	W	L	PCT	ERA	G	IP	H	BB	SO
1955	BROOKLYN (N)	5	3	.625	2.78	21	90.2	81	43	48
1956	BROOKLYN (N)	12	11	.522	3.71	35	199	169	87	109
1957	BROOKLYN (N)	6	9	.400	4.61	32	111.1	102	47	69
1958	LOS ANGELES (N)	2	1	.667	4.50	9	32	30	12	16
1959	LOS ANGELES (N)	11	5	.688	2.06	29	152.2	122	45	76
1960	LOS ANGELES (N)	8	3	.727	3.27	21	115.2	99	43	69
1961	LOS ANGELES (N)	5	6	.455	6.15	40	112.2	130	52	63
1962	New York (N)	10	24	.294	4.51	42	233.1	261	70	118
1963	New York (N)	5	22	.185	3.78	46	236	249	58	108
1964	St. Louis (N)	7	9	.438	3.25	39	166	180	35	84
1965	Cincinnati (N)	1	4	.200	3.64	40	64.1	74	25	30
1966	Philadelphia (N)	2	1	.667	5.56	14	22.2	31	5	13
	Twelve years	74	98	.430	3.83	368	1536.1	1528	522	803
World Series										
	Four years	2	2	.500	6.49	7	26.1	31	16	25

CANNONBALL CRANE B. May, 1862, Boston, Mass.
D. Sept. 19, 1896, Rochester, N.Y.
Right handed, B.R.
5'10½" 204 lbs.

YEAR	CLUB	W	L	PCT	ERA	G	IP	H	BB	SO
1893	BROOKLYN (N)	0	2	.000	7.20	2	7		5	3
	(year totals)	2	6	.250	6.89	12	78.1	103	50	16
	Nine years (totals)	72	95	.431	3.99	204	1550.1	1525	887	720

CLAUDE CROCKER B. July 20, 1924, Caroleen, N.Y.
Right handed, B.R.
6'2" 185 lbs.

YEAR	CLUB	W	L	PCT	ERA	G	IP	H	BB	SO
1944	BROOKLYN (N)	0	0	—	10.80	2	3.1	6	5	1
1945	BROOKLYN (N)	0	0	—	0.00	1	2	2	1	1
	Two years	0	0	—	6.75	3	5.1	8	6	2

JOHN CRONIN B. May 26, 1874, Staten Island, N.Y.
D. July 13, 1929, Middletown, N.Y.
Right handed, B.R.
6' 200 lbs.

YEAR	CLUB	W	L	PCT	ERA	G	IP	H	BB	SO
1895	BROOKLYN (N)	0	0	—	10.80	2	5	10	3	1
1898	Pittsburgh (N)	2	2	.500	3.54	4	28	35	8	9
1899	Cincinnati (N)	2	2	.500	5.49	5	41	56	16	9

YEAR	CLUB	W	L	PCT	ERA	G	IP	H	BB	SO
1901	Detroit (A)	13	15	.464	3.89	30	219.2	261	42	62
1902	Detroit (A)									
1902	Baltimore (A)									
1902	New York (N)									
	(year totals)	8	11	.421	3.09	27	207	197	50	77
1903	New York (N)	6	4	.600	3.81	20	115.2	130	37	50
1904	BROOKLYN (N)	12	23	.343	2.70	40	307	284	79	110
	Seven years	43	57	.430	3.40	128	923.1	973	235	318

BILL CROUCH   B. Aug. 20, 1910, Wilmington, Del.
D. Dec. 26, 1980, Howell, Mich.
Right handed, B.B.
6'1" 180 lbs.

YEAR	CLUB	W	L	PCT	ERA	G	IP	H	BB	SO
1939	BROOKLYN (N)	4	0	1.000	2.58	6	38.1	37	14	10
	Three years (totals)	8	5	.615	3.47	50	155.2	159	52	55

GEORGE CULVER   B. July 8, 1943, Salinas, Calif.
Right handed, B.R.
6'2" 185 lbs.

YEAR	CLUB	W	L	PCT	ERA	G	IP	H	BB	SO
1973	LOS ANGELES (N)	4	4	.500	3.00	28	42		21	23
	Nine years (totals)	48	49	.495	3.62	335	788.1	793	352	451

CLIFF CURTIS   B. July 3, 1883, Delaware, Ohio
D. April 23, 1943, Newark, Ohio
Right handed, B.R.

YEAR	CLUB	W	L	PCT	ERA	G	IP	H	BB	SO
1909	Boston (N)	4	4	.500	1.41	10	83	53	30	22
1910	Boston (N)	6	24	.200	3.55	43	251	251	124	75
1911	Boston (N)									
1911	Chicago (N)									
1911	Philadelphia (N)									
	(year totals)	4	11	.267	3.77	24	129	131	54	40
1912	Philadelphia (N)									
1912	BROOKLYN (N)	5	7	.417	3.94	19	80		37	22
	(year totals)	7	12	.368	3.67	29	130	127	54	42
1913	BROOKLYN (N)	9	9	.500	3.26	30	151.2	145	55	57
	Five years	30	60	.333	3.31	136	744.2	707	317	236

BOB DARNELL   B. Nov. 6, 1930, Wewoka, Okla.
Right handed, B.R.
5'10" 175 lbs.

YEAR	CLUB	W	L	PCT	ERA	G	IP	H	BB	SO
1954	BROOKLYN (N)	0	0	—	3.14	6	14.1	15	7	5
1956	BROOKLYN (N)	0	0	—	0.00	1	1.1	1	0	0
	Two years	0	0	—	2.87	7	15.2	16	7	5

BOBBY DARWIN   B. Feb. 16, 1943, Los Angeles, Calif.
Right handed, B.R.
6'2" 190 lbs.

YEAR	CLUB	W	L	PCT	ERA	G	IP	H	BB	SO
1962	LOS ANGELES (A)	0	1	.000	10.80	1	3.1	8	4	6
1969	LOS ANGELES (N)	0	0	—	9.00	3	4	4	5	0
	Two years	0	1	.000	9.82	4	7.1	12	9	6

The Pitchers' Catalogue • 171

DAN DAUB B. Jan. 12. 1869, Middletown, Ohio
D. March 25, 1951, Bradenton, Fla.
Right handed, B.R.
5'10" 160 lbs.

YEAR	CLUB	W	L	PCT	ERA	G	IP	H	BB	SO
1892	Cincinnati (N)	1	2	.333	2.88	4	25	23	13	7
1893	BROOKLYN (N)	6	6	.500	3.84	12	103	104	61	25
1894	BROOKLYN (N)	9	12	.429	6.32	33	215	285	90	45
1895	BROOKLYN (N)	10	10	.500	4.29	25	184.2	212	51	36
1896	BROOKLYN (N)	12	11	.522	3.60	32	225	255	63	53
1897	BROOKLYN (N)	6	11	.353	6.08	19	137.2	180	48	19
	Six years	44	52	.458	4.79	125	890.1	1057	326	185

CURT DAVIS B. Sept. 7, 1903, Greenfield, Mo.
D. Oct. 13, 1965, Covina, Calif.
Right handed, B.R.
6'2" 185 lbs.

YEAR	CLUB	W	L	PCT	ERA	G	IP	H	BB	SO
1934	Philadelphia (N)	19	17	.528	2.95	51	274.1	283	60	99
1935	Philadelphia (N)	16	14	.533	3.66	44	231	264	47	74
1936	Philadelphia (N)									
1936	Chicago (N)									
	(year totals)	13	13	.500	3.46	34	213.1	217	50	70
1937	Chicago (N)	10	5	.667	4.08	28	123.2	138	30	32
1938	St. Louis (N)	12	8	.600	3.63	40	173.1	187	27	36
1939	St. Louis (N)	22	16	.579	3.63	49	248	279	48	70
1940	St. Louis (N)									
1940	BROOKLYN (N)	8	7	.533	3.81	22	137		19	46
	(year totals)	8	11	.421	4.19	36	191	208	38	58
1941	BROOKLYN (N)	13	7	.650	2.97	28	154.1	141	27	50
1942	BROOKLYN (N)	15	6	.714	2.36	32	206	179	51	60
1943	BROOKLYN (N)	10	13	.435	3.78	31	164.1	182	39	47
1944	BROOKLYN (N)	10	11	.476	3.34	31	194	207	39	49
1945	BROOKLYN (N)	10	10	.500	3.25	24	149.2	171	21	39
1946	BROOKLYN (N)	0	0	—	13.50	1	2	3	2	0
	Thirteen years	158	131	.547	3.42	429	2325	2459	479	684
World Series										
	One year	0	0	.000	5.06	1	5.1	6	3	1

PEA RIDGE DAY B. Aug. 27, 1899, Pea Ridge, Ark.
D. March 21, 1934, Kansas City, Mo.
Right handed, B.R.
6' 190 lbs.

YEAR	CLUB	W	L	PCT	ERA	G	IP	H	BB	SO
1931	BROOKLYN (N)	2	2	.500	4.55	22	57.1	75	13	30
	Four years (totals)	5	7	.417	5.30	46	122.1	163	28	48

ART DECATUR B. Jan. 14, 1894, Cleveland, Ohio
D. April 25, 1966, Talladega, Ala.
Right handed, B.R.
6'1" 190 lbs.

YEAR	CLUB	W	L	PCT	ERA	G	IP	H	BB	SO
1922	BROOKLYN (N)	3	4	.429	2.77	29	87.2	87	29	31
1923	BROOKLYN (N)	3	3	.500	2.67	36	104.2	115	34	27
1924	BROOKLYN (N)	10	9	.526	4.07	31	128.1	158	28	39
1925	BROOKLYN (N)	0	0	.000		1	1		0	0
1925	Philadelphia (N)									
	(year totals)	4	13	.235	5.37	26	129	173	35	31
1926	Philadelphia (N)	0	0	—	6.00	2	3	6	2	0
1927	Philadelphia (N)	3	5	.375	7.26	29	96.2	130	20	27
	Six years	23	34	.404	4.47	153	549.1	669	148	155

WHEEZER DELL

B. June 11, 1887, Tuscarora, Nev.
D. Aug. 24, 1966, Independence, Calif.
Right handed, B.R.
6'4" 210 lbs.

YEAR	CLUB	W	L	PCT	ERA	G	IP	H	BB	SO
1912	St. Louis (N)	0	0	—	11.57	3	2.1	3	3	0
1915	BROOKLYN (N)	11	10	.524	2.34	40	215	166	100	94
1916	BROOKLYN (N)	8	9	.471	2.26	32	155	143	43	76
1917	BROOKLYN (N)	0	4	.000	3.72	17	58	55	25	28
	Four years	19	23	.452	2.55	92	430.1	367	171	198
World Series	One year	0	0	—	0.00	1	1	1	0	0

EDDIE DENT

B. Dec. 8, 1887, Baltimore, Md.
D. Nov. 25, 1974, Birmingham, Ala.
Right handed, B.R.
6'1" 190 lbs.

YEAR	CLUB	W	L	PCT	ERA	G	IP	H	BB	SO
1909	BROOKLYN (N)	2	4	.333	4.29	6	42	47	15	17
1911	BROOKLYN (N)	2	1	.667	3.69	5	31.2	30	10	3
1912	BROOKLYN (N)	0	0	—	36.00	1	1	4	1	1
	Three years	4	5	.444	4.46	12	74.2	81	26	21

RUBE DESSAU

B. March 29, 1883, New Galilee, Pa.
D. May 6, 1952, York, Pa.
Right handed, B.L.
5'11" 175 lbs.

YEAR	CLUB	W	L	PCT	ERA	G	IP	H	BB	SO
1910	BROOKLYN (N)	3	4	.429	5.79	19	51.1	67	29	24
	Two years (totals)	3	5	.375	6.53	21	60.2	80	39	25

LEO DICKERMAN

B. Oct. 31, 1896, DeSoto, Mo.
Right handed, B.R.
6'4" 192 lbs.

YEAR	CLUB	W	L	PCT	ERA	G	IP	H	BB	SO
1923	BROOKLYN (N)									
1924	BROOKLYN (N)	8	12	.400	3.59	35	165.2	185	71	57
	Three years (totals)	19	27	.413	3.95	89	435.2	448	217	134

BILL DOAK

B. Jan. 28, 1891, Pittsburgh, Pa.
D. Nov. 26, 1954, Bradenton, Fla.
Right handed, B.R.
6'½" 165 lbs.

YEAR	CLUB	W	L	PCT	ERA	G	IP	H	BB	SO
1912	Cincinnati (N)	0	0	—	4.50	1	2	4	1	0
1913	St. Louis (N)	2	8	.200	3.10	15	93	79	39	51
1914	St. Louis (N)	20	6	.769	1.72	36	256	193	87	118
1915	St. Louis (N)	16	18	.471	2.64	38	276	263	85	124
1916	St. Louis (N)	12	8	.600	2.63	29	192	177	55	82
1917	St. Louis (N)	16	20	.444	3.10	44	281.1	257	85	111
1918	St. Louis (N)	9	15	.375	2.43	31	211	191	60	74
1919	St. Louis (N)	13	14	.481	3.11	31	202.2	182	55	69
1920	St. Louis (N)	20	12	.625	2.53	39	270	256	80	90
1921	St. Louis (N)	15	6	.714	2.59	32	208.2	224	37	83
1922	St. Louis (N)	11	13	.458	5.54	37	180.1	222	69	73
1923	St. Louis (N)	8	13	.381	3.26	30	185	199	69	53
1924	St. Louis (N)									
1924	BROOKLYN (N)	11	5	.688	3.28	21	149		35	32
	(year totals)	13	6	.684	3.10	32	171.1	155	49	39
1927	BROOKLYN (N)	11	8	.579	3.48	27	145	153	40	32
1928	BROOKLYN (N)	3	8	.273	3.26	28	99.1	104	35	12
1929	St. Louis (N)	1	2	.333	12.00	3	9	17	5	3
	Sixteen years	170	157	.520	2.98	453	2782.2	2676	851	1014

GEORGE DOCKINS

B. May 5, 1917, Clyde, Kan.
Left handed, B.L.
6' 175 lbs.

YEAR	CLUB	W	L	PCT	ERA	G	IP	H	BB	SO
1947	BROOKLYN (N)	0	0	—	11.81	4	5.1	10	2	1
	Two years (totals)	8	6	.571	3.55	35	131.2	142	40	34

WILD BILL DONOVAN

B. Oct. 13, 1876, Lawrence, Mass.
D. Dec. 9, 1923, Forsyth, N.Y.
Right handed, B.R.
5'11" 190 lbs.

YEAR	CLUB	W	L	PCT	ERA	G	IP	H	BB	SO
1898	Washington (N)	1	6	.143	4.30	17	88	88	69	36
1899	BROOKLYN (N)	1	2	.333	4.32	5	25	35	13	11
1900	BROOKLYN (N)	1	2	.333	6.68	5	31	36	18	13
1901	BROOKLYN (N)	25	15	.625	2.77	45	351	324	152	226
1902	BROOKLYN (N)	17	15	.531	2.78	35	297.2	250	111	170
1903	Detroit (A)	17	16	.515	2.29	35	307	247	95	187
1904	Detroit (A)	17	16	.515	2.46	34	293	251	94	137
1905	Detroit (A)	19	14	.576	2.60	34	280.2	236	101	135
1906	Detroit (A)	9	15	.375	3.15	25	211.2	221	72	85
1907	Detroit (A)	25	4	.862	2.19	32	271	222	82	123
1908	Detroit (A)	18	7	.720	2.08	29	242.2	210	53	141
1909	Detroit (A)	8	7	.533	2.31	21	140.1	121	60	76
1910	Detroit (A)	18	7	.720	2.42	26	208.2	184	61	107
1911	Detroit (A)	10	9	.526	3.31	20	168.1	160	64	81
1912	Detroit (A)	0	0	—	0.90	3	10	5	2	6
1915	New York (A)	0	3	.000	4.81	9	33.2	35	10	17
1916	New York (A)	0	0	—	0.00	1	1	1	1	0
1918	Detroit (A)	1	0	1.000	1.50	2	6	5	1	1
	Eighteen years	187	138	.575	2.69	378	2966.2	2631	1059	1552
World Series										
	Three years	1	4	.200	2.70	6	50	41	17	33

JACK DOSCHER

B. July 27 1880, Troy, N.Y.
D. May 22, 1971, Park Ridge, N.J.
Left handed, B.L.
6'1"

YEAR	CLUB	W	L	PCT	ERA	G	IP	H	BB	SO
1903	BROOKLYN (N)	0	0	.000	.000	3	7		9	4
1904	BROOKLYN (N)	0	1	.000	0.00	2	6.1	1	1	2
1905	BROOKLYN (N)	1	5	.167	3.17	12	71	60	30	33
1906	BROOKLYN (N)	0	1	.000	1.29	2	14	12	4	10
	Five years (totals)	2	11	.154	2.84	27	145.2	118	68	61

PHIL DOUGLAS

B. June 17, 1890, Cedartown, Ga.
D. Aug. 1, 1952, Sequatchie Valley, Tenn.
Right handed, B.R.
6'3" 190 lbs.

YEAR	CLUB	W	L	PCT	ERA	G	IP	H	BB	SO
1915	BROOKLYN (N)	5	5	.500	2.61	20	117		17	63
	Nine years (totals)	93	93	.500	2.80	299	1708.1	1626	411	683

AL DOWNING

B. June 28, 1941, Trenton, N.J.
Left handed, B.R.
5'11" 175 lbs.

YEAR	CLUB	W	L	PCT	ERA	G	IP	H	BB	SO
1961	New York (A)	0	1	.000	8.00	5	9	7	12	12
1962	New York (A)	0	0	—	0.00	1	1	0	0	1
1963	New York (A)	13	5	.722	2.56	24	175.2	114	80	171
1964	New York (A)	13	8	.619	3.47	37	244	201	120	217
1965	New York (A)	12	14	.462	3.40	35	212	185	105	179
1966	New York (A)	10	11	.476	3.56	30	200	178	79	152
1967	New York (A)	14	10	.583	2.63	31	201.2	158	61	171
1968	New York (A)	3	3	.500	3.52	15	61.1	54	20	40
1969	New York (A)	7	5	.583	3.38	30	130.2	117	49	85

YEAR	CLUB	W	L	PCT	ERA	G	IP	H	BB	SO
1970	Oakland (A)									
1970	Milwaukee (A)									
	(year totals)	5	13	.278	3.52	27	135.1	118	81	79
1971	LOS ANGELES (N)	20	9	.690	2.68	37	262	245	84	136
1972	LOS ANGELES (N)	9	9	.500	2.98	31	202.2	196	67	117
1973	LOS ANGELES (N)	9	9	.500	3.31	30	193	155	68	124
1974	LOS ANGELES (N)	5	6	.455	3.67	21	98	94	45	63
1975	LOS ANGELES (N)	2	1	.667	2.88	22	75	59	28	39
1976	LOS ANGELES (N)	1	2	.333	3.86	17	46.2	43	18	30
1977	LOS ANGELES (N)	0	1	.000	6.75	12	20	22	16	23
	Seventeen years	123	107	.535	3.22	405	2268	1946	933	1639
League Championship										
	One year	0	0	—	0.00	1	4	1	1	0
World Series										
	Three years	0	3	.000	6.06	5	16.1	20	7	14

CARL DOYLE B. July 30, 1912, Knxoville, Tenn.
D. Sept. 4, 1951, Knoxville, Tenn.
Right handed, B.R.
6'1" 185 lbs.

YEAR	CLUB	W	L	PCT	ERA	G	IP	H	BB	SO
1939	BROOKLYN (N)	1	2	.333	1.02	5	17.2	8	7	7
1940	BROOKLYN (N)	0	0	.000		3	6		6	4
	Four years (totals)	6	15	.286	6.95	51	222.2	277	155	101

TOM DRAKE B. Aug. 7, 1914, Birmingham, Ala.
Right handed, B.R.
6'1" 185 lbs.

YEAR	CLUB	W	L	PCT	ERA	G	IP	H	BB	SO
1941	BROOKLYN (N)	1	1	.500	4.38	10	24.2	26	9	12
	Two years (totals)	1	2	.333	6.13	18	39.2	49	28	13

DON DRYSDALE B. July 23, 1936, Van Nuys, Calif.
Right handed, B.R.
6'5" 190 lbs.

YEAR	CLUB	W	L	PCT	ERA	G	IP	H	BB	SO
1956	BROOKLYN (N)	5	5	.500	2.64	25	99	95	31	55
1957	BROOKLYN (N)	17	9	.654	2.69	34	221	197	61	148
1958	LOS ANGELES (N)	12	13	.480	4.17	44	211.2	214	72	131
1959	LOS ANGELES (N)	17	13	.567	3.46	44	270.2	237	93	242
1960	LOS ANGELES (N)	15	14	.517	2.84	41	269	214	72	246
1961	LOS ANGELES (N)	13	10	.565	3.69	40	244	236	83	182
1962	LOS ANGELES (N)	25	9	.735	2.83	43	314.1	272	78	232
1963	LOS ANGELES (N)	19	17	.528	2.63	42	315.1	287	57	251
1964	LOS ANGELES (N)	18	16	.529	2.18	40	321.1	242	68	237
1965	LOS ANGELES (N)	23	12	.657	2.77	44	308.1	270	66	210
1966	LOS ANGELES (N)	13	16	.448	3.42	40	273.2	279	45	177
1967	LOS ANGELES (N)	13	16	.448	2.74	38	282	269	60	196
1968	LOS ANGELES (N)	14	12	.538	2.15	31	239	201	56	155
1969	LOS ANGELES (N)	5	4	.556	4.43	12	63	71	13	24
	Fourteen years	209	166	.557	2.95	518	3432.1	3084	855	2486

World Series

YEAR	CLUB	W	L	PCT	ERA	G	IP	H	BB	SO
1956	BROOKLYN (N)	0	0	.000	9.00	1	2	2	1	1
1959	LOS ANGELES (N)	1	0	1.000	1.29	1	7	11	4	5
1963	LOS ANGELES (N)	1	0	1.000	0.00	1	9	3	1	9
1965	LOS ANGELES (N)	1	1	.500	3.86	2	11.2	12	3	15
1966	LOS ANGELES (N)	0	2	.000	4.50	2	10	8	3	6
	Five years	3	3	.500	2.95	7	39.2	36	12	36

CLISE DUDLEY

B. Aug. 8, 1903, Graham, N.C.
Right handed, B.L.
6'1" 195 lbs.

YEAR	CLUB	W	L	PCT	ERA	G	IP	H	BB	SO
1929	BROOKLYN (N)	6	14	.300	5.69	35	156.2	202	64	33
1930	BROOKLYN (N)	2	4	.333	6.35	21	66.2	103	27	18
1931	Philadelphia (N)	8	14	.364	3.52	30	179	206	56	50
1932	Philadelphia (N)	1	1	.500	7.13	13	17.2	23	8	5
1933	Pittsburgh (N)	0	0	—	135.00	1	.1	6	1	0
	Five years	17	33	.340	5.03	100	420.1	540	156	106

JOHN DUFFIE

B. Oct. 4, 1945, Greenwood, S.C.
Right handed, B.R.
6'7" 210 lbs.

YEAR	CLUB	W	L	PCT	ERA	G	IP	H	BB	SO
1967	LOS ANGELES (N)	0	2	.000	2.79	2	9.2	11	4	6

JACK DUNN

B. Oct. 6, 1872, Meadville, Pa.
D. Oct. 22, 1928, Baltimore, Md.
Right handed, B.R.

YEAR	CLUB	W	L	PCT	ERA	G	IP	H	BB	SO
1897	BROOKLYN (N)	14	9	.609	4.57	25	216.2	251	66	26
1898	BROOKLYN (N)	16	21	.432	3.60	41	322.2	352	82	66
1899	BROOKLYN (N)	23	13	.639	3.70	41	299.1	323	86	48
1900	BROOKLYN (N)	3	4	.429	3.84	10	60		33	10
1900	Philadelphia (N)									
	(year totals)	8	9	.471	5.16	20	143	175	57	18
1901	Philadelphia (N)									
1901	Baltimore (A)									
	(year totals)	3	4	.429	4.90	11	64.1	85	28	6
1902	New York (N)	0	3	.000	3.71	3	26.2	28	12	6
1904	New York (N)	0	0	—	4.50	1	4	3	3	1
	Seven years	64	59	.520	4.11	142	1076.2	1217	334	171

BULL DURHAM

B. 1881, Bolivar, N.Y.
Right handed

YEAR	CLUB	W	L	PCT	ERA	G	IP	H	BB	SO
1904	BROOKLYN (N)	1	0	1.000	3.27	2	11	10	5	1
	Four years (totals)	1	0	1.000	5.28	9	29	37	12	6

DICK DURNING

B. Oct. 10, 1892, Louisville, Ky.
D. Sept. 23, 1948, Castle Point, N.Y.
Left handed, B.L.
6'2" 178 lbs.

YEAR	CLUB	W	L	PCT	ERA	G	IP	H	BB	SO
1917	BROOKLYN (N)	0	0	—	0.00	1	1	0	0	0
1918	BROOKLYN (N)	0	0	—	13.50	1	2	3	4	0
	Two years	0	0	—	9.00	2	3	3	4	0

GEORGE EARNSHAW

B. Feb. 15, 1900, New York, N.Y.
D. Dec. 1, 1976, Little Rock, Ark.
Right handed, B.R.
6'4" 210 lbs.

YEAR	CLUB	W	L	PCT	ERA	G	IP	H	BB	SO
1928	Philadelphia (A)	7	7	.500	3.81	26	158.1	143	100	117
1929	Philadelphia (A)	24	8	.750	3.29	44	254.2	233	125	149
1930	Philadelphia (A)	22	13	.629	4.44	49	296	299	139	193
1931	Philadelphia (A)	21	7	.750	3.67	43	281.2	255	75	152
1932	Philadelphia (A)	19	13	.594	4.77	36	245.1	262	94	109
1933	Philadelphia (A)	5	10	.333	5.97	21	117.2	153	58	37
1934	Chicago (A)	14	11	.560	4.52	33	277	242	104	97
1935	Chicago (A)									
1935	BROOKLYN (N)	8	12	.400	4.12	25	166		53	72
	(year totals)	9	14	.391	4.60	28	184	201	64	80

YEAR	CLUB	W	L	PCT	ERA	G	IP	H	BB	SO
1936	BROOKLYN (N)	4	9	.308	5.32	19	93		30	40
1936	St. Louis (N)									
	(year totals)	6	10	.375	5.73	39	150.2	193	50	71
	Nine years	127	93	.577	4.38	319	1915.1	1981	809	1005
World Series										
	Three years	4	3	.571	1.58	8	62.2	39	17	56

MAL EASON   B. March 13, 1879, Brookville, Pa.
D. April 16, 1970, Douglas, Ariz.
Right handed

YEAR	CLUB	W	L	PCT	ERA	G	IP	H	BB	SO
1900	Chicago (N)	1	0	1.000	1.00	1	9	9	3	2
1901	Chicago (N)	8	17	.320	3.59	27	220.2	246	60	68
1902	Chicago (N)									
1902	Boston (N)									
	(year totals)	10	12	.455	2.61	29	224.1	258	61	54
1903	Detroit (A)	2	5	.286	3.36	7	56.1	60	19	21
1905	BROOKLYN (N)	5	21	.192	4.30	27	207	230	72	64
1906	BROOKLYN (N)	11	16	.407	3.25	34	227	212	84	64
	Six years	37	71	.343	3.39	125	944.1	1015	289	273

EDDIE EAYRS   B. Nov. 10, 1890, Blackstone, Mass.
D. Nov. 30, 1969, Warwick, R.I.
Left handed, B.L.
5'7" 160 lbs.

YEAR	CLUB	W	L	PCT	ERA	G	IP	H	BB	SO
1921	BROOKLYN (N)	0	0	—	17.36	2	4.2	9	9	1
	Three years (totals)	1	2	.333	6.23	11	39	53	27	13

DICK EGAN   B. March 24, 1937, Berkeley, Calif.
Left handed, B.L.
6'4" 193 lbs.

YEAR	CLUB	W	L	PCT	ERA	G	IP	H	BB	SO
1967	LOS ANGELES (N)	1	1	.500	6.25	20	31.2	34	15	20
	Four years (totals)	1	2	.333	5.15	74	101.1	109	41	68

RUBE EHRHARDT   B. Nov. 20, 1894, Beecher, Ill.
D. April 27, 1980, Chicago Heights, Ill.
Right handed, B.R.
6'2" 190 lbs.

YEAR	CLUB	W	L	PCT	ERA	G	IP	H	BB	SO
1924	BROOKLYN (N)	5	3	.625	2.26	15	83.2	71	17	13
1925	BROOKLYN (N)	10	14	.417	5.03	36	207.2	239	62	47
1926	BROOKLYN (N)	2	5	.286	3.90	44	97	101	35	25
1927	BROOKLYN (N)	3	7	.300	3.57	46	95.2	90	37	22
1928	BROOKLYN (N)	1	3	.250	4.67	28	54	74	27	12
1929	Cincinnati (N)	1	2	.333	4.74	24	49.1	58	22	9
	Six years	22	34	.393	4.15	193	587.1	633	200	128

HARRY EISENSTAT   B. Oct. 10, 1915, Brooklyn, N.Y.
Left handed, B.L.
5'11" 180 lbs.

YEAR	CLUB	W	L	PCT	ERA	G	IP	H	BB	SO
1935	BROOKLYN (N)	0	1	.000	13.50	2	4.2	9	2	2
1936	BROOKLYN (N)	1	2	.333	5.65	5	14.1	22	6	5
1937	BROOKLYN (N)	3	3	.500	3.97	13	47.2	61	11	12
	Eight years (totals)	25	27	.481	3.84	165	478.2	550	114	157

The Pitchers' Catalogue • 177

JUMBO ELLIOTT B. Oct. 22, 1900, St. Louis, Mo.
D. Jan. 7, 1970, Terre Haute, Ind.
Left handed, B.R.
6'3" 235 lbs.

YEAR	CLUB	W	L	PCT	ERA	G	IP	H	BB	SO
1923	St. Louis (A)	0	0	—	27.00	1	1	1	3	0
1925	BROOKLYN (N)	0	2	.000	8.44	3	10.2	17	9	3
1927	BROOKLYN (N)	6	13	.316	3.30	30	188.1	188	60	99
1928	BROOKLYN (N)	9	14	.391	3.89	41	192	194	64	74
1929	BROOKLYN (N)	1	2	.333	6.63	6	19	21	16	7
1930	BROOKLYN (N)	10	7	.588	3.95	35	198.1	204	70	59
1931	Philadelphia (N)	19	14	.576	4.27	52	249	288	83	99
1932	Philadelphia (N)	11	10	.524	5.42	39	166	210	47	62
1933	Philadelphia (N)	6	10	.375	3.84	35	161.2	188	49	43
1934	Philadelphia (N)									
1934	Boston (N)									
	(year totals)	1	2	.333	6.97	10	20.2	27	13	7
	Ten years	63	74	.460	4.24	252	1206.2	1338	414	453

DON ELSTON B. April 26, 1929, Campbellstown, Ohio
Right handed, B.R.
6' 165 lbs.

YEAR	CLUB	W	L	PCT	ERA	G	IP	H	BB	SO
1957	BROOKLYN (N)	0	0	.000	0.00	1	1	1	0	1
	Nine years (totals)	49	54	.476	3.69	450	755.2	702	327	519

JOHNNY ENZMANN B. March 4, 1890, Brooklyn, N.Y.
Right handed, B.R.
5'10" 165 lbs.

YEAR	CLUB	W	L	PCT	ERA	G	IP	H	BB	SO
1914	BROOKLYN (N)	0	0	—	4.74	7	19	21	8	5
	Four years (totals)	10	12	.455	2.84	67	269.2	297	61	91

AL EPPERLY B. May 7, 1918, Glidden, Iowa
Right handed, B.L.
6'2" 194 lbs.

YEAR	CLUB	W	L	PCT	ERA	G	IP	H	BB	SO
1950	BROOKLYN (N)	0	0	—	5.00	5	9	14	5	3
	Two years (totals)	2	0	1.000	4.00	14	36	42	20	13

CARL ERSKINE B. Dec. 13, 1926, Anderson, Ind.
Right handed, B.R.
5'10" 165 lbs.

YEAR	CLUB	W	L	PCT	ERA	G	IP	H	BB	SO
1948	BROOKLYN (N)	6	3	.667	3.23	17	64	51	35	29
1949	BROOKLYN (N)	8	1	.889	4.63	22	79.2	68	51	49
1950	BROOKLYN (N)	7	6	.538	4.72	22	103	109	35	50
1951	BROOKLYN (N)	16	12	.571	4.46	46	189.2	206	78	95
1952	BROOKLYN (N)	14	6	.700	2.70	33	206.2	167	71	131
1953	BROOKLYN (N)	20	6	.769	3.54	39	246.2	213	95	187
1954	BROOKLYN (N)	18	15	.545	4.15	38	260.1	239	92	166
1955	BROOKLYN (N)	11	8	.579	3.79	31	194.2	185	64	84
1956	BROOKLYN (N)	13	11	.542	4.25	31	186.1	189	57	95
1957	BROOKLYN (N)	5	3	.625	3.55	15	66	62	20	26
1958	LOS ANGELES (N)	4	4	.500	5.13	31	98.1	115	35	54
1959	LOS ANGELES (N)	0	3	.000	7.71	10	23.1	33	13	15
	Twelve years	122	78	.610	4.00	335	1718.2	1637	646	981

World Series

		W	L	PCT	ERA	G	IP	H	BB	SO
	Five years	2	2	.500	5.83	11	41.2	36	24	31

World Series

YEAR	CLUB	W	L	PCT	ERA	G	IP	H	BB	SO
1949	BROOKLYN (N)	0	0	.000	16.20	2	1.2		1	0
1952	BROOKLYN (N)	1	1	.500	4.50	3	18		10	10
1953	BROOKLYN (N)	1	0	1.000	5.79	3	14		9	16

YEAR	CLUB	W	L	PCT	ERA	G	IP	H	BB	SO
1955	BROOKLYN (N)	0	0	000	9.00	1	3		2	3
1956	BROOKLYN (N)	0	1	.000	5.40	2	5		2	2
	Five years	2	2	.500	5.83	11	41.2	36	24	31

LEROY EVANS B. March 19, 1874, Knoxville, Tenn.
Deceased
Right handed, B.R.
6' 180 lbs.

YEAR	CLUB	W	L	PCT	ERA	G	IP	H	BB	SO
1902	BROOKLYN (N)	5	6	.455	2.69	13	97		33	35
1903	BROOKLYN (N)	4	8	.333	3.27	15	110		41	42
	Five years (totals)	29	42	.408	3.66	84	614.1	673	233	211

RED EVANS B. Nov. 12, 1906, Chicago, Ill.
Right handed, B.R.
5'11" 168 lbs.

YEAR	CLUB	W	L	PCT	ERA	G	IP	H	BB	SO
1939	BROOKLYN (N)	1	8	.111	5.18	24	64.1	74	26	28
	Two years (totals)	1	11	.083	6.21	41	111.2	144	48	47

CY FALKENBERG B. Dec. 17, 1880, Chicago, Ill.
D. April 14, 1961, San Francisco, Calif.
Right handed, B.R.
6'5" 180 lbs.

YEAR	CLUB	W	L	PCT	ERA	G	IP	H	BB	SO
1915	BROOKLYN (F)									
	(year totals)	12	14	.462	2.86	32	220	206	59	96
	Twelve years (totals)	129	123	.512	2.68	330	2275	2090	690	1164

DICK FARRELL B. April 8, 1934, Boston, Mass.
D. June 11, 1977, Great Yarmouth, England
Right handed, B.R.
6'4" 215 lbs.

YEAR	CLUB	W	L	PCT	ERA	G	IP	H	BB	SO
1961	LOS ANGELES (N)	6	6	.500	5.06	50	89		43	80
	Fourteen years (totals)	106	111	.488	3.45	590	1704.1	1628	468	1177

JIM FAULKNER B. July 27, 1899, Beatrice, Neb.
D. June 1, 1962, West Palm Beach, Fla.
Left handed, B.B.
6'3" 190 lbs.

YEAR	CLUB	W	L	PCT	ERA	G	IP	H	BB	SO
1930	BROOKLYN (N)	0	0	—	81.00	2	.1	2	1	0
	Three years (totals)	10	8	.556	3.75	43	127.1	146	47	34

ALEX FERGUSON B. Feb. 16, 1897, Montclair, N.J.
D. April 28, 1976, Camarillo, Calif.
Right handed, B.R.
6' 180 lbs.

YEAR	CLUB	W	L	PCT	ERA	G	IP	H	BB	SO
1929	BROOKLYN (N)	0	1	.000		3	2		1	1
	Ten years (totals)	61	85	.418	4.91	256	1236	1447	477	396

WES FERRELL
B. Feb. 2, 1908, Greensboro, N.C.
D. Dec. 9, 1976, Sarasota, Fla.
Right handed, B.R.
6'2" 195 lbs.

YEAR	CLUB	W	L	PCT	ERA	G	IP	H	BB	SO
1940	BROOKLYN (N)	0	0	—	6.75	1	4	4	4	4
	Fifteen years (totals)	193	128	.601	4.04	374	2623	2845	1040	985

LOU FETTE
B. March 15, 1907, Alma, Mo.
D. Jan. 3, 1981, Warrensburg, Mo.
Right handed, B.R.
6'1½" 200 lbs.

YEAR	CLUB	W	L	PCT	ERA	G	IP	H	BB	SO
1940	BROOKLYN (N)	0	0	.000	.000	2	3		2	0
	Five years (totals)	41	40	.506	3.15	109	691	658	248	194

PEMBROKE FINLAYSON
B. July 31, 1888, Cheraw, S.C.
D. March 6, 1912, Brooklyn, N.Y.
Right handed, B.R.

YEAR	CLUB	W	L	PCT	ERA	G	IP	H	BB	SO
1908	BROOKLYN (N)	0	0	—	135.00	1	.1	0	4	0
1909	BROOKLYN (N)	0	0	—	5.14	1	7	7	4	2
	Two years	0	0	—	11.05	2	7.1	7	8	2

HAPPY FINNERAN
B. Oct. 29, 1891, East Orange, N.J.
D. Feb. 3, 1942, Orange, N.J.
Right handed, B.B.
5'10½" 169 lbs.

YEAR	CLUB	W	L	PCT	ERA	G	IP	H	BB	SO
1912	Philadelphia (N)	0	2	.000	2.53	14	46.1	50	10	10
1913	Philadelphia (N)	0	0	—	7.20	3	5	12	2	0
1914	BROOKLYN (F)	12	11	.522	3.18	27	175.1	153	60	54
1915	BROOKLYN (F)	12	13	.480	2.80	37	215.1	197	87	68
1918	Detroit (A)									
1918	New York (A)									
	(year totals)	2	8	.200	4.43	28	128	156	43	36
	Five years	26	34	.433	3.30	109	570	568	202	168

CHAUNCEY FISHER
B. Jan. 8, 1872, Anderson, Ind.
D. April 27, 1939, Los Angeles, Calif.
Right handed, B.R.
5'11" 175 lbs.

YEAR	CLUB	W	L	PCT	ERA	G	IP	H	BB	SO
1897	BROOKLYN (N)	9	7	.563	4.23	20	149	184	43	31
	Five years (totals)	21	26	.447	5.37	65	435.2	583	140	80

FREDDIE FITZSIMMONS
B. July 28, 1901, Mishawaka, Ind.
D. Nov. 18, 1979, Yucca Valley, Calif.
Right handed, B.R.
5'11" 185 lbs.

YEAR	CLUB	W	L	PCT	ERA	G	IP	H	BB	SO
1925	New York (N)	6	3	.667	2.65	10	74.2	70	18	17
1926	New York (N)	14	10	.583	2.88	37	219	224	58	48
1927	New York (N)	17	10	.630	3.72	42	244.2	260	67	78
1928	New York (N)	20	9	.690	3.68	40	261.1	264	65	67
1929	New York (N)	15	11	.577	4.10	37	221.2	242	66	55
1930	New York (N)	19	7	.731	4.25	41	224.1	230	59	76
1931	New York (N)	18	11	.621	3.05	35	253.2	242	62	78
1932	New York (N)	11	11	.500	4.43	35	237.2	287	83	65
1933	New York (N)	16	11	.593	2.90	36	251.2	243	72	65
1934	New York (N)	18	14	.563	3.04	38	263.1	266	51	73
1935	New York (N)	4	8	.333	4.02	18	94	104	22	23
1936	New York (N)	10	7	.588	3.32	28	141	147	39	35
1937	New York (N)									

YEAR	CLUB	W	L	PCT	ERA	G	IP	H	BB	SO
1937	BROOKLYN (N)	4	8	.333	4.25	13	91		32	29
	(year totals)	6	10	.375	4.35	19	118	119	40	42
1938	BROOKLYN (N)	11	8	.579	3.02	27	202.2	205	43	38
1939	BROOKLYN (N)	7	9	.438	3.87	27	151.1	178	28	44
1940	BROOKLYN (N)	16	2	.889	2.81	20	134.1	120	25	35
1941	BROOKLYN (N)	6	1	.857	2.07	13	82.2	78	26	19
1942	BROOKLYN (N)	0	0	—	15.00	1	3	6	1	0
1943	BROOKLYN (N)	3	4	.429	5.44	9	44.2	50	21	12
	Nineteen years	217	146	.598	3.51	513	3223.2	3335	846	870
World Series										
	Three years	0	3	.000	3.86	4	25.2	26	5	9

SAM FLETCHER
B. Altoona, Pa.
Right handed
6'2" 210 lbs.

YEAR	CLUB	W	L	PCT	ERA	G	IP	H	BB	SO
1909	BROOKLYN (N)	0	1	.000	8.00	1	9	13	2	5
	Two years (totals)	0	1	.000	10.13	3	18.2	28	13	8

WES FLOWERS
B. Aug. 13, 1913, Vanndale, Ark.
Left handed, B.L.
6'1½" 190 lbs.

YEAR	CLUB	W	L	PCT	ERA	G	IP	H	BB	SO
1940	BROOKLYN (N)	1	1	.500	3.43	5	21	23	10	8
1944	BROOKLYN (N)	1	1	.500	7.79	9	17.1	26	13	3
	Two years	2	2	.500	5.40	14	38.1	49	23	11

TERRY FORSTER
B. Jan. 14, 1952, Sioux, City, S.D.
Left handed, B.L.
6'3" 200 lbs.

YEAR	CLUB	W	L	PCT	ERA	G	IP	H	BB	SO
1978	LOS ANGELES (N)	5	4	.556	1.94	47	65	56	23	46
1979	LOS ANGELES (N)	1	2	.333	5.63	17	16	18	11	8
1980	LOS ANGELES (N)	0	0	—	3.00	9	12	10	4	2
1981	LOS ANGELES (N)	0	1	.000	4.06	21	31	37	15	17
1982	LOS ANGELES (N)	5	6	.455	3.04	56	83	66	31	52
	Twelve years (totals)	43	59	.421	3.40	446	898.2	848	374	662
Divisional Playoff										
	One year	0	0	—	0.00	1	.1	0	0	0
League Championship										
	Two years	1	0	1.000	0.00	2	1.1	1	0	3
World Series										
	Two years	0	0	—	0.00	5	6	6	4	6

ALAN FOSTER
B. Dec. 8, 1946, Pasadena, Calif.
Right handed, B.R.
6' 180 lbs.

YEAR	CLUB	W	L	PCT	ERA	G	IP	H	BB	SO
1967	LOS ANGELES (N)	0	1	.000	2.16	4	16.2	10	3	15
1968	LOS ANGELES (N)	1	1	.500	1.72	3	15.2	11	2	10
1969	LOS ANGELES (N)	3	9	.250	4.37	24	103	119	29	59
1970	LOS ANGELES (N)	10	13	.435	4.25	33	199	200	81	83
1971	Cleveland (A)	8	12	.400	4.15	36	182	158	82	97
1972	California (A)	0	1	.000	4.85	8	13	12	6	11
1973	St. Louis (N)	13	9	.591	3.14	35	203.2	195	63	106
1974	St. Louis (N)	7	10	.412	3.89	31	162	167	61	78
1975	San Diego (N)	3	1	.750	2.40	17	45	41	21	20
1976	San Diego (N)	3	6	.333	3.22	26	86.2	75	35	22
	Ten years	48	63	.432	3.73	217	1026.2	988	383	501

DAVE FOUTZ B. Sept. 7, 1856, Carroll County, Md.
D. March 5, 1897, Waverly, Md.
Right handed, B.R.
6'2" 161 lbs.

YEAR	CLUB	W	L	PCT	ERA	G	IP	H	BB	SO
*1890	BROOKLYN (N)	2	1	.667	1.86	5	29	29	6	4
1891	BROOKLYN (N)	3	2	.600	3.29	6	52	51	16	14
1892	BROOKLYN (N)	13	8	.619	3.41	27	203	210	63	56
1893	BROOKLYN (N)	0	0	—	7.50	6	18	28	8	3
1894	BROOKLYN (N)	0	0	—	13.50	1	2	4	1	0
	Eleven years (totals)	147	66	.690	2.84	251	1997.1	1843	510	790

*1884 St. Louis (AA), 1888 Brooklyn (AA)

ART FOWLER B. July 3, 1922, Converse, S.C.
Right handed, B.R.
5'11" 180 lbs.

YEAR	CLUB	W	L	PCT	ERA	G	IP	H	BB	SO
1954	Cincinnati (N)	12	10	.545	3.83	40	227.2	256	85	93
1955	Cincinnati (N)	11	10	.524	3.90	46	207.2	198	63	94
1956	Cincinnati (N)	11	11	.500	4.05	45	177.2	191	35	86
1957	Cincinnati (N)	3	0	1.000	6.47	33	87.2	111	24	45
1959	LOS ANGELES (N)	3	4	.429	5.31	36	61	70	23	47
1961	Los Angeles (A)	5	8	.385	3.64	53	89	68	29	78
1962	Los Angeles (A)	4	3	.571	2.81	48	77	67	25	38
1963	Los Angeles (A)	5	3	.625	2.42	57	89.1	70	19	53
1964	Los Angeles (A)	0	2	.000	10.29	4	7	8	5	5
	Nine years	54	51	.514	4.03	362	1024	1039	308	539

FRED FRANKHOUSE B. April 9, 1904, Port Royal, Pa.
Right handed, B.R.
5'11" 175 lbs.

YEAR	CLUB	W	L	PCT	ERA	G	IP	H	BB	SO
1927	St. Louis (N)	5	1	.833	2.70	6	50	41	16	20
1928	St. Louis (N)	3	2	.600	3.96	21	84	91	36	29
1929	St. Louis (N)	7	2	.778	4.12	30	133.1	149	43	37
1930	St. Louis (N)									
1930	Boston (N)									
	(year totals)	9	9	.500	5.87	35	130.1	169	54	34
1931	Boston (N)	8	8	.500	4.03	26	127.1	125	43	50
1932	Boston (N)	4	6	.400	3.56	37	108.2	113	45	35
1933	Boston (N)	16	15	.516	3.16	43	244.2	249	77	83
1934	Boston (N)	17	9	.654	3.20	37	233.2	239	77	78
1935	Boston (N)	11	15	.423	4.76	40	230.2	278	81	64
1936	BROOKLYN (N)	13	10	.565	3.65	41	234.1	236	89	84
1937	BROOKLYN (N)	10	13	.435	4.27	33	179.1	214	78	64
1938	BROOKLYN (N)	3	5	.375	4.04	30	93.2	92	44	32
1939	Boston (N)	0	2	.000	2.61	23	38	37	18	12
	Thirteen years	106	97	.522	3.92	402	1888	2033	701	622

JACK FRANKLIN B. Oct. 20, 1919, Paris, Ill.
Right handed, B.R.
5'11½" 170 lbs.

YEAR	CLUB	W	L	PCT	ERA	G	IP	H	BB	SO
1944	BROOKLYN (N)	0	0	—	13.50	1	2	2	4	0

LARRY FRENCH B. Nov. 1, 1907, Visalia, Calif.
Left handed, B.R.
6'1" 195 lbs.

YEAR	CLUB	W	L	PCT	ERA	G	IP	H	BB	SO
1941	BROOKLYN (N)	0	0	.000	3.38	6	16		4	8
1942	BROOKLYN (N)	15	4	.789	1.83	38	147.2	127	36	62
	Fourteen years (totals)	197	171	.535	3.44	570	3152	3375	819	1187
World Series										
	Three years (totals)	0	2	.000	3.00	7	15	16	3	10

CHARLIE FUCHS B. Nov. 18, 1912, Union City, N.J.
D. June 10, 1969, Weehawken, N.J.
Right handed, B.B.
5'8" 168 lbs.

YEAR	CLUB	W	L	PCT	ERA	G	IP	H	BB	SO
1944	BROOKLYN (N)	1	0	1.000	5.74	8	15.2	25	9	5
	Three years (totals)	6	10	.375	4.89	47	165.2	186	73	41

JOHN GADDY B. Feb. 5, 1914, Wadesboro, N.C.
D. May 3, 1966, Albermarle, N.C.
Right handed, B.R.
6'½" 182 lbs.

YEAR	CLUB	W	L	PCT	ERA	G	IP	H	BB	SO
1938	BROOKLYN (N)	2	0	1.000	0.69	2	13	13	4	3

PHIL GALLIVAN B. May 29, 1907, Seattle, Wash.
D. Nov. 24, 1969, St. Paul, Minn.
Right handed, B.R.
6' 180 lbs.

YEAR	CLUB	W	L	PCT	ERA	G	IP	H	BB	SO
1931	BROOKLYN (N)	0	1	.000	5.28	6	15.1	23	7	1
	Three years (totals)	5	11	.313	5.95	54	175.1	227	95	68

MIKE GARMAN B. Sept. 16, 1949, Caldwell, Idaho
Right handed, B.R.
6'3" 195 lbs.

YEAR	CLUB	W	L	PCT	ERA	G	IP	H	BB	SO
1977	LOS ANGELES (N)	4	4	.500	2.71	49	63	60	22	29
1978	LOS ANGELES (N)	0	1	.000	4.50	10	10		3	5
	Nine years	22	27	.449	3.63	303	434	411	202	213
League Championship										
	One year	0	0	—	0.00	2	1.1	0	0	1
World Series										
	One year	0	0	—	0.00	2	4	2	1	3

NED GARVIN B. Jan. 1, 1874, Navasota, Texas
D. June 16, 1908, Fresno, Calif.
Right handed
6'3½" 160 lbs.

YEAR	CLUB	W	L	PCT	ERA	G	IP	H	BB	SO
1896	Philadelphia (N)	0	1	.000	7.62	2	13	19	7	4
1899	Chicago (N)	9	13	.409	2.85	24	199	202	42	69
1900	Chicago (N)	10	18	.357	2.41	30	246.1	225	63	107
1901	Milwaukee (A)	7	20	.259	3.46	37	257.1	258	90	122
1902	Chicago (A)									
1902	BROOKLYN (N)	1	1	.500	1.00	2	18		4	7
	(year totals)	11	12	.478	2.09	25	193.1	184	47	62
1903	BROOKLYN (N)	15	18	.455	3.08	38	298	277	84	154
1904	BROOKLYN (N)	5	15	.250	1.68	23	182		78	86
1904	New York (A)									
	(year totals)	5	16	.238	1.72	25	193.2	155	80	94
	Seven years	57	98	.368	2.72	181	1400.2	1320	413	612

WELCOME GASTON B. Dec. 19, 1874, Senecaville, Ohio
D. Dec. 13, 1944, Columbus, Ohio
Left handed

YEAR	CLUB	W	L	PCT	ERA	G	IP	H	BB	SO
1898	BROOKLYN (N)	1	1	.500	2.81	2	16	17	9	0
1899	BROOKLYN (N)	0	0	—	3.00	1	3	3	4	0
	Two years	1	1	.500	2.84	3	19	20	13	0

HANK GASTRIGHT

B. March 29, 1865, Covington, Ky.
D. Oct. 9, 1937, Cold Springs, Ky.
Right handed, B.R.
6'2" 190 lbs.

YEAR	CLUB	W	L	PCT	ERA	G	IP	H	BB	SO
1894	BROOKLYN (N)	2	6	.250	6.39	16	93	135	55	20
	Seven years (totals)	72	63	.533	4.20	171	1301.1	1337	584	514

BOB GIALLOMBARDO

B. May 20, 1937, Brooklyn, N.Y.
Left handed, B.L.
6' 175 lbs.

YEAR	CLUB	W	L	PCT	ERA	G	IP	H	BB	SO
1958	LOS ANGELES (N)	1	1	.500	3.76	6	26.1	29	15	14

JIM GOLDEN

B. March 20, 1936, Eldon, Mo.
Right handed, B.L.
6' 175 lbs.

YEAR	CLUB	W	L	PCT	ERA	G	IP	H	BB	SO
1960	LOS ANGELES (N)	1	0	1.000	6.43	1	7	6	4	4
1961	LOS ANGELES (N)	1	1	.500	5.79	28	42	52	20	18
	Four years (totals)	9	13	.409	4.54	69	208	233	76	115

DAVE GOLTZ

B. June 23, 1949, Pelican Rapids, Minn.
Right handed, B.R.
6'4" 200 lbs.

YEAR	CLUB	W	L	PCT	ERA	G	IP	H	BB	SO
1972	Minnesota (A)	3	3	.500	2.67	15	91	75	26	38
1973	Minnesota (A)	6	4	.600	5.25	32	106.1	138	32	66
1974	Minnesota (A)	10	10	.500	3.26	28	174	192	45	89
1975	Minnesota (A)	14	14	.500	3.67	32	243	235	72	128
1976	Minnesota (A)	14	14	.500	3.36	36	249.1	239	91	133
1977	Minnesota (A)	20	11	.645	3.36	39	303	284	91	186
1978	Minnesota (A)	15	10	.600	2.49	29	220.1	209	67	116
1979	Minnesota (A)	14	13	.519	4.16	36	251	282	69	132
1980	LOS ANGELES (N)	7	11	.389	4.32	35	171	198	59	91
1981	LOS ANGELES (N)	2	7	.222	4.09	26	77	83	25	48
1982	LOS ANGELES (N)	0	1	.000	4.90	2	3.2	6	0	3
	Eleven years	105	98	.516	3.59	310	1889	1941	577	1030
World Series										
	One year	0	0	—	5.40	2	3.1	4	1	2

RAY GORDONIER

B. April 11, 1892, Rochester, N.Y.
D. Nov. 15, 1960, Rochester, N.Y.
Right handed, B.R.
5'8½" 170 lbs.

YEAR	CLUB	W	L	PCT	ERA	G	IP	H	BB	SO
1921	BROOKLYN (N)	1	0	1.000	5.25	3	12	10	8	4
1922	BROOKLYN (N)	0	0	—	8.74	5	11.1	13	8	5
	Two years	1	0	1.000	6.94	8	23.1	23	16	9

MUDCAT GRANT

B. Aug. 13, 1935, Lacoochee, Fla.
Right handed, B.R.
6'1" 186 lbs.

YEAR	CLUB	W	L	PCT	ERA	G	IP	H	BB	SO
1968	LOS ANGELES (N)	6	4	.600	2.08	37	95	77	19	35
	Fourteen years (totals)	145	119	.549	3.63	571	2441.1	2292	849	1267

HARVEY GREEN B. Feb. 9, 1915, Kenosha, Wis.
D. July 24, 1970, Franklin, La
Right handed, B.B.
6'2½" 185 lbs.

YEAR	CLUB	W	L	PCT	ERA	G	IP	H	BB	SO
1935	BROOKLYN (N)	0	0	—	9.00	2	1	2	3	0

NELSON GREENE B. Sept. 20, 1900, Philadelphia, Pa.
Left handed, B.L.
6' 185 lbs.

YEAR	CLUB	W	L	PCT	ERA	G	IP	H	BB	SO
1924	BROOKLYN (N)	0	1	.000	4.00	4	9	14	2	3
1925	BROOKLYN (N)	2	0	1.000	10.64	11	22	45	7	4
	Two years	2	1	.667	8.71	15	31	59	9	7

KENT GREENFIELD B. July 1, 1902, Guthrie, Ky.
Right handed, B.R.
6'1" 180 lbs.

YEAR	CLUB	W	L	PCT	ERA	G	IP	H	BB	SO
1929	BROOKLYN (N)	0	0	.000	8.00	6	9		3	1
	Six years (totals)	41	48	.461	4.54	152	775.1	871	297	242

HAL GREGG B. July 11, 1921, Anaheim, Calif.
Right handed, B.R.
6'3½" 195 lbs.

YEAR	CLUB	W	L	PCT	ERA	G	IP	H	BB	SO
1943	BROOKLYN (N)	0	3	.000	9.64	5	18.2	21	21	7
1944	BROOKLYN (N)	9	16	.360	5.46	39	197.2	201	137	92
1945	BROOKLYN (N)	18	13	.581	3.47	42	254.1	221	120	139
1946	BROOKLYN (N)	6	4	.600	2.99	26	117.1	103	44	54
1947	BROOKLYN (N)	4	5	.444	5.87	37	104.1	115	55	59
1948	Pittsburgh (N)	2	4	.333	4.60	22	74.1	72	34	25
1949	Pittsburgh (N)	1	1	.500	3.38	8	18.2	20	8	9
1950	Pittsburgh (N)	0	1	.000	13.50	5	5.1	10	7	3
1952	New York (N)	0	1	.000	4.71	16	36.1	42	17	13
	Nine years	40	48	.455	4.54	200	827	805	443	401
World Series										
	One year	0	1	.000	3.55	3	12.2	9	8	10

BURLEIGH GRIMES B. Aug. 18, 1893, Clear Lake, Wis.
Right handed, B.R.
5'10" 175 lbs.

YEAR	CLUB	W	L	PCT	ERA	G	IP	H	BB	SO
1916	Pittsburgh (N)	2	3	.400	2.36	6	45.2	40	10	20
1917	Pittsburgh (N)	3	16	.158	3.53	37	194	186	70	72
1918	BROOKLYN (N)	19	9	.679	2.14	40	269.2	210	76	113
1919	BROOKLYN (N)	10	11	.476	3.47	25	181.1	179	60	82
1920	BROOKLYN (N)	23	11	.676	2.22	40	303.2	271	67	131
1921	BROOKLYN (N)	22	13	.629	2.83	37	302.1	312	76	136
1922	BROOKLYN (N)	17	14	.548	4.76	36	259	324	84	99
1923	BROOKLYN (N)	21	18	.538	3.58	39	327	356	100	119
1924	BROOKLYN (N)	22	13	.629	3.82	38	310.2	351	91	135
1925	BROOKLYN (N)	12	19	.387	5.04	33	246.2	305	102	73
1926	BROOKLYN (N)	12	13	.480	3.71	30	225.1	238	88	64
1927	New York (N)	19	8	.704	3.54	39	259.2	274	87	102
1928	Pittsburgh (N)	25	14	.641	2.99	48	330.2	311	77	97
1929	Pittsburgh (N)	17	7	.708	3.13	33	232.2	245	70	62
1930	Boston (N)									
1930	St. Louis (N)									
	(year totals)	16	11	.593	4.07	33	201.1	246	65	73
1931	St. Louis (N)	17	9	.654	3.65	29	212.1	240	59	67
1932	Chicago (N)	6	11	.353	4.78	30	141.1	174	50	36
1933	Chicago (N)									
1933	St. Louis (N)									
	(year totals)	3	7	.300	3.78	21	83.1	86	37	16
1934	St. Louis (N)									
1934	Pittsburgh (N)									

YEAR	CLUB	W	L	PCT	ERA	G	IP	H	BB	SO
1934	New York (A)									
	(year totals)	4	5	.444	6.11	22	53	63	26	15
	Nineteen years	270	212	.560	3.53	616	4179.2	4412	1295	1512
World Series										
	Four years	3	4	.429	4.29	9	56.2	49	26	28

DAN GRINER B. March 7, 1888, Centerville, Tenn.
D. June 3, 1950, Bishopville, S.C.
Right handed, B.L.
6'1½" 200 lbs.

YEAR	CLUB	W	L	PCT	ERA	G	IP	H	BB	SO
1918	BROOKLYN (N)	1	5	.167	2.15	11	54.1	47	15	22
	Six years (totals)	27	55	.329	3.49	135	673.2	700	202	244

LEE GRISSOM B. Oct. 23, 1907, Sherman, Texas
Left handed, B.B.
6'3" 200 lbs.

YEAR	CLUB	W	L	PCT	ERA	G	IP	H	BB	SO
1940	BROOKLYN (N)	2	5	.286	2.80	14	74		34	56
1941	BROOKLYN (N)	0	0	.000	2.46	4	11		8	5
	Eight years (totals)	29	48	.377	3.89	162	701.2	668	305	379

AD GUMBERT B. Oct. 10, 1868, Pittsburgh, Pa.
D. April 23, 1925, Pittsburgh, Pa.
Right handed

YEAR	CLUB	W	L	PCT	ERA	G	IP	H	BB	SO
*1890	Boston (P)	22	11	.667	3.96	39	277.1	338	86	81
1891	Chicago (N)	17	11	.607	3.58	32	256.1	282	90	73
1892	Chicago (N)	22	19	.537	3.41	46	382.2	399	107	118
1893	Pittsburgh (N)	11	7	.611	5.15	22	162.2	207	78	40
1894	Pittsburgh (N)	15	14	.517	6.02	37	269	372	84	65
1895	BROOKLYN (N)	11	16	.407	5.08	33	234	288	69	45
1896	BROOKLYN (N)	0	4	.000	5.40	5	25		11	7
1896	Philadelphia (N)									
	(year totals)	5	7	.417	4.32	16	108.1	133	34	17
	Nine years	122	101	.547	4.27	262	1985.1	2321	634	546

*1888 Chicago (N)

GEORGE HADDOCK B. Dec. 25, 1866, Portsmouth, N.H.
D. April 18, 1926, Boston, Mass.
Right handed
5'11" 155 lbs.

YEAR	CLUB	W	L	PCT	ERA	G	IP	H	BB	SO
*1890	Buffalo (P)	9	26	.257	5.76	35	290.2	366	149	123
1891	Boston (AA)	34	11	.756	2.49	51	379.2	330	137	169
1892	BROOKLYN (N)	29	13	.690	3.14	46	381.1	340	163	153
1893	BROOKLYN (N)	8	9	.471	5.60	23	151	193	89	37
1894	Philadelphia (N)									
1894	Washington (N)									
	(year totals)	4	7	.364	6.78	14	85	113	51	8
	Seven years	95	87	.522	4.07	204	1580	1650	714	599

*1888 Washington (N)

BILL HALL B. Feb. 22, 1892, Charleston, W. Va.
Right handed, B.R.
6' 180 lbs.

YEAR	CLUB	W	L	PCT	ERA	G	IP	H	BB	SO
1913	BROOKLYN (N)	0	0	—	5.79	3	4.2	4	5	3

186 • **The Complete Dodgers Record Book**

JOHNNY HALL B. Jan. 9, 1924, Muskogee, Okla.
Right handed, B.R.
6'2½" 170 lbs.

YEAR	CLUB	W	L	PCT	ERA	G	IP	H	BB	SO
1948	BROOKLYN (N)	0	0	—	6.23	3	4.1	4	2	2

LUKE HAMLIN B. July 3, 1906, Terris Center, Mich.
D. Feb. 18, 1978, Clare, Mich.
Right handed, B.L.
6'2" 168 lbs.

YEAR	CLUB	W	L	PCT	ERA	G	IP	H	BB	SO
1933	Detroit (A)	1	0	1.000	4.86	3	16.2	20	10	10
1934	Detroit (A)	2	3	.400	5.38	20	75.1	87	44	30
1937	BROOKLYN (N)	11	13	.458	3.59	39	185.2	183	48	93
1938	BROOKLYN (N)	12	15	.444	3.68	44	237.1	243	65	97
1939	BROOKLYN (N)	20	13	.606	3.64	40	269.2	255	54	88
1940	BROOKLYN (N)	9	8	.529	3.06	33	182.1	183	34	91
1941	BROOKLYN (N)	8	8	.500	4.24	30	136	139	41	58
1942	Pittsburgh (N)	4	4	.500	3.94	23	112	128	19	38
1944	Philadelphia (A)	6	12	.333	3.74	29	190	204	38	58
	Nine years	73	76	.490	3.77	261	1405	1442	353	563

GERRY HANNAHS B. March 6, 1953, Binghamton, N.Y.
Left handed, B.L.
6'3" 210 lbs.

YEAR	CLUB	W	L	PCT	ERA	G	IP	H	BB	SO
1978	LOS ANGELES (N)	0	0	—	9.00	1	2	3	0	5
1979	LOS ANGELES (N)	0	2	.000	3.38	4	16	10	13	6
	Four years (totals)	3	7	.300	5.07	16	71	76	42	42

F. C. HANSFORD Deceased.

YEAR	CLUB	W	L	PCT	ERA	G	IP	H	BB	SO
1898	BROOKLYN (N)	0	0	—	3.86	1	7	10	5	0

GEORGE HARPER B. Aug. 17, 1866, Milwaukee, Wis.
D. Dec. 11, 1931, Stockton, Calif.

YEAR	CLUB	W	L	PCT	ERA	G	IP	H	BB	SO
1896	BROOKLYN (N)	4	8	.333	5.55	16	86	106	39	22
	Two years (totals)	10	14	.417	5.43	28	172.1	234	88	46

HARRY HARPER B. April 24, 1895, Hackensack, N.J.
D. April 23, 1963, New York, N.Y.
Left handed, B.L.
6'2" 165 lbs.

YEAR	CLUB	W	L	PCT	ERA	G	IP	H	BB	SO
1923	BROOKLYN (N)	0	1	.000	14.73	1	3.2	8	3	4
	Ten years (totals)	59	76	.437	2.87	219	1256	1100	582	623

BILL HARRIS B. Dec. 3, 1931, Duguayville, New Brunswick, Canada
Right handed, B.L.
5'8" 187 lbs.

YEAR	CLUB	W	L	PCT	ERA	G	IP	H	BB	SO
1957	BROOKLYN (N)	0	1	.000	3.86	1	7	9	1	3
1959	LOS ANGELES (N)	0	0	—	0.00	1	1.2	0	3	0
	Two years	0	1	.000	3.12	2	8.2	9	4	3

BILL HART
B. July 19, 1865, Louisville, Ky.
D. Sept. 19, 1936, Cincinnati, Ohio

YEAR	CLUB	W	L	PCT	ERA	G	IP	H	BB	SO
*1892	BROOKLYN (N)	9	12	.429	3.28	28	195	188	96	65
	Eight years (totals)	66	120	.355	4.65	206	1582	1819	704	431

RAY HATHAWAY
B. Oct. 13, 1916, Greenville, Ohio
Right handed, B.R.
6' 165 lbs.

YEAR	CLUB	W	L	PCT	ERA	G	IP	H	BB	SO
1945	BROOKLYN (N)	0	1	.000	4.00	4	9	11	6	3

JOE HATTEN
B. Nov. 7, 1916, Bancroft, Iowa
Left handed, B.R.
6' 176 lbs.

YEAR	CLUB	W	L	PCT	ERA	G	IP	H	BB	SO
1946	BROOKLYN (N)	14	11	.560	2.84	42	222	207	110	85
1947	BROOKLYN (N)	17	8	.680	3.63	42	225.1	211	105	76
1948	BROOKLYN (N)	13	10	.565	3.58	42	208.2	228	94	73
1949	BROOKLYN (N)	12	8	.600	4.18	37	187.1	194	69	58
1950	BROOKLYN (N)	2	2	.500	4.59	23	68.2	82	31	29
1951	BROOKLYN (N)	1	0	1.000	4.59	11	49		21	22
1951	Chicago (N)									
	(year totals)	3	6	.333	4.91	34	124.2	137	58	45
1952	Chicago (N)	4	4	.500	6.08	13	50.1	65	25	15
	Seven years	65	49	.570	3.87	233	1087	1124	492	381

World Series

YEAR	CLUB	W	L	PCT	ERA	G	IP	H	BB	SO
1947	BROOKLYN (N)	0	0	—	7.00	4	9		7	5
1949	BROOKLYN (N)	0	0	—	16.20	2	1.2		2	0
	Two years	0	0	—	8.44	6	10.2	16	9	5

CHRIS HAUGHEY
B. Oct. 3, 1925, Astoria, N.Y.
Right handed, B.R.
6'1" 180 lbs.

YEAR	CLUB	W	L	PCT	ERA	G	IP	H	BB	SO
1943	BROOKLYN (N)	0	1	.000	3.86	1	7	5	10	0

PHIL HAUGSTAD
B. Feb. 23, 1924, Black River Falls, Wis.
Right handed, B.R.
6'2" 165 lbs.

YEAR	CLUB	W	L	PCT	ERA	G	IP	H	BB	SO
1947	BROOKLYN (N)	1	0	1.000	2.84	6	12.2	14	4	4
1948	BROOKLYN (N)	0	0	—	0.00	1	1	1	0	0
1951	BROOKLYN (N)	0	1	.000	6.46	21	30.2	28	24	22
	Four years (totals)	1	1	.500	5.59	37	56.1	51	41	28

ED HEAD
B. Jan. 25, 1918, Selma, La.
D. Jan. 31, 1980, Bastrop, La.
Right handed, B.R.
6'1" 175 lbs.

YEAR	CLUB	W	L	PCT	ERA	G	IP	H	BB	SO
1940	BROOKLYN (N)	1	2	.333	4.12	13	39.1	40	18	13
1942	BROOKLYN (N)	10	6	.625	3.56	36	136.2	118	47	78
1943	BROOKLYN (N)	9	10	.474	3.66	47	169.2	166	66	83
1944	BROOKLYN (N)	4	3	.571	2.70	9	63.1	54	19	17
1946	BROOKLYN (N)	3	2	.600	3.21	13	56	56	24	17
	Five years	27	23	.540	3.48	118	465	434	174	208

JAKE HEHL   B. Dec. 8, 1899, Brooklyn, N.Y.
D. July 4, 1961, Brooklyn, N.Y.
Right handed, B.R.
5'11" 180 lbs.

YEAR	CLUB	W	L	PCT	ERA	G	IP	H	BB	SO
1918	BROOKLYN (N)	0	0	—	0.00	1	1	0	0	0

FRED HEIMACH   B. Jan. 27, 1901, Camden. N.J.
D. June 1, 1973, Fort Myers, Fla.
Left handed, B.L.
6' 175 lbs.

YEAR	CLUB	W	L	PCT	ERA	G	IP	H	BB	SO
1920	Philadelphia (A)	0	1	.000	14.40	1	5	13	1	0
1921	Philadelphia (A)	1	0	1.000	0.00	1	9	7	1	1
1922	Philadelphia (A)	7	11	.389	5.03	37	171.2	220	63	47
1923	Philadelphia (A)	6	12	.333	4.32	40	208.1	238	69	63
1924	Philadelphia (A)	14	12	.538	4.73	40	198	243	60	60
1925	Philadelphia (A)	0	1	.000	3.98	10	20.1	24	9	6
1926	Philadelphia (A)									
1926	Boston (A)									
	(year totals)	3	9	.250	4.98	33	133.2	147	47	25
1928	New York (A)	2	3	.400	3.31	13	68	66	16	25
1929	New York (A)	11	6	.647	4.01	35	134.2	141	29	26
1930	BROOKLYN (N)	0	2	.000	4.91	9	7.1	14	3	1
1931	BROOKLYN (N)	9	7	.563	3.46	31	135.1	145	23	43
1932	BROOKLYN (N)	9	4	.692	3.97	36	167.2	203	28	30
1933	BROOKLYN (N)	0	1	.000	10.01	10	29.2	49	11	7
	Thirteen years	62	69	.473	4.46	296	1288.2	1510	360	334

HENRY HEITMAN   B. Oct. 6, 1897, New York, N.Y.
D. Dec. 15, 1958, Brooklyn, N.Y.
Right handed, B.R.
6' 175 lbs.

YEAR	CLUB	W	L	PCT	ERA	G	IP	H	BB	SO
1918	BROOKLYN (N)	0	1	.000	108.00	1	.1	4	0	0

GEORGE HEMMING   B. Dec. 15, 1868, Carrollton, Ohio
D. June 3, 1930, Springfield, Mass.
Right handed, B.R.
5'11" 170 lbs.

YEAR	CLUB	W	L	PCT	ERA	G	IP	H	BB	SO
1890	Cleveland (P)									
1890	BROOKLYN (P)	8	4	.667	3.83	19	108		59	31
	(year totals)	8	5	.615	4.25	22	144	142	78	35
1891	BROOKLYN (N)	8	15	.348	4.96	27	199.2	231	84	83
1892	Cincinnati (N)									
1892	Louisivlle (N)									
	(year totals)	2	3	.400	5.05	5	41	46	19	12
1893	Louisville (N)	18	17	.514	5.18	41	332	373	176	79
1894	Louisville (N)									
1894	Baltimore (N)									
	(year totals)	17	19	.472	4.27	41	339.2	406	159	70
1895	Baltimore (N)	20	13	.606	4.05	34	262.1	288	96	43
1896	Baltimore (N)	15	6	.714	4.19	25	202	233	54	33
1897	Louisville (N)	3	4	.429	5.10	9	67	80	25	7
	Eight years	91	82	.526	4.55	204	1587.2	1799	691	362

LAFAYETTE HENION   B. 1899, San Diego, Calif.
D. July 22, 1955, San Luis Obispo, Calif.
Right handed, B.R.
5'11" 154 lbs.

YEAR	CLUB	W	L	PCT	ERA	G	IP	H	BB	SO
1919	BROOKLYN (N)	0	0	—	6.00	1	3	2	2	2

WELDON HENLEY
B. Oct. 20, 1880, Jasper, Ga.
D. Nov. 17, 1960, Palatka, Fla.
Right handed, B.R.
6' 175 lbs.

YEAR	CLUB	W	L	PCT	ERA	G	IP	H	BB	SO
1907	BROOKLYN (N)	1	6	.143	3.05	7	56	54	21	11
	Four years (totals)	33	45	.423	2.94	97	721.2	640	231	309

DUTCH HENRY
B. May 12, 1902, Cleveland, Ohio
D. Aug. 23, 1968, Cleveland, Ohio
Left handed, B.L.
6'1" 173 lbs.

YEAR	CLUB	W	L	PCT	ERA	G	IP	H	BB	SO
1923	BROOKLYN (N)	4	6	.400	3.91	17	94.1	105	28	28
1924	BROOKLYN (N)	1	2	.333	5.67	16	46	69	15	11
	Eight years (totals)	27	43	.386	4.39	164	646.1	809	190	170

ROY HENSHAW
B. July 29, 1911, Chicago, Ill.
Left handed, B.R.
5'8" 155 lbs.

YEAR	CLUB	W	L	PCT	ERA	G	IP	H	BB	SO
1937	BROOKLYN (N)	5	12	.294	5.07	42	156.1	176	69	98
	Eight years (totals)	33	40	.452	4.16	216	742.1	782	327	337

MARTY HERMANN
D. Sept. 11, 1956, Cincinnati, Ohio

YEAR	CLUB	W	L	PCT	ERA	G	IP	H	BB	SO
1918	BROOKLYN (N)	0	0	—	0.00	1	1	0	1	0

ART HERRING
B. March 10, 1907, Altus, Okla.
Right handed, B.R.
5'7" 168 lbs.

YEAR	CLUB	W	L	PCT	ERA	G	IP	H	BB	SO
1929	Detroit (A)	2	1	.667	4.78	4	32	38	19	15
1930	Detroit (A)	3	3	.500	5.33	23	77.2	97	36	16
1931	Detroit (A)	7	13	.350	4.31	35	165	186	67	64
1932	Detroit (A)	1	2	.333	5.24	12	22.1	25	15	12
1933	Detroit (A)	1	2	.333	3.84	24	61	61	20	20
1934	BROOKLYN (N)	2	4	.333	6.20	14	49.1	63	29	15
1939	Chicago (A)	0	0	—	5.65	7	14.1	13	5	8
1944	BROOKLYN (N)	3	4	.429	3.42	12	55.1	59	17	19
1945	BROOKLYN (N)	7	4	.636	3.48	22	124	103	43	34
1946	BROOKLYN (N)	7	2	.778	3.35	35	86	91	29	34
1947	Pittsburgh (N)	1	3	.250	8.44	11	10.2	18	4	6
	Eleven years	34	38	.472	4.32	199	697.2	754	284	243

BILL HERRING
B. Oct. 31, 1893, New York, N.Y.
D. Sept. 10, 1962, Honesdale, Pa.
Right handed, B.R.
6'3" 185 lbs.

YEAR	CLUB	W	L	PCT	ERA	G	IP	H	BB	SO
1915	BROOKLYN (F)	0	0	—	15.00	3	3	5	2	3

GREG HEYDEMAN
B. Jan. 2, 1952, Pocatello, Idaho
Right handed, B.R.
6' 180 lbs.

YEAR	CLUB	W	L	PCT	ERA	G	IP	H	BB	SO
1973	LOS ANGELES (N)	0	0	—	4.50	1	2	2	1	1

JIM HICKMAN
B. May 10, 1937, Henning, Tenn.
Right handed, B.R.
6'3" 192 lbs.

YEAR	CLUB	W	L	PCT	ERA	G	IP	H	BB	SO
1967	LOS ANGELES (N)	0	0	—	4.50	1	2	2	0	0

KIRBY HIGBE
B. April 8, 1915, Columbia, S.C.
Right handed, B.R.
5'11" 190 lbs.

YEAR	CLUB	W	L	PCT	ERA	G	IP	H	BB	SO
1937	Chicago (N)	1	0	1.000	5.40	1	5	4	1	2
1938	Chicago (N)	0	0	—	5.40	2	10	10	6	4
1939	Chicago (N)									
1939	Philadelphia (N)									
	(year totals)	12	15	.444	4.67	43	210	220	123	95
1940	Philadelphia (N)	14	19	.424	3.72	41	283	242	121	137
1941	BROOKLYN (N)	22	9	.710	3.14	48	298	244	132	121
1942	BROOKLYN (N)	16	11	.593	3.25	38	221.2	180	106	115
1943	BROOKLYN (N)	13	10	.565	3.70	35	185	189	95	108
1946	BROOKLYN (N)	17	8	.680	3.03	42	210.2	178	107	134
1947	BROOKLYN (N)	2	0	1.000	3.03	4	16	12	10	
1947	Pittsburgh (N)									
	(year totals)	13	17	.433	3.81	50	240.2	222	122	109
1948	Pittsburgh (N)	8	7	.533	3.36	56	158	140	83	86
1949	Pittsburgh (N)									
1949	New York (N)									
	(year totals)	2	2	.500	5.08	44	95.2	97	53	42
1950	New York (N)	0	3	.000	4.93	18	34.2	37	30	17
	Twelve years	118	101	.539	3.69	418	1952.1	1763	979	971
World Series										
	One year	0	0	—	7.36	1	3.2	6	2	1

STILL BILL HILL
B. Aug. 2, 1874, Chattanooga, Tenn.
D. Jan. 28, 1938, Cincinnati, Ohio
Left handed, B.L.
6'1" 201 lbs.

YEAR	CLUB	W	L	PCT	ERA	G	IP	H	BB	SO
1899	BROOKLYN (N)	1	0	1.000	4.21	2	15		11	9
	Four years (totals)	36	69	.343	4.16	124	925	994	406	280

AL HOLLINGSWORTH
B. Feb. 25, 1908, St. Louis, Mo.
Left handed, B.L.
6' 174 lbs.

YEAR	CLUB	W	L	PCT	ERA	G	IP	H	BB	SO
1939	BROOKLYN (N)	1	2	.333	6.75	8	27		11	11
	Eleven years (totals)	70	104	.402	3.99	315	1520.1	1647	587	608

BONNIE HOLLINGSWORTH
B. Dec. 26, 1895, Knoxville, Tenn.
Right handed, B.R.
5'10½" 170 lbs.

YEAR	CLUB	W	L	PCT	ERA	G	IP	H	BB	SO
1924	BROOKLYN (N)	1	0	1.000	6.75	3	8	7	9	6
	Four years (totals)	4	9	.308	4.94	36	116.2	126	80	49

JIM HOLMES
B. Lawrenceburg, Ky.
D. March 10, 1960, Jacksonville, Fla.

YEAR	CLUB	W	L	PCT	ERA	G	IP	H	BB	SO
1908	BROOKLYN (N)	1	3	.250	3.38	13	40	37	20	10
	Two years (totals)	1	4	.200	3.49	16	49	47	28	11

BURT HOOTON
B. Feb. 7, 1950, Greenville, Texas
Right handed, B.R.
6'1" 210 lbs.

YEAR	CLUB	W	L	PCT	ERA	G	IP	H	BB	SO
1971	Chicago (N)	2	0	1.000	2.14	3	21	8	10	22
1972	Chicago (N)	11	14	.440	2.80	33	218.1	201	81	132
1973	Chicago (N)	14	17	.452	3.68	42	240	248	73	134
1974	Chicago (N)	7	11	.389	4.81	48	176	214	51	94
1975	Chicago (N)	0	2	.000	8.18	3	11	18	4	5
1975	LOS ANGELES (N)	18	7	.720	2.81	31	224	172	64	128
	(year totals)	18	9	.667	3.07	34	234.2	190	68	153
1976	LOS ANGELES (N)	11	15	.423	3.26	33	226.2	203	60	116
1977	LOS ANGELES (N)	12	7	.632	2.62	32	223	184	60	153
1978	LOS ANGELES (N)	19	10	.655	2.71	32	236	196	61	104
1979	LOS ANGELES (N)	11	10	.524	2.97	29	212	191	63	129
1980	LOS ANGELES (N)	14	8	.636	3.65	34	207	194	64	118
1981	LOS ANGELES (N)	11	6	.647	2.28	23	142	124	33	74
1982	LOS ANGELES (N)	4	7	.364	4.03	21	120.2	130	33	51
1983	LOS ANGELES (N)	9	8	.538	4.22	33	160	156	59	87
	Thirteen years	143	122	.545	3.28	397	2417	2239	716	1367
Divisional Playoff										
	One year	1	0	1.000	1.29	1	7	3	3	2
League Championship										
	Three years	2	0	1.000	3.00	4	21	23	10	13

World Series

YEAR	CLUB	W	L	PCT	ERA	G	IP	H	BB	SO
1977	LOS ANGELES (N)	1	1	.500	3.75	2	12	8	2	9
1978	LOS ANGELES (N)	1	1	.500	6.48	2	8.1	13	4	6
1981	LOS ANGELES (N)	1	1	.500	1.59	2	11.1	8	9	3
	Three years	3	3	.500	3.69	6	31.2	29	14	18

LEFTY HOPPER
B. Ridgewood, N.J.
Deceased
Left handed

YEAR	CLUB	W	L	PCT	ERA	G	IP	H	BB	SO
1898	BROOKLYN (N)	0	2	.000	4.91	2	11	14	5	5

ELMER HORTON
B. Sept. 4, 1869, Hamilton, Ohio
Deceased

YEAR	CLUB	W	L	PCT	ERA	G	IP	H	BB	SO
1898	BROOKLYN (N)	0	1	.000	10.00	1	9	16	6	0
	Two years (totals)	0	3	.000	9.75	3	24	38	15	3

BYRON HOUCK
B. Aug. 28, 1887, Prosper, Minn.
D. June 17, 1969, Santa Cruz, Calif.
Right handed, B.R.
6' 175 lbs.

YEAR	CLUB	W	L	PCT	ERA	G	IP	H	BB	SO
1914	BROOKLYN (F)									
	(year totals)	2	6	.250	3.15	20	103	109	49	49
	Four years (totals)	27	24	.529	3.30	118	531.1	462	274	224

CHARLIE HOUGH
B. Jan. 5, 1948, Honolulu, Hawaii
Right handed, B.R.
6'2" 190 lbs.

YEAR	CLUB	W	L	PCT	ERA	G	IP	H	BB	SO
1970	LOS ANGELES (N)	0	0	—	5.29	8	17	18	11	8
1971	LOS ANGELES (N)	0	0	—	4.50	4	4	3	3	4
1972	LOS ANGELES (N)	0	0	—	3.38	2	2.2	2	2	4
1973	LOS ANGELES (N)	4	2	.667	2.76	37	71.2	52	45	70
1974	LOS ANGELES (N)	9	4	.692	3.75	49	96	65	40	63
1975	LOS ANGELES (N)	3	7	.300	2.95	38	61	43	34	34
1976	LOS ANGELES (N)	12	8	.600	2.21	77	142.2	102	77	81
1977	LOS ANGELES (N)	6	12	.333	3.33	70	127	98	70	105

YEAR	CLUB	W	L	PCT	ERA	G	IP	H	BB	SO
1978	LOS ANGELES (N)	5	5	.500	3.29	55	93	69	48	66
1979	LOS ANGELES (N)	7	5	.583	4.77	41	151	152	66	76
1980	LOS ANGELES (N)	1	3	.250	5.63	19	32		21	25
1980	Texas (A)									
	(year totals)	3	5	.375	4.55	35	93	91	58	72
1981	Texas (A)	4	1	.800	2.96	21	82	61	31	69
1982	Texas (A)	16	13	.552	3.95	34	228	217	72	128
1983	Texas (A)	15	13	.532	5.50	34	252	219	95	152
	Fourteen years	84	75	.529	3.58	506	1422	1192	652	962
League Championship										
	Three years	0	0	—	5.68	3	6.1	7	0	6

World Series

YEAR	CLUB	W	L	PCT	ERA	G	IP	H	BB	SO
1974	LOS ANGELES (N)	0	0	—	0.00	1	2		1	4
1977	LOS ANGELES (N)	0	0	—	1.80	2	5		0	5
1978	LOS ANGELES (N)	0	0	—	8.44	2	5.1		2	5
	Three years	0	0	—	4.38	5	12.1	13	3	14

STEVE HOWE B. March 10, 1958, Pontiac, Mich.
Left handed, B.L.
6'1" 180 lbs.

YEAR	CLUB	W	L	PCT	ERA	G	IP	H	BB	SO
1980	LOS ANGELES (N)	7	9	.438	2.65	59	85	83	22	39
1981	LOS ANGELES (N)	5	3	.625	2.50	41	54	51	18	32
1982	LOS ANGELES (N)	7	5	.583	2.08	66	99.1	87	17	49
1983	LOS ANGELES (N)	4	7	.364	4.30	46	68.2	55	29	66
	Four years	23	24	.488	2.35	212	307	276	86	186
Divisional Playoff										
	One year	0	0	—	0.00	2	2	1	0	2
League Championship										
	One year	0	0	—	0.00	2	2	1	0	2
World Series										
	One year	1	0	1.000	3.86	3	7	7	1	4

HARRY HOWELL B. Nov. 14, 1876, Brooklyn, N.Y.
D. May 22, 1956, Spokane, Wash.
Right handed, B.R.

YEAR	CLUB	W	L	PCT	ERA	G	IP	H	BB	SO
1898	BROOKLYN (N)	2	0	1.000	5.00	2	18	15	11	2
1900	BROOKLYN (N)	6	5	.545	3.75	21	110.1	131	36	26
	Thirteen years (totals)	132	146	.475	2.74	340	2567.2	2435	677	986

WAITE HOYT B. Sept. 9, 1899, Brooklyn, N.Y.
Right handed, B.R.
6' 180 lbs.

YEAR	CLUB	W	L	PCT	ERA	G	IP	H	BB	SO
1932	BROOKLYN (N)	1	3	.250	7.67	8	27		12	7
1937	BROOKLYN (N)	7	7	.500	3.23	27	167		30	44
1938	BROOKLYN (N)	0	3	.000	4.96	6	16.1	24	5	3
	Twenty-one years (totals)	237	182	.566	3.59	674	3762.2	4037	1003	1206

BILL HUBBELL B. June 17, 1897, Henderson, Colo.
D. Aug. 3, 1980, Lakewood, Colo.
Right handed, B.R.
6'1½" 195 lbs.

YEAR	CLUB	W	L	PCT	ERA	G	IP	H	BB	SO
1925	BROOKLYN (N)	3	6	.333	5.28	33	87		24	16
	Seven years (totals)	40	63	.388	4.68	204	931	1207	225	167

REX HUDSON B. Aug. 11, 1953, Tulsa, Okla.
Right handed, B.R.
5'11" 165 lbs.

YEAR	CLUB	W	L	PCT	ERA	G	IP	H	BB	SO
1974	LOS ANGELES (N)	0	0	—	22.50	1	2	6	0	0

JIM HUGHES B. Jan. 22, 1874, Sacramento, Calif.
D. June 2, 1924, Sacramento, Calif.

YEAR	CLUB	W	L	PCT	ERA	G	IP	H	BB	SO
1898	Baltimore (N)	23	12	.657	3.20	38	300.2	268	100	81
1899	BROOKLYN (N)	28	6	.824	2.68	35	291.2	250	119	99
1901	BROOKLYN (N)	17	12	.586	3.27	31	250.2	265	102	96
1902	BROOKLYN (N)	15	11	.577	2.87	31	254	228	55	94
	Four years	25	30	.455	4.31	78	440.2	443	205	226

JIM HUGHES B. March 21, 1923, Chicago, Ill.
Right handed, B.R.
6'1" 200 lbs.

YEAR	CLUB	W	L	PCT	ERA	G	IP	H	BB	SO
1952	BROOKLYN (N)	2	1	.667	1.45	6	18.2	16	11	8
1953	BROOKLYN (N)	4	3	.571	3.47	48	85.2	80	41	49
1954	BROOKLYN (N)	8	4	.667	3.22	60	86.2	76	44	58
1955	BROOKLYN (N)	0	2	.000	4.22	24	42.2	41	19	20
1956	BROOKLYN (N)	0	0	.000	5.25	5	12		4	8
1956	Chicago (N)									
	(year totals)	1	3	.250	5.18	30	57.1	53	34	28
1957	Chicago (A)	0	0	—	10.80	4	5	12	3	2
	Six years	15	13	.536	3.83	172	296	278	152	165
World Series										
	One Year	0	0	—	2.25	1	4	3	1	3

MICKEY HUGHES B. Oct. 25, 1866, New York, N.Y.
D. April 10, 1931, Jersey City, N.J.
Right handed

YEAR	CLUB	W	L	PCT	ERA	G	IP	H	BB	SO
*1890	BROOKLYN (N)	4	4	.500	4.20	9	67		33	22
	Three years (totals)	39	28	.582	3.22	75	623.2	594	235	250

*1888 Brooklyn (AA)

GEORGE HUNTER B. July 8, 1886, Buffalo, N.Y.
D. Jan. 11, 1968, Harrisburg, Pa.
Left handed, B.B.
5'8½" 165 lbs.

YEAR	CLUB	W	L	PCT	ERA	G	IP	H	BB	SO
1909	BROOKLYN (N)	3	10	.231	2.46	16	113.1	104	38	43

WILLARD HUNTER B. March 18, 1934, Newark, N.J.
Left handed, B.R.
6'2" 180 lbs.

YEAR	CLUB	W	L	PCT	ERA	G	IP	H	BB	SO
1962	LOS ANGELES (N)	0	0	.000		1	2		4	1
	Two years (totals)	4	9	.308	5.68	69	114	127	47	63

IRA HUTCHINSON B. Aug. 31, 1910, Chicago, Ill.
D. Aug. 21, 1973, Chicago, Ill.
Right handed, B.R.
5'10½" 180 lbs.

YEAR	CLUB	W	L	PCT	ERA	G	IP	H	BB	SO
1939	BROOKLYN (N)	5	2	.714	4.34	41	105.2	103	51	46
	Eight years (totals)	34	33	.507	3.76	209	610.2	628	249	179

BERT INKS B. Jan. 27, 1871, Ligonier, Ind.
D. Oct. 3, 1941, Ligonier, Ind.
Left handed, B.L.
6′3″ 175 lbs.

YEAR	CLUB	W	L	PCT	ERA	G	IP	H	BB	SO
1891	BROOKLYN (N)	3	10	.231	4.02	13	96.1	99	43	47
1892	BROOKLYN (N)	4	2	.667	3.64	9	52		31	26
	Five years (totals)	27	46	.370	5.52	89	603.2	780	266	167

GEORGE JEFFCOAT B. Dec. 24, 1913, New Brookland, S.C.
D. Oct. 13, 1978, Leesville, S.C.
Right handed, B.R.
5′11½″ 175 lbs.

YEAR	CLUB	W	L	PCT	ERA	G	IP	H	BB	SO
1936	BROOKLYN (N)	5	6	.455	4.52	40	95.2	84	63	46
1937	BROOKLYN (N)	1	3	.250	5.13	21	54.1	58	27	29
1939	BROOKLYN (N)	0	0	—	0.00	1	2	2	0	1
	Four years (totals)	7	11	.389	4.51	70	169.2	159	100	86

JACK JENKINS B. Dec. 22, 1942, Covington, Va.
Right handed, B.R.
6′2″ 195 lbs.

YEAR	CLUB	W	L	PCT	ERA	G	IP	H	BB	SO
1969	LOS ANGELES (N)	0	0	—	0.00	1	1	0	0	1
	Three years (totals)	0	3	.000	4.73	8	26.2	28	19	16

TOMMY JOHN B. May 22, 1943, Terre Haute, Ind.
Left handed, B.R.
6′3″ 180 lbs.

YEAR	CLUB	W	L	PCT	ERA	G	IP	H	BB	SO
1963	Cleveland (A)	0	2	.000	2.21	6	20.1	23	6	9
1964	Cleveland (A)	2	9	.182	3.91	25	94.1	97	35	65
1965	Chicago (A)	14	7	.667	3.09	39	183.2	162	58	126
1966	Chicago (A)	14	11	.560	2.62	34	223	195	57	138
1967	Chicago (A)	10	13	.435	2.47	31	178.1	143	47	110
1968	Chicago (A)	10	5	.667	1.98	25	177.1	135	49	117
1969	Chicago (A)	9	11	.450	3.25	33	232.1	230	90	128
1970	Chicago (A)	12	17	.414	3.28	37	269	253	101	138
1971	Chicago (A)	13	16	.448	3.62	38	229	244	58	131
1972	LOS ANGELES (N)	11	5	.688	2.89	29	186.2	172	40	117
1973	LOS ANGELES (N)	16	7	.696	3.10	36	218	202	50	116
1974	LOS ANGELES (N)	13	3	.813	2.59	22	153	133	42	78
1976	LOS ANGELES (N)	10	10	.500	3.09	31	207	207	61	91
1977	LOS ANGELES (N)	20	7	.741	2.78	31	220	225	50	123
1978	LOS ANGELES (N)	17	10	.630	3.30	33	213	230	53	124
1979	New York (A)	21	9	.700	2.97	37	276	268	65	111
1980	New York (A)	22	9	.710	3.43	36	265	270	56	78
1981	New York (A)	9	8	.529	2.64	20	140	135	39	50
*1982	New York–California	14	12	.581	3.69	37	221.2	239	39	68
1983	California (A)	11	13	.462	3.71	34	234.2	287	49	65
	Twenty years	248	184	.578	3.05	614	3941	3850	1045	1983
	Divisional Playoff One year	0	1	.000	6.43	1	7	8	2	0
	League Championship Four years	3	0	1.000	1.02	5	35.1	29	9	21
	World Series Three years	2	1	.667	2.67	6	33.2	34	7	21

*Traded—California Aug. 31, 1982.

ART JONES B. Feb. 7, 1907, Kershaw, S.C.
Right handed, B.R.
6′ 165 lbs.

YEAR	CLUB	W	L	PCT	ERA	G	IP	H	BB	SO
1932	BROOKLYN (N)	0	0	—	18.00	1	1	2	1	0

OSCAR JONES

B. Jan. 21, 1879, London Grove, Pa.
D. Oct. 8, 1946, Perkasie, Pa.
Right handed, B.R.
5'7" 163 lbs.

YEAR	CLUB	W	L	PCT	ERA	G	IP	H	BB	SO
1903	BROOKLYN (N)	20	16	.556	2.94	38	324.1	320	77	95
1904	BROOKLYN (N)	17	25	.405	2.75	46	377	387	92	96
1905	BROOKLYN (N)	8	15	.348	4.66	29	174	197	56	66
	Three years	45	56	.446	3.20	113	875.1	904	225	257

HERB JUUL

B. May 21, 1893, Chicago, Ill.
D. Jan. 4, 1942, Chicago, Ill.
Right handed, B.R.
5'9½" 150 lbs.

YEAR	CLUB	W	L	PCT	ERA	G	IP	H	BB	SO
1914	BROOKLYN (F)	0	3	.000	6.21	9	29	26	31	16

CHET KEHN

B. Oct. 30, 1921, San Diego, Calif.
Right handed, B.R.
5'11" 168 lbs.

YEAR	CLUB	W	L	PCT	ERA	G	IP	H	BB	SO
1942	BROOKLYN (N)	0	0	—	7.04	3	7.2	8	4	3

MIKE KEKICH

B. April 2, 1945, San Diego, Calif.
Left handed, B.R.
6'1" 196 lbs.

YEAR	CLUB	W	L	PCT	ERA	G	IP	H	BB	SO
1965	LOS ANGELES (N)	0	1	.000	9.58	5	10.1	10	13	9
1968	LOS ANGELES (N)	2	10	.167	3.91	25	115	116	46	84
	Nine years (totals)	39	51	.433	4.59	235	860.2	875	442	497

BRICKYARD KENNEDY

B. Oct. 7, 1868, Bellaire, Ohio
D. Sept. 23, 1915, Bellaire, Ohio
Right handed

YEAR	CLUB	W	L	PCT	ERA	G	IP	H	BB	SO
1892	BROOKLYN (N)	13	9	.591	3.86	26	191	189	95	108
1893	BROOKLYN (N)	26	20	.565	3.72	46	382.2	376	168	107
1894	BROOKLYN (N)	22	19	.537	4.92	48	360.2	445	149	107
1895	BROOKLYN (N)	18	13	.581	5.12	39	279.2	335	93	39
1896	BROOKLYN (N)	15	20	.429	4.42	42	305.2	334	130	76
1897	BROOKLYN (N)	19	22	.463	3.91	44	343.1	370	149	81
1898	BROOKLYN (N)	16	21	.432	3.37	40	339.1	360	123	73
1899	BROOKLYN (N)	22	8	.733	2.79	40	277.1	297	86	55
1900	BROOKLYN (N)	20	13	.606	3.91	42	292	316	111	75
1901	BROOKLYN (N)	3	5	.375	3.06	14	85.1	80	24	28
1902	New York (N)	1	4	.200	3.96	6	38.2	44	16	9
1903	Pittsburgh (N)	9	6	.600	3.45	18	125.1	130	57	39
	Twelve years	184	160	.535	3.96	405	3021	3276	1201	797
World Series										
	One year	0	1	.000	5.14	1	7	11	3	3

MAURY KENT

B. Sept. 17, 1885, Marshalltown, Iowa
D. April 19, 1966, Iowa City, Iowa
Right handed, B.B.
6' 168 lbs.

YEAR	CLUB	W	L	PCT	ERA	G	IP	H	BB	SO
1912	BROOKLYN (N)	5	5	.500	4.84	20	93	107	46	24
1913	BROOKLYN (N)	0	0	—	2.45	3	7.1	5	3	1
	Two years	5	5	.500	4.66	23	100.1	112	49	25

NEWT KIMBALL   B. March 27, 1915, Logan, Utah
Right handed, B.R.
6'2½" 190 lbs.

YEAR	CLUB	W	L	PCT	ERA	G	IP	H	BB	SO
1940	BROOKLYN (N)	3	1	.750	3.18	21	34		19	8
1941	BROOKLYN (N)	3	1	.750	3.63	15	52	43	29	17
1942	BROOKLYN (N)	2	0	1.000	3.68	14	29.1	27	19	8
1943	BROOKLYN (N)	1	1	.500	1.64	5	11		5	2
	Six years (totals)	11	9	.550	3.78	94	235.2	219	117	88

CLYDE KING   B. May 23, 1925, Goldsboro, N.C.
Right handed, B.B.
6'1" 175 lbs.

YEAR	CLUB	W	L	PCT	ERA	G	IP	H	BB	SO
1944	BROOKLYN (N)	2	1	.667	3.09	14	43.2	42	12	14
1945	BROOKLYN (N)	5	5	.500	4.09	42	112.1	131	48	29
1947	BROOKLYN (N)	6	5	.545	2.77	29	87.2	85	29	31
1948	BROOKLYN (N)	0	1	.000	8.03	9	12.1	14	6	5
1951	BROOKLYN (N)	14	7	.667	4.15	48	121.1	118	50	33
1952	BROOKLYN (N)	2	0	1.000	5.06	23	42.2	56	12	17
1953	Cincinnati (N)	3	6	.333	5.21	35	76	78	32	21
	Seven years	32	25	.561	4.14	200	496	524	189	150

FRED KIPP   B. Oct. 1, 1931, Piqua, Kan.
Left handed, B.L.
6'4" 200 lbs.

YEAR	CLUB	W	L	PCT	ERA	G	IP	H	BB	SO
1957	BROOKLYN (N)	0	0	—	9.00	1	4	6	0	3
1958	LOS ANGELES (N)	6	6	.500	5.01	40	102.1	107	45	58
1959	LOS ANGELES (N)	0	0	—	0.00	2	2.2	2	3	1
	Four year (totals)	6	7	.462	5.08	47	113.1	119	48	64

FRANK KITSON   B. April 11, 1872, Hopkins, Mich.
D. April 14, 1930, Allegan, Mich.
Right handed, B.L.

YEAR	CLUB	W	L	PCT	ERA	G	IP	H	BB	SO
1898	Baltimore (N)	8	6	.571	3.24	17	119.1	123	35	32
1899	Baltimore (N)	22	16	.579	2.76	40	329.2	329	66	75
1900	BROOKLYN (N)	15	13	.536	4.19	40	253.1	283	56	55
1901	BROOKLYN (N)	19	11	.633	2.98	38	280.2	312	67	127
1902	BROOKLYN (N)	19	12	.613	2.84	31	259.2	251	48	107
1903	Detroit (A)	15	16	.484	2.58	31	257.2	277	38	102
1904	Detroit (A)	8	13	.381	3.07	26	199.2	211	38	69
1905	Detroit (A)	11	14	.440	3.47	33	225.2	230	57	78
1906	Washington (A)	6	16	.273	3.65	30	197	196	57	59
1907	Washington (A)									
1907	New York (A)									
	(year totals)	3	2	.600	3.39	17	93	116	26	25
	Ten years	126	119	.514	3.17	303	2215.2	2328	488	729

JOHNNY KLIPPSTEIN   B. Oct. 17, 1927, Washington, D.C.
Right handed, B.R.
6'1" 173 lbs.

YEAR	CLUB	W	L	PCT	ERA	G	IP	H	BB	SO
1958	LOS ANGELES (N)	3	5	.375	3.80	45	90		44	73
1959	LOS ANGELES (N)	4	0	1.000	5.91	28	45.2	48	33	30
	Eighteen years (totals)	101	118	.461	4.24	711	1967.2	1911	978	1158
World Series										
	Two years (totals)	0	0	—	0.00	3	4.2	3	2	5

ELMER KNETZER

B. July 22, 1885, Carrick, Pa.
D. Oct. 3, 1975, Pittsburgh, Pa.
Right handed, B.R.
5'10" 180 lbs.

YEAR	CLUB	W	L	PCT	ERA	G	IP	H	BB	SO
1909	BROOKLYN (N)	1	3	.250	3.03	5	35.2	33	22	7
1910	BROOKLYN (N)	6	5	.545	3.19	20	132.2	122	60	56
1911	BROOKLYN (N)	11	11	.500	3.49	35	204	202	93	66
1912	BROOKLYN (N)	7	9	.438	4.55	33	140.1	135	70	61
1914	Pittsburgh (F)	19	11	.633	2.88	37	272	257	88	146
1915	Pittsburgh (F)	18	15	.545	2.58	41	279	256	89	120
1916	Boston (N)									
1916	Cincinnati (N)									
	(year totals)	5	14	.263	3.01	38	176.1	172	47	72
1917	Cincinnati (N)	0	0	—	2.96	11	27.1	29	12	7
	Eight years	67	68	.496	3.15	220	1267.1	1206	481	535

HUB KNOLLS

B. Dec. 18, 1883, Medaryville, Ind.
D. July 1, 1946, Chicago, Ill.
Right handed

YEAR	CLUB	W	L	PCT	ERA	G	IP	H	BB	SO
1906	BROOKLYN (N)	0	0	—	4.05	2	6.2	13	2	3

JIM KORWAN

B. March 4, 1874, Brooklyn, N.Y.
D. Aug. 1899, Brooklyn, N.Y.

YEAR	CLUB	W	L	PCT	ERA	G	IP	H	BB	SO
1894	BROOKLYN (N)	0	0	—	14.40	1	5	9	5	2
	Two years (totals)	1	2	.333	6.92	6	39	56	33	14

SANDY KOUFAX

B. Dec. 30, 1935, Brooklyn, N.Y.
Left handed, B.R.
6'2" 210 lbs.

YEAR	CLUB	W	L	PCT	ERA	G	IP	H	BB	SO
1955	BROOKLYN (N)	2	2	.500	3.02	12	41.2	33	28	30
1956	BROOKLYN (N)	2	4	.333	4.91	16	58.2	66	29	30
1957	BROOKLYN (N)	5	4	.556	3.88	34	104.1	83	51	122
1958	LOS ANGELES (N)	11	11	.500	4.48	40	158.2	132	105	131
1959	LOS ANGELES (N)	8	6	.571	4.05	35	153.1	136	92	173
1960	LOS ANGELES (N)	8	13	.381	3.91	37	175	133	100	197
1961	LOS ANGELES (N)	18	13	.581	3.52	42	255.2	212	96	269
1962	LOS ANGELES (N)	14	7	.667	2.54	28	184.1	134	57	216
1963	LOS ANGELES (N)	25	5	.833	1.88	40	311	214	58	306
1964	LOS ANGELES (N)	19	5	.792	1.74	29	223	154	53	223
1965	LOS ANGELES (N)	26	8	.765	2.04	43	335.2	216	71	382
1966	LOS ANGELES (N)	27	9	.750	1.73	41	323	241	77	317
	Twelve years	165	87	.655	2.76	397	2324.1	1754	817	2396

World Series

YEAR	CLUB	W	L	PCT	ERA	G	IP	H	BB	SO
1959	LOS ANGELES (N)	0	1	.500	1.00	2	9	5	1	7
1963	LOS ANGELES (N)	2	0	1.000	1.50	2	18	12	3	23
1965	LOS ANGELES (N)	2	1	.677	0.38	3	24	13	5	29
1966	LOS ANGELES (N)	0	1	.000	1.50	1	6	6	2	2
	Four years	4	3	.571	0.95	8	57	36	11	61

JOE KOUKALIK

B. March 3, 1880, Chicago, Ill.
D. Dec. 27, 1945, Chicago, Ill.
Right handed, B.R.
5'8" 160 lbs.

YEAR	CLUB	W	L	PCT	ERA	G	IP	H	BB	SO
1904	BROOKLYN (N)	0	1	.000	1.13	1	8	10	4	1

LOU KOUPAL
B. Dec. 19, 1898, Tabor, S.D.
D. Dec. 8, 1961, San Gabriel, Calif.
Right handed, B.R.
5'11" 175 lbs.

YEAR	CLUB	W	L	PCT	ERA	G	IP	H	BB	SO
1928	BROOKLYN (N)	1	0	1.000	2.41	17	37.1	43	15	10
1929	BROOKLYN (N)	0	1	.000	5.40	18	40		25	17
	Six years (totals)	10	21	.323	5.58	101	335.1	436	156	87

ABE KRUGER
B. Feb. 14, 1885, Morris Run, Pa.
D. July 4, 1962, Elmira, N.Y.
Right handed, B.R.
6'2" 190 lbs.

YEAR	CLUB	W	L	PCT	ERA	G	IP	H	BB	SO
1908	BROOKLYN (N)	0	1	.000	4.26	2	6.1	5	3	2

CLEM LABINE
B. Aug. 6, 1926, Lincoln, R.I.
Right handed, B.R.
6' 180 lbs.

YEAR	CLUB	W	L	PCT	ERA	G	IP	H	BB	SO
1950	BROOKLYN (N)	0	0	—	4.50	1	2	2	1	0
1951	BROOKLYN (N)	5	1	.833	2.20	14	65.1	52	20	39
1952	BROOKLYN (N)	8	4	.667	5.14	25	77	76	47	43
1953	BROOKLYN (N)	11	6	.647	2.77	37	110.1	92	30	44
1954	BROOKLYN (N)	7	6	.538	4.15	47	108.1	101	56	43
1955	BROOKLYN (N)	13	5	.722	3.24	60	144.1	121	55	67
1956	BROOKLYN (N)	10	6	.625	3.35	62	115.2	111	39	75
1957	BROOKLYN (N)	5	7	.417	3.44	58	104.2	104	27	67
1958	LOS ANGELES (N)	6	6	.500	4.15	52	104	112	33	43
1959	LOS ANGELES (N)	5	10	.333	3.93	56	84.2	91	25	37
1960	LOS ANGELES (N)	0	1	.000	5.82	13	17		8	15
1960	Detroit (A)									
1960	Pittsburgh (N)									
	(year totals)	3	4	.429	3.65	42	66.2	74	31	42
1961	Pittsburgh (N)	4	1	.800	3.69	56	92.2	102	31	49
1962	New York (N)	0	0	—	11.25	3	4	5	1	2
	Thirteen years	77	56	.579	3.63	513	1079.2	1043	396	551
World Series										
	Five years	2	2	.500	3.16	13	31.1	37	7	15

LERRIN LaGROW
B. July 8, 1948, Phoenix, Ariz.
Right handed, B.R.
6'5" 220 lbs.

YEAR	CLUB	W	L	PCT	ERA	G	IP	H	BB	SO
1979	LOS ANGELES (N)	5	1	.833	3.41	31	37		18	22
	Ten years (totals)	34	55	.382	4.11	309	778.2	814	312	375

FRANK LAMANSKE
B. Sept. 30, 1906, Oglesby, Ill.
D. Aug. 4, 1971, Olney, Ill.
Left handed, B.L.
5'11" 170 lbs.

YEAR	CLUB	W	L	PCT	ERA	G	IP	H	BB	SO
1935	BROOKLYN (N)	0	0	—	7.36	2	3.2	5	1	1

WAYNE LaMASTER
B. Feb. 13, 1907, Speed, Ind.
Left handed, B.L.
5'8" 170 lbs.

YEAR	CLUB	W	L	PCT	ERA	G	IP	H	BB	SO
1938	BROOKLYN (N)	0	1	.000	4.91	3	11		3	3
	Two years (totals)	19	27	.413	5.82	71	295.1	352	116	173

RAY LAMB
B. Dec. 28, 1944, Glendale, Calif.
Right handed, B.R.
6'1" 170 lbs.

YEAR	CLUB	W	L	PCT	ERA	G	IP	H	BB	SO
1969	LOS ANGELES (N)	0	1	.000	1.80	10	15	12	7	11
1970	LOS ANGELES (N)	6	1	.857	3.79	35	57	59	27	32
	Five years (totals)	20	23	.465	3.54	154	424	417	174	258

JOE LANDRUM
B. Dec. 13, 1928, Columbia, S.C.
Right handed, B.R.
5'11" 180 lbs.

YEAR	CLUB	W	L	PCT	ERA	G	IP	H	BB	SO
1950	BROOKLYN (N)	0	0	—	8.10	7	6.2	12	1	5
1952	BROOKLYN (N)	1	3	.250	5.21	9	38	46	10	17
	Two years	1	3	.250	5.64	16	44.2	58	11	22

TOMMY LASORDA
B. Sept. 22, 1927, Norristown, Pa.
Left handed, B.L.
5'10" 175 lbs.

YEAR	CLUB	W	L	PCT	ERA	G	IP	H	BB	SO
1954	BROOKLYN (N)	0	0	—	5.00	4	9	8	5	5
1955	BROOKLYN (N)	0	0	—	13.50	4	4	5	6	4
	Three years (totals)	0	4	.000	6.48	26	58.1	53	56	37

BOB LEE
B. Nov. 26, 1937, Ottumwa, Iowa
Right handed, B.R.
6'3" 225 lbs.

YEAR	CLUB	W	L	PCT	ERA	G	IP	H	BB	SO
1967	LOS ANGELES (N)	0	0	.000	5.14	4	7		3	2
	Five years (totals)	25	23	.521	2.71	269	492	402	196	315

KEN LEHMAN
B. June 10, 1928, Seattle, Wash.
Left handed, B.L.
6' 170 lbs.

YEAR	CLUB	W	L	PCT	ERA	G	IP	H	BB	SO
1952	BROOKLYN (N)	1	2	.333	5.28	4	15.1	19	6	7
1956	BROOKLYN (N)	2	3	.400	5.66	25	49.1	65	23	29
1957	BROOKLYN (N)	0	0	.000	0.00	3	7		1	3
	Five years (totals)	14	10	.583	3.91	134	265	273	95	134
World Series										
	One year	0	0	—	0.00	1	2	2	1	0

DUTCH LEONARD
B. March 25, 1909, Auburn, Ill.
Right handed, B.R.
6' 175 lbs.

YEAR	CLUB	W	L	PCT	ERA	G	IP	H	BB	SO
1933	BROOKLYN (N)	2	3	.400	2.93	10	40	42	10	6
1934	BROOKLYN (N)	14	11	.560	3.28	44	183.2	210	34	58
1935	BROOKLYN (N)	2	9	.182	3.92	43	137.2	152	29	41
1936	BROOKLYN (N)	0	0	—	3.66	16	32	34	5	8
1938	Washington (A)	12	15	.444	3.43	33	223.1	221	53	68
1939	Washington (A)	20	8	.714	3.54	34	269.1	273	59	88
1940	Washington (A)	14	19	.424	3.49	35	289	328	78	124
1941	Washington (A)	18	13	.581	3.45	34	256	271	54	91
1942	Washington (A)	2	2	.500	4.11	6	35	28	5	15
1943	Washington (A)	11	13	.458	3.28	31	219.2	218	46	51
1944	Washington (A)	14	14	.500	3.06	32	229.1	222	37	62
1945	Washington (A)	17	7	.708	2.13	31	216	208	35	96
1946	Washington (A)	10	10	.500	3.56	26	161.2	182	36	62
1947	Philadelphia (N)	17	12	.586	2.68	32	235	224	57	103
1948	Philadelphia (N)	12	17	.414	2.51	34	225.2	226	54	92
1949	Chicago (N)	7	16	.304	4.15	33	180	198	43	83
1950	Chicago (N)	5	1	.833	3.77	35	74	70	27	28
1951	Chicago (N)	10	6	.625	2.64	41	81.2	69	28	30

YEAR	CLUB	W	L	PCT	ERA	G	IP	H	BB	SO
1952	Chicago (N)	2	2	.500	2.16	45	66.2	56	24	37
1953	Chicago (N)	2	3	.400	4.60	45	62.2	72	24	27
	Twenty years	191	181	.513	3.25	640	3218.1	3304	738	1170

DENNIS LEWALLYN B. Aug. 11, 1953, Pensacola, Fla.
Right handed, B.R.
6'4" 200 lbs.

YEAR	CLUB	W	L	PCT	ERA	G	IP	H	BB	SO
1975	LOS ANGELES (N)	0	0	—	0.00	2	3	1	0	0
1976	LOS ANGELES (N)	1	1	.500	2.16	4	16.2	12	6	4
1977	LOS ANGELES (N)	3	1	.750	4.24	5	17	22	4	8
1978	LOS ANGELES (N)	0	0	—	0.00	1	2	2	0	0
1979	LOS ANGELES (N)	0	1	.000	5.25	7	12	19	5	1
	Seven years (totals)	4	3	.571	4.13	30	69.2	79	21	25

JIM LINDSEY B. Jan. 24, 1898, Greensburg, La.
D. Oct. 25, 1963, Jackson, La.
Right handed, B.R.
6'1" 175 lbs.

YEAR	CLUB	W	L	PCT	ERA	G	IP	H	BB	SO
1937	BROOKLYN (N)	0	1	.000	3.52	20	38.1	43	12	15
	Nine years (totals)	21	20	.512	4.70	177	431	507	176	175

BILLY LOES B. Dec. 13, 1929, Long Island City, N.Y.
Right handed, B.R.
6'1" 165 lbs.

YEAR	CLUB	W	L	PCT	ERA	G	IP	H	BB	SO
1950	BROOKLYN (N)	0	0	—	7.82	10	12.2	16	5	2
1952	BROOKLYN (N)	13	8	.619	2.69	39	187.1	154	71	115
1953	BROOKLYN (N)	14	8	.636	4.54	32	162.2	165	53	75
1954	BROOKLYN (N)	13	5	.722	4.14	28	147.2	154	60	97
1955	BROOKLYN (N)	10	4	.714	3.59	22	128	116	46	85
1956	BROOKLYN (N)	0	1	.000	9.82	1	1		1	2
1956	Baltimore (a)									
	(year totals)	2	8	.200	5.59	22	58	70	24	24
1957	Baltimore (A)	12	7	.632	3.24	31	155.1	142	37	86
1958	Baltimore (A)	3	9	.250	3.63	32	114	106	44	44
1959	Baltimore (a)	4	7	.364	4.06	37	64.1	58	25	34
1960	San Francisco (N)	3	2	.600	4.93	37	45.2	40	17	28
1961	San Francisco (N)	6	5	.545	4.24	26	114.2	114	39	55
	Eleven years	80	63	.559	3.89	316	1190.1	1135	421	645

World Series

YEAR	CLUB	W	L	PCT	ERA	G	IP	H	BB	SO
1952	BROOKLYN (N)	0	1	.000	4.35	2	10.1	11	5	5
1953	BROOKLYN (N)	1	0	1.000	3.38	1	8	8	2	8
1955	BROOKLYN (N)	0	1	.000	9.82	1	3.2	7	1	5
	Three years	1	2	.333	4.91	4	22	26	8	18

BOB LOGAN B. Feb. 10, 1910, Thompson, Neb.
D. May 20, 1978, Indianapolis, Ind.
Left handed, B.R.
5'10" 170 lbs.

YEAR	CLUB	W	L	PCT	ERA	G	IP	H	BB	SO
1935	BROOKLYN (N)	0	1	.000	3.38	2	2.2	2	1	1
	Five years (totals)	7	15	.318	3.15	57	222.2	245	81	67

BILL LOHRMAN
B. May 22, 1913, Brooklyn, N.Y.
Right handed, B.R.
6′1″ 185 lbs.

YEAR	CLUB	W	L	PCT	ERA	G	IP	H	BB	SO
1943	BROOKLYN (N)	0	2	.000	3.54	6	28		10	5
1944	BROOKLYN (N)	0	0	.000	22.50	2	2		2	0
	Nine years (totals)	60	59	.504	3.69	198	990.2	1048	240	330

VIC LOMBARDI
B. Sept. 20, 1922, Berkeley, Calif.
Left handed, B.L.
5′7″ 158 lbs.

YEAR	CLUB	W	L	PCT	ERA	G	IP	H	BB	SO
1945	BROOKLYN (N)	10	11	.476	3.31	38	203.2	195	86	64
1946	BROOKLYN (N)	13	10	.565	2.89	41	193	170	84	60
1947	BROOKLYN (N)	12	11	.522	2.99	33	174.2	156	65	72
1948	Pittsburgh (N)	10	9	.526	3.70	38	163	156	67	54
1949	Pittsburgh (N)	5	5	.500	4.57	34	134	149	68	64
1950	Pittsburgh (N)	0	5	.000	6.60	39	76.1	93	48	26
	Six years	50	51	.495	3.68	223	944.2	919	418	340
World Series										
	One year	0	1	.000	12.15	2	6.2	14	1	5

TOM LONG
B. April 22, 1898, Memphis, Tenn.
D. Sept. 16, 1973, Louisville, Ky.
Left handed, B.L.
5′9″ 154 lbs.

YEAR	CLUB	W	L	PCT	ERA	G	IP	H	BB	SO
1924	BROOKLYN (N)	0	0	—	9.00	1	2	2	2	0

TOM LOVETT
B. Dec. 7, 1863, Providence, R.I.
D. March 20, 1928, Providence, R.I.
B.R.

YEAR	CLUB	W	L	PCT	ERA	G	IP	H	BB	SO
*1890	BROOKLYN (N)	30	11	.732	2.78	44	372	327	141	124
1891	BROOKLYN (N)	23	19	.548	3.69	44	365.2	361	129	129
1893	BROOKLYN (N)	3	5	.375	6.56	14	96	134	35	15
1894	Boston (N)	8	6	.571	5.97	15	104	155	36	23
	Six years	88	59	.599	3.94	162	1305.1	1341	444	439

*1885 Philadelphia (AA), 1889 Brooklyn (AA)

RAY LUCAS
B. Oct. 2, 1908, Springfield, Ohio
D. Oct. 9, 1969, Harrison, Mich.
Right handed, B.R.
6′2″ 175 lbs.

YEAR	CLUB	W	L	PCT	ERA	G	IP	H	BB	SO
1933	BROOKLYN (N)	0	0	—	7.20	2	5	6	4	0
1934	BROOKLYN (N)	1	1	.500	6.75	10	30.2	39	14	3
	Five years (totals)	1	1	.500	5.79	22	56	58	32	5

CON LUCID
B. Feb. 24, 1869, Dublin, Ireland
Deceased

YEAR	CLUB	W	L	PCT	ERA	G	IP	H	BB	SO
1893	Louisville (N)	0	1	.000	15.00	2	6	10	10	0
1894	BROOKLYN (N)	5	3	.625	6.56	10	71.1	87	44	15
1895	BROOKLYN (N)	10	7	.580	5.23	21	148		62	29
1895	Philadelphia (N)									
	(year totals)	16	10	.615	5.66	31	206.2	244	107	43
1896	Philadelphia (N)	1	4	.200	8.36	5	42	75	17	3
1897	St. Louis (N)	1	5	.167	3.67	6	49	66	26	4
	Five years	23	23	.500	6.02	54	375	482	204	65

DOLF LUQUE
B. Aug. 4, 1890, Havana, Cuba
D. July 3, 1957, Havana, Cuba
Right handed, B.R.
5'7" 160 lbs.

YEAR	CLUB	W	L	PCT	ERA	G	IP	H	BB	SO
1914	Boston (N)	0	1	.000	4.15	2	8.2	5	4	1
1915	Boston (N)	0	0	—	3.60	2	5	6	4	3
1918	Cincinnati (N)	6	3	.667	3.80	12	83	84	32	26
1919	Cincinnati (N)	10	3	.769	2.63	30	106	89	36	40
1920	Cincinnati (N)	13	9	.591	2.51	37	207.2	168	60	72
1921	Cincinnati (N)	17	19	.472	3.38	41	304	318	64	102
1922	Cincinnati (N)	13	23	.361	3.31	39	261	266	72	79
1923	Cincinnati (N)	27	8	.771	1.93	41	322	279	88	151
1924	Cincinnati (N)	10	15	.400	3.16	31	219.1	229	53	86
1925	Cincinnati (N)	16	18	.471	2.63	36	291	263	78	140
1926	Cincinnati (N)	13	16	.448	3.43	34	233.2	231	77	83
1927	Cincinnati (N)	13	12	.520	3.20	29	230.2	225	56	76
1928	Cincinnati (N)	11	10	.524	3.57	33	234.1	254	84	72
1929	Cincinnati (N)	5	16	.238	4.50	32	176	213	56	43
1930	BROOKLYN (N)	14	8	.636	4.30	31	199	221	58	62
1931	BROOKLYN (N)	7	6	.538	4.56	19	102.2	122	27	25
1932	New York (N)	6	7	.462	4.01	38	110	128	32	32
1933	New York (N)	8	2	.800	2.69	35	80.1	75	19	23
1934	New York (N)	4	3	.571	3.83	26	42.1	54	17	12
1935	New York (N)	1	0	1.000	0.00	2	3.2	1	1	2
	Twenty years	194	179	.520	3.24	550	3220.1	3231	918	1130
World Series										
	Two years	1	0	1.000	0.00	3	9.1	3	2	11

MAX MACON
B. Oct. 14, 1915, Pensacola, Fla.
Left handed, B.L.
6'3" 175 lbs.

YEAR	CLUB	W	L	PCT	ERA	G	IP	H	BB	SO
1940	BROOKLYN (N)	1	0	1.000	22.50	2	2	5	0	1
1942	BROOKLYN (N)	5	3	.625	1.93	14	84	67	33	27
1943	BROOKLYN (N)	7	5	.583	5.96	25	77	89	32	21
	Six years (totals)	17	19	.472	4.24	81	297.1	305	128	90

SAL MAGLIE
B. April 26, 1917, Niagara Falls, N.Y.
Right handed, B.R.
6'2" 180 lbs.

YEAR	CLUB	W	L	PCT	ERA	G	IP	H	BB	SO
1956	BROOKLYN (N)									
	(year totals)	13	5	.722	2.89	30	196	160	54	110
1957	BROOKLYN (N)	6	6	.500	2.94	19	101		26	50
	Ten years (totals)	119	62	.657	3.15	303	1723	1591	562	862
World Series										
	Three years (totals)	1	2	.333	3.41	4	29	29	10	20

DUSTER MAILS
B. Oct. 1, 1895, San Quentin, Calif.
D. July 5, 1974, San Francisco, Calif.
Left handed, B.L.
6' 195 lbs.

YEAR	CLUB	W	L	PCT	ERA	G	IP	H	BB	SO
1915	BROOKLYN (N)	0	1	.000	3.60	2	5	6	5	3
1916	BROOKLYN (N)	0	1	.000	3.63	11	17.1	15	9	13
	Seven years (totals)	32	25	.561	4.10	104	516	554	220	232

MAL MALLETTE
B. Jan. 30, 1922, Syracuse, N.Y.
Left handed, B.L.
6'2" 200 lbs.

YEAR	CLUB	W	L	PCT	ERA	G	IP	H	BB	SO
1950	BROOKLYN (N)	0	0	—	0.00	2	1.1	2	1	2

AL MAMAUX

B. May 30, 1894, Pittsburgh, Pa.
D. Jan. 2, 1963, Santa Monica, Calif.
Right handed, B.R.
6'1½" 168 lbs.

YEAR	CLUB	W	L	PCT	ERA	G	IP	H	BB	SO
1913	Pittsburgh (N)	0	0	—	3.00	1	3	2	2	2
1914	Pittsburgh (N)	5	2	.714	1.71	13	63	41	24	30
1915	Pittsburgh (N)	21	8	.724	2.04	38	251.2	182	96	152
1916	Pittsburgh (N)	21	15	.583	2.53	45	310	264	136	163
1917	Pittsburgh (N)	2	11	.154	5.25	16	85.2	92	50	22
1918	BROOKLYN (N)	0	1	.000	6.75	2	8	14	2	2
1919	BROOKLYN (N)	10	12	.455	2.66	30	199.1	174	66	80
1920	BROOKLYN (N)	12	8	.600	2.69	41	190.2	172	63	101
1921	BROOKLYN (N)	3	3	.500	3.14	12	43	36	13	21
1922	BROOKLYN (N)	1	4	.200	3.70	37	87.2	97	33	35
1923	BROOKLYN (N)	0	2	.000	8.31	5	13	20	6	5
1924	New York (A)	1	1	.500	5.68	14	38	44	20	12
	Twelve years	76	67	.531	2.90	254	1293	1138	511	625
World Series										
	One year	0	0	—	4.50	3	4	2	0	5

JUAN MARICHAL

B. Oct. 24, 1937, Laguna Verde, Dominican Republic
Right handed, B.R.
6' 185 lbs.

YEAR	CLUB	W	L	PCT	ERA	G	IP	H	BB	SO
1975	LOS ANGELES (N)	0	1	.000	13.50	2	6	11	5	1
	Sixteen years (totals)	243	142	.631	2.89	471	3509.1	3153	709	2303

DAN MARION

B. 1890
D. Jan. 19, 1933, Milwaukee, Wis.
Right handed, B.R.
6'1" 187 lbs.

YEAR	CLUB	W	L	PCT	ERA	G	IP	H	BB	SO
1914	BROOKLYN (F)	3	2	.600	3.93	17	89.1	97	38	41
1915	BROOKLYN (F)	10	9	.526	3.20	35	208.1	193	64	46
	Two years	13	11	.542	3.42	52	297.2	290	102	87

RUBE MARQUARD

B. Oct. 9, 1889, Cleveland, Ohio
D. June 1, 1980, Baltimore, Md.
Left handed, B.B.
6'3" 180 lbs.

YEAR	CLUB	W	L	PCT	ERA	G	IP	H	BB	SO
1908	New York (N)	0	1	.000	3.60	1	5	6	2	2
1909	New York (N)	5	13	.278	2.60	29	173	155	73	109
1910	New York (N)	4	4	.500	4.46	13	70.2	65	40	52
1911	New York (N)	24	7	.774	2.50	45	277.2	221	106	237
1912	New York (N)	26	11	.703	2.57	43	294.2	286	80	175
1913	New York (N)	23	10	.697	2.50	42	288	248	49	151
1914	New York (N)	12	22	.353	3.06	39	268	261	47	92
1915	New York (N)									
1915	BROOKLYN (N)	2	2	.500	6.12	6	25		5	13
	(year totals)	11	10	.524	4.04	33	193.2	207	38	92
1916	BROOKLYN (N)	13	6	.684	1.58	36	205	169	38	107
1917	BROOKLYN (N)	19	12	.613	2.55	37	232.2	200	60	117
1918	BROOKLYN (N)	9	18	.333	2.64	34	239	231	59	89
1919	BROOKLYN (N)	3	3	.500	2.29	8	59	54	10	29
1920	BROOKLYN (N)	10	7	.588	3.23	28	189.2	181	35	89
1921	Cincinnati (N)	17	14	.548	3.39	39	265.2	291	50	88
1922	Boston (N)	11	15	.423	5.09	39	198	255	66	57
1923	Boston (N)	11	14	.440	3.73	38	239	265	65	78
1924	Boston (N)	1	2	.333	3.00	6	36	33	13	10
1925	Boston (N)	2	8	.200	5.75	26	72	105	27	19
	Eighteen years	201	177	.532	3.08	536	3306.2	3233	858	1593
World Series										
	Five years	2	5	.286	2.76	11	58.2	52	15	35

BUCK MARROW

B. Aug. 29, 1909, Tarboro, N.C.
Right handed, B.R.
6'4" 200 lbs.

YEAR	CLUB	W	L	PCT	ERA	G	IP	H	BB	SO
1937	BROOKLYN (N)	1	2	.333	6.61	6	16.1	19	9	2
1938	BROOKLYN (N)	0	1	.000	4.58	15	19.2	23	11	6
	Three years (totals)	3	8	.273	5.06	39	99.2	112	49	39

MIKE MARSHALL

B. Jan. 15, 1943, Adrian, Mich.
Right handed, B.R.
5'10" 180 lbs.

YEAR	CLUB	W	L	PCT	ERA	G	IP	H	BB	SO
1967	Detroit (A)	1	3	.250	1.98	37	59	51	20	41
1969	Seattle (A)	3	10	.231	5.13	20	87.2	99	35	47
1970	Houston (N)									
1970	Montreal (N)									
	(year totals)	3	8	.273	3.86	28	70	64	33	43
1971	Montreal (N)	5	8	.385	4.30	66	111	100	50	85
1972	Montreal (N)	14	8	.636	1.78	65	116	82	47	95
1973	Montreal (N)	14	11	.560	2.66	92	179	163	75	124
1974	LOS ANGELES (N)	15	12	.556	2.42	106	208	191	56	143
1975	LOS ANGELES (N)	9	14	.391	3.30	57	109	98	39	64
1976	LOS ANGELES (N)	4	3	.571	4.43	30	63		25	39
1976	Atlanta (N)									
	(year totals)	6	4	.600	3.99	54	99.1	99	39	56
1977	Atlanta (N)									
1977	Texas (A)									
	(year totals)	3	2	.600	4.71	16	42	54	15	24
1978	Minnesota (A)	10	12	.455	2.36	54	99	80	37	56
1979	Minnesota (A)	10	15	.400	2.64	90	143	132	48	81
1980	Minnesota (A)	1	3	.250	6.19	18	32	42	12	13
1981	New York (N)	3	2	.600	2.61	20	31	26	8	8
	Four years	97	112	.464	3.14	723	1386	1281	514	880
League Championship										
	One year	0	0	—	0.00	2	3	0	0	1
World Series										
	One year	0	1	.000	1.00	5	9	6	1	10

MORRIE MARTIN

B. Sept. 3, 1922, Dixon, Mo.
Left handed, B.L.
6' 173 lbs.

YEAR	CLUB	W	L	PCT	ERA	G	IP	H	BB	SO
1949	BROOKLYN (N)	1	3	.250	7.04	10	30.2	39	15	15
	Ten years (totals)	38	34	.528	4.29	250	604.2	607	251	245

EARL MATTINGLY

B. Nov. 4, 1904, Newport, Md.
Right handed, B.R.
5'10½" 164 lbs.

YEAR	CLUB	W	L	PCT	ERA	G	IP	H	BB	SO
1933	BROOKLYN (N)	0	1	.000	2.51	8	14.1	15	10	6

AL MAUL

B. Oct. 9, 1865, Philadelphia, Pa.
D. May 3, 1958, Philadelphia, Pa.
Right handed, B.R.
6' 175 lbs.

YEAR	CLUB	W	L	PCT	ERA	G	IP	H	BB	SO
1899	BROOKLYN (N)	2	0	1.000	4.50	4	26	35	6	2
	Fifteen years (totals)	84	79	.515	4.43	187	1431.2	1659	518	346

RALPH MAURIELLO

B. Aug. 25, 1934, Brooklyn, N.Y.
Right handed, B.R.
6'3" 195 lbs.

YEAR	CLUB	W	L	PCT	ERA	G	IP	H	BB	SO
1958	LOS ANGELES (N)	1	1	.500	4.63	3	11.2	10	8	11

BERT MAXWELL
B. Oct. 17, 1886, Texarkana, Ark.
D. Dec. 10, 1967, Brady, Texas
Right handed, B.B.

YEAR	CLUB	W	L	PCT	ERA	G	IP	H	BB	SO
1914	BROOKLYN (F)	3	4	.429	3.28	12	71.1	76	24	19
	Four years (totals)	4	7	.364	4.16	21	123.1	144	42	35

AL McBEAN
B. May 15, 1938, Charlotte Amalie, Virgin Islands
Right handed, B.R.
5'11½" 165 lbs.

YEAR	CLUB	W	L	PCT	ERA	G	IP	H	BB	SO
1969	LOS ANGELES (N)	2	6	.250	3.94	31	48		21	26
	Ten years (totals)	67	50	.573	3.13	409	1072.1	1058	365	575

GENE McCANN
B. June 13, 1876, Baltimore, Md.
D. April 26, 1943, New York, N.Y.
Right handed

YEAR	CLUB	W	L	PCT	ERA	G	IP	H	BB	SO
1901	BROOKLYN (N)	2	3	.400	3.44	6	34	34	16	9
1902	BROOKLYN (N)	1	2	.333	2.40	3	30	32	12	9
	Two years	3	5	.375	2.95	9	64	66	28	18

DANNY McDEVITT
B. Nov. 18, 1932, New York, N.Y.
Left handed, B.L.
5'10" 175 lbs.

YEAR	CLUB	W	L	PCT	ERA	G	IP	H	BB	SO
1957	BROOKLYN (N)	7	4	.636	3.25	22	119	105	72	90
1958	LOS ANGELES (N)	2	6	.250	7.45	13	48.1	71	31	26
1959	LOS ANGELES (N)	10	8	.556	3.97	39	145	149	51	106
1960	LOS ANGELES (N)	0	4	.000	4.25	24	53	51	42	30
1961	New York (A)									
1961	Minnesota (A)									
	(year totals)	2	2	.500	4.08	24	39.2	38	27	23
1962	Kansas City (A)	0	3	.000	5.82	33	51	47	41	28
	Six years	21	27	.438	4.40	155	456	461	264	303

JOHN McDOUGAL
Deceased.

YEAR	CLUB	W	L	PCT	ERA	G	IP	H	BB	SO
1895	BROOKLYN (N)	0	0	—	12.00	1	3	3	5	2

DAN McFARLAN
B. Nov. 26, 1874, Gainesville, Texas
D. Sept. 24, 1924, Louisville, Ky.

YEAR	CLUB	W	L	PCT	ERA	G	IP	H	BB	SO
1899	BROOKLYN (N)	0	0	.000	3.60	1	5		1	1
	Two years (totals)	8	25	.242	5.02	40	263.2	354	82	51

CHAPPIE McFARLAND
D. Dec. 15, 1924, Houston, Texas
Right handed

YEAR	CLUB	W	L	PCT	ERA	G	IP	H	BB	SO
1906	BROOKLYN (N)	0	1	.000	8.00	1	9		5	5
	Five years (totals)	34	59	.366	3.35	106	841	893	192	307

JOE McGINNITY
B. March 19, 1871, Rock Island, Ill.
D. Nov. 14, 1929, Brooklyn, N.Y.
Right handed, B.R.
5'11" 206 lbs.

YEAR	CLUB	W	L	PCT	ERA	G	IP	H	BB	SO
1900	BROOKLYN (N)	29	9	.763	2.90	45	347	350	113	93
	Ten years (totals)	247	145	.630	2.64	466	3458.2	3276	812	1068

PAT McGLOTHIN B. Oct. 20, 1920, Coalfield, Tenn.
Right handed, B.L.
6'3½" 180 lbs.

YEAR	CLUB	W	L	PCT	ERA	G	IP	H	BB	SO
1949	BROOKLYN (N)	1	1	.500	4.60	7	15.2	13	5	11
1950	BROOKLYN (N)	0	0	—	13.50	1	2	5	1	2
	Two years	1	1	.500	5.60	8	17.2	18	6	13

BOB McGRAW B. April 10, 1895, La Veta, Colo.
D. June 2, 1978, Seal Beach, Calif.
Right handed, B.R.
6'2" 160 lbs.

YEAR	CLUB	W	L	PCT	ERA	G	IP	H	BB	SO
1917	New York (A)	0	1	.000	0.82	2	11	9	3	3
1918	New York (A)	0	1	.000	—	1		0	4	0
1919	New York (A)									
1919	Boston (A)									
	(year totals)	1	2	.333	5.44	16	43	44	27	9
1920	New York (A)	0	0	—	4.67	15	27	24	20	11
1925	BROOKLYN (N)	0	2	.000	3.20	2	19.2	14	13	3
1926	BROOKLYN (N)	9	13	.409	4.59	33	174.1	197	67	49
1927	BROOKLYN (N)	0	1	—	9.00	1	4		2	2
1927	St. Louis (N)									
	(year totals)	4	6	.400	5.23	19	98	126	32	39
1928	Philadelphia (N)	7	8	.467	4.64	39	132	150	56	28
1929	Philadelphia (N)	5	5	.500	5.73	41	86.1	113	43	22
	Nine years	26	38	.406	4.89	168	591.1	677	265	164

JIM McGRAW B. 1890
D. Nov. 14, 1918, Cleveland, Ohio
Right handed, B.R.

YEAR	CLUB	W	L	PCT	ERA	G	IP	H	BB	SO
1914	BROOKLYN (F)	0	0	—	0.00	1	2	0	0	2

HARRY McINTYRE B. Jan. 11, 1879, Detroit, Mich.
D. Jan. 9, 1949, Daytona Beach, Fla.
Right handed, B.R.
5'11" 180 lbs.

YEAR	CLUB	W	L	PCT	ERA	G	IP	H	BB	SO
1905	BROOKLYN (N)	8	25	.242	3.70	40	309	340	101	135
1906	BROOKLYN (N)	12	21	.364	2.97	39	276	254	89	121
1907	BROOKLYN (N)	7	15	.318	2.39	28	199.2	178	79	49
1908	BROOKLYN (N)	11	20	.355	2.69	40	288	259	90	108
1909	BROOKLYN (N)	8	17	.320	3.63	32	228	200	91	84
1910	Chicago (N)	13	9	.591	3.07	28	176	152	50	65
1911	Chicago (N)	11	7	.611	4.11	25	149	147	33	56
1912	Chicago (N)	1	2	.333	3.80	4	23.2	22	6	8
1913	Cincinnati (N)	0	1	.000	27.00	1	1	3	0	0
	Nine years	71	117	.378	3.22	237	1650.1	1555	539	626
World Series										
	One year	0	1	.000	6.75	2	5.1	4	3	3

DOC McJAMES B. Aug. 27, 1873, Williamsburg, S.C.
D. Sept. 23, 1901, Charleston, S.C.
Right handed

YEAR	CLUB	W	L	PCT	ERA	G	IP	H	BB	SO
1895	Washington (N)	1	1	.500	1.59	2	17	17	16	9
1896	Washington (N)	12	20	.375	4.27	37	280.1	310	135	103
1897	Washington (N)	15	23	.395	3.61	44	323.2	361	137	156
1898	Baltimore (N)	27	15	.643	2.36	45	374	327	113	178
1899	BROOKLYN (N)	19	15	.559	3.50	37	275.1	295	122	105
1901	BROOKLYN (N)	5	6	.455	4.75	13	91	104	40	42
	Six years	79	80	.497	3.43	178	1361.1	1414	563	593

KIT McKENNA

B. Feb. 10, 1873, Lynchburg, Va.
D. March 31, 1941, Lynchburg, Va.

YEAR	CLUB	W	L	PCT	ERA	G	IP	H	BB	SO
1898	BROOKLYN (N)	2	6	.250	5.63	14	100.2	118	57	27
	Two years (totals)	4	9	.308	5.31	22	145.2	184	76	34

CAL McLISH

B. Dec. 1, 1925, Anadarko, Okla.
Right handed, B.R.
6' 179 lbs.

YEAR	CLUB	W	L	PCT	ERA	G	IP	H	BB	SO
1944	BROOKLYN (N)	3	10	.231	7.82	23	84	110	48	24
1946	BROOKLYN (N)	0	0	—	—	1	1	0	0	0
	Fifteen years (totals)	92	92	.500	4.01	352	1609	1684	552	713

SADIE McMAHON

B. Sept. 19, 1867, Wilmington, Del.
D. Feb. 20, 1954, Delaware City, Del.
Right handed, B.R.
5'9" 185 lbs.

YEAR	CLUB	W	L	PCT	ERA	G	IP	H	BB	SO
1890	BROOKLYN-Balt. (AA)	7	3			12				
1897	BROOKLYN (N)	0	5	.000	5.86	9	63	75	29	13
	Nine years (totals)	177	125	.586	3.49	323	2647	2761	947	967

JOHN McMAKIN

B. March 6, 1878, Spartanburg, S.C.
D. Sept. 25, 1956, Lyman, S.C.
Right handed, B.R.
5'11" 165 lbs.

YEAR	CLUB	W	L	PCT	ERA	G	IP	H	BB	SO
1902	BROOKLYN (N)	2	2	.500	3.09	4	32	34	11	6

DOUG McWEENY

B. Aug. 17, 1896, Chicago, Ill.
D. Jan. 1, 1953, Chicago, Ill.
Right handed, B.R.
6'2" 180 lbs.

YEAR	CLUB	W	L	PCT	ERA	G	IP	H	BB	SO
1921	Chicago (A)	3	6	.333	6.08	27	97.2	127	45	46
1922	Chicago (A)	0	1	.000	5.91	4	10.2	13	7	5
1924	Chicago (A)	1	3	.250	4.57	13	43.1	47	18	17
1926	BROOKLYN (N)	11	13	.458	3.04	42	216.1	213	84	96
1927	BROOKLYN (N)	4	8	.333	3.56	34	164.1	167	70	73
1928	BROOKLYN (N)	14	14	.500	3.17	42	244	218	114	79
1929	BROOKLYN (N)	4	10	.286	6.10	36	146	167	93	59
1930	Cincinnati (N)	0	2	.000	7.36	8	25.2	28	20	10
	Eight years	37	57	.394	4.17	206	948	980	450	386

RUBE MELTON

B. Feb. 27, 1917, Cramerton, N.C.
D. Sept. 11, 1971, Greer, S.C.
Right handed, B.R.
6'5" 205 lbs.

YEAR	CLUB	W	L	PCT	ERA	G	IP	H	BB	SO
1941	Philadelphia (N)	1	5	.167	4.73	25	83.2	81	47	57
1942	Philadelphia (N)	9	20	.310	3.70	42	209.1	180	114	107
1943	BROOKLYN (N)	5	8	.385	3.92	30	119.1	102	79	63
1944	BROOKLYN (N)	9	13	.409	3.46	37	187.1	178	96	91
1946	BROOKLYN (N)	6	3	.667	1.99	24	99.2	72	52	44
1947	BROOKLYN (N)	0	1	.000	13.50	4	4.2	7	7	1
	Six years	30	50	.375	3.62	162	704	620	395	363

ANDY MESSERSMITH

B. Aug. 6, 1945, Toms River, N.J.
Right handed, B.R.
6'1" 200 lbs.

YEAR	CLUB	W	L	PCT	ERA	G	IP	H	BB	SO
1968	California (A)	4	2	.667	2.21	28	81.1	44	35	74
1969	California (A)	16	11	.593	2.52	40	250	169	100	211
1970	California (A)	11	10	.524	3.00	37	195	144	78	162
1971	California (A)	20	13	.606	2.99	38	277	224	121	179
1972	California (A)	8	11	.421	2.81	25	170	125	68	142
1973	LOS ANGELES (N)	14	10	.583	2.70	33	249.2	196	77	177
1974	LOS ANGELES (N)	20	6	.769	2.59	39	292	227	94	221
1975	LOS ANGELES (N)	19	14	.576	2.29	42	322	244	96	213
1976	Atlanta (N)	11	11	.500	3.04	29	207	166	74	135
1977	Atlanta (N)	5	4	.556	4.41	16	102	101	39	69
1978	New York (A)	0	3	.000	5.64	6	22.1	24	15	16
1979	LOS ANGELES (N)	2	4	.333	4.94	11	62	55	34	26
	Twelve years	130	99	.568	2.86	344	2230.1	1719	831	1625
League Championship										
	One year	1	0	1.000	2.57	1	7	8	3	0
World Series										
	One year	0	2	.000	4.50	2	14	11	7	12

RUSS MEYER

B. Oct. 25, 1923, Peru, Ill.
Right handed, B.B.
6'1" 175 lbs.

YEAR	CLUB	W	L	PCT	ERA	G	IP	H	BB	SO
1946	Chicago (N)	0	0	—	3.18	4	17	21	10	10
1947	Chicago (N)	3	2	.600	3.40	23	45	43	14	22
1948	Chicago (N)	10	10	.500	3.66	29	164.2	157	77	89
1949	Philadelphia (N)	17	8	.680	3.08	37	213	199	70	78
1950	Philadelphia (N)	9	11	.450	5.30	32	159.2	193	67	74
1951	Philadelphia (N)	8	9	.471	3.48	28	168	172	55	65
1952	Philadelphia (N)	13	14	.481	3.14	37	232.1	235	65	92
1953	BROOKLYN (N)	15	5	.750	4.56	34	191.1	201	63	106
1954	BROOKLYN (N)	11	6	.647	3.99	36	180.1	193	49	70
1955	BROOKLYN (N)	6	2	.750	5.42	18	73	86	31	26
1956	Chicago (N)									
1956	Cincinnati (N)									
	(year totals)	1	6	.143	6.21	21	58	72	26	29
1957	Boston (A)	0	0	—	5.40	2	5	10	3	1
1959	Kansas City (A)	1	0	1.000	4.50	18	24	24	11	10
	Thirteen years	94	73	.563	3.99	319	1531.1	1606	541	672
World Series										
	Three years	0	1	.000	3.09	4	11.2	16	6	10

GLENN MICKENS

B. July 26, 1930, Wilmar, Calif.
Right handed, B.R.
6' 175 lbs.

YEAR	CLUB	W	L	PCT	ERA	G	IP	H	BB	SO
1953	BROOKLYN (N)	0	1	.000	11.37	4	6.1	11	4	5

PETE MIKKELSEN

B. Oct. 25, 1939, Staten Island, N.Y.
Right handed, B.R.
6'2" 210 lbs.

YEAR	CLUB	W	L	PCT	ERA	G	IP	H	BB	SO
1964	New York (A)	7	4	.636	3.56	50	86	79	41	63
1965	New York (A)	4	9	.308	3.28	41	82.1	78	36	69
1966	Pittsburgh (N)	9	8	.529	3.07	71	126	106	51	76
1967	Pittsburgh (N)									
1967	Chicago (N)									
	(year totals)	1	2	.333	4.55	39	63.1	59	24	30
1968	Chicago (N)									
1968	St. Louis (N)									
	(year totals)	0	0	—	2.61	8	20.2	17	8	13
1969	LOS ANGELES (N)	7	5	.583	2.78	48	81	57	30	51
1970	LOS ANGELES (N)	4	2	.667	2.76	33	62	48	20	47
1971	LOS ANGELES (N)	8	5	.615	3.65	41	74	67	17	46

YEAR	CLUB	W	L	PCT	ERA	G	IP	H	BB	SO
1972	LOS ANGELES (N)	5	5	.500	4.06	33	57.2	65	23	41
	Nine years	45	40	.529	3.38	364	653	576	250	436
World Series										
	One year	0	1	.000	5.79	4	4.2	4	2	4

JOHNNY MILJUS B. June 30, 1895, Pittsburgh, Pa.
D. Feb. 11, 1976, Polson, Mont.
Right handed, B.R.
6'1" 178 lbs.

YEAR	CLUB	W	L	PCT	ERA	G	IP	H	BB	SO
1917	BROOKLYN (N)	0	1	.000	0.60	4	15	14	8	9
1920	BROOKLYN (N)	1	0	1.000	3.09	9	23.1	24	4	9
1921	BROOKLYN (N)	6	3	.667	4.23	28	93.2	115	27	37
	Seven years (totals)	29	26	.527	3.92	127	457.1	526	173	166

BOB MILLER B. Feb. 18, 1939, St. Louis, Mo.
Right handed, B.R.
6'1" 180 lbs.

YEAR	CLUB	W	L	PCT	ERA	G	IP	H	BB	SO
1957	St. Louis (N)	0	0	—	7.00	5	9	13	5	7
1959	St. Louis (N)	4	3	.571	3.31	11	70.2	66	21	43
1960	St. Louis (N)	4	3	.571	3.42	15	52.2	53	17	33
1961	St. Louis (N)	1	3	.250	4.24	34	74.1	82	46	39
1962	New York (N)	1	12	.077	4.89	33	143.2	146	62	91
1963	LOS ANGELES (N)	10	8	.556	2.89	42	187	171	65	125
1964	LOS ANGELES (N)	7	7	.500	2.62	74	137.2	115	63	94
1965	LOS ANGELES (N)	6	7	.462	2.97	61	103	82	26	77
1966	LOS ANGELES (N)	4	2	.667	2.77	46	84.1	70	29	58
1967	LOS ANGELES (N)	2	9	.182	4.31	52	85.2	88	27	32
1968	Minnesota (A)	0	3	.000	2.74	45	72.1	65	24	41
1969	Minnesota (A)	5	5	.500	3.02	48	119.1	118	32	57
1970	Cleveland (A)									
1970	Chicago (N)									
1970	Chicago (A)									
	(year totals)	6	8	.429	4.79	37	107	129	54	55
1971	Chicago (N)									
1971	San Diego (N)									
1971	Pittsburgh (N)									
	(year totals)	8	5	.615	1.64	56	98.2	83	40	51
1972	Pittsburgh (N)	5	2	.714	2.65	36	54.1	54	24	18
1973	Detroit (A)									
1973	San Diego (N)									
1973	New York (N)									
	(year totals)	4	2	.667	3.67	41	73.2	63	34	39
1974	New York (N)	2	2	.500	3.58	58	78	89	39	35
	Seventeen years	69	81	.460	3.37	694	1551.1	1487	608	895
League Championship										
	Two years	0	1	.000	5.79	2	4.2	8	3	3
World Series										
	Three years	0	1	.000	2.00	6	9	9	3	3

FRED MILLER B. June 28, 1886, Fairfield, Ind.
D. May 2, 1953, Brookville, Ind.

YEAR	CLUB	W	L	PCT	ERA	G	IP	H	BB	SO
1910	BROOKLYN (N)	1	1	.500	4.71	6	21	25	13	2

LARRY MILLER B. June 19, 1937, Topeka, Kan.
Left handed, B.L.
6' 195 lbs.

YEAR	CLUB	W	L	PCT	ERA	G	IP	H	BB	SO
1964	LOS ANGELES (N)	4	8	.333	4.18	16	79.2	87	28	50
	Three years (totals)	5	14	.263	4.71	48	145.1	162	57	93

RALPH MILLER   B. March 15, 1873, Cincinnati, Ohio
D. Cincinnati, Ohio
Right handed, B.R.
5'11" 170 lbs.

YEAR	CLUB	W	L	PCT	ERA	G	IP	H	BB	SO
1898	BROOKLYN (N)	4	14	.222	5.34	23	151.2	161	86	43
	Two years (totals)	5	17	.227	5.24	28	185.2	203	99	46

WALT MILLER   B. Oct. 19, 1884, Gas City, Ind.
D. March 1, 1956, Marion, Ind.
Right handed, B.R.
5'11½" 180 lbs.

YEAR	CLUB	W	L	PCT	ERA	G	IP	H	BB	SO
1911	BROOKLYN (N)	0	1	.000	6.55	3	11	16	6	0

BOB MILLIKEN   B. Aug. 25, 1926, Majorsville, W. Va.
Right handed, B.R.
6' 195 lbs.

YEAR	CLUB	W	L	PCT	ERA	G	IP	H	BB	SO
1953	BROOKLYN (N)	8	4	.667	3.37	37	117.2	94	42	65
1954	BROOKLYN (N)	5	2	.714	4.02	24	62.2	58	18	25
	Two years	13	6	.684	3.59	61	180.1	152	60	90
World Series										
	One year	0	0	—	0.00	1	2	2	1	0

PAUL MINNER   B. July 30, 1923, New Wilmington, Pa.
Left handed, B.L.
6'5" 200 lbs.

YEAR	CLUB	W	L	PCT	ERA	G	IP	H	BB	SO
1946	BROOKLYN (N)	0	1	.000	6.75	3	4	6	3	3
1948	BROOKLYN (N)	4	3	.571	2.44	28	62.2	61	26	23
1949	BROOKLYN (N)	3	1	.750	3.80	27	47.1	49	18	17
	Ten years (totals)	69	84	.451	3.94	253	1310.1	1428	393	481
World Series										
	One year	0	0	—	0.00	1	1	1	0	0

CLARENCE MITCHELL   B. Feb. 22, 1891, Franklin, Neb.
D. Nov. 6, 1963, Grand Island, Neb.
Left handed, B.L.
5'11½" 190 lbs.

YEAR	CLUB	W	L	PCT	ERA	G	IP	H	BB	SO
1911	Detroit (A)	1	0	1.000	8.16	5	14.1	20	7	4
1916	Cincinnati (N)	11	10	.524	3.14	29	194.2	211	45	52
1917	Cincinnati (N)	9	15	.375	3.22	32	159.1	166	34	37
1918	BROOKLYN (N)	0	1	.000	108.00	1	1	4	0	0
1919	BROOKLYN (N)	7	5	.583	3.06	23	108.2	123	23	43
1920	BROOKLYN (N)	5	2	.714	3.09	19	78.2	85	23	18
1921	BROOKLYN (N)	11	9	.550	2.89	37	190	206	46	39
1922	BROOKLYN (N)	0	3	.000	14.21	5	12.2	28	7	1
1923	Philadelphia (N)	9	10	.474	4.72	29	139.1	170	46	42
1924	Philadelphia (N)	6	13	.316	5.62	30	165	223	58	36
1925	Philadelphia (N)	10	17	.370	5.28	32	199.1	245	51	46
1926	Philadelphia (N)	9	14	.391	4.58	28	178.2	232	55	52
1927	Philadelphia (N)	6	3	.667	4.09	13	94.2	99	28	17
1928	Philadelphia (N)									
1928	St. Louis (N)									
	(year totals)	8	9	.471	3.53	22	155.2	162	40	31
1929	St. Louis (N)	8	11	.421	4.27	25	173	221	60	39
1930	St. Louis (N)									
1930	New York (N)									
	(year totals)	11	3	.786	4.02	25	132	156	38	41
1931	New York (N)	13	11	.542	4.07	27	190.1	221	52	39
1932	New York (N)	1	3	.250	4.15	8	30.1	41	11	7
	Eighteen years	125	139	.473	4.12	390	2217	2613	624	544
World Series										
	Two years	0	0	—	0.87	2	10.1	5	5	3

FRED MITCHELL B. June 5, 1878, Cambridge, Mass.
D. Oct. 13, 1970, Newton, Mass.
Right handed, B.R.
5'9½" 185 lbs.

YEAR	CLUB	W	L	PCT	ERA	G	IP	H	BB	SO
1904	BROOKLYN (N)	2	5	.286	3.82	8	66		23	16
1905	BROOKLYN (N)	3	7	.300	4.78	12	96	107	38	44
	Five years (totals)	30	48	.385	4.10	97	718	806	303	216

JOE MOELLER B. Feb. 15, 1943, Blue Island, Ill.
Right handed, B.R.
6'5" 192 lbs.

YEAR	CLUB	W	L	PCT	ERA	G	IP	H	BB	SO
1962	LOS ANGELES (N)	6	5	.545	5.25	19	85.2	87	58	46
1964	LOS ANGELES (N)	7	13	.350	4.21	27	145.1	153	31	97
1966	LOS ANGELES (N)	2	4	.333	2.52	29	78.2	73	14	31
1967	LOS ANGELES (N)	0	0	—	9.00	6	5	9	3	2
1968	LOS ANGELES (N)	1	1	.500	5.06	3	16	17	2	11
1969	LOS ANGELES (N)	1	0	1.000	3.35	23	51	54	13	25
1970	LOS ANGELES (N)	7	9	.438	3.93	31	135	131	43	63
1971	LOS ANGELES (N)	2	4	.333	3.82	28	66	72	12	32
	Eight years	26	36	.419	4.02	166	582.2	596	176	307
World Series										
	One year	0	0	—	4.50	1	2	1	1	0

GEORGE MOHART B. March 6, 1892, Buffalo, N.Y.
D. Oct. 2, 1970, Silver Creek, N.Y.
Right handed, B.R.
5'9" 165 lbs.

YEAR	CLUB	W	L	PCT	ERA	G	IP	H	BB	SO
1920	BROOKLYN (N)	0	1	.000	1.77	13	35.2	33	7	13
1921	BROOKLYN (N)	0	0	—	3.86	2	7	8	1	1
	Two years	0	1	.000	2.11	15	42.2	41	8	14

CY MOORE B. Feb. 7, 1905, Elberton, Ga.
D. March 28, 1972, Augusta, Ga.
Right handed, B.R.
6'1" 178 lbs.

YEAR	CLUB	W	L	PCT	ERA	G	IP	H	BB	SO
1929	BROOKLYN (N)	3	3	.500	5.56	32	68	87	31	17
1930	BROOKLYN (N)	0	0	—	0.00	1		2	0	0
1931	BROOKLYN (N)	1	2	.333	3.79	23	61.2	62	13	35
1932	BROOKLYN (N)	0	3	.000	4.81	20	48.2	56	17	23
	Six years (totals)	16	26	.381	4.86	147	466.1	547	168	183

RAY MOORE B. June 1, 1926, Meadows, Md.
Right handed, B.R.
6' 195 lbs.

YEAR	CLUB	W	L	PCT	ERA	G	IP	H	BB	SO
1952	BROOKLYN (N)	1	2	.333	4.76	14	28.1	29	26	11
1953	BROOKLYN (N)	0	1	.000	3.38	1	8	6	4	4
	Eleven years (totals)	63	59	.516	4.06	365	1072.2	935	560	612

JOHNNY MORRISON B. Oct. 22, 1895, Pelleville, Ky.
D. March 20, 1966, Louisville, Ky.
Right handed, B.R.
5'11" 188 lbs.

YEAR	CLUB	W	L	PCT	ERA	G	IP	H	BB	SO
1929	BROOKLYN (N)	13	7	.650	4.48	39	136.2	150	61	57
1930	BROOKLYN (N)	1	2	.333	5.45	16	34.2	47	16	11
	Ten years (totals)	103	80	.563	3.65	297	1535	1574	506	546

RAY MOSS
B. Dec. 5, 1901, Chattanooga, Tenn.
Right handed, B.R.
6'1" 185 lbs.

YEAR	CLUB	W	L	PCT	ERA	G	IP	H	BB	SO
1926	BROOKLYN (N)	0	0	—	9.00	1	1	3	0	0
1927	BROOKLYN (N)	1	0	1.000	3.24	1	8.1	11	1	1
1928	BROOKLYN (N)	0	3	.000	4.92	22	60.1	62	35	5
1929	BROOKLYN (N)	11	6	.647	5.04	39	182	214	81	59
1930	BROOKLYN (N)	9	6	.600	5.10	36	118.1	127	55	30
1931	BROOKLYN (N)	0	0	.000	0.00	1	0	0	0	0
1931	Boston (N)									
	(year totals)	1	3	.250	4.50	13	46	57	17	14
	Six years	22	18	.550	4.95	112	416	474	189	109

EARL MOSSOR
B. July 21, 1925, Forbes, Tenn.
Right handed, B.L.
6'1" 175 lbs.

YEAR	CLUB	W	L	PCT	ERA	G	IP	H	BB	SO
1951	BROOKLYN (N)	0	0	—	32.40	3	1.2	2	7	1

GLEN MOULDER
B. Sept. 28, 1917, Cleveland, Okla.
Right handed, B.R.
6' 180 lbs.

YEAR	CLUB	W	L	PCT	ERA	G	IP	H	BB	SO
1946	BROOKLYN (N)	0	0	—	4.50	1	2	2	1	1
	Three years (totals)	7	8	.467	5.21	66	160.2	188	98	50

VAN MUNGO
B. June 8, 1911, Pageland, S.C.
Right handed, B.R.
6'2" 185 lbs.

YEAR	CLUB	W	L	PCT	ERA	G	IP	H	BB	SO
1931	BROOKLYN (N)	3	1	.750	2.32	5	31	27	13	12
1932	BROOKLYN (N)	13	11	.542	4.43	39	223.1	224	115	107
1933	BROOKLYN (N)	16	15	.516	2.72	41	248	223	84	110
1934	BROOKLYN (N)	18	16	.529	3.37	45	315.1	300	104	184
1935	BROOKLYN (N)	16	10	.615	3.65	37	214.1	205	90	143
1936	BROOKLYN (N)	18	19	.486	3.35	45	311.2	275	118	238
1937	BROOKLYN (N)	9	11	.450	2.91	25	161	136	56	122
1938	BROOKLYN (N)	4	11	.267	3.92	24	133.1	133	72	72
1939	BROOKLYN (N)	4	5	.444	3.26	14	77.1	70	33	34
1940	BROOKLYN (N)	1	0	1.000	2.45	7	22	24	10	9
1941	BROOKLYN (N)	0	0	—	4.50	2	2	1	2	0
1942	New York (N)	1	2	.333	5.94	9	36.1	38	21	27
1943	New York (N)	3	7	.300	3.91	45	154.1	140	79	83
1945	New York (N)	14	7	.667	3.20	26	183	161	71	101
	Fourteen years	120	115	.511	3.47	364	2113	1957	868	1242

LES MUNNS
B. Dec. 1, 1908, Grand Forks, N.D.
Right handed, B.R.
6'5" 212 lbs.

YEAR	CLUB	W	L	PCT	ERA	G	IP	H	BB	SO
1934	BROOKLYN (N)	3	7	.300	4.71	33	99.1	106	60	41
1935	BROOKLYN (N)	1	3	.250	5.55	21	58.1	74	33	13
	Three years (totals)	4	13	.235	4.76	61	181.2	203	105	58

CON MURPHY
B. Oct. 15, 1863, Worcester, Mass.
D. Aug. 1, 1914, Worcester, Mass.
5'9" 130 lbs.

YEAR	CLUB	W	L	PCT	ERA	G	IP	H	BB	SO
1890	BROOKLYN (P)									
1890	BROOKLYN-Balt. (AA)									
	(year totals)	7	19	.269	5.17	32	235	289	128	55
	Two years (totals)	12	28	.300	4.88	49	372.2	467	143	111

JIM MURRAY
B. Dec. 31, 1898, Scranton, Pa.
D. July 15, 1973, New York, N.Y.
Left handed, B.L.
6'2" 210 lbs.

YEAR	CLUB	W	L	PCT	ERA	G	IP	H	BB	SO
1922	BROOKLYN (N)	0	0	—	4.50	4	6	8	3	3

SAM NAHEM
B. Oct. 19, 1915, New York, N.Y.
Right handed, B.R.
6'1½" 190 lbs.

YEAR	CLUB	W	L	PCT	ERA	G	IP	H	BB	SO
1938	BROOKLYN (N)	1	0	1.000	3.00	1	9	6	4	2
	Four years (totals)	10	8	.556	4.69	90	224.1	222	127	101

RON NEGRAY
B. Feb. 26, 1930, Akron, Ohio
Right handed, B.R.
6'1" 185 lbs.

YEAR	CLUB	W	L	PCT	ERA	G	IP	H	BB	SO
1952	BROOKLYN (N)	0	0	—	3.46	4	13	15	5	5
1958	LOS ANGELES (N)	0	0	—	7.15	4	11.1	12	7	2
	Four years (totals)	6	6	.500	4.04	66	162.2	170	57	81

DON NEWCOMBE
B. June 14, 1926, Madison, N.J.
Right handed, B.R.
6'4" 220 lbs.

YEAR	CLUB	W	L	PCT	ERA	G	IP	H	BB	SO
1949	BROOKLYN (N)	17	8	.680	3.17	38	244.1	223	73	149
1950	BROOKLYN (N)	19	11	.633	3.70	40	267.1	258	75	130
1951	BROOKLYN (N)	20	9	.690	3.28	40	272	235	91	164
1954	BROOKLYN (N)	9	8	.529	4.55	29	144.1	158	49	82
1955	BROOKLYN (N)	20	5	.800	3.20	34	233.2	222	38	143
1956	BROOKLYN (N)	27	7	.794	3.06	38	268	219	46	139
1957	BROOKLYN (N)	11	12	.478	3.48	28	198.2	199	33	90
1958	LOS ANGELES (N)	0	6	.000	7.94	11	34		8	16
1958	Cincinnati (N)									
	(year totals)	7	13	.350	4.67	31	167.2	212	36	69
1959	Cincinnati (N)	13	8	.619	3.16	30	222	216	27	100
1960	Cincinnati (N)									
1960	Cleveland (A)									
	(year totals)	6	9	.400	4.48	36	136.2	160	22	63
	Ten years	149	90	.623	3.56	344	2154.2	2102	490	1129

World Series

YEAR	CLUB	W	L	PCT	ERA	G	IP	H	BB	SO
1949	BROOKLYN (N)	0	2	.000	3.09	2	11.2	10	3	11
1955	BROOKLYN (N)	0	1	.000	9.53	1	5.2	8	2	4
1956	BROOKLYN (N)	0	1	.000	21.21	2	4.2	11	3	4
	Three years	0	4	.000	8.59	5	22	29	8	19

BOBO NEWSOM
B. Aug. 11, 1907, Hartsville, S.C.
D. Dec. 7, 1962, Orlando, Fla.
Right handed, B.R.
6'3" 200 lbs.

YEAR	CLUB	W	L	PCT	ERA	G	IP	H	BB	SO
1929	BROOKLYN (N)	0	3	.000	10.61	3	9.1	15	5	6
1930	BROOKLYN (N)	0	0	—	0.00	2	3	2	2	1
1942	BROOKLYN (N)	2	2	.500	3.38	6	32		14	21
1943	BROOKLYN (N)	9	4	.692	3.02	22	125		57	75
	Twenty years (totals)	211	222	.487	3.98	600	3759.1	3771	1732	2082

DOC NEWTON B. Oct. 26, 1877, Indianapolis, Ind.
D. May 14, 1931, Memphis, Tenn.
Left handed, B.L.
6' 185 lbs.

YEAR	CLUB	W	L	PCT	ERA	G	IP	H	BB	SO
1900	Cincinnati (N)	9	15	.375	4.14	35	234.2	255	100	88
1901	Cincinnati (N)									
1901	BROOKLYN (N)	6	5	.545	2.83	13	105		30	45
	(year totals)	10	19	.345	3.62	33	273.1	300	89	100
1902	BROOKLYN (N)	15	14	.517	2.42	31	264.1	208	87	107
1905	New York (A)	3	2	.600	2.11	11	59.2	61	24	15
1906	New York (A)	6	4	.600	3.17	21	125	118	33	52
1907	New York (A)	7	10	.412	3.18	19	133	132	31	70
1908	New York (A)	4	6	.400	2.95	23	88.1	78	41	49
1909	New York (A)	0	3	.000	2.82	4	22.1	27	11	11
	Eight years	54	73	.425	3.22	177	1200.2	1179	416	502

TOM NIEDENFUER B. Aug. 13, 1959, St. Louis Park, Minn.
Right handed, B.R.
6'5" 225 lbs.

YEAR	CLUB	W	L	PCT	ERA	G	IP	H	BB	SO
1981	LOS ANGELES (N)	3	1	.750	3.81	17	26	25	6	12
1982	LOS ANGELES (N)	3	4	.429	2.71	55	69.2	71	25	60
1983	LOS ANGELES (N)	8	3	.729	2.75	66	94.2	55	29	66
	Three years	14	8	.636	3.00	138	190	151	60	138
League Championship										
	One year	0	0	—	0.00	1	.1	2	0	0
World Series										
	One year	0	0	—	0.00	2	5	3	1	0

OTHO NITCHOLAS B. Sept. 13, 1908, McKinney, Texas
Right handed, B.R.
6' 190 lbs.

YEAR	CLUB	W	L	PCT	ERA	G	IP	H	BB	SO
1945	BROOKLYN (N)	1	0	1.000	5.30	7	18.2	19	1	4

JERRY NOPS B. June 23, 1875, Toledo, Ohio
D. March 26, 1937, Camden, N.J.
Left handed

YEAR	CLUB	W	L	PCT	ERA	G	IP	H	BB	SO
1900	BROOKLYN (N)	4	4	.500	3.84	9	68	79	18	22
	Six years (totals)	71	41	.634	3.70	136	988.1	1083	281	294

FRED NORMAN B. Aug. 20, 1942, San Antonio, Texas
Left handed, B.L.
5'8" 155 lbs.

YEAR	CLUB	W	L	PCT	ERA	G	IP	H	BB	SO
1970	LOS ANGELES (N)	2	0			30	62			
	Sixteen years (totals)	104	103	.502	3.64	403	1938.6	1790	815	1303

BOB O'BRIEN B. April 23, 1949, Pittsburgh, Pa.
Left handed, B.L.
5'10" 170 lbs.

YEAR	CLUB	W	L	PCT	ERA	G	IP	H	BB	SO
1971	LOS ANGELES (N)	2	2	.500	3.00	14	42	42	13	15

JOE OESCHGER B. May 24, 1891, Chicago, Ill.
Right handed, B.R.
6' 190 lbs.

YEAR	CLUB	W	L	PCT	ERA	G	IP	H	BB	SO
1925	BROOKLYN (N)	1	2	.333	6.08	21	37	60	19	6
	Twelve years (totals)	83	116	.417	3.81	365	1818	1936	651	535

PHIL ORTEGA B. Oct. 7, 1939, Gilbert, Ariz.
Right handed, B.R.
6'2" 170 lbs.

YEAR	CLUB	W	L	PCT	ERA	G	IP	H	BB	SO
1960	LOS ANGELES (N)	0	0	—	17.05	3	6.1	12	5	4
1961	LOS ANGELES (N)	0	2	.000	5.54	4	13	10	2	15
1962	LOS ANGELES (N)	0	2	.000	6.88	24	53.2	60	39	30
1963	LOS ANGELES (N)	0	0	—	18.00	1	1	2	0	1
1964	LOS ANGELES (N)	7	9	.438	4.00	34	157.1	149	56	107
	Ten years (totals)	46	62	.426	4.43	204	951.2	884	378	549

TINY OSBORNE B. April 9, 1893, Porterdale, Ga.
D. Jan. 5, 1969, Atlanta, Ga.
Right handed, B.L.
6'4½" 215 lbs.

YEAR	CLUB	W	L	PCT	ERA	G	IP	H	BB	SO
1922	Chicago (N)	9	5	.643	4.50	41	184	183	95	81
1923	Chicago (N)	8	15	.348	4.56	37	179.2	174	89	69
1924	Chicago (N)									
1924	BROOKLYN (N)	6	5	.545						
	(year totals)	6	5	.545	5.03	23	107.1	126	56	54
1925	BROOKLYN (N)	8	15	.348	4.94	41	175	210	75	59
	Four years	31	40	.437	4.72	142	646	693	315	263

CHARLIE OSGOOD B. Nov. 23, 1926, Somerville, Mass.
Right handed, B.R.
5'10" 180 lbs.

YEAR	CLUB	W	L	PCT	ERA	G	IP	H	BB	SO
1944	BROOKLYN (N)	0	0	—	3.00	1	3	2	3	0

CLAUDE OSTEEN B. Aug. 9, 1939, Caney Springs, Tenn.
Left handed, B.L.
5'11" 160 lbs.

YEAR	CLUB	W	L	PCT	ERA	G	IP	H	BB	SO
1957	Cincinnati (N)	0	0	—	2.25	3	4	4	3	3
1959	Cincinnati (N)	0	0	—	7.04	2	7.2	11	9	3
1960	Cincinnati (N)	0	1	.000	5.03	20	48.1	53	30	15
1961	Cincinnati (N)									
1961	Washington (A)									
	(year totals)	1	1	.500	4.82	4	18.2	14	9	14
1962	Washington (A)	8	13	.381	3.65	28	150.1	140	47	59
1963	Washington (A)	9	14	.391	3.35	40	212.1	222	60	109
1964	Washington (A)	15	13	.536	3.33	37	257	256	64	133
1965	LOS ANGELES (N)	15	15	.500	2.79	40	287	253	78	162
1966	LOS ANGELES (N)	17	14	.548	2.85	39	240.1	238	65	137
1967	LOS ANGELES (N)	17	17	.500	3.22	39	288.1	298	52	152
1968	LOS ANGELES (N)	12	18	.400	3.08	39	254	267	54	119
1969	LOS ANGELES (N)	20	15	.571	2.66	41	321	293	74	183
1970	LOS ANGELES (N)	16	14	.533	3.82	37	259	280	52	114
1971	LOS ANGELES (N)	14	11	.560	3.51	38	259	262	63	109
1972	LOS ANGELES (N)	20	11	.645	2.64	33	252	232	69	100
1973	LOS ANGELES (N)	16	11	.593	3.31	33	236.2	227	61	86
1974	Houston (N)									
1974	St. Louis (N)									
	(year totals)	9	11	.450	3.80	31	161	184	58	51
1975	Chicago (A)	7	16	.304	4.36	37	204.1	237	92	63
	Eighteen years	196	195	.501	3.30	541	3461	3471	940	1612

World Series

YEAR	CLUB	W	L	PCT	ERA	G	IP	H	BB	SO
1965	LOS ANGELES (N)	1	1	.500	0.64	2	14	9	5	4
1966	LOS ANGELES (N)	0	1	.000	1.29	1	7	3	1	3
	Two years	1	2	.333	0.86	3	21	12	6	7

FRITZ OSTERMUELLER

B. Sept. 15, 1907, Quincy, Ill.
D. Dec. 17, 1957, Quincy, Ill.
Left handed, B.L.
5'11" 175 lbs.

YEAR	CLUB	W	L	PCT	ERA	G	IP	H	BB	SO
1943	BROOKLYN (N)	1	1	.500	3.33	7	27		12	15
1944	BROOKLYN (N)	2	1	.667	3.21	10	42		12	17
	Fifteen years (totals)	114	115	.498	3.99	390	2067	2170	835	774

PHIL PAGE

B. Aug. 23, 1905, Springfield, Mass.
D. June 26, 1958, Springfield, Mass.
Left handed, B.R.
6'2" 175 lbs.

YEAR	CLUB	W	L	PCT	ERA	G	IP	H	BB	SO
1934	BROOKLYN (N)	1	0	1.000	5.40	6	10	13	6	4
	Four years (totals)	3	3	.500	6.23	31	69.1	86	44	15

ERV PALICA

B. Feb. 9, 1928, Lomita, Calif.
Right handed, B.R.
6'1½" 180 lbs.

YEAR	CLUB	W	L	PCT	ERA	G	IP	H	BB	SO
1947	BROOKLYN (N)	0	1	.000	3.00	3	3	2	2	1
1948	BROOKLYN (N)	6	6	.500	4.45	41	125.1	111	58	74
1949	BROOKLYN (N)	8	9	.471	3.62	49	97	93	49	44
1950	BROOKLYN (N)	13	8	.619	3.58	43	201.1	176	98	131
1951	BROOKLYN (N)	2	6	.250	4.75	19	53	55	20	15
1953	BROOKLYN (N)	0	0	—	12.00	4	6	10	8	3
1954	BROOKLYN (N)	3	3	.500	5.32	25	67.2	77	31	25
1955	Baltimore (A)	5	11	.313	4.14	33	169.2	165	83	68
1956	Baltimore (A)	4	11	.267	4.49	29	116.1	117	50	62
	Nine years	41	55	.427	4.22	246	839.1	806	399	423
World Series										
	One year	0	0	—	0.00	1	2	1	1	1

ED PALMQUIST

B. June 10, 1933, Los Angeles, Calif.
Right handed, B.R.
6'3" 195 lbs.

YEAR	CLUB	W	L	PCT	ERA	G	IP	H	BB	SO
1960	LOS ANGELES (N)	0	1	.000	2.54	22	39	34	16	23
1961	LOS ANGELES (N)	0	1	—	6.00	5	9		7	5
	Two years (totals)	1	3	.250	5.11	36	68.2	77	36	41

CAMILO PASCUAL

B. Jan. 20, 1934, Havana, Cuba
Right handed, B.R.
5'11" 165 lbs.

YEAR	CLUB	W	L	PCT	ERA	G	IP	H	BB	SO
1970	LOS ANGELES (N)	0	0	—	2.57	10	14	12	5	8
	Eighteen years (totals)	174	170	.506	3.63	529	2930	2703	1069	2167

JIM PASTORIUS

B. July 12, 1881, Pittsburgh, Pa.
D. May 10, 1941, Pittsburgh, Pa.
Left handed, B.L.

YEAR	CLUB	W	L	PCT	ERA	G	IP	H	BB	SO
1906	BROOKLYN (N)	9	14	.391	3.61	29	211.2	225	69	58
1907	BROOKLYN (N)	16	12	.571	2.35	28	222	218	77	70
1908	BROOKLYN (N)	4	20	.167	2.44	28	213.2	171	74	54
1909	BROOKLYN (N)	1	9	.100	5.76	12	79.2	91	58	23
	Four years	30	55	.353	3.12	97	727	705	278	205

DAVE PATTERSON
B. July 25, 1956, Springfield, Mo.
Right handed, B.R.
6' 170 lbs.

YEAR	CLUB	W	L	PCT	ERA	G	IP	H	BB	SO
1979	LOS ANGELES (N)	4	1	.800	5.26	36	53	62	22	34

JIMMY PATTISON
B. Dec. 18, 1908, Brooklyn, N.Y.
Left handed, B.L.
6' 185 lbs.

YEAR	CLUB	W	L	PCT	ERA	G	IP	H	BB	SO
1929	BROOKLYN (N)	0	1	.000	4.63	6	11.2	9	4	5

HARLEY PAYNE
B. Jan. 9, 1866, Windsor, Ontario, Canada
D. Dec. 29, 1935, Orwell, Ohio
Left handed

YEAR	CLUB	W	L	PCT	ERA	G	IP	H	BB	SO
1896	BROOKLYN (N)	14	16	.467	3.39	34	241.2	284	58	52
1897	BROOKLYN (N)	14	17	.452	4.63	40	280	350	71	86
1898	BROOKLYN (N)	1	0	1.000	4.00	1	9	11	3	2
1899	Pittsburgh (N)	1	3	.250	3.76	5	26.1	33	4	8
	Four years	30	36	.455	4.04	80	557	678	136	148

ALEJANDRO PENA
B. June 25, 1959, Cambiaso Puerto Plata, Dominican Republic
Right handed, B.R.
6'3" 200 lbs.

YEAR	CLUB	W	L	PCT	ERA	G	IP	H	BB	SO
1981	LOS ANGELES (N)	1	1	.500	2.88	14	25	18	11	14
1982	LOS ANGELES (N)	0	2	—	4.79	29	35.2	37	21	20
	Two years	1	3	.250	4.01	43	60.2	55	32	34
League Championship										
	One year	0	0	—	0.00	2	2.1	1	0	0

JOSE PENA
B. Dec. 3, 1942, Ciudad Juyarez, Mexico
Right handed, B.R.
6'2" 190 lbs.

YEAR	CLUB	W	L	PCT	ERA	G	IP	H	BB	SO
1970	LOS ANGELES (N)	4	3	.571	4.42	29	57	51	29	31
1971	LOS ANGELES (N)	2	0	1.000	3.56	21	43	32	18	44
1972	LOS ANGELES (N)	0	0		8.59	5	7.1	13	6	4
	Four years (totals)	7	4	.636	4.97	61	112.1	106	58	82

CHARLIE PERKINS
B. Sept. 9, 1905, Birmingham, Ala.
Left handed, B.R.
6' 175 lbs.

YEAR	CLUB	W	L	PCT	ERA	G	IP	H	BB	SO
1934	BROOKLYN (N)	0	3	.000	8.51	11	24.1	37	14	5
	Two years (totals)	0	3	.000	7.50	19	48	62	29	20

RON PERRANOSKI
B. April 1, 1936, Paterson, N.J.
Left handed, B.L.
6' 180 lbs.

YEAR	CLUB	W	L	PCT	ERA	G	IP	H	BB	SO
1961	LOS ANGELES (N)	7	5	.583	2.65	53	91.2	82	41	56
1962	LOS ANGELES (N)	6	6	.500	2.85	70	107.1	103	36	68
1963	LOS ANGELES (N)	16	3	.842	1.67	69	129	112	43	75
1964	LOS ANGELES (N)	5	7	.417	3.09	72	125.1	128	46	79
1965	LOS ANGELES (N)	6	6	.500	2.24	59	104.2	85	40	53
1966	LOS ANGELES (N)	6	7	.462	3.18	55	82	82	31	50
1967	LOS ANGELES (N)	6	7	.462	2.45	70	110	97	45	75
1968	Minnesota (A)	8	7	.533	3.10	66	87	86	38	65
1969	Minnesota (A)	9	10	.474	2.11	75	119.2	85	52	62

218 • The Complete Dodgers Record Book

YEAR	CLUB	W	L	PCT	ERA	G	IP	H	BB	SO
1970	Minnesota (A)	7	8	.467	2.43	67	111	108	42	55
1971	Minnesota (A)									
1971	Detroit (A)									
	(year totals)	1	5	.167	5.49	47	60.2	76	31	29
1972	Detroit (A)									
1972	LOS ANGELES (N)	2	0	1.000	2.65	9	9		8	5
	(year totals)	2	1	.667	5.30	26	35.2	42	16	15
1973	California (A)	0	2	.000	4.09	8	11	11	7	5
	Thirteen years	79	74	.516	2.79	737	1175	1097	468	687
League Championship										
	Two years	0	1	.000	10.29	5	7	13	1	5

World Series

YEAR	CLUB	W	L	PCT	ERA	G	IP	H	BB	SO
1963	LOS ANGELES (N)	0	0	—	0.00	1	.2	1	0	0
1965	LOS ANGELES (N)	0	0	—	7.36	2	3.2	3	1	4
1966	LOS ANGELES (N)	0	0	—	5.40	2	3.1	4	2	1
	Three years	0	0	—	5.87	5	7.2	8	5	4

RUBE PETERS   B. March 15, 1886, Grand Fork, Ill.
Right handed, B.R.
6' 185 lbs.

YEAR	CLUB	W	L	PCT	ERA	G	IP	H	BB	SO
1914	BROOKLYN (F)	2	2	.500	3.82	11	37.2	52	16	13
	Two years (totals)	7	8	.467	4.06	39	146.1	186	49	52

JIM PETERSON   B. Aug. 18, 1908, Philadelphia, Pa.
D. April 8, 1975, Palm Beach, Fla.
Right handed, B.R.
6'½" 200 lbs.

YEAR	CLUB	W	L	PCT	ERA	G	IP	H	BB	SO
1937	BROOKLYN (N)	0	0	—	7.94	3	5.2	8	2	4
	Three years (totals)	2	6	.250	5.27	41	109.1	140	42	29

JESSE PETTY   B. Nov. 23, 1894, Orr, Okla.
D. Oct. 23, 1971, St. Paul, Minn.
Left handed, B.R.
6' 195 lbs.

YEAR	CLUB	W	L	PCT	ERA	G	IP	H	BB	SO
1921	Cleveland (A)	0	0		2.00	4	9	10	0	0
1925	BROOKLYN (N)	9	9	.500	4.88	28	153	188	47	39
1926	BROOKLYN (N)	17	17	.500	2.84	38	275.2	246	79	101
1927	BROOKLYN (N)	13	18	.419	2.98	42	271.2	263	53	101
1928	BROOKLYN (N)	15	15	.500	4.04	40	234	264	56	74
1929	Pittsburgh (N)	11	10	.524	3.71	36	184.1	197	42	58
1930	Pittsburgh (N)									
1930	Chicago (N)									
	(year totals)	2	9	.182	5.69	19	80.2	118	19	34
	Seven years	67	78	.462	3.68	207	1208.1	1286	296	407

JEFF PFEFFER   B. March 4, 1888, Seymour, Ill.
D. Aug. 15, 1972, Chicago, Ill.
Right handed, B.R.
6'3" 210 lbs.

YEAR	CLUB	W	L	PCT	ERA	G	IP	H	BB	SO
1911	St. Louis (A)	0	0	—	7.20	2	10	11	4	4
1913	BROOKLYN (N)	0	1	.000	3.33	5	24.1	28	13	13
1914	BROOKLYN (N)	23	12	.657	1.97	43	315	264	91	135
1915	BROOKLYN (N)	19	14	.576	2.10	40	291.2	243	76	84
1916	BROOKLYN (N)	25	11	.694	1.92	41	328.2	274	63	128
1917	BROOKLYN (N)	11	15	.423	2.23	30	266	225	66	115
1918	BROOKLYN (N)	1	0	1.000	0.00	1	9	2	3	1
1919	BROOKLYN (N)	17	13	.567	2.66	30	267	270	49	92
1920	BROOKLYN (N)	16	9	.640	3.01	30	215	225	45	80
1921	BROOKLYN (N)	1	5	.167	4.50	6	32		9	8

YEAR	CLUB	W	L	PCT	ERA	G	IP	H	BB	SO
1921	St. Louis (N)									
	(year totals)	10	8	.556	4.35	24	130.1	151	37	30
1922	St. Louis (N)	19	12	.613	3.58	44	261.1	286	58	83
1923	St. Louis (N.)	8	9	.471	4.02	26	152.1	171	40	32
1924	St. Louis (N)									
1924	Pittsburgh (N)									
	(year totals)	9	8	.529	4.35	31	136.2	170	47	39
	Thirteen years	158	112	.585	2.77	347	2407.1	2320	592	836

World Series

YEAR	CLUB	W	L	PCT	ERA	G	IP	H	BB	SO
1916	BROOKLYN (N)	0	1	.000	1.69	3	10.2	7	5	4
1920	BROOKLYN (N)	0	0	—	3.00	1	3	4	1	2
	Two years	0	1	.000	2.63	4	13.2	11	6	6

LEE PFUND B. Oct. 10, 1919, Oak Park, Ill.
Right handed, B.R.
6'1" 185 lbs.

YEAR	CLUB	W	L	PCT	ERA	G	IP	H	BB	SO
1945	BROOKLYN (N)	3	2	.600	5.20	15	62.1	69	35	27

RAY PHELPS B. Dec. 11, 1903, Dunlap, Tenn.
D. July 7, 1971, Fort Pierce, Fla.
Right handed, B.R.
6'2" 200 lbs.

YEAR	CLUB	W	L	PCT	ERA	G	IP	H	BB	SO
1930	BROOKLYN (N)	14	7	.667	4.11	36	179.2	198	52	64
1931	BROOKLYN (N)	7	9	.438	5.00	28	149.1	184	44	50
1932	BROOKLYN (N)	4	5	.444	5.90	20	79.1	101	27	21
1935	Chicago (A)	4	8	.333	4.82	27	125	126	55	38
1936	Chicago (A)	4	6	.400	6.03	15	68.2	91	42	17
	Five years	33	35	.485	4.93	126	602	700	220	190

ED PIPGRAS B. June 15, 1904, Schleswig, Iowa
D. April 13, 1964, Currie, Minn.
Right handed, B.R.
6'2½" 175 lbs.

YEAR	CLUB	W	L	PCT	ERA	G	IP	H	BB	SO
1932	BROOKLYN (N)	0	1	.000	5.40	5	10	16	6	5

NORMAN PLITT B. Feb. 21, 1893, York, Pa.
D. Feb. 1, 1954, New York, N.Y.
Right handed, B.R.
5'11" 170 lbs.

YEAR	CLUB	W	L	PCT	ERA	G	IP	H	BB	SO
1918	BROOKLYN (N)	0	0	—	4.50	1	2	3	1	0
1927	BROOKLYN (N)	2	6	.250	4.93	19	62		36	9
	Two years (totals)	3	6	.333	4.77	23	71.2	85	38	9

BUD PODBIELAN B. March 6, 1924, Curlew, Wash.
Right handed, B.R.
6'1½" 170 lbs.

YEAR	CLUB	W	L	PCT	ERA	G	IP	H	BB	SO
1949	BROOKLY(N)	0	1	.000	3.65	7	12.1	9	9	5
1950	BROOKLYN (N)	5	4	.556	5.33	20	72.2	93	29	28
1951	BROOKLYN (N)	2	2	.500	3.50	27	79.2	67	36	26
1952	BROOKLYN (N)	0	0	.000		3	2		3	1
	Nine years (totals)	25	42	.373	4.49	172	641	693	245	242

JOHNNY PODRES
B. Sept. 30, 1932, Witherbee, N.Y.
Left handed, B.L.
5'11" 170 lbs.

YEAR	CLUB	W	L	PCT	ERA	G	IP	H	BB	SO
1953	BROOKLYN (N)	9	4	.692	4.23	33	115	126	64	82
1954	BROOKLYN (N)	11	7	.611	4.27	29	151.2	147	53	79
1955	BROOKLYN (N)	9	10	.474	3.95	27	159.1	160	57	114
1957	BROOKLYN (N)	12	9	.571	2.66	31	196	168	44	109
1958	LOS ANGELES (N)	13	15	.464	3.72	39	210.1	208	78	143
1959	LOS ANGELES (N)	14	9	.609	4.11	34	195	192	74	145
1960	LOS ANGELES (N)	14	12	.538	3.08	34	227.2	217	71	159
1961	LOS ANGELES (N)	18	5	.783	3.74	32	182.2	192	51	124
1962	LOS ANGELES (N)	15	13	.536	3.81	40	255	270	71	178
1963	LOS ANGELES (N)	14	12	538	3.54	37	198.1	196	64	134
1964	LOS ANGELES (N)	0	2	.000	16.88	2	2.2	5	3	0
1965	LOS ANGELES (N)	7	6	.538	3.43	27	134	126	39	63
1966	LOS ANGELES (N)	0	0	.000	0.00	1	2		1	1
1966	Detroit (A)									
	(year totals)	4	5	.444	3.38	37	109.1	108	35	54
1967	Detroit (A)	3	1	.750	3.84	21	63.1	58	11	34
1969	San Diego (N)	5	6	.455	4.29	17	65	66	28	17
	Fifteen years	148	116	.561	3.67	440	2265.1	2239	743	1435

World Series

YEAR	CLUB	W	L	PCT	ERA	G	IP	H	BB	SO
1953	BROOKLYN (N)	0	1	.000	3.38	1	2.2	1	1	0
1955	BROOKLYN (N)	2	0	1.000	1.00	2	18	15	4	10
1959	LOS ANGELES (N)	1	0	1.000	4.82	2	9.1	7	6	4
1963	LOS ANGELES (N)	1	0	1.000	1.08	1	8.2	6	2	4
	Four years	4	1	.800	2.11	6	38.1	29	13	18

BOOTS POFFENBERGER
B. July 1, 1915, Williamsport, Md.
Right handed, B.R.
5'10" 178 lbs.

YEAR	CLUB	W	L	PCT	ERA	G	IP	H	BB	SO
1939	BROOKLYN (N)	0	0	—	5.40	3	5	7	4	2
	Three years (totals)	16	12	.571	4.75	57	267.1	301	149	65

ED POOLE
B. Sept. 7, 1877, Wheeling, W. Va.
D. March 23, 1920, Carrollton, Ohio
Right handed, B.R.
5'10" 175 lbs.

YEAR	CLUB	W	L	PCT	ERA	G	IP	H	BB	SO
1904	BROOKLYN (N)	8	13	.381	3.39	25	178	178	74	67
	Five years (totals)	34	34	.500	3.04	80	595	584	238	226

BILL POSEDEL
B. Aug. 2, 1906, San Francisco, Calif.
Right handed, B.R.
5'11" 175 lbs.

YEAR	CLUB	W	L	PCT	ERA	G	IP	H	BB	SO
1938	BROOKLYN (N)	8	9	.471	5.66	33	140	178	46	49
	Five years (totals)	41	43	.488	4.56	138	679.1	757	248	227

DYKES POTTER
B. Sept. 7, 1910, Ashland, Ky.
Right handed, B.R.
6' 185 lbs.

YEAR	CLUB	W	L	PCT	ERA	G	IP	H	BB	SO
1938	BROOKLYN (N)	0	0	—	4.50	2	2	4	0	1

BILL POUNDS   B. Paterson, N.J.

YEAR	CLUB	W	L	PCT	ERA	G	IP	H	BB	SO
1903	BROOKLYN (N)									
	(year totals)	0	0	—	8.18	2	11	16	2	4

TED POWER   B. Jan. 31, 1955, Guthrie, Okla.
Right handed, B.R.
6'4" 220 lbs.

YEAR	CLUB	W	L	PCT	ERA	G	IP	H	BB	SO
1981	LOS ANGELES (N)	1	3	.250	3.21	5	14	16	7	7
1982	LOS ANGELES (N)	1	1	.500	6.68	12	33.2	38	23	15
	Two years	2	4	.333	5.66	17	47.2	54	30	22

TOT PRESNELL   B. Aug. 8, 1906, Findlay, Ohio
Right handed, B.R.
5'10½" 175 lbs.

YEAR	CLUB	W	L	PCT	ERA	G	IP	H	BB	SO
1938	BROOKLYN (N)	11	14	.440	3.56	43	192	209	56	57
1939	BROOKLYN (N)	9	7	.563	4.02	31	156.2	171	33	43
1940	BROOKLYN (N)	6	5	.545	3.69	24	68.1	58	17	21
1941	Chicago (N)	5	3	.625	3.09	29	70	69	23	27
1942	Chicago (N)	1	1	.500	5.49	27	39.1	40	5	9
	Five years	32	30	.516	3.80	154	526.1	547	134	157

JOHN PURDIN   B. July 16, 1942, Lynx, Ohio
Right handed, B.R.

YEAR	CLUB	W	L	PCT	ERA	G	IP	H	BB	SO
1964	LOS ANGELES (N)	2	0	1.000	0.56	3	16	6	6	8
1965	LOS ANGELES (N)	2	1	.667	6.75	11	22.2	26	13	16
1968	LOS ANGELES (N)	2	3	.400	3.07	35	55.2	42	21	38
1969	LOS ANGELES (N)	0	0	—	6.19	9	16	19	12	6
	Four years	6	4	.600	3.92	58	110.1	93	52	68

JACK QUINN   B. July 5, 1884, Jeanesville, Pa.
D. April 17, 1946, Pottsville, Pa.
Right handed, B.R.
6' 196 lbs.

YEAR	CLUB	W	L	PCT	ERA	G	IP	H	BB	SO
1931	BROOKLYN (N)	5	4	.556	2.66	39	64.1	65	24	25
1932	BROOKLYN (N)	3	7	.300	3.30	42	87.1	102	24	28
	Twenty-three years (totals)	247	216	.533	3.27	755	3934.2	4234	859	1329

STEVE RACHUNOK   B. Dec. 5, 1916, Rittman, Ohio
Right handed, B.R.
6'4½" 205 lbs.

YEAR	CLUB	W	L	PCT	ERA	G	IP	H	BB	SO
1940	BROOKLYN (N)	0	1	.000	4.50	2	10	9	5	10

PAT RAGAN   B. Nov. 15, 1888, Blanchard, Iowa
D. Sept. 4, 1956, Los Angeles, Calif.
Right handed, B.R.
5'10½" 185 lbs.

YEAR	CLUB	W	L	PCT	ERA	G	IP	H	BB	SO
1909	Cincinnati (N)									
1909	Chicago (N)									
	(year totals)	0	1	.000	3.09	4	11.2	11	5	4
1911	BROOKLYN (N)	4	3	.571	2.11	22	93.2	81	31	39
1912	BROOKLYN (N)	6	18	.250	3.63	36	208	211	65	101
1913	BROOKLYN (N)	15	18	.455	3.77	44	264.2	284	64	109
1914	BROOKLYN (N)	10	15	.400	2.98	38	208.1	214	85	106
1915	BROOKLYN (N)	1	0	1.000	0.90	5	20		8	7

YEAR	CLUB	W	L	PCT	ERA	G	IP	H	BB	SO
1915	Boston (N)									
	(year totals)	15	12	.556	2.34	38	246.2	219	67	88
1916	Boston (N)	9	9	.500	2.08	28	182	143	47	94
1917	Boston (N)	7	9	.438	2.93	30	147.2	138	35	61
1918	Boston (N)	8	17	.320	3.23	30	206.1	212	54	68
1919	Boston (N)									
1919	New York (N)									
1919	Chicago (A)									
	(year totals)	1	2	.333	3.44	12	36.2	36	17	10
1923	Philadelphia (N)	0	0	—	6.00	1	3	6	0	0
	Eleven years	75	104	.419	2.99	283	1608.2	1555	470	680

ED RAKOW B. May 30, 1936, Pittsburgh, Pa.
Right handed, B.B.
5'11" 178 lbs.

YEAR	CLUB	W	L	PCT	ERA	G	IP	H	BB	SO
1960	LOS ANGELES (N)	0	1	.000	7.36	9	22	30	11	9
	Seven years (totals)	36	47	.434	4.33	195	761.1	771	304	484

WILLIE RAMSDELL B. April 4, 1918, Williamsburg, Kan.
D. Oct. 8, 1969, Wichita, Kan.
Right handed, B.R.
5'11" 165 lbs.

YEAR	CLUB	W	L	PCT	ERA	G	IP	H	BB	SO
1947	BROOKLYN (N)	1	1	.500	6.72	2	2.2	4	3	3
1948	BROOKLYN (N)	4	4	.500	5.19	27	50.1	48	41	34
1950	BROOKLYN (N)	1	2	.333	3.00	5	6		2	2
	Five years (totals)	24	39	.381	3.83	111	479.2	455	215	240

DOUG RAU B. Dec. 15, 1948, Columbus, Texas
Left handed, B.L.
6'2" 175 lbs.

YEAR	CLUB	W	L	PCT	ERA	G	IP	H	BB	SO
1972	LOS ANGELES (N)	2	2	.500	2.20	7	32.2	18	11	19
1973	LOS ANGELES (N)	4	2	.667	3.96	31	63.2	64	28	51
1974	LOS ANGELES (N)	13	11	.542	3.73	36	198	191	70	126
1975	LOS ANGELES (N)	15	9	.625	3.10	38	258	227	61	151
1976	LOS ANGELES (N)	16	12	.571	2.57	34	231	221	69	98
1977	LOS ANGELES (N)	14	8	.636	3.44	32	212	232	49	126
1978	LOS ANGELES (N)	15	9	.625	3.26	30	199	219	68	95
1979	LOS ANGELES (N)	1	5	.167	5.30	11	56	73	22	28
1981	California (A)	1	2	.333	9.00	3	10	14	4	3
	Nine years	81	60	.574	3.35	222	1260.1	1259	382	697
League Championship										
	Three years	0	1	.000	6.75	3	6.2	8	3	2

World Series

YEAR	CLUB	W	L	PCT	ERA	G	IP	H	BB	SO
1977	LOS ANGELES (N)	0	1	.000	15.88	2	1.2		0	1
1978	LOS ANGELES (N)	0	0	—	0.00	1	2		0	3
	Two years	0	1	.000	6.23	3	4.1	5	0	4

LANCE RAUTZHAN B. Aug. 20, 1952, Pottsville, Pa.
Left handed, B.R.
6'1" 195 lbs.

YEAR	CLUB	W	L	PCT	ERA	G	IP	H	BB	SO
1977	LOS ANGELES (N)	4	1	.800	4.29	25	21	25	7	13
1978	LOS ANGELES (N)	2	1	.667	2.95	43	61	61	19	25
1979	LOS ANGELES (N)	0	2	.000	7.20	12	10		11	5
	Three years	6	4	.600	3.88	83	95	98	47	45
League Championship										
	Two years	1	0	1.000	5.40	2	1.2	3	2	0

World Series

YEAR	CLUB	W	L	PCT	ERA	G	IP	H	BB	SO
1977	LOS ANGELES (N)	0	0	—	0.00	1	0.1	0	2	0
1978	LOS ANGELES (N)	0	0	—	13.50	2	2	4	0	0
	Two years	0	0	—	11.57	3	2.1	4	2	0

HOWIE REED B. Dec. 21, 1936, Dallas, Texas
Right handed, B.R.
6'1" 195 lbs.

YEAR	CLUB	W	L	PCT	ERA	G	IP	H	BB	SO
1964	LOS ANGELES (N)	3	4	.429	3.20	26	90	79	36	52
1965	LOS ANGELES (N)	7	5	.583	3.12	38	78	73	27	47
1966	LOS ANGELES (N)	0	0	—	0.00	1	2		0	0
	Ten years (totals)	26	29	.473	3.72	229	515.2	510	208	268

World Series

	One year	0	0	—	8.10	2	3.1	2	2	4

PHIL REGAN B. April 6, 1937, Otsego, Mich.
Right handed, B.R.
6'3" 200 lbs.

YEAR	CLUB	W	L	PCT	ERA	G	IP	H	BB	SO
1960	Detroit (A)	0	4	.000	4.50	17	68	70	25	38
1961	Detroit (A)	10	7	.588	5.25	32	120	134	41	46
1962	Detroit (A)	11	9	.550	4.04	35	171.1	169	64	87
1963	Detroit (A)	15	9	.625	3.86	38	189	179	59	115
1964	Detroit (A)	5	10	.333	5.03	32	146.2	162	49	91
1965	Detroit (A)	1	5	.167	5.05	16	51.2	57	20	37
1966	LOS ANGELES (N)	14	1	.933	1.62	65	116.2	85	24	88
1967	LOS ANGELES (N)	6	9	.400	2.99	55	96.1	108	32	53
1968	LOS ANGELES (N)	2	0	1.000	3.38	5	8		1	7
1968	Chicago (N)									
	(year totals)	12	5	.706	2.27	73	134.2	119	25	67
1969	Chicago (N)	12	6	.667	3.70	71	112	120	35	56
1970	Chicago (N)	5	9	.357	4.74	54	76	81	32	31
1971	Chicago (N)	5	5	.500	3.95	48	73	84	33	28
1972	Chicago (N)									
1972	Chicago (A)									
	(year totals)	0	2	.000	3.63	15	17.1	24	8	6
	Thirteen years	96	81	.542	3.84	551	1372.2	1392	447	743

World Series

	One year	0	0	—	0.00	2	1.2	0	1	2

BILL REIDY B. Oct. 9, 1873, Cleveland, Ohio
D. Oct. 14, 1915, Cleveland, Ohio
Right handed

YEAR	CLUB	W	L	PCT	ERA	G	IP	H	BB	SO
1899	BROOKLYN (N)	1	0	1.000	2.57	2	7	9	2	2
1903	BROOKLYN (N)	7	6	.538		15				
1904	BROOKLYN (N)	0	4	.000	4.46	6	38.1	49	6	11
	Six years (totals)	28	39	.418	4.17	79	601.2	740	106	109

BOBBY REIS B. Jan. 2, 1909, Woodside, N.Y.
D. May 1, 1973, St. Paul, Minn.
Right handed, B.R.
6'1" 175 lbs.

YEAR	CLUB	W	L	PCT	ERA	G	IP	H	BB	SO
1935	BROOKLYN (N)	3	2	.600	2.83	14	41.1	46	24	7
	Four years (totals)	10	13	.435	4.27	69	242.2	262	144	52

DOC REISLING B. July 25, 1874, Martins Ferry, Ohio
D. March 4, 1955, Tulsa, Okla.
Right handed, B.R.

YEAR	CLUB	W	L	PCT	ERA	G	IP	H	BB	SO
1904	BROOKLYN (N)	3	4	.429	2.12	7	51	45	10	19
1905	BROOKLYN (N)	0	1	.000	3.00	2	3	3	4	2
	Four years (totals)	15	19	.441	2.45	49	311.2	303	75	100

ED REULBACH B. Dec. 1, 1882, Detroit, Mich.
D. July 17, 1961, Glens Falls, N.Y.
Right handed, B.R.
6'1" 190 lbs.

YEAR	CLUB	W	L	PCT	ERA	G	IP	H	BB	SO
1905	Chicago (N)	18	13	.581	1.42	34	292	208	73	152
1906	Chicago (N)	20	4	.833	1.65	33	218	129	92	94
1907	Chicago (N)	17	4	.810	1.69	27	192	147	64	96
1908	Chicago (N)	24	7	.774	2.03	46	297.2	227	106	133
1909	Chicago (N)	19	9	.679	1.78	35	262.2	194	82	105
1910	Chicago (N)	14	8	.636	3.12	24	173.1	161	49	55
1911	Chicago (N)	16	9	.640	2.96	33	221.2	191	103	79
1912	Chicago (N)	11	6	.647	3.78	39	169	161	60	75
1913	Chicago (N)									
1913	BROOKLYN (N)	7	6	.538	2.05	15	110		34	46
	(year totals)	8	9	.471	2.66	25	148.2	118	55	56
1914	BROOKLYN (N)	11	18	.379	2.64	44	256	228	83	119
1915	Newark (F)	20	10	.667	2.23	33	270	233	69	117
1916	Boston (N)	7	6	.538	2.47	21	109.1	99	41	47
1917	Boston (N)	0	1	.000	2.82	5	22.1	21	15	9
	Thirteen years	185	104	.640	2.28	399	2632.2	2117	892	1137
World Series										
	Four years	2	0	1.000	3.03	7	32.2	24	14	13

JERRY REUSS B. June 19, 1949, St. Louis, Mo.
Left handed, B.L.
6'5" 200 lbs.

YEAR	CLUB	W	L	PCT	ERA	G	IP	H	BB	SO
1969	St. Louis (N)	1	0	1.000	0.00	1	7	2	3	3
1970	St. Louis (N)	7	8	.467	4.11	20	127	132	49	74
1971	St. Louis (N)	14	14	.500	4.78	36	211	228	109	131
1972	Houston (N)	9	13	.409	4.17	33	192	177	83	174
1973	Houston (N)	16	13	.552	3.74	41	279.1	271	117	177
1974	Pittsburgh (N)	16	11	.593	3.50	35	260	259	101	105
1975	Pittsburgh (N)	18	11	.621	2.54	32	237	224	78	131
1976	Pittsburgh (N)	14	9	.609	3.53	31	209.1	209	51	108
1977	Pittsburgh (N)	10	13	.435	4.11	33	208	225	71	116
1978	Pittsburgh (N)	3	2	.600	4.88	23	83	97	23	42
1979	LOS ANGELES (N)	7	14	.333	3.54	39	160	178	60	83
1980	LOS ANGELES (N)	18	6	.750	2.52	37	229	193	40	111
1981	LOS ANGELES (N)	10	4	.714	2.29	22	153	138	27	51
1982	LOS ANGELES (N)	18	11	.621	3.11	39	254.2	232	50	138
1983	LOS ANGELES (N)	12	11	.522	2.94	32	223.1	233	50	143
	Fifteen years	173	140	.550	3.47	454	2833.1	2798	912	1587
Divisional Playoff										
	One year	1	0	1.000	0.00	2	18	10	5	7
League Championship										
	Three years	0	4	.000	5.59	4	19.1	18	13	6
World Series										
	One year	1	1	.500	3.86	2	11.2	10	3	8

RICK RHODEN B. May 16, 1953, Boynton Beach, Fla.
Right handed, B.R.
6'3" 195 lbs.

YEAR	CLUB	W	L	PCT	ERA	G	IP	H	BB	SO
1974	LOS ANGELES (N)	1	0	1.000	2.00	4	9	5	4	7
1975	LOS ANGELES (N)	3	3	.500	3.09	26	99	94	32	40
1976	LOS ANGELES (N)	12	3	.800	2.98	27	181	165	53	77
1977	LOS ANGELES (N)	16	10	.615	3.75	31	216	223	63	122
1978	LOS ANGELES (N)	10	8	.556	3.65	30	165	160	51	79
1979	Pittsburgh (N)	0	1	.000	7.20	1	5	5	2	2

YEAR	CLUB	W	L	PCT	ERA	G	IP	H	BB	SO
1980	Pittsburgh (N)	7	5	.583	3.83	20	127	133	40	70
1981	Pittsburgh (N)	9	4	.692	3.90	21	136	147	53	76
1982	Pittsburgh (N)	11	14	.440	4.14	35	230.1	239	70	128
1983	Pittsburgh (N)	13	13	.500	4.04	36	244.1	256	68	153
	Ten years	82	61	.590	3.69	231	1412	1427	436	754
League Championship										
	Two years	0	0	—	1.08	2	8.1	4	3	3
World Series										
	One year	0	1	.000	2.57	2	7	4	1	5

PETE RICHERT B. Oct. 29, 1939, Floral Park, N.Y.
Left handed, B.L.
5'11" 165 lbs.

YEAR	CLUB	W	L	PCT	ERA	G	IP	H	BB	SO
1962	LOS ANGELES (N)	5	4	.556	3.87	19	81.1	77	45	75
1963	LOS ANGELES (N)	5	3	.625	4.50	20	78	80	28	54
1964	LOS ANGELES (N)	2	3	.400	4.15	8	34.2	38	18	25
1965	Washington (A)	15	12	.556	2.60	34	194	146	84	161
1966	Washington (A)	14	14	.500	3.37	36	245.2	196	69	195
1967	Washington (A)									
1967	Baltimore (A)									
	(year totals)	9	16	.360	3.47	37	186.2	156	56	131
1968	Baltimore (A)	6	3	.667	3.47	36	62.1	51	12	47
1969	Baltimore (A)	7	4	.636	2.20	44	57.1	42	14	54
1970	Baltimore (A)	7	2	.778	1.96	50	55	36	24	66
1971	Baltimore (A	3	5	.375	3.50	35	36	26	22	35
1972	LOS ANGELES (N)	2	3	.400	2.25	37	52	42	18	38
1973	LOS ANGELES (N)	3	3	.500	3.18	39	51	44	19	31
1974	St. Louis (N)									
1974	Philadelphia (N)									
	(year totals)	2	1	.667	2.27	34	31.2	25	15	13
	Thirteen years	80	73	.523	3.19	429	1165.2	959	424	925
League Championship										
	One year	0	0	—	0.00	1	1	0	2	2
World Series										
	Three years	0	0	—	0.00	3	1	0	0	1

JIM ROBERTS B. Oct. 13, 1895, Artesia, Miss.
Right handed, B.R.
6'3" 205 lbs.

YEAR	CLUB	W	L	PCT	ERA	G	IP	H	BB	SO
1924	BROOKLYN (N)	0	3	.000	7.46	11	25.1	41	8	10
1925	BROOKLYN (N)	0	0	—	0.00	1	1	1	0	0
	Two years	0	3	.000	7.18	12	26.1	42	8	10

DICK ROBERTSON B. 1891, Washington, D.C.
Right handed, B.R.
5'9" 160 lbs.

YEAR	CLUB	W	L	PCT	ERA	G	IP	H	BB	SO
1918	BROOKLYN (N)	3	6	.333	2.59	13	87	87	28	18
	Three years (totals)	3	8	.273	2.89	22	124.2	125	46	26

PREACHER ROE B. Feb. 26, 1915, Ashflat, Ark.
Left handed, B.R.
6'2" 170lbs.

YEAR	CLUB	W	L	PCT	ERA	G	IP	H	BB	SO
1938	St. Louis (N)	0	0	—	13.50	1	2.2	6	2	1
1944	Pittsburgh (N)	13	11	.542	3.11	39	185.1	182	59	88
1945	Pittsburgh (N)	14	13	.519	2.87	33	235	228	46	148
1946	Pittsburgh (N)	3	8	.273	5.14	21	70	83	25	28
1947	Pittsburgh (N)	4	15	.211	5.25	38	144	156	63	59
1948	BROOKLYN (N)	12	8	.600	2.63	34	177.2	156	33	86
1949	BROOKLYN (N)	15	6	.714	2.79	30	212.2	201	44	109
1950	BROOKLYN (N)	19	11	.633	3.30	36	250.2	245	66	125
1951	BROOKLYN (N)	22	3	.880	3.04	34	257.2	247	64	113

YEAR	CLUB	W	L	PCT	ERA	G	IP	H	BB	SO
1952	BROOKLYN (N)	11	2	.846	3.12	27	158.2	163	39	83
1953	BROOKLYN (N)	11	3	.786	4.36	25	157	171	40	85
1954	BROOKLYN (N)	3	4	.429	5.00	15	63	69	23	31
	Twelve years	127	84	.602	3.43	333	1914.1	1907	504	956

World Series

YEAR	CLUB	W	L	PCT	ERA	G	IP	H	BB	SO
1949	BROOKLYN (N)	1	0	1.000	0.00	1	9	6	0	3
1952	BROOKLYN (N)	1	0	1.000	3.18	3	11.1	9	6	7
1953	BROOKLYN (N)	0	1	.000	4.50	1	8	5	4	4
	Three years	2	1	.667	2.54	5	28.1	20	10	14

ED ROEBUCK
B. July 3, 1931, East Millsboro, Pa.
Right handed, B.R.
6'2" 185 lbs.

YEAR	CLUB	W	L	PCT	ERA	G	IP	H	BB	SO
1955	BROOKLYN (N)	5	6	.455	4.71	47	84	96	24	33
1956	BROOKLYN (N)	5	4	.556	3.93	43	89.1	83	29	60
1957	BROOKLYN (N)	8	2	.800	2.71	44	96.1	70	46	73
1958	LOS ANGELES (N)	0	1	.000	3.48	32	44	45	15	26
1960	LOS ANGELES (N)	8	3	.727	2.78	58	116.2	109	38	77
1961	LOS ANGELES (N)	2	0	1.000	5.00	5	9	12	2	9
1962	LOS ANGELES (N)	10	2	.833	3.09	64	119.1	102	54	72
1963	LOS ANGELES (N)	2	4	.333	4.25	29	40		21	26
1963	Washington (A)									
	(year totals)	4	5	.444	3.69	55	97.2	117	50	51
1964	Washington (A)									
1964	Philadelphia (N)									
	(year totals)	5	3	.625	2.30	62	78.1	55	27	42
1965	Philadelphia (N)	5	3	.625	3.40	44	50.1	55	15	29
1966	Philadelphia (N)	0	2	.000	6.00	6	6	9	2	5
	Eleven years	52	31	.627	3.35	460	791	753	302	477

World Series

YEAR	CLUB	W	L	PCT	ERA	G	IP	H	BB	SO
1955	BROOKLYN (N)	0	0	—	0.00	1	2	1	0	0
1956	BROOKLYN (N)	0	0	—	2.08	3	4.1	1	0	5
	Two years	0	0	—	1.42	4	6.1	2	0	5

LEE ROGERS
B. Oct. 8, 1913, Tuscaloosa, Ala.
Left handed, B.R.
5'11" 170 lbs.

YEAR	CLUB	W	L	PCT	ERA	G	IP	H	BB	SO
1938	BROOKLYN (N)	0	2	—	5.63	12	24		10	11

JIM ROMANO
B. April 6, 1927, Brooklyn, N.Y.
Right handed, B.R.
6'4" 190 lbs.

YEAR	CLUB	W	L	PCT	ERA	G	IP	H	BB	SO
1950	BROOKLYN (N)	0	0	—	5.68	3	6.1	8	2	8

VICENTE ROMO
B. April 12, 1943, Santa Rosalia, Mexico
Right handed, B.R.
6'1" 180 lbs.

YEAR	CLUB	W	L	PCT	ERA	G	IP	H	BB	SO
1968	LOS ANGELES (N)	0	0	—	0.00	1	1		1	1
	Seven years (totals)	31	31	.500	3.38	320	610	544	267	392

KEN ROWE
B. Dec. 31, 1933, Ferndale, Mich.
Right handed, B.R.
6'2" 185 lbs.

YEAR	CLUB	W	L	PCT	ERA	G	IP	H	BB	SO
1963	LOS ANGELES (N)	1	1	.500	2.93	14	27.2	28	11	12
	Three years (totals)	2	1	.667	3.57	26	45.1	55	14	19

SCHOOLBOY ROWE
B. Jan. 11, 1910, Waco, Texas
D. Jan. 8, 1961, El Dorado, Ark.
Right handed, B.R.
6'4½" 210 lbs.

YEAR	CLUB	W	L	PCT	ERA	G	IP	H	BB	SO
1942	BROOKLYN (N)	1	0	1.000	5.40	9	30		12	6
	Fifteen years (totals)	158	101	.610	3.87	382	2219.1	2330	558	913

JEAN PIERRE ROY
B. June 26, 1920, Montreal, Quebec, Canada
Right handed, B.B.
5'10" 160 lbs.

YEAR	CLUB	W	L	PCT	ERA	G	IP	H	BB	SO
1946	BROOKLYN (N)	0	0	—	9.95	3	6.1	5	5	6

LUTHER ROY
B. July 29, 1902, Ooltewah, Tenn.
D. July 24, 1963, Grand Rapids, Mich.
Right handed, B.R.
5'10½" 161 lbs.

YEAR	CLUB	W	L	PCT	ERA	G	IP	H	BB	SO
1929	BROOKLYN (N)	0	0	—	4.50	2	4		4	0
	Four years (totals)	6	12	.333	7.17	56	170.2	231	92	36

NAP RUCKER
B. Sept. 30, 1884, Crabapple, Ga.
D. Dec. 19, 1970, Alpharetta, Ga.
Left handed, B.R.
5'11" 190 lbs.

YEAR	CLUB	W	L	PCT	ERA	G	IP	H	BB	SO
1907	BROOKLYN (N)	15	13	.536	2.06	37	275.1	242	80	131
1908	BROOKLYN (N)	18	20	.474	2.08	42	333.1	265	125	199
1909	BROOKLYN (N)	13	19	.406	2.24	38	309.1	245	101	201
1910	BROOKLYN (N)	17	19	.472	2.58	41	320.1	293	84	147
1911	BROOKLYN (N)	22	18	.550	2.71	48	315.2	255	110	190
1912	BROOKLYN (N)	18	21	.462	2.21	45	297.2	272	72	151
1913	BROOKLYN (N)	14	15	.483	2.87	41	260	236	67	111
1914	BROOKLYN (N)	7	6	.538	3.39	16	103.2	113	27	35
1915	BROOKLYN (N)	9	4	.692	2.42	19	122.2	134	28	38
1916	BROOKLYN (N)	2	1	.667	1.69	9	37.1	34	7	14
	Ten years	135	136	.498	2.42	336	2375.1	2089	701	1217
World Series										
	One year	0	0	—	0.00	1	2	1	0	3

ERNIE RUDOLPH
B. Feb. 13, 1910, Black River Falls, Wis.
Right handed, B.L.
5'8" 165 lbs.

YEAR	CLUB	W	L	PCT	ERA	G	IP	H	BB	SO
1945	BROOKLYN (N)	1	0	1.000	5.19	7	8.2	12	7	3

DUTCH RUETHER
B. Sept. 13, 1893, Alameda, Calif.
D. May 16, 1970, Phoenix, Ariz.
Left handed, B.L.
6'1½" 180 lbs.

YEAR	CLUB	W	L	PCT	ERA	G	IP	H	BB	SO
1917	Chicago (N)									
1917	Cincinnati (N)									
	(year totals)	3	2	.600	3.00	17	72	80	26	35

228 • The Complete Dodgers Record Book

YEAR	CLUB	W	L	PCT	ERA	G	IP	H	BB	SO
1918	Cincinnati (N)	0	1	.000	2.70	2	10	10	3	10
1919	Cincinnati (N)	19	6	.760	1.82	33	242.2	195	83	78
1920	Cincinnati (N)	16	12	.571	2.47	37	265.2	235	96	99
1921	BROOKLYN (N)	10	13	.435	4.26	36	211.1	247	67	78
1922	BROOKLYN (N)	21	12	.636	3.53	35	267.1	290	92	89
1923	BROOKLYN (N)	15	14	.517	4.22	34	275	308	86	87
1924	BROOKLYN (N)	8	13	.381	3.94	30	166.2	189	45	65
1925	Washington (A)	18	7	.720	3.87	30	223.1	241	105	68
1926	Washington (A)									
1926	New York (A)									
	(year totals)	14	9	.609	4.60	28	205.1	246	84	56
1927	New York (A)	13	6	.684	3.38	27	184	202	52	45
	Eleven years	137	95	.591	3.50	309	2123.1	2243	739	710
World Series										
	Two years	1	1	.500	3.93	3	18.1	19	6	2

ANDY RUSH B. Dec. 26, 1889, Longton, Kan.
D. March 16, 1969, Fresno, Calif.
Right handed, B.R.
6'3" 180 lbs.

YEAR	CLUB	W	L	PCT	ERA	G	IP	H	BB	SO
1925	BROOKLYN (N)	0	1	.000	9.31	4	9.2	16	5	4

JOHN RUSSELL B. Oct. 20, 1895, San Mateo, Calif.
D. Nov. 20, 1930, Ely, Nev.
Left handed, B.L.
6'2" 195 lbs.

YEAR	CLUB	W	L	PCT	ERA	G	IP	H	BB	SO
1917	BROOKLYN (N)	0	1	.000	4.50	5	16	12	6	1
1918	BROOKLYN (N)	0	0	—	18.00	1	1	2	1	0
	Four years (totals)	2	7	.222	5.40	21	90	103	46	19

JOHNNY RUTHERFORD B. May 5, 1925, Belleville, Ontario, Canada
Right handed, B.L.
5'10½" 170 lbs.

YEAR	CLUB	W	L	PCT	ERA	G	IP	H	BB	SO
1952	BROOKLYN (N)	7	7	.500	4.25	22	97.1	97	29	29
World Series										
	One year	0	0	—	9.00	1	1	1	1	1

JACK RYAN B. Sept. 19, 1884, Lawrenceville, Ill.
D. Oct. 16, 1949, Hondsboro, Miss.
Right handed

YEAR	CLUB	W	L	PCT	ERA	G	IP	H	BB	SO
1911	BROOKLYN (N)	0	1	.000	3.00	3	6	9	4	1
	Three years (totals)	4	5	.444	2.88	24	103	101	26	32

ROSY RYAN B. March 15, 1898, Worcester, Mass.
D. Dec. 10, 1980, Scottsdale, Ariz.
Right handed, B.L.
6' 185 lbs.

YEAR	CLUB	W	L	PCT	ERA	G	IP	H	BB	SO
1933	BROOKLYN (N)	1	1	.500	4.55	30	61.1	69	16	22
	Ten years (totals)	51	47	.520	4.14	248	881	941	278	315

BILL SAYLES B. July 27, 1917, Portland, Ore.
Right handed, B.R.
6'2" 175 lbs.

YEAR	CLUB	W	L	PCT	ERA	G	IP	H	BB	SO
1943	BROOKLYN (N)	0	0	—	7.50	5	12		10	5
	Two years (totals)	1	3	.250	5.61	28	78.2	87	46	52

DOC SCANLAN
B. March 7, 1881, Syracuse, N.Y.
D. May 29, 1949, Brooklyn, N.Y.
Right handed, B.L.
5'8" 165 lbs.

YEAR	CLUB	W	L	PCT	ERA	G	IP	H	BB	SO
1903	Pittsburgh (N)	0	1	.000	4.00	1	9	5	6	0
1904	Pittsburgh (N)									
1904	BROOKLYN (N)	7	6	.538	2.16	13	104		40	40
	(year totals)	8	9	.471	2.64	17	126	115	60	50
1905	BROOKLYN (N)	14	12	.538	2.92	33	250	220	104	135
1906	BROOKLYN (N)	19	14	.576	3.19	38	288	230	127	120
1907	BROOKLYN (N)	6	7	.462	3.20	17	107	90	61	59
1909	BROOKLYN (N)	8	7	.533	2.93	19	141.1	125	65	72
1910	BROOKLYN (N)	8	12	.400	2.61	34	217.1	175	116	102
1911	BROOKLYN (N)	3	10	.231	3.64	22	113.2	101	69	45
	Eight years	66	72	.478	3.00	181	1252.1	1061	608	584

BILL SCHARDT
B. Jan. 20, 1886, Cleveland, Ohio
D. July 26, 1964, Vermillion, Ohio
Right handed, B.R.
6'4" 210 lbs.

YEAR	CLUB	W	L	PCT	ERA	G	IP	H	BB	SO
1911	BROOKLYN (N)	5	16	.238	3.59	39	195.1	190	91	77
1912	BROOKLYN (N)	0	1	.000	4.35	7	20.2	25	6	7
	Two years	5	17	.227	3.67	46	216	215	97	84

HENRY SCHMIDT
B. June 26, 1873, Brownsville, Texas
D. April 23, 1926, Nashville, Tenn.
Right handed
5'8" 150 lbs.

YEAR	CLUB	W	L	PCT	ERA	G	IP	H	BB	SO
1903	BROOKLYN (N)	21	13	.618	3.83	40	301	321	120	96

JOHNNY SCHMITZ
B. Nov. 27, 1920, Wausau, Wis.
Left handed, B.R.
6' 170 lbs.

YEAR	CLUB	W	L	PCT	ERA	G	IP	H	BB	SO
1951	BROOKLYN (N)	1	4	.200	5.30	16	56		28	20
1952	BROOKLYN (N)	1	1	.500	4.36	10	33		18	11
	Thirteen years (totals)	93	114	.449	3.55	366	1812.2	1766	757	746

CHARLIE SCHMUTZ
B. Jan. 1, 1891, San Diego, Calif.
D. June 27, 1962, Seattle, Wash.
Right handed, B.R.
6'1½" 195 lbs.

YEAR	CLUB	W	L	PCT	ERA	G	IP	H	BB	SO
1914	BROOKLYN (N)	1	3	.250	3.30	18	57.1	57	13	21
1915	BROOKLYN (N)	0	0	—	6.75	1	4	7	1	1
	Two years	1	3	.250	3.52	19	61.1	64	14	22

FRANK SCHNEIBERG
B. March 12, 1882, Milwaukee, Wis.
D. May 18, 1948, Milwaukee, Wis.

YEAR	CLUB	W	L	PCT	ERA	G	IP	H	BB	SO
1910	BROOKLYN (N)	0	0	—	63.00	1	1	5	4	0

GENE SCHOTT
B. July 14, 1913, Batavia, Ohio
Right handed, B.R.
6'2" 185 lbs.

YEAR	CLUB	W	L	PCT	ERA	G	IP	H	BB	SO
1939	BROOKLYN (N)	0	1	.000	4.91	4	11	14	5	1
	Five years (totals)	28	41	.406	3.72	136	587.1	590	222	192

PAUL SCHREIBER
B. Oct. 8, 1902, Jacksonville, Fla.
Right handed, B.R.
6'2" 180 lbs.

YEAR	CLUB	W	L	PCT	ERA	G	IP	H	BB	SO
1922	BROOKLYN (N)	0	0	—	0.00	1	1	2	0	0
1923	BROOKLYN (N)	0	0	—	4.20	9	15	16	8	4
	Three years (totals)	0	0	—	3.98	12	20.1	22	10	5

FERDIE SCHUPP
B. Jan. 16, 1891, Louisville, Ky.
D. Dec. 16, 1971, Los Angeles, Calif.
Left handed, B.R.
5'10" 150 lbs.

YEAR	CLUB	W	L	PCT	ERA	G	IP	H	BB	SO
1921	BROOKLYN (N)	3	4	.429	4.57	20	61		27	26
	Ten years (totals)	62	39	.614	3.32	216	1054	938	464	553

DICK SCOTT
B. March 15, 1933, Portsmouth, N.H.
Left handed, B.R.
6'2" 185 lbs.

YEAR	CLUB	W	L	PCT	ERA	G	IP	H	BB	SO
1963	LOS ANGELES (N)	0	0	—	6.75	9	12	17	3	6
	Two years (totals)	0	0	—	8.27	12	16.1	27	4	7

TOM SEATON
B. Aug. 30, 1889, Blair, Neb.
D. April 10, 1940, El Paso, Texas
Right handed, B.L.
6' 175 lbs.

YEAR	CLUB	W	L	PCT	ERA	G	IP	H	BB	SO
1912	Philadelphia (N)	16	12	.571	3.28	44	255	246	106	118
1913	Philadelphia (N)	27	12	.692	2.60	52	322.1	262	136	168
1914	BROOKLYN (F)	25	13	.658	3.03	44	302.2	299	102	172
1915	BROOKLYN (F)									
1915	Newark (F)									
	(year totals)	15	17	.469	3.92	44	264.1	260	120	114
1916	Chicago (N)	5	6	.455	3.27	31	121	108	43	45
1917	Chicago (N)	5	4	.556	2.53	16	74.2	60	23	27
	Six years	93	64	.592	3.14	231	1340	1235	530	644

TOM SEATS
B. Sept. 24, 1911, Farmington, N.C.
Left handed, B.R.
5'11" 190 lbs.

YEAR	CLUB	W	L	PCT	ERA	G	IP	H	BB	SO
1945	BROOKLYN (N)	10	7	.588	4.36	31	121.2	127	37	44
	Two years (totals)	12	9	.571	4.47	57	177.1	194	58	69

DAVE SELLS
B. Sept. 18, 1946, Vacaville, Calif.
Right handed, B.R.
5'11" 175 lbs.

YEAR	CLUB	W	L	PCT	ERA	G	IP	H	BB	SO
1975	LOS ANGELES (N)	0	2	.000	3.86	5	7		3	1
	Four years (totals)	11	7	.611	3.90	90	138.1	146	67	49

ELMER SEXAUER
B. May 21, 1926, St. Louis County, Mo.
Right handed, B.R.
6'4" 220 lbs.

YEAR	CLUB	W	L	PCT	ERA	G	IP	H	BB	SO
1948	BROOKLYN (N)	0	0	—	13.50	2	.2	0	2	0

GREG SHANAHAN
B. Dec. 11, 1947, Eureka, Calif.
Right handed, B.R.
6'2" 190 lbs.

YEAR	CLUB	W	L	PCT	ERA	G	IP	H	BB	SO
1973	LOS ANGELES (N)	0	0	—	3.45	7	15.2	14	4	11
1974	LOS ANGELES (N)	0	0	—	3.86	4	7	7	5	2
	Two years	0	0	—	3.57	11	22.2	21	9	13

GEORGE SHARROTT
B. Nov. 2, 1869, Staten Island, N.Y.
D. Jan. 6, 1932, Jamaica, N.Y.

YEAR	CLUB	W	L	PCT	ERA	G	IP	H	BB	SO
1893	BROOKLYN (N)	4	6	.400	5.87	13	95	114	58	24
1894	BROOKLYN (N)	0	1	.000	7.00	2	9	7	5	2
	Two years	4	7	.364	5.97	15	104	121	63	26

JOE SHAUTE
B. Aug. 1, 1899, Peckville, Pa.
D. Feb. 21, 1970, Scranton, Pa.
Left handed, B.L.
6' 190 lbs.

YEAR	CLUB	W	L	PCT	ERA	G	IP	H	BB	SO
1922	Cleveland (A)	0	0	—	19.64	3	3.2	7	3	3
1923	Cleveland (A)	10	8	.556	3.51	33	172	176	53	61
1924	Cleveland (A)	20	17	.541	3.75	46	283	317	83	68
1925	Cleveland (A)	4	12	.250	5.43	26	131	160	44	34
1926	Cleveland (A)	14	10	.583	3.53	34	206.2	215	65	47
1927	Cleveland (A)	9	16	.360	4.22	45	230.1	255	75	63
1928	Cleveland (A)	13	17	.433	4.04	36	253.2	295	68	81
1929	Cleveland (A)	8	8	.500	4.28	26	162	211	52	43
1930	Cleveland (A)	0	0	—	15.43	4	4.2	8	4	2
1931	BROOKLYN (N)	11	8	.579	4.83	25	128.2	162	32	50
1932	BROOKLYN (N)	7	7	.500	4.62	34	117	147	21	32
1933	BROOKLYN (N)	3	4	.429	3.49	41	108.1	125	31	26
1934	Cincinnati (N)	0	2	.000	4.15	8	17.1	19	3	2
	Thirteen years	99	109	.476	4.15	360	1818.1	2097	534	512

LARRY SHERRY
B. Juily 25, 1935, Los Anegeles, Calif.
Right handed, B.R.
6'2" 180 lbs.

YEAR	CLUB	W	L	PCT	ERA	G	IP	H	BB	SO
1958	LOS ANGELES (N)	0	0	—	12.46	5	4.1	10	7	2
1959	LOS ANGELES (N)	7	2	.778	2.19	23	94.1	75	43	72
1960	LOS ANGELES (N)	14	10	.583	3.79	57	142.1	125	82	114
1961	LOS ANGELES (N)	4	4	.500	3.90	53	94.2	90	39	79
1962	LOS ANGELES (N)	7	3	.700	3.20	58	90	81	44	71
1963	LOS ANGELES (N)	2	6	.250	3.73	36	79.2	82	24	47
1964	Detroit (A)	7	5	.583	3.66	38	66.1	52	37	58
1965	Detroit (A)	3	6	.333	3.10	39	78.1	71	40	46
1966	Detroit (A)	8	5	.615	3.82	55	77.2	66	36	63
1967	Detroit (A)									
1967	Houston (N)									
	(year totals)	1	3	.250	5.50	49	68.2	88	20	52
1968	California (A)	0	0	—	6.00	3	3	7	2	2
	Eleven years	53	44	.546	3.67	416	799.1	747	374	606
World Series										
	One year	2	0	1.000	0.71	4	12.2	8	2	5

STEVE SHIRLEY
B. Nov. 12, 1956, San Francisco, Calif.
Left handed, B.L.
6' 185 lbs.

YEAR	CLUB	W	L	PCT	ERA	G	IP	H	BB	SO
1982	LOS ANGELES	1	1	.500	4.26	11	12	15	21	20

HARRY SHRIVER B. Sept. 2, 1896, Wadestown, W. Va.
D. Jan. 1, 1970, Morgantown, W. Va.
Right handed, B.R.
6'2" 180 lbs.

YEAR	CLUB	W	L	PCT	ERA	G	IP	H	BB	SO
1922	BROOKLYN (N)	4	6	.400	2.99	25	108.1	114	48	38
1923	BROOKLYN (N)	0	0	—	6.75	1	4	8	0	1
	Two years	4	6	.400	3.12	26	112.1	122	48	39

BILL SINGER B. April 24, 1944, Los Angeles, Calif.
Right handed, B.R.
6'4" 184 lbs.

YEAR	CLUB	W	L	PCT	ERA	G	IP	H	BB	SO
1964	LOS ANGELES (N)	0	1	.000	3.21	2	14	11	12	3
1965	LOS ANGELES (N)	0	0	—	0.00	2	1	2	2	1
1966	LOS ANGELES (N)	0	0	—	0.00	3	4	4	2	4
1967	LOS ANGELES (N)	12	8	.600	2.64	32	204.1	185	61	169
1968	LOS ANGELES (N)	13	17	.433	2.88	37	256.1	227	78	227
1969	LOS ANGELES (N)	20	12	.625	2.34	41	316	244	74	247
1970	LOS ANGELES (N)	8	5	.615	3.14	16	106	79	32	93
1971	LOS ANGELES (N)	10	17	.370	4.17	31	203	195	71	144
1972	LOS ANGELES (N)	6	16	.273	3.67	26	169.1	148	60	101
1973	California (A)	20	14	.588	3.22	40	315.2	280	130	241
1974	California (A)	7	4	.636	2.97	14	109	102	43	77
1975	California A)	7	15	.318	4.98	29	179	17	81	78
1976	Texas (A)									
1976	Minnesota (A)									
	(year totals)	13	10	.565	3.69	36	236.2	233	96	97
1977	Toronto (A)	2	8	.200	6.75	13	60	71	39	33
	Fourteen years	118	127	.482	3.39	322	2174.1	1952	781	1515

DWAIN SLOAT B. Dec. 1, 1918, Nokomis, Ill.
Left handed, B.R.
6' 168 lbs.

YEAR	CLUB	W	L	PCT	ERA	G	IP	H	BB	SO
1948	BROOKLYN (N)	0	1	.000	6.14	4	7.1	7	8	1
	Two years (totals)	0	1	.000	6.61	9	16.1	21	11	4

FRANK SMITH B. Oct. 28, 1879, Pittsburgh, Pa.
D. Nov. 3, 1952, Pittsburgh, Pa.
Right handed, B.R.
5'10½" 194 lbs.

YEAR	CLUB	W	L	PCT	ERA	G	IP	H	BB	SO
1915	BROOKLYN (F)									
	Eleven years (totals)	136	112	.548	2.59	354	2273	1975	676	1051

GEORGE SMITH B. May 31, 1892, Byram, Conn.
D. Jan. 7, 1965, Greenwich, Conn.
Right handed, B.R.
6'2" 163 lbs.

YEAR	CLUB	W	L	PCT	ERA	G	IP	H	BB	SO
1918	BROOKLYN (N)	4	1	.800	2.34	8	50		5	18
1923	BROOKLYN (N)	3	6	.333	3.66	25	91	99	28	15
	Eight years (totals)	39	81	.325	3.89	229	1143.1	1321	255	263

JACK SMITH B. Nov. 15, 1935, Pikeville, Ky.
Right handed, B.R.
6' 185 lbs.

YEAR	CLUB	W	L	PCT	ERA	G	IP	H	BB	SO
1962	LOS ANGELES (N)	0	0	—	4.50	8	10	10	4	7
1963	LOS ANGELES (N)	0	0	—	7.56	4	8.1	10	2	5
	Three years (totals)	2	2	.500	4.56	34	49.1	48	17	31

SHERRY SMITH

B. Feb. 18, 1891, Monticello, Ga.
D. Sept. 12, 1949, Reidsville, Ga.
Left handed, B.L.
6'1" 170 lbs.

YEAR	CLUB	W	L	PCT	ERA	G	IP	H	BB	SO
1911	Pittsburgh (N)	0	0	—	54.00	1	.2	4	1	0
1912	Pittsburgh (N)	1	0	1.000	6.75	3	4	6	1	3
1915	BROOKLYN (N)	14	8	.636	2.59	29	173.2	169	42	52
1916	BROOKLYN (N)	14	10	.583	2.34	36	219	193	45	67
1917	BROOKLYN (N)	12	12	.500	3.32	38	211.1	210	51	58
1919	BROOKLYN (N)	7	12	.368	2.24	30	173	181	29	40
1920	BROOKLYN (N)	11	9	.550	1.85	33	136.1	134	27	33
1921	BROOKLYN (N)	7	11	.389	3.90	35	175.1	232	34	36
1922	BROOKLYN (N)	4	8	.333	4.55	28	109		35	15
1922	Cleveland (A)									
	(year totals)	5	8	.385	4.42	30	124.1	146	38	19
1923	Cleveland (A)	9	6	.600	3.27	30	124	129	37	23
1924	Cleveland (A)	12	14	.462	3.02	39	247.2	267	42	34
1925	Cleveland (A)	11	14	.440	4.86	31	237	296	48	30
1926	Cleveland (A)	11	10	.524	3.73	27	188.1	214	31	25
1927	Cleveland (A)	1	4	.200	5.45	11	38	53	14	8
	Fourteen years	115	118	.494	3.32	373	2052.2	2234	440	428

World Series

YEAR	CLUB	W	L	PCT	ERA	G	IP	H	BB	SO
1916	BROOKLYN (N)	0	1	.000	1.35	1	13.1	7	6	2
1920	BROOKLYN (N)	1	1	.500	0.52	2	17	10	3	3
	Two years	1	2	.333	0.89	3	30.1	17	9	5

HARRY SMYTHE

B. Oct. 24, 1904, Augusta, Ga.
Left handed, B.L.
5'10½" 179 lbs.

YEAR	CLUB	W	L	PCT	ERA	G	IP	H	BB	SO
1934	BROOKLYN (N)	1	1	.500	6.00	8	21		8	5
	Three years (totals)	5	12	.294	6.40	60	154.2	232	62	33

GENE SNYDER

B. March 31, 1931, York, Pa.
Left handed, B.R.
5'11" 175 lbs.

YEAR	CLUB	W	L	PCT	ERA	G	IP	H	BB	SO
1959	LOS ANGELES (N)	1	1	.500	5.47	11	26.1	32	20	20

EDDIE SOLOMON

B. Feb. 9, 1952, Houston County, Ga.
Right handed, B.R.
6'2" 185 lbs.

YEAR	CLUB	W	L	PCT	ERA	G	IP	H	BB	SO
1973	LOS ANGELES (N)	0	0	—	7.11	4	6.1	10	4	6
1974	LOS ANGELES (N)	0	0	—	1.35	4	6.2	5	2	2
	Nine years (totals)	33	36	.478	3.80	174	665	688	227	317

RUDY SOMMERS

B. Oct. 30, 1886, Cincinnati, Ohio
D. March 18, 1949, Louisville, Ky.
Left handed, B.L.
5'11" 165 lbs.

YEAR	CLUB	W	L	PCT	ERA	G	IP	H	BB	SO
1914	BROOKLYN (F)	4	7	.364	4.06	23	82	88	34	40
	Four years (totals)	4	8	.333	4.81	33	101	113	53	44

ANDY SOMMERVILLE

B. Feb. 6, 1876, Brooklyn, N.Y.
D. June 16, 1931, Richmond Hill, N.Y.

YEAR	CLUB	W	L	PCT	ERA	G	IP	H	BB	SO
1894	BROOKLYN (N)	0	1	.000	162.00	1	1	1	5	0

ELIAS SOSA
B. June 10, 1950, La Vega, Dominican Republic
Right handed, B.R.
6'2" 186 lbs.

YEAR	CLUB	W	L	PCT	ERA	G	IP	H	BB	SO
1976	LOS ANGELES (N)	2	4	.333	3.44	24	34		12	20
1977	LOS ANGELES (N)	2	2	.500	1.97	44	64	42	12	47
	Eleven years (totals)	58	47	.552	3.23	560	847.2	801	304	493
Divisional Playoff										
	One year	0	0	—	3.00	2	3	4	0	1
League Championship										
	Two years	0	1	.000	9.00	3	3	6	1	0
World Series										
	One year	0	0	—	11.57	2	2.1	3	1	1

KARL SPOONER
B. June 23, 1931, Oriskany Falls, N.Y.
Left handed, B.R.
6' 185 lbs.

YEAR	CLUB	W	L	PCT	ERA	G	IP	H	BB	SO
1954	BROOKLYN (N)	2	0	1.000	0.00	2	18	7	6	27
1955	BROOKLYN (N)	8	6	.571	3.65	29	98.2	79	41	78
	Two years	10	6	.625	3.09	31	116.2	86	47	105
World Series										
	One year	0	1	.000	13.50	2	3.1	4	3	6

EDDIE STACK
B. Oct. 24, 1887, Chicago, Ill.
D. Aug. 28, 1958, Chicago, Ill.
Right handed, B.R.

YEAR	CLUB	W	L	PCT	ERA	G	IP	H	BB	SO
1912	BROOKLYN (N)	7	5	.583	3.36	28	142	139	55	45
1913	BROOKLYN (N)	4	4	.500	2.38	23	87		32	34
	Five years (totals)	26	24	.520	3.52	102	491	469	188	200

DON STANHOUSE
B. Feb. 12, 1951, DuQuion, Ill.
Right handed, B.R.
6'2½" 185 lbs.

YEAR	CLUB	W	L	PCT	ERA	G	IP	H	BB	SO
1980	LOS ANGELES (N)	2	2	.500	5.04	21	25	30	16	5
	Nine years (totals)	38	53	.418	3.78	277	733.2	678	440	400

BILL STEELE
B. Oct. 5, 1885, Milford, Pa.
D. Oct. 19, 1949, Overland, Mo.
Right handed, B.R.

YEAR	CLUB	W	L	PCT	ERA	G	IP	H	BB	SO
1914	BROOKLYN (N)	1	1	.500	5.63	8	16		7	3
	Five years (totals)	37	43	.463	4.02	129	676.2	733	235	236

ELMER STEELE
B. May 17, 1884, Muitzeskill, N.Y.
D. March 9, 1966, Rhinebeck, N.Y.
Right handed, B.B.
5'11" 200 lbs.

YEAR	CLUB	W	L	PCT	ERA	G	IP	H	BB	SO
1911	BROOKLYN (N)	0	0	—	3.13	5	23		23	24
	Five years (totals)	20	23	.465	2.41	75	418	367	68	147

ED STEIN
B. Sept. 5, 1869, Detroit, Mich.
D. May 10, 1928, Detroit, Mich.
5'11" 170 lbs.

YEAR	CLUB	W	L	PCT	ERA	G	IP	H	BB	SO
1890	Chicago (N)	12	6	.667	3.81	20	160.2	147	83	65
1891	Chicago (N)	7	6	.538	3.74	14	101	99	57	38
1892	BROOKLYN (N)	27	16	.628	2.84	48	377.1	310	150	190

YEAR	CLUB	W	L	PCT	ERA	G	IP	H	BB	SO
1893	BROOKLYN (N)	19	15	.559	3.77	37	298.1	294	119	81
1894	BROOKLYN (N)	27	14	.659	4.54	45	359	396	171	84
1895	BROOKLYN (N)	15	13	.536	4.72	32	255.1	282	93	55
1896	BROOKLYN (N)	3	6	.333	4.88	17	90.1	130	51	16
1898	BROOKLYN (N)	0	2	.000	5.48	3	23	39	9	6
	Eight years	110	78	.585	3.96	216	1665	1697	733	535

JERRY STEPHENSON   B. Oct. 6, 1943, Detroit, Mich.
Right handed, B.L.
6'2" 185 lbs.

YEAR	CLUB	W	L	PCT	ERA	G	IP	H	BB	SO
1970	LOS ANGELES (N)	0	0	—	9.00	3	7	11	5	6
	Seven years (totals)	8	19	.296	5.69	67	238.2	265	145	184

DAVE STEWART   B. Feb. 19, 1957, Oakland, Calif.
Right handed, B.R.
6'2" 200 lbs.

YEAR	CLUB	W	L	PCT	ERA	G	IP	H	BB	SO
1978	LOS ANGELES (N)	0	0	—	0.00	1	2	1	0	1
1981	LOS ANGELES (N)	4	3	.571	2.51	32	43	40	14	29
1982	LOS ANGELES (N)	9	8	.529	3.81	45	146.1	137	49	80
1983	LOS ANGELES (N)	5	2	.714	2.96	46	76	67	33	54
	Four years	18	13	.615	3.28	124	267.1	245	96	164
Divisional Playoff										
	One year	0	2	.000	40.50	2	.2	4	0	1
World Series										
	One year	0	0	—	0.00	2	1.2	1	2	1

MIKE STRAHLER   B. March 14, 1947, Chicago, Ill.
Right handed, B.R.
6'4" 180 lbs.

YEAR	CLUB	W	L	PCT	ERA	G	IP	H	BB	SO
1970	LOS ANGELES (N)	1	1	.500	1.42	6	19	13	10	11
1971	LOS ANGELES (N)	0	0	—	2.77	6	13	10	8	7
1972	LOS ANGELES (N)	1	2	.333	3.26	19	47	42	22	25
	Four years (totals)	6	8	.429	3.57	53	159	149	79	80

ELMER STRICKLETT   B. Aug. 29, 1876, Glasco, Kan.
Right handed, B.R.
5'6" 140 lbs.

YEAR	CLUB	W	L	PCT	ERA	G	IP	H	BB	SO
1905	BROOKLYN (N)	9	18	.333	3.34	33	237	259	71	77
1906	BROOKLYN (N)	14	18	.438	2.72	41	291.2	273	77	88
1907	BROOKLYN (N)	12	14	.462	2.27	29	229.2	211	65	69
	Four years (totals)	35	51	.407	2.85	104	765.1	755	215	237

DUTCH STRYKER   B. July 29, 1895, Atlantic Highlands, N.J.
D. Nov. 5, 1964, Red Bank, N.J.
Right handed, B.R.
5'11½" 180 lbs.

YEAR	CLUB	W	L	PCT	ERA	G	IP	H	BB	SO
1926	BROOKLYN (N)	0	0	—	27.00	2	2	8	1	0
	Two years (totals)	3	8	.273	6.57	22	75.1	98	23	22

TOM SUNKEL   B. Aug. 9, 1912, Paris, Ill.
Left handed, B.L.
6'1" 190 lbs.

YEAR	CLUB	W	L	PCT	ERA	G	IP	H	BB	SO
1944	BROOKLYN (N)	1	3	.250	7.50	12	24	39	10	6
	Six years (totals)	9	15	.375	4.34	63	230.1	218	133	112

RICK SUTCLIFFE B. June 21, 1956, Independence, Mo.
Right handed, B.L.
6'7" 215 lbs.

YEAR	CLUB	W	L	PCT	ERA	G	IP	H	BB	SO
1976	LOS ANGELES (N)	0	0	—	0.00	1	5	2	1	3
1978	LOS ANGELES (N)	0	0	—	0.00	2	2	2	1	0
1979	LOS ANGELES (N)	17	10	.630	3.46	39	242	217	97	117
1980	LOS ANGELES (N)	3	9	.250	5.56	42	110	122	55	59
1981	LOS ANGELES (N)	2	2	.500	4.02	14	47	41	20	16
1982	Cleveland (A)	14	8	.636	2.96	34	216	174	98	142
1983	Cleveland (A)	17	11	.633	4.29	36	243.1	251	102	160
	Seven years	53	40	.580	3.96	168	865.1	809	374	497

DON SUTTON B. April 2, 1945, Clio, Ala.
Right handed, B.R.
6'1" 185 lbs.

YEAR	CLUB	W	L	PCT	ERA	G	IP	H	BB	SO
1966	LOS ANGELES (N)	12	12	.500	2.99	37	225.2	192	52	209
1967	LOS ANGELES (N)	11	15	.423	3.95	37	232.2	223	57	169
1968	LOS ANGELES (N)	11	15	.423	2.60	35	207.2	179	59	162
1969	LOS ANGELES (N)	17	18	.486	3.47	41	293	269	91	217
1970	LOS ANGELES (N)	15	13	.536	4.08	38	260	251	78	201
1971	LOS ANGELES (N)	17	12	.586	2.55	38	265	231	55	194
1972	LOS ANGELES (N)	19	9	.679	2.08	33	272.2	186	63	207
1973	LOS ANGELES (N)	18	10	.643	2.42	33	256.1	196	56	200
1974	LOS ANGELES (N)	19	9	.679	3.23	40	276	241	80	179
1975	LOS ANGELES (N)	16	13	.552	2.87	35	254	202	62	175
1976	LOS ANGELES (N)	21	10	.677	3.06	35	267.2	231	82	161
1977	LOS ANGELES (N)	14	8	.636	3.19	33	240	207	69	150
1978	LOS ANGELES (N)	15	11	.577	3.55	34	238	228	54	154
1979	LOS ANGELES (N)	12	15	.444	3.82	33	226	201	61	146
1980	LOS ANGELES (N)	13	5	.722	2.21	32	212	163	47	128
1981	Houston (N)	11	9	.550	2.60	23	159	132	29	104
*1982	Houston-Milwaukee (A)	17	9	.570	3.29	34	249.2	224	64	175
	Seventeen years	258	193	.572	3.05	591	4136	3556	1059	2931
League Championship										
	Three years	3	1	.750	1.71	4	31.2	23	4	17

*Traded Aug. 31, 1982
World Series

YEAR	CLUB	W	L	PCT	ERA	G	IP	H	BB	SO
1974	LOS ANGELES (N)	1	0	1.000	2.77	2	13	9	3	12
1977	LOS ANGELES (N)	1	0	1.000	3.94	2	16	17	1	6
1978	LOS ANGELES (N)	0	2	.000	7.49	2	12	17	4	8
	Three years	2	2	.500	4.61	6	41	43	8	26

BILL SWIFT B. Jan. 10, 1908, Elmira, N.Y.
D. Feb. 23, 1969, Bartow, Fla.
Right handed, B.R.
6'1½" 192 lbs.

YEAR	CLUB	W	L	PCT	ERA	G	IP	H	BB	SO
1941	BROOKLYN (N)	3	0	1.000	3.27	9	22	26	7	9
	Eleven years (totals)	95	82	.537	3.58	336	1637.2	1682	351	636

VITO TAMULIS B. July 11, 1911, Cambridge, Mass.
D. May 5, 1974, Nashville, Tenn.
Left handed, B.L.
5'9" 170 lbs.

YEAR	CLUB	W	L	PCT	ERA	G	IP	H	BB	SO
1934	New York (A)	1	0	1.000	0.00	1	9	7	1	5
1935	New York (A)	10	5	.667	4.09	30	160.2	178	55	57
1938	St. Louis (A)									
1938	BROOKLYN (N)	12	6	.667		38	160		40	70
	(year totals)	12	9	.571	4.17	41	175	207	50	81
1939	BROOKLYN (N)	9	8	.529	4.37	39	158.2	177	45	83
1940	BROOKLYN (N)	8	5	.615	3.09	41	154.1	147	34	55

YEAR	CLUB	W	L	PCT	ERA	G	IP	H	BB	SO
1941	Philadelphia (N)				3.68	12	24		10	8
1941	BROOKLYN (N)	0	0	—						
	(year totals)	0	1	.000	5.56	18	34	42	17	13
	Six years	40	28	.588	3.97	170	691.2	758	202	294

HARRY TAYLOR   B. May 20, 1919, East Glenn, Ind.
Right handed, B.R.
6'1" 175 lbs.

YEAR	CLUB	W	L	PCT	ERA	G	IP	H	BB	SO
1946	BROOKLYN (N)	0	0	—	3.86	4	4.2	5	1	6
1947	BROOKLYN (N)	10	5	.667	3.11	33	162	130	83	58
1948	BROOKLYN (N)	2	7	.222	5.36	17	80.2	90	61	32
	Six years (totals)	19	21	.475	4.10	90	357.2	344	201	127
World Series										
	One year	0	0	—	0.00	1		2	1	0

CHUCK TEMPLETON   B. June 1, 1932, Detroit, Mich.
Left handed, B.R.
6'3" 210 lbs.

YEAR	CLUB	W	L	PCT	ERA	G	IP	H	BB	SO
1955	BROOKLYN (N)	0	1	.000	11.57	4	4.2	5	5	3
1956	BROOKLYN (N)	0	1	.000	6.61	6	16.1	20	10	8
	Two years	0	2	.000	7.71	10	21	25	15	11

ADONIS TERRY   B. Aug. 7, 1864, Westfield, Mass.
D. Feb. 24, 1915, Milwaukee, Wis.
Right handed, B.R.

YEAR	CLUB	W	L	PCT	ERA	G	IP	H	BB	SO
*1890	BROOKLYN (N)	26	16	.619	2.94	46	370	362	133	185
1891	BROOKLYN (N)	6	16	.273	4.22	25	194	207	8;	65
1892	Baltimore (N)									
1892	Pittsburgh (N)									
	(.year totals)	17	8	.680	2.57	31	249	192	113	98
1893	Pittsburgh (N)	12	8	.600	4.45	26	170	177	99	52
1894	Pittsburgh (N)									
1894	Chicago (N)									
	(year totals)	5	12	.294	6.09	24	164	234	127	39
1895	Chicago (N)	21	14	.600	4.80	38	311.1	346	131	88
1896	Chicago (N)	15	13	.536	4.28	30	235.1	268	88	74
1897	Chicago (N)	0	1	.000	10.13	1	8	11	6	1
	Fourteen years	197	195	.503	3.72	441	3523	3521	1301	1555

*1884 Brooklyn (AA)

GRANT THATCHER   B. Feb. 23, 1877, Maytown, Pa.
D. March 17, 1936, Lancaster, Pa.
Right handed
5'10½" 180 lbs.

YEAR	CLUB	W	L	PCT	ERA	G	IP	H	BB	SO
1903	BROOKLYN (N)	3	1	.750	2.89	4	28	33	7	9
1904	BROOKLYN (N)	1	0	1.000	4.00	1	9	9	2	4
	Two years	4	1	.800	3.16	5	37	42	9	13

HENRY THIELMAN   B. Oct. 30, 1880, St. Cloud, Minn.
D. Sept. 2, 1942
Right handed, B.R.
5'11" 175 lbs.

YEAR	CLUB	W	L	PCT	ERA	G	IP	H	BB	SO
1903	BROOKLYN (N)	0	3	.000	4.66	4	29	31	14	10
	Two years (totals)	8	19	.296	3.37	31	246	240	98	64

FAY THOMAS
B. Oct. 10, 1904, Holyrood, Kan.
Right handed, B.R.
6'2" 195 lbs.

YEAR	CLUB	W	L	PCT	ERA	G	IP	H	BB	SO
1932	BROOKLYN (N)	0	1	.000	7.41	7	14	22	8	9
	Four years (totals)	9	20	.310	4.95	81	229	269	133	112

HANK THORMAHLEN
B. July 5, 1896, Jersey City, N.J.
D. Feb. 6, 1955, Hollywood, Calif.
Left handed, B.L.
6' 180 lbs.

YEAR	CLUB	W	L	PCT	ERA	G	IP	H	BB	SO
1925	BROOKLYN (N)	0	3	.000	3.94	5	16	22	9	7
	Six years (totals)	30	30	.500	3.33	104	565	550	203	148

SLOPPY THURSTON
B. June 2, 1899, Fremont, Neb.
D. Sept. 14, 1973, Los Angeles, Calif.
Right handed, B.R.
5'11' 165 lbs.

YEAR	CLUB	W	L	PCT	ERA	G	IP	H	BB	SO
1923	St. Louis (A)									
1923	Chicago (A)									
	(year totals)	7	8	.467	3.13	46	195.2	231	38	55
1924	Chicago (A)	20	14	.588	3.80	38	291	330	60	37
1925	Chicago (A)	10	14	.417	6.17	36	175	250	47	35
1926	Chicago (A)	6	8	.429	5.02	31	134.1	164	36	35
1927	Washington (A)	13	13	.500	4.47	29	205.1	254	60	38
1930	BROOKLYN (N)	6	4	.600	3.40	24	106	110	17	26
1931	BROOKLYN (N)	9	9	.500	3.97	24	143	175	39	23
1932	BROOKLYN (N)	12	8	.600	4.06	28	153	174	38	35
1933	BROOKLYN (N)	6	8	.429	4.52	32	131.1	171	34	22
	Nine years	89	86	.509	4.26	288	1534.2	1859	369	306

FRED UNDERWOOD
B. 1869, Kansas
D. Jan. 26, 1906, Kansas City, Mo.

YEAR	CLUB	W	L	PCT	ERA	G	IP	H	BB	SO
1894	BROOKLYN (N)	2	4	.333	7.85	7	47	80	30	10

BILL UPHAM
B. April 4, 1888, Akron, Ohio
D. Sept. 14, 1959, Newark, N.J.
Right handed, B.R.
6' 178 lbs.

YEAR	CLUB	W	L	PCT	ERA	G	IP	H	BB	SO
1915	BROOKLYN (F)	7	8	.467	3.05	33	121	129	40	46
	Two years (totals)	8	9	.471	3.37	36	141.2	157	41	54

RENE VALDES
B. June 2, 1929, Guanabocco, Cuba
Right handed, B.R.
6'3" 175 lbs.

YEAR	CLUB	W	L	PCT	ERA	G	IP	H	BB	SO
1957	BROOKLYN (N)	1	1	.500	5.54	5	13	13	7	10

FERNANDO VALENZUELA
B. Nov. 1, 1960, Sonora, Mexico
Left handed, B.L.
5'11" 180 lbs.

YEAR	CLUB	W	L	PCT	ERA	G	IP	H	BB	SO
1980	LOS ANGELES (N)	2	0	1.000	0.00	10	18	8	5	16
1981	LOS ANGELES (N)	13	7	.650	2.48	25	192	140	61	180
1982	LOS ANGELES (N)	19	13	.593	2.87	37	285	247	83	199
1983	LOS ANGELES (N)	15	10	.600	3.75	35	257	245	99	189
	Four years	49	30	.645	3.00	107	752	640	248	554

YEAR	CLUB	W	L	PCT	ERA	G	IP	H	BB	SO
Divisional Playoff										
	One year	1	0	1.000	1.06	2	17	10	3	10
League Championship										
	One year	1	1	.500	2.45	2	14.2	10	5	10
World Series										
	One year	1	0	1.000	4.00	1	9	9	7	6

DAZZY VANCE B. March 4, 1891, Orient, Iowa
D. Feb. 16, 1961, Homosassa Springs, Fla.
Right handed, B.R.
6'2" 200 lbs.

YEAR	CLUB	W	L	PCT	ERA	G	IP	H	BB	SO
1915	Pittsburgh (N)									
1915	New York (A)									
	(year totals)	0	4	.000	4.11	9	30.2	26	21	18
1918	New York (A)	0	0	—	15.43	2	2.1	9	2	0
1922	BROOKLYN (N)	18	12	.600	3.70	36	245.2	259	94	134
1923	BROOKLYN (N)	18	15	.545	3.50	37	280.1	263	100	197
1924	BROOKLYN (N)	28	6	.824	2.16	35	308.2	238	77	262
1925	BROOKLYN (N)	22	9	.710	3.53	31	265.1	247	66	221
1926	BROOKLYN (N)	9	10	.474	3.89	24	169	172	58	140
1927	BROOKLYN (N)	16	15	.516	2.70	34	273.1	242	69	184
1928	BROOKLYN (N)	22	10	.688	2.09	38	280.1	226	72	200
1929	BROOKLYN (N)	14	13	.519	3.89	31	231.1	244	47	126
1930	BROOKLYN (N)	17	15	.531	2.61	35	258.2	241	55	173
1931	BROOKLYN (N)	11	13	.458	3.38	30	218.2	221	53	150
1932	BROOKLYN (N)	12	11	.522	4.20	27	275.2	171	57	103
1933	St. Louis (N)	6	2	.750	3.55	28	99	105	28	67
1934	St. Louis (N)									
1934	Cincinnati (N)									
	(year totals)	1	3	.250	4.56	25	77	90	25	42
1935	BROOKLYN (N)	3	2	.600	4.41	20	51	55	16	28
	Sixteen years	197	140	.585	3.24	442	2967	2809	840	2045
World Series										
	One year	0	0	—	0.00	1	1.1	2	1	3

SANDY VANCE B. Jan. 5, 1947, Lamar, Colo.
Right handed, B.R.
6'2" 180 lbs.

YEAR	CLUB	W	L	PCT	ERA	G	IP	H	BB	SO
1970	LOS ANGELES (N)	7	7	.500	3.13	20	115	109	37	45
1971	LOS ANGELES (N)	2	1	.667	6.92	10	26	38	9	11
	Two years	9	8	.529	3.83	30	141	147	46	56

CHRIS VAN CUYK B. March 1, 1927, Kimberly, Wis.
Left handed, B.L.
6'6" 215 lbs.

YEAR	CLUB	W	L	PCT	ERA	G	IP	H	BB	SO
1950	BROOKLYN (N)	1	3	.250	4.86	12	33.1	33	12	21
1951	BROOKLYN (N)	1	2	.333	5.52	9	29.1	33	11	16
1952	BROOKLYN (N)	5	6	.455	5.16	23	97.2	104	40	66
	Three years	7	11	.389	5.16	44	160.1	63	170	103

JOHNNY VAN CUYK B. July 7, 1921, Little Chute, Wis.
Left handed, B.L.
6'1" 190 lbs.

YEAR	CLUB	W	L	PCT	ERA	G	IP	H	BB	SO
1947	BROOKLYN (N)	0	0	—	5.40	2	3.1	5	1	2
1948	BROOKLYN (N)	0	0	—	3.60	3	5	4	1	1
1949	BROOKLYN (N)	0	0	—	9.00	2	2	3	1	0
	Three years	0	0	—	5.23	7	10.1	12	3	3

GEORGE VAN HALTREN
B. March 30, 1866, St. Louis, Mo.
D. Sept. 29, 1945, Oakland, Calif.
Left handed, B.L.
5'11" 170 lbs.

YEAR	CLUB	W	L	PCT	ERA	G	IP	H	BB	SO
1890	BROOKLYN (P)	15	10	.600	4.28	28	223	272	89	48
	Nine years (totals)	40	31	.563	4.05	93	689.1	809	244	281

JOE VERNON
B. Nov. 25, 1889, Mansfield, Mass.
D. March 13, 1955, Philadelphia, Pa.
Right handed, B.R.

YEAR	CLUB	W	L	PCT	ERA	G	IP	H	BB	SO
1914	BROOKLYN (F)	0	0	—	10.80	1	3.1	4	5	0
	Two years (totals)	0	0	—	11.05	2	7.1	8	11	1

RUBE VICKERS
B. May 17, 1878, Pittsford, Mich.
D. Dec. 9, 1958, Belleville, Mich.
Right handed, B.R.
6'2" 225 lbs.

YEAR	CLUB	W	L	PCT	ERA	G	IP	H	BB	SO
1903	BROOKLYN (N)	0	1	.000	10.93	4	14	27	9	5
	Five years (totals)	23	28	.451	3.04	88	441	426	119	213

PAUL WACHTEL
B. April 30, 1888, Myersville, Md.
D. Dec. 15, 1964, San Antonio, Texas
Right handed, B.R.
5'11" 175 lbs.

YEAR	CLUB	W	L	PCT	ERA	G	IP	H	BB	SO
1917	BROOKLYN (N)	0	0	—	10.50	2	6	9	4	3

BEN WADE
B. Nov. 26, 1922, Morehead City, N.C.
Right handed, B.R.
6'3" 195 lbs.

YEAR	CLUB	W	L	PCT	ERA	G	IP	H	BB	SO
1948	Chicago (N)	0	1	.000	7.20	2	5	4	4	1
1952	BROOKLYN (N)	11	9	.550	3.60	37	180	166	94	118
1953	BROOKLYN (N)	7	5	.583	3.79	32	90.1	79	33	65
1954	BROOKLYN (N)	1	1	.500	8.20	23	45		21	25
1954	St. Louis (N)									
	(year totals)	1	1	.500	7.28	36	68	89	36	44
1955	Pittsburgh (N)	0	1	.000	3.21	11	28	26	14	7
	Five years	19	17	.528	4.34	118	371.1	364	181	235
World Series										
	One year	0	0	—	15.43	2	2.1	4	1	2

BULL WAGNER
B. Jan. 1, 1887, Lillie, Mich.
D. Oct. 2, 1967, Muskegon, Mich.
Right handed, B.R.
6'½" 225 lbs.

YEAR	CLUB	W	L	PCT	ERA	G	IP	H	BB	SO
1913	BROOKLYN (N)	3	2	.600	5.48	18	70.2	77	30	11
1914	BROOKLYN (N)	0	1	.000	6.57	6	12.1	14	12	4
	Two years	3	3	.500	5.64	24	83	91	42	15

MYSTERIOUS WALKER
B. March 21, 1884, Utica, Neb.
D. Feb. 1, 1958, Oak Park, Ill.
Right handed, B.R.

YEAR	CLUB	W	L	PCT	ERA	G	IP	H	BB	SO
1913	BROOKLYN (N)	1	3	.250	3.55	11	58.1	44	35	35
1915	BROOKLYN (N)	2	4	.333	3.70	13	65.2	61	22	28
	Four years (totals)	6	23	.207	4.01	60	296.1	306	135	143

STAN WALL B. June 15, 1951, Butler, Mo.
Left handed, B.L.
6'1" 175 lbs.

YEAR	CLUB	W	L	PCT	ERA	G	IP	H	BB	SO
1975	LOS ANGELES (N)	0	1	.000	1.69	10	16	12	7	6
1976	LOS ANGELES (N)	2	2	.500	3.60	31	50	50	15	27
1977	LOS ANGELES (N)	2	3	.400	5.34	25	32	36	13	22
	Three years	4	6	.400	3.86	66	98	98	35	55

TOMMY WARREN B. July 5, 1920, Tulsa, Okla.
D. Jan. 2, 1968, Tulsa, Okla.
Right handed, B.L.
6'1" 190 lbs.

YEAR	CLUB	W	L	PCT	ERA	G	IP	H	BB	SO
1944	BROOKLYN (N)	1	4	.200	4.98	22	68.2	74	40	18

HANK WEBB B. May 21, 1950, Amityville, N.Y.
Right handed, B.R.
6'3" 175 lbs.

YEAR	CLUB	W	L	PCT	ERA	G	IP	H	BB	SO
1977	LOS ANGELES (N)	0	0	—	2.25	5	8	5	1	2
	Six years (totals)	7	9	.438	4.31	53	169	159	91	71

LES WEBBER B. May 6, 1915, Lakeport, Calif.
Right handed, B.R.
6'1½" 185 lbs.

YEAR	CLUB	W	L	PCT	ERA	G	IP	H	BB	SO
1942	BROOKLYN (N)	3	2	.600	2.96	19	51.2	46	22	23
1943	BROOKLYN (N)	2	2	.500	3.81	54	115.2	112	69	24
1944	BROOKLYN (N)	7	8	.467	4.94	48	140.1	157	64	42
1945	BROOKLYN (N)	7	3	.700	3.58	17	75.1	69	25	30
1946	BROOKLYN (N)	3	3	.500	2.30	11	43		15	16
1946	Cleveland (A)									
	(year totals)	4	4	.500	4.66	15	48.1	47	20	21
1948	Cleveland (A)	0	0	—	40.50	1	.2	3	1	1
	Six years	23	19	.548	4.19	154	432	434	201	141

BOB WELCH B. Nov. 3, 1956, Detroit, Mich.
Right handed, B.R.
6'3" 190 lbs.

YEAR	CLUB	W	L	PCT	ERA	G	IP	H	BB	SO
1978	LOS ANGELES (N)	7	4	.636	2.03	23	111	92	26	66
1979	LOS ANGELES (N)	5	6	.455	4.00	25	81	82	32	64
1980	LOS ANGELES (N)	14	9	.609	3.28	32	214	190	79	141
1981	LOS ANGELES (N)	9	5	.643	3.45	23	141	141	41	88
1982	LOS ANGELES (N)	16	11	.593	3.36	36	235.2	199	81	176
	Five years	51	35	.593	3.23	139	782.2	704	259	535

Divisional Playoff
| | One year | 0 | 0 | — | 0.00 | 1 | 1 | 0 | 1 | 1 |

League Championship
| | Two years | 1 | 0 | 1.000 | 3.00 | 4 | 6 | 4 | 0 | 7 |

World Series

YEAR	CLUB	W	L	PCT	ERA	G	IP	H	BB	SO
1978	LOS ANGELES (N)	0	1	.000	6.23	3	4.1	4	2	6
1981	LOS ANGELES (N)	1	0	1.000	—	1	0	3	1	0
	Two years	1	1	.500		4	4.1	7	3	6

JOHN WELLS

B. Nov. 25, 1923, Junction City, Kan.
Right handed, B.R.
5'11½" 180 lbs.

YEAR	CLUB	W	L	PCT	ERA	G	IP	H	BB	SO
1944	BROOKLYN (N)	0	2	.000	5.40	4	15	18	11	7

GUS WEYHING

B. Sept. 29, 1866, Louisville, Ky.
D. Sept. 3, 1955, Louisville, Ky.
Right handed, B.R.
5'10" 145 lbs.

YEAR	CLUB	W	L	PCT	ERA	G	IP	H	BB	SO
*1890	BROOKLYN (N)	30	16	.652	3.60	49	390	419	179	177
1891	Philadelphia (AA)	31	20	.608	3.18	52	450	428	161	219
1892	Philadelphia (N)	32	21	.604	2.66	59	469.2	411	168	202
1893	Philadelphia (N)	23	16	.590	4.74	42	345.1	399	145	101
1894	Philadelphia (N)	16	14	.533	5.81	38	266.1	365	116	81
1895	Philadelphia (N)									
1895	Pittsburgh (N)									
1895	Louisville (N)									
	(year totals)	8	21	.276	5.81	31	231	318	84	61
1896	Louisville (N)	2	3	.400	6.64	5	42	62	15	9
1898	Washington (N)	15	26	.366	4.51	45	361	428	84	92
1899	Washington (N)	17	23	.425	4.54	43	334.2	414	76	96
1900	St. Louis (N)									
1900	BROOKLYN (N)	3	4	.429	4.40	8	47		21	8
	(year totals)	6	6	.500	4.47	15	94.2	126	41	14
1901	Cleveland (A)									
1901	Cincinnati (N)									
	(year totals)	0	1	.000	5.75	3	20.1	31	7	3
	Fourteen years	264	234	.530	3.89	538	4324.1	4562	1566	1665

*1887 Philadelphia (AA)

JESSE WHITING

B. Unknown

YEAR	CLUB	W	L	PCT	ERA	G	IP	H	BB	SO
1906	BROOKLYN (N)	1	1	.500	2.92	3	24.2	26	6	7
1907	BROOKLYN (N)	0	0	—	12.00	1	3	3	3	2
	Three years (totals)	1	2	.333	4.17	5	36.2	42	15	9

KEMP WICKER

B. Aug. 13, 1906, Kernersville, N.C.
D. June 11, 1973, Kernersville, N.C.
Left handed, B.R.
5'11" 182 lbs.

YEAR	CLUB	W	L	PCT	ERA	G	IP	H	BB	SO
1941	BROOKLYN (N)	1	2	.333	3.66	16	32	30	14	8
	Four years (totals)	10	7	.588	4.66	40	141	168	52	27
World Series										
	One year	0	0	—	0.00	1	1	0	0	0

HOYT WILHELM

B. July 26, 1923, Huntersville, N.C.
Right handed, B.R.
6' 190 lbs.

YEAR	CLUB	W	L	PCT	ERA	G	IP	H	BB	SO
1971	LOS ANGELES (N)	0	1	—	1.00	9	18		4	15
1972	LOS ANGELES (N)	0	1	.000	4.62	16	25.1	20	15	9
	Twenty-one years (totals)	143	122	.540	2.52	1070	2254	1757	778	1610

KAISER WILHELM

B. Jan. 26, 1874, Wooster, Ohio
D. May 21, 1936, Rochester, N.Y.
Right handed, B.R.
6' 162 lbs.

YEAR	CLUB	W	L	PCT	ERA	G	IP	H	BB	SO
1903	Pittsburgh (N)	5	4	.556	3.24	12	86	88	25	20
1904	Boston (N)	14	22	.389	3.69	39	288	316	74	73
1905	Boston (N)	4	22	.154	4.54	34	242	287	75	76
1908	BROOKLYN (N)	15	21	.417	1.87	42	332	266	83	99
1909	BROOKLYN (N)	3	13	.188	3.26	22	163	176	59	45
1910	BROOKLYN (N)	3	6	.333	4.74	15	68.1	88	18	17
1914	Baltimore (F)	13	17	.433	4.03	47	243.2	263	81	113
1915	Baltimore (F)	0	0	—	0.00	1	1	0	0	0
1921	Philadelphia (N)	0	0	—	3.38	4	8	11	3	1
	Nine years	57	105	.352	3.44	216	1432	1495	418	444

NICK WILLHITE

B. Jan. 27, 1941, Tulsa, Okla.
Left handed, B.L.
6'2" 190 lbs.

YEAR	CLUB	W	L	PCT	ERA	G	IP	H	BB	SO
1963	LOS ANGELES (N)	2	3	.400	3.79	8	38	44	10	28
1964	LOS ANGELES (N)	2	4	.333	3.71	10	43.2	43	13	24
1965	LOS ANGELES (N)	2	2	.500	5.36	15	42		22	28
1966	LOS ANGELES (N)	0	0	—	2.08	6	4.1	3	5	4
	Five years (totals)	6	12	.333	4.55	58	182	195	75	118

LEON WILLIAMS

B. Dec. 2, 1905, Macon, Ga.
Left handed, B.L.
5'10½" 154 lbs.

YEAR	CLUB	W	L	PCT	ERA	G	IP	H	BB	SO
1926	BROOKLYN (N)	0	0	—	5.40	8	8.1	16	2	3

STAN WILLIAMS

B. Sept. 14, 1936, Enfield, N.H.
Right handed, B.R.
6'5" 230 lbs.

YEAR	CLUB	W	L	PCT	ERA	G	IP	H	BB	SO
1958	LOS ANGELES (N)	9	7	.563	4.01	27	119	99	65	80
1959	LOS ANGELES (N)	5	5	.500	3.97	35	124.2	102	86	89
1960	LOS ANGELES (N)	14	10	.583	3.00	38	207.1	162	72	175
1961	LOS ANGELES (N)	15	12	.556	3.90	41	235.1	213	108	205
1962	LOS ANGELES (N)	14	12	.538	4.46	40	185.2	184	98	108
1963	New York (A)	9	8	.529	3.20	29	146.1	137	57	98
1964	New York (A)	1	5	.167	3.84	21	82	76	38	54
1965	Cleveland (A)	0	0	—	6.23	3	4.1	6	3	1
1967	Cleveland (A)	6	4	.600	2.62	16	79	64	24	75
1968	Cleveland (A)	13	11	.542	2.50	44	194.1	163	51	147
1969	Cleveland (A)	6	14	.300	3.94	61	178.1	155	67	139
1970	Minnesota (A)	10	1	.909	1.99	68	113	85	32	76
1971	Minnesota (A)									
1971	St. Louis (N)									
	(year totals)	7	5	.583	3.76	56	91	76	46	55
1972	Boston (A)	0	0	—	6.75	3	4	5	1	3
	Fourteen years	109	94	.537	3.48	482	1764.1	1527	748	1305
League Championship										
	One year	0	0	—	0.00	2	6	2	1	2
World Series										
	Two years	0	0	—	0.00	2	5	1	2	6

FIN WILSON

B. Dec. 9, 1891, East Cork, Ky.
D. March 9, 1959, Coral Gables, Fla.
Left handed, B.L.
6'1" 194 lbs.

YEAR	CLUB	W	L	PCT	ERA	G	IP	H	BB	SO
1914	BROOKLYN (F)	0	1	.000	7.71	2	7	7	11	4
1915	BROOKLYN (F)	1	7	.125	3.78	18	102.1	85	53	47
	Two years	1	8	.111	4.03	20	109.1	92	64	51

TEX WILSON
B. July 8, 1901, Trenton, Texas
D. Sept. 15, 1946, Sulphur Springs, Texas
Left handed, B.R.
5'10" 170 lbs.

YEAR	CLUB	W	L	PCT	ERA	G	IP	H	BB	SO
1924	BROOKLYN (N)	0	0	—	14.73	2	3.2	7	1	1

HOOKS WILTSE
B. Sept. 7, 1880, Hamilton, N.Y.
D. Jan. 21, 1959, Long Beach, N.Y.
Left handed, B.R.
6' 185 lbs.

YEAR	CLUB	W	L	PCT	ERA	G	IP	H	BB	SO
1915	BROOKLYN (F)	3	5	.375	2.28	18	59.1	49	7	17
	Twelve years (totals)	141	90	.610	2.47	357	2112.1	1892	498	965

JIM WINFORD
B. Oct. 9, 1909, Shelbyville, Tenn.
D. Dec. 16, 1970, Oakland, Calif.
Right handed, B.R.
6'1" 180 lbs.

YEAR	CLUB	W	L	PCT	ERA	G	IP	H	BB	SO
1938	BROOKLYN (N)	0	1	.000	11.12	2	5.2	9	4	4
	Six years (totals)	14	18	.438	4.56	68	276.1	307	115	109

LAVE WINHAM
B. 1881, Brooklyn, N.Y.
D. Sept. 11, 1951, Brooklyn, N.Y.
Left handed

YEAR	CLUB	W	L	PCT	ERA	G	IP	H	BB	SO
1902	BROOKLYN (N)	0	0	—	0.00	1	3	4	2	1
	Two years (totals)	3	1	.750	2.08	6	39	37	23	23

TOM WINSETT
B. Nov. 24, 1909, McKenzie, Tenn.
Right handed, B.L.
6'2" 190 lbs.

YEAR	CLUB	W	L	PCT	ERA	G	IP	H	BB	SO
1937	BROOKLYN (N)	0	0	—	18.00	1	1	3	2	0

HANK WINSTON
B. June 15, 1904, Youngsville, N.C.
D. Feb. 7, 1974, Jacksonville, Fla.
Right handed, B.L.
6'3½" 226 lbs.

YEAR	CLUB	W	L	PCT	ERA	G	IP	H	BB	SO
1936	BROOKLYN (N)	1	3	.250	6.12	14	32.1	40	16	8
	Two years (totals)	1	3	.250	6.23	15	39	47	22	10

PETE WOJEY
B. Dec. 1, 1919, Stowe, Pa.
Right handed, B.R.
5'11" 185 lbs.

YEAR	CLUB	W	L	PCT	ERA	G	IP	H	BB	SO
1954	BROOKLYN (N)	1	1	.500	3.25	14	27.2	24	14	21
	Three years (totals)	1	1	.500	3.00	18	33	27	15	22

CLARENCE WRIGHT
B. Dec. 11, 1878, Cleveland, Ohio
D. Oct. 29, 1930, Barbeton, Ohio
Right handed, B.R.

YEAR	CLUB	W	L	PCT	ERA	G	IP	H	BB	SO
1901	BROOKLYN (N)	1	0	1.000	1.00	1	9	6	1	6
	Four years (totals)	14	26	.350	4.50	46	323.2	361	152	140

FRANK WURM

B. April 27, 1924, Cambridge, N.Y.
Left handed, B.B.
6'1" 175 lbs.

YEAR	CLUB	W	L	PCT	ERA	G	IP	H	BB	SO
1944	BROOKLYN (N)	0	0	—	108.00	1	.1	1	5	1

WHIT WYATT

B. Sept. 27, 1907, Kensington, Ga.
Right handed, B.R.
6'1" 185 lbs.

YEAR	CLUB	W	L	PCT	ERA	G	IP	H	BB	SO
1929	Detroit (A)	0	1	.000	6.75	4	25.1	30	18	14
1930	Detroit (A)	4	5	.444	3.57	21	85.2	76	35	68
1931	Detroit (A)	0	2	.000	8.44	4	21.1	30	12	8
1932	Detroit (A)	9	13	.409	5.03	43	205.2	228	102	82
1933	Detroit (A)									
1933	Chicago (A)									
	(year totals)	3	5	.375	4.56	36	104.2	111	54	40
1934	Chicago (A)	4	11	.267	7.18	23	67.2	83	37	36
1935	Chicago (A)	4	3	.571	6.75	30	52	65	25	22
1936	Chicago (A)	0	0	—	0.00	3	3	3	0	0
1937	Cleveland (A)	2	3	.400	4.44	29	73	67	40	52
1939	BROOKLYN (N)	8	3	.727	2.31	16	109	88	39	52
1940	BROOKLYN (N)	15	14	.517	3.46	37	239.1	233	62	124
1941	BROOKLYN (N)	22	10	.688	2.34	38	288.1	223	82	176
1942	BROOKLYN (N)	19	7	.731	2.73	31	217.1	185	63	104
1943	BROOKLYN (N)	14	5	.737	2.49	26	180.2	139	43	80
1944	BROOKLYN (N)	2	6	.250	7.17	9	37.2	51	16	4
1945	Philadelphia (N)	0	7	.000	5.26	10	51.1	72	14	10
	Sixteen years	106	95	.527	3.78	360	1762	1684	642	872
World Series										
	One year	1	1	.500	2.50	2	18	15	10	14

RUBE YARRISON

B. March 9, 1896, Montgomery, Pa.
Right handed, B.R.
5'11" 165 lbs.

YEAR	CLUB	W	L	PCT	ERA	G	IP	H	BB	SO
1924	BROOKLYN (N)	0	2	.000	6.55	3	11	12	3	2
	Two years	1	4	.200	7.86	21	44.2	62	15	12

JOE YEAGER

B. Aug. 28, 1875, Philadelphia, Pa.
D. July 2, 1937, Detroit, Mich.
Right handed

YEAR	CLUB	W	L	PCT	ERA	G	IP	H	BB	SO
1898	BROOKLYN (N)	12	22	.353	3.65	36	291.1	333	80	70
1899	BROOKLYN (N)	2	2	.500	4.72	10	47.2	56	16	6
1900	BROOKLYN (N)	1	1	.500	6.88	2	17	21	5	2
1901	Detroit (A)	12	11	.522	2.61	26	199.2	209	46	38
1902	Detroit (A)	6	12	.333	4.82	19	140	171	41	28
1903	Detroit (A)	0	1	.000	4.00	1	9	15	0	1
	Six years	33	49	.402	3.74	94	704.2	805	188	145

EARL YINGLING

B. Oct. 29, 1888, Chillicothe, Ohio
D. Oct. 2, 1962, Columbus, Ohio
Left handed, B.L.
5'11½" 180 lbs.

YEAR	CLUB	W	L	PCT	ERA	G	IP	H	BB	SO
1911	Cleveland (A)	1	0	1.000	4.43	4	22.1	30	9	6
1912	BROOKLYN (N)	6	11	.353	3.59	25	163	186	56	51
1913	BROOKLYN (N)	8	8	.500	2.58	26	146.2	158	10	40
1914	Cincinnati (N)	8	13	.381	3.45	34	198	207	54	80
1918	Washington (A)	1	2	.333	2.13	5	38	30	12	15
	Five years	24	34	.414	3.22	94	568	611	141	192

CHINK ZACHARY B. Oct. 19, 1917, Brooklyn, N.Y.
Right handed, B.R.
5'11" 182 lbs.

YEAR	CLUB	W	L	PCT	ERA	G	IP	H	BB	SO
1944	BROOKLYN (N)	0	2	.000	9.58	4	10.1	10	7	3

TOM ZACHARY B. May 7, 1896, Graham, N.C.
D. Jan. 24, 1969, Graham, N.C.
Left handed, B.L.
6'1" 187 lbs.

YEAR	CLUB	W	L	PCT	ERA	G	IP	H	BB	SO
1935	BROOKLYN (N)	7	12	.368	3.59	25	158	193	35	33
1936	BROOKLYN (N)	0	0	—		1	1		1	
	Nineteen years (totals)	185	191	.492	3.72	533	3134	3590	914	720

GEOFF ZAHN B. Dec. 19, 1946, Baltimore, Md.
Left handed, B.L.
6'1" 180 lbs.

YEAR	CLUB	W	L	PCT	ERA	G	IP	H	BB	SO
1973	LOS ANGELES (N)	1	0	1.000	1.35	6	13.1	5	2	9
1974	LOS ANGELES (N)	3	5	.375	2.03	21	80	78	16	33
1975	LOS ANGELES (N)	0	1	—	9.00	2	3		5	1
	Ten years (totals)	87	86	.503	3.88	240	1409	1522	413	549

THE DODGERS YEAR-BY-YEAR RECORD AND ROSTER

This section contains (1) the Dodgers National League record at a glance and (2) a capsulated compilation of the roster of players on the Dodger ballclub from 1890 to 1983, inclusive. The year-by-year statistical charts include:

The manager
Games won
Games lost
League standing
Team roster
Pitchers' records and batting averages
Players' positions, games played, and batting averages

For more detailed records or individual players, see Chapter II.

THE DODGERS NATIONAL LEAGUE RECORD AT A GLANCE

YEAR	TOTAL GAMES	WON	LOST	PERCENTAGE	FINISH	MANAGER
1890	129	86	43	.667	1	William McGunnigle
1891	137	61	76	.445	6	John Montgomery Ward
1892	154	95	59	.617	3	John Montgomery Ward
1893	128	65	63	.508	6	Dave Luther Foutz
1894	131	70	61	.534	5	Dave Luther Foutz
1895	131	71	60	.542	5	Dave Luther Foutz
1896	131	58	73	.443	9	Dave Luther Foutz
1897	132	61	71	.462	6	William Barnie
1898	145	54	91	.372	10	William Barnie
						Mike Griffin
						Charles Ebbets
1899	103	88	42	.667	1	Edward Hanlon
1900	136	82	54	.603	1	Edward Hanlon
1901	136	79	57	.581	3	Edward Hanlon
1902	138	75	63	.543	2	Edward Hanlon
1903	136	70	66	.515	5	Edward Hanlon
1904	153	56	97	.366	6	Edward Hanlon
1905	152	48	104	.316	8	Edward Hanlon
1906	152	66	86	.434	5	Patrick Donovan
1907	148	65	83	.439	5	Patrick Donovan
1908	154	53	101	.344	7	Patrick Donovan
1909	153	55	98	.359	6	Harry Lumley
1910	154	64	90	.416	6	William Dahlen
1911	150	64	86	.427	7	William Dahlen
1912	153	58	95	.379	7	William Dahlen
1913	149	65	84	.436	6	William Dahlen
1914	154	75	79	.487	5	Wilbert Robinson
1915	152	80	72	.527	3	Wilbert Robinson
1916	154	94	60	.610	1	Wilbert Robinson
1917	151	70	81	.464	7	Wilbert Robinson
1918	126	57	69	.452	5	Wilbert Robinson
1919	140	69	71	.493	5	Wilbert Robinson
1920	154	93	61	.604	1	Wilbert Robinson
1921	152	77	75	.507	5	Wilbert Robinson
1922	154	76	78	.494	6	Wilbert Robinson
1923	154	76	78	.494	6	Wilbert Robinson
1924	154	92	62	.597	2	Wilbert Robinson
1925	153	68	85	.444	6	Wilbert Robinson
1926	153	71	82	.464	6	Wilbert Robinson
1927	153	65	88	.425	6	Wilbert Robinson
1928	153	77	76	.503	6	Wilbert Robinson
1929	153	70	83	.458	6	Wilbert Robinson
1930	154	86	68	.558	4	Wilbert Robinson
1931	152	79	73	.520	4	Wilbert Robinson
1932	154	81	73	.526	3	Wilbert Robinson
1933	153	65	88	.425	6	Max Carey
1934	152	71	81	.467	6	Casey Stengel
1935	153	70	83	.458	5	Casey Stengel
1936	154	67	87	.435	7	Casey Stengel
1937	153	62	91	.405	6	Burleigh Grimes
1938	149	69	80	.463	7	Burleigh Grimes
1939	153	84	69	.549	3	Leo Durocher
1940	153	88	65	.575	2	Leo Durocher

250 • The Complete Dodgers Record Book

YEAR	TOTAL GAMES	WON	LOST	PERCENTAGE	FINISH	MANAGER
1941	154	100	54	.649	1	Leo Durocher
1942	154	104	50	.675	2	Leo Durocher
1943	153	81	72	.529	3	Leo Durocher
1944	154	63	91	.409	7	Leo Durocher
1945	154	87	67	.565	3	Leo Durocher
1946	156	96	60	.615	2	Leo Durocher
1947	154	94	60	.610	1	Clyde Sukeforth
1948						Burt Shotton
1948	154	84	70	.545	3	Leo Durocher
						Burt Shotton
1949	154	97	57	.630	1	Burt Shotton
1950	154	89	65	.578	2	Burt Shotton
1951	157	97	60	.618	2	Charlie Dressen
1952	153	96	57	.627	1	Charlie Dressen
1953	154	105	49	.682	1	Charlie Dressen
1954	154	92	62	.597	2	Walter Alston
1955	153	98	55	.641	1	Walter Alston
1956	154	93	61	.604	1	Walter Alston
1957	154	84	70	.545	3	Walter Alston
1958	154	71	83	.461	7	Walter Alston
1959	156	88	68	.564	1	Walter Alston
1960	154	82	72	.532	4	Walter Alston
1961	154	89	65	.578	2	Walter Alston
1962	165	102	63	.618	2	Walter Alston
1963	162	99	63	.611	1	Walter Alston
1964	162	80	82	.494	6	Walter Alston
1965	162	97	65	.599	1	Walter Alston
1966	162	95	67	.586	1	Walter Alston
1967	162	73	89	.451	8	Walter Alston
1968	162	76	86	.469	7	Walter Alston
1969	162	85	77	.525	4	Walter Alston
1970	161	87	74	.540	2	Walter Alston
1971	162	89	73	.549	2	Walter Alston
1972	155	85	70	.548	3	Walter Alston
1973	161	95	66	.590	2	Walter Alston
1974	162	102	60	.628	1	Walter Alston
1975	162	88	74	.543	2	Walter Alston
1976	162	92	70	.567	2	Walter Alston
1977	162	98	64	.604	1	Tommy Lasorda
1978	162	95	67	.586	1	Tommy Lasorda
1979	162	79	83	.487	3	Tommy Lasorda
1980	163	92	71	.564	2	Tommy Lasorda
1981	110	63	47	.572		Tommy Lasorda
(Splitseason: first half)		36	21		1	Tommy Lasorda
(Splitseason: second half)		27	26		4	
1982	162	88	74			
1983	162	91	71	.560	1	Tommy Lasorda

**The 1981 baseball strike shortened the season, which was played in two halves. **1981

THE YEAR-BY-RECORD AND ROSTER

1890 (First place)

WON—86
LOST—43
William Henry McGunnigle, Mgr.

PLAYER	POS.	W	L	G	BA
Pitchers					
Baldwin, C.		1	0	2	.000
Caruthers, R.		22	11	71	.265
Foutz, D.		3	1	129	.303
Hughes, M.		3	5	8	.043
Lovett, T.		30	11	44	.201
Terry, W.		26	15	99	.278

PLAYER	POS.	W	L	G	BA
Burns, O.	OF			119	.284
Bushong, A.	C			16	.234
Clark, R.	C			43	.218
Collins, H.	2B			129	.278
Corkhill, P.	OF			51	.225
Daly, T.	C			82	.243
Donovan, P.	OF			26	.380
O'Brien, W.	OF			85	.314
Pinckney, G.	3B			126	.309
Reynolds, C.		(Did not play)			
Smith, G.	SS			129	.191
Stallings, G.	C			4	.000

1891 (Sixth place)

WON—61
LOST—76
John Montgomery Ward, Mgr.

PLAYER	POS.	W	L	G	BA
Pitchers					
Caruthers, G.		18	14	47	.291
Foutz, D.		3	3	130	.257
Hemming, G.		8	15	22	.169
Inks, A.		3	10	13	.272
Lovett, T.		23	19	42	.184
Terry, W.		6	16	25	.202
Burdock, J.	2B			3	.083
Burns, O.	OF			122	.285
Collins, H.	2B			107	.276
Dailey, C.	C			53	.320
Daly, T.	C			61	.293
Ely, F.	SS			31	.171
Esterbrook, T.	2B			3	.375
Griffin, M.	OF			133	.272
Kinslow, T.	C			59	.238
O'Brien, J.	2B			43	.251
O'Brien, W.	OF			102	.260
Pinckney, G.	3B			135	.273
Ward, J. Mgr.	SS			104	.277

1892 (Third place)

WON—95
LOST—59
John Montgomery Ward, Mgr.

PLAYER	POS.	W	L	G	BA
Pitchers					
Foutz, D.	P-OF	13	8	53	.199
Haddock, G.		29	13	44	.173
Hart, W.		9	12	29	.187
Inks, A.		5	1	9	.375
Kennedy, W.		13	9	22	.188
Stein, E.		27	16	45	.218
Brouthers, D.	1B			152	.335
Burns, T.	OF			139	.315

PLAYER	POS.	W	L	G	BA
Collins, H.	OF			20	.302
Corcoran, T.	SS			151	.237
Dailey, C.	C			78	.243
Daly, T.	3B			120	.255
Griffin, M.	OF			129	.276
Joyce, W.	3B			97	.245
Kinslow, T.	C			63	.309
O'Brien, W.	OF			121	.245
Ward, J. Mgr.	2B			148	.265

1893 (Sixth place)

WON—65
LOST—63
David Luther Foutz, Mgr.

PLAYER	POS.	W	L	G	BA
Pitchers					
Crane, E.		0	2	6	.600
Daub, D.		6	6	12	.205
Haddock, G.		8	9	26	.250
Kennedy, W.		26	20	45	.275
Lovett, T.		3	6	18	.212
Sharrott, G.		4	6	11	.207
Stein, E.		19	15	35	.243
Brouthers, D.	1B			75	.337
Burns, T.	OF			107	.270
Corcoran, T.	SS			115	.275
Dailey, C.	C			58	.265
Daly, T.	2B			126	.289
Griffin, M.	OF			93	.293
Hatfield, G.	3B			33	.292
Keeler, W.	3B			19	.313
Kinslow, T.	C			77	.259
LaChance, G.	C			11	.176
Richardson, D.	2B			51	.223
Shoch, G.	OF			93	.263
Stovey, H.	OF			45	.251

1894 (Fifth place)

WON—70
LOST—61
David Luther Foutz, Mgr.

PLAYER	POS.	W	L	G	BA
Pitchers					
Daub, D.		9	12	28	.226
Gastright, H.				16	.184
Kennedy, W.		22	19	44	.300
Korwan, J.		0	0	1	.000
Lucid, C.		4	3	10	.212
Sharrott, G.		1	1	3	.570
Sommerville, A.		0	1	1	.000
Stein, E.		27	14	41	.260
Underwood, F.		2	3	7	.389

PLAYER	POS.	W	L	G	BA
Anderson, J.	OF			16	.301
Browning, L.	OF			1	1.000
Burns, T.	OF			126	.361
Corcoran, T.	SS			129	.300
Dailey, C.	C			65	.256
Daly, T.	2B			123	.341
Earle, W.	C			14	.321
Foutz, D. Mgr.	1B			73	.307
Gilbert, P.	3B			6	.000
Griffin, M.	OF			106	.365
Kinslow, T.	C			61	.305
LaChance, G.	1B			65	.323
Shindle, W.	3B			117	.300
Shoch, G.	OF			63	.320
Treadway, G.	OF			122	.328

1895 (Fifth place)

WON—71
LOST—60
David Luther Foutz, Mgr.

PLAYER	POS.	W	L	G	BA
Pitchers					
Abbey, B.		4	3	8	.263
Cronin, J.		0	0	2	.500
Daub, D.		10	10	20	.217
Gumbert, A.		11	16	26	.344
Kennedy, W.		18	13	36	.321
Lucid, C.		10	7	21	.283
McDougal, J.		0	0	5	.000
Stein, E.		15	13	28	.283
Anderson, J.	OF			103	.286
Burns, T.	OF			17	.192
Burrell, F.	C			10	.160
Corcoran, T.	SS			128	.277
Dailey, C.	C			40	.211
Daly, T.	2B			122	.281
Foutz, D. Mgr.	OF			28	.296
Griffin, M.	OF			132	.335
Grim, J.	C			90	.280
Hines, H.	OF			2	.250
LaChance, G.	1B			128	.312
Mulvey, J.	3B			13	.327
Shindle, W.	3B			118	.278
Shoch, G.	OF			58	.259
Treadway, G.	OF			85	.257

1896 (Ninth place)

WON—58
LOST—73
David Luther Foutz, Mgr.

PLAYER	POS.	W	L	G	BA
Pitchers					
Abbey, B.		8	8	19	.174
Daub, D.		12	11	27	.229

PLAYER	POS.	W	L	G	BA
Gumbert, A.		0	4	5	.182
Harper, G.		4	8	16	.176
Kennedy, W.		15	20	37	.197
Payne, H.		14	16	32	.218
Stein, E.		3	7	17	.250
Anderson, J.	OF			104	.314
Bonner, F.	2B			7	.185
Burrell, F.	C			58	.301
Corcoran, T.	SS			132	.289
Dailey, C.	C			1	.000
Daly, T.	2B			64	.281
Foutz, D. Mgr.	1B			2	.250
Griffin, M.	OF			122	.314
Grim, J.	C			80	.267
Jones, F.	OF			102	.353
LaChance, G.	1B			89	.284
McCarthy, T.	OF			101	.249
Shindle, W.	3B			131	.279
Shoch, G.	2B			75	.292

1897 (Sixth place)

WON–61
LOST–71
Wm. S. Barnie, Mgr.

PLAYER	POS.	W	L	G	BA
Pitchers					
Brown, John J.		0	2	2	.500
Daub, Daniel W.		6	11	18	.244
Dunn, Jack		14	9	34	.228
Fisher, Chauncey		9	7	18	.200
Kennedy, Brickyard		19	22	42	.269
McMahon, John J.		0	0	9	.167
Payne, Harley F.		14	17	39	.232
Anderson, John J.	OF			116	.325
Burrell, Buster	C			31	.238
Canavan, James E.	2B			63	.217
Griffin, Michael	OF			134	.318
Grim, Jack	C			76	.248
Hanifin, Patrick	OF			9	.200
Jones, Fielder	OF			135	.322
LaChance, George	1B			125	.308
Sheckard, Samuel	SS			13	.326
Shindle, W.	3B			134	.284
Shoch, George	2B			79	.278
Smith, Alexander	C			61	.300
Smith, Germany	SS			113	.201

1898 (Tenth place)

WON—54
LOST—91
Wm. S. Barnie, Michael J. Griffin, Chas. H. Ebbets, Mgrs.

PLAYER	POS.	W	L	G	BA
Pitchers					
Dunn, J.		16	21	45	.250
Gaston, W.		1	1	2	.125
Hansford, F.		0	1	1	.000
Hopper, C.		0	2	2	.000
Horton, E.		0	1	1	.250
Howell, H.		2	0	2	.250
Kennedy, W.		16	21	38	.259
Miller, R.		4	14	21	.197
McKenna, J.		2	6	14	.256
Payne, H.		1	0	1	.750
Stein, E.		0	2	3	.400
Yeager, J.		12	22	36	.178
Daly, T.	2B			23	.329
Dresser, E.	SS			1	.250
Griffin, M. Mgr.	OF			134	.296
Grim, J.	C			50	.281
Hallman, W.	2B			133	.244
Jones, F.	OF			147	.304
LaChance, G.	1B			135	.247
Magoon, G.	SS			93	.224
Ryan, J.	C			82	.189
Sheckard, S.	OF			105	.291
Shindle, W.	3B			120	.225
Smith, A.	OF			48	.261
Tucker, T.	1B			73	.279
Wagner, A.	3B			11	.237

1899 (First place)

WON—88
LOST—62
Edward Hugh Hanlon, Mgr.

PLAYER	POS.	W	L	G	BA
Pitchers					
Donovan, W.		1	2	4	.231
Dunn, J.		23	13	39	.244
Gaston, W.		0	1	1	1.000
Hill, W.		1	0	1	.500
Hughes, J.		28	6	35	.261
Kennedy, W.		22	8	37	.241
Maul, A.		2	0	4	.273
McFarlan, A.		0	0	1	.000
McJames, J.		19	15	33	.162
Reidy, W.		0	0	2	.000
Yeager, J.		3	2	15	.209
Anderson, J.	OF			112	.269
Beck, E.	SS			7	.158
Casey, J.	3B			136	.269
Cassidy, P.	3B			6	.150
Dahlen, W.	SS			122	.283

PLAYER	POS.	W	L	G	BA
Daly, T.	2B			143	.313
Farrell, C.	C			78	.299
Grim, J.	C			14	.271
Jennings, H.	1B			67	.296
Jones, F.	OF			95	.285
Keeler, W.	OF			143	.377
Kelley, J.	OF			144	.330
McGann, D.	1B			63	.243
McGuire, J.	C			43	.318
Smith, A.	C			16	.164
Wrigley, G.	SS			15	.229

1900 (First place)

WON—82
LOST—54
Edward Hugh Hanlon, Mgr.

PLAYER	POS.	W	L	G	BA
Pitchers					
Donovan, W.		1	2	5	.000
Dunn, J.		3	5	8	.273
Howell, H.		6	5	21	.309
Kennedy, W.		20	13	37	.301
Kitson, F.		15	13	33	.283
McGinnity, J.		29	9	41	.185
Nops, J.		3	4	9	.160
Weyhing, A.		3	2	8	.222
Yeager, J.		1	1	3	.333
Casey, J.	3B			1	.333
Cross, L.	3B			117	.293
Dahlen, W.	SS			134	.259
Daly, T.	2B			98	.312
DeMontreville, E.	2B			63	.244
Farrell, C.	C			73	.275
Jennings, H.	1B			112	.270
Jones, F.	OF			136	.309
Keeler, W.	OF			137	.368
Kelley, J.	OF			118	.319
McGuire, J.	C			68	.286
Sheckard, S.	OF			75	.300
Smith, A.	3B			7	.240
Steelman, M.	C			1	.000

1901 (Third place)

WON—79
LOST—57
Edward Hugh Hanlon, Mgr.

PLAYER	POS.	W	L	G	BA
Pitchers					
Carsey, W.		1	0	2	.000
Donovan, W.		25	15	41	.200
Hughes, J.		17	12	30	.178
Kennedy, W.		3	5	14	.167

PLAYER	POS.	W	L	G	BA
Kitson, F.		19	11	32	.281
McCann, H.		2	3	6	.000
McJames, J.		5	6	13	.029
Newton, E.		6	5	13	.220
Wright, C.		1	0	1	.333
Dahlen, W.	SS			130	.266
Daly, T.	2B			132	.315
Davis, A.	OF			25	.209
Dolan, P.	OF			62	.261
Farrell, C.	C			76	.296
Gatins, F.	3B			49	.229
Gochnaur, J.	SS			3	.363
Hearne, H.	C			2	.500
Irwin, C.	3B			64	.223
Keeler, W.	OF			136	.355
Kelley, J.	1B			120	.309
McCreery, T.	OF			84	.335
McGuire, J.	C			84	.296
Sheckard, S.	OF			133	.353
Steelman, M.	C			1	.333

1902 (Second place)

WON—75
LOST—63
Edward Hugh Hanlon, Mgr.

PLAYER	POS.	W	L	G	BA
Pitchers					
Donovan, W.		17	15	46	.169
Evans, L.		5	6	13	.265
Garvin, V.		1	1	2	.142
Hughes, J.		15	11	29	.202
Kitson, F.		19	12	31	.266
McCann, H.		1	2	3	.083
McMackin, J.		2	2	4	.153
Newton, E.		15	14	32	.174
Winham, L.		0	0	1	.000
Dahlen, W.	SS			136	.267
Deisel, E.	C			1	.667
Dolan, P.	OF			140	.280
Farrell, C.	C			72	.242
Flood, T.	2B			131	.218
Fuller, C.	C			3	.000
Hearne, H.	C			62	.281
Hildebrand, G.	OF			11	.227
Irwin, C.	3B			131	.273
Keeler, W.	OF			132	.336
Latimer, C.	C			8	.041
McCreery, T.	1B			111	.244
Ritter, L.	C			16	.250
Sheckard, S.	OF			122	.265
Wall, J.	C			5	.176
Ward, J.	OF			13	.290
Wheeler, E.	3B			24	.128

1903 (Fifth place)

WON—70
LOST—66
Edward Hugh Hanlon, Mgr.

PLAYER	POS.	W	L	G	BA
Pitchers					
Doscher, J.		0	0	3	.000
Evans, L.		4	8	15	.172
Garvin, V.		15	18	38	.075
Jones, O.		20	16	38	.256
Pounds, W.		0	0	1	.667
Reidy, W.		7	6	15	.243
Schmidt, H.		21	13	41	.196
Thatcher, U.		3	1	4	.182
Thielman, H.		0	3	8	.217
Vickers, H.		0	1	3	.000
Broderick, M.	2B			2	.000
Dahlen, W.	SS			138	.262
Dobbs, J.	OF			110	.237
Doyle, J.	1B			139	.313
Flood, T.	2B			87	.249
Gessler, H.	OF			43	.247
Hearne, H.	C			19	.281
Householder, E.	OF			12	.209
Hug, E.	C			1	.000
Jacklitsch, F.	C			55	.267
Jennings, H.	OF			6	.235
Jordan, A.	2B			77	.236
McCreedie, W.	OF			56	.324
McCreery, T.	OF			38	.262
McManus, F.	C			2	.000
Ritter, L.	C			75	.236
Sheckard, S.	OF			139	.332
Strang, S.	3B			135	.272

1904 (Sixth place)

WON—56
LOST—97
Edward Hugh Hanlon, Mgr.

PLAYER	POS.	W	L	G	BA
Pitchers					
Cronin, J.		12	23	40	.157
Doscher, J.		0	1	2	.333
Durham, L.		1	0	2	.250
Garvin, V.		5	15	23	.127
Jones, O.		17	25	46	.175
Koukalik, J.		0	1	1	.000
Mitchell, F.		2	4	8	.292
Poole, E.		8	13	24	.129
Reidy, W.		0	4	11	.196
Reisling, F.		3	3	7	.000
Scanlan, W.		7	6	14	.143
Thatcher, U.		1	0	1	.250
Babb, C.	SS			151	.265
Batch, E.	3B			28	.255

PLAYER	POS.	W	L	G	BA
Bergen, W.	C			94	.182
Dillon, F.	1B			134	.258
Dobbs, J.	OF			95	.248
Doyle, J.	1B			8	.227
Gessler, H.	OF			89	.290
Jacklitsch, F.	C			23	.234
Jordan, A.	2B			85	.179
Loudenschlager, C.	2B			1	.000
Lumley, H.	OF			150	.279
McCormick, M.	3B			105	.184
Ritter, L.	C			63	.248
Sheckard, S.	OF			143	.239
Strang, S.	2B			76	.192
Van Buren, E.	OF			1	1.000

1905 (Eighth place)

WON—48
LOST—104
Edward Hugh Hanlon, Mgr.

PLAYER	POS.	W	L	G	BA
Pitchers					
Doscher, J.		1	5	11	.095
Eason, M.		5	21	29	.173
Jones, O.		8	15	30	.200
Mitchell, F.		3	7	25	.190
McIntire, H.		8	25	45	.246
Reisling, F.		0	0	2	.000
Scanlan, W.		14	12	33	.167
Stricklett, E.		9	18	33	.148
Babb, C.	SS			74	.187
Batch, E.	3B			145	.252
Bergen, W.	C			76	.190
Dobbs, J.	OF			123	.254
Gessler, H.	1B			119	.290
Hall, R.	OF			52	.236
Hummel, J.	2B			30	.266
Lewis, P.	SS			118	.254
Lumley, H.	OF			129	.293
Malay, C.	2B			101	.252
McGamwell, E.	1B			4	.267
Owens, T.	2B			43	.215
Ritter, L.	C			90	.219
Sheckard, S.	OF			129	.292
Yale, W.	1B			4	.076

1906 (Fifth place)

WON—66
LOST—86
Patrick Joseph Donovan, Mgr.

PLAYER	POS.	W	L	G	BA
Pitchers					
Doscher, J.		0	1	2	.000
Eason, M.		11	16	36	.091
Knolls, O.		0	0	2	.500

PLAYER	POS.	W	L	G	BA
McFarland, C.		0	1	1	.000
McIntire, H.		12	21	42	.175
Pastorius, J.		9	14	5	.071
Scanlan, W.		19	14	38	.186
Stricklett, E.		14	18	41	.206
Whiting, J.		1	1	3	.300
Alperman, C.	2B			127	.252
Batch, E.	OF			52	.256
Bergen, W.	C			103	.161
Butler, J.	C			1	.000
Casey, J.	3B			149	.233
Donovan, P. Mgr.	OF			7	.238
Gessler, H.	1B			9	.242
Hummel, J.	2B			86	.199
Jordan, T.	2B			126	.262
Lewis, P.	SS			135	.243
Lumley, H.	OF			131	.324
Maloney, W.	OF			151	.221
McCarthy, J.	OF			86	.304
Reardon, P.	OF			5	.071
Ritter, L.	C			67	.208

1907 (Fifth place)

WON—65
LOST—83
Patrick Joseph Donovan, Mgr.

PLAYER	POS.	W	L	G	BA
Pitchers					
Bell, G.		8	16	35	.095
Henley, W.		1	5	7	.222
McIntire, H.		7	15	28	.217
Pastorius, J.		16	12	28	.205
Rucker, G.		15	13	37	.155
Scanlan, W.		6	7	17	.265
Stricklett, E.		12	14	30	.148
Whiting, J.		0	0	2	.000
Alperman, C.	2B			138	.233
Batch, E.	OF			106	.247
Bergen, W.	C			51	.159
Burch, A.	OF			36	.292
Butler, J.	C			29	.127
Casey, J.	3B			138	.231
Donovan, P.	OF			1	.000
Hummel, J.	2B			97	.234
Hurley, P.	C			1	.000
Jordan, T.	1B			143	.274
Lewis, P.	SS			136	.248
Lumley, H.	OF			118	.267
Maloney, W.	OF			144	.229
McCarthy, J.	OF			25	.220
McLane, E.	OF			1	.000
Ritter, L.	C			89	.203

1908 (Seventh place)

WON—53
LOST—101
Patrick Joseph Donovan, Mgr.

PLAYER	POS.	W	L	G	BA
Pitchers					
Bell, G.		4	16	29	.170
Finlayson, P.		0	0	1	.000
Holmes, J.		1	4	13	.077
Kruger, A.		0	1	1	.000
McIntire, H.		11	20	40	.200
Pastorius, J.		4	20	28	.129
Rucker, G.		18	20	42	.179
Wilhelm, I.		15	21	42	.108
Alperman, C.	2B			57	.197
Bergen, W.	C			99	.175
Burch, A.	OF			116	.243
Catterson, T.	OF			18	.191
Dunn, J.	C			20	.172
Farmer, A.	C			12	.167
Hummell, J.	OF			154	.241
Jordan, T.	1B			146	.247
Lewis, P.	SS			116	.219
Lumley, H.	OF			116	.216
Maloney, W.	OF			107	.195
Murch, S.	1B			6	.181
McMillan, T.	SS			43	.238
Pattee, H.	2B			74	.216
Ritter, L.	C			37	.192
Sheehan, T.	3B			145	.214

1909 (Sixth place)

WON—55
LOST—98
Harry G. Lumley, Mgr.

PLAYER	POS.	W	L	G	BA
Pitchers					
Bell, G.		16	15	33	.166
Dent, E.		2	4	6	.067
Finlayson, P.		0	0	1	.000
Fletcher, S.		0	1	1	.000
Hunter, G.		3	10	39	.228
Knetzer, E.		1	3	5	.000
McIntire, H.		8	17	32	.171
Pastorius, J.		1	9	12	.080
Rucker, G.		13	19	38	.118
Scanlan, W.		8	7	19	.273
Wilhelm, I.		3	13	22	.228
Alperman, C.	2B			108	.248
Bergen, W.	C			112	.139
Burch, A.	OF			152	.271
Catterson, T.	OF			9	.222
Clement, W.	OF			88	.256
Downey, A.	OF			19	.256

PLAYER	POS.	W	L	G	BA
Dunn, J.	C			7	.160
Hummel, J.	1B			145	.280
Jordan, T.	1B			95	.273
Kustus, J.	OF			50	.145
Lennox, J.	3B			121	.262
Lumley, H. Mgr.	OF			52	.250
Marshall, W.	C			47	.202
Meyer, L.	SS			7	.130
McElveen, P.	3B			67	.198
McMillan, T.	SS			108	.212
Myers, H.	OF			6	.227
Redmond, H.	2B			6	.100
Sebring, J.	OF			25	.099
Wheat, Z.	OF			26	.304

1910 (Sixth place)

WON—64
LOST—90
Wm. Frederick Dahlen, Mgr.

PLAYER	POS.	W	L	G	BA
Pitchers					
Barger, E.		15	15	35	.231
Bell, G.		10	27	44	.134
Burk, C.		0	3	4	.000
Crable, G.		0	0	2	.000
Dessau, F.		2	3	19	.067
Knetzer, E.		6	5	20	.053
Miller, F.		1	1	3	.000
Rucker, G.		17	19	41	.209
Scanlan, W.		8	12	34	.203
Schneiberg, F.		0	0	1	.000
Wilhelm, I.		3	7	15	.316
Bergen, W.	C			89	.161
Burch, A.	OF			83	.236
Coulson, R.	OF			25	.247
Dahlen, W. Mgr.				3	.000
Dalton, T.	OF			72	.227
Daubert, J.	1B			144	.264
Davidson, W.	OF			131	.238
Erwin, R.	C			68	.188
Hummel, J.	2B			153	.244
Hunter, G.	OF			1	.000
Jordan, T.	1B			5	.200
Lennox, J.	3B			100	.259
Lumley, H.	OF			8	.100
Miller, L.	C			28	.167
McElveen, P.	3B			64	.225
McMillan, T.	SS			23	.176
Smith, H.	OF			16	.237
Smith, T.	SS			106	.181
Stark, M.	SS			30	.165
Wheat, Z.	OF			156	.284

1911 (Seventh place)

WON—64
LOST—86
Wm. Frederick Dahlen, Mgr.

PLAYER	POS.	W	L	G	BA
Pitchers					
Aitchison, R.		0	1	1	.000
Barger, E.		11	15	42	.228
Bell, G.		5	6	19	.121
Burk, C.		1	3	13	.095
Dent, E.		2	1	5	.143
Knetzer, E.		11	11	35	.097
Miller, W.		0	1	3	.000
Ragan, D.		4	3	22	.138
Rucker, G.		22	18	48	.202
Ryan, J.		0	1	3	.000
Scanlan, W.		3	10	22	.121
Schardt, W.		5	16	39	.169
Steele, E.		0	0	5	.000
Bergen, W.	C			84	.132
Browne, G.	OF			7	.333
Burch, A.	OF			46	.228
Coulson, R.	OF			145	.234
Dahlen, W. Mgr.	SS			1	.000
Daley, J.	OF			16	.231
Daubert, J.	1B			149	.307
Davidson, W.	OF			74	.233
Erwin, R.	C			74	.271
Higgins, R.	C			4	.300
Hummel, J.	2B			133	.270
Humphrey, A.	OF			8	.143
LeJeune, S.	OF			6	.157
Miller, L.	C			22	.210
Myers, H.	OF			12	.179
McElveen, P.	2B			16	.193
Northen, H.	OF			19	.316
Smith, A.	SS			12	.138
Smith, J.	3B			28	.261
Stark, M.	SS			55	.295
Tooley, A.	SS			114	.206
Wheat, Z.	OF			136	.287
Zimmerman, E.	3B			122	.185

1912 (Seventh place)

WON—58
LOST—95
Wm. Frederick Dahlen, Mgr.

PLAYER	POS.	W	L	G	BA
Pitchers					
Allen, F.		3	9	20	.167
Barger, E.		1	9	17	.189
Burk, C.		0	0	2	.250
Curtis, C.		5	7	19	.308
Dent, E.		0	0	1	.000
Kent, M.		5	5	20	.229

PLAYER	POS.	W	L	G	BA
Knetzer, E.		7	9	33	.135
Ragan, D.		6	18	36	.060
Rucker, G.		18	21	45	.245
Schardt, W.		0	1	7	.000
Stack, W.		7	5	28	.135
Yingling, E.		6	11	25	.250
Cutshaw, G.	2B			102	.280
Daley, J.	OF			61	.256
Daubert, J.	1B			145	.308
Downs, J.	2B			9	.250
Erwin, R.	C			59	.211
Fisher, R.	SS			82	.233
Higgins, R.	C			1	.000
Hummel, J.	2B			122	.282
Kirkpatrick, E.	3B			32	.191
Miller, L.	C			98	.278
Moran, J.	OF			130	.276
Northen, H.	OF			118	.282
Phelps, E.	C			52	.288
Smith, R.	3B			128	.286
Stark, M.	SS			8	.182
Stengel, C.	OF			17	.316
Tooley, A.	SS			77	.234
Wheat, Z.	OF			123	.305

1913 (Sixth place)

WON—65
LOST—84
Wm. Frederick Dahlen, Mgr.

PLAYER	POS.	W	L	G	BA
Pitchers					
Allen, F.		4	18	34	.137
Brown, E.		0	0	3	.000
Curtis, C.		9	9	30	.122
Hall, W.		0	0	3	.000
Kent, M.		0	0	5	.000
Pfeffer, E.		0	1	5	.000
Ragan, D.		15	18	44	.165
Reulbach, E.		7	6	16	.103
Rucker, G.		14	15	41	.241
Stack, W.		4	4	23	.154
Wagner, W.		4	2	18	.231
Walker, F.		1	3	10	.167
Yingling, E.		8	8	26	.383
Callahan, L.	OF			33	.171
Collins, W.	OF			32	.189
Cutshaw, G.	2B			147	.267
Daubert, J.	1B			139	.350
Erwin, R.	C			20	.258
Fischer, W.	C			62	.267
Fisher, R.	SS			132	.262
Heckinger, M.	C			9	.222
Hummel, J.	OF			67	.242
Kirkpatrick, E.	1B			48	.247
Meyer, B.	OF			38	.195
Miller, D.	C			104	.272

PLAYER	POS.	W	L	G	BA
Moran, H.	OF			132	.266
Mowe, R.	SS			5	.111
McCarty, G.	C			9	.192
Phelps, E.	C			15	.222
Scheer, A.	OF			6	.272
Smith, R.	3B			151	.296
Stengel, C.	OF			124	.272
Wheat, Z.	OF			138	.301

1914 (Fifth place)

WON—75
LOST—79
Wilbert Robinson, Mgr.

PLAYER	POS.	W	L	G	BA
Pitchers					
Aitchison, R.		12	7	26	.196
Allen, F.		8	14	37	.128
Brown, E.		1	2	11	.083
Enzmann, J.		1	0	7	.000
Pfeffer, E.		23	12	44	.198
Ragan, D.		10	15	38	.133
Reulbach, E.		11	18	44	.122
Rucker, G.		7	6	16	.265
Schmutz, C.		1	3	18	.187
Steele, W.		1	1	8	.333
Wagner, W.		0	1	6	.000
Cutshaw, G.	2B			153	.257
Dalton, T.	OF			128	.319
Daubert, J.	1B			126	.329
Egan, R.	SS			106	.226
Elberfeld, N.	SS			30	.226
Erwin, R.	C			7	.500
Fischer, W.	C			43	.257
Getz, G.	3B			55	.248
Hummel, J.	1B			73	.264
Miller, O.	C			54	.231
Myers, H.	OF			70	.286
McCarty, L.	C			90	.254
O'Mara, O.	SS			67	.263
Riggert, J.	OF			27	.190
Smith, R.	3B			90	.245
Stengel, C.	OF			126	.316
Wheat, Z.	OF			145	.319

1915 (Third place)

WON—80
LOST—72
Wilbert Robinson, Mgr.

PLAYER	POS.	W	L	G	BA
Pitchers					
Aitchison, R.		0	4	7	.000
Appleton, E.		4	10	34	.159
Brown, E.		0	0	1	.000

PLAYER	POS.	W	L	G	BA
Cadore, L.		0	2	7	.000
Cheney, L.		0	2	5	.143
Coombs, J.		14	10	29	.280
Dell, W.		11	10	40	.152
Douglas, P.		5	5	20	.154
Mails, J.		0	1	2	.000
Marquard, R.		2	2	6	.125
Pfeffer, E.		19	14	40	.255
Ragan, D.		1	0	4	.167
Rucker, G.		9	4	19	.214
Schmutz, C.		0	0	1	.000
Smith, S.		14	8	29	.246
Cutshaw, G.	2B			154	.246
Daubert, J.	1B			150	.301
Egan, R.	2B			3	.000
Getz, G.	3B			130	.258
Hummel, J.	OF			53	.230
Karst, J.	3B			1	.000
Miller, L.	C			84	.224
Myers, H.	OF			153	.248
McCarty, G.	C			84	.239
Nixon, A.	OF			14	.231
Olson, I.	3B			18	.077
O'Mara, O.	SS			149	.244
Schultz, J.	3B			56	.292
Smyth, J.	OF			19	.136
Stengel, C.	OF			132	.237
Wheat, M.	C			8	.071
Wheat, Z.	OF			146	.258
Zimmerman, W.	OF			22	.281

1916 (First place)

WON—94
LOST—60
Wilbert Robinson, Mgr.

PLAYER	POS.	W	L	G	BA
Pitchers					
Appleton, E.		1	2	14	.167
Cadore, L.		0	0	1	.000
Cheney, L.		18	12	41	.114
Coombs, J.		13	8	27	.180
Dell, W.		8	9	32	.091
Mails, J.		0	1	11	.250
Marquard, R.		13	6	36	.143
Pfeffer, E.		25	11	43	.279
Rucker, G.		2	1	9	.091
Smith, S.		14	10	38	.273
Cutshaw, G.	2B			154	.260
Daubert, J.	1B			127	.316
Dede, A.	C			1	.000
Fabrique, A.	SS			2	.000
Getz, G.	3B			40	.219
Hickman, D.	OF			9	.200
Johnston, J.	OF			118	.252

PLAYER	POS.	W	L	G	BA
Kelleher, J.	3B			2	.000
Merkle, F.	1B			23	.208
Meyers, C.	C			80	.247
Miller, L.	OF			3	.333
Miller, O.	C			73	.255
Mowrey, H.	3B			144	.244
Myers, H.	OF			113	.262
McCarty, G.	C			55	.311
Nixon, A.	OF			1	1.000
Olson, I.	SS			108	.254
O'Mara, O.	SS			72	.202
Smyth, J.	OF			2	.000
Stengel, C.	OF			127	.279
Wheat, M.	C			2	.000
Wheat, Z.	OF			149	.312

1917 (Seventh place)

WON—70
LOST—81
Wilbert Robinson, Mgr.

PLAYER	POS.	W	L	G	BA
Pitchers					
Cadore, L.		13	13	37	.261
Cheney, L.		8	12	35	.206
Coombs, J.		7	11	32	.227
Dell, W.		0	4	17	.063
Durning, R.		0	0	1	.000
Marquard, R.		19	12	37	.200
Miljus, J.		0	1	4	.000
Pfeffer, E.		11	15	31	.130
Russell, J.		0	1	5	.250
Smith, S.		12	12	43	.195
Wachtel, P.		0	0	2	.333
Cutshaw, G.	2B			135	.259
Daubert, J.	1B			125	.261
Fabrique, A.	SS			25	.205
Hickman, D.	OF			114	.219
Johnston, J.	OF			103	.270
Krueger, E.	C			31	.272
Leard, W.	2B			3	.000
Malone, L.				1	.000
Merkle, F.	1B			2	.125
Meyers, J.	C			47	.214
Miller, O.	C			92	.230
Mowrey, H.	3B			83	.214
Myers, H.	OF			120	.268
Olson, I.	SS			139	.269
O'Rourke, F.	3B			64	.237
Smyth, J.	OF			29	.120
Snyder, J.	C			7	.273
Stengel, C.	OF			150	.257
Wheat, M.	C			29	.133
Wheat, Z.	OF			109	.312

1918 (Fifth place)

WON—57
LOST—69
Wilbert Robinson, Mgr.

PLAYER	POS.	W	L	G	BA
Pitchers					
Cadore, L.		1	0	2	.000
Cheney, L.		11	13	33	.242
Coombs, J.		8	14	46	.168
Durning, R.		0	0	1	.000
Grimes, B.		19	9	41	.200
Griner, D.		1	5	12	.071
Hehl, H.		0	0	1	.000
Heitman, H.		0	1	1	.000
Hermann, M.		0	0	1	.000
Mamaux, A.		0	1	2	.000
Marquard, R.		9	18	34	.171
Mitchell, C.		0	1	10	.250
Pfeffer, E.		1	0	1	.250
Plitt, N.		0	0	1	1.000
Robertson, R.		3	6	14	.300
Russell, J.		0	0	1	.000
Smith, G.		4	1	8	.064
Archer, J.	C			9	.273
Bashang, A.	OF			2	.200
Daubert, J.	1B			108	.308
Doolan, M.	2B			92	.179
Hickman, D.	OF			53	.234
Johnston, J.	OF			123	.281
Krueger, E.	C			30	.289
Miller, D.	C			75	.193
Myers, H.	OF			107	.256
Nixon, A.	OF			6	.454
Olson, I.	SS			126	.239
O'Mara, O.	3B			121	.213
O'Rourke, F.	2B			4	.167
Schmandt, R.	2B			34	.307
Sheridan, E.	2B			2	.250
Ward, C.	SS			2	.333
Wheat, M.	C			57	.217
Wheat, Z.	OF			105	.335

1919 (Fifth place)

WON—69
LOST—71
Wilbert Robinson, Mgr.

PLAYER	POS.	W	L	G	BA
Pitchers					
Cadore, L.		14	12	37	.161
Cheney, L.		1	3	9	.182
Grimes, B.		10	11	26	.246
Henion, L.		0	0	1	.000
Mamaux, A.		10	12	30	.175
Marquard, R.		3	3	8	.261
Mitchell, C.		7	5	34	.367

PLAYER	POS.	W	L	G	BA
Pfeffer, E.		17	13	30	.206
Smith, S.		7	12	30	.148
Allen, H.	OF			4	.000
Baird, H.	3B			20	.167
Fitzsimmons, T.	3B			4	.000
Griffith, T.	OF			125	.281
Hickman, D.	OF			57	.192
Johnston, J.	2B			117	.281
Kilduff, P.	3B			32	.301
Konetchy, E.	1B			132	.298
Krueger, E.	C			80	.248
Magee, L.	2B			45	.238
Malone, L.	3B			51	.204
Miller, O.	C			51	.226
Myers, H.	OF			133	.307
Olson, I.	SS			140	.278
O'Mara, O.	3B			2	.000
Schmandt, R.	2B			47	.165
Ward, C.	3B			45	.233
Wheat, M.	C			41	.205
Wheat, Z.	OF			137	.297

1920 (First place)

WON—93
LOST—61
Wilbert Robinson, Mgr.

PLAYER	POS.	W	L	G	BA
Pitchers					
Cadore, L.		15	14	35	.220
Grimes, B.		23	11	43	.306
Mamaux, A.		12	8	41	.167
Marquard, R.		10	7	28	.169
Miljus, J.		1	0	10	.333
Mitchell, C.		5	2	55	.234
Mohart, G.		0	1	13	.125
Pfeffer, E.		16	9	30	.243
Smith, S.		11	9	33	.233
Baird, H.				6	.333
Elliott, H.	C			41	.241
Griffith, T.	OF			93	.260
Hood, W.	OF				.154
Johnston, J.	3B			155	.291
Kilduff, P.	2B			141	.272
Konetchy, E.	1B			131	.308
Krueger, E.	C			52	.288
Lamar, W.	OF			24	.273
Miller, O.	C			90	.289
Myers, H.	OF			154	.304
McCabe, W.	OF			41	.147
Neis, B.	OF			95	.253
Olson, I.	SS			143	.254
Schmandt, R.	1B			28	.238
Sheehan, J.	3B			4	.400
Sheridan, E.	SS			2	.000
Taylor, J.	C			5	.167

270 • The Complete Dodgers Record Book

PLAYER	POS.	W	L	G	BA
Ward, C.	SS			19	.155
Wheat, Z.	OF			148	.328

1921 (Fifth place)

WON—77
LOST—75
Wilbert Robinson, Mgr.

PLAYER	POS.	W	L	G	BA
Pitchers					
Bailey, A.		0	0	7	.000
Cadore, L.		13	14	35	.187
Eayrs, E.		0	0	8	.167
Gordonier, R.		1	0	3	.250
Grimes, B.		22	13	37	.237
Mamaux, A.		3	3	12	.182
Miljus, J.		6	3	28	.167
Mitchell, C.		11	9	46	.264
Mohart, G.		0	0	2	.500
Pfeffer, E.		1	5	6	.000
Ruether, W.		10	13	49	.351
Schupp, F.		3	4	20	.083
Smith, S.		7	11	35	.228
Griffith, T.	OF			129	.312
Hood, W.	OF			56	.262
Janvrin, H.	1B			44	.196
Johnston, J.	3B			152	.325
Kilduff, P.	2B			107	.288
Konetchy, E.	1B			55	.269
Krueger, E.	C			65	.264
Lamar, W.	OF			3	.333
Miller, L.	C			91	.234
Myers, H.	OF			144	.288
Nels, B.	OF			102	.257
Olson, I.	SS			151	.267
Schmandt, R.	1B			95	.306
Sheehan, J.	3B			5	.000
Taylor, J.	C			30	.196
Ward, C.	SS			12	.071
Wheat, Z.	OF			148	.320

1922 (Sixth place)

WON—76
LOST—78
Wilbert Robinson, Mgr.

PLAYER	POS.	W	L	G	BA
Pitchers					
Cadore, L.		8	15	29	.267
Decatur, A.		3	4	29	.080
Gordonier, R.		0	0	5	.000
Grimes, B.		17	14	36	.237
Mamaux, A.		1	4	37	.235
Mitchell, C.		0	3	56	.290
Murray, J.		0	0	4	.500
Ruether, W.		21	12	67	.208

PLAYER	POS.	W	L	G	BA
Schreiber, P.		0	0	1	.000
Shriver, H.		4	6	25	.037
Smith, S.		4	8	28	.257
Vance, C.		18	12	36	.224
Crane, S.	SS			3	.250
DeBerry, J.	C			85	.301
Griffith, B.	OF			106	.308
Griffith, T.	OF			99	.316
High, A.	3B			153	.283
Hood, W.	OF			2	.000
Hungling, B.	C			39	.225
Janvrin, H.	2B			30	.298
Johnston, J.	2B			138	.319
Miller, L.	C			59	.261
Myers, H.	OF			153	.317
Neis, B.	OF			61	.229
Olson, I.	2B			136	.272
Post, S.	1B			9	.280
Schmandt, R.	1B			110	.267
Taylor, J.	C			7	.214
Ward, C.	SS			33	.274
Wheat, Z.	OF			152	.335
Whitted, G.	OF			1	.000

1923 (Sixth place)

WON—76
LOST—78
Wilbert Robinson, Mgr.

PLAYER	POS.	W	L	G	BA
Pitchers					
Cadore, L.		4	1	9	.077
Decatur, A.		3	3	36	.000
Dickerman, L.		8	12	35	.250
Grimes, B.		21	18	40	.238
Harper, H.		0	1	1	.000
Henry, F.		4	6	17	.229
Mamaux, A.		0	2	5	.500
Ruether, W.		15	14	49	.274
Schreiber, P.		0	0	9	.000
Shriver, H.		0	0	1	.000
Smith, G.		3	6	25	.192
Vance, C.		18	15	37	.084
Ainsmith, E.	C			2	.200
Bailey, A.	OF			127	.265
Barber, S.	OF			13	.217
Berg, M.	SS			49	.186
DeBerry, J.	C			78	.285
Fournier, J.	1B			133	.351
French, R.	SS			43	.219
Griffith, B.	OF			79	.294
Griffith, T.	OF			131	.293
Hargreaves, C.	C			20	.281
High, A.	3B			123	.270
Hungling, B.	C			2	.000
Johnston, J.	2B			151	.325
Mullen, W.	3B			4	.273

PLAYER	POS.	W	L	G	BA
McCarren, W.	3B			69	.245
Neis, B.	OF			126	.274
Olson, I.	2B			82	.260
Schliebner, F.	1B			19	.250
Stewart, J.	2B			4	.364
Taylor, J.	C			96	.288
Wheat, Z.	OF			98	.375

1924 (Second place)

WON—92
LOST—62
Wilbert Robinson, Mgr.

PLAYER	POS.	W	L	G	BA
Pitchers					
Decatur, A.		10	9	31	.114
Dickerman, L.		0	0	7	.167
Doak, W.		11	5	21	.179
Ehrhardt, W.		5	3	15	.138
Greene, N.		0	1	4	.000
Grimes, B.		22	13	40	.298
Henry, F.		1	2	16	.250
Hollingsworth, J.		1	0	2	.000
Long, T.		0	0	1	.000
Osborne, E.		6	5	21	.250
Roberts, J.		0	3	11	.143
Ruether, W.		8	13	33	.242
Vance, C.		28	6	35	.151
Wilson, G.		0	0	2	.000
Yarrison, B.		0	2	3	.000
Bailey, A.	OF			18	.239
Brown, E.	OF			114	.308
DeBerry, J.	C			77	.243
Fournier, J.	1B			154	.334
Griffith, T.	OF			140	.251
Hargreaves, C.	C			15	.407
High, A.	2B			144	.328
Johnston, J.	SS			86	.298
Johnston, W.	2B			4	.250
Jones, J.	SS			10	.108
Klugman, J.	2B			31	.165
Loftus, R.	OF			46	.272
Mitchell, J.	SS			64	.263
Neis, B.	OF			80	.303
Olson, I.	SS			10	.222
Stock, M.	3B			142	.242
Taylor, J.	C			99	.290
Wheat, Z.	OF			141	.375

1925 (Sixth place)

WON—68
LOST—85
Wilbert Robinson, Mgr.

PLAYER	POS.	W	L	G	BA
Pitchers					
Brown, L.		0	3	17	.087
Cantrell, G.		1	0	14	.000
Decatur, A.		0	0	1	.000
Ehrhardt, W.		10	14	36	.211
Elliott, J.		0	2	3	.000
Greene, N.		2	0	11	.286
Grimes, B.		12	19	34	.250
Hubbell, W.		3	6	33	.150
McGraw, R.		0	2	2	.167
Oeschger, J.		1	2	21	.125
Osborne, E.		8	15	41	.246
Petty, J.		9	9	28	.140
Roberts, J.		0	0	1	.000
Rush, J.		0	1	4	.000
Thormahlen, H.		0	3	5	.200
Vance, C.		22	9	31	.143
Barrett, R.				1	.000
Brown, E.	OF			153	.306
Corgan, C.	SS			14	.170
Cox, E.	OF			122	.329
DeBerry, J.	C			67	.259
Ford, H.	SS			66	.273
Fournier, J.	1B			145	.350
Griffith, T.	OF			7	.000
Hargreaves, C.	C			45	.277
High, A.	2B			44	.200
Hutson, R.	OF			7	.500
Johnston, J.	3B			123	.297
Loftus, R.	OF			51	.237
Mitchell, J.	SS			97	.250
Standaert, J.				1	.000
Stock, M.	2B			146	.328
Taylor, J.	C			109	.310
Tierney, J.	3B			93	.257
Wheat, Z.	OF			150	.359

1926 (Sixth place)

WON—71
LOST—82
Wilbert Robinson, Mgr.

PLAYER	POS.	W	L	G	BA
Pitchers					
Barnes, J.		10	11	31	.237
Boehler, G.		1	0	11	.250
Ehrhardt, W.		2	5	44	.250
Grimes, B.		12	13	31	.222
Moss, R.		0	0	1	.000
McGraw, R.		9	13	33	.145
McWeeney, D.		11	13	42	.109

PLAYER	POS.	W	L	G	BA
Petty, J.		17	17	38	.175
Stryker, S.		0	0	2	.000
Vance, C.		9	10	22	.182
Williams, L.		0	0	12	.200
Bohne, S.	SS			47	.200
Butler, J.	SS			147	.269
Carey, M.	OF			27	.260
Clabaugh, J.	OF			11	.071
Cox, E.	OF			124	.296
DeBerry, J.	C			48	.287
Dowd, R.	2B			2	.000
Felix, A.	OF			134	.280
Fewster, W.	2B			105	.243
Fournier, J.	1B			87	.284
Hargreaves, C.	C			85	.250
Herman, F.	1B			137	.319
Jacobson, M.	OF			110	.247
Maranville, W.	SS			78	.235
Marriott, W.	3B			109	.267
Standaert, J.	2B			66	.345
Stock, M.	2B			3	.000
Wheat, Z.	OF			111	.290
Witt, L.	OF			63	.259

1927 (Sixth place)

WON—65
LOST—88
Wilbert Robinson, Mgr.

PLAYER	POS.	W	L	G	BA
Pitchers					
Barnes, J.		2	10	18	.217
Cantrell, G.		0	0	6	.333
Clark, W.		7	2	27	.143
Doak, W.		11	8	27	.128
Ehrhardt, W.		3	7	46	.250
Elliott, J.		6	13	30	.141
Moss, R.		1	0	1	.333
McGraw, R.		0	1	1	.000
McWeeney, D.		4	8	34	.043
Petty, J.		13	18	42	.099
Plitt, N.		2	6	19	.222
Vance, C.		16	15	34	.167
Barrett, R.	3B			99	.259
Butler, J.	SS			149	.238
Carey, M.	OF			144	.266
Corgan, C.	2B			19	.263
DeBerry, J.	C			68	.234
Felix, A.	OF			130	.265
Fewster, W.				4	.000
Flowers, D.	SS			67	.234
Hargreaves, C.	C			46	.286
Hendrick, H.	OF			128	.310
Henline, W.	C			67	.266
Herman, F.	1B			130	.272
Jacobson, M.	OF			11	.000
Marriott, W.	3B			6	.111

PLAYER	POS.	W	L	G	BA
Meusel, E.	OF			42	.243
Partridge, J.	2B			146	.260
Roettger, O.	OF			5	.000
Statz, A.	OF			130	.274
Tremper, C.	OF			26	.233

1928 (Sixth place)

WON—77
LOST—76
Wilbert Robinson, Mgr.

PLAYER	POS.	W	L	G	BA
Pitchers					
Clark, W.		12	9	40	.152
Doak, W.		3	8	28	.111
Ehrhardt, W.		1	3	28	.286
Elliott, J.		9	14	41	.176
Koupal, L.		1	0	17	.111
Moss, R.		0	3	24	.320
McWeeney, D.		14	14	42	.173
Petty, J.		15	15	40	.111
Vance, C.		22	10	38	.177
Bancroft, D.	SS			149	.247
Bissonette, A.	1B			155	.320
Bressler, R.	OF			145	.295
Carey, M.	OF			108	.247
DeBerry, J.	C			82	.252
Flowers, D.	2B			103	.274
Freigau, H.	SS			17	.206
Gilbert, W.	3B			39	.203
Gooch, J.	C			42	.317
Hargreaves, C.	C			20	.197
Harris, J.	OF			55	.236
Hendrick, H.	3B			126	.318
Henline, W.	C			55	.212
Herman, F.	OF			134	.340
Lopez, A.	C			3	.000
Partridge, J.	2B			37	.247
Riconda, H.	2B			92	.224
Statz, A.	OF			77	.234
Tremper, C.	OF			10	.194
Tyson, A.	OF			59	.271
West, W.	OF			7	.286

1929 (Sixth place)

WON—70
LOST—83
Wilbert Robinson, Mgr.

PLAYER	POS.	W	L	G	BA
Pitchers					
Ballou, N.		2	3	25	.063
Blethen, C.		0	0	2	.000
Bradshaw, J.		0	0	2	.000
Clark, W.		16	19	42	.165
Dudley, E.		6	14	36	.098

PLAYER	POS.	W	L	G	BA
Elliott, J.		1	2	6	.250
Ferguson, J.		0	1	3	1.000
Greenfield, K.		0	0	7	.000
Koupal, L.		0	1	18	.071
Moore, W.		3	3	32	.188
Morrison, J.		13	7	39	.163
Moss, R.		11	6	42	.076
McWeeney, D.		4	10	36	.104
Newsom, L.		0	3	3	.000
Pattison, J.		0	1	6	.500
Roy, L.		0	0	2	.000
Vance, C.		14	13	31	.135
Bancroft, D.	SS			104	.277
Bissonette, A.	1B			116	.281
Bressler, R.	OF			136	.318
Carey, M.	OF			19	.304
Cullop, H.	OF			13	.195
DeBerry, J.	C			68	.262
Flowers, D.	2B			46	.200
Frederick, J.	OF			148	.328
Gilbert, W.	3B			143	.304
Gooch, J.				1	.000
Hendrick, H.	OF			110	.354
Henline, W.	C			27	.242
Herman, F.	OF			146	.381
Moore, G.	2B			111	.296
Picinich, V.	C			93	.260
Rhiel, W.	2B			76	.278
Warner, J.	SS			17	.274
West, W.	OF			5	.250
Wright, F.	SS			24	.200

1930 (Fourth place)

WON—86
LOST—68
Wilbert Robinson, Mgr.

PLAYER	POS.	W	L	G	BA
Pitchers					
Clark, W.		13	13	44	.206
Dudley, E.		2	4	21	.208
Elliott, J.		10	7	35	.147
Faulkner, J.		0	0	2	.000
Heimach, F.		0	2	13	.250
Luque, A.		14	8	31	.240
Moore, W.		0	0	1	.000
Morrison, J.		1	2	16	.000
Moss, R.		9	6	36	.154
Newsom, L.		0	0	2	.000
Phelps, R.		14	7	36	.147
Thurston, H.		6	4	36	.200
Vance, C.		17	15	35	.135
Bissonette, A.	1B			146	.336
Boone, I.	OF			40	.297
Bressler, R.	OF			109	.299
DeBerry, J.	C			35	.295

PLAYER	POS.	W	L	G	BA
Finn, C.	2B			87	.278
Flowers, D.	2B			89	.320
Frederick, J.	OF			142	.334
Gilbert, W.	3B			150	.294
Hendrick, H.	OF			68	.257
Herman, F.	OF			153	.393
Lee, H.	OF			22	.162
Lopez, A.	C			128	.309
Moore, G.	2B			76	.281
Picinich, V.	C			23	.217
Slade, G.	SS			25	.216
Warner, J.	3B			21	.320
Wright, F.	SS			135	.321

1931 (Fourth place)

WON—79
LOST—73
Wilbert Robinson, Mgr.

PLAYER	POS.	W	L	G	BA
Pitchers					
Clark, W.		14	10	34	.250
Day, C.		2	2	22	.222
Gallivan, P.		0	1	6	.000
Heimach, F.		9	7	39	.197
Luque, A.		7	6	19	.133
Mattingly, L.		0	1	8	.000
Moore, W.		1	2	23	.154
Moss, R.		0	0	1	.000
Mungo, V.		3	1	5	.250
Phelps, R.		7	9	28	.157
Quinn, J.		5	4	39	.200
Shaute, J.		11	8	25	.178
Thurston, H.		9	9	24	.217
Vance, C.		11	13	30	.134
Bissonette, A.	1B			152	.290
Boone, I.				6	.200
Bressler, R.	OF			67	.281
Cohen, A.	OF			1	.667
Finn, C.	2B			118	.274
Flowers, D.	2B			22	.226
Frederick, J.	OF			146	.270
Gilbert, W.	3B			145	.266
Hendrick, H.				1	.000
Herman, F.	OF			151	.313
Lombardi, E.	C			73	.297
Lopez, A.	C			111	.269
O'Doul, F.	OF			134	.336
Picinich, V.	C			24	.267
Reis, R.	3B			6	.294
Rosenfeld, M.	OF			3	.222
Slade, G.	SS			85	.239
Sothern, D.	OF			19	.161
Thompson, L.	2B			74	.265
Warner, J.	3B			9	.500
Wright, F.	SS			77	.284

1932 (Third place)

WON—81
LOST—73
Max George Carey, Mgr.

PLAYER	POS.	W	L	G	BA
Pitchers					
Clark, W.		20	12	40	.216
Heimach, F.		9	4	37	.164
Hoyt, W.		1	3	8	.000
Jones, A.		0	0	1	.000
Moore, W.		0	3	21	.214
Mungo, V.		13	11	39	.203
Phelps, R.		4	5	20	.087
Pipgras, E.		0	1	5	.000
Quinn, J.		3	7	42	.200
Shaute, J.		7	7	35	.200
Thomas, F.		0	1	7	.000
Thurston, H.		12	8	29	.304
Vance, C.		12	11	27	.089
Boone, I.	OF			13	.143
Caldwell, B.	1B			7	.091
Clancy, J.	1B			53	.306
Cohen, A.	OF			9	.156
Cuccinello, A.	2B			154	.281
Finn, C.	3B			65	.238
Frederick, J.	OF			118	.299
Kelly, G.	1B			64	.243
Lopez, A.	C			126	.275
O'Doul, F.	OF			148	.368
Picinich, V.	C			41	.257
Reis, R.	3B			1	.250
Richards, P.	C			3	.000
Rosenfeld, M.	OF			34	.359
Siebert, R.	1B			6	.286
Slade, G.	SS			79	.240
Stripp, J.	3B			138	.303
Sukeforth, C.	C			59	.234
Taylor, D.	OF			105	.324
Thompson, L.				3	.000
Wilson, L.	OF			135	.297
Wright, F.	SS			127	.274

1933 (Sixth place)

WON—65
LOST—88
Max George Carey, Mgr.

PLAYER	POS.	W	L	G	BA
Pitchers					
Beck, W.		12	20	43	.189
Benge, R.		10	17	37	.184
Carroll, O.		13	15	34	.149
Clark, W.		2	4	11	.154
Heimach, F.		0	1	10	.200
Leonard, E.		2	3	10	.000
Lucas, R.		0	0	2	.000
Mungo, V.		16	15	41	.179

PLAYER	POS.	W	L	G	BA
Ryan, W.		1	1	30	.154
Shaute, J.		3	4	41	.222
Thurston, H.		6	8	32	.159
Bissonette, A.	1B			35	.246
Blue, L.	1B			1	.000
Boyle, R.	OF			93	.299
Cuccinello, A.	2B			134	.252
Delmas, B.	2B			12	.250
Flowers, D.	SS			78	.233
Frederick, J.	OF			147	.308
Frey, L.	SS			34	.319
Hutcheson, J.	OF			55	.234
Jordan, J.	SS			70	.256
Judge, J.	1B			42	.214
Leslie, S.	1B			96	.283
Lopez, A.	C			126	.301
O'Doul, F.	OF			43	.252
Outen, W.	C			93	.248
Picinich, V.	C			6	.167
Rosenfeld, M.	OF			5	.111
Stripp, J.	3B			141	.277
Sukeforth, C.	C			20	.056
Taylor, D.	OF			103	.285
Wilson, L.	OF			117	.267
Wright, F.	SS			71	.255

1934 (Sixth place)

WON—71
LOST—81
Chas. Dillon Stengel, Mgr.

PLAYER	POS.	W	L	G	BA
Pitchers					
Babich, J.		7	11	25	.140
Beck, W.		2	6	22	.235
Benge, R.		14	12	36	.169
Carroll, O.		1	3	28	.240
Clark, W.		2	0	17	.125
Herring, A.		2	4	14	.143
Leonard, E.		14	11	44	.179
Lucas, R.		1	1	10	.333
Mungo, V.		18	16	46	.248
Munns, L.		3	7	34	.241
Page, P.		1	0	6	.000
Perkins, C.		0	3	11	.286
Smythe, W.		1	1	10	.333
Zachary, J.		5	6	24	.184
Berres, R.	C			39	.215
Boyle, R.	OF			128	.305
Bucher, J.	2B			47	.226
Chapman, G.	OF			67	.280
Cuccinello, A.	2B			140	.261
Frederick, J.	OF			104	.296
Frey, L.	SS			125	.284
Hogg, W.	3B			2	.000
Jordan, J.	SS			97	.266
Koenecke, L.	OF			123	.320

PLAYER	POS.	W	L	G	BA
Leslie, S.	1B			146	.332
Lopez, A.	C			140	.273
Millies, W.	C			2	.000
McCarthy, J.	1B			17	.179
Stripp, J.	3B			104	.315
Sukeforth, C.	C			27	.163
Taylor, D.	OF			120	.299
Tremark, N.	OF			17	.250
Wilson, L.	OF			67	.262

1935 (Fifth place)

WON—70
LOST—83
Chas. Dillon Stengel, Mgr.

PLAYER	POS.	W	L	G	BA
Pitchers					
Babich, J.		7	14	37	.184
Baker, T.		1	0	11	.474
Barr, R.		0	0	2	.000
Benge, R.		9	9	23	.191
Clark, W.		13	8	34	.177
Earnshaw, G.		8	12	25	.217
Eisenstat, H.		0	1	2	.000
Green, H.		0	0	2	.000
Lamanske, F.		0	0	2	.000
Leonard, E.		2	9	43	.025
Logan, R.		0	1	2	.000
Mungo, V.		16	10	44	.289
Munns, L.		1	3	22	.188
Reis, R.		3	2	52	.247
Vance, C.		3	2	20	.059
Zachary, J.		7	12	25	.135
Bordagaray, S.	OF			120	.282
Boyle, R.	OF			127	.272
Bucher, J.	2B			123	.302
Cooney, J.	OF			10	.310
Cuccinello, A.	2B			102	.292
Dedeaux, R.	SS			2	.250
Frey, L.	SS			131	.262
Jordan, J.	2B			94	.278
Koenecke, L.	OF			100	.283
Leslie, S.	1B			142	.308
Lopez, A.	C			128	.251
Mills, C.	OF			17	.214
McCarthy, J.	1B			22	.250
Ock, H.	C			1	.000
Onis, H.	C			1	1.000
Phelps, E.	C			47	.364
Sherlock, V.	2B			9	.462
Skaff, F.	3B			6	.545
Stripp, J.	3B			109	.306
Taylor, D.	OF			112	.290
Taylor, J.	C			26	.130
Tremark, N.	OF			10	.231

1936 (Seventh place)

WON—67
LOST—87
Chas. Dillon Stengel, Mgr.

PLAYER	POS.	W	L	G	BA
Pitchers					
Baker, T.		1	8	37	.233
Brandt, E.		11	13	43	.190
Butcher, A.		6	6	42	.125
Clark, W.		7	11	33	.231
Earnshaw, G.		4	9	19	.242
Eisenstat, H.		1	2	5	.333
Frankhouse, F.		13	10	42	.143
Jeffcoat, G.		5	6	40	.130
Leonard, E.		0	0	16	.400
Mungo, V.		18	19	50	.179
Winston, H.		1	3	14	.091
Zachary, J.		0	0	1	.000
Berres, R.	C			105	.240
Bordagaray, S.	OF			125	.315
Bucher, J.	3B			110	.251
Cooney, J.	OF			130	.282
Eckhardt, O.	OF			16	.182
Frey, L.	SS			148	.279
Gautreaux, S.	C			75	.268
Geraghty, B.	SS			51	.194
Hassett, J.	1B			156	.310
Hudson, J.	SS			6	.167
Jordan, J.	2B			115	.234
Lindstrom, F.	OF			26	.264
Moore, R.	OF			42	.239
Phelps, E.	C			115	.367
Radtke, J.	2B			33	.097
Siebert, R.	OF			2	.000
Stripp, J.	3B			110	.317
Taylor, D.	OF			43	.293
Tremark, N.	OF			8	.250
Watkins, G.	OF			105	.256
Wilson, E.	OF			52	.347
Winsett, J.	OF			22	.235

1937 (Sixth place)

WON—62
LOST—91
Burleigh Arland Grimes, Mgr.

PLAYER	POS.	W	L	G	BA
Pitchers					
Baker, T.		0	1	7	.000
Birkofer, R.		0	2	12	.273
Butcher, A.		11	15	40	.161
Cantwell, B.		0	0	13	.167
Clark, W.		0	0	2	.000
Eisenstat, H.		3	3	13	.000
Fitzsimmons, F.		4	8	13	.167
Frankhouse, F.		10	13	39	.190
Hamlin, L.		11	13	41	.186

PLAYER	POS.	W	L	G	BA
Henshaw, R.		5	12	43	.167
Hoyt, W.		7	7	27	.083
Jeffcoat, G.		1	3	21	.000
Lindsey, J.		0	1	20	.167
Marrow, C.		1	2	6	.000
Mungo, V.		9	11	28	.250
Peterson, J.		0	0	3	.000
Winsett, J.		0	0	118	.237
Brack, G.	OF			112	.274
Brown, J.	SS			48	.270
Bucher, J.	2B			125	.253
Chervinko, P.	C			30	.146
Cisar, G.	OF			20	.207
Cooney, J.	OF			120	.293
Daniel, H.	1B			12	.185
English, E.	SS			129	.238
Fallon, G.	2B			4	.250
Gautreaux, S.	C			11	.100
Haas, B.	1B			16	.400
Hassett, J.	1B			137	.304
Hudson, J.	SS			13	.185
Klumpp, E.	C			5	.091
Lavagetto, H.	2B			149	.282
Malinosky, A.	3B			35	.228
Manush, H.	OF			132	.333
Moore, R.	C			13	.136
Morgan, E.	OF			31	.188
Parks, A.	OF			7	.313
Phelps, E.	C			121	.313
Polly, N.	3B			10	.222
Rosen, G.	OF			22	.312
Spencer, R.	C			51	.205
Stripp, J.	3B			90	.243
Wilson, E.	OF			36	.222

1938 (Seventh place)

WON—69
LOST—80
Burleigh Arland Grimes, Mgr.

PLAYER	POS.	W	L	G	BA
Pitchers					
Butcher, A.		5	4	25	.160
Fitzsimmons, F		11	8	27	.171
Frankhouse, F.		3	5	31	.154
Gaddy, J.		2	0	2	.000
Hamlin, L.		12	15	44	.141
Hoyt, W.		0	3	6	.000
LaMaster, W.		0	1	5	.167
Marrow, C.		0	1	15	.000
Mungo, V.		4	11	32	.191
Nahem, S.		1	0	1	.400
Posedel, W.		8	9	33	.227
Potter, M.		0	0	2	.000
Pressnell, F.		11	14	43	.143
Rogers, L.		0	2	14	.000
Tamulis, V.		12	6	39	.127
Winford, J.		0	1	2	.000

PLAYER	POS.	W	L	G	BA
Brack, G.	OF			40	.214
Camilli, A.	1B			146	.251
Campbell, W.	C			54	.246
Chervinko, P.	C			12	.148
Coscarart, P.	2B			32	.152
Cuyler, H.	OF			82	.273
Durocher, L.	SS			141	.219
English, E.	3B			34	.250
George, C.	C			7	.200
Haas, B.				1	.000
Hassett, J.	OF			115	.293
Hayworth, R.	C			5	.000
Hockett, O.	OF			21	.329
Hudson, J.	2B			135	.261
Koy, E.	OF			142	.299
Lavagetto, H.	3B			137	.273
Manush, H.	OF			17	.235
Phelps, E.	C			66	.308
Rogers, S.	3B			23	.189
Rosen, G.	OF			138	.281
Shea, M.	C			48	.183
Sington, F.	OF			17	.358
Spencer, R.	C			16	.267
Stainback, G.	OF			35	.327
Thomas, R.	C			1	.333
Williams, W.	SS			20	.333
Winsett, J.	OF			12	.300

1939 (Third place)

WON—84
LOST—69
Leo Ernest Durocher, Mgr.

PLAYER	POS.	W	L	G	BA
Pitchers					
Casey, H.		15	10	40	.203
Crouch, W.		4	0	6	.133
Doyle, W.		1	2	5	.167
Evans, R.		1	8	24	.308
Fitzsimmons, F.		7	9	27	.234
Hamlin, L.		20	13	40	.126
Hollingsworth, A.		1	2	9	.125
Hutchinson, I.		5	2	41	.037
Jeffcoat, G.		0	0	1	.000
Mungo, V.		4	5	29	.345
Poffenberger, C.		0	0	3	.000
Pressnell, F.		9	7	31	.196
Schott, E.		0	0	1	.000
Tamulis, V.		9	8	39	.182
Wyatt, J.		8	3	16	.167
Almada, M.	OF			39	.214
Camilli, A.	1B			157	.290
Coscarart, P.	2B			115	.277
Deal, F.	OF			4	.000
Durocher, L. Mgr.	SS			116	.277
Hartje, C.	C			9	.313
Hayworth, R.	C			21	.154
Hockett, O.	OF			9	.231

PLAYER	POS.	W	L	G	BA
Hudson, J.	SS			109	.254
Koy, E.	OF			125	.278
Lary, L.	SS			29	.161
Lavagetto, H.	3B			153	.300
Lazzeri, A.	2B			14	.282
Moore, E.	OF			107	.225
Parks, A.	OF			71	.272
Phelps, E.	C			98	.285
Ripple, J.	OF			28	.330
Rosen, G.	OF			54	.251
Sewell, J.		(DID NOT PLAY)			
Sington, F.	OF			32	.274
Stainback, G.	OF			68	.269
Todd, A.	C			86	.277
Walker, F.	OF			61	.280

1940 (Second place)

WON—88
LOST—65
Leo Ernest Durocher, Mgr.

PLAYER	POS.	W	L	G	BA
Pitchers					
Carleton, J.		6	6	34	.186
Casey, H.		11	8	45	.250
Davis, C.		8	7	22	.128
Doyle, W.		0	0	3	1.000
Fette, L.		0	0	2	.000
Fitzsimmons, F.		16	2	20	.106
Ferrell, W.		0	0	2	.000
Flowers, C.		1	1	5	.200
Grissom, L.		2	5	14	.217
Hamlin, L.		9	8	35	.086
Head, E.		1	2	14	.182
Kimball, N.		3	1	21	.000
Macon, M.		1	0	21	.000
Mungo, V.		1	0	8	.000
Pressnell, F.		6	5	24	.000
Rachunok, S.		0	1	2	.000
Tamulis, V.		8	5	42	.130
Wyatt, J.		15	14	37	.175
Camilli, A.	1B			142	.287
Coscarart, P.	2B			143	.237
Cullenbine, R.	OF			22	.180
Durocher, L. Mgr.	SS			62	.231
Franks, H.	C			65	.183
Gallagher, J.	OF			57	.264
Gilbert, C.	OF			57	.246
Giuliani, A.	C			1	.000
Hudson, J.	SS			85	.218
Koy, E.	OF			24	.229
Lavagetto, H.	3B			118	.257
Mancuso, A.	C			60	.229
Medwick, J.	OF			106	.300
Moore, E.	OF			10	.269
Phelps, E.	C			118	.295

PLAYER	POS.	W	L	G	BA
Reese, H.	SS			84	.272
Reiser, H.	3B			58	.293
Ripple, J.	OF			7	.231
Ross, D.	3B			10	.289
Vosmik, J.	OF			116	.282
Walker, F.	OF			143	.308
Wasdell, J.	OF			77	.278

1941 (First place)

WON—100
LOST—54
Leo Ernest Durocher, Mgr.

PLAYER	POS.	W	L	G	BA
Pitchers					
Albosta, E.		0	2	2	.000
Allen, J.		3	0	11	.050
Brown, M		3	2	24	.000
Casey, H.		14	11	45	.120
Chipman, R.		1	0	1	.000
Davis, C.		13	7	31	.186
Drake, T.		1	1	11	.400
Fitzsimmons, F.		6	1	13	.143
French, L.		0	0	6	.250
Grissom, L.		0	0	4	.500
Hamlin, L.		8	8	30	.146
Higbe, W.		22	9	48	.188
Kimball, N.		3	1	15	.214
Mungo, V.		0	0	2	.000
Swift, W.		3	0	9	.200
Tamulis, V.		0	0	12	.000
Wicker, K.		1	2	16	.250
Wyatt, J.		22	10	40	.239
Camilli, A.	1B			149	.285
Coscarart, P.	2B			43	.127
Durocher, L. Mgr.	SS			18	.286
Franks, H.	C			57	.201
Galan, A.	OF			17	.259
Giuliani, A.	OF			3	.000
Herman, W.	2B			133	.291
Kampouris, A.	2B			16	.314
Lavagetto, H.	3B			132	.277
Medwick, J.	OF			133	.318
Owen, A.	C			128	.231
Pfister, G.	C			1	.000
Phelps, E.	C			16	.233
Reese, H.	SS			152	.228
Reiser, H.	OF			137	.343
Riggs, L.	3B			77	.305
Tatum, T.	OF			8	.167
Vosmik, J.	OF			25	.196
Walker, F.	OF			148	.311
Waner, P.	OF			11	.171
Wasdell, J.	OF			94	.299

1942 (Second place)

WON—104
LOST—50
Leo Ernest Durocher, Mgr.

PLAYER	POS.	W	L	G	BA
Pitchers					
Allen, J.		10	6	27	.179
Casey, H.		6	3	50	.148
Chipman, R.		0	0	2	.000
Davis, C.		15	6	32	.176
Fitzsimmons, F.		0	0	1	.500
French, L.		15	4	38	.300
Head, E.		10	6	36	.333
Higbe, W.		16	11	38	.104
Kehn, C.		0	0	3	1.000
Kimball, N.		2	0	14	.200
Macon, M.		5	3	26	.279
Newsom, L.		2	2	6	.000
Rowe, L.		1	0	14	.211
Webber, L.		3	2	19	.071
Wyatt, J.		19	7	31	.182
Bordagaray, S.	OF			48	.241
Camilli, A.	1B			150	.252
Dahlgren, E.	1B			17	.173
Dapper, C.	C			8	.471
Galan, A.	OF			69	.263
Herman, W.	2B			155	.256
Kampouris, A.	2B			10	.238
Medwick, J.	OF			142	.300
Owen, A.	C			133	.259
Reese, H.	SS			151	.255
Reiser, H.	OF			125	.310
Riggs, L.	3B			70	.278
Rizzo, J.	OF			78	.230
Rojek, S.				1	.000
Sullivan, W.	C			43	.267
Vaughan, J.	3B			128	.277
Walker, F.	OF			118	.290

1943 (Third place)

WON—81
LOST—72
Leo Ernest Durocher, Mgr.

PLAYER	POS.	W	L	G	BA
Pitchers					
Allen, J.		5	1	17	.429
Barney, R.		2	2	9	.058
Chipman, R.		0	0	1	.000
Davis, C.		10	13	31	.164
Fitzsimmons, F.		3	4	9	.071
Gregg, H.		0	3	5	.000
Haughey, C.		0	1	1	.000
Head, E.		9	10	47	.152
Higbe, W.		13	10	35	.138
Kimball, N.		1	1	5	.000
Lohrman, W.		0	2	6	.143

PLAYER	POS.	W	L	G	BA
Macon, M.		7	5	45	.164
Melton, R.		5	8	30	.105
Newsom, L.		9	4	22	.250
Ostermueller, F.		1	1	8	.000
Sayles, W.		0	0	6	.500
Webber, L.		2	2	54	.120
Wyatt, J.		14	5	27	.283
Ankeman, F.	SS			1	.500
Barkley, J.	SS			20	.314
Bordagaray, S.	OF			89	.302
Bragan, R.	C			74	.264
Camilli, A.	1B			95	.247
Campanis, A.	2B			7	.100
Cooney, J.	1B			37	.206
Durocher, L. Mgr.	SS			6	.222
Galan, A.	OF			139	.287
Gillenwater, C.	OF			8	.176
Glossop, A.	SS			87	.171
Hart, W.	SS			8	.158
Herman, W.	2B			153	.330
Hermanski, E.	OF			18	.300
Hodges, G.	SS			1	.000
Kampouris, A.	2B			19	.227
Medwick, J.	OF			48	.272
Moore, D.	C			37	.253
Olmo, L.	OF			57	.303
Orengo, J.	3B			7	.200
Owen, A.	C			106	.260
Peck, H.				1	.000
Schultz, H.	1B			45	.269
Vaughan, J.	SS			149	.305
Walker, F.	OF			138	.302
Waner, P.	OF			82	.311

1944 (Seventh place)

WON—63
LOST—91
Leo Ernest Durocher, Mgr.

PLAYER	POS.	W	L	G	BA
Pitchers					
Branca, R.		0	2	21	.000
Chapman, W.		5	3	20	.368
Chipman, R.		3	1	11	.182
Crocker, C.		0	0	2	1.000
Davis, C.		10	11	31	.159
Flowers, C.		1	1	9	.600
Franklin, J.		0	0	1	.000
Fuchs, C.		1	0	8	.000
Gregg, H.		9	16	42	.206
Head, E.		4	3	9	.263
Herring, A.		3	4	12	.200
King, C.		2	1	14	.200
Lohrman, W.		0	0	3	.000
Melton, R.		9	13	37	.123
McLish, C.		3	10	31	.219
Osgood, C.		0	0	1	.000
Ostermueller, F.		2	1	11	.154

PLAYER	POS.	W	L	G	BA
Sunkel, T.		1	3	12	.000
Warren, T.		1	4	41	.256
Webber, L.		7	8	48	.205
Wells, J.		0	2	4	.250
Wurm, F.		0	0	1	.000
Wyatt, J.		2	6	11	.154
Zachary, A.		0	2	4	.000
Anderholt, M.	OF			17	.271
Andrews, S.	C			4	.125
Ankeman, F.	2B			13	.250
Basinski, E.	2B			39	.257
Bolling, J.	1B			56	.351
Bordagaray, S.	3B			130	.281
Bragan, R.	SS			94	.267
Brown, T.	SS			46	.164
Cooney, J.	OF			7	.750
Dantonio, J.	C			3	.143
Durrett, E.	OF			11	.156
English, G.	SS			27	.152
Galan, A.	OF			151	.318
Hart, W.	SS			29	.178
Hayworth, R.	C			7	.000
Jarvis, L.	C			1	.000
Koch, B.	2B			33	.219
Mauch, E.	SS			5	.133
Miksis, E.	3B			26	.220
Olmo, L.	OF			136	.258
Owen, A.	C			130	.273
Rochelli, L.	2B			5	.176
Rosen, G.	OF			89	.261
Schultz, H.	1B			138	.255
Smyres, C.				5	.000
Stanky, E.	2B			89	.276
Walker, F.	OF			147	.357
Waner, L.	OF			15	.286
Waner, P.	OF			83	.287

1945 (Third place)

WON—87
LOST—67
Leo Ernest Durocher, Mgr.

PLAYER	POS.	W	L	G	BA
Pitchers					
Branca, R.		5	6	16	.000
Buker, C.		7	2	42	.188
Chapman, W.		3	3	13	.136
Crocker, C.		0	0	1	.000
Davis, C.		10	10	24	.137
Gregg, H.		18	13	42	.220
Hathaway, R.		0	1	4	.000
Herring, A.		7	4	23	.095
King, C.		5	5	43	.125
Lombardi, V.		10	11	45	.183
Nicholas, O.		1	0	7	.250
Pfund, L.		3	2	15	.182

PLAYER	POS.	W	L	G	BA
Rudolph, E.		1	0	7	.000
Seats, T.		10	7	31	.209
Webber, L.		7	3	17	.091
Aderholt, M.	OF			39	.217
Andrews, S.	C			21	.163
Basinski, E.	SS			108	.262
Bordagaray, S.	3B			113	.256
Brown, T.	SS			57	.245
Corbitt, C.	3B			2	.500
Dantonio, J.	C			47	.250
Douglas, J.	1B			5	.000
Durocher, L. Mgr.	2B			2	.200
Durrett, E.	OF			8	.125
Galan, A.	1B			152	.307
Hart, W.	3B			58	.230
Hayworth, R.	C			2	.000
Herman, F.	OF			2	.000
Lund, D.				4	.000
Olmo, L.	OF			141	.313
Owen, A.	C			24	.286
Palica, E.				2	.000
Peacock, J.	C			48	.255
Rosen, G.	OF			145	.325
Sandlock, M.	C			80	.282
Schultz, H.	1B			39	.239
Stanky, E.	2B			153	.258
Stevens, E.	1B			55	.274
Sukeforth, C.	C			18	.294
Walker, F.	OF			154	.300
White, W.	SS			4	.000

1946 (Second place)

WON—96
LOST—60
Leo Ernest Durocher, Mgr.

PLAYER	POS.	W	L	G	BA
Pitchers					
Barney, R.		2	5	16	.235
Behrman, H.		11	5	47	.095
Branca, R.		3	1	24	.111
Casey, H.		11	5	46	.136
Davis, C.		0	0	1	.000
Gregg, H.		6	4	26	.125
Hatten, J.		14	11	42	.076
Head, E.		3	2	13	.313
Herring, A.		7	2	35	.182
Higbe, W.		17	8	42	.130
Lombardi, V.		13	10	43	.230
Melton, R.		6	3	24	.107
Minner, P.		0	1	3	.000
Moulder, G.		0	0	1	.000
McLish, C.		0	0	1	.000
Roy, J.		0	0	3	.000
Taylor, J.		0	0	4	.000
Webber, L.		3	3	11	.100

PLAYER	POS.	W	L	G	BA
Anderson, F.	C			79	.256
Corriden, J.				1	.000
Davis, O.				1	.000
Edwards, C.				92	.267
Furillo, C.	OF			117	.284
Galan, A.	OF			99	.310
Graham, J.	1B			2	.200
Herman, W.	3B			47	.288
Hermanski, E.	OF			64	.200
Lavagetto, H.	3B			88	.236
Medwick, J.	OF			41	.312
Miksis, E.	3B			23	.146
Naylor, E.				3	.000
Padgett, D.	C			19	.167
Ramazzotti, R.	3B			62	.208
Reese, H.	SS			152	.284
Reiser, H.	OF			122	.277
Riggs, L.	3B			1	.000
Rojek, S.	SS			45	.277
Rosen, G.	OF			3	.333
Sandlock, M.	C			19	.147
Schultz, H.	1B			90	.253
Stanky, E.	2B			144	.273
Stevens, E.	1B			103	.242
Tepsic, J.	OF			15	.000
Walker, F.	OF			150	.319
Whitman, D.	OF			104	.260

1947 (First place)

WON—94
LOST—60
Clyde Leroy Sukeforth and Burton Edwin Shotton, Mgrs.

PLAYER	POS.	W	L	G	BA
Pitchers					
Bankhead, D.		0	0	6	.250
Banta, J.		0	1	3	.000
Barney, R.		5	2	28	.111
Behrman, H.		5	3	40	.231
Branca, R.		21	12	43	.124
Casey, H.		10	4	46	.056
Chandler, E.		0	1	15	.000
Dockins, G.		0	0	4	.000
Gregg, H.		4	5	37	.265
Hatten, J.		17	8	42	.205
Haugstad, P.		1	0	6	.000
Higbe, W.		2	0	4	.200
King, C.		6	5	29	.115
Lombardi, V.		12	11	36	.242
Melton, R.		0	1	4	1.000
Palica, E.		0	1	3	.000
Ramsdell, J.		1	1	2	1.000
Taylor, J.		10	5	33	.129
Van Cuyk, J.		0	0	2	.000
Bragan, R.	C			25	.194
Brown, T.	3B			15	.235
Edwards, C.	C			130	.296
Furillo, C.	OF			124	.295

PLAYER	POS.	W	L	G	BA
Gionfriddo, A.	OF			37	.177
Hermanski, E.	OF			79	.275
Hodges, G.	C			28	.156
Jorgensen, J.	3B			129	.274
Lavagetto, H.	3B			41	.261
Lund, D.	OF			11	.300
Miksis, E.	2B			45	.267
Rackley, M.	OF			18	.222
Reese, H.	SS			142	.284
Reiser, H.	OF			110	.309
Robinson, J.	1B			151	.296
Rojek, S.	SS			32	.263
Schultz, H.	1B			2	.000
Snider, E.	OF			40	.241
Stanky, E.	2B			146	.252
Stevens, E.	1B			5	.154
Tatum, T.	OF			4	.000
Vaughan, J.	OF			64	.325
Walker, F.	OF			148	.306
Whitman, D.	OF			4	.400

1948 (Third place)

WON—84
LOST—70
Leo Ernest Durocher and Burton Edwin Shotton, Mgrs.

PLAYER	POS.	W	L	G	BA
Pitchers					
Banta, J.		0	1	2	.000
Barney, R.		15	13	44	.167
Behrman, H.		5	4	34	.107
Branca, R.		14	9	36	.203
Casey, H.		3	0	22	.000
Erskine, C.		6	3	17	.095
Hall, J.		0	0	3	.000
Hatten, J.		13	10	43	.206
Haugstad, P.		0	0	1	.000
King, C.		0	1	9	.000
Minner, P.		4	3	31	.190
Palica, E.		6	6	45	.128
Ramsdell, J.		4	4	27	.091
Roe, E.		12	8	34	.098
Sexauer, E.		0	0	2	.000
Sloat, D.		0	1	4	.000
Taylor, J.		2	7	17	.273
Van Cuyk, J.		0	0	3	.000
Bragan, R.	C			9	.167
Brown, T.	3B			54	.241
Campanella, R.	C			83	.258
Cox, W.	3B			88	.249
Edwards, C.	C			96	.276
Furillo, C.	OF			108	.297
Hermanski, E.	OF			133	.290
Hodges, G.	1B			134	.249
Jorgensen, J.	3B			31	.300
Lund, D.	OF			27	.188
Mauch, E.	2B			12	.154
Miksis, E.	2B			86	.213

PLAYER	POS.	W	L	G	BA
Rackley, M.	OF			88	.327
Ramazzotti, R.	2B			4	.000
Reese, H.	SS			151	.274
Reiser, H.	OF			64	.236
Robinson, J.	2B			147	.296
Shuba, G.	OF			63	.267
Snider, E.	OF			53	.244
Vaughan, J.	OF			65	.244
Ward, P.	1B			42	.260
Whitman, D.	OF			60	.291

1949 (First place)

WON—97
LOST—57
Burton Edwin Shotton, Mgr.

PLAYER	POS.	W	L	G	BA
Pitchers					
Banta, J.		10	6	48	.109
Barney, R.		9	8	38	.213
Branca, R.		13	5	34	.081
Erskine, C.		8	1	22	.115
Hatten, J.		12	8	39	.179
Martin, M.		1	3	10	.200
Minner, P.		3	1	27	.214
McGlothin, E.		1	1	7	.000
Newcombe, D.		17	8	39	.229
Palica, E.		8	9	49	.158
Podbielan, C.		0	1	7	.000
Roe, E.		15	6	30	.114
Van Cuyk, J.		0	0	2	.000
Abrams, C.	OF			8	.083
Brown, T.	OF			41	.303
Campanella, R.	C			130	.287
Connors, K.				1	.000
Cox, W.	3B			100	.234
Edwards, C.	C			64	.209
Furillo, C.	OF			142	.324
Hermanski, E.	OF			87	.299
Hodges, G.	1B			156	.285
Hopp, J.	OF			8	.000
Jorgensen, J.	3B			53	.269
Miksis, E.	3B			50	.221
McCormick, M.	OF			55	.209
Olmo, L.	OF			38	.305
Rackley, M.	OF			9	.444
Ramazzotti, R.	3B			5	.154
Reese, H.	SS			155	.342
Robinson, J.	2B			156	.342
Shuba, G.				1	.000
Snider, E.	OF			146	.292
Whitman, D.	OF			23	.184

1950 (Second place)

WON—89
LOST—65
Burton Edwin Shotton, Mgr.

PLAYER	POS.	W	L	G	BA
Pitchers					
Bankhead, D.		9	4	41	.231
Banta, J.		4	4	16	.167
Barney, R.		2	1	20	.125
Branca, R.		7	9	43	.118
Epperly, A.		0	0	5	.000
Erskine, C.		7	6	22	.243
Hatten, J.		2	2	27	.111
Labine, C.		0	0	1	.000
Landrum, J.		0	0	7	.000
Loes, W.		0	0	10	.000
Mallette, M.		0	0	2	.000
McGlothin, E.		0	0	1	.000
Newcombe, D.		19	11	40	.247
Palica, E.		13	8	48	.221
Podbielan, C.		5	4	20	.107
Ramsdell, J.		1	2	5	.000
Roe, E.		19	11	36	.154
Romano, J.		0	0	3	.000
Van Cuyk, C.		1	3	12	.100
Abrams, C.	OF			38	.205
Belardi, C.	1B			10	.000
Brown, T.	OF			48	.291
Campanella, R.	C			126	.281
Cox, W.	3B			119	.257
Edwards, C.	C			50	.183
Furillo, C.	OF			153	.305
Hermanski, E.	OF			94	.298
Jorgensen, J.	3B			2	.000
Lembo, S.	C			5	.167
Miksis, E.	2B			51	.250
Morgan, R.	3B			67	.226
Reese, H.	SS			141	.260
Robinson, J.	2B			144	.328
Russell, J.	OF			77	.229
Shuba, G.	OF			34	.207
Snider, E.	OF			152	.321

1951 (Second place)

WON—97
LOST—60
Chas. Walter Dressen, Mgr.

PLAYER	POS.	W	L	G	BA
Pitchers					
Bankhead, D.		0	1	15	.000
Branca, R.		13	12	42	.175
Erskine, C.		16	12	46	.131
Hatten, J.		1	0	11	.135
Haugstad, P.		0	1	21	.000
King, C.		14	7	48	.138
Labine, C.		5	1	14	.143

294 • The Complete Dodgers Record Book

PLAYER	POS.	W	L	G	BA
Mossor, E.		0	0	3	1.000
Newcombe, D.		20	9	40	.223
Palica, E.		2	6	20	.154
Podbielan, C.		2	2	27	.304
Roe, E.		22	3	34	.112
Schmitz, J.		1	4	16	.222
Van Cuyk, C.		1	2	9	.250
Abrams, C.	OF			67	.280
Belardi, C.				3	.333
Bridges, E.	3B			63	.254
Brown, T.	OF			11	.160
Campanella, R.	C			143	.325
Cox, W.	3B			142	.279
Edwards, C.	C			17	.250
Edwards, H.				35	.226
Furillo, C.	OF			158	.295
Hermanski, E.	OF			31	.250
Hodges, G.	1B			158	.268
Livingston, T.	C			2	.400
Miksis, E.	3B			19	.200
Pafko, A.	OF			84	.249
Reese, H.	SS			154	.286
Robinson, J.	2B			153	.338
Russell, J.	OF			16	.000
Snider, E.	OF			150	.277
Terwilliger, W.	2B			37	.280
Thompson, D.	OF			80	.229
Walker, A.	C			36	.243
Williams, R.	OF			23	.200

1952 (First place)

WON—96
LOST—57
Chas. Walter Dressen, Mgr.

PLAYER	POS.	W	L	G	BA
Pitchers					
Black, J.		15	4	57	.139
Branca, R.		4	2	16	.158
Erskine, C.		14	6	34	.152
Hughes, J.		2	1	6	.000
King, C.		2	0	23	.000
Labine, C.		8	4	26	.045
Landrum, J.		1	3	9	.125
Lehman, K.		1	2	4	.000
Loes, W.		13	8	39	.092
Moore, R.		1	2	14	.000
Negray, R.		0	0	4	.000
Podbielan, C.		0	0	4	.000
Roe, E.		11	2	27	.070
Rutherford, J.		7	7	22	.290
Schmitz, J.		1	1	10	.125
Van Cuyk, C.		5	6	23	.242
Wade, B.		11	9	37	.117
Abrams, C.	OF			10	.200
Amoros, E.	OF			20	.250

PLAYER	POS.	W	L	G	BA
Bridges, E.	2B			51	.196
Campanella, R.	C			128	.269
Cox, W.	3B			116	.259
Furillo, C.	OF			134	.247
Hodges, G.	1B			153	.254
Holmes, T.	OF			31	.111
Lembo, S.	C			2	.200
Morgan, R.	3B			67	.236
Nelson, G.	1B			37	.256
Pafko, A.	OF			150	.287
Reese, H.	SS			149	.272
Robinson, J.	2B			149	.308
Shuba, G.	OF			94	.305
Snider, E.	OF			144	.303
Walker, A.	C			46	.259
Williams, R.	OF			36	.309

1953 (First place)

WON—105
LOST—49
Chas. Walter Dressen, Mgr.

PLAYER	POS.	W	L	G	BA
Pitchers					
Black, J.		6	3	40	.163
Branca, R.		0	0	7	.000
Erskine, C.		20	6	43	.215
Hughes, J.		4	3	48	.286
Labine, C.		11	6	37	.071
Loes, W.		14	8	32	.125
Meyer, R.		15	5	34	.147
Mickens, G.		0	1	4	.000
Milliken, R.		8	4	37	.118
Moore, R.		0	1	1	.000
Palica, E.		0	0	4	1.000
Podres, J.		9	4	34	.306
Roes, E.		11	3	25	.053
Wade, B.		7	5	32	.167
Antonello, W.	OF			40	.163
Belardi, C.	1B			69	.239
Campanella, R.	C			144	.312
Cox, W.	3B			100	.291
Furillo, C.	OF			132	.344
Howell, H.				1	.000
Mauro, C.	OF			8	.000
Morgan, R.	3B			69	.260
Reese, H.	SS			140	.271
Robinson, J.	OF			136	.329
Shuba, G.	OF			74	.254
Snider, E.	OF			153	.336
Teed, R.				1	.000
Thompson, D.	OF			96	.242
Walker, A.	C			43	.242
Williams, R.	OF			30	.218

1954 (Second place)

WON—92
LOST—62
Walter Emmons Alston, Mgr.

PLAYER	POS.	W	L	G	BA
Pitchers					
Black, J.		0	0	5	.000
Darnell, R.		0	0	6	.000
Erskine, C.		18	15	39	.159
Hughes, J.		8	4	60	.188
Labine, C.		7	6	47	.033
Lasorda, T.		0	0	4	.000
Loes, W.		13	5	28	.118
Meyer, R.		11	6	36	.043
Milliken, R.		5	2	24	.176
Newcombe, D.		9	8	31	.319
Palica, E.		3	3	28	.250
Podres, J.		11	7	38	.283
Roe, E.		3	4	15	.143
Spooner, K.		2	0	2	.167
Wade, B.		1	1	23	.000
Wojey, P.		1	1	14	.000
Amoros, E.	OF			79	.274
Belardi, C.				11	.222
Campanella, R.	C			111	.207
Cox, W.	3B			77	.235
Furillo, C.	OF			150	.294
Gilliam, J.	2B			146	.282
Hoak, D.	3B			88	.245
Hodges, G.	1B			154	.304
Kress, C.	1B			13	.083
Moryn, W.	OF			48	.275
Reese, H.	SS			141	.309
Robinson, J.	OF			124	.311
Shuba, G.	OF			45	.154
Snider, E.	OF			149	.341
Thompson, C.	C			10	.154
Thompson, D.	OF			34	.040
Walker, A.	C			50	.181
Williams, R.	OF			16	.147
Zimmer, D.	SS			24	.182

1955 (First place)

WON—98
LOST—55
Walter Emmons Alston, Mgr.

PLAYER	POS.	W	L	G	BA
Pitchers					
Bessent, F.		8	1	24	.100
Black, J.		1	0	6	.333
Craig, R.		5	3	21	.077
Erskine, C.		11	8	42	.203
Hughes, J.		0	2	24	.000
Koufax, S.		2	2	12	.000
Labine, C.		13	5	60	.097
Lasorda, T.		0	0	4	.000

PLAYER	POS.	W	L	G	BA
Loes, W.		10	4	22	.091
Meyer, R.		6	2	18	.037
Newcombe, D.		20	5	57	.359
Podres, J.		9	10	32	.183
Roebuck, E.		5	6	47	.111
Spooner, K.		8	6	29	.286
Templeton, C.		0	1	4	.000
Amoros, E.	OF			119	.247
Borkowski, R.	OF			9	.105
Campanella, R.	C			123	.318
Furillo, C.	OF			140	.314
Gilliam, J.	2B			147	.249
Hamric, O.				2	.000
Hoak, D.	3B			94	.240
Hodges, G.	1B			150	.289
Howell, H.	C			16	.262
Kellert, F.	1B			39	.325
Moryn, W.	OF			11	.263
Reese, H.	SS			145	.282
Robinson, J.	3B			105	.256
Shuba, G.	OF			44	.275
Snider, E.	OF			148	.309
Walker, A.	C			48	.252
Zimmer, D.	2B			88	.239

1956 (First place)

WON—93
LOST—61
Walter Emmons Alston, Mgr.

PLAYER	POS.	W	L	G	BA
Pitchers					
Bessent, F.		4	3	38	.111
Branca, R.		0	0	1	.000
Craig, R.		12	11	35	.016
Darnell, R.		0	0	1	.000
Drysdale, D.		5	5	26	.192
Erskine, C.		13	11	32	.121
Hughes, J.		0	0	5	.000
Koufax, S.		2	4	16	.118
Labine, C.		10	6	62	.087
Lehman, K.		2	3	25	.300
Loes, W.		0	1	1	.000
Maglie, S.		13	5	28	.129
Newcombe, D.		27	7	52	.234
Roebuck, E.		5	4	43	.333
Templeton, C.		0	1	6	.000
Amoros, E.	OF			114	.260
Aspromonte, R.				1	.000
Campanella, R.	C			124	.219
Cimoli, G.	OF			73	.111
Demeter, D.	OF			3	.333
Fernandez, H.	SS			34	.227
Furillo, C.	OF			149	.289
Gilliam, J.	2B			153	.300
Hodges, G.	1B			153	.265
Howell, H.	C			7	.231

PLAYER	POS.	W	L	G	BA
Jackson, R.	3B			101	.274
Mitchell, L.	OF			19	.292
Neal, C.	2B			62	.287
Nelson, G.	1B			31	.208
Reese, H.	SS			147	.257
Robinson, J.	3B			117	.275
Snider, E.	OF			151	.292
Walker, A.	C			54	.212
Williams, R.				7	.286
Zimmer, D.	SS			17	.300

1957 (Third place)

WON—84
LOST—70
Walter Emmons Alston, Mgr.

PLAYER	POS.	W	L	G	BA
Pitchers					
Bessent, F.		1	3	27	.250
Collum, J.		0	0	3	.000
Craig, R.		6	9	32	.138
Drysdale, D.		17	9	37	.123
Elston, D.		0	0	1	.000
Erskine, C.		5	3	21	.091
Harris, W.		0	1	1	.500
Kipp, F.		0	0	1	.000
Koufax, S.		5	4	34	.000
Labine, C.		5	7	58	.100
Lehman, K.		0	0	3	.500
Maglie, S.		6	6	19	.034
McDevitt, D.		7	4	22	.154
Newcombe, D.		11	12	34	.230
Podres, J.		12	9	35	.208
Roebuck, E.		8	2	44	.238
Valdes, R.		1	1	5	.000
Amoros, E.	OF			106	.277
Campanella, R.	C			103	.242
Cimoli, G.	OF			142	.293
Furillo, C.	OF			119	.306
Gentile, J.	1B			4	.167
Gilliam, J.	2B			149	.250
Hodges, G.	1B			150	.299
Jackson, R.	3B			48	.198
Kennedy, R.	OF			19	.129
Miller, R.				1	.000
Neal, C.	SS			128	.270
Pignatano, J.	C			8	.214
Reese, H.	3B			103	.224
Roseboro, J.	C			35	.145
Snider, E.	OF			139	.274
Valo, E.	OF			81	.273
Walker, A.	C			60	.181
Zimmer, D.	3B			84	.219

1958 (Seventh place)

WON—71
LOST—83
Walter Emmons Alston, Mgr.

PLAYER	POS.	W	L	G	BA
Pitchers					
Bessent, F.		1	0	19	.000
Birrer, W.		0	0	16	.571
Collum, J.		0	0	2	.000
Craig, R.		2	1	9	.000
Drysdale, D.		12	13	47	.227
Erskine, C.		4	4	32	.037
Giallombardo, R.		1	1	8	.167
Kipp, F.		6	6	42	.250
Klippstein, J.		3	5	45	.050
Koufax, S.		11	11	40	.122
Labine, C.		6	6	52	.056
Mauriello, R.		1	1	3	.000
McDevitt, D.		2	6	13	.133
Negray, R.		0	0	4	.000
Newcombe, D.		0	6	11	.417
Podres, J.		13	15	42	.127
Roebuck, E.		0	1	32	.500
Sherry, L.		0	0	5	.000
Williams, S.		9	7	27	.050
Bilko, S.	1B			47	.208
Cimoli, G.	OF			109	.246
Demeter, D.	OF			43	.189
Fairly, R.	OF			15	.283
Furillo, C.	OF			122	.290
Gentile, J.	1B			12	.133
Gilliam, J.	OF			147	.261
Gray, R.	3B			58	.249
Hodges, G.	1B			141	.259
Howard, F.	OF			8	.241
Jackson, R.	3B			35	.185
Larker, N.	OF			99	.277
Lillis, R.	SS			20	.391
Miles, D.	OF			8	.182
Neal, C.	2B			140	.254
Pignatano, J.	C			63	.218
Reese, H.	SS			59	.224
Robinson, E.	3B			8	.200
Roseboro, J.	C			114	.271
Snider, E.	OF			106	.312
Valo, E.	OF			65	.248
Walker, A.	C			25	.114
Wilson, R.	OF			3	.200
Zimmer, D.	SS			127	.262

1959 (First place)

WON—88
LOST—68
Walter Emmons Alston, Mgr.

PLAYER	POS.	W	L	G	BA
Pitchers					
Churn, C.		3	2	14	.167
Craig, R.		11	5	29	.058
Drysdale, D.		17	13	46	.165
Erskine, C.		0	3	10	.000
Fowler, A.		3	4	36	.083
Harris, W.		0	0	1	.000
Kipp, F.		0	0	2	.000
Klippstein, J.		4	0	28	.143
Koufax, S.		8	6	35	.111
Labine, C.		5	10	56	.000
McDevitt, D.		10	8	39	.109
Podres, J.		14	9	34	.246
Sherry, L.		7	2	23	.219
Snyder, E.		1	1	11	.000
Williams, S.		5	5	35	.194
Amoros, E.				5	.200
Baxes, D.	3B			11	.303
Davis, H.				1	.000
Demeter, D.	OF			139	.256
Drake, S.	OF			9	.250
Essegian, C.	OF			24	.304
Fairly, R.	OF			118	.238
Furillo, C.	OF			50	.290
Gilliam, J.	3B			145	.282
Gray, R.	3B			21	.154
Hodges, G.	1B			124	.276
Howard, F.	OF			9	.143
Larker, N.	1B			108	.289
Lillis, R.	SS			30	.229
Moon, W.	OF			145	.302
Neal, C.	2B			151	.287
Pignatano, J.	C			52	.237
Repulski, E.	OF			53	.255
Roseboro, J.	C			118	.232
Sherry, N.	C			2	.333
Snider, E.	OF			126	.308
Wills, M.	SS			83	.260
Zimmer, D.	SS			97	.165

1960 (Fourth place)

WON—82
LOST—72
Walter Emmons Alston, Mgr.

PLAYER	POS.	W	L	G	BA
Pitchers					
Craig, R.		8	3	21	.056
Drysdale, D.		15	14	41	.157
Golden, J.		1	0	1	.333
Koufax, S.		8	13	37	.123
Labine, C.		0	1	13	.500

PLAYER	POS.	W	L	G	BA
McDevitt, D.		0	4	24	.200
Ortega, F.		0	0	3	.000
Palmquist, E.		0	1	22	.000
Podres, J.		14	12	34	.136
Rakow, E.		0	1	9	.333
Roebuck, E.		8	3	58	.167
Sherry, L.		14	10	57	.162
Williams, S.		14	10	38	.141
Amoros, E.	OF			9	.143
Aspromonte, R.	SS			21	.182
Camilli, D.	C			6	.333
Davis, H.	OF			110	.276
Davis, W.	OF			22	.318
Demeter, D.	OF			64	.274
Essegian, C.	OF			52	.215
Fairly, R.	OF			14	.108
Furillo, C.	OF			8	.200
Gilliam, J.	3B			151	.248
Hodges, G.	1B			101	.198
Howard, F.	OF			117	.268
Larker, N.	1B			133	.323
Lillis, R.	SS			48	.267
Moon, W.	OF			138	.299
Neal, C.	2B			139	.256
Noren, I.				26	.200
Pignatano, J.	C			58	.233
Repulski, E.	OF			4	.200
Roseboro, J.	C			103	.213
Sherry, N.	C			47	.283
Smith, C.	3B			18	.167
Snider, E.	OS			101	.243
Wills, M.	SS			148	.295

1961 (Second place)

WON—89
LOST—65
Walter Emmons Alston, Mgr.

PLAYER	POS.	W	L	G	BA
Pitchers					
Craig, R.		5	6	40	.148
Drysdale, D.		13	10	40	.193
Farrell, R.		6	6	50	.000
Golden, J.		1	1	28	.000
Koufax, S.		18	13	42	.065
Ortega, F.		0	2	4	.250
Palmquist, E.		0	1	5	.000
Perranoski, R.		7	5	53	.083
Podres, J.		18	5	32	.232
Roebuck, E.		2	0	5	.000
Sherry, L.		4	4	53	.154
Williams, S.		15	12	41	.167
Aspromonte, R.	3B			47	.241
Camilli, D.	C			13	.133
Davis, H.	OF			132	.278
Davis, W.	OF			128	.254
Demeter, D.	OF			15	.172

PLAYER	POS.	W	L	G	BA
Fairly, R.	OF			111	.322
Gilliam, J.	3B			144	.244
Harkness, T.	1B			5	.500
Hodges, G.	1B			109	.242
Howard, F.	OF			92	.295
Larker, N.	1B			97	.270
Lillis, R.	3B			19	.111
Moon, W.	OF			134	.328
Neal, C.	2B			108	.235
Roseboro, J.	C			128	.251
Sherry, N.	C			47	.256
Smith, C.	3B			9	.250
Snider, E.	OF			85	.296
Spencer, D.	3B			60	.243
Warwick, C.	OF			19	.091
Wills, M.	SS			148	.282
Windhorn, G.	OF			34	.242

1962 (Second place)

WON—102
LOST—63
Walter Emmons Alston, Mgr.

PLAYER	POS.	W	L	G	BA
Pitchers					
Drysdale, D.		25	9	43	.198
Hunter, W.		0	0	1	.000
Koufax, S.		14	7	28	.087
Moeller, J.		6	5	19	.212
Ortega, F.		0	2	24	.000
Perranoski, R.		6	6	70	.071
Podres, J.		15	13	40	.159
Richert, P.		5	4	19	.080
Roebuck, E.		10	2	64	.214
Sherry, L.		7	3	58	.118
Smith, J.		0	0	8	.000
Williams, S.		14	12	40	.076
Burright, L.	2B			115	.205
Camilli, D.	C			45	.284
Carey, A.	3B			53	.234
Davis, H.	OF			163	.346
Davis, W.	OF			157	.285
Fairly, R.	1B			147	.278
Gilliam, J.	2B			160	.270
Harkness, T.	1B			92	.258
Howard, F.	OF			141	.296
McMullen, K.	OF			6	.273
Moon, W.	OF			95	.242
Roseboro, J.	C			128	.249
Sherry, N.	C			35	.182
Snider, E.	OF			80	.278
Spencer, D.	3B			77	.236
Tracewski, R.	SS			15	.000
Walls, R.	OF			60	.266
Wills, M.	SS			165	.299

1963 (First place)

WON—99
LOST—63
Walter Emmons Alston, Mgr.

PLAYER	POS.	W	L	G	BA
Pitchers					
Calmus, R.		3	1	21	.000
Drysdale, D.		19	17	42	.167
Koufax, S.		25	5	40	.054
Miller, R.		10	8	42	.070
Ortega, F.		0	0	1	.000
Perranoski, R.		16	3	69	.125
Podres, J.		14	12	37	.141
Richert, P.		5	3	20	.181
Roebuck, E.		2	4	29	.250
Rowe, K.		1	1	14	.000
Sherry, L.		2	6	36	.111
Smith, J.		0	0	4	.000
Willhite, J.		2	3	8	.300
Breeding, M.	2B			20	.167
Camilli, D.	C			49	.162
Davis, H.	OF			146	.326
Davis, W.	OF			156	.245
Fairly, R.	1B			152	.271
Ferrara, A.	OF			21	.159
Gilliam, J.	2B			148	.282
Gleason, R.				8	1.000
Griffith, R.	2B			1	.000
Howard, F.	OF			123	.273
McMullen, K.	3B			79	.236
Moon, W.	OF			122	.262
Nen, R.	1B			7	.125
Oliver, N.	2B			65	.239
Roseboro, J.	C			135	.236
Skowron, W.	1B			89	.203
Spencer, D.	3B			7	.111
Tracewski, R.	SS			104	.226
Walls, R.	OF			64	.233
Wills, M.	SB			134	.302
Zimmer, D.	3B			22	.217

1964 (Sixth place)

WON—80
LOST—82
Walter Emmons Alston, Mgr.

PLAYER	POS.	W	L	G	BA
Pitchers					
Brewer, J.		4	3	34	.273
Drysdale, D.		18	16	40	.173
Koufax, S.		19	5	29	.095
Miller, L.		4	8	16	.269
Miller, R.		7	7	74	.158
Moeller, J.		7	13	27	.067
Ortega, F.		7	9	35	.136
Perranoski, R.		5	7	72	.105

PLAYER	POS.	W	L	G	BA
Podres, J.		0	2	2	.000
Purdin, J.		2	0	3	.200
Reed, H.		3	4	26	.100
Richert, P.		2	3	8	.091
Singer, W.		0	1	2	.167
Willhite, J.		2	4	10	.000
Camilli, D.	C			50	.179
Crawford, W.	OF			10	.313
Davis, H.	OF			152	.275
Davis, W.	OF			157	.294
Fairly, R.	1B			150	.256
Gilliam, J.	3B			116	.228
Griffith, R.	3B			78	.290
Howard, F.	OF			134	.226
McMullen, K.	1B			24	.209
Moon, W.	OF			68	.220
Oliver, N.	2B			99	.243
Parker, M.	OF			124	.257
Roseboro, J.	C			134	.287
Shirley, B.	3B			18	.274
Torborg, J.	C			28	.233
Tracewski, R.	2B			106	.247
Walls, R.	OF			37	.179
Werhas, J.	3B			20	.193
Wills, M.	SS			158	.275

1965 (First place)

WON—97
LOST—65
Walter Emmons Alston, Mgr.

PLAYER	POS.	W	L	G	BA
Pitchers					
Brewer, J.		3	2	20	.000
Drysdale, D.		23	12	58	.300
Kekich, M.		0	1	5	.000
Koufax, S.		26	8	43	.177
Miller, R.		6	7	61	.000
Osteen, C.		15	15	42	.121
Perranoski, R.		6	6	59	.158
Podres, J.		7	6	27	.178
Purdin, J.		2	1	11	.000
Reed, H.		7	5	38	.000
Singer, W.		0	0	2	.000
Willhite, J.		2	2	15	.400
Crawford, W.	OF			52	.148
Davis, H.	OF			17	.250
Davis, W.	OF			142	.238
Fairly, R.	OF			158	.274
Ferrara, A.	OF			41	.210
Gilliam, J.	3B			111	.280
Griffith, R.	OF			22	.171
Johnson, L.	OF			131	.259
Kennedy, J.	3B			104	.171
Lefebvre, J.	2B			157	.250
Le John, D.	3B			34	.256
Moon, W.	OF			53	.202

PLAYER	POS.	W	L	G	BA
Oliver, N.	2B			8	1.000
Parker, M.	1B			154	.238
Roseboro, J.	C			136	.233
Smith, R.	OF			10	.000
Torborg, J.	C			56	.240
Tracewski, R.	3B			78	.215
Valle, H.	C			9	.308
Werhas, J.	1B			4	.000
Wills, M.	SS			158	.286

1966 (First place)

WON—95
LOST—67
Walter Emmons Alston, Mgr.

PLAYER	POS.	W	L	G	BA
Pitchers					
Brewer, J.		0	2	13	.000
Drysdale, D.		13	16	46	.189
Koufax, S.		27	9	41	.076
Miller, R.		4	2	46	.077
Moeller, J.		2	4	29	.167
Osteen, C.		17	14	39	.211
Perranoski, R.		6	7	55	.250
Podres, J.		0	0	1	.000
Reed, H.		0	0	1	.000
Regan, P.		14	1	65	.143
Singer, W.		0	0	3	.000
Sutton, D.		12	12	38	.183
Willhite, J.		0	0	6	.000
Barbieri, J.	OF			39	.280
Campanis, J.	C			1	.000
Covington, J.	OF			37	.121
Crawford, W.				6	.000
Davis, H.	OF			100	.313
Davis, W.	OF			153	.284
Fairly, R.	OF			117	.288
Ferrara, A.	OF			63	.270
Gilliam, J.	3B			88	.217
Griffith, R.	OF			23	.067
Hutton, T.	1B			3	.000
Johnson, L.	OF			152	.272
Kennedy, J.	3B			125	.201
Lefebvre, J.	2B			152	.274
Oliver, N.	2B			80	.193
Parker, M.	1B			156	.253
Roseboro, J.	C			142	.276
Schofield, J.	3B			20	.257
Shirley, B.	SS			12	.200
Stuart, R.	1B			38	.264
Torborg, J.	C			46	.225
Wills, M.	SS			143	.273

1967 (Eighth place)

WON—73
LOST—89
Walter Emmons Alston, Mgr.

PLAYER	POS.	W	L	G	BA
Pitchers					
Brewer, J.		5	4	30	.045
Brubaker, B.		0	0	1	.000
Drysdale, D.		13	16	38	.129
Duffie, J.		0	2	2	.000
Egan, R.		1	1	20	.000
Foster, A.		0	1	4	.000
Hickman, J.		0	0	65	.163
Lee, R.		0	0	4	.000
Miller, R.		2	9	52	.125
Moeller, J.		0	0	6	.000
Osteen, C.		17	17	42	.178
Perranoski, R.		6	7	70	.100
Regan, P.		6	9	55	.100
Singer, W.		12	8	34	.090
Sutton, D.		11	15	43	.133
Alcaraz, A.	2B			17	.233
Bailey, R.	3B			116	.227
Campanis, J.	C			41	.161
Crawford, W.	OF			4	.250
Davis, W.	OF			143	.257
Dean, T.	SS			12	.143
Fairly, R.	OF			153	.220
Ferrara, A.	OF			122	.277
Gabrielson, L.	OF			90	.261
Hunt, R.	2B			110	.263
Johnson, L.	OF			104	.270
Lefebvre, J.	3B			136	.261
Michael, E.	SS			98	.202
Oliver, N.	2B			77	.237
Parker, M.	1B			139	.247
Roseboro, J.	C			116	.272
Schofield, J.	SS			84	.216
Torborg, J.	C			76	.214
Werhas, J.				7	.143

1968 (Seventh place)

WON—76
LOST—86
Walter Emmons Alston, Mgr.

PLAYER	POS.	W	L	G	BA
Pitchers					
Aguirre, H.		1	2	25	.000
Billingham, J.		3	0	50	.000
Brewer, J.		8	3	54	.222
Drysdale, D.		14	12	31	.177
Foster, A.		1	1	3	.250
Grant, J.		6	4	43	.129
Kekich, M.		2	10	25	.081
Moeller, J.		1	1	3	.000
Osteen, C.		12	18	40	.179

PLAYER	POS.	W	L	G	BA
Purdin, J.		2	3	36	.500
Regan, P.		2	0	5	.000
Romo, V.		0	0	1	.000
Singer, W.		13	17	37	.148
Sutton, D.		11	15	36	.177
Alcaraz, A.	2B			41	.151
Bailey. R.	3B			105	.227
Boyer, K.	3B			83	.271
Campanis, J.	C			4	.091
Colavito, R.	OF			40	.204
Crawford, W.	OF			61	.251
Davis, W.	OF			160	.250
Fairey, J.	OF			99	.199
Fairly, R.	OF			141	.234
Ferrara, A.	OF			2	.143
Gabrielson, L.	OF			108	.270
Haller, T.	C			144	.285
James, C.	OF			10	.200
Lefebvre, J.	2B			84	.241
Parker, M.	1B			135	.239
Popovich, P.	2B			134	.232
Savage, T.	OF			61	.206
Shirley, B.	SS			39	.148
Sudakis, W.	3B			24	.276
Torborg, J.	C			37	.161
Versalles, Z.	SS			122	.196

1969 (Fourth place)

WON—85
LOST—77
Walter Emmons Alston, Mgr.

PLAYER	POS.	W	L	G	BA
Pitchers					
Brewer, J.		7	6	59	.091
Bunning, J.		3	1	9	.111
Darwin, A.		0	0	6	.000
Drysdale, D.		5	4	12	.136
Foster, A.		3	9	24	.074
Jenkins, W.		0	0	1	.000
Lamb, R.		0	1	10	.000
McBean, A.		2	6	31	.000
Mikkelsen, P.		7	5	48	.167
Moeller, J.		1	0	23	.200
Osteen, C.		20	15	44	.216
Purdin, J.		0	0	9	.000
Singer, W.		20	12	41	.102
Sutton, D.		17	18	41	.153
Boyer, K.	1B			25	.206
Buckner, W.				1	.000
Crawford, W.	OF			129	.247
Davis, W.	OF			129	.311
Fairly, R.	1B			30	.219
Gabrielson, L.	OF			83	.270
Garvey, S.				3	.333
Grabarkewitz, B.	SS			34	.092
Haller, T.	C			134	.263

PLAYER	POS.	W	L	G	BA
Hutton, T.	1B			16	.271
Joshua, V.	OF			14	.250
Kosco, A.	OF			120	.248
Lefebvre, J.	3B			95	.236
Miller, J.	OF			26	.211
Mota, M.	OF			85	.323
Parker, M.	1B			132	.278
Popovich, P.	2B			28	.200
Russell, W.	OF			98	.226
Sizemore, T.	2B			159	.271
Stinson, G.	C			4	.375
Sudakis, W.	1B			132	.234
Torborg, J.	C			51	.185
Valentine, R.				5	.000
Wills, M.	SS			104	.297

1970 (Second place)

WON—87
LOST—74
Walter Emmons Alston, Mgr.

PLAYER	POS.	W	L	G	BA
Pitchers					
Brewer, J.		7	6	58	.083
Foster, A.		10	13	33	.109
Hough, C.		0	0	8	.333
Lamb, R.		6	1	35	.000
McBean, A.		0	0	1	.000
Mikkelsen, P.		4	2	33	.333
Moeller, J.		7	9	31	.154
Norman, F.		2	0	30	.143
Osteen, C.		16	14	39	.204
Pascual, C.		0	0	10	.000
Pena, J.		4	3	29	.125
Singer, W.		8	5	16	.132
Stephenson, J.		0	0	3	.000
Strahler, M.		1	1	6	.250
Sutton, D.		15	13	40	.155
Vance, G.		7	7	20	.189
Buckner, W.	OF			28	.191
Crawford, W.	OF			109	.234
Davis, W.	OF			146	.305
Ferguson, J.	C			5	.250
Gabrielson, L.	OF			43	.190
Garvey, S.	3B			34	.269
Grabarkewitz, B.	3B			156	.289
Haller, T.	C			112	.286
Joshua, V.	OF			72	.266
Kosco, A.	OF			74	.228
Lefebvre, J.	2B			109	.252
Moore, G.	OF			7	.188
Mota, M.	OF			124	.305
Paciorek, T.	OF			8	.222
Parker, M.	1B			161	.319
Russell, W.	OF			81	.259
Sizemore, T.	2B			96	.306
Stinson, G.	C			4	.000
Sudakis, W.	C			94	.264

PLAYER	POS.	W	L	G	BA
Torborg, J.	C			64	.231
Wills, M.	SS			132	.270

1971 (Second place)

WON—89
LOST—73
Walter Emmons Alston, Mgr.

PLAYER	POS.	W	L	G	BA
Pitchers					
Alexander, D.		6	6	17	.273
Brewer, J.		6	5	55	.333
Downing, A.		20	9	37	.174
Hough, C.		0	0	4	.000
Mikkelsen, P.		8	5	41	.200
Moeller, J.		2	4	28	.000
O'Brien, R.		2	2	14	.111
Osteen, C.		14	11	39	.186
Pena, J.		2	0	21	.667
Singer, W.		10	17	31	.103
Strahler, M.		0	0	6	.000
Sutton, D.		17	12	39	.216
Vance, G.		2	1	10	.000
Wilhelm, J.		0	1	9	.000
Allen, R.	3B			155	.295
Buckner, W.	OF			108	.277
Cey, R.				2	.000
Crawford, W.	OF			114	.281
Darwin, A.	OF			11	.250
Davis, W.	OF			158	.309
Ferguson, J.	C			36	.216
Garvey, S.	3B			81	.227
Grabarkewitz, B.	2B			44	.225
Haller, T.	C			84	.267
Joshua, V.	OF			11	.000
Lefebvre, J.	2B			119	.245
Mota, M.	OF			91	.312
Paciorek, T.	OF			2	.500
Parker, M.	1B			157	.274
Russell, W.	2B			91	.227
Sims, D.	C			90	.274
Sudakis, W.	C			41	.193
Valentine, R.	SS			101	.249
Wills, M.	SS			149	.281

1972 (Third place)

WON—85
LOST—70
Walter Emmons Alston, Mgr.

PLAYER	POS.	W	L	G	BA
Pitchers					
Brewer, J.		8	7	51	.000
Downing, A.		9	9	31	.121
Hough, C.		0	0	2	.000
John, T.		11	5	29	.159

PLAYER	POS.	W	L	G	BA
Pitchers					
Mikkelsen, P.		5	5	33	.000
Osteen, C.		20	11	36	.273
Pena, J.		0	0	5	.000
Perranoski, R.		2	0	9	.000
Rau, D.		2	2	7	.143
Richert, P.		2	3	37	.500
Singer, W.		6	16	26	.073
Strahler, M.		1	2	19	.182
Sutton, D.		19	9	33	.143
Wilhelm, J.		0	1	16	.000
Buckner, W.	OF			105	.319
Cannizzaro, C.	C			73	.240
Cey, R.	3B			11	.270
Crawford, W.	OF			96	.251
Davis, W.	OF			149	.289
Dietz, R.	C			27	.161
Ferguson, J.	C			8	.292
Garvey, S.	3B			96	.269
Grabarkewitz, B.	3B			53	.167
Lacy, L.	2B			60	.259
Lefebvre, J.	2B			70	.201
Lopes, D.	2B			11	.214
McDermott, T.	1B			9	.130
Mota, M.	OF			118	.323
Paciorek, T.	1B			11	.255
Parker, M.	1B			130	.279
Robinson, F.	OF			103	.251
Russell, W.	SS			129	.272
Sims, D.	C			51	.192
Valentine, R.	2B			119	.274
Wills, M.	SS			71	.129
Yeager, S.	C			35	.274

1973 (Second place)

WON—95
LOST—66
Walter Alston, Mgr.

PLAYER	POS.	W	L	G	BA
Pitchers					
Brewer, J.		6	8	56	.400
Downing, A.		9	9	30	.088
Haydeman, G.		0	0	1	.000
Hough, C.		4	2	37	.214
John, T.		16	7	36	.203
Messersmith, A.		14	10	33	.169
Osteen, C.		16	11	33	.154
Rau, D.		4	2	31	.091
Richert, P.		3	3	39	.200
Shanahan, G.		0	0	7	.000
Solomon, E.		0	0	4	.000
Sutton, D.		18	10	33	.119
Zahn, G.		1	0	6	.000
Agee, T.	OF			109	.222
Alvarez, O.	OF			4	.250

PLAYER	POS.	W	L	G	BA
Buckner, W.	OF			140	.275
Cey, R.	3B			152	.245
Crawford, W.	OF			145	.295
Ferguson, J.	C			136	.263
Garvey, S.	1B			114	.304
Joshua, V.	OF			75	.252
Lacy, L.	2B			57	.207
Lopes, D.	2B			142	.275
McMullen, K.	3B			42	.247
Mota, M.	OF			89	.314
Paciorek, T.	OF			96	.262
Pasley, K.	C			0	.000
Royster, J.	2B			10	.211
Russell, W.	SS			162	.265
Wynn, J.	OF			139	.220
Yeager, S.	C			54	.254

1974 (First place)

WON—102
LOST—60
Walter Alston, Mgr.

PLAYER	POS.	W	L	G	BA
Pitchers					
Brewer, J.		4	4	24	.000
Downing, A.		5	6	21	.172
Hough, C.		9	4	49	.000
Hudson, R.		0	0	1	.000
John, T.		13	3	22	.118
Marshall, M.		15	12	106	.235
Messersmith, A.		20	6	39	.240
Rau, D.		13	11	36	.141
Rhoden, R.		1	0	4	.500
Solomon, E.		0	0	4	.000
Sutton, D.		19	9	40	.184
Wall, S.		0	0	0	.000
Zahn, G.		3	5	21	.174
Alvarez, O.	OF			1	.000
Auerbach, R.	IF			45	.342
Buckner, B.	OF			145	.314
Cey, R.	3B			159	.262
Crawford, W.	OF			139	.295
De Jesus, I.	SS			3	.333
Ferguson, J.	C			111	.252
Garvey, S.	1B			156	.312
Hale, J.	OF			4	1.000
Lacy, L.	2B			48	.282
Lopes, D.	2B			145	.266
McMullen, K.	3B			49	.250
Mota, M.	OF			66	.281
Paciorek, T.	OF			85	.240
Pasley, K.	C			1	.000
Russell, W.	SS			160	.269
Royster, J.	2B			0	.000
Wynn, J.	OF			150	.271
Yeager, S.	C			94	.266

1975 (Second place)

WON—88
LOST—74
Walter Alston, Mgr.

PLAYER	POS.	W	L	G	BA
Pitchers					
Downing, A.		2	1	22	.000
Hooton, B.		18	7	31	.123
Hough, C.		3	7	38	.333
John, T.		On Disabled List Entire Season			
Lewellyn, D.		0	0	2	.000
Marshall, M.		9	14	57	.067
Messersmith, A.		19	14	42	.157
Rau, D.		15	9	38	.195
Rhoden, R.		3	3	26	.071
Sutton, D.		16	13	35	.138
Wall, S.		0	1	10	.000
Alvarez, O.	OF			4	.000
Auerbach, R.	IF			85	.224
Buckner, W.	OF			92	.243
Cey, R.	3B			158	.283
Crawford, W.	OF			124	.263
Cruz, H.	OF			53	.266
DeJesus, I.	2B			63	.184
Ferguson, J.	C			66	.208
Garvey, S.	1B			160	.319
Hale, J.	OF			71	.211
Lacy, L.	OF			48	.256
Lopes, D.	2B			155	.262
McMullen, K.	3B			39	.239
Mota, M.	OF			52	.265
Russell, W.	SS			84	.206
Simpson, J.	OF			9	.333
Yeager, S.	C			135	.228

1976 (Second place)

WON—92
LOST—70
Tom Lasorda, Mgr.

PLAYER	POS.	W	L	G	BA
Pitchers					
Downing, A.		1	2	17	.000
Hooton, B.		11	15	33	.097
Hough, C.		12	8	77	.286
John, T.		10	10	31	.109
Lewellyn, D.		1	1	4	.000
Marshall, M.		4	3	30	.091
Rau, D.		16	12	34	.150
Rhoden, R.		12	3	27	.308
Sosa, E.		2	4	24	.143
Sutcliffe, R.		0	0	1	.000
Sutton, D.		21	10	35	.083
Wall, S.		2	2	31	.000
Baker, D.	OF			112	.242
Burke, G.	OF			25	.239

PLAYER	POS.	W	L	G	BA
Cey, R.	3B			145	.277
Garvey, S.	1B			162	.317
Goodson, E.	3B			83	.229
Hale, J.	OF			44	.154
Lacy, L.	OF			53	.266
Lopes, D.	2B			117	.241
Mota, M.	OF			50	.288
Pasley, K.	C			23	.231
Rodriguez, E.	C			36	.212
Russell, W.	SS			149	.274
Simpson, J.	OF			23	.133
Smith, R.	OF			65	.280
Yeager, S.	C			117	.214

1977 (First place)

WON—91
LOST—57
Tom Lasorda, Mgr.

PLAYER	POS.	W	L	G	BA
Pitchers					
Castillo, R.		1	0	6	.000
Garman, M.		4	4	49	.000
Hooton, B.		12	7	32	.123
Hough, C.		6	12	70	.182
John, T.		20	7	31	.177
Rau, D.		14	8	32	.141
Rautzhan, L.		4	1	25	.000
Rhoden, R.		16	10	31	.231
Sutton, D.		14	8	33	.151
Webb, H.		0	0	5	.000
Baker, D.	OF			153	.291
Burke, G.	OF			83	.254
Cey, R.	3B			153	.241
Davalillo, V.	OF			24	.313
Garvey, S.	1B			162	.297
Goodson, E.	IF			61	.167
Grote, J.	C			18	.259
Lacy, L.	IF			75	.266
Landestoy, R.	IF			15	.278
Leonard, J.	OF			11	.300
Lopes, D.	2B			134	.283
Martinez, T.	2B			67	.299
Monday, R.	OF			118	.230
Mota, M.	OF			49	.395
Oates, J.	C			60	.269
Russell, W.	SS			153	.278
Simpson, J.	OF			29	.174
Smith, R.	OF			148	.307
Washington, R.	SS			10	.368
Yeager, S.	C			125	.256

1978 (First place)

WON—95
LOST—67
Tom Lasorda, Mgr.

PLAYER	POS.	W	L	G	BA
Pitchers					
Castillo, R.		0	4	18	.000
Forster, T.		5	4	47	.500
Hannahs, G.		0	0	1	.000
Hooton, B.		19	10	32	.149
Hough, C.		5	5	55	.333
Rau, D.		15	9	30	.143
Rautzhan, L.		2	1	43	.000
Rhoden, R.		10	8	30	.135
Stewart, D.		0	0	1	.000
Sutcliffe, R.		0	0	2	.000
Sutton, D.		15	11	34	.083
Welch, B.		7	4	23	.172
Baker, D.	OF			149	.262
Cey, R.	3B			159	.270
Davalillo, V.	OF			75	.312
Ferguson, J.	C			67	.237
Garvey, S.	1B			162	.316
Gulden, B.	C			3	.000
Guerrero, P.	IF			5	.625
Law, R.	OF			11	.250
Lopes, D.	2B			151	.278
Martinez, T.	2B			54	.255
Monday, R.	OF			119	.254
Mota, M.	OF			37	.303
Oates, J.	C			40	.307
Russell, W.	SS			155	.286
Simpson, J.	OF			10	.400
Smith, R.	OF			128	.295
White, M.	OF			7	.500
Yeager, S.	C			94	.193

1979 (Third place)

WON—79
LOST—83
Tom Lasorda, Mgr.

PLAYER	POS.	W	L	G	BA
Pitchers					
Beckwith, J.		1	2	17	.000
Brett, K.		4	3	30	273
Castillo, R.		2	0	19	.000
Forster, T.		1	2	17	.000
Hooton, B.		11	10	29	.147
Hough, C.		7	5	42	.158
La Grow, L.		5	1	31	.333
Patterson, D.		4	1	36	.143
Rau, D.		1	5	11	.143
Reuss, J.		7	14	39	.167
Sutcliffe, R.		17	10	39	.247
Sutton, D.		12	15	33	.143
Welch, B.		5	6	25	.158

PLAYER	POS.	W	L	G	BA
Baker, D.	OF			151	.274
Cey, R.	3B			150	.281
Ferguson, J.	C			122	.252
Garvey, S.	1B			162	.315
Guerrero, P.	OF			25	.242
Hatcher, M.	3B			33	.269
Lopes, D.	2B			153	.265
Martinez, T.	IF			81	.268
Monday, R.	OF			12	.303
Oates, J.	C			26	.130
Russell, W.	SS			153	.271
Smith, R.	OF			68	.274
Thomas, D.	OF			140	.256
Thomasson, G.	OF			115	.248
Yeager, S.	C			105	.216

1980 (Second place)

WON—92
LOST—71
Tom Lasorda, Mgr.

PLAYER	POS.	W	L	G	BA
Pitchers					
Beckwith, J.		3	3	38	.000
Castillo, R.		8	6	61	.111
Forster, T.		0	0	9	.000
Goltz, D.		7	11	35	.128
Hooton, B.		14	8	34	.063
Howe, S.		7	9	59	.091
Reuss, J.		18	6	37	.088
Stanhouse, D.		2	2	21	.000
Sutcliffe, R.		3	9	42	.148
Sutton, D.		13	5	32	.078
Valenzuela, F.		2	0	10	.000
Welch, B.		14	9	32	.243
Baker, D.	OF			153	.294
Cey, R.	3B			157	.254
Ferguson, J.	C			77	.238
Garvey, S.	1B			163	.304
Guerrero, P.	OF			75	.322
Hatcher, M.	3B			57	.226
Johnstone, J.	OF			109	.307
Frias, P.	SS			14	.222
Law, R.	OF			128	.260
Lopes, D.	2B			141	.251
Mitchell, B.	OF			9	.333
Monday, R.	OF			96	.268
Perconte, J.	2B			14	.235
Russell, W.	SS			130	.264
Scioscia, M.	C			54	.254
Smith, R.	OF			92	.322
Thomas, D.	OF			112	.266
Weiss, G.	SS			8	.000
Yeager, S.	C			96	.211

1981 (First place)

WON—63
LOST—47
Tom Lasorda, Mgr.

PLAYER	POS.	W	L	G	BA
Pitchers					
Castillo, R.		2	4	33	
Forster, T.		0	1	21	.000
Goltz, D.		2	7	26	.059
Hooton, B.		11	6	23	.190
Howe, S.		5	3	41	.000
Niedenfuer, T.		3	1	17	.000
Pena, A.		1	1	14	.000
Power, T.		1	3	5	.000
Ruess, J.		10	4	22	.196
Stewart, D.		4	3	32	.400
Sutcliffe, R.		2	2	14	
Valenzuela, F.		13	7	25	.250
Welch, B.		9	5	23	.222
Baker, D.	OF			103	.320
Bradley, M.	OF			9	.167
Cey, R.	3B			85	.288
Garvey, S.	1B			110	.283
Guerrero, P.	OF			98	.300
Johnstone, J.	OF			61	.205
Landreaux, K.	OF			99	.251
Maldonado, C.	OF			11	.083
Marshall, M.	3B			14	.200
Mitchell, R.	OF			26	.125
Monday, R.	OF			66	.315
Perconte, J.	2B			8	.222
Roenicke, R.	OF			22	.234
Russell, W.	SS			82	.233
Sax, S.	2B			31	.277
Scioscia, M.	C			93	.276
Smith, R.	OF			40	.212
Thomas, D.	OF			80	.248
Yeager, S.	C			42	.209

1982 (Second place)

WON—88
LOST—74
Tommy Lasorda, Mgr.

PLAYER	POS.	W	L	G	BA
Pitchers					
Beckwith, J.		2	1	19	.000
Forster, T.		5	6	56	.000
Goltz, D.		0	1	2	.000
Hooton, B.		4	7	21	.086
Howe, S.		7	5	66	.000
Niedenfuer, T.		3	4	55	.000
Pena, A.		0	2	29	.000
Power, T.		1	1	12	.000
Reuss, J.		18	11	39	.221
Romo, V.		1	2	15	.200
Shirley, S.		1	1	11	1.000

PLAYER	POS.	W	L	G	BA
Stewart, D.		9	8	45	.179
Welch, B.		16	11	36	.141
Wright, R.		2	1	14	.125
Baker, D.	OF			147	.300
Belanger, M.	SS			54	.240
Bradley, M.	OF			8	.333
Brock, G.	3B			18	.118
Cey, R.	3B			150	.254
Garvey, S.	1B			162	.282
Guerrero, P.	OF			150	.304
Landreaux, K.	OF			129	.284
Maldonado, C.	OF			6	.000
Marshall, M.	OF			49	.242
Monday, R.	OF			104	.257
Morales, J.	C			35	.300
Orta, J.	OF			86	.217
Roenicke, R.	OF			109	.259
Russell, B.	SS			153	.274
Sax, S.	2B			150	.282
Scioscia, M.	C			129	.219
Taveras, A.	2B			11	.333
Thomas, D.	2B			66	.265
Yeager, S.	C			82	.245

1983 (First place)

WON—91
LOST—71
Tommy Lasorda, Mgr.

PLAYER	POS.	W	L	G	BA
Pitchers					
Beckwith, J.		3	4	42	.200
Fernandez, S.		0	1	2	1.000
Hershiser, O.		0	0	8	—
Honeycutt, R.		2	3	9	.083
Hooton, B.		9	8	33	.160
Howe, S.		4	7	46	.125
Niedenfuer, T.		8	3	66	.000
Pena, A.		12	9	34	.100
Reuss, J.		12	11	32	.282
Rodas, R.		0	0	7	—
Stewart, D.		5	2	46	.143
Valenzuela, F.		15	10	35	.187
Welch, B.		15	12	31	.096
White, L.		0	0	4	—
Wright, R.		0	0	6	—
Zachry, T.		6	1	40	.500
Anderson, D.	2B			61	.165
Baker, D.	OF			149	.260
Bream, S.				15	.182
Brock, G.	1B			146	.224
Espy, C.	2B			20	.273
Fimple, J.	C			54	.250
Guerrero, P.	3B-OF			160	.298
Landestoy, R.	2B			71	.159
Landreaux, K.	OF			141	.281
Maldonado, C.	OF			42	.194

PLAYER	POS.	W	L	G	BA
Marshall, M.	1B			140	.284
Monday, R.	OF			99	.247
Morales, J.	C			47	.283
Reyes, G.	C			19	.161
Reynolds, R.	OF			24	.236
Rivera, G.				13	.353
Roenicke, R.	OF			81	.222
Russell, B.	SS			131	.246
Sax, D.	C			7	.000
Sax, S.	2B			155	.281
Scioscia, M.	C			12	.314
Taveras, A.	2B			10	.000
Thomas, D.	3B-2B			118	.250
Yeager, S.	C			113	.203

THE WORLD SERIES

PROFESSIONAL BASEBALL dates all the way back to the year 1868, when Harry Wright signed four ballplayers for his Cincinnati Red Stocking team, and by 1869 the entire squad was being paid a salary to play ball. As a result, Wright did attract the best players to his team and they won an amazing 65 games out of 66.

The team barnstormed from Massachusetts to California, defeating teams throughout the nation and a tournament was arranged in 1868 with teams from Detroit, Pittsburgh, Albany, Boston, New York, Brooklyn, Chicago, Montreal, Quebec, Philadelphia, Cleveland, and Hamilton, Ontario. The tournament winner—and the "first world championship"—was won by the Hamilton team.

Interest in baseball was so great that a number of leagues were organized. The National Association of Baseball Players and the National League were formed, and then the American Association.

By 1882 the two league winners, Chicago in the National League and the Cincinnati Reds of the American Association, met in a series that went two games. Each team won one game and then furious arguments among the team owners broke off the championship play.

The Series of 1882 ended when Denny McKnight, the president of the American Association, threatened to expel all Cincinnati players if they persisted in their Series against the White Sox, and so the Series ended unresolved.

By 1884, Colonel Art Mills, president of the National League, brought about peace between the two leagues and the first authorized World Series was organized. The Providence Grays of the National League met the New York Metropolitans of the American Association. The Providence Grays, behind the superlative pitching of Charles Radbourne, who won 60 games during the regular season, beat the Mets three days in a row, 6–0, 3–1, and 11–2.

That "World Series" arrangement continued in 1885, when Cap Anson's White Sox won the National League title and the St. Louis Browns won the American Association flag. A seven-game series was arranged, but it concluded after each club had won three games and the seventh game ended in a tie. (One of the Chicago victories was a 9–0 forfeit.)

That Series was a historic curiosity for many reasons, but one highlight was the fact that both teams committed a record number of errors: the Browns made 43 while the White Sox committed 57—a startling total of 100 errors for the seven games played.

St. Louis and Chicago met again for the championship in 1886 and it was agreed by Chris Von Der Ahe, owner of the Browns, and Charles Comiskey of the White Sox that the Series would be played on a "winner-take-all" basis. The players for both teams agreed to these terms.

The deciding game of the Series went to ten innings, when Curt Welch, the Brownies' center fielder, walked and then worked his way around to third base. King Kelly, catching for the White Sox, signaled his pitcher for a "pitch out" but Welch tore in safely from third base, for a clean steal of home with the run that won the game and the Series for the Browns. That slide of Welch's became known as "Welch's $15,000 slide." That was the amount of money that the Browns collected for winning the "winner-take-all" series.

The following year, 1887, Detroit of the National League defeated the Browns, 10 games to five, in a traveling circus World Series. In addition to playing in the contending cities, Detroit and St. Louis, the World Series caravan was played in Chicago, Pittsburgh, New York, Brooklyn, Boston, Philadelphia, Washington, and Baltimore.

In 1888 the New York Giants won their first National League championship and faced the challenge of the strong St. Louis Browns, winners of the American Association title for the fourth straight time.

The first three games were played at the Polo Grounds in New York City, and the fourth game was played in Brooklyn. The fifth game was back at the Polo Grounds. The sixth game was played at Philadelphia, and then the traveling World Series circus went to St. Louis for the final games. The Giants won five of the first six games and won the championship in St. Louis by defeating the Browns, 11–3, in the eighth game of the Series. The Giants won seven of the first eight games played.

The Giants repeated in 1889 and defeated their neighbors from Brooklyn in the first interborough World Series. This Series preceded the first modern New York–Brooklyn Series by 52 years, but there was tremendous rivalry between the teams even at that early date. Brooklyn took the first game, a sensational one, that saw them score four runs in the ninth inning to win a slugfest, 12–10. The Giants took the second game, 6–2, as Brooklyn committed eight errors. But Brooklyn came back to win the next two games from the Giants, 8–7 and 10–7. Then the Giants won four of the next five games and the championship.

In 1890 most of the stars in the National League and the American association jumped to the newly formed Players' League and there was much feuding and fighting during the next several years.

In 1894 Colonel William Temple, a minority stockholder of the Pirates, donated a large, expensive cup to the winner of a series between the first place and second place teams in the National League. The series was to be decided by winning four games out of the seven played, with the players of the contending teams sharing in the receipts. The Temple Cup Series lasted four years and was discontinued after 1897, because the second-place clubs defeated the champions in three of the four series.

A disastrous two-year war—a period wracked by backbiting and name-calling between the National and American Leagues—ended with the Cincinnati peace pact of January 1903. Ban Johnson's fighting, aggressive, young American League, which took the field in 1901 and 1902, had won recognition as a full major league, with all the rights and prerogatives of the older National League.

In the summer of 1903 with both the Pirates and the Red Sox way out in front in their respective leagues, Barney Dreyfuss, the Pirates' owner, talked with Henry Killilea, a Milwaukee lawyer, who owned the Red Sox (they were known as the Puritans then) about the possibility of a postseason game between the two clubs.

Killilea went to Ban Johnson's office in Chicago and

told Johnson, "Dreyfuss is willing to meet us in a World Series. What do you think of the idea?"

"Do you think you can beat the Pirates?" asked Johnson.

"They've got stars like Honus Wagner, George Beaumont, Fred Clarke, and some other great hitters, but my manager, Collins, thinks he can beat them."

"Then play them. By all means. And if we beat them, it will be the best thing in the world for the American League."

Dreyfuss and Killilea made all the arrangements for what amounts to the first modern World Series. Dreyfuss suggested that the winning team take five victories in a nine-game series. The two owners agreed to split the gate receipts; the players would draw two extra weeks salary and a bonus for the Series.

Although Boston trailed in the Series, one game to three, the Puritans came back to win four games in a row. Bill Dineen and Cy Young pitched the entire Series for Boston and won the five games and the World Series.

The winning Boston players each received $1,316, and the Pittsburgh players received $1,182. Dreyfuss gave his Pittsburgh players his share of the receipts. The nine-game Series attracted 100,429 spectators and total receipts amounted to $55,000. Tickets were sold for 50 cents and $1, and despite the small ball parks, the receipts were considered sensational.

The following year, 1904, there was no World Series, due to the stubbornness of John Brush, owner of the New York Giants and his manager, John J. McGraw. Both Brush and McGraw hated the rival American League, calling it a "bush league." They were particularly angry at the New York Highlanders (now the Yankees) for moving a team into their territory and they wanted nothing to do with either the team or the league.

In 1904 the Giants won the National League pennant and the Red Sox repeated in the American League, but there was no Series.

But by 1905 an agreement was reached and peace was declared by all parties. The World Series between the Giants and the Athletics marked a new era in baseball, and the popularity of the game soon made the World Series an annual event of national and, later, international interest.

DODGERS WORLD SERIES RESULTS AT A GLANCE

YEAR	WINNER	LOSER	GAMES
1916	Boston	BROOKLYN	4 GAMES TO 1
1920	Cleveland	BROOKLYN	5 GAMES TO 2
1941	New York	BROOKLYN	4 GAMES TO 1
1947	New York	BROOKLYN	4 GAMES TO 3
1949	New York	BROOKLYN	4 GAMES TO 1
1952	New York	BROOKLYN	4 GAMES TO 1
1953	New York	BROOKLYN	4 GAMES TO 2
1955	BROOKLYN	New York	4 GAMES TO 3
1956	New York	BROOKLYN	4 GAMES TO 3
1959	LOS ANGELES	Chicago	4 GAMES TO 2
1963	LOS ANGELES	New York	4 GAMES TO 0
1965	LOS ANGELES	Minnesota	4 GAMES TO 3
1966	Baltimore	LOS ANGELES	4 GAMES TO 0
1974	Oakland	LOS ANGELES	4 GAMES TO 1
1977	New York	LOS ANGELES	4 GAMES TO 2
1978	New York	LOS ANGELES	4 GAMES TO 2
1981	LOS ANGELES	New York	4 GAMES TO 2

COLUMN HEADINGS

The following is a key to the abbreviated column headings that appear in the complete box scores of each World Series game.

AB	At bat
R	Runs scored
H	Hits
O	Putouts
A	Assists
E	Errors

The World Series • 323

The following is a key to the abbreviated column headings that appear in the composite batting averages at the end of each World Series section.

G	Number of games played	3b	Triples
AB	At bats	Hr	Home runs
R	Runs	RBI	Runs batted in
H	Hits	BA	Batting average
2b	Doubles	PH	Pinch hitter

The following is an explanation of the column headings that appear in the composite pitching averages at the end of each World Series section.

G	Games pitched	SO	Strikeouts
IP	Innings pitched	BB	Bases on balls
H	Hits allowed	W	Games won
R	Runs allowed	L	Games lost
Er	Earned runs	ERA	Earned run average

WORLD SERIES HIGHLIGHTS: 1916

BOSTON (AL) DEFEATS BROOKLYN (NL), 4 GAMES TO 1

FIRST GAME (Oct. 7, at Boston)
BROOKLYN 000 100 004   5 10 4
BOSTON 001 010 31x   6 8 1
Marquard, Pfeffer (8th)
Shore, Mays (9th)

Rube Marquard, the Dodgers' star left hander, handcuffed the hard-hitting Red Sox for six innings, as Ernie Shore, the Sox hurler, matched him in an exciting 2–1 ball game. Then in the sixth inning the Red Sox struck with three runs and they were off to a 5–1 lead over the Dodgers. In the ninth inning, the Dodgers rallied, scoring four runs and had the bases full. Carl Mays relieved Shore for the Red Sox and then Jake Daubert smashed a hard line drive to the left of shortstop Everett Scott. Scott dove for the ball, caught it in the web of his glove, and the Dodger rally fell short as the Red Sox took the game, 6 to 5.

SECOND GAME (Oct. 9, at Boston)
BROOKLYN 100 000 000 000 00   1 6 2
BOSTON 001 000 000 000 01   2 7 1
Smith
Ruth

The Dodgers scored in the first inning and the Sox matched the run in the third. Pitchers Sherry Smith of the Dodgers and the great Red Sox left hander Babe Ruth pitched magnificently for 13½ innings. In the 14th inning, pinch hitter Del Gainor of the Sox doubled down the left-field line to score Earl McNally for the winning Red Sox run and a 2–1 victory.

THIRD GAME (Oct. 10, at Brooklyn)
BOSTON 000 002 100   3 7 1
BROOKLYN 001 120 00x   4 10 0
Mays, Foster (6th)
Coombs, Pfeffer (7th)

Ivy Olson's triple in the fifth inning with two men on base was the thin margin of victory for the Dodgers, as pitcher Jack Pfeffer held the Sox in check during the seventh, eighth, and ninth innings for a close and exciting Dodger win, 4 to 3.

FOURTH GAME (Oct. 11, at Brooklyn)
BOSTON 030 110 100   6 10 1
BROOKLYN 200 000 000   2 5 4
Leonard
Marquard, Cheney (5th), Rucker (8th)

The Dodgers quickly scored two runs in the very first inning to take the lead. In the third inning, Larry Gardner, hard-hitting third baseman of the Sox, smashed a home run with two men on base to give the Sox a 3–2 margin. They increased their lead over the Dodgers with runs in the fourth, fifth, and seventh innings to run up a 6 to 2 victory as Dutch Leonard held the Dodgers to 5 hits.

FIFTH GAME (Oct. 12, at Boston)
BROOKLYN 010 000 000   1 3 3
BOSTON 012 010 00x   4 7 2
Pfeffer, Dell (8th)
Shore

In the fifth and deciding game, Ernie Shore, brilliant left hander for the Sox, held the Dodgers to three scattered hits as the Sox bunched seven hits for a decisive 4 to 1 triumph and the World Championship.

WORLD SERIES BOX SCORES: 1916 (FIVE GAMES)

GAME 1

BROOKLYN (N.L.)	AB	R	H	O	A	E	BOSTON (A.L.)	AB	R	H	O	A	E
Myers, cf	5	0	2	1	0	0	Hooper, rf	4	2	1	1	1	0
Daubert, 1b	4	0	0	5	1	0	Janvrin, 2b	4	1	2	2	8	1
Stengel, rf	4	2	2	1	0	1	Walker, cf	4	1	2	0	0	0
Wheat, lf	4	1	2	3	0	0	Hoblitzel, 1b	5	2	1	14	0	0
Cutshaw, 2b	3	1	0	5	2	1	Lewis, lf	3	0	1	0	0	0
Mowrey, 3b	3	1	1	1	2	0	Gardner, 3b	4	0	1	1	3	0
Olson, ss	4	0	1	2	1	2	Scott, ss	2	0	0	2	4	0
Meyers, c	4	0	1	6	3	0	Cady, c	1	0	0	7	0	0
Marquad, p	2	0	0	0	0	0	Thomas, c	0	0	0	0	0	0
*Johnston	1	0	1	0	0	0	Shore, p	4	0	0	0	3	0
Pfeffer, p	0	0	0	0	0	0	Mays, p	0	0	0	0	0	0
†Merkle	0	0	0	0	0	0	Totals	31	6	8	27	19	1
Totals	34	5	10	24	9	4							

Brooklyn   0 0 0   1 0 0   0 0 4—5
Boston   0 0 1   0 1 0   3 1 x—6

*Singled for Marquard in eighth.
†Walked for Pfeffer in ninth.
Two-base hits—Lewis, Hooper, Janvrin. Wheat, Meyers. Runs batted in—Myers, Wheat, Mowrey, Merkle, Walker, Hoblitzel, Lewis, Gardner, Scott. Sacrifice hits—Scott, Janvrin, Lewis. Sacrifice fly—Scott. Double plays—Janvrin, Scott and Hoblitzel; Hooper and Cady; Gardner, Janvrin and Hoblitzel; Shore, Scott, Janvrin and Hoblitzel. Left on bases—Boston 11, Brooklyn 6. Earned runs—Boston 4, Brooklyn 3. Struck out—By Marquard 6, by Shore 5. Bases on balls—Off Marquard 4, off Pfeffer 2, off Shore 3. Hit by pitcher—By Shore (Cutshaw). Passed ball—Myers. Hits—Off Marquard 7 in 7 innings, off Pfeffer 1 in 1 inning, off Shore 9 in 8⅔ innings, off Mays 1 in ⅓ inning. Winning pitcher—Shore. Losing pitcher—Marquard.

GAME 2

BOSTON (A.L.)	AB	R	H	O	A	E	BROOKLYN (N.L.)	AB	R	H	O	A	E
Hooper, rf	6	0	1	2	1	0	Johnston, rf	5	0	1	1	0	0
Janvrin, 2b	6	0	1	4	5	0	Daubert, 1b	5	0	0	18	1	0
Walker, cf	3	0	0	2	1	0	Myers, cf	6	1	1	4	1	0
Walsh, cf	3	0	0	1	0	0	Wheat, lf	5	0	0	2	0	0
Hoblitzel, 1b	2	0	0	21	1	0	Cutshaw, 2b	5	0	0	5	6	1
*McNally	0	1	0	0	0	0	Mowrey, 3b	5	0	1	3	5	1
Lewis, lf	3	0	1	1	0	0	Olson, ss	2	0	1	2	4	0
Gardner, 3b	5	0	0	3	7	1	Miller, c	5	0	1	4	1	0
†Gainor	1	0	1	0	0	0	Smith, p	5	0	1	1	7	0
Scott, ss	4	1	2	1	8	0	Totals	43	1	6‡	40	25	2
Thomas, c	4	0	1	5	4	0							
Ruth, p	5	0	0	2	4	0							
Totals	42	2	7	42	31	1							

```
Brooklyn    1 0 0  0 0 0  0 0 0  0 0 0  0 0—1
Boston      0 0 1  0 0 0  0 0 0  0 0 0  0 1—2
```

*Ran for Hoblitzel in fourteenth.
†Singled for Gardner in fourteenth.
‡One out when winning run scored.
Two-base hits—Smith, Janvrin. Three-base hits—Scott, Thomas. Home run—Myers. Runs batted in—Gainor, Ruth, Myers. Sacrifice hits—Lewis 2, Thomas, Olson 2. Double plays—Scott, Janvrin and Hoblitzel; Mowrey, Cutshaw and Daubert; Myers and Miller. Left on bases—Boston 9, Brooklyn 5. Earned runs—Boston 2, Brooklyn 1. Struck out—By Smith 2, by Ruth 4. Bases on balls—Off Smith 6, off Ruth 3.

GAME 3

BROOKLYN (N.L.)	AB	R	H	O	A	E	BOSTON (A.L.)	AB	R	H	O	A	E
Myers, cf	3	0	0	3	0	0	Hooper, rf	4	1	2	1	0	0
Daubert, 1b	4	1	3	7	0	0	Janvrin, 2b	4	0	0	1	0	0
Stengel, rf	3	0	1	2	1	0	Shorten, cf	4	0	3	0	0	0
Wheat, lf	2	1	1	4	0	0	Hoblitzel, 1b	4	0	1	12	2	0
Cutshaw, 2b	4	0	1	4	0	0	Lewis, lf	4	0	0	1	1	0
Mowrey, 3b	3	1	0	2	1	0	Gardner, 3b	3	1	1	2	0	1
Olson, ss	4	1	2	1	2	0	Scott, ss	3	0	0	1	7	0
Miller, c	3	0	0	4	2	0	Thomas, c	3	0	0	5	0	0
Coombs, p	3	0	1	0	2	0	Mays, p	1	0	0	0	4	0
Pfeffer, p	1	0	1	0	1	0	*Henriksen	0	1	0	0	0	0
							Foster, p	1	0	0	1	2	0
Totals	30	4	10	27	9	0	Totals	31	3	7	24	16	1

```
Boston     0 0 0  0 0 2  1 0 0—3
Brooklyn   0 0 1  1 2 0  0 0 x—4
```

*Walked for Mays in sixth.
Three-base hits—Olson, Daubert, Hooper. Home run—Gardner. Runs batted in—Cutshaw, Olson 2, Coombs, Hooper, Shorten, Gardner. Sacrifice hits—Stengel, Miller, Myers. Stolen base—Wheat. Left on bases—Brooklyn 9, Boston 2. Earned runs—Brooklyn 3, Boston 3. Struck out—By Mays 2, by Foster 1, by Coombs 1, by Pfeffer 3. Bases on balls—Off Mays 3, off Coombs 1. Hit by pitcher—By Mays (Myers). Wild pitch—Foster. Hits—Off Mays 7 in 5 innings, off Foster 3 in 3 innings, off Coombs 7 in 6⅓ innings, off Pfeffer 0 in 2⅔ innings. Winning pitcher—Coombs. Losing pitcher—Mays.

GAME 4

BROOKLYN (N.L.)	AB	R	H	O	A	E	BOSTON (A.L.)	AB	R	H	O	A	E
Johnston, rf	4	1	1	0	0	1	Hooper, rf	4	1	2	3	0	0
Myers, cf	4	1	1	1	0	0	Janvrin, 2b	5	1	0	1	2	1
Merkle, 1b	3	0	1	9	1	1	Walker, cf	4	0	1	2	0	0
Wheat, lf	4	0	1	0	0	1	Hoblitzel, 1b	3	1	2	8	0	0
Cutshaw, 2b	4	0	1	3	2	0	Lewis, lf	4	2	2	6	0	0
Mowrey, 3b	3	0	0	1	4	0	Gardner, 3b	3	1	1	1	3	0
Olson, ss	3	0	0	2	2	0	Scott, ss	4	0	0	3	3	0
Meyers, c	3	0	0	11	3	0	Carrigan, c	3	0	2	3	1	0
‡Stengel	0	0	0	0	0	0	Leonard, p	3	0	0	0	1	0
Marquard, p	1	0	0	0	2	0	Totals	33	6	10	27	10	1
*Pfeffer	1	0	0	0	0	0							
Cheney, p	0	0	0	0	0	1							
†O'Mara	1	0	0	0	0	0							
Rucker, p	0	0	0	0	0	0							
§Getz	1	0	0	0	0	0							
Totals	32	2	5	27	14	4							

```
Boston     0 3 0  1 1 0  1 0 0—6
Brooklyn   2 0 0  0 0 0  0 0 0—2
```

*Fanned for Marquard in fourth.
†Struck out for Cheney in seventh.
‡Ran for Meyers in ninth.
§Grounded out for Rucker in ninth.
Two-base hits—Lewis, Cutshaw, Hoblitzel. Three-base hit—Johnston. Home run—Gardner. Runs batted in—Myers, Cutshaw, Hoblitzel, Gardner 3, Carrigan. Sacrifice hits—Carrigan, Gardner. Stolen base—Hooper. Left on bases—Brooklyn 7, Boston 5. Earned runs—Boston 5, Brooklyn 1. Struck out—By Leonard 3, by Marquard 3, by Cheney 5, by Rucker 3. Bases on balls—Off Leonard 4, off Marquard 2, off Cheney 1. Wild pitch—Leonard. Passed ball—Meyers. Hits—Off Marquard 5 in 4 innings, off Cheney 4 in 3 innings, off Rucker 1 in 2 innings. Losing pitcher—Marquard.

GAME 5

BROOKLYN (N.L.)	AB	R	H	O	A	E	BOSTON (A.L.)	AB	R	H	O	A	E
Myers, cf	4	0	0	0	0	0	Hooper, rf	3	2	1	1	0	0
Daubert, 1b	4	0	0	10	1	0	Janvrin, 2b	4	0	2	0	1	0
Stengel, rf	4	0	1	0	0	0	Shorten, cf	3	0	1	3	0	0
Wheat, lf	4	0	0	5	0	0	Hoblitzel, 1b	3	0	0	14	1	0
Cutshaw, 2b	3	1	0	2	3	0	Lewis, lf	3	1	2	1	0	0
Mowrey, 3b	3	0	1	1	3	1	Gardner, 3b	2	0	0	0	5	0
Olson, 3b	3	0	0	2	3	2	Scott, ss	3	0	0	2	3	2
Meyers, c	3	0	1	4	2	0	Cady, c	3	1	1	4	1	0
Pfeffer, p	2	0	0	0	1	0	Shore, p	3	0	0	2	3	0
*Merkle	1	0	0	0	0	0	Totals	27	4	7	27	14	2
Dell, p	0	0	0	0	0	0							
Totals	31	1	3	24	13	3							

Brooklyn   0 1 0   0 0 0   0 0 0—1
Boston   0 1 2   0 1 0   0 0 x—4

*Flied out for Pfeffer in eighth.
Two-base hit—Janvrin. Three-base hit—Lewis. Runs batted in—Janvrin, Shorten, Gardner. Sacrifice hits—Mowrey, Lewis, Shorten. Sacrifice fly—Gardner. Left on bases—Brooklyn 5, Boston 4. Earned runs—Boston 2, Brooklyn 0. Struck out—By Pfeffer 2, by Shore 4. Bases on balls—Off Pfeffer 2, off Shore 1. Wild pitches—Pfeffer 2. Passed ball—Cady. Hits—Off Pfeffer 6 in 7 innings, off Dell 1 in 1 inning. Losing pitcher—Pfeffer.

WORLD SERIES COMPOSITE BOX SCORE: 1916

PITCHING SUMMARY

Boston Red Sox PITCHER	G	IP	H	R	ER	SO	BB	W	L	ERA	Brooklyn Dodgers PITCHER	G	IP	H	R	ER	SO	BB	W	L	ERA
Foster	1	3	3	0	0	1	0	0	0	0.00	Rucker	1	2	1	0	0	3	0	0	0	0.00
Ruth	1	14	6	1	1	4	3	1	0	0.64	Dell	1	1	1	0	0	0	0	0	0	0.00
Leonard	1	9	5	2	1	3	4	1	0	1.00	Smith	1	13⅓	7	2	2	2	6	0	1	1.35
Shore	2	17⅔	12	6	3	9	4	2	0	1.53	Pfeffer	3	10⅔	7	5	2	5	4	0	1	1.69
Mays	2	5⅓	8	4	3	2	3	0	1	5.06	Cheney	1	3	4	2	1	5	1	0	0	3.00
											Coombs	1	6⅓	7	3	3	1	1	1	0	4.26
											Marquard	2	11	12	9	8	9	6	0	2	6.55
Totals	5	49	34	13	8	19	14	4	1	1.46	Totals	5	47⅓	39	21	16	25	18	1	4	3.04

BATTING SUMMARY

Boston Red Sox PLAYER-POS.	G	AB	R	H	2B	3B	HR	RBI	BA	Brooklyn Dodgers PLAYER-POS.	G	AB	R	H	2B	3B	HR	RBI	BA
Gainor, ph	1	1	0	1	0	0	0	1	1.000	Stengel, rf-ph	4	11	2	4	0	0	0	0	.364
Carrigan, c	1	3	0	2	0	0	0	1	.667	Coombs, p	1	3	0	1	0	0	0	1	.333
Shorten, cf	2	7	0	4	0	0	0	2	.571	Johnston, ph-rf	3	10	1	3	0	1	0	0	.300
Lewis, lf	5	17	3	6	2	1	0	1	.353	Olson, ss	5	16	1	4	0	1	0	2	.250
Hooper, rf	5	21	6	7	1	1	0	1	.333	Pfeffer, p-ph	4	4	0	1	0	0	0	0	.250
Walker, cf	3	11	1	3	0	1	0	1	.273	Merkle, ph-1b	3	4	0	1	0	0	0	1	.250
Cady, c	2	4	1	1	0	0	0	0	.250	Wheat, lf	5	19	2	4	0	1	0	1	.211
Hoblitzel, 1b	5	17	3	4	1	1	0	2	.235	Meyers, c	3	10	0	2	0	1	0	0	.200
Janvrin, 2b	5	23	2	5	3	0	0	1	.217	Smith, p	1	5	0	1	1	0	0	0	.200
Gardner, 3b	5	17	2	3	0	0	2	6	.176	Myers, cf	5	22	2	4	0	0	1	3	.182
Thomas, c	3	7	0	1	0	1	0	0	.143	Daubert, 1b	4	17	1	3	0	1	0	0	.176
Scott, ss	5	16	1	2	0	1	0	1	.125	Mowrey, 3b	5	17	2	3	0	0	0	1	.176
Shore, p	2	7	0	0	0	0	0	0	.000	Miller, c	2	8	0	1	0	0	0	0	.125
Mays, p	2	1	0	0	0	0	0	0	.000	Cutshaw, 2b	5	19	2	2	1	0	0	2	.105
Walsh, cf	1	3	0	0	0	0	0	0	.000	Marquard, p	2	3	0	0	0	0	0	0	.000
McNally, pr	1	0	0	0	0	0	0	0	.000	O'Mara, ph	1	1	0	0	0	0	0	0	.000
Ruth, p	1	5	0	0	0	0	0	1	.000	Rucker, p	1	0	0	0	0	0	0	0	.000
Henriksen, ph	1	0	1	0	0	0	0	0	.000	Getz, ph	1	1	0	0	0	0	0	0	.000
Foster, p	1	1	0	0	0	0	0	0	.000	Cheney, p	1	0	0	0	0	0	0	0	.000
Leonard, p	1	3	0	0	0	0	0	0	.000	Dell, p	1	0	0	0	0	0	0	0	.000
Totals	5	164	21	39	7	6	2	18	.238	Totals	5	170	13	34	2	5	1	11	.200

WORLD SERIES HIGHLIGHTS: 1920

CLEVELAND (AL) DEFEATS BROOKLYN (NL), 5 GAMES TO 2

FIRST GAME (Oct. 5, at Brooklyn)
CLEVELAND 020 100 000   3 5 0
BROOKLYN 000 000 100   1 5 1
Coveleski
Marquard, Mamaux (7th), Cadore (9th)

Stan Coveleski, the outstanding spitball pitcher of the Indians, held the Dodgers scoreless for six innings and limited the hard-hitting Brooklynites to six hits as the Indians scored three runs off the pitching of Rube Marquard, Al Mamaux, and Leon Cadore to win the game, 3–1.

SECOND GAME (Oct. 6, at Brooklyn)
CLEVELAND 000 000 000   0 7 1
BROOKLYN 101 010 00x   3 7 0
Bagby, Uhle (7th)
Grimes

Another spitball pitcher, Burleigh Grimes, the Dodger ace, shut out Tris Speaker's Indians, allowing them seven safeties as the Dodgers defeated the Indians 3–0 to even the Series.

THIRD GAME (Oct. 7, at Brooklyn)
CLEVELAND 000 100 000   1 3 1
BROOKLYN 200 000 00x   2 6 1
Caldwell, Mails (1st), Uhle (8th)
Smith

The Dodgers jumped off to a quick 2–0 lead in the first inning and were never headed as Sherry Smith allowed the Cleveland Indians only three hits. Speaker's double scored the only run for Cleveland as Smith's brilliant pitching set the Indians down in order. Final score: 2–1.

FOURTH GAME (Oct. 9, at Cleveland)
BROOKLYN 000 100 000   1 5 1
CLEVELAND 202 001 00x   5 12 2
Cadore, Mamaux (2d), Marquard (3d), Pfeffer (6th)
Coveleski

The Indians pounded four Dodger pitchers for 12 hits and five runs as they beat Brooklyn, 5–1. Stan Coveleski, matching his first-game performance, won his second World Series game over the Dodgers.

FIFTH GAME (Oct. 10, at Cleveland)
BROOKLYN 000 000 001   1 13 1
CLEVELAND 400 310 00x   8 12 2
Grimes, Mitchell (4th)
Bagby

The fifth game was a free-hitting contest with both teams combining for a total of 25 hits. The Indians jumped on Grimes in the first inning as Elmer Smith of the Indians hit the first grand slam in World Series history. The Indians added three more runs in the 4th inning off Clarence Mitchell, who relieved Grimes. The game was also highlighted by Bill Wambsganss' unassisted triple play in the fifth inning. The unique triple play, the first in World Series play, killed a Dodger rally and the Indians went on to win, 8–1.

SIXTH GAME (Oct. 11, at Cleveland)
BROOKLYN 000 000 000   0 3 0
CLEVELAND 000 001 00x   1 7 3
Smith
Mails

Sherry Smith of the Dodgers and Duster Mails locked horns in a scoreless pitching duel until Tris Speaker of the Indians singled with two out in the sixth inning and scored on a two-base hit by George Burns for the only run of the game.

SEVENTH GAME (Oct. 12, at Cleveland)
```
BROOKLYN ................... 000 000 000   0 5 2
CLEVELAND .................. 000 110 10x   3 7 3
```
Grimes, Mamaux (8th)
Coveleski

Once again Stan Coveleski baffled the Dodgers with a fine pitching effort, allowing Brooklyn only five scattered singles as he shut them out in the final game of a seesaw Series, 3–0.

WORLD SERIES BOX SCORES: 1920 (SEVEN GAMES)

GAME 1

CLEVELAND (A.L.)	AB	R	H	O	A	E	BROOKLYN (N.L.)	AB	R	H	O	A	E
Evans, lf	2	0	0	1	0	0	Olson, ss	3	0	2	0	3	0
†Jamieson, lf	1	0	0	0	0	0	J. Johnston, 3b	3	0	0	1	3	0
Wambsganss, 2b	3	0	0	0	2	0	Griffith, rf	4	0	1	1	0	0
Speaker, cf	4	0	0	4	0	0	Wheat, lf	4	1	1	4	0	0
Burns, 1b	3	1	1	9	1	0	Myers, cf	4	0	0	1	0	0
xE. Smith, rf	1	0	0	0	0	0	Konetchy, 1b	4	0	0	12	1	1
Gardner, 3b	4	0	0	1	3	0	Kilduff, 2b	3	0	0	1	3	0
Wood, rf	2	2	1	4	0	0	Krueger, c	3	0	0	7	1	0
yW. Johnston, 1b	1	0	0	0	1	0	Marquard, p	1	0	0	0	0	0
Sewell, ss	3	0	1	3	4	0	*Lamar	1	0	0	0	0	0
O'Neill, c	3	0	2	3	0	0	Mamaux, p	0	0	0	0	1	0
Coveleski, p	3	0	0	2	2	0	‡Mitchell	1	0	1	0	0	0
Totals	30	3	5	27	13	0	§Neis	0	0	0	0	0	0
							Cadore, p	0	0	0	0	1	0
							Totals	31	1	5	27	13	1

```
Cleveland     0 2 0  1 0 0  0 0 0—3
Brooklyn      0 0 0  0 0 0  1 0 0—1
```

*Popped out for Marquard in sixth.
†Grounded out for Evans in eighth.
‡Singled for Mamaux in eighth.
§Ran for Mitchell in eighth.
xGrounded out for Burns in ninth.
yGrounded out for Wood in ninth.
Runs batted in—O'Neill 2, Konetchy. Two-base hits—O'Neill 2, Wood, Wheat. Sacrifice hits—Wambsganss, J. Johnston. Double play—Konetchy, Krueger and J. Johnston. Left on bases—Brooklyn 5, Cleveland 3. Earned runs—Brooklyn 1, Cleveland 1. Struck out—By Marquard 4, by Mamaux 3, by Coveleski 3. Bases on balls—Off Marquard 2, off Coveleski 1. Hits—Off Marquard 5 in 6 innings, off Mamaux 0 in 2 innings, off Cadore 0 in 1 inning. Losing pitcher—Marquard.

GAME 2

CLEVELAND (A.L.)	AB	R	H	O	A	E	BROOKLYN (N.L.)	AB	R	H	O	A	E
Jamieson, lf	4	0	1	2	0	0	Olson, ss	4	1	1	3	2	0
Wambsganss, 2b	3	0	0	3	0	0	J. Johnston, 3b	4	1	1	0	1	0
†Burns	0	0	0	0	0	0	Griffith, rf	4	0	2	3	0	0
Lunte, 2b	0	0	0	0	0	0	Wheat, lf	3	0	1	3	0	0
Speaker, cf	3	0	2	2	0	0	Myers, cf	3	0	1	2	0	0
E. Smith, rf	4	0	0	3	0	0	Konetchy, 1b	3	0	0	10	1	0
Gardner, 3b	3	0	2	1	2	0	Kilduff, 2b	3	0	0	2	3	0
W. Johnston, 1b	4	0	0	3	3	0	Miller, c	3	0	0	3	1	0
Sewell, ss	4	0	0	1	1	0	Grimes, p	3	1	1	1	4	0
O'Neill, c	4	0	1	7	2	0	Totals	30	3	7	27	12	0
Bagby, p	2	0	0	2	1	1							
*Graney	1	0	0	0	0	0							
Uhle, p	0	0	0	0	0	0							
‡Nunamaker	1	0	1	0	0	0							
Totals	33	0	7	24	9	1							

```
Cleveland     0 0 0  0 0 0  0 0 0—0
Brooklyn      1 0 1  0 1 0  0 0 x—3
```

*Struck out for Bagby in seventh.
†Walked for Wambsganss in eighth.
‡Singled for Uhle in ninth.
Runs batted in—Griffith 2, Wheat. Two-base hits—Wheat, Gardner, Griffith, Speaker. Stolen bases—J. Johnston. Double play—Gardner, O'Neill, W. Johnston and O'Neill. Left on bases—Cleveland 10, Brooklyn 4. Earned runs—Brooklyn 2. Struck out—By Uhle 3, by Grimes 2. Bases on balls—Off Bagby 1, off Grimes 4. Hits—Off Bagby 7 in 6 innings, off Uhle 0 in 2 innings. Losing pitcher—Bagby.

GAME 3

BROOKLYN (N.L.)	AB	R	H	O	A	E	CLEVELAND (A.L.)	AB	R	H	O	A	E
Olson, ss	2	1	1	0	6	0	Evans, lf	4	0	0	2	0	0
J. Johnston, 3b	3	0	0	0	4	0	Wambsganss, 2b	3	0	0	2	2	0
Griffith, rf	1	1	0	2	0	0	Speaker, cf	4	1	1	2	0	0
*Neis, rf	3	0	0	0	0	0	Burns, 1b	3	0	0	12	0	0
Wheat, lf	4	0	3	1	0	1	Gardner, 3b	3	0	0	0	0	0
Myers, cf	4	0	2	1	0	0	Wood, rf	3	0	0	1	0	0
Konetchy, 1b	3	0	0	17	2	0	Sewell, ss	2	0	0	2	3	1
Kilduff, 2b	1	0	0	2	6	0	O'Neill, c	3	0	2	2	2	0
Miller, c	1	0	0	2	0	0	†Jamieson	0	0	0	0	0	0
S. Smith, p	3	0	0	2	2	0	Uhle, p	0	0	0	0	1	0
Totals	25	2	6	27	20	1	Caldwell, p	0	0	0	0	0	0
							Mails, p	2	0	0	1	3	0
							‡Nunamaker, c	1	0	0	0	0	0
							Totals	28	1	3	24	11	1

```
Cleveland    0 0 0  1 0 0  0 0 0—1
Brooklyn     2 0 0  0 0 0  0 0 x—2
```

*Grounded out for Griffith in third.
†Ran for O'Neill in eighth.
‡Hit into double play for Mails in eighth.
Runs batted in—Wheat, Myers, Two-base hit—Speaker. Sacrifice hits—J. Johnston, Kilduff, Miller. Double plays—Mails and Burns; Olson, Kilduff and Konetchy; Wambsganss, Sewell and Burns; J. Johnston, Kilduff and Konetchy. Left on bases—Brooklyn 7, Cleveland 2. Earned runs—Brooklyn 1, Cleveland 0. Struck out—by Mails 2, by S. Smith 2. Bases on balls—Off Caldwell 1, off Mails 4. off S. Smith 2. Hits—Off Caldwell 2 in ⅓ inning, off Mails 3 in 6⅔ innings, off Uhle 1 in 1 inning. Losing pitcher—Caldwell.

GAME 4

BROOKLYN (N.L.)	AB	R	H	O	A	E	CLEVELAND (A.L.)	AB	R	H	O	A	E
Olson, ss	4	0	1	1	3	0	Jamieson, lf	2	0	0	1	0	0
J. Johnston, 3b	4	1	2	1	0	0	‡Evans, lf	3	0	1	0	0	0
yNeis	0	0	0	0	0	0	Wambsganss, 2b	4	2	2	4	6	0
Griffith, rf	4	0	1	1	0	0	Speaker, cf	5	2	2	3	0	0
Wheat, lf	4	0	0	0	0	1	E. Smith, rf	1	0	1	1	0	0
Myers, cf	3	0	0	6	1	0	*Burns, 1b	2	0	1	7	0	1
Konetchy, 1b	2	0	0	5	0	0	Gardner, 3b	3	0	1	2	3	0
Kilduff, 2b	3	0	1	2	3	0	W. Johnston, 1b	1	0	0	4	0	0
Miller, c	3	0	0	7	0	0	†Wood, rf	2	0	0	0	0	0
Cadore, p	0	0	0	1	0	0	xGraney, rf	1	0	0	0	0	0
Mamaux, p	1	0	0	0	0	0	Sewell, ss	4	0	2	1	7	1
Marquard, p	0	0	0	0	1	0	O'Neill, c	2	0	1	4	0	0
§Lamar	1	0	0	0	0	0	Coveleski, p	4	1	1	0	2	0
Pfeffer, p	1	0	0	0	0	0	Totals	34	5	12	27	18	2
Totals	30	1	5	24	8	1							

```
Brooklyn     0 0 0  1 0 0  0 0 0—1
Cleveland    2 0 2  0 0 1  0 0 x—5
```

*Singled for E. Smith in third.
†Flied out for W. Johnston in third.
‡Flied out for Jamieson in fourth.
§Grounded out for Marquard in sixth.
xForced runner for Wood in seventh.
yRan for J. Johnston in ninth.
Runs batted in—Griffith, Wambsganss, E. Smith, Burns, Gardner. Two-base hit—Griffith. Sacrifice fly—Gardner. Double plays—Myers, Olson and Kilduff; Sewell, Wambsganss and Burns; Gardner, Wambsganss and Burns. Left on bases—Cleveland 10, Brooklyn 3. Earned runs—Cleveland 4, Brooklyn 1. Struck out—By Cadore 1, by Mamaux 1, by Coveleski 4, by Marquard 2, by Pfeffer 1. Bases on balls—Off Cadore 1, off Marquard 1, off Coveleski 1, off Pfeffer 2. Wild pitch—Pfeffer. Hits—Off Cadore 4 in 1 (pitched to two batters in second inning), off Mamaux 2 in 1 (pitched to two batters in third inning), off Marquard 2 in 3 innings, off Pfeffer 4 in 3 innings. Passed ball—Miller. Losing pitcher—Cadore.

GAME 5

BROOKLYN (N.L.)	AB	R	H	O	A	E	CLEVELAND (A.L.)	AB	R	H	O	A	E
Olson, ss	4	0	2	3	5	0	Jamieson, lf	4	1	2	2	1	0
Sheehan, 3b	3	0	1	1	1	1	*Graney, lf	1	0	0	0	0	0
Griffith, rf	4	0	0	0	0	0	Wambsganss, 2b	5	1	1	7	2	0
Wheat, lf	4	1	2	3	0	0	Speaker, cf	3	2	1	1	0	0
Myers, cf	4	0	2	0	0	0	E. Smith, rf	4	1	3	0	0	0
Konetchy, 1b	4	0	2	9	2	0	Gardner, 3b	4	0	1	2	2	1
Kilduff, 2b	4	0	1	5	6	0	W. Johnston, 1b	3	1	2	9	1	0
Miller, c	2	0	2	0	1	0	Sewell, ss	3	0	0	2	4	0
Krueger, c	2	0	1	2	1	0	O'Neill, c	2	1	0	3	1	1
Grimes, p	1	0	0	0	1	0	Thomas, c	0	0	0	1	0	0
Mitchell, p	2	0	0	1	0	0	Bagby, p	4	1	2	0	2	0
Totals	34	1	13	24	17	1	Totals	33	8	12	27	13	2

```
Brooklyn     0 0 0   0 0 0   0 0 1—1
Cleveland    4 0 0   3 1 0   0 0 x—8
```

*Struck out for Jamieson in eighth.
Runs batted in—E. Smith 4, Bagby 3, Gardner, Konetchy. Three-base hits—Konetchy, E. Smith. Home Runs—E. Smith, Bagby. Sacrifice hits—Sheehan, W. Johnston. Double plays—Olson, Kilduff and Konetchy; Jamieson and O'Neill; Gardner, Wambsganss and W. Johnston; W. Johnston, Sewell and W. Johnston. Triple play—Wambsganss, unassisted. Left on bases—Brooklyn 7, Cleveland 6. Earned runs—Cleveland 7, Brooklyn 1. Struck out—By Bagby 3, by Mitchell 1. Bases on balls—Off Grimes 1, off Mitchell 3. Wild pitch—Bagby. Hits—Off Grimes 9 in 3⅓ innings, off Mitchell 3 in 4⅔ innings. Passed ball—Miller. Losing pitcher—Grimes.

GAME 6

BROOKLYN (N.L.)	AB	R	H	O	A	E	CLEVELAND (A.L.)	AB	R	H	O	A	E
Olson, ss	4	0	1	4	1	0	Evans, lf	4	0	3	4	0	0
Sheehan, 3b	4	0	0	0	3	0	Wambsganss, 2b	4	0	0	1	2	0
Neis, rf	2	0	0	3	0	0	Speaker, cf	3	1	1	3	0	0
*Krueger	1	0	0	0	0	0	Burns, 1b	2	0	1	10	0	0
Griffith, rf	0	0	0	0	0	0	Gardner, 3b	3	0	0	2	2	1
Wheat, lf	4	0	0	2	0	0	Wood, rf	3	0	1	2	0	0
Myers, cf	4	0	1	1	0	0	Sewell, ss	3	0	1	2	3	2
Konetchy, 1b	3	0	1	9	0	0	O'Neill, c	3	0	0	3	2	0
‡McCabe	0	0	0	0	0	0	Mails, p	3	0	0	0	1	0
Kilduff, 2b	4	0	0	2	2	0	Totals	28	1	7	27	10	3
Miller, c	3	0	0	3	3	0							
S. Smith, p	3	0	0	0	3	0							
Totals	32	0	3	24	12	0							

```
Brooklyn     0 0 0   0 0 0   0 0 0—0
Cleveland    0 0 0   0 0 1   0 0 x—1
```

*Forced runner for Neis in eighth.
†Ran for Konetchy in ninth.
Run batted in—Burns. Two-base hits—Burns, Olson. Left on bases—Brooklyn 7, Cleveland 4. Earned runs—Cleveland 1. Struck out—By Mails 4, by S. Smith 1. Bases on balls—Off Mails 2, off S. Smith 1. Losing pitcher—Smith.

GAME 7

BROOKLYN (N.L.)	AB	R	H	O	A	E	CLEVELAND (A.L.)	AB	R	H	O	A	E
Olson, ss	4	0	0	1	1	0	Jamieson, lf	4	1	2	3	0	0
Sheehan, 3b	4	0	1	2	1	1	Wambsganss, 2b	4	0	1	4	3	0
Griffith, rf	4	0	0	3	0	0	Speaker, cf	3	0	1	3	0	0
Wheat, lf	4	0	2	3	0	0	E. Smith, rf	3	0	0	3	1	0
Myers, cf	4	0	0	3	0	0	Gardner, 3b	4	1	1	1	3	0
Konetchy, 1b	4	0	1	8	0	0	W. Johnston, 1b	2	0	1	11	1	0
Kilduff, 2b	3	0	0	1	4	0	Sewell, ss	4	0	0	0	6	2
Miller, c	2	0	0	2	1	0	O'Neill, C.	4	0	1	1	0	0
†Lamar	1	0	0	0	0	0	Coveleski, p	3	1	0	0	1	1
Krueger, c	0	0	0	1	0	0	Totals	31	3	7*	26	15	3
Grimes, p	2	0	1	0	2	1							

GAME 7 (continued)

BROOKLYN (N.L.)	AB	R	H	O	A	E	CLEVELAND (A.L.)	AB	R	H	O	A	E
‡Schmandt	1	0	0	0	0	0							
Mamaux, p	0	0	0	0	0	0							
Totals	33	0	5	24	9	2							

	Brooklyn	0 0 0 0 0 0 0 0 0—0
	Cleveland	0 0 0 1 1 0 1 0 x—3

*Olson out; hit by batted ball in third.
†Grounded out for Miller in seventh.
‡Grounded out for Grimes in eighth.
Runs batted in—Jamieson, Speaker. Two-base hits—O'Neill, Jamieson. Three-base hit—Speaker. Stolen bases—W. Johnston, Jamieson. Left on bases—Cleveland 8, Brooklyn 6. Earned runs—Cleveland 2, Brooklyn 0. Struck out—By Coveleski 1, by Grimes 2, by Mamaux 1. Bases on balls—Off Grimes 4. Hits—Off Grimes 7 in 7 innings, off Mamaux 0 in 1 inning. Losing pitcher—Grimes.

WORLD SERIES COMPOSITE BOX SCORE: 1920

PITCHING SUMMARY

Cleveland Indians PITCHER	G	IP	H	R	ER	SO	BB	W	L	ERA	Brooklyn Dodgers PITCHER	G	IP	H	R	ER	SO	BB	W	L	ERA
Mails	2	15⅔	6	0	0	6	6	1	0	0.00	Mitchell	1	4⅔	3	1	0	1	3	0	0	0.00
Uhle	2	3	1	0	0	3	0	0	0	0.00	S. Smith	2	17	10	2	1	3	3	1	1	0.52
Coveleski	3	27	15	2	2	8	2	3	0	0.67	Marquard	2	9	7	3	1	6	3	0	1	1.00
Bagby	2	15	20	4	3	3	1	1	1	1.80	Pfeffer	1	3	4	1	1	2	0	0	0	3.00
Caldwell	1	⅓	2	2	1	0	1	0	1	27.00	Grimes	3	19⅓	23	10	9	4	9	1	2	4.19
											Mamaux	3	4	2	2	2	5	0	0	0	4.50
											Cadore	2	2	4	2	2	1	1	0	1	9.00
Totals	7	61	44	8	6	20	10	5	2	0.88	Totals	7	59	53	21	16	21	21	2	5	2.44

BATTING SUMMARY

Cleveland Indians PLAYER-POS.	G	AB	R	H	2B	3B	HR	RBI	BA	Brooklyn Dodgers PLAYER-POS.	G	AB	R	H	2B	3B	HR	RBI	BA
Nunamaker, ph-c	2	2	0	1	0	0	0	0	.500	Mitchell, ph	2	3	0	1	0	0	0	0	.333
O'Neill, c	7	21	1	7	3	0	0	2	.333	Grimes, p	3	6	1	2	0	0	0	0	.333
Bagby, p	2	6	1	2	0	0	1	3	.333	Wheat, lf	7	27	2	9	2	0	0	2	.333
Jamieson, ph-lf	6	15	2	5	1	0	0	1	.333	Olson, ss	7	25	2	8	1	0	0	0	.320
Speaker, cf	7	25	6	8	2	1	0	1	.320	Myers, cf	7	26	0	6	0	0	0	1	.231
E. Smith, ph-rf	5	13	1	4	0	1	1	5	.308	J. Johnston, 3b	4	14	2	3	0	0	0	0	.214
Evans, lf-ph	4	13	0	4	0	0	0	0	.308	Griffith, rf	7	21	1	4	2	0	0	3	.190
Burns, 1b-ph	5	10	1	3	1	0	0	3	.300	Sheehan, 3b	3	11	0	2	0	0	0	0	.182
W. Jo'ton, ph-1b	5	11	1	3	0	0	0	0	.273	Konetchy, 1b	7	23	0	4	0	1	0	2	.174
Gardner, 3b	7	24	1	5	1	0	0	2	.208	Krueger, c-ph	4	6	0	1	0	0	0	0	.167
Wood, rf-ph	4	10	2	2	1	0	0	0	.200	Miller, c	6	14	0	2	0	0	0	0	.143
Sewell, ss	7	23	0	4	0	0	0	0	.174	Kilduff, 2b	7	21	0	2	0	0	0	0	.095
Wambsganss, 2b	7	26	3	4	0	0	0	1	.154	Lamar, ph	3	3	0	0	0	0	0	0	.000
Coveleski, p	3	10	2	1	0	0	0	0	.100	Neis, pr-rf	4	5	0	0	0	0	0	0	.000
Lunte, 2b	1	0	0	0	0	0	0	0	.000	Marquard, p	2	1	0	0	0	0	0	0	.000
Graney, ph-rf-lf	3	3	0	0	0	0	0	0	.000	Mamaux, p	3	1	0	0	0	0	0	0	.000
Uhle, p	2	0	0	0	0	0	0	0	.000	Cadore, p	2	0	0	0	0	0	0	0	.000
Caldwell, p	1	0	0	0	0	0	0	0	.000	S. Smith, p	2	6	0	0	0	0	0	0	.000
Mails, p	2	5	0	0	0	0	0	0	.000	Pfeffer, p	1	1	0	0	0	0	0	0	.000
Thomas, c	1	0	0	0	0	0	0	0	.000	McCabe, pr	1	1	0	0	0	0	0	0	.000
										Schmandt, ph	1	1	0	0	0	0	0	0	.000
Totals	7	217	21	53	9	2	2	18	.244	Totals	7	215	8	44	5	1	0	8	.205

WORLD SERIES HIGHLIGHTS: 1941

NEW YORK (AL) DEFEATS BROOKLYN (NL), 4 GAMES TO 1

FIRST GAME (Oct. 1, at New York)
BROOKLYN 000 010 100 2 6 0
NEW YORK. 010 101 00x 3 6 1
Davis, Casey (6th), Allen (7th)
Ruffing

Joe Gordon, Yankee second baseman, homered off Dodger pitcher Curt Davis in the second inning as the Yankees jumped off to a 1–0 lead. Bill Dickey also homered, giving the Yanks a 3–1 lead going into the seventh inning. The Dodgers came within a run of tying the game in the seventh, but Pee Wee Reese was caught trying to advance to third base after Wasdell's foul fly was caught ending the Dodger threat.

SECOND GAME (Oct. 2, at New York)
BROOKLYN 000 021 000 3 6 2
NEW YORK. 011 000 000 2 9 1
Wyatt
Chandler, Murphy (6th)

The Dodgers came from behind, scoring two runs in the fifth inning and another in the sixth to move ahead of the Yankees by a 3–2 score. Whit Wyatt pitched six scoreless innings to hold the Yanks in check. Dolf Camilli's single in the sixth inning scored Dixie Walker with the game's deciding run.

THIRD GAME (Oct. 4, at Brooklyn)
NEW YORK. 000 000 020 2 8 0
BROOKLYN 000 000 010 1 4 0
Russo
Fitzsimmons, Casey (8th), French (8th), Allen (9th)

Fred Fitzsimmons held the Yankees scoreless into the seventh inning. Then Marius Russo, the Yankee pitcher, hit a line drive that struck Fitzsimmons above the knee, and he was taken out of the game. The Yanks then scored twice off Hugh Casey on hits by Red Rolfe, Tommy Henrich, Joe DiMaggio, and Charlie Keller to win the game, 2–1.

FOURTH GAME (Oct. 5, at Brooklyn)
NEW YORK. 100 200 004 7 12 0
BROOKLYN 000 220 000 4 9 1
Donald, Breuer (5th), Murphy (8th)
Higbe, French (4th), Allen (5th), Casey (5th)

With the Yanks leading 3–0, Pistol Pete Reiser homered with a man on base in the fourth inning to give the Dodgers two runs. They scored two more in the fifth and seemingly were on their way to a 4–3 win. Then in the ninth inning with two out, Henrich swung at a third strike. Dodger catcher Mickey Owen allowed the ball to go through him to the fence, and Henrich made it safely to first base. The Yankees then went on to score four runs on a single by DiMaggio, a double by Keller, and a double by Joe Gordon, for a crucial turnabout 7–4 win.

FIFTH GAME (Oct. 6, at Brooklyn)
NEW YORK 020 010 000 3 6 0
BROOKLYN 001 000 000 1 4 1
Bonham
Wyatt

Ernie Bonham limited the Dodgers to one hit after the third inning to outpitch Whit Wyatt in the fifth and deciding game of the Series, 3–1. Bonham gave up only four hits over nine innings. The Dodgers lone run was scored on a double by pitcher Wyatt, a single by Lew Riggs, and Pete Reiser's long sacrifice fly ball.

WORLD SERIES BOX SCORES: 1941 (FIVE GAMES)

GAME 1

BROOKLYN (N.L.)	AB	R	H	O	A	E
Walker, rf	3	0	0	3	0	0
Herman, 2b	3	0	0	0	6	0
Reiser, cf	3	0	0	4	0	0
Camilli, 1b	4	0	0	7	2	0
Medwick, lf	4	0	1	4	0	0
Lavagetto, 3b	4	1	0	0	0	0
Reese, ss	4	1	3	4	2	0
Owen, c	2	0	1	1	0	0
*Riggs	1	0	1	0	0	0
Franks, c	1	0	0	0	1	0
Davis, p	2	0	0	1	0	0
Casey, p	0	0	0	0	0	0
†Wasdell	1	0	0	0	0	0
Allen, p	0	0	0	0	0	0
Totals	32	2	6	24	11	0

NEW YORK (A.L.)	AB	R	H	O	A	E
Sturm, 1b	3	0	1	7	0	0
Rolfe, 3b	3	0	1	2	2	0
Henrich, rf	4	0	0	0	0	0
DiMaggio, cf	4	0	0	5	0	0
Keller, lf	2	2	0	4	0	0
Dickey, c	4	0	2	6	0	0
Gordon, 2b	2	1	2	0	2	0
Rizzuto, ss	4	0	0	3	5	1
Ruffing, p	3	0	0	0	0	0
Totals	29	3	6	27	9	1

Brooklyn 0 0 0 0 1 0 1 0 0—2
New York 0 1 0 1 0 1 0 0 x—3

*Singled for Owen in seventh.
†Fouled out for Casey in seventh.
Runs batted in—Gordon 2, Dickey, Owen, Riggs. Two-base hit—Dickey. Three-base hit—Owen. Home run—Gordon. Double plays—Rolfe and Rizzuto; Gordon, Rizzuto and Sturm. Left on bases—New York 8, Brooklyn 6. Earned runs—New York 3, Brooklyn 1. Struck out—By Ruffing 5, by Davis 1. Bases on balls—Off Ruffing 3, off Davis 3, off Allen 2. Hit by pitcher—By Allen (Sturm). Hits—Off Davis 6 in 5⅓ innings, off Casey 0 in ⅔ innings, off Allen 0 in 2 innings. Losing pitcher—Davis.

GAME 2

BROOKLYN (N.L.)	AB	R	H	O	A	E
Walker, rf	4	1	0	4	0	0
Herman, 2b	4	0	1	4	4	0
Reiser, cf	4	0	0	2	1	0
Camilli, 1b	3	1	1	8	1	0
Medwick, lf	4	1	2	0	0	0
Lavagetto, 3b	3	0	1	1	1	0
Reese, ss	4	0	0	2	4	2
Owen, c	2	0	1	6	1	0
Wyatt, p	3	0	0	0	1	0
Totals	31	3	6	27	13	2

NEW YORK (A.L.)	AB	R	H	O	A	E
Sturm, 1b	5	0	1	11	0	0
Rolfe, 3b	5	0	1	1	2	0
Henrich, rf	4	1	1	0	0	0
DiMaggio, cf	3	0	0	4	0	0
Keller, lf	4	1	2	1	0	0
Dickey, c	4	0	0	5	1	0
*Bordagaray	0	0	0	0	0	0
Rosar, c	0	0	0	0	0	0
Gordon, 2b	1	0	1	2	7	1
Rizzuto, ss	4	0	1	3	5	0
Chandler, p	2	0	1	0	0	0
Murphy, p	1	0	0	0	0	0
†Selkirk	1	0	1	0	0	0
Totals	34	2	9	27	15	1

Brooklyn 0 0 0 0 2 1 0 0 0—3
New York 0 1 1 0 0 0 0 0 0—2

*Ran for Dickey in eighth.
†Singled for Murphy in ninth.
Runs batted in—Chandler, Keller, Reese, Owen, Camilli. Two-base hits—Henrich, Medwick. Double plays—Reese, Herman and Camilli; Gordon, Rizzuto and Sturm 2; Dickey and Gordon. Left on bases—New York 10, Brooklyn 4. Earned runs—Brooklyn 2, New York 2. Struck out—By Wyatt 5, by Chandler 2, by Murphy 2. Bases on balls—Off Wyatt 5, off Chandler 2, off Murphy 1. Hits—Off Chandler 4 in 5 innings (pitched to two batters in sixth), off Murphy 2 in 4 innings. Losing pitcher—Chandler.

GAME 3

NEW YORK (A.L.)	AB	R	H	O	A	E
Sturm, 1b	4	0	1	12	0	0
Rolfe, 3b	4	1	2	1	2	0
Henrich, rf	3	1	1	2	0	0

BROOKLYN (N.L.)	AB	R	H	O	A	E
Reese, ss	4	0	1	3	1	0
Herman, 2b	1	0	0	0	1	0
Coscarart, 2b	2	0	0	0	3	0

GAME 3 (continued)

NEW YORK (A.L.)	AB	R	H	O	A	E	BROOKLYN (N.L.)	AB	R	H	O	A	E
DiMaggio, cf	4	0	2	2	0	0	Reiser, cf	4	0	1	5	0	0
Keller, lf	4	0	1	2	0	0	Medwick, lf	4	0	1	3	0	0
Dickey, c	4	0	0	4	1	0	Lavagetto, 3b	3	0	0	1	0	0
Gordon, 2b	3	0	1	2	4	0	Camilli, 1b	3	0	0	11	0	0
Rizzuto, ss	3	0	0	2	3	0	Walker, rf	3	1	1	2	0	0
Russo, p	4	0	0	0	4	0	Owen, c	3	0	0	2	1	0
Totals	33	2	8	27	14	0	Fitzsimmons, p	2	0	0	0	2	0
							Casey, p	0	0	0	0	0	0
							French, p	0	0	0	0	0	0
							*Galan	1	0	0	0	0	0
							Allen, p	0	0	0	0	0	0
							Totals	30	1	4	27	8	0

```
New York      0 0 0   0 0 0   0 2 0—2
Brooklyn      0 0 0   0 0 0   0 1 0—1
```

*Fanned for French in eighth.
Runs batted in—DiMaggio, Keller, Reese. Two-base hits—Reiser, Walker. Three-base hit—Gordon. Stolen bases—Rizzuto, Sturm. Double plays—Rizzuto and Sturm; Reese and Camilli. Left on bases—New York, Brooklyn 4. Earned runs—New York 2, Brooklyn 1. Struck out—By Russo 5, by Fitzsimmons 1. Bases on balls—Off Russo 2, off Fitzsimmons 3. Hits—Off Fitzsimmons 4 in 7 innings, off Casey 4 in 1/3 inning, off French 0 in 2/3 inning, off Allen 0 in 1 inning. Losing pitcher—Casey.

GAME 4

NEW YORK (A.L.)	AB	R	H	O	A	E	BROOKLYN (N.L.)	AB	R	H	O	A	E
Sturm, 1b	5	0	2	9	1	0	Reese, ss	5	0	0	2	4	0
Rolfe, 3b	5	1	2	0	2	0	Walker, rf	5	1	2	5	0	0
Henrich, rf	4	1	0	3	0	0	Reiser, cf	5	1	2	1	0	0
DiMaggio, cf	4	1	2	2	0	0	Camilli, 1b	4	0	2	10	1	0
Keller, lf	5	1	4	1	0	0	Riggs, 3b	3	0	0	0	2	0
Dickey, c	2	2	0	7	0	0	Medwick, lf	2	0	0	1	0	0
Gordon, 2b	5	1	2	2	3	0	Allen, p	0	0	0	0	0	0
Rizzuto, ss	4	0	0	2	3	0	Casey, p	2	0	1	0	3	0
Donald, p	2	0	0	0	1	0	Owen, c	2	1	0	2	1	1
Breuer, p	1	0	0	0	1	0	Coscarart, 2b	3	1	0	4	2	0
†Selkirk	1	0	0	0	0	0	Higbe, p	1	0	1	0	1	0
Murphy, p	1	0	0	1	0	0	French, p	0	0	0	0	0	0
Totals	39	7	12	27	11	0	*Wasdell, lf	3	0	1	2	0	0
							Totals	35	4	9	27	14	1

```
New York      1 0 0   2 0 0   0 0 4—7
Brooklyn      0 0 0   2 2 0   0 0 0—4
```

*Doubled for French in fourth.
†Grounded out for Breuer in eighth.
Runs batted in—Keller 3, Sturm 2, Gordon 2, Wasdell 2, Reiser 2. Two-base hits—Keller 2, Walker, Camilli, Wasdell, Gordon. Home run—Reiser. Double play—Gordon, Rizzuto and Sturm. Left on bsdes—New York 11, Brooklyn 8. Earned runs—Brooklyn 4, New York 3. Struck out—By Donald 2, by Breuer 2, by Murphy 1, by Higbe 1, by Casey 1. Bases on balls—Off Donald 3, off Breuer 1, off Higbe 2, off Casey 2, off Allen 1. Hit by pitcher—By Allen (Henrich). Hits—Off Donald 6 in 4 innings (pitched to two batters in fifth), off Breuer 3 in 3 innings, off Murphy 0 in 2 innings, off Higbe 6 in 3 2/3 innings, off French 0 in 1/3 inning, off Allen 1 in 2/3 inning, off Casey 5 in 4 1/3 innings. Winning pitcher—Murphy. Losing pitcher—Casey.

GAME 5

NEW YORK (A.L.)	AB	R	H	O	A	E	BROOKLYN (N.L.)	AB	R	H	O	A	E
Sturm, 1b	4	0	1	9	0	0	Walker, rf	3	0	1	0	0	0
Rolfe, 3b	3	0	0	3	0	0	Riggs, 3b	4	0	1	1	3	0
Henrich, rf	3	1	1	1	0	0	Reiser, cf	4	0	1	2	0	0
DiMaggio, cf	4	0	1	6	0	0	Camilli, 1b	4	0	0	9	1	0
Keller, lf	3	1	0	4	0	0	Medwick, lf	3	0	0	0	0	0
Dickey, c	4	1	1	2	0	0	Reese, ss	3	0	0	2	3	1
Gordon, 2b	3	0	1	0	3	0	†Wasdell	1	0	0	0	0	0
Rizzuto, ss	3	0	1	2	2	0	Owen, c	3	0	0	9	1	0

GAME 5 (continued)

NEW YORK (A.L.)	AB	R	H	O	A	E
Bonham, p	4	0	0	0	1	0
Totals	31	3	6	27	6	0

BROOKLYN (N.L.)	AB	R	H	O	A	E
Coscarart, 2b	2	0	0	3	3	0
*Galan	1	0	0	0	0	0
Herman, 2b	0	0	0	0	2	0
Wyatt, p	3	1	1	1	1	0
Totals	31	1	4	27	14	1

```
New York    0 2 0  0 1 0  0 0 0—3
Brooklyn    0 0 1  0 0 0  0 0 0—1
```

*Fouled out for Coscarart in seventh.
†Flied out for Reese in ninth.
Runs batted in—Gordon, Reiser, Henrich. Two-base hit—Wyatt. Three-base hit—Reiser. Home run—Henrich. Left on bases—New York 6, Brooklyn 5. Earned runs—New York 3, Brooklyn 1. Double plays—Owen and Riggs; Reese, Coscarart and Camilli; Herman, Reese and Camilli. Struck out—By Bonham 2, by Wyatt 9. Bases on balls—Off Bonham 2, off Wyatt 5. Wild pitch—Wyatt.

WORLD SERIES COMPOSITE BOX SCORE: 1941

PITCHING SUMMARY

New York Yankees

PITCHER	G	IP	H	R	ER	SO	BB	W	L	ERA
Murphy	2	6	2	0	0	3	1	1	0	0.00
Breuer	1	3	3	0	0	2	1	0	0	0.00
Ruffing	1	9	6	2	1	5	3	1	0	1.00
Bonham	1	9	4	1	1	2	2	1	0	1.00
Russo	1	9	4	1	1	5	2	1	0	1.00
Chandler	1	5	4	3	2	2	2	0	1	3.60
Donald	1	4	6	4	4	2	3	0	0	9.00
Totals	5	45	29	11	9	21	14	4	1	1.89

Brooklyn Dodgers

PITCHER	G	IP	H	R	ER	SO	BB	W	L	ERA
Fitzsimmons	1	7	4	0	0	1	3	0	0	0.00
Allen	3	3⅔	1	0	0	3	0	0	0	0.00
French	2	1	0	0	0	0	0	0	0	0.00
Wyatt	2	18	15	5	5	14	10	1	1	2.50
Casey	3	5⅓	9	6	2	1	2	0	2	3.40
Davis	1	5⅓	6	3	3	1	3	0	1	5.10
Higbe	1	3⅔	6	3	3	1	2	0	0	7.50
Totals	5	44	41	17	13	18	23	1	4	2.65

BATTING SUMMARY

New York Yankees

PLAYER-POS.	G	AB	R	H	2B	3B	HR	RBI	BA
Gordon, 2b	5	14	2	7	1	1	1	5	.500
Chandler, p	1	2	0	1	0	0	0	1	.500
Selkirk, ph	2	2	0	1	0	0	0	0	.500
Keller, lf	5	18	5	7	2	0	0	5	.380
Rolfe, 3b	5	20	2	6	0	0	0	0	.300
Sturm, 1b	5	21	0	6	0	0	0	2	.286
DiMaggio, cf	5	19	1	5	0	0	0	1	.263
Henrich, rf	5	18	4	3	1	0	1	1	.167
Dickey, c	5	18	3	3	1	0	0	1	.167
Rizzuto, ss	5	18	0	2	0	0	0	0	.111
Rosar, c	1	0	0	0	0	0	0	0	.000
Ruffing, p	1	3	0	0	0	0	0	0	.000
Murphy, p	2	2	0	0	0	0	0	0	.000
Russo, p	1	4	0	0	0	0	0	0	.000
Donald, p	1	2	0	0	0	0	0	0	.000
Breuer, p	1	1	0	0	0	0	0	0	.000
Bonham, p	1	4	0	0	0	0	0	0	.000
Bordagaray, pr	1	0	0	0	0	0	0	0	.000
Totals	5	166	17	41	5	1	2	16	.247

Brooklyn Dodgers

PLAYER-POS.	G	AB	R	H	2B	3B	HR	RBI	BA
Higbe, p	1	1	0	1	0	0	0	0	1.000
Riggs, ph-3b	3	8	0	2	0	0	0	1	.250
Medwick, lf	5	17	1	4	1	0	0	0	.235
Walker, rf	5	18	3	4	2	0	0	0	.222
Reiser, cf	5	20	1	4	1	1	1	3	.200
Reese, ss	5	20	1	4	0	0	0	2	.200
Wasdell, ph-lf	3	5	0	1	1	0	0	2	.200
Camilli, 1b	5	18	1	3	0	0	0	1	.167
Owen, c	5	12	1	2	0	1	0	2	.167
Wyatt, p	2	6	1	1	1	0	0	0	.167
Herman, 2b	4	8	1	1	0	0	0	0	.125
Lavagetto, 3b	3	10	1	1	0	0	0	0	.100
Coscarart, 2b	3	7	1	0	0	0	0	0	.000
Franks, c	1	1	0	0	0	0	0	0	.000
Davis, p	1	2	0	0	0	0	0	0	.000
Casey, p	3	2	0	1	0	0	0	0	.000
Allen, p	3	0	0	0	0	0	0	0	.000
Fitzsimmons, p	1	2	0	0	0	0	0	0	.000
French, p	2	0	0	0	0	0	0	0	.000
Galan, ph	2	2	0	0	0	0	0	0	.000
Totals	5	159	11	29	7	2	1	11	.182

WORLD SERIES HIGHLIGHTS: 1947

NEW YORK (AL) DEFEATS BROOKLYN (NL), 4 GAMES TO 3

FIRST GAME (Sept. 30, at New York)
BROOKLYN 100 001 100   3 6 0
NEW YORK.................. 000 050 00x   5 4 0
Branca, Behrman (5th), Casey (7th)
Shea, Page (6th)

Ralph Branca started by retiring the first 12 Yankees, but Ralph weakened in the fifth inning and the Yanks pounded him for five runs to defeat the Dodgers, 5–3. Spec Shea, pitching for the Yanks, allowed the Dodgers only six hits.

SECOND GAME (Oct. 1, at New York)
BROOKLYN 001 100 001   3 9 2
NEW YORK.................. 101 121 40x 10 15 1
Lombardi, Gregg (5th), Behrman (7th), Barney (7th)
Reynolds

Allie Reynolds struck out 10 Dodgers and evenly spaced the nine Dodger hits as the Yanks fell upon Vic Lombardi, Hal Gregg, Hank Behrman, and Rex Barney for 15 hits in a 10–3 drubbing.

THIRD GAME (Oct. 2, at Brooklyn)
NEW YORK.................. 002 221 100   8 13 0
BROOKLYN 061 200 00x   9 13 1
Newsom, Raschi (2d), Drews (3d), Chandler (4th), Page (6th)
Hatten, Branca (5th), Casey (7th)

The underdog Dodgers jumped on Bobo Newsom and Vic Raschi, scoring six runs in the second inning and continued to pound Yankee pitchers Karl Drews and Spud Chandler to eke out a 13-hit, 9–8 win in a slugfest.

FOURTH GAME (Oct. 3, at Brooklyn)
NEW YORK.................. 100 100 000   2 8 1
BROOKLYN 000 010 002   3 1 3
Bevens
Taylor, Gregg (1st), Behrman (8th), Casey (9th)

Floyd Bevens, the Yankee pitcher, was just one out away from a great World Series win. He had pitched a no-hit game going into the ninth inning, when with two out Cookie Lavagetto slammed a double that scored two runs and gave the Dodgers a hard-fought win, 3–2, to even the series.

FIFTH GAME (Oct. 4, at Brooklyn)
NEW YORK.................. 000 110 000   2 5 0
BROOKLYN 000 001 000   1 4 1
Shea
Barney, Hatten (5th), Behrman (7th), Casey (8th)

Spec Shea pitched and batted the Yankees to a 2–1 win in a tight pitching duel. Joe DiMaggio's homer in the fifth inning provided the winning margin as the Yankees garnered five hits off five Dodger pitchers, while the Dodgers got only four hits off Shea.

SIXTH GAME (Oct. 5, at New York)
BROOKLYN 202 004 000   8 12 1
NEW YORK.................. 004 100 001   6 15 2
Lombardi, Branca (3d), Hatten (6th), Casey (9th)
Reynolds, Drews (3d), Page (5th), Newsom (6th), Raschi (7th),
   Wensloff (8th)

The Dodgers tied the Series at three games each, as they came from behind to score four runs in the sixth inning to defeat the Yankees 8–6. The Yankees pounded Vic Lombardi, Branca, Joe Hatten, and Hugh Casey for 15 hits, while the Dodgers slammed six Yankee pitchers for 12 hits. Al Gionfriddo's sensational catch saved the game for the Dodgers.

Gionfriddo had gone into the game as a defensive measure in the sixth inning, and pulled down DiMaggio's 415-foot drive with two men on base after a long run.

SEVENTH GAME (Oct. 6, at New York)
BROOKLYN 020 000 000   2 7 0
NEW YORK 010 201 10x   5 7 0
Gregg, Behrman (4th), Hatten (6th), Barney (6th), Casey (7th)
Shea, Bevens (2d), Page (5th)

The Dodgers knocked out Spec Shea in the second inning and led the Yankees 2–1 until the fourth inning, when Bobby Brown doubled in the tying run. Tommy Henrich singled to score the go-ahead run and the Yanks led 3–2. The Yankees scored again in the sixth and seventh innings. The final score was 5–2, and another World Series went to the Yankees.

WORLD SERIES BOX SCORES: 1947 (SEVEN GAMES)

GAME 1

BROOKLYN (N. L.)	AB	R	H	O	A	E	NEW YORK (A.L.)	AB	R	H	O	A	E
Stanky, 2b	4	0	1	0	4	0	Stirnweiss, 2b	4	0	0	3	1	0
Robinson, 1b	2	1	0	8	1	0	Henrich, rf	4	0	1	3	0	0
Reiser, cf-lf	4	1	1	3	0	0	Berra, c	4	0	0	5	0	0
Walker, rf	4	0	2	1	0	0	DiMaggio, cf	4	1	1	2	0	0
Hermanski, lf	2	0	0	2	0	0	McQuinn, 1b	3	1	0	7	2	0
†Furillo, cf	1	0	1	2	0	0	Johnson, 3b	2	1	0	1	2	0
Edwards, c	4	0	0	8	0	0	Lindell, lf	3	0	1	3	0	0
Jorgensen, 3b	2	0	0	0	1	0	Rizzuto, ss	2	1	1	1	3	0
‡Lavagetto, 3b	2	0	0	0	0	0	Shea, p	1	0	0	1	2	0
Reese, ss	4	1	1	0	2	0	*Brown	0	1	0	0	0	0
Branca, p	2	0	0	0	0	0	Page, p	1	0	0	1	2	0
Behrman, p	0	0	0	0	1	0	Totals	28	5	4	27	12	0
§Miksis	1	0	0	0	0	0							
Casey, p	0	0	0	0	0	0							
Totals	32	3	6	24	9	0							

Brooklyn   1 0 0   0 0 1   1 0 0—3
New York   0 0 0   0 5 0   0 0 x—5

*Walked for Shea in fifth.
†Singled for Hermanski in sixth.
‡Popped out for Jorgensen in seventh.
§Struck out for Behrman in seventh.
Two-base hit—Lindell. Runs batted in—Walker, Lindell 2, Brown, Henrich 2, Furillo. Stolen bases—Robinson, Reese. Double play—Johnson and McQuinn. Bases on balls—Off Shea 2; off Branca 3; off Page 1. Struck out—By Shea 3; by Branca 5; by Page 2; by Casey 1. Hit by pitcher—By Branca 1 (Johnson). Pitching record—Off Shea 2 hits, 1 run in 5 innings; off Page 4 hits, 2 runs in 4 innings; off Branca 2 hits, 5 runs in 4 innings (pitched to six batters in fifth); off Behrman 1 hit, no runs in 2 innings; off Casey 1 hit, no runs in 2 innings. Earned runs—New York 5, Brooklyn 3. Left on bases—Brooklyn 5, New York 3. Wild pitch—Page. Balk—Shea. Winning pitcher—Shea. Losing pitcher—Branca.

GAME 2

BROOKLYN (N.L.)	AB	R	H	O	A	E	NEW YORK (A. L.)	AB	R	H	O	A	E
Stanky, 2b	4	0	1	3	2	1	Stirnweiss, 2b	4	2	3	1	2	0
Robinson, 1b	4	0	2	5	0	0	Henrich, rf	4	1	2	3	0	0
Reiser, cf	4	0	1	4	0	1	Lindell, lf	4	1	2	2	0	0
Walker, rf	4	1	1	1	0	0	DiMaggio, cf	4	0	1	4	0	0
Hermanski, lf	3	1	0	3	0	0	McQuinn, 1b	5	1	2	6	1	0
Edwards, c	4	0	1	5	1	0	Johnson, 3b	5	2	2	1	2	0
Reese, ss	3	1	2	0	0	0	Rizzuto, ss	5	0	1	3	4	0
Jorgensen, 3b	4	0	1	3	5	0	Berra, c	3	1	0	6	1	1
Lombardi, p	2	0	0	0	0	0	Reynolds, p	4	2	2	1	0	0
Gregg, p	0	0	0	0	2	0	Totals	38	10	15	27	10	1
*Vaughan	1	0	0	0	0	0							
Behrman, p	0	0	0	0	0	0							

GAME 2 (continued)

BROOKLYN (N.L.)	AB	R	H	O	A	E	NEW YORK (A. L.)	AB	R	H	O	A	E
Barney, p	0	0	0	0	0	0							
†Gionfriddo	1	0	0	0	0	0							
Totals	34	3	9	24	10	2							

```
Brooklyn     0 0 1  1 0 0  0 0 1— 3
New York     1 0 1  1 2 1  4 0 x—10
```

*Flied out for Gregg in seventh.
†Forced Jorgenson while batting for Barney in ninth.
Two-base hits—Rizzuto, Lindell, Robinson. Three-base hits—Stirnweiss, Lindell, Johnson. Home runs—Walker, Henrich. Sacrifice hit—Henrich. Runs batted in—Robinson, Lindell 2, Walker, Rizzuto, Henrich, McQuinn, Reynolds, Johnson, Stirnweiss, Jorgensen. Stolen base—Reese. Double plays—Jorgensen, Stanky and Robinson; Stirnweiss, Rizzuto and McQuinn. Bases on balls—Off Lombardi 1; off Gregg 1; off Behrman 1; off Barney 1; off Reynolds 2. Struck out—By Reynolds 6; by Lombardi 3; by Gregg 2. Pitching record—Off Lombardi 9 hits, 5 runs in 4 innings (pitched to two batters in fifth); off Gregg 2 hits, 1 run in 2 innings; off Behrman 3 hits, 4 runs in ⅓ inning; off Barney 1 hit, no runs in 1⅔ innings. Wild pitches—Behrman, Barney. Earned runs—New York 10, Brooklyn 3. Left on bases—New York 9, Brooklyn 6. Losing pitcher—Lombardi.

GAME 2

BROOKLYN (N.L.)	AB	R	H	O	A	E	NEW YORK (A. L.)	AB	R	H	O	A	E
Stirnweiss, 2b	5	0	2	2	3	0	Stanky, 2b	4	2	1	4	5	0
Henrich, rf	4	0	1	0	0	0	Robinson, 1b	4	1	2	10	1	0
Lindell, lf	4	1	2	0	0	0	Reiser, cf	0	0	0	0	0	0
DiMaggio, cf	4	1	2	3	0	0	*Furillo, cf	3	1	2	0	0	1
McQuinn, 1b	4	0	0	8	1	0	Walker, rf	5	0	2	1	0	0
Johnson, 3b	4	1	1	2	1	0	Hermanski, lf	3	2	1	4	0	0
Rizzuto, ss	5	0	1	5	2	0	Edwards, c	4	1	1	5	0	0
Lollar, c	3	2	2	2	1	0	Reese, ss	3	1	1	1	3	0
xBerra, c	2	1	1	2	0	0	Jorgensen, 3b	4	0	2	1	3	0
Newsom, p	0	0	0	0	1	0	Hatten, p	2	1	1	0	0	0
Raschi, p	0	0	0	0	0	0	Branca, p	1	0	0	0	0	0
†Clark	0	1	0	0	0	0	Casey, p	1	0	0	1	1	0
Drews, p	0	0	0	0	2	0	Totals	34	9	13	27	13	1
‡Phillips	1	0	0	0	0	0							
Chandler, p	0	0	0	0	0	0							
§Brown	1	1	1	0	0	0							
Page, p	1	0	0	0	0	0							
Totals	38	8	13	24	11	0							

```
New York     0 0 2  2 2 1  1 0 0—8
Brooklyn     0 6 1  2 0 0  0 0 x—9
```

*Doubled for Reiser in second.
†Walked for Raschi in third.
‡Flied out for Drews in fourth.
§Doubled for Chandler in sixth.
xHomered for Lollar in seventh.
Two-base hits—Edwards, Stanky, Furillo, Lollar, Brown, Henrich, Jorgensen. Home runs—DiMaggio, Berra. Sacrifice hit—Robinson. Runs batted in—Edwards, Reese, Stanky 2, Furillo 2, Lindell, DiMaggio 3, Jorgensen, Lollar, Stirnweiss, Walker, Hermanski, Henrich, Berra. Stolen bases—Robinson, Walker. Double plays—Reese, Stanky and Robinson; Stanky and Robinson. Bases on balls—Off Newsom 2; off Hatten 3; off Chandler 3; off Branca 2; off Page 1; off Casey 1. Struck out—By Hatten 3; by Branca 1; by Chandler 1; by Page 3; by Casey 1. Hit by pitcher—Drews 1 (Hermanski). Pitching record—Off Newsom 5 hits, 5 runs in 1⅔ innings; off Raschi 2 hits, 1 run in ⅓ inning; off Drews 1 hit, 1 run in 1 inning; off Chandler 2 hits, 2 runs in 2 innings; off Page 3 hits, no runs in 3 innings; off Hatten 8 hits, 6 runs in 4⅓ innings; off Branca 4 hits, 2 runs in 2 innings; off Casey 1 hit, no runs in 2⅔ innings. Wild pitches—Drews, Page. Passed ball—Lollar. Earned runs—Brooklyn 9, New York 8. Left on bases—Brooklyn 9, New York 9. Winning pitcher—Casey. Losing pitcher—Newsom.

GAME 4

NEW YORK (A.L.)	AB	R	H	O	A	E	BROOKLYN (N.L.)	AB	R	H	O	A	E
Stirnweiss, 2b	4	1	2	2	1	0	Stanky, 2b	1	0	0	2	3	0
Henrich, rf	5	0	1	2	0	0	xLavagetto	1	0	1	0	0	0
Berra, c	4	0	0	6	1	1	Reese, ss	4	0	0	3	5	1
DiMaggio, cf	2	0	0	2	0	0	Robinson, 1b	4	0	0	11	1	0
McQuinn, 1b	4	0	1	7	0	0	Walker, rf	2	0	0	0	1	0
Johnson, 3b	4	1	1	3	2	0	Hermanski, lf	4	0	0	2	0	0
Lindell, lf	3	0	2	3	0	0	Edwards, c	4	0	0	7	1	1

GAME 4 (continued)

NEW YORK (A.L.)	AB	R	H	O	A	E
Rizzuto, ss	4	0	1	1	2	0
Bevens, p	3	0	0	0	1	0
Totals	33	2		26	7	1

BROOKLYN (N.L.)	AB	R	H	O	A	E
Furillo, cf	3	0	0	2	0	0
†Gionfriddo	0	1	0	0	0	0
Jorgensen, 3b	2	1	0	0	1	1
Taylor, p	0	0	0	0	0	0
Gregg, p	1	0	0	0	1	0
*Vaughan	0	0	0	0	0	0
Behrman, p	0	0	0	0	1	0
Casey, p	0	0	0	0	1	0
‡Reiser	0	0	0	0	0	0
§Miksis	0	1	0	0	0	0
Totals	26	3	1	27	15	3

```
New York    1 0 0   1 0 0   0 0 0—2
Brooklyn    0 0 0   0 1 0   0 0 2—3
```

*Walked for Gregg in seventh.
†Ran for Furillo in ninth.
‡Walked for Casey in ninth.
§Ran for Reiser in ninth.
xDoubled for Stanky in ninth.
yTwo out when winning run was scored.
Two-base hits—Lindell, Lavagetto. Three-base hit—Johnson. Sacrifice hits—Stanky, Bevens. Runs batted in—DiMaggio, Lindell, Reese, Lavagetto 2. Stolen bases—Rizzuto, Reese, Gionfriddo. Double plays—Reese, Stanky and Robinson; Gregg, Reese and Robinson; Casey, Edwards and Robinson. Bases on balls—Off Taylor 1; off Gregg 3; off Bevens 10. Struck out—By Gregg 5; by Bevens 10. Pitching record—Off Taylor 2 hits, 1 run in 0 inning (pitched to four batters); off Gregg 4 hits, 1 run in 7 innings; off Berman 2 hits, 0 runs in 1⅓ innings; off Casey 0 hits, 0 runs in ⅔ inning. Wild pitch—Bevens. Earned runs—Brooklyn 3, New York 1. Left on bases—New York 9, Brooklyn 8. Winning pitcher—Casey.

GAME 5

NEW YORK (A.L.)	AB	R	H	O	A	E
Stirnweiss, 2b	3	0	0	3	4	0
Henrich, rf	4	0	2	1	0	0
Lindell, lf	2	0	0	3	0	0
DiMaggio, cf	4	1	1	3	0	0
McQuinn, 1b	4	0	0	7	0	0
Johnson, 3b	3	0	0	2	1	0
A. Robinson, c	3	1	0	7	0	0
Rizzuto, ss	2	0	0	1	1	0
Shea, p	4	0	2	0	1	0
Totals	29	2	5	27	7	0

BROOKLYN (N.L.)	AB	R	H	O	A	E
Stanky, 2b	3	0	0	2	2	0
‡Reiser	0	0	0	0	0	0
§Miksis, 2b	0	0	0	1	1	1
Reese, ss	2	0	0	2	3	0
J. Robinson, 1b	4	0	1	5	0	0
Walker, rf	4	0	0	0	0	0
Hermanski, lf	4	0	1	2	0	0
Edwards, c	3	0	1	9	2	0
xLombardi	0	0	0	0	0	0
Furillo, cf	3	0	0	2	0	0
Jorgensen, 3b	4	0	0	3	0	0
Barney, p	1	0	0	0	1	0
Hatten, p	0	0	0	0	0	0
*Gionfriddo	0	1	0	0	0	0
Behrman, p	0	0	0	0	1	0
†Vaughan	1	0	1	0	0	0
Casey, p	0	0	0	1	0	0
yLavagetto	1	0	0	0	0	0
Totals	30	1	4	27	10	1

```
New York    0 0 0   1 1 0   0 0 0—2
Brooklyn    0 0 0   0 0 1   0 0 0—1
```

*Walked for Hatten in sixth.
†Doubled for Behrman in seventh.
‡Walked for Stanky in seventh.
§Ran for Reiser in seventh.
xRan for Edwards in ninth.
yFanned for Casey in ninth.
Two-base hits—Henrich, Vaughan, Shea. Home run—DiMaggio. Sacrifice hit—Furillo. Runs batted in—Shea, DiMaggio, J. Robinson. Double plays—Reese, Stanky and J. Robinson; Reese, Miksis and J. Robinson. Bases on balls—Off Barney 9; off Shea 5; off Behrman 1. Struck out—By Barney 3; by Shea 7; by Hatten 1; by Behrman 2; by Casey 1. Hit by pitcher—By Casey (Lindell). Pitching record—Off Barney 3 hits, 2 runs in 4⅔ innings; off Hatten 0 hits, 0 runs in 1⅓ innings; off Behrman 1 hit, 0 runs in 1 inning; off Casey 1 hit, 0 runs in 2 innings. Wild pitch—Barney. Passed balls—Edwards 2. Earned runs—New York 2, Brooklyn 1. Left on bases—New York 11, Brooklyn 8. Losing pitcher—Barney.

GAME 6

BROOKLYN (N.L.)	AB	R	H	O	A	E	NEW YORK (A.L.)	AB	R	H	O	A	E
Stanky, 2b	5	2	2	4	2	0	Stirnweiss, 2b	5	0	0	1	6	0
Reese, ss	4	2	3	2	1	0	Henrich, rf-lf	5	1	2	1	0	0
J. Robinson, 1b	5	1	2	7	1	0	Lindell, lf	2	1	2	0	0	0
Walker, rf	5	0	1	3	0	0	Berra, rf	3	0	2	1	0	0
Hermanski, lf	1	0	0	0	0	0	DiMaggio, cf	5	1	1	5	0	0
†Miksis, lf	1	0	0	0	0	0	Johnson, 3b	5	1	2	1	5	0
Gionfriddo, lf	2	0	0	1	0	0	Phillips, 1b	1	0	0	4	0	0
Edwards, c	4	1	1	5	0	0	*Brown	1	0	1	0	0	0
Furillo, cf	4	1	2	4	1	0	McQuinn, 1b	1	0	0	6	0	1
Jorgensen, 3b	2	0	0	1	1	1	Rizzuto, ss	4	0	1	6	1	0
‡Lavagetto, 3b	2	0	0	0	1	0	Lollar, c	1	1	1	0	0	0
Lombardi, p	1	0	0	0	0	0	A. Robinson, c	4	1	2	2	0	1
Branca, p	1	0	0	0	1	0	Reynolds, p	0	0	0	0	0	0
§Bragan	1	0	1	0	0	0	Drews, p	2	0	0	0	1	0
xBankhead	0	1	0	0	0	0	Page, p	0	0	0	0	0	0
Hatten, p	1	0	0	0	0	0	Newsom, p	0	0	0	0	0	0
Casey, p	0	0	0	0	1	0	yClark	1	0	0	0	0	0
Totals	39	8	12	27	9	1	Raschi, p	0	0	0	0	0	0
							zHouk	1	0	1	0	0	0
							Wensloff, p	0	0	0	0	1	0
							aFrey	1	0	0	0	0	0
							Totals	42	6	15	27	14	2

```
Brooklyn     2 0 2  0 0 4  0 0 0—8
New York     0 0 4  1 0 0  0 0 1—6
```

*Singled for Phillips in third.
†Popped out for Hermanski in fifth.
‡Flied out for Jorgensen in sixth.
§Doubled for Branca in sixth.
xRan for Bragan in sixth.
yLined out for Newsom in sixth.
zSingled for Raschi in seventh.
aForced A. Robinson for Wensloff in ninth.

Two-base hits—Reese, J. Robinson, Walker, Lollar, Furillo, Bragan. Runs batted in—J. Robinson, Walker, Stirnweiss, Lindell, Johnson, Brown, Berra, Lavagetto, Reese 2, Frey, Bragan. Double play—Rizzuto and Phillips. Bases on balls—Off Reynolds 1; off Drews 1; off Hatten 4. Struck out—By Lombardi 2; by Branca 2; by Page 1; by Raschi 1. Pitching record—Off Reynolds 6 hits, 4 runs in 2⅓ innings; off Drews 1 hit, 0 runs in 2 innings; off Page 4 hits, 4 runs in 1 inning; off Newsom 1 hit, 0 runs in ⅔ inning; off Raschi 0 hits, 0 runs in 1 inning; off Wensloff 0 hits, 0 runs in 2 innings; off Lombardi 5 hits, 4 runs in 2⅔ innings; off Branca 6 hits, 1 run in 2⅓ innings; off Hatten 3 hits, 1 run in 3 innings (pitched to two batters in ninth); off Casey 1 hit, 0 runs in 1 inning. Wild pitch—Lombardi. Passed ball—Lollar. Earned runs—Brooklyn 7, New York 6. Left on bases—New York 13, Brooklyn 6. Winning pitcher—Branca. Losing pitcher—Page.

GAME 7

BROOKLYN (N.L.)	AB	R	H	O	A	E	NEW YORK (A.L.)	AB	R	H	O	A	E
Stanky, 2b	4	0	1	3	1	0	Stirnweiss, 2b	2	0	0	5	4	0
Reese, ss	3	0	0	0	1	0	Henrich, lf	5	0	1	2	0	0
J. Robinson, 1b	4	0	0	3	2	0	Berra, rf	3	0	0	1	0	0
Walker, rf	3	0	0	3	0	0	‡Clark, rf	1	0	1	2	0	0
Hermanski, lf	2	1	1	2	0	0	DiMaggio, cf	3	0	0	3	0	0
†Miksis, lf	2	0	1	2	0	0	McQuinn, 1b	2	1	0	7	0	0
Edwards, c	4	1	2	5	0	0	Johnson, 3b	3	2	1	1	1	0
Furillo, cf	3	0	1	4	0	0	A. Robinson, c	3	0	0	4	2	0
Jorgensen, 3b	2	0	1	0	1	0	Rizzuto, ss	4	2	3	2	2	0
§Lavagetto, 3b	1	0	0	0	0	0	Shea, p	0	0	0	0	0	0
Gregg, p	2	0	0	1	0	0	Bevens, p	1	0	0	0	0	0
Behrman, p	0	0	0	1	0	0	*Brown	1	0	1	0	0	0
Hatten, p	0	0	0	0	0	0	Page, p	2	0	0	0	0	0
Barney, p	0	0	0	0	0	0	Totals	30	5	7	27	9	0
xHodges	1	0	0	0	0	0							
Casey, p	0	0	0	0	0	0							
Totals	31	2	7	24	5	0							

GAME 7 (continued)

```
Brooklyn    0 2 0  0 0 0  0 0 0—2
New York    0 1 0  2 0 1  1 0 x—5
```

*Doubled for Bevens in fourth.
†Grounded out for Hermanski in sixth.
‡Singled for Berra in sixth.
§Popped out for Jorgensen in seventh.
xStruck out for Barney in seventh.

Two-base hits—Jorgensen, Brown. Three-base hits—Hermanski, Johnson. Sacrifice hit—McQuinn. Runs batted in—Edwards, Jorgensen, Rizzuto, Brown, Henrich, Clark, A. Robinson. Stolen base—Rizzuto. Double play—Rizzuto, Stirnweiss and McQuinn. Bases on balls—Off Shea 1; off Bevens 1; off Gregg 4; off Behrman 3. Struck out—By Gregg 3; by Bevens 2; by Behrman 1; by Page 1; by Hatten 1. Pitching record—Off Gregg 3 hits, 3 runs in 3⅔ innings; off Behrman 2 hits, 1 run in 1⅔ innings; off Hatten 1 hit, 0 runs in ⅓ inning; off Barney 0 hits, 0 runs in ⅓ inning; off Barney 0 hits, 0 runs in ⅓ inning; off Casey 1 hit, 1 run in 2 innings; off Shea 4 hits, 2 runs in 1⅓ innings; off Bevens 2 hits, 0 runs in 2⅔ innings; off Page 1 hit, 0 runs in 5 innings. Earned runs—New York 5, Brooklyn 2. Left on bases—New York 9, Brooklyn 4. Winning pitcher—Page. Losing pitcher—Gregg.

WORLD SERIES COMPOSITE BOX SCORE: 1947

PITCHING SUMMARY

New York Yankees

PITCHER	G	IP	H	R	ER	SO	BB	W	L	ERA
Wensloff	1	2	0	0	0	0	0	0	0	0.00
Shea	3	15⅓	10	4	4	10	8	2	0	2.35
Bevens	2	11⅓	3	3	3	7	11	0	1	2.38
Drews	2	3	2	1	1	0	1	0	0	3.00
Page	4	13	12	6	6	7	2	1	1	4.15
Reynolds	2	11⅓	15	7	6	6	3	1	0	4.76
Raschi	2	1⅓	2	1	1	1	0	0	0	7.50
Chandler	1	2	2	2	2	1	3	0	0	9.00
Newsom	2	2⅓	6	5	5	0	2	0	1	19.29
Totals	7	61⅔	52	29	28	32	30	4	3	3.50

Brooklyn Dodgers

PITCHER	G	IP	H	R	ER	SO	BB	W	L	ERA
Taylor	1	0	2	1	0	0	1	0	0	0.00
Casey	6	10⅓	5	1	1	3	1	2	0	0.87
Barney	3	6⅔	4	2	2	3	10	0	1	2.71
Gregg	3	12⅔	9	5	5	10	8	0	1	3.56
Hatten	4	9	12	7	7	5	7	0	0	7.00
Behrman	5	6⅓	9	5	5	3	5	0	0	7.14
Branca	3	8⅓	12	8	8	8	5	1	1	8.67
Lombardi	2	6⅔	14	9	9	5	1	0	1	12.14
Totals	7	60	67	38	37	37	38	3	4	5.55

BATTING SUMMARY

New York Yankees

PLAYER-POS.	G	AB	R	H	2B	3B	HR	RBI	BA
Brown, ph	4	3	2	3	2	0	0	3	1.000
Houk, ph	1	1	0	1	0	0	0	0	1.000
Lollar, c	2	4	3	3	2	0	0	1	.750
Reynolds, p	2	4	2	2	0	0	0	1	.500
Lindell, lf	6	18	3	9	3	1	0	7	.500
Clark, ph-rf	3	2	1	1	0	0	0	1	.500
Shea, p	3	5	0	2	1	0	0	1	.400
Henrich, rf-lf	7	31	2	10	2	0	1	5	.323
Rizzuto, ss	7	26	3	8	1	0	0	2	.308
Johnson, 3b	7	26	8	7	0	3	0	2	.269
Stirnweiss, 2b	7	27	3	7	0	1	0	3	.259
DiMaggio, cf	7	26	4	6	0	0	2	5	.231
A. Robinson, c	3	10	2	2	0	0	0	1	.200
Berra, c-ph-rf	6	19	2	3	0	0	1	2	.158
McQuinn, 1b	7	23	3	3	0	0	0	1	.130
Page, p	4	4	0	0	0	0	0	0	.000
Newsom, p	2	0	0	0	0	0	0	0	.000
Raschi, p	2	0	0	0	0	0	0	0	.000
Drews, p	2	2	0	0	0	0	0	0	.000
Phillips, ph-1b	2	2	0	0	0	0	0	0	.000
Chandler, p	1	0	0	0	0	0	0	0	.000
Bevens, p	2	4	0	0	0	0	0	0	.000
Wensloff, p	1	0	0	0	0	0	0	0	.000
Frey, ph	1	1	0	0	0	0	0	1	.000
Totals	7	238	38	67	11	5	4	36	.282

Brooklyn Dodgers

PLAYER-POS.	G	AB	R	H	2B	3B	HR	RBI	BA
Bragan, ph	1	1	0	1	1	0	0	1	1.000
Vaughan, ph	3	2	0	1	1	0	0	0	.500
Furillo, ph-cf	6	17	2	6	2	0	0	3	.353
Hatten, p	4	3	1	1	0	0	0	0	.333
Reese, ss	7	23	5	7	1	0	0	4	.304
Robinson, 1b	7	27	3	7	2	0	0	3	.259
Miksis, ph-2b-lf	5	4	1	1	0	0	0	0	.255
Reiser, cf-lf-ph	5	8	1	2	0	0	0	0	.250
Stanky, 2b	7	25	4	6	1	0	0	2	.240
Walker, rf	7	27	1	6	1	0	1	4	.222
Edwards, c	7	27	3	6	1	0	0	2	.222
Jorgensen, 3b	7	20	1	4	2	0	0	3	.200
Hermanski, lf	7	19	4	3	0	1	0	1	.158
Lavagetto, ph-3b	5	7	0	1	1	0	0	3	.143
G'friddo, ph-pr-lf	4	3	2	0	0	0	0	0	.000
Branca, p	3	4	0	0	0	0	0	0	.000
Casey, p	6	1	0	0	0	0	0	0	.000
Gregg, p	3	3	0	0	0	0	0	0	.000
Barney, p	3	1	0	0	0	0	0	0	.000
Taylor, p	1	0	0	0	0	0	0	0	.000
Lombardi, p-pr	3	3	0	0	0	0	0	0	.000
Bankhead, pr	1	0	1	0	0	0	0	0	.000
Hodges, ph	1	1	0	0	0	0	0	0	.000
Totals	7	226	29	52	13	1	1	26	.230

WORLD SERIES HIGHLIGHTS: 1949

NEW YORK (AL) DEFEATS BROOKLYN (NL) 4 GAMES TO 1

FIRST GAME (Oct. 5, at New York)
BROOKLYN 000 000 000 0 2 0
NEW YORK....................000 000 001 1 5 1
Newcombe
Reynolds

Dodger ace Don Newcombe and Yankee star Allie Reynolds pitched scoreless ball for eight innings. Reynolds struck out nine Dodgers, while Newcombe fanned 11. But the big Dodger hurler made just one bad pitch in the ninth inning—to Tommy Henrich. The Yankee first baseman slammed the ball out of the park for a home run and the victory.

SECOND GAME (Oct. 6, at New York)
BROOKLYN 010 000 000 1 7 2
NEW YORK....................000 000 000 0 6 1
Roe
Raschi, Page (9th)

Jackie Robinson scored the only Dodger run in the second inning as Gil Hodges singled him home, but that run was enough to win Game 2 for the Dodgers. Preacher Roe allowed the hard-hitting Yankees just 6 hits as he outpitched Vic Raschi and Yankee relief star Joe Page in another 1–0 pitching duel.

THIRD GAME (Oct. 7, at Brooklyn)
NEW YORK....................001 000 003 4 5 0
BROOKLYN 000 100 002 3 5 0
Byrne, Page (4th)
Branca, Banta (9th)

Pee Wee Reese, Luis Olmo, and Roy Campanella homered for the Dodgers, but they were the only runs the Dodgers were able to manage off the combined pitching efforts of Tommy Byrne and Joe Page. The Yankees scored three runs in the ninth inning to break a 1–1 deadlock.

FOURTH GAME (Oct. 8, at Brooklyn)
NEW YORK....................000 330 000 6 10 0
BROOKLYN 000 004 000 4 9 1
Lopat, Reynolds (6th)
Newcombe, Hatten (4th), Erskine (6th), Banta (7th)

Bobby Brown was the star of the game as he batted in three runs with a double and triple to give the Yankees a 6–4 triumph. The Dodgers came back strong in the sixth inning, scoring four runs, but starter Allie Reynolds came in to relieve Eddie Lopat and held the Dodgers in check the rest of the way.

FIFTH GAME (Oct. 9, at Brooklyn)
NEW YORK.................... 203 113 000 10 11 1
BROOKLYN 001 001 400 6 11 2
Raschi, Page (7th)
Barney, Banta (3d), Erskine (6th), Hatten (6th), Palica (7th),
   Minner (9th)

The Yankees scored early, knocking Rex Barney out of the box as they reached him for five runs. Barney walked six Yankees in 2⅔ innings, to add to his troubles. The Dodgers came back in the seventh inning with four runs, but they still trailed by a 10–6 margin. Joe Page held them in check for the rest of the game, which meant another World Series victory for the Bronx Bombers.

WORLD SERIES BOX SCORES: 1949 (FIVE GAMES)

GAME 1

BROOKLYN (N.L.)	AB	R	H	O	A	E	NEW YORK (A.L.)	AB	R	H	O	A	E
Reese, ss	4	0	1	2	2	0	Rizzuto, ss	4	0	0	1	2	0
Jorgensen, 3b	3	0	1	0	2	0	Henrich, 1b	4	1	1	9	0	0
Snider, cf	4	0	0	3	0	0	Berra, c	3	0	0	9	0	0
Robinson, 2b	4	0	0	4	0	0	DiMaggio, cf	3	0	0	1	0	0
Hermanski, lf	3	0	0	0	0	0	Lindell, lf	3	0	1	0	0	0
Furillo, rf	3	0	0	0	0	0	Johnson, 3b	3	0	0	2	3	0
Hodges, 1b	2	0	0	4	0	0	Mapes, rf	3	0	0	4	0	0
Campanella, c	2	0	0	11	0	0	Coleman, 2b	3	0	1	1	2	1
Newcombe, p	3	0	0	0	0	0	Reynolds, p	3	0	2	0	1	0
Totals	28	0	2	*24	4	0	Totals	29	1	5	27	8	1

Brooklyn   0 0 0 0 0 0 0 0 0—0
New York   0 0 0 0 0 0 0 0 1—1

*None out when winning run scored.
Two-base hits—Jorgensen, Reynolds, Coleman. Home run—Henrich. Run batted in—Heinrich. Stolen base—Reese. Sacrifice hit—Hodges. Double play—Reynolds, Coleman and Henrich. Bases on balls—Off Reynolds 4. Struck out—By Reynolds 9, by Newcombe 11. Earned run—New York 1. Left on bases—Brooklyn 6, New York 4. Winning pitcher—Reynolds. Losing pitcher—Newcombe.

GAME 2

BROOKLYN (N.L.)	AB	R	H	O	A	E	NEW YORK (A.L.)	AB	R	H	O	A	E
Reese, ss	4	0	0	1	3	1	Rizzuto, ss	3	0	1	0	6	0
Jorgensen, 3b	4	0	1	1	4	0	Henrich, 1b	4	0	0	11	1	0
Snider, cf	4	0	1	3	1	0	Bauer, rf	4	0	1	1	0	0
Robinson, 2b	3	1	1	3	1	0	DiMaggio, cf	4	0	1	1	0	0
Hermanski, rf	3	0	1	2	0	0	Lindell, lf	4	0	0	2	1	1
§Furillo	1	0	0	0	0	0	Johnson, 3b	4	0	1	0	2	0
McCormick, rf	0	0	0	1	0	0	Coleman, 2b	4	0	1	6	3	0
Rackley, lf	2	0	0	0	0	0	Silvera, c	2	0	0	6	0	0
Olmo, lf	2	0	1	2	0	0	*Mize	1	0	1	0	0	0
Hodges, 1b	3	0	1	9	1	0	†Stirnweiss	0	0	0	0	0	0
Campanella, c	2	0	1	4	0	0	Niarhos, c	0	0	0	0	0	0
Roe, p	3	0	0	1	1	1	Raschi, p	2	0	0	0	0	0
							‡Brown	1	0	0	0	0	0
							Page, p	0	0	0	0	0	0
Totals	31	1	7	27	11	2	Totals	33	0	6	27	13	1

Brooklyn   0 1 0 0 0 0 0 0 0—1
New York   0 0 0 0 0 0 0 0 0—0

*Singled for Silvera in eighth.
†Ran for Mize in eighth.
‡Struck out for Raschi in eighth.
§Popped out for Hermanski in ninth.
Two-base hits—Robinson, Coleman, Jorgensen. Three-base hit—Hermanski. Run batted in—Hodges. Sacrifice hits—Rizzuto, Robinson. Stolen bases—Rizzuto, Johnson. Double play—Rizzuto, Coleman and Henrich. Base on balls—Off Raschi 1. Struck out—By Raschi 4, by Roe 3. Pitching record—Off Raschi 6 hits, 1 run in 8 innings; off Page 1 hit, no runs in 1 inning. Earned run—Brooklyn 1. Left on bases—Brooklyn 5, New York 7. Winning pitcher—Roe. Losing pitcher—Raschi.

GAME 3

NEW YORK (A.L.)	AB	R	H	O	A	E	BROOKLYN (N.L.)	AB	R	H	O	A	E
Rizzuto, ss	4	0	0	0	0	0	Reese, ss	2	1	1	1	2	0
Henrich, 1b	3	0	0	10	0	0	Miksis, 3b	4	0	1	3	1	0
Berra, c	3	1	0	7	2	0	Furillo, rf	4	0	1	2	0	0
DiMaggio, cf	4	0	0	4	0	0	Robinson, 2b	2	0	0	2	3	0
Brown, 3b	4	1	1	0	2	0	Hodges, 1b	3	0	0	8	0	0

GAME 3 (continued)

NEW YORK (A.L.)	AB	R	H	O	A	E	BROOKLYN (N.L.)	AB	R	H	O	A	E
Woodling, lf	3	1	1	2	0	0	Olmo, lf	4	1	1	0	0	0
Mapes, rf	2	1	0	2	0	0	Snider, cf	4	0	0	3	0	0
*Mize	1	0	1	0	0	0	Campanella, c	4	1	1	7	0	0
†Bauer, rf	0	0	0	0	0	0	Branca, p	3	0	0	1	0	0
Coleman, 2b	4	0	1	2	4	0	Banta, p	0	0	0	0	0	0
Byrne, p	1	0	1	0	0	0	‡Edwards	1	0	0	0	0	0
Page, p	3	0	0	0	1	0	Totals	31	3	5	27	6	0
Totals	32	4	5	27	9	0							

```
New York    0 0 1   0 0 0   0 0 3—4
Brooklyn    0 0 0   1 0 0   0 0 2—3
```

*Singled for Mapes in ninth.
†Ran for Mize in ninth.
‡Struck out for Banta in ninth.
Two-base hit—Woodling. Home runs—Reese, Olmo, Campanella. Runs batted in—Rizzuto, Reese, Mize 2, Coleman, Olmo, Campanella. Double play—Berra and Coleman. Bases on balls—Off Branca 4, off Byrne 2, off Page 2. Struck out—By Branca 6, by Byrne 1, by Page 4, by Banta 1. Pitching record—Off Byrne 2 hits, 1 run in 3⅓ innings; off Page 3 hits, 2 runs in 5⅔ innings; off Branca 4 hits, 4 runs in 8⅔ innings; off Banta 1 hit, 0 runs in ⅓ inning. Hit by pitcher—By Byrne 1 (Reese). Earned runs—New York 4, Brooklyn 3. Left on bases—New York 5, Brooklyn 6. Winning pitcher—Page. Losing pitcher—Branca.

GAME 4

NEW YORK (A.L.)	AB	R	H	O	A	E	BROOKLYN (N.L.)	AB	R	H	O	A	E
Rizzuto, ss	4	0	2	1	4	0	Reese, ss	4	1	2	0	2	0
Henrich, 1b	4	1	3	10	0	0	Miksis, 3b	2	0	0	0	2	1
Berra, c	5	1	1	10	1	0	‡Cox, 3b	2	0	1	1	0	0
DiMaggio, cf	3	1	0	1	0	0	Snider, cf	4	0	0	4	0	0
R. Brown, 3b	3	1	2	0	3	0	Robinson, 2b	3	1	1	2	3	0
Woodling, lf	3	1	0	2	0	0	Hodges, 1b	4	1	1	8	1	0
Mapes, rf	2	1	1	1	0	0	Olmo, lf	4	1	1	2	1	0
*Bauer, rf	2	0	0	2	0	0	Campanella, c	4	0	1	5	2	0
Coleman, 2b	4	0	0	0	0	0	Hermanski, rf	4	0	2	4	0	0
Lopat, p	3	0	1	0	1	0	Newcombe, p	1	0	0	1	1	0
Reynolds, p	1	0	0	0	0	0	Hatten, p	0	0	0	0	0	0
Totals	34	6	10	27	9	0	†T. Brown	1	0	0	0	0	0
							Erskine, p	0	0	0	0	0	0
							§Jorgensen	1	0	0	0	0	0
							Banta, p	0	0	0	0	0	0
							xWhitman	1	0	0	0	0	0
							Totals	35	4	9	27	12	1

```
New York    0 0 0   3 3 0   0 0 0—6
Brooklyn    0 0 0   0 0 4   0 0 0—4
```

*Flied out for Mapes in fifth.
†Flied out for Hatten in fifth.
‡Singled for Miksis in sixth.
§Struck out for Erskine in sixth.
xStruck out for Banta in ninth.
Two-base hits—Reese, R. Brown, Mapes, Lopat. Three-base hit—R. Brown. Runs batted in—Mapes 2, Lopat, R. Brown 3, Robinson, Olmo, Campanella, Hermanski. Double plays—Miksis, Campanella and Robinson; Rizzuto and Henrich. Bases on balls—Off Newcombe 3; off Lopat 1; off Hatten 2; off Banta 1. Struck out—By Lopat 4; by Reynolds 5; by Banta 1. Pitching record—Off Newcombe 5 hits, 3 runs in 3⅔ innings; off Hatten 3 hits, 3 runs in 1⅓ innings; off Erskine 1 hit, 0 runs in 1 inning; off Banta 1 hit, 0 runs in 3 innings; off Lopat 9 hits, 4 runs in 5⅔ innings; off Reynolds 0 hits, 0 runs in 3⅓ innings. Earned runs—New York 6, Brooklyn 4. Left on bases—New York 7, Brooklyn 5. Winning pitcher—Lopat. Losing pitcher—Newcombe.

GAME 5

NEW YORK (A.L.)	AB	R	H	O	A	E	BROOKLYN (N.L.)	AB	R	H	O	A	E
Rizzuto, ss	3	2	0	3	3	0	Reese, ss	5	0	2	1	0	0
Henrich, 1b	4	2	1	8	0	0	Jorgensen, 3b	3	1	0	0	0	0
Berra, c	5	0	0	11	0	0	xMiksis	1	0	1	0	0	0

GAME 5 (continued)

NEW YORK (A.L.)	AB	R	H	O	A	E		BROOKLYN (N.L.)	AB	R	H	O	A	E
DiMaggio, cf	4	1	1	0	0	0		Snider, cf	5	2	2	5	0	0
R. Brown, 3b	4	2	3	0	1	0		Robinson, 2b	4	0	1	1	2	1
Woodling, lf	4	2	3	3	0	0		Hermanski, rf	3	1	1	1	0	0
Mapes, rf	3	1	0	1	0	1		Hodges, 1b	5	1	2	9	1	0
Coleman, 2b	5	0	2	1	0	0		Rackley, lf	3	0	0	2	0	0
Raschi, p	3	0	1	0	0	0		§Olmo, lf	1	0	0	2	0	0
Page, p	1	0	0	0	1	0		Campanella, c	3	1	1	5	0	0
Totals	36	10	11	27	5	1		Barney, p	0	0	0	1	1	1
								Banta, p	1	0	0	0	1	0
								*T. Brown	1	0	0	0	0	0
								Erskine, p	0	0	0	0	0	0
								Hatten, p	0	0	0	0	0	0
								†Cox	1	0	0	0	0	0
								Palica, p	0	0	0	0	1	0
								Edwards	1	0	1	0	0	0
								Minner, p	0	0	0	0	1	0
								Totals	37	6	11	27	7	2

```
New York     2 0 3   1 1 3   0 0 0 — 10
Brooklyn     0 0 1   0 0 1   4 0 0 —  6
```

*Struck out for Banta in fifth.
†Struck out for Hatten in sixth.
‡Struck out for Rackley in seventh.
§Singled for Palica in eigth.
xDoubled for Jorgensen in ninth.

Two-base hits—Campanella, Woodling 2, Snider, Coleman, Miksis. Three-base hit—R. Brown. Home runs—DiMaggio, Hodges. Runs batted in—DiMaggio 2, R. Brown 2, Coleman 3, Raschi, Berra, Reese, Hermanski, Robinson, Hodges 3. Sacrifice hits—Rizzuto, Mapes. Double play—Page, Rizzuto and Henrich. Bases on balls—Off Barney 6; off Erskine 1; off Palica 1; off Raschi 4; off Page 1. Struck out—By Barney 2; by Banta 2; by Palica 1; by Raschi 7; by Page 4. Pitching record—Off Barney 3 hits, 5 runs in 2⅔ innings; off Banta 3 hits, 2 runs in 2⅓ innings; off Erskine 2 hits 3 runs in ⅔ inning; off Hatten 1 hit, 0 runs in 1⅓ inning; off Palica 1 hit, 0 runs in 2 innings; off Minner 1 hit, 0 runs in 1 inning; off Raschi 9 hits, 6 runs in 6⅔ innings; off Page 2 hits, 0 runs in 2⅓ innings. Earned runs—New York 10, Brooklyn 6. Left on bases—New York 9, Brooklyn 9. Winning pitcher—Raschi. Losing pitcher—Barney.

WORLD SERIES COMPOSITE BOX SCORE: 1949

PITCHING SUMMARY

New York Yankees PITCHER	G	IP	H	R	ER	SO	BB	W	L	ERA		Brooklyn Dodgers PITCHER	G	IP	H	R	ER	SO	BB	W	L	ERA
Reynolds	2	12⅓	2	0	0	14	4	1	0	0.00		Roe	1	9	6	0	0	3	0	1	0	0.00
Raschi	2	14⅔	15	7	7	11	5	1	1	4.30		Palica	1	2	1	0	0	1	1	0	0	0.00
Page	3	9	6	2	2	8	3	1	0	2.00		Minner	1	1	1	0	0	0	0	0	0	0.00
Byrne	1	3⅓	2	1	1	1	2	0	0	2.70		Newcombe	2	11⅔	10	4	4	11	3	0	2	3.09
Lopat	1	5⅔	9	4	4	4	1	1	0	6.35		Banta	3	5⅔	5	2	2	4	1	0	0	3.18
Totals	5	45	34	14	14	38	15	4	1	2.80		Branca	1	8⅔	4	4	4	6	4	0	1	4.15
												Hatten	2	1⅓	4	3	3	0	2	0	0	16.20
												Erskine	2	1⅔	3	3	3	0	1	0	0	16.20
												Barney	1	2⅔	3	5	5	2	6	0	1	16.88
												Totals	5	44	37	21	21	27	18	1	4	4.29

BATTING SUMMARY

New York Yankees PLAYER-POS.	G	AB	R	H	2B	3B	HR	RBI	BA		Brooklyn Dodgers PLAYER-POS.	G	AB	R	H	2B	3B	HR	RBI	BA
Rizzuto, ss	5	18	2	3	0	0	0	1	.167		Reese, ss	5	19	2	6	1	0	1	2	.316
Henrich, 1b	5	19	4	5	0	0	1	1	.263		Jorgensen, 3b-ph	4	11	1	2	2	0	0	0	.182
Berra, c	4	16	2	1	0	0	0	1	.063		Snider, cf	5	21	2	3	1	0	0	0	.143
DiMaggio, cf	5	18	2	2	0	0	1	2	.111		Robinson, 2b	5	16	2	3	1	0	0	2	.188
Lindell, lf	2	7	0	1	0	0	0	0	.143		Hermanski, lf-rf	4	13	1	4	0	1	0	2	.308
Johnson, 3b	2	7	0	1	0	0	0	0	.143		Furillo, rf-ph	3	8	0	1	0	0	0	0	.125
Mapes, rf	4	10	3	1	0	0	0	2	.100		Hodges, 1b	5	17	2	4	0	0	1	4	.235

BATTING SUMMARY

New York Yankees

PLAYER-POS.	G	AB	R	H	2B	3B	HR	RBI	BA
Coleman, 2b	5	20	0	5	3	0	0	4	.250
Reynolds, p	2	4	0	2	1	0	0	0	.500
Bauer, rf-pr-ph	3	6	0	1	0	0	0	0	.167
Silvera, c	1	2	0	0	0	0	0	0	.000
Mize, ph	2	2	0	2	0	0	0	2	1.000
Stirnweiss, pr	1	0	0	0	0	0	0	0	.000
Niarhos, c	1	0	0	0	0	0	0	0	.000
Raschi, p	2	5	0	1	0	0	0	1	.200
R. Brown, ph-3b	4	12	4	6	1	2	0	5	.500
Page, p	3	4	0	0	0	0	0	0	.000
Woodling, lf	3	10	4	4	3	0	0	0	.400
Byrne, p	1	1	0	1	0	0	0	0	1.000
Lopat, p	1	3	0	1	1	0	0	1	.333
Totals	5	164	21	37	10	2	2	20	.226

Brooklyn Dodgers

PLAYER-POS.	G	AB	R	H	2B	3B	HR	RBI	BA
Campanella, c	5	15	2	4	1	0	1	2	.267
Newcombe, p	2	4	0	0	0	0	0	0	.000
McCormick, rf	1	0	0	0	0	0	0	0	.000
Rackley, lf	2	5	0	0	0	0	0	0	.000
Olmo, lf	4	11	2	3	0	0	1	2	.273
Roe, p	1	3	0	0	0	0	0	0	.000
Miksis 3b-ph	3	7	0	2	1	0	0	0	.286
Branca, p	1	3	0	0	0	0	0	0	.000
Banta, p	3	1	0	0	0	0	0	0	.000
Edwards, ph	2	2	0	1	0	0	0	0	.500
Cox, ph-3b	2	3	0	1	0	0	0	0	.333
Hatten, p	2	0	0	0	0	0	0	0	.000
T. Brown, ph	2	2	0	0	0	0	0	0	.000
Erskine, p	2	0	0	0	0	0	0	0	.000
Whitman, ph	1	1	0	0	0	0	0	0	.000
Barney, p	1	0	0	0	0	0	0	0	.000
Palica, p	1	0	0	0	0	0	0	0	.000
Minner, p	1	0	0	0	0	0	0	0	.000
Totals	5	162	14	34	7	1	4	14	.210

WORLD SERIES HIGHLIGHTS: 1952

NEW YORK (AL) DEFEATS BROOKLYN (NL), 4 GAMES TO 3

FIRST GAME (Oct. 1, at Brooklyn)
NEW YORK......................001 000 010 2 6 2
BROOKLYN 010 002 01x 4 6 0
Reynolds, Scarborough (8th)
Black

Jackie Robinson, Duke Snider, and Pee Wee Reese homered off Yankee pitchers Allie Reynolds and Ray Scarborough for a 4–2 Dodger win over the Yankees as Joe Black continued the brilliant pitching that brought him a 15 and 4 record during the regular season. Black limited the Yanks to six hits.

SECOND GAME (Oct. 2, at Brooklyn)
NEW YORK......................000 115 000 7 10 0
BROOKLYN 001 000 000 1 3 1
Raschi
Erskine, Loes (6th), Lehman (8th)

The Yankees were leading 2–1 going into the sixth inning, when a home run by second baseman Billy Martin broke open the game. The Yankees went on to score five runs for an easy 7–1 win. Vic Raschi allowed the Dodgers three scattered hits.

THIRD GAME (Oct. 3, at New York)
BROOKLYN 001 010 012 5 11 0
NEW YORK......................010 000 011 3 6 2
Roe
Lopat, Gorman (9th)

Preacher Roe out-lasted Eddie Lopat and Tom Gorman in a fine exhibition of clutch pitching as the Dodgers won by a 5–3 score. Pee Wee Reese played brilliantly in the field and was the offensive star as well, getting three hits and scoring one run. Yogi Berra and John Mize homered for the Yankees.

FOURTH GAME (Oct. 4, at New York)
BROOKLYN 000 000 010 0 4 1
NEW YORK...................... 000 100 01X 2 4 1
Black, Rutherford (8th)
Reynolds

Mickey Mantle and John Mize provided the Yankee power as the Bronx Bombers eked out a 2–0 win over the Dodgers. Mantle tripled and scored and Mize homered for the games only runs in a pitcher's battle that featured Joe Black of the Dodgers opposing Allie Reynolds.

FIFTH GAME (Oct. 5, at New York)
BROOKLYN 010 030 100 01 6 10 0
NEW YORK................ 000 050 000 00 5 5 1
Erskine
Blackwell, Sain (6th)

Carl Erskine held the Yankees scoreless for five innings and then weakened to allow the Bombers to explode for five runs in the fifth inning and take a 5–4 lead over the Dodgers. Then Erskine settled down and retired the next 19 Yankee batters in order as the Dodgers squeaked out a 6–5 win on Duke Snider's single in the eleventh inning that scored Billy Cox with the game-winning run.

SIXTH GAME (Oct. 6, at Brooklyn)
NEW YORK................ 000 000 210 3 9 0
BROOKLYN 000 001 010 2 8 1
Raschi, Reynolds (8th)
Loes, Roe (9th)

Duke Snider powered 2 home runs in a game that saw all the runs but one come on home runs. Mickey Mantle and Yogi Berra were the heroes in this impressive display of power in a key game in which both teams used starters in relief. Mantle's homer in the eighth was the deciding blow.

SEVENTH GAME (Oct. 7, at Brooklyn)
NEW YORK................ 000 111 100 4 10 4
BROOKLYN 000 110 000 2 8 1
Lopat, Reynolds (4th), Raschi (7th), Kuzava (7th)
Black, Roe (6th), Erskine (8th)

Mickey Mantle and Gene Woodling homered to give the Yankees a 4–2 victory. Mickey also drove in two runs as Bob Kuzava nailed down the Yankee win by retiring the last six Dodger batters in order as the Yankees wrapped up another World Series win over the game Dodgers.

WORLD SERIES BOX SCORES: 1952 (SEVEN GAMES)

GAME 1

NEW YORK (A.L.)	AB	R	H	O	A	E	BROOKLYN (N.L.)	AB	R	H	O	A	E
Bauer, rf	4	0	0	2	0	0	Cox, 3b	3	0	0	1	2	0
Rizzuto, ss	4	0	1	2	1	0	Reese, ss	4	2	2	4	1	0
Mantle, cf	4	0	2	2	0	0	Snider, cf	4	1	2	2	0	0
Berra, c	4	0	0	7	2	0	Robinson, 2b	2	1	1	1	4	0
Collins, 1b	4	0	0	8	0	0	Campanella, c	3	0	1	6	0	0
Noren, lf	3	0	0	1	0	0	Pafko, lf	3	0	0	3	1	0
McDougald, 3b	2	1	1	0	4	1	Hodges, 1b	3	0	0	6	3	0
Martin, 2b	3	0	1	2	1	0	Furillo, rf	3	0	0	3	0	0
Reynolds, p	2	0	0	0	1	1	Black, p	3	0	0	1	0	0
*Woodling	1	1	1	0	0	0	Totals	28	4	6	27	11	0
Scarborough, p	0	0	0	0	1	0							
Totals	31	2	6	26	10	2							

```
              New York     0 0 1  0 0 0  0 1 0—2
              Brooklyn     0 1 0  0 0 2  0 1 x—4
```

*Tripled for Reynolds in eighth.
Runs batted in—Robinson, McDougald, Snider 2, Bauer, Reese. Two-base hit—Snider. Three-base hit—Woodling. Home runs—Robinson, McDougald, Snider, Reese. Double plays—Martin and Collins; Cox, Robinson and Hodges. Left on bases—New York 4, Brooklyn 2. Earned runs—New York 2, Brooklyn 4. Bases on balls—Off Reynolds 4, off Black 2. Struck out—by Reynolds 4, by Scarborough 1, by Black 6. Pitching records—Off Reynolds 5 hits, 3 runs in 7 innings; off Scarborough 1 hit, 1 run in 1 inning. Wild pitch—Reynolds. Winning pitcher—Black. Losing pitcher—Reynolds.

GAME 2

NEW YORK (A.L.)	AB	R	H	O	A	E	BROOKLYN (N.L.)	AB	R	H	O	A	E
Bauer, rf	4	0	1	3	0	0	Cox, 3b	4	0	0	1	0	0
Rizzuto, ss	4	0	0	2	2	0	Reese, ss	3	1	1	2	5	0
Mantle, cf	5	2	3	2	0	0	Snider, cf	4	0	1	1	0	0
Woodling, lf	4	1	1	2	0	0	Robinson, 2b	3	0	0	3	3	0
Berra, c	3	0	2	10	2	0	Campanella, c	4	0	1	7	3	0
Collins, 1b	3	1	0	8	1	0	Pafko, lf	4	0	0	2	0	0
McDougald, 3b	3	2	1	0	1	0	Hodges, 1b	3	0	0	9	0	1
Martin, 2b	4	1	2	0	1	0	Furillo, rf	3	0	0	2	0	0
Raschi, p	3	0	0	0	0	0	Erskine, p	2	0	0	0	1	0
Totals	33	7	10	27	7	0	Loes, p	0	0	0	0	0	0
							*Nelson	0	0	0	0	0	0
							Lehman, p	0	0	0	0	1	0
							Totals	30	1	3	27	13	1

```
New York     0 0 0  1 1 5  0 0 0—7
Brooklyn     0 0 1  0 0 0  0 0 0—1
```

*Walked for Loes in seventh inning.
Runs batted in—Campanella, Berra, Martin 4, McDougald. Two-base hit—Mantle. Home run—Martin. Stolen base—McDougald. Double play—Reese, Robinson and Hodges. Left on bases—New York 6, Brooklyn 7. Earned runs—New York 6, Brooklyn 1. Bases on balls—Off Raschi 5, off Erskine 6, off Lehman 1. Struck out—By Raschi 9, by Erskine 4, by Loes 2. Pitching records—Off Erskine 6 hits, 4 runs in 5 innings (none out in sixth); off Loes 2 hits, 3 runs in 2 innings; off Lehman 2 hits, 0 runs in 2 innings. Wild pitch—Erskine. Winning pitcher—Raschi. Losing pitcher—Erskine.

GAME 3

BROOKLYN (N.L.)	AB	R	H	O	A	E	NEW YORK (A.L.)	AB	R	H	O	A	E
Furillo, rf	5	1	1	0	0	0	Rizzuto, ss	4	0	0	4	4	0
Reese, ss	5	1	3	1	4	0	Collins, 1b	4	0	0	7	0	0
Robinson, 2b	4	2	2	2	3	0	†Sain	1	0	0	0	0	0
Campanella, c	5	0	1	9	1	0	Mantle, cf	4	0	0	6	0	0
Pafko, lf	5	0	2	2	0	0	Woodling, lf	4	0	1	2	0	0
Snider, cf	5	0	1	3	0	0	Berra, c	4	1	3	1	1	1
Hodges, 1b	3	0	0	9	2	0	Bauer, rf	2	1	0	3	0	0
Cox, 3b	2	1	1	0	2	0	McDougald, 3b	4	0	0	1	2	1
Roe, p	2	0	0	1	0	0	Martin, 2b	1	0	0	3	3	0
Totals	36	5	11	27	12	0	Lopat, p	2	0	1	0	0	0
							Gorman, p	0	0	0	0	0	0
							*Mize	1	1	1	0	0	0
							Totals	31	3	6	27	10	2

```
Brooklyn     0 0 1  0 1 0  0 1 2—5
New York     0 1 0  0 0 0  0 1 1—3
```

*Homered for Gorman in ninth.
†Flied out for Collins in ninth.
Runs batted in—Lopat, Robinson, Reese, Pafko, Berra, Mize. Two-base hits—Furillo, Berra. Home runs—Berra, Mize. Sacrifice hits—Bauer, Roe 2. Stolen bases—Snider, Reese, Robinson. Double plays—Rizzuto and Martin; McDougald and Collins. Left on bases—Brooklyn 10, New York 8. Earned runs—Brooklyn 5, New York 3. Bases on balls—Off Roe 5, off Lopat 4. Struck out—By Roe 5. Pitching records—Off Lopat 10 hits 5 runs in 8⅓ innings; off Gorman 1 hit, 0 runs in ⅔ inning. Hit by pitched ball—By Roe 1 (Martin). Passed ball—Berra. Winning pitcher—Roe. Losing pitcher—Lopat.

GAME 4

BROOKLYN (N.L.)	AB	R	H	O	A	E	NEW YORK (A.L.)	AB	R	H	O	A	E
Cox, 3b	3	0	0	2	2	0	McDougald, 3b	3	0	0	0	1	0
†Nelson	1	0	0	0	0	0	Rizzuto, ss	2	0	0	1	3	0
Morgan, 3b	0	0	0	1	0	0	Mantle, cf	3	1	1	4	0	0
Reese, ss	4	0	2	0	3	1	Mize, 1b	3	1	2	4	2	0
Snider, cf	4	0	0	5	0	0	‡Collins, 1b	0	0	0	1	0	0

GAME 4 (continued)

BROOKLYN (N.L.)	AB	R	H	O	A	E		NEW YORK (A.L.)	AB	R	H	O	A	E
Robinson, 2b	4	0	0	0	2	0		Berra, c	4	0	0	12	1	0
Campanella, c	3	0	0	4	0	0		Woodling, lf	3	0	1	1	0	0
Pafko, lf	3	0	1	2	0	0		Bauer, rf	4	0	0	1	0	0
Hodges, 1b	2	0	0	10	0	0		Martin, 2b	3	0	0	2	1	1
Furillo, rf	2	0	1	1	0	0		Reynolds, p	3	0	0	1	0	0
Black, p	1	0	0	0	2	0		Totals	28	2	4	27	8	1
Shuba	1	0	0	0	0	0								
Rutherford, p	0	0	0	0	0	0								
Totals	28	0	4	24	10	1								

```
Brooklyn    0 0 0  0 0 0  0 0 0—0
New York    0 0 0  1 0 0  0 1 x—2
```

*Flied out for Black in eighth.
†Struck out for Cox in eighth.
‡Ran for Mize in eighth.
Run batted in—Mize. Two-base hits—Woodling, Mize. Three-base hit—Mantle. Home run—Mize. Sacrifice—Furillo. Double play—Rizzuto, Martin and Mize. Left on bases—Brooklyn 5, New York 8. Earned runs—New York 2. Bases on balls—Off Black 5, off Rutherford 1, off Reynolds 3. Struck out—By Reynolds 10, by Black 2, by Rutherford 1. Pitching records—Off Black 3 hits, 1 run in 7 innings; off Rutherford 1 hit, 1 run in 1 inning. Winning pitcher—Reynolds. Losing pitcher—Black.

GAME 5

BROOKLYN (N.L.)	AB	R	H	O	A	E		NEW YORK (A.L.)	AB	R	H	O	A	E
Cox 3b	5	2	3	2	2	0		McDougald, 3b	4	1	0	0	2	0
Reese, ss	5	0	1	1	1	0		Rizzuto, ss	5	1	1	1	4	1
Snider, cf	5	1	3	4	0	0		Mantle, cf	5	0	1	1	0	0
Robinson, 2b	2	1	0	2	1	0		Mize, 1b	5	1	1	9	1	0
Shuba, lf	2	0	1	4	0	0		Berra, c	4	0	0	10	1	0
Furillo, rf	4	0	1	3	0	0		Woodling, lf	4	0	0	5	0	0
Campanella, c	5	0	0	6	1	0		Bauer, rf	3	1	0	1	0	0
Pafko, rf-lf	4	0	1	3	0	0		Martin, 2b	4	1	1	6	3	0
Holmes, lf	1	0	0	2	0	0		Blackwell, p	1	0	0	0	1	0
Hodges, 1b	3	1	0	6	0	0		*Noren	1	0	1	0	0	0
Erskine, p	4	1	0	0	1	0		Sain, p	2	0	0	0	2	0
Totals	40	6	10	33	6	0		Totals	38	5	5	33	14	1

```
Brooklyn    0 1 0  0 3 0  1 0 0  0 1—6
New York    0 0 0  0 5 0  0 0 0  0 0—5
```

*Singled for Blackwell in fifth.
Runs batted in—Pafko, Reese, Snider 4, Noren, McDougald, Mize 3. Two-base hits—Furillo, Snider. Home runs Snider, Mize. Stolen base—Robinson. Sacrifices—Erskine, Cox, Reese. Double plays—Martin, Rizzuto and Mize; McDougald, Berra and Mize. Left on bases—Brooklyn 11, New York 3. Earned runs—Brooklyn 6, New York 5. Bases on balls—Off Erskine 3, off Blackwell 3, off Sain 3. Struck out—By Erskine 6, by Blackwell 4, by Sain 3. Pitching records—Off Blackwell 4 hits, 4 runs in 5 innings; off Sain 6 hits, 2 runs in 6 innings. Hit by pitched ball—By Sain 1 (Snider). Winning pitcher—Erskine. Losing pitcher—Sain.

GAME 6

NEW YORK (A.L.)	AB	R	H	O	A	E		BROOKLYN (N.L.)	AB	R	H	O	A	E
McDougald, 3b	4	0	1	1	2	0		Cox, 3b	5	0	2	1	3	0
Rizzuto, ss	4	0	1	2	2	0		Reese, ss	4	0	0	5	2	1
Mantle, cf	3	1	1	0	0	0		Snider, cf	3	2	2	4	0	0
Mize, 1b	3	0	0	7	0	0		Robinson, 2b	4	0	0	2	2	0
Collins, 1b	1	0	0	2	0	0		Shuba, lf	4	0	1	2	0	0
Berra, c	5	1	1	12	0	0		*Amoros	0	0	0	0	0	0
Woodling, lf	3	1	2	3	0	0		Holmes, lf	0	0	0	0	0	0
Noren, rf	4	0	2	0	0	0		Campanella, c	4	0	1	5	0	0
Bauer, rf	0	0	0	0	0	0		Hodges, lb	3	0	0	7	1	0
Martin, 2b	4	0	0	0	3	0		†Nelson	1	0	0	0	0	0

GAME 6 (continued)

NEW YORK (A.L.)	AB	R	H	O	A	E	BROOKLYN (N.L.)	AB	R	H	O	A	E
Raschi, p	3	0	1	0	1	0	Furillo, rf	3	0	1	1	0	0
Reynolds, p	1	0	0	0	0	0	Loes, p	3	0	1	0	2	0
Totals	35	3	9	27	8	0	Roe, p	0	0	0	0	0	0
							‡Pafko	1	0	0	0	0	0
							Totals	35	2	8	27	10	1

```
New York    0 0 0  0 0 0  2 1 0—3
Brooklyn    0 0 0  0 0 1  0 1 0—2
```

*Ran for Shuba in eighth.
†Struck out for Hodges in ninth.
‡Popped out for Roe in ninth.
Runs batted in—Snider 2, Berra, Raschi, Mantle. Two-base hits—Cox, Shuba. Home runs—Snider 2, Berra, Mantle. Stolen base—Loes. Double play—Hodges, Reese and Robinson. Left on bases—New York 11, Brooklyn 8. Earned runs—New York 3, Brooklyn 2. Bases on balls—Off Raschi 1, off Reynolds 1, off Loes 5, off Roe 1. Struck out—By Raschi 9, by Reynolds 2, by Loes 3, by Roe 1. Pitching records—Off Raschi 8 hits, 2 runs in 7⅔ innings; off Reynolds 0 hits, 0 runs in 1⅓ innings; off Loes 9 hits, 3 runs in 8⅓ innings; off Roe 0 hits, 0 runs in ⅔ inning. Balk—Loes. Winning pitcher—Raschi. Losing pitcher—Loes.

GAME 7

NEW YORK (A.L.)	AB	R	H	O	A	E	BROOKLYN (N.L.)	AB	R	H	O	A	E
McDougald, 3b	5	1	2	2	3	2	Cox, 3b	5	1	2	2	3	1
Rizzuto, ss	4	1	1	1	1	0	Reese, ss	4	0	1	2	2	0
Mantle, cf	5	1	2	1	0	0	Snider, cf	4	1	1	4	0	0
Mize, 1b	3	0	2	6	0	0	Robinson, 2b	4	0	1	0	4	0
Collins, 1b	0	0	0	1	0	0	Campanella, c	4	0	2	2	0	0
Berra, c	4	0	0	7	0	0	Hodges, 1b	4	0	0	13	0	0
Woodling, lf	4	1	2	5	0	1	Shuba, lf	3	0	1	1	0	0
Noren, rf	2	0	0	1	0	0	§Pafko	1	0	0	0	0	0
*Bauer, rf	1	0	0	0	0	0	Holmes, lf	0	0	0	0	0	0
Martin, 2b	4	0	1	2	4	0	Furillo, rf	3	0	0	3	0	0
Lopat, p	1	0	0	0	1	0	Black, p	2	0	0	0	0	0
Reynolds, p	1	0	0	1	0	1	Roe, p	0	0	0	0	0	0
†Houk	1	0	0	0	0	0	‡Nelson	1	0	0	0	0	0
Raschi, p	0	0	0	0	0	0	Erskine, p	0	0	0	0	0	0
Kuzava, p	1	0	0	0	0	0	xMorgan	1	0	0	0	0	0
Totals	36	4	10	27	9	4	Totals	36	2	8	27	9	1

```
New York    0 0 0  1 1 1  1 0 0—4
Brooklyn    0 0 0  1 1 0  0 0 0—2
```

*Safe on error for Noren in sixth.
†Grounded out for Reynolds in seventh.
‡Popped out for Roe in seventh.
§Struck out for Shuba in eighth.
xFlied out for Erskine in ninth.
Runs batted in—Mize, Hodges, Woodling, Reese, Mantle 2. Two-base hits—Rizzuto, Cox. Home runs—Woodling, Mantle. Sacrifice—Rizzuto. Double plays—Robinson, Reese and Hodges; Rizzuto, Martin and Mize. Left on bases—New York 8, Brooklyn 9. Earned runs—New York 4, Brooklyn 2. Bases on balls—Off Raschi 2, off Black 1, off Erskine 1. Struck out—By Lopat 3, by Reynolds 2, by Kuzava 2, by Black 1, by Roe 1. Pitching records—Off Lopat 4 hits, 1 run in 3 innings (pitched to three batters in fourth); off Reynolds 3 hits, 1 run in 3 innings; off Raschi 1 hit, 0 runs in ⅓ inning; off Kuzava 0 hits, 0 runs in 2⅔ innings; off Black 6 hits, 3 runs in 5⅓ innings; off Roe 3 hits, 1 run in 1⅔ innings; off Erskine 1 hit, 0 runs in 2 innings. Winning pitcher—Reynolds. Losing pitcher—Black.

WORLD SERIES COMPOSITE BOX SCORE: 1952

PITCHING SUMMARY

New York Yankees PITCHER	G	IP	H	R	ER	SO	BB	W	L	ERA	Brooklyn Dodgers PITCHER	G	IP	H	R	ER	SO	BB	W	L	ERA
Kuzava	1	2⅔	0	0	0	2	0	0	0	0.00	Lehman	1	2	2	0	0	0	1	0	0	0.00
Gorman	1	⅔	1	0	0	0	0	0	0	0.00	Black	3	21⅓	15	6	6	9	8	1	2	2.53
Raschi	3	17	12	3	3	18	8	2	0	1.59	Roe	3	11⅓	9	4	4	7	6	1	0	3.18
Reynolds	4	20⅓	12	4	4	18	6	2	1	1.77	Loes	2	10⅓	11	6	5	5	0	1	1	4.35
Sain	1	6	6	2	2	3	3	0	1	3.00	Erskine	3	18	12	9	9	10	10	1	1	4.50

PITCHING SUMMARY (continued)

New York Yankees											Brooklyn Dodgers										
PITCHER	G	IP	H	R	ER	SO	BB	W	L	ERA	PITCHER	G	IP	H	R	ER	SO	BB	W	L	ERA
Lopat	2	11⅓	14	6	6	3	4	0	1	4.76	Rutherford	1	1	1	1	1	1	1	0	0	9.00
Blackwell	1	5	4	4	4	3	0	0	0	7.20	Totals	7	64	50	26	25	32	31	3	4	3.52
Scarborough	1	1	1	1	1	1	0	0	0	9.00											
Totals	7	64	50	20	20	49	24	4	3	2.81											

BATTING SUMMARY

New York Yankees									Brooklyn Dodgers								
PLAYER-POS.	G	AB	R	H	2B	3B	HR	RBI	BA	PLAYER-POS.	G	AB	R	H	2B	3B	HR	RBI	BA
Mize, ph-1b	5	15	3	6	1	0	3	6	.400	Snider, cf	7	29	5	10	2	0	4	8	.345
Woodling, ph-lf	7	23	4	8	1	1	1	1	.348	Reese, ss	7	29	4	10	0	0	1	4	.345
Mantle, cf	7	29	5	10	1	1	2	3	.345	Loes, p	2	3	0	1	0	0	0	0	.333
Lopat, p	2	3	0	1	0	0	0	1	.333	Shuba, ph-lf	4	10	0	3	1	0	0	0	.300
Noren, lf-ph-rf	4	10	0	3	0	0	0	1	.300	Cox, 3b	7	27	4	8	2	0	0	0	.296
Martin, 2b	7	23	2	5	0	0	1	4	.217	Campanella, c	7	28	0	6	0	0	0	1	.214
Berra, c	7	28	2	6	1	0	2	3	.214	Pafko, lf-rf-ph	7	21	0	4	0	0	0	2	.190
McDougald, 3b	7	25	5	5	0	0	1	3	.200	Robinson, 2b	7	23	4	4	0	0	1	2	.174
Raschi, p	3	6	0	1	0	0	0	0	.167	Furillo, rf	7	23	1	4	2	0	0	0	.174
Rizzuto, ss	7	27	2	4	1	0	0	0	.148	Holmes, lf	3	1	0	0	0	0	0	0	.000
Bauer, rf-ph	7	18	2	1	0	0	0	1	.056	Morgan, 3b-ph	2	1	0	0	0	0	0	0	.000
Collins, 1b-pr	6	12	1	0	0	0	0	0	.000	Hodges, 1b	7	21	1	0	0	0	0	1	.000
Reynolds, p	4	7	0	0	0	0	0	0	.000	Black, p	3	6	0	0	0	0	0	0	.000
Scarborough, p	1	0	0	0	0	0	0	0	.000	Erskine, p	3	6	1	0	0	0	0	0	.000
Gorman, p	1	0	0	0	0	0	0	0	.000	Lehman, p	1	0	0	0	0	0	0	0	.000
Blackwell, p	1	1	0	0	0	0	0	0	.000	Roe, p	3	2	0	0	0	0	0	0	.000
Kuzava, p	1	1	0	0	0	0	0	0	.000	Rutherford, p	1	0	0	0	0	0	0	0	.000
Sain, ph-p	2	3	0	0	0	0	0	0	.000	Amoros, pr	1	0	0	0	0	0	0	0	.000
Houk, ph	1	1	0	0	0	0	0	0	.000	Nelson, ph	4	3	0	0	0	0	0	0	.000
Totals	7	232	26	50	5	2	10	24	.216	Totals	7	233	20	50	7	0	6	18	.215

WORLD SERIES HIGHLIGHTS: 1953

NEW YORK (AL) DEFEATS BROOKLYN, 4 GAMES TO 2

FIRST GAME (Sept. 30, at New York)
BROOKLYN 000 013 100   5 12 2
NEW YORK 400 010 13x   9 12 0
Erskine, Hughes (2d), Labine (6th), Wade (7th)
Reynolds, Sain (6th)

The Yankees pounded four Dodger pitchers for a total of 12 hits, including home runs by Berra and Joe Collins. Billy Martin continued his World Series heroics, contributing three hits to the Yankee victory. Gilliam, Hodges, and George Shuba homered for the Dodgers.

SECOND GAME (Oct. 1, at New York)
BROOKLYN 000 200 000   2 9 1
NEW YORK 100 000 12x   4 5 0
Roe
Lopat

Preacher Roe and Eddie Lopat battled each other through seven thrilling innings of a 2–2 tie, until Mickey Mantle homered in the eighth with a man on base. Mantle's homer was only the fifth hit off Roe.

THIRD GAME (Oct. 2, at Brooklyn)
NEW YORK 000 010 010   2 6 0
BROOKLYN 000 011 01x   3 9 0
Raschi
Erskine

Roy Campanella homered, Jackie Robinson had three hits, and Carl Erskine pitched one of the finest World Series games on record, striking out 14 Yankees while yielding only six hits to win a 3–2 squeaker.

FOURTH GAME (Oct. 3, at Brooklyn)
NEW YORK.....................000 020 001   3 9 0
BROOKLYN 300 102 10x   7 12 0
Ford, Gorman (2d), Sain (5th), Schallock (7th)
Loes, Labine (9th)

The Dodgers, led by Duke Snider's big bat, tied the Series at two all. Snider had a home run and two doubles as the Dodgers scored three runs in the first inning, then added another run in the fourth, two more in the sixth inning, and another run in the seventh for an easy 7–3 victory.

FIFTH GAME (Oct. 4, at Brooklyn)
NEW YORK.....................105 000 311 11 11 1
BROOKLYN 010 010 041   7 14 1
McDonald, Kuzava (8th), Reynolds (9th)
Podres, Meyer (3d), Wade (8th), Black (9th)

Mickey Mantle homered with the bases full in the third inning as the Yankees scored five runs for an early lead. They increased their lead in the seventh, scoring 3 more runs and easily defeated the Dodgers in a free-swinging contest to go one game up in the Series.

SIXTH GAME (Oct. 5, at New York)
BROOKLYN 000 001 002   3 8 3
NEW YORK.....................210 000 001   4 13 0
Erskine, Milliken (5th), Labine (7th)
Ford, Reynolds (8th)

The score was tied at 3–3 when Billy Martin came to bat in the ninth inning and cracked out his 12th hit of the Series, a home run, to give the Yankees a hard-fought 4–3 win in the final game of the Series.

WORLD SERIES BOX SCORES: 1953 (SIX GAMES)

GAME 1

NEW YORK (A.L.)	AB	R	H	O	A	E	BROOKLYN (N.L.)	AB	R	H	O	A	E
McDougald, 3b	5	0	0	3	2	0	Gilliam, 2b	5	1	2	3	3	0
Collins, 1b	4	2	2	6	0	0	Reese, ss	3	0	0	3	3	0
Bauer, rf	5	1	2	4	0	0	Snider, cf	5	0	2	3	0	0
Berra, c	4	1	2	8	2	0	Robinson, lf	4	0	0	0	0	0
Mantle, cf	3	1	1	0	0	0	Campanella, c	4	1	1	6	3	0
Woodling, lf	3	1	1	4	0	0	Hodges, 1b	5	1	3	7	0	0
Martin, 2b	4	1	3	1	2	0	Furillo, rf	4	0	1	2	0	1
Rizzuto, ss	3	1	0	1	1	0	Cox, 3b	5	1	2	0	1	0
Reynolds, p	1	0	0	0	0	0	Erskine, p	0	0	0	0	0	0
Sain, p	2	1	1	0	0	0	*Belardi	1	0	0	0	0	0
Totals	34	9	12	27	7	0	Hughes, p	1	0	0	0	0	1
							†Shuba	1	1	1	0	0	0
							Labine, p	1	0	0	0	1	0
							Wade, p	0	0	0	0	0	0
							Totals	39	5	12	24	11	2

Brooklyn   0 0 0   0 1 3   1 0 0—5
New York   4 0 0   0 1 0   1 3 x—9

*Struck out for Erskine in second.
†Homered for Hughes in sixth.
Runs batted in—Bauer, Martin 3, Gilliam, Berra, Hodges, Shuba 2, Furillo, Collins 2, Sain 2. Two-base hits—Cox, Snider, Sain. Three-base hits—Bauer, Martin. Home runs—Gilliam, Berra, Hodges, Shuba, Collins. Stolen base—Martin. Left on bases—Brooklyn 12, New York 6. Earned runs—Brooklyn 5, New York 9. Bases on balls—Off Reynolds 3, off Sain 1, off Erskine 3, off Hughes 1, off Wade 1. Struck out—By Reynolds 6, by Erskine 1, by Hughes 3, by Labine 1, by Wade 2. Pitching records—Off Erskine 2 hits, 4 runs in 1 innings; off Labine 4 hits, 1 run in 1⅔ innings; off Wade 3 hits, 3 runs in 1⅓ innings; off Reynolds 7 hits, 4 runs in 5⅓ innings; off Sain 5 hits, 1 run in 3⅔ innings. Hit by pitcher—By Reynolds 1 (Campanella). Winning pitcher—Sain. Losing pitcher—Labine.

GAME 2

NEW YORK (A.L.)	AB	R	H	O	A	E	BROOKLYN (N.L.)	AB	R	H	O	A	E
Woodling, lf	3	1	0	1	0	0	Gilliam, 2b	5	0	0	1	2	0
Collins, 1b	3	0	0	15	0	0	Reese, ss	3	0	2	0	1	0
Bauer, rf	4	1	1	1	0	0	Snider, cf	5	0	0	2	0	0
Berra, c	3	0	0	4	0	0	Robinson, lf	4	0	1	3	0	0
Mantle, cf	3	1	1	4	0	0	Campanella, c	4	0	0	5	3	0
McDougald, 3b	3	0	0	0	3	0	Hodges, 1b	3	1	2	9	1	0
Martin, 2b	3	1	2	1	5	0	Furillo, rf	4	1	2	3	0	1
Rizzuto, ss	2	0	1	1	5	0	Cox, 3b	3	0	1	0	2	0
Lopat, p	3	0	0	0	2	0	Roe, p	3	0	0	1	1	0
							*Williams	1	0	1	0	0	0
Totals	27	4	5	27	15	0	Totals	35	2	9	24	10	1

```
Brooklyn    0 0 0  2 0 0  0 0 0—2
New York    1 0 0  0 0 0  1 2 x—4
```

*Singled for Roe in ninth.
Runs batted in—Berra, Cox 2, Martin, Mantle 2. Two-base hits—Rizzuto, Cox, Furillo. Three-base hit—Reese. Home runs—Martin, Mantle. Sacrifice hit—Rizzuto. Stolen base—Hodges. Double play—Martin, Rizzuto and Collins. Left on bases—Brooklyn 10, New York 5. Earned runs—Brooklyn 2, New York 4. Bases on balls—Off Lopat 4, off Roe 4. Struck out—By Lopat 3, by Roe 4. Hit by pitcher—By Roe 1 (McDougald). Winning pitcher—Lopat. Losing pitcher—Roe.

GAME 3

BROOKLYN (N.L.)	AB	R	H	O	A	E	NEW YORK (A.L.)	AB	R	H	O	A	E
Gilliam, 2b	4	0	1	1	2	0	McDougald, 3b	4	0	1	2	3	0
Reese, ss	4	0	1	1	4	0	‡Noren	0	0	0	0	0	0
Snider, cf	3	1	1	0	0	0	Collins, 1b	5	0	0	8	0	0
Hodges, 1b	2	0	1	8	1	0	Bauer, rf	4	1	1	1	0	0
Campanella, c	4	1	1	14	0	0	Berra, c	1	0	1	4	1	0
Furillo, rf	4	0	0	1	0	0	Mantle, cf	4	0	0	2	0	0
Robinson, lf	4	1	3	1	0	0	Woodling, lf	4	0	1	0	0	0
Thompson, lf	0	0	0	0	0	0	Martin, 2b	3	1	1	3	4	0
Cox, 3b	3	0	0	0	1	0	Rizzuto, ss	3	0	1	3	3	0
Erskine, p	3	0	1	1	2	0	*Bollweg	1	0	0	0	0	0
							Raschi, p	2	0	0	1	1	0
							†Mize	1	0	0	0	0	0
Totals	31	3	9	27	10	0	Totals	32	2	6	24	12	0

```
New York    0 0 0  0 1 0  0 1 0—2
Brooklyn    0 0 0  0 1 1  0 1 x—3
```

*Struck out for Rizzuto in ninth.
†Struck out for Raschi in ninth.
‡Walked for McDougald in ninth.
Runs batted in—McDougald, Cox, Robinson, Woodling, Campanella. Two-base hit—Robinson. Home run—Campanella. Sacrifice hits—Raschi, Cox. Double play—Rizzuto, RMartin and Collins. Left on bases—New York 9, Brooklyn 8. Earned runs—New York 2, Brooklyn 3. Bases on balls—Off Erskine 3, off Rachi 3. Struck out—By Erskine 14, by Raschi 4. Hit by pitcher—By Erskine (Berra 2). Wild pitch—Erskine. Balk—Raschi. Winning pitcher—Erskine. Losing pitcher—Raschi.

GAME 4

BROOKLYN (N.L.)	AB	R	H	O	A	E	NEW YORK (A.L.)	AB	R	H	O	A	E
Gilliam, 2b	5	1	3	2	2	0	Mantle, cf	5	0	1	1	0	0
Reese, ss	5	0	0	2	1	0	Collins, 1b	4	0	0	9	1	0
Robinson, lf	4	0	1	1	0	0	Bauer, rf	4	0	1	4	0	0
Thompson, lf	0	0	0	0	1	0	Berra, c	4	0	2	4	0	0
Hodges, 1b	4	0	1	5	1	0	Woodling, lf	3	1	1	1	0	0
Campanella, c	2	2	0	10	0	0	Martin, 2b	4	1	2	4	2	0
Snider, cf	4	1	3	5	0	0	McDougald, 3b	3	1	1	0	5	0
Furillo, rf	4	1	1	2	0	0	Rizzuto, ss	4	0	1	0	2	0
Cox, 3b	4	1	2	0	1	0	Ford, p	0	0	0	0	0	0

GAME 4 (continued)

BROOKLYN (N.L.)	AB	R	H	O	A	E		NEW YORK (A.L.)	AB	R	H	O	A	E
Loes, p	3	0	2	0	0	0		Gorman, p	1	0	0	1	0	0
Labine, p	0	0	0	0	0	0		*Bollweg	1	0	0	0	0	0
Totals	35	7	12	27	6	0		Sain, p	0	0	0	0	0	0
								†Noren	1	0	0	0	0	0
								Schallock, p	0	0	0	0	1	0
								‡Mize	1	0	0	0	0	0
								Totals	35	3	9	24	11	0

```
New York     0 0 0   0 2 0   0 0 1—3
Brooklyn     3 0 0   1 0 2   1 0 x—7
```

*Struck out for Gorman in fifth.
†Popped out for Sain in seventh.
‡Flied out for Schallock in ninth.
Runs batted in—Robinson, Snider 4, Gilliam 2, McDougald 2, Mantle. Two-base hits—Gilliam 3, Snider 2, Cox. Three-base hit—Martin. Home runs—McDougald, Snider. Sacrifice hit—Loes. Left on bases—New York 7, Brooklyn 7. Earned runs—New York 3, Brooklyn 7. Bases on balls—Off Loes 2, off Ford 1, off Schallock 1. Struck out—By Loes 8, by Gorman 1, by Sain 1, by Schallock 1, by Labine 1. Pitching records—Off Ford 3 hits, 3 runs in 1 inning; off Gorman 4 hits, 1 run in 3 innings; off Sain 3 hits, 2 runs in 2 innings; off Schallock 2 hits, 1 run in 2 innings; off Loes 8 hits, 3 runs in 8 innings (pitched to three batters in ninth); off Labine 1 hit, 0 runs in 1 inning. Wild pitch—Ford. Winning pitcher—Loes. Losing pitcher—Ford.

GAME 5

NEW YORK (A.L.)	AB	R	H	O	A	E		BROOKLYN (N.L.)	AB	R	H	O	A	E
Woodling, lf	3	1	1	2	1	0		Gilliam, 2b	4	2	2	4	3	0
Collins, 1b	5	2	1	6	2	0		Reese, ss	5	0	1	0	1	0
Bauer, rf	3	1	0	1	0	0		Snider, cf	5	0	2	3	0	0
Berra, c	4	2	2	6	0	0		Robinson, lf	5	1	1	0	0	0
Mantle, cf	5	1	1	2	0	0		Campanella, c	4	2	3	8	3	0
Martin, 2b	5	1	2	3	2	0		Hodges, 1b	4	0	2	11	1	1
McDougald, 3b	5	1	2	0	1	0		Furillo, rf	4	1	1	0	0	0
Rizzuto, ss	3	2	1	4	6	1		Cox, 3b	4	1	1	1	4	0
McDonald, p	2	0	1	3	0	0		Podres, p	1	0	1	0	1	0
Kuzava, p	1	0	0	0	0	0		Meyer, p	1	0	0	0	1	0
Reynolds, p	0	0	0	0	0	0		*Belardi	1	0	0	0	0	0
Totals	36	11	11	27	12	1		Wade, p	0	0	0	0	0	0
								†Shuba	0	0	0	0	0	0
								‡Williams	1	0	0	0	0	0
								Black, p	0	0	0	0	0	0
								Totals	39	7	14	27	14	1

```
New York     1 0 5   0 0 0   3 1 1—11
Brooklyn     0 1 0   0 1 0   0 4 1— 7
```

*Grounded out for Meyer in seventh.
†Announced for Wade in eighth.
‡Struck out for Shuba in eighth.
Runs batted in—Woodling, Mantle 4, Snider, Martin 2, McDonald, Berra, Furillo, Cox 3, McDougald, Gilliam. Two-base hits—McDonald, Collins. Three-base hit—McDougald. Home runs—Woodling, Mantle, Martin, Cox, McDougald, Gilliam. Sacrifice hits—McDonald, Bauer. Stolen base—Rizzuto. Double plays—Woodling and Berra; Rizzuto and Collins; Martin, Rizzuto and Collins. Left on bases—New York 7, Brooklyn 6. Earned runs—New York 6, Brooklyn 6. Bases on balls—Off Podres 2, off Meyer 4. Struck out—By Meyer 5, by Black 2, by McDonald 3, by Kuzava 1. Pitching records—Off Podres 1 hit, 5 runs in 2⅔ innings; off Meyer 8 hits, 4 runs in 4⅓ innings; off Wade 1 hit, 1 run in 1 inning; off Black 1 hit. 1 run in 1 inning; off McDonald 12 hits, 6 runs in 7⅔ innings; off Kuzava 2 hits, 1 run in ⅔ inning; off Reynolds 0 hits, 0 runs in ⅔ inning. Hit by pitcher—By Podres (Bauer), by McDonald (Gilliam). Winning pitcher—McDonald. Losing pitcher—Podres.

GAME 6

BROOKLYN (N.L.)	AB	R	H	O	A	E		NEW YORK (A.L.)	AB	R	H	O	A	E
Gilliam, 2b	4	0	0	4	4	1		Woodling, lf	4	1	2	1	0	0
Reese, ss	4	0	1	1	4	0		Collins, 1b	3	0	1	5	1	0
Robinson, lf	4	1	2	3	0	0		‡Mize	1	0	0	0	0	0
Campanella, c	4	0	1	4	0	0		Bollweg, 1b	0	0	0	0	0	0
Hodges, 1b	4	0	0	7	0	0		Bauer, rf	3	2	1	3	0	0
Snider, cf	3	1	0	4	1	0		Berra, c	5	0	2	10	0	0

GAME 6 (continued)

BROOKLYN (N.L.)	AB	R	H	O	A	E	NEW YORK (A.L.)	AB	R	H	O	A	E
Furillo, rf	4	1	3	2	0	0	Mantle, cf	4	0	1	5	0	0
Cox, 3b	4	0	1	0	1	1	Martin, 2b	5	0	2	1	0	0
Erskine, p	1	0	0	0	0	1	McDougald, 3b	4	0	0	0	0	0
*Williams	0	0	0	0	0	0	Rizzuto, ss	4	1	2	2	2	0
Milliken, p	0	0	0	0	0	0	Ford, p	3	0	1	0	1	0
†Morgan	1	0	0	0	0	0	Reynolds, p	1	0	1	0	0	0
Labine, p	1	0	0	0	1	0	Totals	37	4	13	27	4	0
Totals	34	3	8	§25	11	3							

```
Brooklyn    0 0 0   0 0 1   0 0 2—3
New York    2 1 0   0 0 0   0 0 1—4
```

*Walked for Erskine in fifth.
†Lined out for Milliken in seventh.
‡Grounded out for Collins in eighth.
§One out when winning run scored.
Runs batted in—Berra, Martin 2, Woodling. Campanella, Furillo 2. Two-base hits—Berra, Furillo, Martin, Robinson. Home run—Furillo. Stolen base—Robinson. Double plays—Cox, Gilliam and Hodges; Snider, Gilliam and Campanella; Labine, Gilliam and Hodges. Left on bases—Brooklyn 6, New York 13. Earned runs—Brooklyn 3, New York 4. Bases on balls—Off Erskine 3, off Milliken 1, off Labine 1, off Ford 1, off Reynolds 1. Struck out—By Ford 7, by Reynolds 3, by Erskine 1, by Labine 1. Pitching records—Off Erskine 6 hits, 3 runs in 4 innings; off Milliken 2 hits, 0 runs in 2 innings; off Labine 5 hits, 1 run in 2⅓ innings; off Ford 6 hits, 1 run in 7 innings; off Reynolds 2 hits, 2 runs in 2 innings. Winning pitcher—Reynolds. Losing pitcher—Labine.

WORLD SERIES COMPOSITE BOX SCORE: 1953

PITCHING SUMMARY

New York Yankees

PITCHER	G	IP	H	R	ER	SO	BB	W	L	ERA
Reynolds	3	8	9	6	6	9	4	1	0	6.75
Sain	2	5⅔	8	3	3	1	1	1	0	4.50
Lopat	1	9	9	2	2	3	4	1	0	2.00
Raschi	1	8	9	3	3	4	3	0	1	3.38
Ford	2	8	9	4	4	7	2	0	1	4.50
Gorman	1	3	4	1	1	1	0	0	0	3.00
Schallock	1	2	2	1	1	1	1	0	0	4.50
McDonald	1	7⅔	12	6	5	3	0	1	0	5.63
Kuzava	1	⅔	2	1	1	0	0	0	0	13.50
Totals	6	52	64	27	26	30	15	4	2	4.50

Brooklyn Dodgers

PITCHER	G	IP	H	R	ER	SO	BB	W	L	ERA
Erskine	3	14	14	9	9	16	9	1	0	5.79
Hughes	1	4	3	1	1	3	1	0	0	2.25
Labine	3	5	10	2	2	3	1	0	2	2.25
Wade	2	2⅓	4	4	4	2	1	0	0	15.43
Roe	1	8	5	4	4	4	0	0	1	4.56
Loes	1	8	8	3	3	8	2	1	0	3.38
Podres	1	2⅔	1	5	1	0	2	0	1	3.38
Meyer	1	4⅓	8	4	3	5	4	0	0	6.23
Black	1	1	1	1	1	2	0	0	0	9.00
Milliken	1	2	2	0	0	0	1	0	0	0.00
Totals	6	51⅓	56	33	28	43	25	2	4	4.94

BATTING SUMMARY

New York Yankees

PLAYER-POS.	G	AB	R	H	2B	3B	HR	RBI	BA
McDougald, 3b	6	24	2	4	0	1	2	4	.167
Collins, 1b	6	24	4	4	1	0	1	2	.167
Bauer, rf	6	23	6	6	0	1	0	1	.261
Berra, c	6	21	3	9	1	0	1	4	.429
Mantle, cf	6	24	3	5	0	0	2	7	.208
Woodling, lf	6	20	5	6	0	0	1	3	.300
Martin, 2b	6	24	5	12	1	2	2	8	.500
Rizzuto, ss	6	19	4	6	1	0	0	0	.316
Reynolds, p	3	2	0	1	0	0	0	0	.500
Sain, p	2	2	1	1	1	0	0	2	.500
Lopat, p	1	3	0	0	0	0	0	0	.000
Noren, ph	2	1	0	0	0	0	0	0	.000
Bollweg, ph-1b	3	2	0	0	0	0	0	0	.000
Raschi, p	1	2	0	0	0	0	0	0	.000
Mize, ph	3	3	0	0	0	0	0	0	.000
Ford, p	2	3	0	1	0	0	0	0	.333
Gorman, p	1	1	0	0	0	0	0	0	.000
Schallock, p	1	0	0	0	0	0	0	0	.000

Brooklyn Dodgers

PLAYER-POS.	G	AB	R	H	2B	3B	HR	RBI	BA
Gilliam, 2b	6	27	4	8	3	0	2	4	.296
Reese, ss	6	24	0	5	0	1	0	0	.208
Snider, cf	6	25	3	8	3	0	1	5	.320
Robinson, lf	6	25	3	8	2	0	0	2	.320
Campanella, c	6	22	6	6	0	0	1	2	.273
Hodges, 1b	6	22	3	8	0	0	1	1	.364
Furillo, rf	6	24	4	8	2	0	1	4	.333
Cox, 3b	6	23	3	7	3	0	1	6	.304
Erskine, p	3	4	0	1	0	0	0	0	.250
Belardi, ph	2	2	0	0	0	0	0	0	.000
Hughes, p	1	1	0	0	0	0	0	0	.000
Shuba, ph	2	1	1	1	0	0	1	2	1.000
Labine, p	3	2	0	0	0	0	0	0	.000
Wade, p	2	0	0	0	0	0	0	0	.000
Roe, p	1	3	0	0	0	0	0	0	.000
Williams, ph	3	2	0	1	0	0	0	0	.500
Thompson, lf	2	0	0	0	0	0	0	0	.000
Loes, p	1	3	0	2	0	0	0	0	.667

BATTING SUMMARY (continued)

New York Yankees PLAYER-POS.	G	AB	R	H	2B	3B	HR	RBI	BA
McDonald, p	1	2	0	1	1	0	0	1	.500
Kuzava, p	1	1	0	0	0	0	0	0	.000
Totals	6	201	33	56	6	4	9	32	.279

Brooklyn Dodgers PLAYER-POS.	G	AB	R	H	2B	3B	HR	RBI	BA
Podres, p	1	1	0	1	0	0	0	0	1.000
Meyer, p	1	1	0	0	0	0	0	0	.000
Black, p	1	0	0	0	0	0	0	0	.000
Milliken, p	1	0	0	0	0	0	0	0	.000
Morgan, ph	1	1	0	0	0	0	0	0	.000
Totals	6	213	27	64	13	1	8	26	.300

WORLD SERIES HIGHLIGHTS: 1955

BROOKLYN (NL) DEFEATS NEW YORK (AL), 4 GAMES TO 3

FIRST GAME (Sept. 28, at New York)
BROOKLYN 021 000 020   5 10 0
NEW YORK 021 102 00x   6 9 1
Newcombe, Bessent (6th), Labine (8th)
Ford, Grim (9th)

Joe Collins' second homer in the sixth inning with a man on base put the Yankees ahead, 6–3. Carl Furillo and Duke Snider homered for the Dodgers and Jackie Robinson tripled and stole home in the eighth inning to put the Dodgers within one run of the Yanks. But that wasn't quite enough, and the Yankees took the opening game of the Series, 6–5.

SECOND GAME (Sept. 29, at New York)
BROOKLYN 000 110 000   2 5 2
NEW YORK 000 400 00x   4 8 0
Loes, Bessent (4th), Spooner (5th), Labine (8th)
Byrne

Tommy Byrne of the Yankees allowed the Dodgers only 5 hits and won his own game when he singled in the fourth inning with the bases loaded. Byrne's hit paved the way for four Yankee runs and a 4–2 Yankee victory.

THIRD GAME (Sept. 30, at Brooklyn)
NEW YORK 020 000 100   3 7 0
BROOKLYN 220 200 20x   8 11 1
Turley, Morgan (2d), Kucks (5th), Sturdivant (7th)
Podres

Roy Campanella drove in three runs with three hits to lead the Dodgers to an 8–3 triumph over the Yankees. Johnny Podres allowed the Yankees only seven hits as he outpitched four Yankee hurlers for the Dodgers' first Series victory.

FOURTH GAME (Oct. 1, at Brooklyn)
NEW YORK 110 102 000   5 9 0
BROOKLYN 001 330 10x   8 14 0
Larsen, Kucks (5th), R. Coleman (6th), Morgan (7th),
Sturdivant (8th)
Erskine, Bessent (4th), Labine (5th)

Home runs by Roy Campanella and Gil Hodges gave the Dodgers a 4–3 lead in the fourth inning. Duke Snider's home run with two men on base in the fifth inning gave the Dodgers a 7–3 lead, which they never relinquished. Final score: Dodgers 8, Yankees 5.

FIFTH GAME (Oct. 2, at Brooklyn)
NEW YORK 000 100 110   3 6 0
BROOKLYN 021 010 01x   5 9 2
Grim, Turley (7th)
Craig, Labine (7th)

Duke Snider continued his torrid hitting pace with two home runs to give the Dodgers an early 3–1 lead over the Yankees in the fourth inning. Sandy Amoros also homered to give the Dodgers a 5–3 victory as Clem Labine limited the Yanks to six hits.

SIXTH GAME (Oct. 3, at New York)
BROOKLYN 000 100 000 1 4 1
NEW YORK.................... 500 000 00x 5 8 0
Spooner, Meyer (1st), Roebuck (7th)
Ford

The Yankees knocked out Karl Spooner in the first inning, scoring five runs on singles by Berra and Bauer and Bill Skowron's home run. Whitey Ford held the Dodgers to one run on four hits.

SEVENTH GAME (Oct. 4, at New York)
BROOKLYN 000 101 000 2 5 0
NEW YORK.................... 000 000 000 0 8 1
Podres
Byrne, Grim (6th), Turley (8th)

The Dodgers, behind the brilliant pitching of lefty Johnny Podres, shut out the Yankees as they battled their way to their first World Series championship in history. Gil Hodges drove in both Dodger runs and Sandy Amoros saved the game in the sixth inning with a spectacular running catch of Yogi Berra's drive down the left-field line to choke off a Yankee rally.

WORLD SERIES BOX SCORES: 1955 (SEVEN GAMES)

GAME 1

NEW YORK (A.L.)	AB	R	H	O	A	E	BROOKLYN (N.L.)	AB	R	H	O	A	E
Bauer, rf	4	0	2	3	0	0	Gilliam, lf	3	0	0	2	0	0
McDougald, 3b	4	0	1	2	1	1	Reese, ss	5	0	1	2	5	0
Noren, cf	4	0	0	4	0	0	Snider, cf	5	1	2	1	0	0
Berra, c	3	1	1	5	0	0	Campanella, c	5	0	0	5	1	0
Collins, 1b	3	3	2	6	1	0	Furillo, rf	4	2	3	1	0	0
Howard, lf	3	1	1	1	0	0	Hodges, 1b	4	0	1	12	1	0
Martin, 2b	3	0	2	2	3	0	J. Robinson, 3b	4	2	1	0	2	0
Rizzuto, ss	2	0	0	3	2	0	Zimmer, 2b	2	0	1	1	3	0
*E. Robinson	0	0	0	0	0	0	Newcombe, p	3	0	0	0	1	0
Coleman, ss	1	0	0	0	0	0	Bessent, p	0	0	0	0	1	0
Ford, p	2	1	0	1	3	0	†Kellert	1	0	1	0	0	0
Grim, p	0	0	0	0	0	0	‡Hoak	0	0	0	0	0	0
							Labine, p	0	0	0	0	0	0
Totals	29	6	9	27	10	1	Totals	36	5	10	24	14	0

```
Brooklyn      0 2 1  0 0 0  0 2 0—5
New York      0 2 1  1 0 2  0 0 x—6
```

*Batted for Rizzuto in sixth when Martin was out attempting to steal home.
†Singled for Bessent in eighth.
‡Ran for Kellert in eighth.
Runs batted in—Furillo, Zimmer 2, Howard 2, Snider, Noren, Collins 3. Three-base hits—J. Robinson, Martin. Home runs—Furillo, Howard, Snider, Collins 2. Stolen base—Robinson. Sacrifice fly—Zimmer. Double plays—Zimmer and Hodges; Martin, Rizzuto and Collins; Hodges, Reese and Hodges. Left on bases—Brooklyn 9, New York 2. Earned runs—Brooklyn 3, New York 6. Bases on balls—Off Ford 4, off Newcombe 2, off Labine 1. Struck out—By Ford 2, by Newcombe 4, by Grim 2. Pitching records—Off Newcombe 8 hits, 6 runs in 5⅔, off Bessent 0 hits, 0 runs in 1⅓, off Ford 9 hits, 5 runs in 8, off Labine 1 hit, 0 runs in 1, off Grim 1 hit, 0 runs in 1. Winner—Ford. Loser—Newcombe.

GAME 2

NEW YORK (A.L.)	AB	R	H	O	A	E	BROOKLYN (N.L.)	AB	R	H	O	A	E
Bauer, rf	1	0	1	3	0	0	Gilliam, lf	4	0	1	0	1	0
Cerv, cf	3	0	0	0	0	0	Reese, ss	4	1	2	2	3	0
McDougald, 3b	4	0	0	1	0	0	Snider, cf	4	0	1	2	0	0
Noren, cf-lf	3	0	0	4	0	0	Campanella, c	3	0	0	11	2	0
Berra, c	3	1	2	6	1	0	Furillo, rf	3	0	0	0	0	0

GAME 2 (continued)

NEW YORK (A.L.)	AB	R	H	O	A	E	BROOKLYN (N.L.)	AB	R	H	O	A	E
Collins, 1b	3	1	0	5	0	0	Hodges, 1b	3	0	0	6	1	0
Howard, lf-rf	4	1	1	2	1	0	J. Robinson, 3b	2	1	0	1	1	0
Martin, 2b	3	1	1	2	3	0	Zimmer, 2b	3	0	1	2	2	2
Rizzuto, ss	1	0	1	2	1	0	Loes, p	1	0	0	0	0	0
*E. Robinson	0	0	0	0	0	0	Bessent, p	0	0	0	0	0	0
†J. Coleman, ss	1	0	0	2	2	0	‡Kellert	1	0	0	0	0	0
Byrne, p	3	0	1	0	0	0	Spooner, p	0	0	0	0	1	0
Totals	29	4	8	27	8	0	§Hoak	0	0	0	0	0	0
							Labine, p	0	0	0	0	0	0
							Totals	28	2	5	24	11	2

```
Brooklyn     0 0 0   1 1 0   0 0 0 — 2
New York     0 0 0   4 0 0   0 0 x — 4
```

*Hit by pitch for Rizzuto in fourth.
†Ran for E. Robinson in fourth.
‡Hit into double play for Bessent in fifth.
§Walked for Spooner in eighth.
Runs batted in—Snider, Howard, Martin, Byrne 2, Gilliam. Two-base hit—Reese. Double plays—Campanella and Zimmer; Zimmer, Reese and Hodges; Hodges and Reese; J. Coleman, Martin and Collins; Berra and Martin; Martin, J. Coleman and Collins. Left on bases—Brooklyn 4, New York 5. Earned runs—New York 4, Brooklyn 2. Bases on balls—Off Byrne 5, off Loes 1, off Spooner 1. Struck out—By Byrne 6, by Loes 5, by Spooner 5, by Labine 1. Pitching records—Off Loes 7 hits, 4 runs in 3⅔, off Bessent 0 hits, 0 runs in ⅓, off Spooner 1 hit, 0 runs in 3, off Labine 0 hits, 0 runs in 1. Hit by pitcher—By Loes (Berra, E. Robinson). Winner—Byrne. Loser—Loes.

GAME 3

BROOKLYN (N.L.)	AB	R	H	O	A	E	NEW YORK (A.L.)	AB	R	H	O	A	E
Gilliam, 2b	3	1	1	2	3	0	Cerv, lf-cf	4	0	0	3	0	0
Reese, ss	3	1	1	1	2	0	McDougald, 3b	4	0	1	0	3	0
Snider, cf	4	1	1	1	0	0	Berra, c	4	0	1	4	0	0
Campanella, c	5	1	3	6	0	1	Mantle, cf-rf	4	1	1	2	0	0
Furillo, rf	5	0	1	1	0	0	Skowron, 1b	4	1	2	5	2	0
Hodges, 1b	5	0	0	14	0	0	Howard, rf-lf	4	0	0	5	0	0
Robinson, 3b	5	2	2	0	7	0	Martin, 2b	4	0	0	3	0	0
Amoros, lf	1	1	1	2	1	0	Rizzuto, ss	2	1	1	2	1	0
Podres, p	3	1	1	0	1	0	Turley, p	1	0	0	0	0	0
Totals	34	8	11	27	14	1	Morgan, p	0	0	0	0	0	0
							*Bauer	1	0	0	0	0	0
							Kucks, p	0	0	0	0	0	0
							†Carey	1	0	1	0	0	0
							Sturdivant, p	0	0	0	0	1	0
							Totals	33	3	7	24	7	0

```
New York     0 2 0   0 0 0   1 0 0 — 3
Brooklyn     2 2 0   2 0 0   2 0 x — 8
```

*Flied out for Morgan in fifth.
†Tripled for Kucks in seventh.
Runs batted in—Campanella 3, Mantle, Gilliam, Reese 2, Furillo, Carey, Amoros. Two-base hits—Skowron, Furillo, Robinson, Campanella. Three-base hit—Carey. Home runs—Campanella, Mantle. Sacrifice hit—Podres. Double play—Reese, Gilliam and Hodges. Left on bases—Brooklyn 11, New York 5. Earned runs—Brooklyn 8, New York 2. Bases on balls—Off Podres 2, off Turley 2, off Morgan 3, off Kucks 1, off Sturdivant 1. Struck out—By Podres 6, by Turley 1, by Morgan 1. Pitching records—Off Turley 3 hits, 4 runs in 1⅓, off Morgan 3 hits, 2 runs in 2⅔, off Kucks 1 hit, 0 runs in 2, off Sturdivant 4 hits, 2 runs in 2. Hit by pitcher—By Turley (Amoros). Winner—Podres. Loser—Turley.

GAME 4

BROOKLYN (N.L.)	AB	R	H	O	A	E	NEW YORK (A.L.)	AB	R	H	O	A	E
Gilliam, 2b	4	1	2	1	4	0	Noren, cf	5	0	1	3	0	0
Reese, ss	4	1	2	1	2	0	McDougald, 3b	5	1	1	1	1	0
Snider, cf	4	1	1	6	0	0	Mantle, rf	5	0	1	2	0	0
Campanella, c	5	2	3	4	0	0	Berra, c	3	0	1	4	1	0
Furillo, rf	5	1	2	1	0	0	Collins, 1b	2	2	0	11	1	0

GAME 4 (continued)

BROOKLYN (N.L.)	AB	R	H	O	A	E
Hodges, 1b	4	1	3	11	0	0
J. Robinson, 3b	4	0	0	1	2	0
Amoros, lf	3	1	1	2	0	0
Erskine, p	1	0	0	0	1	0
Bessent, p	1	0	0	0	1	0
Labine, p	2	0	0	0	2	0
Totals	37	8	14	27	12	0

NEW YORK (A.L.)	AB	R	H	O	A	E
Howard, lf	3	1	1	0	0	0
Martin, 2b	4	1	2	1	3	0
Rizzuto, ss	3	0	1	2	2	0
Larsen, p	2	0	0	0	1	0
Kucks, p	0	0	0	0	1	0
*E. Robinson	1	0	1	0	0	0
†Carroll	0	0	0	0	0	0
R. Coleman, p	0	0	0	0	0	0
Morgan, p	0	0	0	0	0	0
‡Skowron	1	0	0	0	0	0
Sturdivant, p	0	0	0	0	0	0
Totals	34	5	9	24	10	0

```
New York    1 1 0  1 0 2  0 0 0—5
Brooklyn    0 0 1  3 3 0  1 0 x—8
```

*Singled for Kucks in sixth.
†Ran for E. Robinson in sixth.
‡Flied out for Morgan in eighth.
Runs batted in—McDougald, Rizzuto, Gilliam, Martin 2, Campanella, Hodges 3, Snider 3, E. Robinson. Two-base hits—Gilliam, Campanella, Martin. Home runs—McDougald, Campanella, Hodges, Snider. Stolen bases—Rizzuto, Collins, Gilliam. Sacrifice hits—Howard, Reese. Double play—J. Robinson, Gilliam and Hodges. Left on bases—Brooklyn 9, New York 7. Earned runs—Brooklyn 8, New York 5. Bases on balls—Off Erskine 2, off Bessent 1, off Labine 1, off Larsen 2, off Sturdivant 1. Struck out—By Erskine 3, by Bessent 1, by Larsen 2, by Kucks 1, by R. Coleman 1. Pitching records—Off Erskine 3 hits, 3 runs in 3 (pitched to two batters in fourth), off Bessent 3 hits, 0 runs in 1⅔, off Larsen 5 hits, 5 runs in 4 (pitched to one batter in fifth), off Kucks 3 hits, 2 runs in 1, off R. Coleman 5 hits, 1 run in 1 (pitched to three batters in seventh), off Morgan 0 hits, 0 runs in 1, off Sturdivant 1 hit, 0 runs in 1, off Labine 3 hits, 2 runs in 4⅓. Winner—Labine. Loser—Larsen.

GAME 5

BROOKLYN (N.L.)	AB	R	H	O	A	E
Gilliam, 2b	3	0	1	1	5	0
Reese, ss	3	0	0	4	3	1
Snider, cf	4	2	3	0	0	0
Campanella, c	3	0	0	6	0	0
Furillo, rf	4	1	1	1	0	0
Hodges, 1b	3	1	2	14	1	0
J. Robinson, 3b	3	0	1	0	3	1
Amoros, lf	4	1	1	1	0	0
Craig, p	0	0	0	0	1	0
Labine, p	2	0	0	0	1	0
Totals	29	5	9	27	14	2

NEW YORK (A.L.)	AB	R	H	O	A	E
Howard, lf	4	0	1	0	0	0
Noren, cf	4	0	0	2	0	0
McDougald, 3b	3	0	0	1	2	0
Berra, c	4	2	2	9	1	0
Collins, rf-1b	3	0	0	0	0	0
E. Robinson, 1b	2	0	1	6	0	0
‡Carroll	0	0	0	0	0	0
Bauer, rf	0	0	0	0	0	0
Martin, 2b	4	0	1	4	3	0
Rizzuto, ss	1	0	0	2	0	0
*Skowron	1	0	0	0	0	0
J. Coleman, ss	1	0	0	0	1	0
§Carey	1	0	0	0	0	0
Grim, p	2	0	0	0	1	0
†Cerv	1	1	1	0	0	0
Turley, p	0	0	0	0	1	0
xByrne	1	0	0	0	0	0
Totals	32	3	6	24	9	0

```
New York    0 0 0  1 0 0  1 1 0—3
Brooklyn    0 2 1  0 1 0  0 1 x—5
```

*Fouled out for Rizzuto in fourth.
†Homered for Grim in seventh.
‡Ran for E. Robinson in eighth.
§Grounded out for J. Coleman in ninth.
xGrounded out for Turley in ninth.
Runs batted in—Amoros 2, Snider 2, Martin, Cerv, Berra, J. Robinson. Two-base hit—Snider. Home runs—Amoros, Snider 2, Cerv, Berra. Sacrifice hits—Craig, Hodges. Double plays—Gilliam, Reese and Hodges; Martin and E. Robinson; J. Coleman, Martin and E. Robinson; Hodges, Reese and Hodges; J. Robinson, Gilliam and Hodges. Left on bases—New York 5, Brooklyn 7. Earned runs—New York 5, Brooklyn 1. Bases on balls—Off Craig 5, off Grim 4, off Turley 1. Struck out—By Craig 4, by Labine 1, by Grim 5, by Turley 5. Pitching records—Off Craig 4 hits, 2 runs in 6 (pitched to two batters in seventh), off Grim 6 hits, 4 runs in 6, off Turley 3 hits, 1 run in 2, off Labine 2 hits, 1 run in 3. Winner—Craig. Loser—Grim.

GAME 6

NEW YORK (A.L.)	AB	R	H	O	A	E	BROOKLYN (N.L.)	AB	R	H	O	A	E
Rizzuto, ss	3	1	0	1	5	0	Gilliam, 2b-lf	3	0	1	0	0	0
Martin, 2b	4	0	1	4	2	0	Reese, ss	4	1	1	3	2	0
McDougald, 3b	3	1	0	0	5	0	Snider, cf	1	0	0	1	0	0
Berra, c	3	1	2	8	0	0	*Zimmer, 2b	2	0	0	1	1	0
Bauer, rf	4	1	3	0	0	0	Campanella, c	3	0	0	5	0	0
Skowron, 1b	2	1	1	6	0	0	Furillo, rf	3	0	1	1	0	0
†Collins, 1b	1	0	0	5	1	0	Hodges, 1b	3	0	0	7	1	0
Cerv, cf	4	0	1	2	0	0	J. Robinson, 3b	4	0	0	2	3	1
Howard, lf	4	0	0	1	0	0	Amoros, lf-cf	4	0	1	2	0	0
Noren, lf	0	0	0	0	0	0	Spooner, p	0	0	0	0	0	0
Ford, p	4	0	0	0	1	0	Meyer, p	2	0	0	0	1	0
Totals	32	5	8	27	14	0	‡Kellert	1	0	0	0	0	0
							Roebuck, p	0	0	0	2	0	0
							Totals	30	1	4	24	8	1

```
Brooklyn      0 0 0  1 0 0  0 0 0—1
New York      5 0 0  0 0 0  0 0 x—5
```

*Struck out for Snider in fourth.
†Walked for Skowron in fifth.
‡Popped out for Meyer in seventh.
Runs batted in—Berra, Bauer, Skowron 3, Furillo. Home run—Skowron. Stolen base—Rizzuto. Double plays—McDougald, Martin and Skowron; J. Robinson and Hodges. Left on bases—Brooklyn 7, New York 7. Bases on balls—Off Ford 4, off Spooner 2, off Meyer 2. Struck out—By Ford 8, by Spooner 1, by Meyer 4. Pitching records—Off Spooner 3 hits, 5 runs in ⅓, Meyer 4 hits, 0 runs in 5⅔, Roebuck 1 hit, 0 runs in 2. Runs and earned runs—Spooner 5-5, Meyer 0-0, Roebuck 0-0, Ford 1-1. Hit by pitcher—By Ford (Furillo). Wild pitch—Ford. Winner—Ford. Loser—Spooner.

GAME 7

BROOKLYN (N.L.)	AB	R	H	O	A	E	NEW YORK (A.L.)	AB	R	H	O	A	E
Gilliam, lf-2b	4	0	1	2	0	0	Rizzuto, ss	3	0	1	1	3	0
Reese, ss	4	1	1	2	6	0	Martin, 2b	3	0	1	1	6	0
Snider, cf	3	0	0	2	0	0	McDougald, 3b	4	0	3	1	1	0
Campanella, c	3	1	1	5	0	0	Berra, c	4	0	1	4	1	0
Furillo, rf	3	0	0	3	0	0	Bauer, rf	4	0	0	1	0	0
Hodges, 1b	2	0	1	10	0	0	Skowron, 1b	4	0	1	11	1	1
Hoak, 3b	3	0	1	1	1	0	Cerv, cf	4	0	0	5	0	0
Zimmer, 2b	2	0	0	0	2	0	Howard, lf	4	0	1	2	0	0
*Shuba	1	0	0	0	0	0	Byrne, p	2	0	0	0	2	0
Amoros, lf	0	0	0	2	1	0	Grim, p	0	0	0	1	0	0
Podres, p	4	0	0	0	1	0	†Mantle	1	0	0	0	0	0
Totals	29	2	5	27	11	0	Turley, p	0	0	0	0	0	0
							Totals	33	0	8	27	14	1

```
Brooklyn      0 0 0  1 0 1  0 0 0—2
New York      0 0 0  0 0 0  0 0 0—0
```

*Grounded out for Zimmer in sixth.
†Popped out for Grim in seventh.
Runs batted in—Hodges 2. Two-base hits—Skowron, Campanella, Berra. Sacrifice hits—Snider, Campanella. Sacrifice fly—Hodges. Double play—Amoros, Reese and Hodges. Left on bases—Brooklyn 8, New York 8. Earned runs—Brooklyn 1, New York 0. Bases on balls—Off Byrne 3, off Grim 1, off Turley 1, off Podres 2. Struck out—By Byrne 2, by Grims 1, by Turley 1, by Podres 4. Pitching records—Off Byrne 3 hits, 2 runs in 5⅓; off Grim 1 hit, 0 runs in 1⅔; off Turley 1 hit, 0 runs in 2. Wild pitch—Grim. Winner—Podres. Loser—Byrne.

WORLD SERIES COMPOSITE BOX SCORE: 1955

PITCHING SUMMARY

Brooklyn Dodgers

PITCHER	G	IP	H	R	ER	SO	BB	W	L	ERA
Meyer	1	5⅔	4	0	0	4	2	0	0	0.00
Bessent	3	3⅓	3	0	0	1	0	0	0	0.00
Roebuck	1	2	1	0	0	0	0	0	0	0.00

New York Yankees

PITCHER	G	IP	H	R	ER	SO	BB	W	L	ERA
Ford	2	17	13	6	4	10	8	2	0	2.12
Grim	3	8⅔	8	4	4	8	5	0	1	4.15
Byrne	2	14⅓	8	4	3	8	8	1	1	1.88

PITCHING SUMMARY (continued)

Brooklyn Dodgers

PITCHER	G	IP	H	R	ER	SO	BB	W	L	ERA
Podres	2	18	15	3	2	10	4	2	0	1.00
Labine	4	9⅓	6	3	3	2	2	1	0	2.89
Craig	1	6	4	2	2	4	5	1	0	3.00
Erskine	1	3	3	3	3	2	0	0	0	9.00
Newcombe	1	5⅔	8	6	6	4	2	0	1	9.53
Loes	1	3⅔	7	4	4	5	1	0	1	9.82
Spooner	2	3⅓	4	5	5	6	3	0	1	13.50
Totals	7	60	55	26	25	39	22	4	3	3.75

New York Yankees

PITCHER	G	IP	H	R	ER	SO	BB	W	L	ERA
Turley	3	5⅓	7	5	5	7	4	0	1	8.44
Morgan	2	3⅔	3	2	2	1	3	0	0	4.91
Kucks	2	3	4	2	2	1	1	0	0	6.00
Sturdivant	2	3	5	2	2	0	2	0	0	6.00
Larsen	1	4	5	5	5	2	2	0	1	11.25
R. Coleman	1	1	5	1	1	1	0	0	0	9.00
Totals	7	60	58	31	28	38	33	3	4	4.20

BATTING SUMMARY

Brooklyn Dodgers

PLAYER-POS.	G	AB	R	H	2B	3B	HR	RBI	BA
Amoros, lf-cf	5	12	3	4	0	0	1	3	.333
Kellert, ph	3	3	0	1	0	0	0	0	.333
Hoak, pr-ph-3b	3	3	0	1	0	0	0	0	.333
Snider, cf	7	25	5	8	1	0	4	7	.320
Reese, ss	7	27	5	8	1	0	0	2	.296
Furillo, rf	7	27	4	8	1	0	1	3	.296
Gilliam, lf-2b	7	24	2	7	1	0	0	3	.292
Hodges, 1b	7	24	2	7	0	0	1	5	.292
Campanella, c	7	27	4	7	3	0	2	4	.259
Zimmer, 2b-ph	4	9	0	2	0	0	0	2	.222
J. Robinson, 3b	6	22	5	4	1	1	0	1	.182
Podres, p	2	7	1	1	0	0	0	0	.143
Newcombe, p	1	3	0	0	0	0	0	0	.000
Bessent, p	3	1	0	0	0	0	0	0	.000
Labine, p	4	4	0	0	0	0	0	0	.000
Loes, p	1	1	0	0	0	0	0	0	.000
Spooner, p	2	0	0	0	0	0	0	0	.000
Erskine, p	1	1	0	0	0	0	0	0	.000
Craig, p	1	0	0	0	0	0	0	0	.000
Meyer, p	1	2	0	0	0	0	0	0	.000
Roebuck, p	1	1	0	0	0	0	0	0	.000
Shuba, ph	1	1	0	0	0	0	0	0	.000
Totals	7	223	31	58	8	1	9	30	.260

New York Yankees

PLAYER-POS.	G	AB	R	H	2B	3B	HR	RBI	BA
E. Rob'son, ph-1b	4	3	0	2	0	0	0	1	.667
Carey, ph	2	2	0	1	0	1	0	1	.500
Bauer, rf-ph	6	14	1	6	0	0	0	1	.429
Berra, c	7	24	5	10	1	0	1	2	.417
Skowron, 1b-ph	5	12	2	4	2	0	1	3	.333
Martin, 2b	7	25	2	8	1	1	0	4	.320
Rizzuto, ss	7	15	2	4	0	0	0	1	.267
McDougald, 3b	7	27	2	7	0	0	1	1	.259
Mantle, cf-rf-ph	3	10	1	2	0	0	1	1	.200
Howard, lf-rf	7	26	3	5	0	0	1	3	.192
Collins, 1b-rf-ph	5	12	6	2	0	0	0	3	.167
Byrne, p-ph	3	6	0	1	0	0	0	2	.167
Cerv cf-lf	5	16	1	2	0	0	1	1	.125
Noren, cf-lf	5	16	0	1	0	0	0	1	.063
J. Coleman, ss-pr	3	3	0	0	0	0	0	0	.000
Ford, p	2	6	1	0	0	0	0	0	.000
Grim, p	3	2	0	0	0	0	0	0	.000
Turley, p	3	1	0	0	0	0	0	0	.000
Morgan, p	2	0	0	0	0	0	0	0	.000
Kucks, p	2	0	0	0	0	0	0	0	.000
Sturdivant, p	2	0	0	0	0	0	0	0	.000
Larsen, p	1	2	0	0	0	0	0	0	.000
R. Coleman, p	1	0	0	0	0	0	0	0	.000
Carroll, pr	2	0	0	0	0	0	0	0	.000
Totals	7	222	26	55	4	2	8	25	.248

WORLD SERIES HIGHLIGHTS: 1956

NEW YORK (AL) DEFEATS BROOKLYN (NL), 4 GAMES TO 3

FIRST GAME (Oct. 3, at Brooklyn)
NEW YORK....................200 100 000   3 9 1
BROOKLYN 023 100 00x   6 9 0
Ford, Kucks (4th), Morgan (6th), Turley (8th)
Maglie

Sal Maglie beat the Yankees 6–3 in the opening game of the Series, striking out 10 batters and scattering nine hits. Gil Hodges' home run with two men on base in the third inning broke the game open for the Dodgers. Jackie Robinson also homered for Brooklyn, while Mantle and Billy Martin homered for New York.

SECOND GAME (Oct. 5, at Brooklyn)
NEW YORK....................150 100 001   8 12 2
BROOKLYN 061 220 02x 13 12 0
Larsen, Kucks (2d), Byrne (2d), Sturdivant (3d), Morgan (3d),
  Turley (5th), McDermott (6th)
Newcombe, Roebuck (2d), Bessent (3d)

The Yankees scored early, highlighted by Berra's home run with the bases full as they knocked out Newcombe in the 2nd inning with a barrage of hits. Don Bessent relieved Newcombe and held the Yankees for the rest of the way in a 13 to 8 slugfest. Duke Snider homered with two men on as the Dodgers scored 6 runs in the second inning, and then continued to score against the combined pitching of six Yankee relievers.

THIRD GAME (Oct. 6, at New York)
BROOKLYN 010 001 100   3 8 1
NEW YORK.....................010 003 01x   5 8 1
Craig, Labine (7th)
Ford

Billy Martin and Enos Slaughter homered for the Yankees in the sixth inning and Whitey Ford scattered eight Dodger hits as the Yankees took a 5–3 victory in a tense seesaw game.

FOURTH GAME (Oct. 7, at New York)
BROOKLYN 000 100 001   2 6 0
NEW YORK.....................100 201 20x   6 7 2
Erskine, Roebuck (5th), Drysdale (7th)
Sturdivant

Mickey Mantle and Hank Bauer homered to give the Yankees a 6–2 victory to even the Series at two games each. The Yankees' Tom Sturdivant outpitched Drysdale, Erskine, and Roebuck, as he struck out seven Dodgers and held them to six hits.

FIFTH GAME (Oct. 8, at New York)
BROOKLYN 000 000 000   0 0 0
NEW YORK.....................000 101 00x   2 5 0
Maglie
Larsen

Don Larsen pitched the only perfect no-hit game in World Series history, setting down 27 Dodgers, in a row and winning, 2–0.

SIXTH GAME (Oct. 9, at Brooklyn)
NEW YORK.....................000 000 000 0   0 7 0
BROOKLYN 000 000 000 1   1 4 0
Turley
Labine

Jackie Robinson singled in the 10th inning of a pitchers' duel to score Junior Gilliam with the only run, giving the Dodgers a 1–0 victory over the Yankees. Clem Labine scattered seven hits in pitching one of his best games of the year against Bob Turley.

SEVENTH GAME (Oct. 10, at Brooklyn)
NEW YORK.....................202 100 400   9 10 0
BROOKLYN 000 000 000   0 3 1
Kucks
Newcombe, Bessent (4th), Craig (7th), Roebuck (7th),
Erskine (9th)

The Yankees pounded five Dodger pitchers for 10 hits, including a grand slam home run by Bill Skowron. Johnny Kucks pitched the best game of his big-league career, shutting out the Dodgers with 3 hits and racking up a 9–0 triumph for yet another Yankee World Series victory.

WORLD SERIES BOX SCORES: 1956 (SEVEN GAMES)

GAME 1

NEW YORK (A.L.)	AB	R	H	O	A	E	BROOKLYN (N.L.)	AB	R	H	O	A	E
Bauer, rf	5	0	2	3	0	0	Gilliam, 2b	3	0	0	3	1	0
Slaughter, lf	5	1	3	3	0	0	Reese, ss	4	1	2	1	1	0
Mantle, cf	3	1	1	4	1	0	Snider, cf	3	1	1	1	0	0

GAME 1 (continued)

NEW YORK (A.L.)	AB	R	H	O	A	E
Berra, c	3	0	0	4	0	0
Skowron, 1b	4	0	0	5	3	1
McDougald, ss	4	0	0	2	6	0
Martin, 2b-3b	3	1	1	2	1	0
Carey, 3b	3	0	1	0	1	0
cCollins	1	0	0	0	0	0
Turley, p	0	0	0	0	0	0
Ford, p	1	0	0	1	0	0
aWilson	1	0	0	0	0	0
Kucks, p	0	0	0	0	0	0
bCerv	1	0	1	0	0	0
Morgan, p	0	0	0	0	0	0
dByrne	1	0	0	0	0	0
G. Coleman, 2b	0	0	0	0	0	0
Totals	35	3	9	24	12	1

BROOKLYN (N.L.)	AB	R	H	O	A	E
Robinson, 3b	4	1	1	2	2	0
Hodges, 1b	4	2	2	4	0	0
Furillo, rf	4	0	1	2	0	0
Campanella, c	4	1	1	11	1	0
Amoros, lf	3	0	1	3	0	0
Maglie, p	3	0	0	0	0	0
Totals	32	6	9	27	5	0

```
New York    2 0 0   1 0 0   0 0 0 — 3
Brooklyn    0 2 3   1 0 0   0 0 x — 6
```

aStruck out for Ford in fourth.
bSingled for Kucks in sixth.
cStruck out for Carey in eighth.
dFouled out for Morgan in eighth.
Runs batted in—Mantle 2, Robinson, Furillo, Hodges 3, Martin, Amoros. Two-base hits—Furillo, Campanella. Home runs—Mantle, Robinson, Hodges, Martin. Stolen base—Gilliam. Double plays—Skowron, McDougald and Martin; Gilliam, Reese and Hodges. Left on bases—New York 9, Brooklyn 4. Earned runs—Brooklyn 6, New York 3. Bases on balls—Off Maglie 4, off Morgan 2. Struck out—By Maglie 10, by Ford 1, by Kucks 1, by Turley 2. Pitching records—Off Ford 6 hits, 5 runs in 3 innings; off Kucks 2 hits, 1 run in 2 innings; off Morgan 1 hit, 0 runs in 2 innings; off Turley 0 runs, 0 hits in 1 inning. Winning pitcher—Maglie. Losing pitcher—Ford.

GAME 2

NEW YORK (A.L.)	AB	R	H	O	A	E
McDougald, ss	3	0	1	1	0	0
Slaughter, lf	4	3	2	1	0	0
Mantle, cf	4	1	1	2	0	0
Berra, c	4	1	2	10	0	0
Collins, 1b	4	0	1	3	0	1
Bauer, rf	5	0	1	2	0	1
Martin, 3b-2b	4	1	1	3	2	0
G. Coleman, 2b	2	0	0	2	2	0
dSkowron	1	0	0	0	0	0
Carey, 3b	0	0	0	0	1	0
Larsen, p	1	1	1	0	0	0
Kucks, p	0	0	0	0	0	0
Byrne, p	0	0	0	0	0	0
Sturdivant, p	0	0	0	0	0	0
Morgan, p	1	1	1	0	0	0
Turley, p	0	0	0	0	0	0
bSiebern	1	0	0	0	0	0
McDermott, p	1	0	1	0	0	0
Totals	35	8	12	24	5	2

BROOKLYN (N.L.)	AB	R	H	O	A	E
Gilliam, 2b	3	1	1	5	3	0
Reese, ss	6	1	1	2	5	0
Snider, cf	4	3	2	6	0	0
Robinson, 3b	4	2	2	0	2	0
Hodges, 1b	3	2	3	6	0	0
Amoros, lf	4	1	0	0	0	0
cJackson	1	0	0	0	0	0
Cimoli, lf	0	0	0	1	0	0
Furillo, rf	4	2	2	2	0	0
Campanella, c	3	1	0	5	0	0
Newcombe, p	0	0	0	0	1	0
Roebuck, p	0	0	0	0	0	0
aMitchell	1	0	0	0	0	0
Bessent, p	2	0	1	0	0	0
Totals	35	13	12	27	11	0

```
New York    1 5 0   1 0 0   0 0 1 —  8
Brooklyn    0 6 1   2 2 0   0 2 x — 13
```

aFouled out for Roebuck in second.
bFlied out for Turley in sixth.
cStruck out for Amoros in seventh.
dStruck out for G. Coleman in eighth.
Runs batted in—Collins 2, Larsen, Berra 4, Campanella, Reese 2, Snider 3, Bessent, Slaughter, Hodges 4, Gilliam 2. Two-base hits—Hodges 2. Home runs—Berra, Snider. Sacrifice hits—G. Coleman, McDougald, Bessent. Sacrifice flies—Campanella, Slaughter. Double plays—Martin and Collins; Reese, Gilliam and Hodges. Left on bases—Brooklyn 11, New York 7. Earned runs—New York 8, Brooklyn 6. Bases on balls—Off Newcombe 2, off Bessent 2, off Larsen 4, off Sturdivant 2, off Morgan 2, off McDermott 3. Struck out—By Bessent 4, by Byrne 1, by Sturdivant 2, by Morgan 3, by Turley 1, by McDermott 3. Pitching records—Off Newcombe 6 hits, 6 runs in 1⅔ innings; off Roebuck 0 hits, 0 runs in ⅓ inning; off Bessent 6 hits, 2 runs in 7 innings; off Larsen 1 hit, 4 runs in 1⅔ innings; off Kucks 1 hit, 1 run in 0 inning (pitched to one batter in second); off Byrne 1 hit, 1 run in ⅓ inning; off Sturdivant 2 hits, 1 run in ⅔ inning; off Morgan 5 hits, 4

GAME 2 (continued)

runs in 2 innings; off Turley 0 hits, 0 runs in 1/3 inning; off McDermott 2 hits, 2 runs in 3 innings. Wild pitch—Bessent. Winning pitcher—Bessent. Losing pitcher—Morgan.

GAME 3

BROOKLYN (N.L.)	AB	R	H	O	A	E	NEW YORK (A.L.)	AB	R	H	O	A	E
Gilliam, lf	4	0	0	2	0	0	Bauer, rf	4	1	1	2	1	0
Reese, ss	4	1	2	2	3	0	Collins, 1b	4	1	0	8	0	0
Snider, cf	3	0	0	4	0	0	Mantle, cf	4	0	1	2	0	0
Robinson, 3b	3	1	1	0	0	0	Berra, c	4	1	2	8	1	0
Hodges, 1b	3	1	1	5	1	0	Slaughter, lf	3	1	2	1	0	0
Furillo, rf	4	0	2	1	0	0	Martin, 2b	4	1	1	3	3	0
Campanella, c	3	0	1	7	0	0	McDougald, ss	2	0	1	4	2	0
Neal, 2b	4	0	0	2	2	1	Carey, 3b	3	0	0	1	5	1
Craig, p	2	0	1	1	1	0	Ford, p	3	0	0	0	0	0
aJackson	1	0	0	0	0	0	Totals	31	5	8	27	12	1
Labine, p	0	0	0	0	0	0							
Totals	31	3	8	24	7	1							

Brooklyn   0 1 0 0 0 1 1 0 0—3
New York   0 1 0 0 0 3 0 1 x—5

aFlied out for Craig in seventh.
Runs batted in—Campanella, Martin, Snider, Slaughter 3, Berra. Two-base hits—Berra, Furillo. Three-base hit—Reese. Home runs—Martin, Slaughter. Sacrifice flies—Campanella, Snider. Double plays—Martin, McDougald and Collins. Craig, Reese and Hodges; Neal, Reese and Hodges. Left on bases—Brooklyn 5, New York 4. Earned runs—New York 4, Brooklyn 2. Bases on balls—Off Ford 2, off Craig 1, off Labine 1. Struck out—By Ford 7, by Craig 4, by Labine 2. Pitching records—Off Craig 7 hits, 4 runs in 6 innings; off Labine 1 hit, 1 run in 2 innings. Winning pitcher—Ford. Losing pitcher—Craig.

GAME 4

BROOKLYN (N.L.)	AB	R	H	O	A	E	NEW YORK (A.L.)	AB	R	H	O	A	E
Gilliam, 2b	4	0	0	1	4	0	Bauer, rf	4	1	1	1	0	0
Reese, ss	4	0	1	1	2	0	Collins, 1b	3	1	1	8	2	1
Snider, cf	4	1	1	3	0	0	Mantle, cf	3	2	1	4	0	0
Robinson, 3b	3	1	1	0	2	0	Berra, c	4	0	1	8	1	0
Hodges, 1b	4	0	1	10	1	0	Slaughter, lf	3	1	0	1	0	0
Amoros, lf	3	0	0	2	0	0	Martin, 2b	4	0	1	0	3	0
Furillo, rf	3	0	0	0	0	0	McDougald, ss	2	0	0	3	3	0
Campanella, c	2	0	2	6	0	0	Carey, 3b	3	1	1	0	0	1
Erskine, p	1	0	0	1	2	0	Sturdivant, p	3	0	1	2	0	0
aWalker	1	0	0	0	0	0	Totals	29	6	7	27	9	2
Roebuck, p	0	0	0	0	0	0							
bMitchell	1	0	0	0	0	0							
Drysdale, p	0	0	0	0	0	0							
cJackson	1	0	0	0	0	0							
Totals	31	2	6	24	11	0							

Brooklyn   0 0 0 1 0 0 0 0 1—2
New York   1 0 0 2 0 1 2 0 x—6

aHit into double play for Erskine in fifth.
bFlied out for Roebuck in seventh.
cCalled out on strikes for Drysdale in ninth.
Runs batted in—Berra, Hodges, Martin, McDougald, Mantle, Bauer 2, Campanella. Two-base hits—Collins, Snider, Robinson. Home runs—Mantle, Bauer. Stolen base—Mantle. Sacrifice fly—McDougald. Double plays—Gilliam, Reese and Hodges; Collins (unassisted); Martin, McDougald and Collins. Left on bases—Brooklyn 8, New York 3. Earned runs—New York 6, Brooklyn 2. Bases on balls—Off Sturdivant 6, off Erskine 2, off Drysdale 1. Struck out—By Sturdivant 7, by Erskine 2, by Roebuck 2, by Drysdale 1. Pitching records—Off Erskine 4 hits, 3 runs in 4 innings; off Roebuck 1 hit, 1 run in 2 innings; off Drysdale 2 hits, 2 runs in 2 innings. Winning pitcher, Sturdivant. Losing pitcher Erskine.

GAME 5

BROOKLYN (N.L.)	AB	R	H	O	A	E	NEW YORK (A.L.)	AB	R	H	O	A	E
Gilliam, 2b	3	0	0	2	0	0	Bauer, rf	4	0	1	4	0	0
Reese, ss	3	0	0	4	2	0	Collins, 1b	4	0	1	7	0	0
Snider, cf	3	0	0	1	0	0	Mantle, cf	3	1	1	4	0	0
Robinson, 3b	3	0	0	2	4	0	Berra, c	3	0	0	7	0	0

GAME 5 (continued)

BROOKLYN (N.L.)	AB	R	H	O	A	E		NEW YORK (A.L.)	AB	R	H	O	A	E
Hodges, 1b	3	0	0	5	1	0		Slaughter, lf	2	0	0	1	0	0
Amoros, lf	3	0	0	3	0	0		Martin, 2b	3	0	1	3	4	0
Furillo, rf	3	0	0	0	0	0		McDougald, ss	2	0	0	0	2	0
Campanella, c	3	0	0	7	2	0		Carey, 3b	3	1	1	1	1	0
Maglie, p	2	0	0	0	1	0		Larsen, p	2	0	0	0	1	0
aMitchell	1	0	0	0	0	0		Totals	26	2	5	27	8	0
Totals	27	0	0	24	10	0								

```
Brooklyn     0 0 0  0 0 0  0 0 0—0
New York     0 0 0  1 0 1  0 0 x—2
```

aCalled out on strikes for Maglie in ninth.
Runs batted in—Mantle, Bauer. Home run—Mantle. Sacrific hit—Larsen. Double plays—Reese and Hodges; Hodges, Campanella, Robinson, Campanella and Robinson. Left on bases—Brooklyn 0, New York 3. Earned runs—New York 2, Brooklyn 0. Bases on balls—Off Maglie 2. Struck out—By Larsen 7, by Maglie 5. Winning pitcher—Larsen. Losing pitcher—Maglie.

GAME 6

NEW YORK (A.L.)	AB	R	H	O	A	E		BROOKLYN (N.L.)	AB	R	H	O	A	E
Bauer, rf	5	0	2	2	0	0		Gilliam, 2b	3	1	1	0	7	0
Collins, 1b	5	0	2	4	1	0		Reese, ss	4	0	0	2	3	0
Mantle, cf	3	0	0	2	0	0		Snider, cf	2	0	1	4	0	0
Berra, c	4	0	2	12	0	0		Robinson, 3b	4	0	1	1	1	0
Slaughter, lf	3	0	0	1	1	0		Hodges, 1b	3	0	0	14	0	0
Martin, 2b	4	0	1	3	1	0		Amoros, lf	3	0	0	2	0	0
McDougald, ss	4	0	0	3	0	0		Furillo, rf	4	0	0	2	0	0
Carey, 3b	4	0	0	2	0	0		Campanella, c	4	0	0	5	0	0
Turley, p	4	0	0	0	2	0		Labine, p	4	0	1	0	3	0
Totals	36	0	7	a29	5	0		Totals	31	1	4	30	14	0

```
New York     0 0 0  0 0 0  0 0 0 0—0
Brooklyn     0 0 0  0 0 0  0 0 0 1—1
```

aTwo out when winning run scored.
Run batted in—Robinson. Two-base hits—Berra, Collins, Labine. Sacrifice hit—Reese. Double play—Gilliam, Reese and Hodges. Left on base—Dodgers 10, Yankees 8. Bases on ball—Off Labine 2, off Turley 8. Struck out—By Labine 5, by Turley 11. Winning pitcher—Labino. Losing pitcher—Turley.

GAME 7

NEW YORK (A.L.)	AB	R	H	O	A	E		BROOKLYN (N.L.)	AB	R	H	O	A	E
Bauer, rf	5	1	1	0	0	0		Gilliam, 2b	4	0	0	6	2	0
Martin, 2b	5	2	2	2	6	0		Reese, ss	2	0	0	2	5	1
Mantle, cf	4	1	1	0	0	0		Snider, cf	4	0	2	1	0	0
Berra, c	3	3	2	1	1	0		Robinson, 3b	3	0	0	0	1	0
Skowron, 1b	5	1	1	16	1	0		Hodges, 1b	3	0	0	10	2	0
Howard, lf	5	1	2	2	0	0		Amoros, lf	3	0	0	0	0	0
McDougald, ss	4	0	1	3	3	0		Furillo, rf	3	0	1	0	0	0
Carey, 3b	3	0	0	2	2	0		Campanella, c	3	0	0	8	0	0
Kucks, p	3	0	0	1	2	0		Newcombe, p	1	0	0	0	1	0
Totals	37	9	10	27	15	0		Bessent, p	0	0	0	0	0	0
								aMitchell	1	0	0	0	0	0
								Craig, p	0	0	0	0	0	0
								Roebuck, p	0	0	0	0	0	0
								bWalker	1	0	0	0	0	0
								Erskine, p	0	0	0	0	0	0
								Totals	28	0	3	27	11	1

```
New York     2 0 2  1 0 0  4 0 0—9
Brooklyn     0 0 0  0 0 0  0 0 0—0
```

aGrounded out for Bessent in sixth.
bGrounded out for Roebuck in eighth.
Runs batted in—Berra 4, Howard, Skowron 4. Two-base hits—Mantle, Howard. Home runs—Berra 2, Howard, Skowron. Stolen base—

Bauer. Sacrifice hit—Kucks. Double plays—Kucks, Martin and Skowron; McDougald and Skowron. Left on base—Yankees 6, Dodgers 4. Bases on balls—Off Newcombe 1, off Bessent 1, off Craig 2, off Kucks 3. Struck out—By Newcombe 4, by Bessent 1, by Roebuck 3, by Kucks 1. Pitching records—Off Newcombe 5 hits, 5 runs in 3 innings (pitched to one batter in fourth); off Bessent 2 hits, 0 runs in 3 innings; off Craig 3 hits, 4 runs in 0 inning (pitched to 5 batters in seventh); off Roebuck 0 hits, 0 runs in 2 innings; off Erskine 0 hits, 0 runs in 1 inning. Wild pitch—Craig. Winning pitcher—Kucks. Losing pitcher—Newcombe.

WORLD SERIES COMPOSITE BOX SCORE: 1956

PITCHING SUMMARY

New York Yankees PITCHER	G	IP	H	R	ER	SO	BB	W	L	ERA	Brooklyn Dodgers PITCHER	G	IP	H	R	ER	SO	BB	W	L	ERA
Turley	3	11	4	1	1	14	8	0	1	0.82	Maglie	2	17	14	5	5	15	6	1	1	2.65
Ford	2	12	14	8	7	8	2	1	1	5.25	Newcombe	2	4⅔	11	11	11	4	3	0	1	21.21
Kucks	3	11	6	2	1	2	3	1	0	0.82	Roebuck	3	4⅓	1	1	1	5	0	0	0	2.08
Morgan	2	4	6	4	4	3	4	0	1	9.00	Bessent	2	10	8	2	2	5	3	1	0	1.80
Larsen	2	10⅔	1	4	0	7	4	1	0	0.00	Craig	2	6	10	8	8	4	3	0	1	12.00
Byrne	1	⅓	1	1	0	1	0	0	0	0.00	Labine	2	12	8	1	0	7	3	1	0	0.00
Sturdivant	2	9⅔	8	3	3	9	8	1	0	2.79	Erskine	2	5	4	3	3	2	2	0	1	5.40
McDermott	1	3	2	2	1	3	3	0	0	3.00	Drysdale	1	2	2	2	2	1	1	0	0	9.00
Totals	7	61⅔	42	25	17	47	32	4	3	2.48	Totals	7	61	58	33	32	43	21	3	4	4.72

BATTING SUMMARY

New York Yankees PLAYER-POS.	G	AB	R	H	2B	3B	HR	RBI	BA	Brooklyn Dodgers PLAYER-POS.	G	AB	R	H	2B	3B	HR	RBI	BA
Bauer, rf	7	32	3	9	0	0	1	3	.281	Gilliam, 2b-lf	7	24	2	2	0	0	0	2	.083
Slaughter, lf	6	20	6	7	0	0	1	4	.350	Reese, ss	7	27	3	6	0	1	0	2	.222
Mantle, cf	7	24	6	6	1	0	3	4	.250	Snider, cf	7	23	5	7	1	0	1	4	.304
Berra, c	7	25	5	9	2	0	3	10	.360	Robinson, 3b	7	24	5	6	1	0	1	2	.250
Skowron, 1b-ph	3	10	1	1	0	0	1	4	.100	Hodges, 1b	7	23	5	7	2	0	1	8	.304
McDougald, ss	7	21	0	3	0	0	0	1	.143	Furillo, rf	7	25	2	6	2	0	0	1	.240
Martin, 2b-3b	7	27	5	8	0	0	2	3	.296	Campanella, c	7	22	2	4	1	0	0	3	.182
Carey, 3b	7	19	2	3	0	0	0	0	.158	Amoros, lf	6	19	1	1	0	0	0	1	.053
Collins, ph-1b	6	21	2	5	2	0	0	2	.238	Maglie, p	2	5	0	0	0	0	0	0	.000
Turley, p	3	4	0	0	0	0	0	0	.000	Jackson, ph	3	3	0	0	0	0	0	0	.000
Ford, p	2	4	0	0	0	0	0	0	.000	Cimoli, lf	1	0	0	0	0	0	0	0	.000
Wilson, ph	1	1	0	0	0	0	0	0	.000	Newcombe, p	2	1	0	0	0	0	0	0	.000
Kucks, p	3	3	0	0	0	0	0	0	.000	Roebuck, p	3	0	0	0	0	0	0	0	.000
Cerv, ph	1	1	0	1	0	0	0	0	1.000	Mitchell, ph	4	4	0	0	0	0	0	0	.000
Morgan, p	2	1	1	1	0	0	0	0	1.000	Bessent, p	2	2	0	1	0	0	0	1	.500
Byrne, ph-p	2	1	0	0	0	0	0	0	.000	Neal, 2b	1	4	0	0	0	0	0	0	.000
G. Coleman, 2b	2	2	0	0	0	0	0	0	.000	Craig, p	2	2	0	1	0	0	0	0	.500
Larsen, p	2	3	1	1	0	0	0	1	.333	Labine, p	2	4	0	1	1	0	0	0	.250
Sturdivant, p	2	3	0	1	0	0	0	0	.333	Erskine, p	2	1	0	0	0	0	0	0	.000
Siebern, ph	1	1	0	0	0	0	0	0	.000	Walker, ph	2	2	0	0	0	0	0	0	.000
McDermott, p	1	1	0	1	0	0	0	0	1.000	Drysdale, p	1	0	0	0	0	0	0	0	.000
Howard, lf	1	5	1	2	1	0	1	1	.400	Totals	7	215	25	42	8	1	3	24	.195
Totals	7	228	33	58	6	0	12	33	.253										

WORLD SERIES HIGHLIGHTS: 1959

LOS ANGELES (NL) DEFEATS CHICAGO (AL), 4 GAMES TO 2

FIRST GAME (Oct. 1, at Chicago)
LOS ANGELES 000 000 000   0 8 3
CHICAGO 207 200 00x 11 11 0
Craig, Churn (3d), Labine (4th), Koufax (5th), Klippstein (7th)
Wynn, Staley (8th)

Ted Kluszewski was the offensive star, hitting two home runs and batting in five runs as the White Sox routed the Dodgers, 11–0. Pitchers Early Wynn and Gerry Staley combined to limit the Dodgers to eight scattered hits.

SECOND GAME (Oct. 2, at Chicago)
LOS ANGELES 000 010 300   4 9 1
CHICAGO 200 000 010   3 8 0
Podres, Sherry (7th)
Shaw, Lown (7th)

Dodger second baseman Charley Neal belted two home runs and a pinch-hit homer by Chuck Essegian with a man on base provided the winning margin as the Dodgers came from behind to tie the Series with the White Sox.

THIRD GAME (Oct. 4, at Los Angeles)
CHICAGO 000 000 010   1 12 0
LOS ANGELES 000 000 21x   3 5 0
Donovan, Staley (7th)
Drysdale, Sherry (8th)

Carl Furillo's single in the seventh inning with the bases full scored two runs, and Larry Sherry's outstanding relief work gave the Dodgers a 3–1 victory over the Pale Hose. The Sox pounded starter Don Drysdale for 11 hits, but could score only one run.

FOURTH GAME (Oct. 5, at Los Angeles)
CHICAGO 000 000 400   4 10 3
LOS ANGELES 004 000 01x   5 9 0
Wynn, Lown (3d), Pierce (4th), Staley (7th)
Craig, Sherry (8th)

The Dodgers got to Early Wynn for four runs in the third inning to take an early lead, but the White Sox bounced back in the seventh as Sherm Lollar, the White Sox catcher, homered with two men on base to tie the score at 4–4. In the eighth inning, Gil Hodges homered and Larry Sherry once again relieved and stopped the White Sox.

FIFTH GAME (Oct. 6, at Los Angeles)
CHICAGO 000 100 000   1 5 0
LOS ANGELES 000 000 000   0 9 0
Shaw, Pierce (8th), Donovan (8th)
Koufax, Williams (8th)

A record crowd of more than 92,000 spectators saw one of the most exciting World Series games, as Sandy Koufax and Bob Shaw hooked up in a tight pitchers' duel. Chicago scored the only run of the game in the fourth inning when Lollar hit into a double play and Nellie Fox scored the game-winning run.

SIXTH GAME (Oct. 8, at Chicago)
LOS ANGELES 002 600 001   9 13 0
CHICAGO 000 300 000   3 6 1
Podres, Sherry (4th)
Wynn, Donovan (4th), Lown (4th), Staley (5th), Pierce (8th),
  Moore (9th)

Home runs by Duke Snider, Wally Moon, and Chuck Essegian powered the Dodgers to a 9–3 win over the White Sox to give them their first World Series championship in Los Angeles. Once again Larry Sherry pitched superbly in relief and limited the Sox to just 4 hits and no runs in 5½ innings.

WORLD SERIES BOX SCORES: 1959 (SIX GAMES)

GAME 1

LOS ANGELES (N.L.)	AB	R	H	O	A	E	CHICAGO (A.L.)	AB	R	H	O	A	E
Gilliam, 3b	4	0	1	0	1	0	Aparicio, ss	5	0	0	3	3	0
Neal, 2b	4	0	2	0	3	1	Fox, 2b	4	2	1	2	2	0
Moon, lf	4	0	1	2	0	0	Landis, cf	4	3	3	1	0	0
Snider, cf	2	0	0	2	0	2	Kluszewski, 1b	4	2	3	8	2	0
Demeter, cf	1	0	0	0	0	0	Lollar, c	3	1	0	7	0	0
Larker, rf	4	0	1	4	0	0	Goodman, 3b	2	1	1	0	0	0
Hodges, 1b	4	0	2	10	0	0	Esposito, 3b	2	0	0	1	0	0

GAME 1 (continued)

LOS ANGELES (N.L.)	AB	R	H	O	A	E	CHICAGO (A.L.)	AB	R	H	O	A	E
Roseboro, c	4	0	0	5	0	0	Smith, lf	4	1	2	2	0	0
Wills, ss	3	0	1	1	2	0	Rivera, rf	4	1	0	2	0	0
‡Furillo	1	0	0	0	0	0	Wynn, p	3	0	1	1	1	0
Craig, p	1	0	0	0	1	0	Staley, p	1	0	0	0	1	0
Churn, p	0	0	0	0	1	0	Totals	36	11	11	27	9	0
Labine, p	0	0	0	0	0	0							
*Essegian	1	0	0	0	0	0							
Koufax, p	0	0	0	0	0	0							
†Fairly	1	0	0	0	0	0							
Klippstein, p	0	0	0	0	1	0							
Totals	34	0	8	24	9	3							

```
Los Angeles    0 0 0  0 0 0  0 0 0— 0
Chicago        2 0 7  2 0 0  0 0 x—11
```

*Struck out for Labine in fifth.
†Grounded out for Koufax in seventh.
‡Flied out for Wills in ninth.
Runs batted in—Landis, Kluszewski 5, Lollar, Goodman, Wynn. Two-base hits—Fox, Smith 2, Wynn. Home runs—Kluszewski 2. Stolen base—Neal. Sacrifice fly—Lollar. Double play—Aparicio, Fox and Kluszewski. Left on bases—Los Angeles 8, Chicago 3. Earned runs—Chicago 7, Los Angeles 0. Bases on balls—Off Wynn 1, off Craig 1. Struck out—By Wynn 6, by Staley 1, by Craig 1, by Labine 1, by Koufax 1, by Klippstein 2. Pitching records—Off Wynn 6 hits, 0 runs in 7 innings (pitched to one batter in eighth); off Staley 2 hits, 0 runs in 2 innings; off Craig 5 hits, 5 runs in 2⅓ innings; off Churn 5 hits, 6 runs in ⅔ innings (pitched to two batters in fourth); off Labine 0 hits, 0 runs in 1 inning; off Koufax 0 hits, 0 runs in 2 innings; off Klippstein 1 hit, 0 runs in 2 innings. Winner—Wynn. Loser—Craig.

GAME 2

LOS ANGELES (N.L.)	AB	R	H	O	A	E	CHICAGO (A.L.)	AB	R	H	O	A	E
Gilliam, 3b	4	1	1	1	1	0	Aparicio, ss	5	1	2	3	1	0
Neal, 2b	5	2	2	2	4	0	Fox, 2b	4	0	0	0	5	0
Moon, lf	3	0	1	1	1	0	Landis, cf	3	1	0	2	0	0
Snider, cf	4	0	1	1	0	0	Kluszewski, 1b	4	0	1	9	0	0
Demeter, cf	0	0	0	0	0	0	†Torgeson, 1b	0	1	0	0	0	0
Larker, rf	3	0	0	4	0	0	Lollar, c	4	0	2	4	0	0
Sherry, p	1	0	0	1	1	0	Smith, lf	3	0	1	2	0	0
Hodges, 1b	4	0	0	10	1	0	Phillips, 3b	3	0	1	2	0	0
Roseboro, c	4	0	1	6	0	0	‡Goodman, 3b	1	0	0	0	0	0
Wills, ss	4	0	1	1	6	1	McAnany, rf	3	0	0	3	0	0
Podres, p	2	0	1	0	0	0	Rivera, rf	1	0	0	2	0	0
*Essegian	1	1	1	0	0	0	Shaw, p	3	0	1	0	1	0
Fairly, rf	1	0	0	0	0	0	Lown, p	0	0	0	0	0	0
Totals	36	4	9	27	14	1	§Cash	1	0	0	0	0	0
							Totals	35	3	8	27	7	0

```
Los Angeles    0 0 0  0 1 0  3 0 0—4
Chicago        2 0 0  0 0 0  0 1 0—3
```

*Hit home run for Podres in seventh.
†Ran for Kluszewski in eighth.
‡Struck out for Phillips in eighth.
§Grounded out for Lown in ninth.
Runs batted in—Neal 3, Essegian, Kluszewski, Lollar, Smith. Two-base hits—Aparicio, Phillips, Smith. Home runs—Neal 2, Essegian. Stolen bases—Moon, Gilliam. Left on bases—Chicago 8, Los Angeles 7. Earned runs—Los Angeles 4, Chicago 3. Bases on balls—Off Podres 3, off Shaw 1, off Lown 1. Struck out—By Podres 3, by Sherry 1, by Shaw 1, by Lown 3. Pitching records—Off Podres 5 hits, 2 runs in 6 innings; off Sherry 3 hits, 1 run in 3 innings; off Shaw 8 hits, 4 runs in 6⅔ innings; off Lown 1 hit, 0 runs in 2⅓ innings. Winner—Podres. Loser—Shaw.

GAME 3

CHICAGO (A.L.)	AB	R	H	O	A	E	LOS ANGELES (N.L.)	AB	R	H	O	A	E
Aparicio, ss	4	0	2	0	3	0	Gilliam, 3b	4	0	0	3	2	0
Fox, 2b	4	0	3	3	6	0	Neal, 2b	4	1	2	3	2	0
Landis, cf	5	0	1	2	0	0	Moon, rf	4	0	0	1	0	0
Kluszewski, 1b	3	1	1	11	1	0	Larker, lf	2	1	0	1	0	0

GAME 3 (continued)

CHICAGO (A.L.)	AB	R	H	O	A	E	LOS ANGELES (N.L.)	AB	R	H	O	A	E
Lollar, c	4	0	2	5	1	0	Hodges, 1b	2	0	1	6	1	0
Goodman, 3b	3	0	2	1	1	0	Demeter, cf	2	0	0	0	0	0
‡Esposito, 3b	0	0	0	0	0	0	*Furillo	1	0	1	0	0	0
Smith, lf	4	0	0	0	0	0	†Fairly, cf	0	0	0	0	0	0
Rivera, rf	3	0	0	1	0	0	Roseboro, c	3	0	0	9	3	0
Donovan, p	3	0	1	1	1	0	Wills, ss	3	1	1	3	2	0
Staley, p	0	0	0	0	0	0	Drysdale, p	2	0	0	1	1	0
§Cash	1	0	0	0	0	0	Sherry, p	0	0	0	0	0	0
Totals	34	1	12	24	13	0	Totals	27	3	5	27	11	0

```
Chicago        0 0 0   0 0 0   0 1 0—1
Los Angeles    0 0 0   0 0 0   2 1 x—3
```

*Singled for Demeter in seventh.
†Ran for Furillo in seventh.
‡Ran for Goodman in eighth.
§Struck out for Staley in ninth.
Runs batted in—Furillo 2, Neal. Two-base hit—Neal. Stolen base—Landis. Sacrifice hit—Sherry. Double plays—Aparicio, Fox and Kluszewski; Roseboro and Neal; Gilliam, Neal and Hodges; Wills, Neal and Hodges. Left on bases—Chicago 11, Los Angeles 3. Earned runs—Chicago 1, Los Angeles 3. Bases on balls—Off Drysdale 4, off Donovan 2. Struck out—By Drysdale 5, by Sherry 3, by Donovan 5. Pitching records—Off Drysdale 11 hits, 1 run in 7 innings (pitched to two batters in eighth); off Sherry 1 hit, 0 runs in 2 innings; off Donovan 2 hits, 2 runs in 6⅔ innings; off Staley 3 hits 1 run in 1⅓ innings. Hit by pitcher—By Sherry (Goodman). Winner—Drysdale. Loser—Donovan.

GAME 4

CHICAGO (A.L.)	AB	R	H	O	A	E	LOS ANGELES (N.L.)	AB	R	H	O	A	E
Landis, cf	5	1	1	0	0	1	Gilliam, 3b	4	0	0	0	1	0
Aparicio, ss	3	0	1	0	2	1	Neal, 2b	4	0	0	4	4	0
Fox, 2b	5	1	3	3	4	0	Moon, rf-lf	4	1	2	3	0	0
Kluszewski, 1b	4	1	2	9	0	0	Larker, lf	2	1	1	0	0	0
Lollar, c	4	1	1	6	2	0	†Furillo, rf	1	0	0	0	0	0
Goodman, 3b	4	0	0	0	0	0	Fairly, rf	1	0	0	0	0	0
Smith, lf	3	0	2	3	0	0	Hodges, 1b	4	2	2	10	0	0
Rivera, rf	3	0	0	3	1	0	Demeter, cf	3	1	2	1	0	0
Wynn, p	1	0	0	0	1	0	Roseboro, c	3	0	1	7	0	0
Lown, p	0	0	0	0	0	0	Wills, ss	4	0	1	2	6	0
*Cash	1	0	0	0	0	0	Craig, p	2	0	0	0	1	0
Pierce, p	0	0	0	0	0	1	Sherry, p	0	0	0	0	0	0
‡Torgeson	1	0	0	0	0	0	Totals	32	5	9	27	12	0
Staley, p	0	0	0	0	0	0							
Totals	34	4	10	24	10	3							

```
Chicago        0 0 0   0 0 0   4 0 0—4
Los Angeles    0 0 4   0 0 0   0 1 x—5
```

*Struck out for Lown in fourth.
†Struck out for Larker in fifth.
‡Grounded out for Pierce in seventh.
Runs batted in—Kluszewski, Lollar 3, Hodges 2, Roseboro. Two-base hit—Fox. Home runs—Lollar, Hodges. Stolen bases—Aparicio, Wills. Sacrifice hits—Roseboro, Craig, Aparicio. Double plays—Wills, Neal and Hodges; Neal, Wills and Hodges. Left on bases—Chicago 9, Los Angeles 6. Earned runs—Los Angeles 4, Chicago 4. Bases on balls—Of Craig 4, off Sherry 1, off Pierce 1. Struck out—By Craig 7, by Wynn 2, by Pierce 2, by Staley 2. Pitching records—Off Craig 10 hits, 4 runs in 7 innings; off Sherry 0 hits, 0 runs in 2 innings; off Wynn 8 hits, 4 runs in 2⅔ innings; off Lown 0 hits, 0 runs in ⅓ inning; off Pierce 0 hits, 0 runs in 3 innings; off Staley 1 hit, 1 run in 2 innings. Passed ball—Lollar. Winner—Sherry. Loser—Staley.

GAME 5

CHICAGO (A.L.)	AB	R	H	O	A	E	LOS ANGELES (N.L.)	AB	R	H	O	A	E
Aparicio, ss	4	0	2	3	5	0	Gilliam, 3b	5	0	4	0	3	0
Fox, 2b	3	1	1	4	4	0	Neal, 2b	5	0	1	5	2	0
Landis, cf	4	0	1	2	0	0	Moon, rf-cf	4	0	1	0	0	0
Lollar, c	4	0	0	1	0	0	Larker, lf	4	0	0	3	1	0

GAME 5 (continued)

CHICAGO (A.L.)	AB	R	H	O	A	E	LOS ANGELES (N.L.)	AB	R	H	O	A	E
Kluszewski, 1b	4	0	0	12	0	0	Hodges, 1b	4	0	3	7	1	0
Smith, rf-lf	4	0	0	1	0	0	Demeter, cf	3	0	0	4	0	0
Phillips, 3b	3	0	1	1	2	0	xFairly	0	0	0	0	0	0
McAnany, lf	1	0	0	1	0	0	yRepulski, rf	0	0	0	0	0	0
Rivera, rf	0	0	0	2	0	0	Roseboro, c	3	0	0	6	1	0
Shaw, p	1	0	0	0	3	0	zFurillo	1	0	0	0	0	0
Pierce, p	0	0	0	0	0	0	Pignatano, c	0	0	0	1	0	0
Donovan, p	0	0	0	0	0	0	Wills, ss	2	0	0	1	2	0
Totals	28	1	5	27	14	0	*Essegian	0	0	0	0	0	0
							†Zimmer, ss	1	0	0	0	1	0
							Koufax, p	2	0	0	0	0	0
							‡Snider	1	0	0	0	0	0
							§Podres	0	0	0	0	0	0
							Williams, p	0	0	0	0	0	0
							aSherry	1	0	0	0	0	0
							Totals	36	0	9	27	11	0

```
Chicago       0 0 0  1 0 0  0 0 0—1
Los Angeles   0 0 0  0 0 0  0 0 0—0
```

*Walked for Wills in seventh.
†Ran for Essegian in seventh.
‡Hit into force play for Koufax in seventh.
§Ran for Snider in seventh.
xAnnounced as batter for Demeter in eighth.
yWalked intentionally for Fairly in eighth.
zPopped out for Roseboro in eighth.
aGrounded out for Williams in ninth.

Runs batted in—None (run scored on Lollar's double play). Three-base hit—Hodges. Stolen base—Gilliam. Sacrifice hits—Shaw 2. Double play—Neal and Hodges. Left on bases—Chicago 5, Los Angeles 11. Earned runs—Chicago 1, Los Angeles 0. Bases on balls—Off Koufax 1, off Williams 2, off Shaw 1, off Pierce 1. Struck out—By Koufax 6, by Williams 1, by Shaw 1. Pitching records—Off Koufax 5 hits, 1 run in 7 innings; off Williams 0 hits, 0 runs in 2 innings; off Shaw 9 hits, 0 runs in 7⅓ innings; off Pierce 0 hits, 0 runs in 0 innings (pitched to one batter in eighth); off Donovan 0 hits, 0 runs in 1⅔ innings. Wild pitch—Shaw. Winner—Shaw. Loser—Koufax.

GAME 6

LOS ANGELES (N.L.)	AB	R	H	O	A	E	CHICAGO (A.L.)	AB	R	H	O	A	E
Gilliam, 3b	4	1	0	0	2	0	Aparicio, ss	5	0	1	1	2	1
Neal, 2b	5	1	3	4	4	0	Fox, 2b	4	0	1	2	2	0
Moon, lf	4	2	1	3	0	0	Landis, cf	3	1	1	2	0	0
Snider, cf-rf	3	1	1	2	0	0	Lollar, c	3	1	0	5	2	0
xEssegian	1	1	1	0	0	0	Kluszewski, 1b	4	1	2	10	0	0
Fairly, rf	0	0	0	0	0	0	Smith, lf	2	0	0	2	0	0
Hodges, 1b	5	0	1	10	0	0	Phillips, 3b-rf	4	0	1	3	1	0
Larker, rf	1	0	1	0	0	0	McAnany, rf	1	0	0	1	0	0
*Demeter, cf	3	1	1	4	0	0	†Goodman, 3b	3	0	0	0	1	0
Roseboro, c	4	0	0	2	0	0	Wynn, p	1	0	0	0	1	0
Wills, ss	4	1	1	2	3	0	Donovan, p	0	0	0	0	0	0
Podres, p	2	1	1	0	1	0	Lown, p	0	0	0	0	0	0
Sherry, p	2	0	2	0	2	0	‡Torgeson	0	0	0	0	0	0
Totals	38	9	13	27	12	0	Staley, p	0	0	0	1	0	0
							§Romano	1	0	0	0	0	0
							Pierce, p	0	0	0	0	0	0
							Moore, p	0	0	0	0	0	0
							yCash	1	0	0	0	0	0
							Totals	32	3	6	27	9	1

```
Los Angeles   0 0 2  6 0 0  0 0 1—9
Chicago       0 0 0  3 0 0  0 0 0—3
```

*Ran for Larker in fourth.
†Struck out for McAnany in fourth.
‡Walked for Lown in fourth.
§Grounded out for Staley in seventh.
xHomered for Snider in ninth.
yFlied out for Moore in ninth.

Runs batted in—Neal 2, Moon 2, Snider 2, Essegian, Wills, Podres, Kluszewski 3. Two-base hits—Podres, Neal, Fox, Kluszewski. Home runs—Snider, Moon, Kluszewski, Essegian. Sacrifice hit—Roseboro. Double play—Podres, Neal and Hodges. Left on bases—Los Angeles 7, Chicago 7. Earned runs—Los Angeles 9, Chicago 3. Bases on balls—Off Wynn 3, off Donovan 1, off Podres 3, off Sherry 1. Struck out—By Wynn 2, by Pierce 1, by Moore 1, by Podres 1, by Sherry 1. Pitching records—Off Wynn 5 hits, 5 runs in 3⅓ innings; off Donovan 2 hits, 3 runs in 0 innings (pitched to three batters in fourth); off Lown 1 hit, 0 runs in ⅔ innings; off Staley 2 hits, 0 runs in 3 innings; off Pierce 2 hits, 0 runs in 1 inning; off Moore 1 hit, 1 run in 1 inning; off Podres 2 hits, 3 runs in 3⅓ innings; off Sherry 4 hits, 0 runs in 5⅔ innings. Hit by pitcher—By Podres (Landis). Winner—Sherry. Loser—Wynn.

WORLD SERIES COMPOSITE BOX SCORE: 1959

PITCHING SUMMARY

Los Angeles Dodgers PITCHER	G	IP	H	R	ER	SO	BB	W	L	ERA
Craig	2	9⅓	15	9	9	8	5	0	1	8.68
Churn	1	⅔	5	6	2	0	0	0	0	27.00
Labine	1	1	0	0	0	1	0	0	0	0.00
Koufax	2	9	5	1	1	7	1	0	1	1.00
Klippstein	1	2	1	0	0	2	0	0	0	0.00
Podres	2	9⅓	7	5	5	4	6	1	0	4.82
Sherry	4	12⅔	8	1	1	5	2	2	0	0.71
Drysdale	1	7	11	1	1	5	4	1	0	1.29
Williams	1	2	0	0	0	1	2	0	0	0.00
Totals	6	53	52	23	19	33	20	4	2	3.23

Chicago White Sox PITCHER	G	IP	H	R	ER	SO	BB	W	L	ERA
Wynn	3	13	19	9	8	10	4	1	1	5.54
Staley	4	8⅓	8	2	2	3	0	0	1	2.16
Shaw	2	14	17	4	4	2	2	1	1	2.57
Lown	3	3⅓	2	0	0	3	1	0	0	0.00
Donovan	3	8⅓	4	5	5	5	3	0	1	5.40
Pierce	3	4	2	0	0	3	2	0	0	0.00
Moore	1	1	1	1	1	1	0	0	0	9.00
Totals	6	52	53	21	20	27	12	2	4	3.46

BATTING SUMMARY

Los Angeles Dodgers PLAYER-POS.	G	AB	R	H	2B	3B	HR	RBI	BA
Gilliam, 3b	6	25	2	6	0	0	0	0	.240
Neal, 2b	6	27	4	10	2	0	2	6	.370
Moon, lf-rf-cf	6	23	3	6	0	0	1	2	.261
Snider, cf-ph-rf	4	10	1	2	0	0	1	2	.200
Demeter, cf-pr	6	12	2	3	0	0	0	0	.250
Larker, rf-lf	6	16	2	3	0	0	0	0	.188
Hodges, 1b	6	23	2	9	0	1	1	2	.391
Roseboro, c	6	21	0	2	0	0	0	1	.095
Wills, ss	6	20	2	5	0	0	0	1	.250
Furillo, pf-rf	4	4	0	1	0	0	0	2	.250
Craig, p	2	3	0	0	0	0	0	0	.000
Churn, p	1	0	0	0	0	0	0	0	.000
Labine, p	1	0	0	0	0	0	0	0	.000
Essegian, ph	4	3	2	2	0	0	2	2	.667
Koufax, p	2	2	0	0	0	0	0	0	.000
Fairly, ph-rf-pr	6	3	0	0	0	0	0	0	.000
Klippstein, p	1	0	0	0	0	0	0	0	.000
Sherry, p-ph	5	4	0	2	0	0	0	0	.500
Podres, p-pr	3	4	1	2	1	0	0	1	.500
Drysdale, p	1	2	0	0	0	0	0	0	.000
Repulski, ph	1	0	0	0	0	0	0	0	.000
Pignatano, c	1	0	0	0	0	0	0	0	.000
Zimmer, pr-ss	1	1	0	0	0	0	0	0	.000
Williams, p	1	0	0	0	0	0	0	0	.000
Totals	6	203	21	53	3	1	7	19	.261

Chicago White Sox PLAYER-POS.	G	AB	R	H	2B	3B	HR	RBI	BA
Aparicio, ss	6	26	1	8	1	0	0	0	.308
Fox, 2b	6	24	4	9	3	0	0	0	.375
Landis, cf	6	24	6	7	0	0	0	1	.292
Kluszewski, 1b	6	23	5	9	1	0	3	10	.391
Lollar, c	6	22	3	5	0	0	1	5	.227
Goodman, 3b-ph	5	13	1	3	0	0	0	1	.231
Esposito, 3b-pr	2	2	0	0	0	0	0	0	.000
Smith, lf-rf	6	20	1	5	3	0	0	1	.250
Rivera, rf	5	11	1	0	0	0	0	0	.000
Wynn, p	3	5	0	1	0	0	0	1	.200
Staley, p	4	1	0	0	0	0	0	0	.000
Tor'son, pr-1b-ph	3	1	1	0	0	0	0	0	.000
Phillips, 3b-rf	3	10	0	3	1	0	0	0	.300
McAnany, rf	3	5	0	0	0	0	0	0	.000
Shaw, p	2	4	0	1	0	0	0	0	.250
Lown, p	3	0	0	0	0	0	0	0	.000
Cash, ph	4	4	0	0	0	0	0	0	.000
Donovan, p	3	3	0	1	0	0	0	0	.333
Pierce, p	3	0	0	0	0	0	0	0	.000
Romano, ph	2	1	0	0	0	0	0	0	.000
Moore, p	1	0	0	0	0	0	0	0	.000
Totals	6	199	23	52	10	0	4	19	.261

WORLD SERIES HIGHLIGHTS: 1963

LOS ANGELES (NL) DEFEATS NEW YORK (AL), 4 GAMES TO 0

FIRST GAME (Oct. 2, at New York)
LOS ANGELES 041 000 000   5 9 0
NEW YORK 000 000 020   2 6 0
Koufax
Ford, Williams (6th), Hamilton (9th)

Sandy Koufax pitched superbly, fanning 15 Yankees and setting them down with only six hits as the Dodgers won, 5–2. Johnny Roseboro, the Dodgers' catcher, homered with two men on in the second inning as the Dodgers scored four runs. Tommy Tresh, Yankee outfielder, homered with a man on base in the eighth inning for the Yankee runs.

SECOND GAME (Oct. 3, at New York)
LOS ANGELES 200 100 010   4 10 1
NEW YORK. 000 000 001   1 7 0
Podres, Perranoski (9th)
Downing, Terry (6th), Reniff (9th)

Lefty Johnny Podres outpitched three Yankees hurlers, allowing the Bronx Bombers just six hits in the 8⅓ innings he worked. He was relieved in the ninth inning by Ron Perranoski. The Dodgers scored two runs in the first inning when Willie Davis doubled with two men on base and that was enough to win the ball game.

THIRD GAME (Oct. 5, at Los Angeles)
NEW YORK. 000 000 000   0 3 0
LOS ANGELES 100 000 00x   1 4 1
Bouton, Reniff (8th)
Drysdale

Don Drysdale pitched one of his greatest games as he went the distance to shut out the Yankees on three hits. Drysdale struck out nine Yankees and walked just one batter. The Dodgers scored the only run of the game in the first inning, when Tommy Davis singled to drive in Gilliam as the Dodgers took their third Series game in a row, 1–0.

FOURTH GAME (Oct. 6, at Los Angeles)
NEW YORK. 000 000 100   1 6 1
LOS ANGELES 000 010 10x   2 2 1
Ford, Reniff (8th)
Koufax

Sandy Koufax allowed the Yankees six hits, including a Mickey Mantle homer, and struck out eight batters as the Dodgers won a thrilling 2–1 game to sweep the Series. Koufax and Whitey Ford were a perfect match for this pitching duel. It was a 1–1 tie until the seventh inning, when Junior Gilliam scored on Willie Davis' sacrifice fly to give the Dodgers their most coveted World Series win.

WORLD SERIES BOX SCORES: 1963 (FOUR GAMES)

GAME 1

LOS ANGELES (N.L.)	AB	R	H	O	A	E	NEW YORK (A.L.)	AB	R	H	O	A	E
Wills, ss	5	0	0	2	0	0	Kubek, ss	4	1	1	1	5	0
Gilliam, 3b	4	0	1	1	1	0	Richardson, 2b	3	0	0	2	2	0
W. Davis, cf	3	1	0	1	0	0	Tresh lf	3	1	1	0	0	0
T. Davis, lf	4	0	3	0	0	0	Mantle, cf	3	0	0	1	0	0
F. Howard, rf	4	1	1	0	0	0	Maris, rf	4	0	0	2	0	0
Fairly, rf	0	0	0	0	0	0	E. Howard, c	4	0	1	11	0	0
Skowron, 1b	3	1	2	3	0	0	Pepitone, 1b	4	0	2	8	0	0
Tracewski, 2b	4	1	1	2	2	0	Boyer, 3b	4	0	1	1	2	0
Roseboro, c	4	1	1	18	0	0	Ford, p	1	0	0	1	2	0
Koufax, p	4	0	0	0	1	0	*Lopez	1	0	0	0	0	0
Totals	35	5	9	27	4	0	Williams, p	0	0	0	0	0	0
							†Linz	1	0	0	0	0	0
							Hamilton, p	0	0	0	0	0	0
							‡Bright	1	0	0	0	0	0
							Totals	33	2	6	27	11	0

Los Angeles   0 4 1 0 0 0 0 0 0—5
New York   0 0 0 0 0 0 0 2 0—2

*Struck out for Ford in fifth.
†Struck out for Williams in eighth.
‡Struck out for Hamilton in ninth.
Runs batted in—Skowron 2, Roseboro 3, Tresh 2. Two-base hit—F. Howard. Home runs—Roseboro, Tresh. Stolen base—T. Davis. Sac-

rifice hit—W. Davis. Left on bases—Los Angeles 6, New York 7. Earned runs—Los Angeles 5, New York 2. Bases on balls—Off Koufax 3, off Ford 2. Struck out—By Koufax 15, by Ford 4, by Williams 5, by Hamilton 1. Pitching records—Off Ford 8 hits and 5 runs in 5 innings; off Williams 1 hit and 0 runs in 3 innings; off Hamilton 0 hits and 0 runs in 1 inning. Losing pitcher—Ford.

GAME 2

LOS ANGELES (N.L.)	AB	R	H	O	A	E	NEW YORK (A.L.)	AB	R	H	O	A	E
Wills, ss	4	1	2	2	3	0	Kubek, ss	4	0	0	2	4	0
Gilliam, 3b	4	1	1	1	1	0	Richardson, 2b	4	0	1	3	5	0
W. Davis, cf	4	1	2	3	0	0	Tresh, lf	4	0	2	0	0	0
T. Davis, lf	4	0	2	6	0	0	Mantle, cf	4	0	0	0	0	0
F. Howard, rf	3	0	0	2	0	0	Maris, rf	1	0	0	1	0	0
†Fairly, rf	0	0	0	0	0	0	Lopez, rf	3	1	2	1	0	0
Skowron, 1b	4	1	2	8	1	0	E. Howard, c	4	0	2	6	0	0
Tracewski, 2b	3	0	0	0	1	0	Pepitone, 1b	3	0	0	13	1	0
Roseboro, c	4	0	0	5	0	0	Boyer, 3b	4	0	0	3	0	0
Podres, p	4	0	1	0	2	1	Downing, p	1	0	0	0	1	0
Perranoski, p	0	0	0	0	0	0	*Bright	1	0	0	0	0	0
Totals	34	4	10	27	8	1	Terry, p	0	0	0	1	1	0
							‡Linz	1	0	0	0	0	0
							Reniff, p	0	0	0	0	0	0
							Totals	34	1	7	27	15	0

```
Los Angeles     2 0 0  1 0 0  0 1 0—4
New York        0 0 0  0 0 0  0 0 1—1
```

*Called out on strikes for Downing in fifth.
†Walked intentionally for F. Howard in eighth.
‡Lined out for Terry in eighth.
Runs batted in—W. Davis 2, T. Davis, Skowron, E. Howard. Two-base hits—W. Davis 2, Lopez 2. Three-base hits—T. Davis 2. Home run—Skowron. Stolen base—Wills. Double plays—Richardson, Kubek and Pepitone; Kubek, Richardson and Pepitone; Terry, Richardson and Pepitone. Left on bases—Los Angeles 5, New York 7. Earned runs—Los Angeles 4, New York 1. Bases on balls—Off Podres 1, off Downing 1, off Terry 1. Struck out—By Podres 4, by Perranoski 1, by Downing 6. Pitching record—Off Podres 6 hits and 1 run in 8⅓ innings; of Perranoski 1 hit and 0 runs in ⅔ inning; off Downing 7 hits and 3 runs in 5 innings; off Terry 3 hits and 1 run in 3 innings; off Reniff 0 hits and 0 runs in 1 inning. Winning pitcher—Podres. Losing pitcher—Downing.

GAME 3

NEW YORK (A.L.)	AB	R	H	O	A	E	LOS ANGELES (N.L.)	AB	R	H	O	A	E
Kubek, ss	4	0	2	2	2	0	Wills, ss	4	0	0	1	2	1
Richardson, 2b	3	0	0	1	3	0	Gilliam, 3b	2	1	0	0	0	0
Tresh, lf	4	0	0	2	0	0	W. Davis, cf	3	0	0	0	0	0
Mantle, cf	4	0	1	1	0	0	T. Davis, lf	4	0	1	0	0	0
Pepitone, 1b	3	0	0	8	2	0	Fairly, rf	1	0	0	3	0	0
E. Howard, c	3	0	0	7	1	0	Skowron, 1b	3	0	1	10	2	0
Blanchard, rf	3	0	0	1	0	0	Roseboro, c	3	0	1	9	0	0
Boyer, 3b	2	0	0	1	1	0	Tracewski, 2b	3	0	1	3	3	0
Bouton, p	2	0	0	1	2	0	Drysdale, p	1	0	0	1	3	0
*Berra	1	0	0	0	0	0	Totals	24	1	4	27	10	1
Reniff, p	0	0	0	0	0	0							
Totals	29	0	3	24	11	0							

```
New York        0 0 0  0 0 0  0 0 0—0
Los Angeles     1 0 0  0 0 0  0 0 x—1
```

*Lined out for Bouton in eighth.
Run batted in—T. Davis. Sacrifice hits—Richardson, W. Davis. Double plays—Pepitone, Kubek and Pepitone; Richardson, Pepitone and Kubek. Left on bases—New York 5, Los Angeles 6. Earned run—Los Angeles 1. Bases on balls—Off Bouton 5, off Reniff 1, off Drysdale 1. Struck out—By Bouton 4, by Reniff 1, by Drysdale 9. Hit by pitcher—By Drysdale (Pepitone). Wild pitches—Bouton 2. Pitching record—Off Bouton 4 hits and 1 run in 7 innings; off Reniff 0 hits and 0 runs in 1 inning. Losing pitcher—Bouton.

GAME 4

NEW YORK (A.L.)	AB	R	H	O	A	E	LOS ANGELES (N.L.)	AB	R	H	O	A	E
Kubek, ss	4	0	0	0	2	0	Wills, ss	2	0	0	0	5	0
Richardson, 2b	4	0	2	1	4	0	Gilliam, 3b	3	1	0	0	0	0
Tresh, lf	4	0	0	1	0	0	W. Davis, cf	2	0	0	2	0	0

374 • The Complete Dodgers Record Book

GAME 4 (continued)

NEW YORK (A.L.)	AB	R	H	O	A	E	LOS ANGELES (N.L.)	AB	R	H	O	A	E
Mantle, cf	4	1	1	4	0	0	T. Davis, lf	3	0	0	0	0	0
E. Howard, c	4	0	2	6	1	0	F. Howard, rf	3	1	2	2	0	0
Lopez, rf	4	0	0	1	0	0	Fairly, rf	0	0	0	0	0	0
Pepitone, 1b	3	0	0	8	3	1	Skowron, 1b	3	0	0	9	1	0
Boyer, 3b	3	0	0	0	2	0	Roseboro, c	3	0	0	11	0	0
Ford, p	2	0	0	2	0	0	Tracewski, 2b	3	0	0	2	1	1
*Linz	1	0	1	0	0	0	Koufax, p	2	0	0	1	2	0
Reniff, p	0	0	0	1	0	0	Totals	24	2	2	27	9	1
Totals	33	1	6	24	12	1							

```
New York       0 0 0  0 0 0  1 0 0—1
Los Angeles    0 0 0  0 1 0  1 0 x—2
```

*Singled for Ford in eighth.
Runs batted in—Mantle, W. Davis, Howard. Two-base hit—Richardson. Home run—F. Howard, Mantle. Sacrifice fly—W. Davis. Double plays—E. Howard and Pepitone; Kubek, Richardson and Pepitone; Tracewski and Skowron. Left on bases—New York 5, Los Angeles 0. Earned runs—New York 1, Los Angeles 1. Bases on balls—Off Ford 1. Struck out—By Ford 4, by Koufax 8. Pitching record—Off Ford 2 hits and 2 runs in 7 innings; off Reniff 0 hits and 0 runs in 1 inning. Losing pitcher—Ford.

WORLD SERIES COMPOSITE BOX SCORE: 1963

PITCHING SUMMARY

Los Angeles Dodgers

PITCHER	G	IP	H	R	ER	SO	BB	W	L	ERA
Perranoski	1	⅔	1	0	0	1	0	0	0	0.00
Drysdale	1	9	3	0	0	9	1	1	0	0.00
Podres	1	8⅓	6	1	1	4	1	1	0	1.08
Koufax	2	18	12	3	3	23	3	2	0	1.50
Totals	4	36	22	4	4	37	5	4	0	1.00

New York Yankees

PITCHER	G	IP	H	R	ER	SO	BB	W	L	ERA
Williams	1	3	1	0	0	5	0	0	0	0.00
Reniff	3	3	0	0	0	1	1	0	0	0.00
Hamilton	1	1	0	0	0	1	0	0	0	0.00
Bouton	1	7	4	1	1	4	5	0	1	1.29
Terry	1	3	3	1	1	0	1	0	0	3.00
Ford	2	12	10	7	6	8	3	0	2	4.50
Downing	1	5	7	3	3	6	1	0	1	5.40
Totals	4	34	25	12	11	25	11	0	4	2.91

BATTING SUMMARY

Los Angeles Dodgers

PLAYER-POS.	G	AB	R	H	2B	3B	HR	RBI	BA
T. Davis, lf	4	15	0	6	0	2	0	2	.400
Skowron, 1b	4	13	2	5	0	0	1	3	.385
F. Howard, rf	3	10	2	3	1	0	1	1	.300
Podres, p	1	4	0	1	0	0	0	0	.250
W. Davis, cf	4	12	2	2	2	0	0	3	.167
Gilliam, 3b	4	13	3	2	0	0	0	0	.154
Tracewski, 2b	4	13	1	2	0	0	0	0	.154
Roseboro, c	4	14	1	2	0	0	1	3	.143
Wills, ss	4	15	1	2	0	0	0	0	.133
Koufax, p	2	6	0	0	0	0	0	0	.000
Perranoski, p	1	0	0	0	0	0	0	0	.000
Drysdale, p	1	1	0	0	0	0	0	0	.000
Fairly, rf-pr	4	1	0	0	0	0	0	0	.000
Totals	4	117	12	25	3	2	3	12	.214

New York Yankees

PLAYER-POS.	G	AB	R	H	2B	3B	HR	RBI	BA
Linz, ph	3	3	0	1	0	0	0	0	.333
E. Howard, c	4	15	0	5	0	0	0	1	.333
Lopez, ph-rf	3	8	1	2	2	0	0	0	.250
Tresh, lf	4	15	1	3	0	0	1	2	.200
Richardson, 2b	4	14	0	3	1	0	0	0	.214
Kubek, ss	4	16	1	3	0	0	0	0	.188
Pepitone, 1b	4	13	0	2	0	0	0	0	.154
Mantle, cf	4	15	1	2	0	0	1	1	.133
Boyer, 3b	4	13	0	1	0	0	0	0	.077
Maris, rf	2	5	0	0	0	0	0	0	.000
Ford, p	2	3	0	0	0	0	0	0	.000
Williams, p	1	0	0	0	0	0	0	0	.000
Hamilton, p	1	0	0	0	0	0	0	0	.000
Bright, ph	2	2	0	0	0	0	0	0	.000
Downing, p	1	1	0	0	0	0	0	0	.000
Terry, p	1	0	0	0	0	0	0	0	.000
Reniff, p	3	0	0	0	0	0	0	0	.000
Blanchard, rf	1	3	0	0	0	0	0	0	.000
Bouton, p	1	2	0	0	0	0	0	0	.000
Berra, ph	1	1	0	0	0	0	0	0	.000
Totals	4	129	4	22	3	0	2	4	.171

WORLD SERIES HIGHLIGHTS: 1965

LOS ANGELES (NL) DEFEATS MINNESOTA (AL), 4 GAMES TO 3

FIRST GAME (Oct. 6, at Minnesota)
LOS ANGELES 010 000 001 2 10 1
MINNESOTA....................016 001 00x 8 10 0
Drysdale, Reed (3d), Brewer (5th), Perranoski (7th)
Grant

Zoilo Versalles homered in the third inning with two men on base and the Twins jumped out to a 7–1 lead over the Dodgers. Both teams had 10 hits, but Mudcat Grant scattered the Dodgers hits and struck out five batters on the way to an 8–2 victory.

SECOND GAME (Oct. 7, at Minnesota)
LOS ANGELES 000 000 100 1 7 3
MINNESOTA....................000 002 12x 5 9 0
Koufax, Perranoski (7th), Miller (8th)
Kaat

The Twins continued to pound Dodger pitching in the second game of the Series. The Twins roughed up Sandy Koufax for six hits and two runs in the sixth inning, driving him out of the box. Perranoski relieved Koufax and was belted for three hits and three runs as the Twins took another game by a 5 to 1 score.

THIRD GAME (Oct. 9, at Los Angeles)
MINNESOTA....................000 000 000 0 5 0
LOS ANGELES 000 211 00x 4 10 1
Pascual, Merritt (6th), Klippstein (8th)
Osteen

Claude Osteen held the hard-hitting Twins to five hits and shut them out as the Dodgers came out of their batting slump, cracking 10 hits. Lou Johnson led the attack with two doubles. Ron Fairly, Wills, and Gilliam also slammed two-base hits as the Dodgers rolled over Minnesota, 4–0.

FOURTH GAME (Oct. 10, at Los Angeles)
MINNESOTA....................000 101 000 2 5 2
LOS ANGELES 110 103 01x 7 10 0
Grant, Worthington (6th), Pleis (8th)
Drysdale

Don Drysdale came back with an outstanding pitching effort as he held the Twins to five hits while striking out 11, as the Dodgers continued their heavy hitting in a 7–2 win over the Twins. Killebrew and Oliva homered for the Twins, while Wes Parker and Lou Johnson slammed home runs for the Dodgers. Ron Fairly, the Dodger right fielder, drove in three runs.

FIFTH GAME (Oct. 11, at Los Angeles)
MINNESOTA....................000 000 000 0 4 1
LOS ANGELES 202 100 20x 7 14 0
Kaat, Boswell (3d), Perry (6th)
Koufax

Sandy Koufax regained his pitching form, shutting out the Twins on 4 hits while striking out 10 and notching a 7–0 shutout victory. Maury Wills had four hits, including two doubles, and scored twice as the Dodgers easily took their third straight Series win.

SIXTH GAME (Oct. 13, at Minnesota)
LOS ANGELES 000 000 100 1 6 1
MINNESOTA....................000 203 00x 5 6 1
Osteen, Reed (6th), Miller (8th)
Grant

Jim "Mudcat" Grant held the Dodgers scoreless for six; in the seventh, they scored their only run on Fairly's homer. Grant won his own game with a three-run homer as he pitched and batted the Twins to a 5 to 1 triumph.

SEVENTH GAME (Oct. 14, at Minnesota)
LOS ANGELES 000 200 000 2 7 0
MINNESOTA 000 000 000 0 3 1
Koufax
Kaat, Worthington (4th), Klippstein (6th), Merritt (7th), Perry (9th)

Sandy Koufax was brilliant, fanning 10 Minnesota batters and holding the twins to three base hits as the Dodgers won both a 2–0 victory and another World Series championship. Lou Johnson homered for the Dodgers.

WORLD SERIES BOX SCORES: 1965 (SEVEN GAMES)

GAME 1

LOS ANGELES (N.L.)	AB	R	H	O	A	E	MINNESOTA (A.L.)	AB	R	H	O	A	E
Wills, ss	5	0	2	3	2	0	Versalles, ss	5	1	2	3	2	0
Gilliam, 3b	5	0	1	0	1	0	Valdespino, lf	4	1	1	4	0	0
W. Davis, cf	4	0	1	2	0	0	Oliva, rf	4	0	0	7	0	0
Fairly, rf	4	1	1	2	0	0	Killebrew, 3b	3	1	1	3	0	0
Johnson, lf	4	0	1	4	0	0	Hall, cf	3	0	1	1	0	0
Lefebvre, 2b	4	1	1	0	4	1	Mincher, 1b	3	2	1	3	0	0
Parker, 1b	3	0	1	7	0	0	Battey, c	4	0	1	5	0	0
Roseboro, c	4	0	1	6	0	0	Quilici, 2b	4	1	2	1	1	0
Drysdale, p	1	0	0	0	1	0	Grant, p	3	2	1	0	0	0
Reed, p	0	0	0	0	0	0	Totals	33	8	10	27	3	0
*Crawford	1	0	1	0	0	0							
Brewer, p	0	0	0	0	0	0							
†Moon	1	0	0	0	0	0							
Perranoski, p	0	0	0	0	1	0							
‡LeJohn	1	0	0	0	0	0							
Totals	37	2	10	24	9	1							

```
Los Angeles    0 1 0  0 0 0  0 0 1—2
Minnesota      0 1 6  0 0 1  0 0 x—8
```

*Singled for Reed in fifth.
†Fouled out for Brewer in seventh.
‡Struck out for Perranoski in ninth.
Runs batted in—Wills, Fairly, Versalles 4, Mincher, Battery 2, Quilici. Two-base hits—Quilici, Valdespino, Grant. Home runs—Fairly, Mincher, Versalles. Stolen base—Versalles. Sacrifice hit—Grant. Double play—Perranoski, Wills and Parker. Left on bases—Los Angeles 9, Minnesota 5. Earned runs—Los Angeles 2. Minnesota 4. Bases on balls—Off Drysdale 1, off Perranoski 2, off Grant 1. Struck out—By Drysdale 4, by Reed 1, by Brewer 1, by Grant 5. Pitching records—Off Drysdale 7 hits and 7 runs in 2⅔ innings; off Reed 0 hits and 0 runs in 1⅓ inning; off Brewer 3 hits and 1 run in 2 innings; off Perranoski 0 hits and 0 runs in 2 innings. Wild pitch—Brewer. Losing pitcher—Drysdale.

GAME 2

LOS ANGELES (N.L.)	AB	R	H	O	A	E	MINNESOTA (A.L.)	AB	R	H	O	A	E
Wills, ss	4	0	1	1	2	0	Versalles, ss	5	2	1	0	0	0
Gilliam, 3b	4	0	0	0	0	2	Nossek, cf	3	0	1	4	0	0
W. Davis, cf	4	0	0	1	0	0	Oliva, rf	4	1	1	3	0	0
Johnson, lf	4	0	0	3	0	1	Killebrew, 3b	3	0	2	2	1	0
Fairly, rf	4	1	2	1	0	0	Battey, c	4	0	1	3	1	0
Lefebvre, 2b	4	0	2	2	0	0	Allison, lf	4	1	1	2	0	0
Parker, 1b	1	0	1	3	1	0	Mincher, 1b	4	1	1	7	4	0
Roseboro, c	4	0	1	12	1	0	Quilici, 2b	2	0	0	1	3	0
Koufax, p	2	0	0	1	2	0	Kaat, p	4	0	1	5	0	0
*Drysdale	1	0	0	0	0	0	Totals	33	5	9	27	9	0
Perranoski, p	0	0	0	0	0	0							
Miller, p	0	0	0	0	0	0							
†Tracewski	1	0	0	0	0	0							
Totals	33	1	7	24	6	3							

```
Los Angeles    0 0 0  0 0 0  1 0 0—1
Minnesota      0 0 0  0 0 2  1 2 x—5
```

*Struck out for Koufax in seventh.
†Lined out for Miller in ninth.
Runs batted in—Roseboro, Oliva, Killebrew, Kaat 2. Two-base hits—Oliva, Allison. Three-base hit—Versalles. Sacrifice hits—Parker, Nossek. Left on bases—Los Angeles 8, Minnesota 8. Earned runs—Los Angeles 1, Minnesota 4. Bases on balls—Off Koufax 1, off Perranoski 2, off Kaat 1. Struck out—By Koufax 9, by Perranoski 1, Kaat 3. Pitching records—Off Koufax 6 hits and 2 runs in 6 innings; off Perranoski 3 hits and 3 runs in 1⅔ innings; off Miller 0 hits and 0 runs in ⅓ inning. Hit by pitcher—By Kaat (Parker). Wild pitch—Perranoski. Balk—Perranoski. Losing pitcher Koufax.

GAME 3

MINNESOTA (A.L.)	AB	R	H	O	A	E	LOS ANGELES (N.L.)	AB	R	H	O	A	E
Versalles, ss	3	0	2	3	3	0	Wills, ss	4	0	1	2	5	0
Nossek, cf	4	0	1	3	0	0	Gilliam, 3b	4	0	1	1	1	0
Oliva, rf	4	0	1	2	0	0	Kennedy, 3b	0	0	0	0	0	1
Killebrew, 3b	3	0	0	1	1	0	W. Davis, cf	4	1	1	2	0	0
Battey, c	3	0	0	0	0	0	Fairly, rf	4	1	1	1	0	0
Zimmerman, c	1	0	0	1	1	0	Johnson, lf	2	0	2	0	0	0
Allison, lf	3	0	0	3	0	0	Lefebvre, 2b	2	1	1	1	3	0
Mincher, 1b	3	0	1	7	0	0	Tracewski, 2b	2	0	0	2	3	0
Quilici, 2b	3	0	0	4	2	0	Parker, 1b	3	1	1	14	2	0
Pascual, p	1	0	0	0	1	0	Roseboro, c	3	0	1	2	2	0
*Rollins	1	0	0	0	0	0	Osteen, p	2	0	1	2	2	0
Merritt, p	0	0	0	0	2	0	Totals	30	4	10	27	18	1
†Valdespino	1	0	0	0	0	0							
Klippstein, p	0	0	0	0	0	0							
Totals	30	0	5	24	10	0							

```
Minnesota      0 0 0   0 0 0   0 0 0—0
Los Angeles    0 0 0   2 1 1   0 0 x—4
```

*Grounded out for Pascual in sixth.
†Popped out for Merritt in eighth.
Runs batted in—Wills, Johnson, Roseboro 2. Two-base hits—Versalles, Gilliam, Johnson 2, Fairly, Wills. Stolen bases—Wills, Parker, Roseboro. Sacrifice hits—Johnson, Osteen. Double plays—Tracewski and Parker; Zimmerman and Versalles; Wills and Parker. Left on bases—Minnesota 5, Los Angeles 6. Earned runs—Minnesota 0, Los Angeles 4. Bases on balls—Off Pascual 1, off Klippstein 1, off Osteen 2. Struck out—By Klippstein 1, by Osteen 2. Pitching records—Off Pascual 8 hits and 3 runs in 5 innings; off Merrit 2 hits and 1 run in 2 innings; off Klippstein 0 hits and 0 runs in 1 inning. Losing pitcher—Pascual.

GAME 4

MINNESOTA (A.L.)	AB	R	H	O	A	E	LOS ANGELES (N.L.)	AB	R	H	O	A	E
Versalles, ss	4	0	1	3	2	0	Wills, ss	4	1	2	1	2	0
Valdespino, lf	4	0	1	2	0	0	Gilliam, 3b	2	1	0	1	1	0
Oliva, rf	4	1	1	2	0	0	*Kennedy, 3b	0	0	0	0	1	0
Killebrew, 3b	2	1	1	1	0	0	W. Davis, cf	4	1	2	3	0	0
Hall, cf	4	0	0	1	0	0	Fairly, rf	4	1	1	1	0	0
Mincher, 1b	4	0	0	8	0	0	Johnson, lf	4	1	2	1	1	0
Battey, c	3	0	0	3	2	0	Parker, 1b	4	2	2	8	0	0
Zimmerman, c	0	0	0	1	0	0	Roseboro, c	3	0	1	10	1	0
Quilici, 2b	3	0	0	3	3	1	Tracewski, 2b	4	0	0	2	3	0
Grant, p	2	0	0	0	0	0	Drysdale, p	3	0	0	0	1	0
Worthington, p	0	0	0	0	0	1	Totals	32	7	10	27	10	0
†Nossek	1	0	1	0	0	0							
Pleis, p	0	0	0	0	1	0							
Totals	31	2	5	24	8	2							

```
Minnesota      0 0 0   1 0 1   0 0 0—2
Los Angeles    1 1 0   1 0 3   0 1 x—7
```

*Ran for Gilliam in seventh.
†Singled for Worthingotn in eighth.
Runs batted in—Oliva, Killebrew, Fairly 3, Johnson, Parker. Home runs—Killebrew, Parker, Oliva, Johnson. Stolen bases—Wills, Parker. Double play—Battey and Versalles. Left on bases—Minnesota 4, Los Angeles 4. Earned runs—Minnesota 2, Los Angeles 5. Bases on balls—Off Grant 1, off Worthington 1, off Drysdale 2. Struck out—By Grant 2, by Worthington 2, by Drysdale 11. Pitching records—Off Grant 6 hits and 5 runs in 5 innings (pitched to two batters in sixth); off Worthington 2 hits and 1 run in 2 innings; off Pleis 2 hits and 1 run in 1 inning. Hit by pitcher—By Worthington (Gilliam). Wild pitch—Grant. Losing pitcher—Grant.

GAME 5

MINNESOTA (A.L.)	AB	R	H	O	A	E	LOS ANGELES (N.L.)	AB	R	H	O	A	E
Versalles, ss	4	0	0	2	0	0	Wills, ss	5	2	4	1	7	0
Nossek, cf	4	0	1	2	0	0	Gilliam, 3b	4	1	2	0	0	0
Oliva, rf	3	0	0	2	0	0	Kennedy, 3b	1	0	0	0	0	0
Killebrew, 3b	3	0	1	1	2	0	W. Davis, cf	4	1	2	1	0	0
Battey, c	3	0	0	7	1	0	Johnson, lf	5	1	1	2	0	0
Allison, lf	2	0	0	3	0	0	Fairly, rf	5	1	3	2	0	0
Mincher, 1b	3	0	0	5	0	0	Parker, 1b	4	0	0	7	0	0
Quilici, 2b	3	0	1	2	3	1	Tracewski, 2b	3	0	1	4	2	0
Kaat, p	1	0	0	0	1	0	Roseboro, c	2	1	0	10	0	0
Boswell, p	0	0	0	0	0	0	Koufax, p	4	0	1	0	1	0
*Rollins	1	0	0	0	0	0	Totals	37	7	14	27	10	0
Perry, p	0	0	0	0	1	0							
†Valdespino	1	0	1	0	0	0							
Totals	28	0	4	24	8	1							

```
Minnesota      0 0 0  0 0 0  0 0 0—0
Los Angeles    2 0 2  1 0 0  2 0 x—7
```

*Flied out for Boswell in sixth.
†Singled for Perry in ninth.
Runs batted in—Wills, Gilliam 2, Johnson, Fairly, Koufax. Two-base hits—Wills 2, Fairly. Stolen bases—W. Davis 3, Wills. Sacrifice hits—W. Davis, Parker. Double plays—Wills, Tracewski and Parker 2; Wills and Tracewski. Left on bases—Minnesota 2, Los Angeles 11. Earned runs—Minnesota 0, Los Angeles 6. Bases on balls—Off Boswell 2, off Perry 1, off Koufax 1. Struck out—By Kaat 1, by Boswell 3, by Perry 3, by Koufax 10. Pitching records—off Kaat 6 hits and 4 runs in 2⅓ innings; off Boswell 3 hits and 1 run in 2⅔ innings; off Perry 5 hits and 2 runs in 3 innings. Losing pitcher—Kaat.

GAME 6

LOS ANGELES (N.L.)	AB	R	H	O	A	E	MINNESOTA (A.L.)	AB	R	H	O	A	E
Wills, ss	4	0	1	4	4	0	Versalles, ss	3	0	1	2	3	0
Gilliam, 3b	4	0	0	0	3	0	Nossek, cf	4	0	0	4	0	0
W. Davis, cf	4	0	0	1	0	0	Oliva, rf	4	0	2	0	0	0
Fairly, rf	4	1	2	1	0	0	Killebrew, 3b	4	0	0	1	1	1
Johnson, lf	4	0	1	0	0	0	Battey, c	4	1	1	5	1	0
Parker, 1b	4	0	0	10	1	0	Allison, lf	3	2	1	2	0	0
Roseboro, c	3	0	1	5	0	0	Mincher, 1b	3	0	0	11	0	0
Tracewski, 2b	3	0	1	2	3	1	Quilici, 2b	2	1	0	2	4	0
Osteen, p	1	0	0	0	1	0	Grant, p	3	1	1	0	1	0
*Crawford	1	0	0	0	0	0	Totals	30	5	6	27	10	1
Reed, p	0	0	0	1	0	0							
†Moon	1	0	0	0	0	0							
Miller, p	0	0	0	0	0	0							
Totals	33	1	6	24	12	1							

```
Los Angeles    0 0 0  0 0 0  1 0 0—1
Minnesota      0 0 0  2 0 3  0 0 x—5
```

*Struck out for Osteen in sixth.
†Grounded out for Reed in eighth.
Runs batted in—Fairly, Allison 2, Grant 3. Three-base hit—Battey. Home runs—Fairly, Allison, Grant. Stolen base—Allison. Double plays—Osteen, Wills and Parker; Battey and Versalles. Left on bases—Los Angeles 5, Minnesota 6. Earned runs—Los Angeles 1, Minnesota 4. Bases on balls—Off Osteen 3, off Reed 2. Struck out—By Osteen 2, by Reed 3, by Grant 5. Pitching records—Off Osteen 4 hits and 2 runs in 5 innings; off Reed 2 hits and 3 runs in 2 innings; off Miller 0 hits and 0 runs in 1 inning. Losing pitcher—Osteen.

GAME 7

LOS ANGELES (N.L.)	AB	R	H	O	A	E	MINNESOTA (A.L.)	AB	R	H	O	A	E
Wills, ss	4	0	0	2	4	0	Versalles, ss	4	0	1	0	2	0
Gilliam, 3b	5	0	2	2	1	0	Nossek, cf	4	0	0	0	0	0
Kennedy, 3b	0	0	0	0	1	0	Oliva, rf	3	0	0	4	0	1
W. Davis, cf	2	0	0	1	0	0	Killebrew, 3b	3	0	1	2	2	0
Johnson, lf	4	1	1	3	0	0	Battey, c	4	0	0	8	1	0
Fairly, rf	4	1	1	0	0	0	Allison, lf	4	0	0	1	0	0
Parker, 1b	4	0	2	6	0	0	Mincher, 1b	3	0	0	10	0	0

GAME 7 (continued)

LOS ANGELES (N.L.)	AB	R	H	O	A	E	MINNESOTA (A.L.)	AB	R	H	O	A	E
Tracewski, 2b	4	0	0	1	0	0	Quilici, 2b	3	0	1	1	3	0
Roseboro, c	2	0	1	12	0	0	Kaat, p	1	0	0	0	1	0
Koufax, p	3	0	0	0	1	0	Worthington, p	0	0	0	1	1	0
							*Rollins	0	0	0	0	0	0
Totals	32	2	7	27	7	0	Klippstein, p	0	0	0	0	0	0
							Merritt, p	0	0	0	0	0	0
							†Valdespino	1	0	0	0	0	0
							Perry, p	0	0	0	0	0	0
							Totals	30	0	3	27	10	1

```
Los Angeles     0 0 0   2 0 0   0 0 0—2
Minnesota       0 0 0   0 0 0   0 0 0—0
```

*Walked for Worthington in fifth.
†Flied out for Merritt in eighth.

Runs batted in—Johnson, Parker. Two-base hits—Roseboro, Fairly, Quilici. Three-base hit—Parker. Home run—Johnson. Sacrifice hit—W. Davis. Left on bases—Los Angeles 9, Minnesota 6. Earned runs—Los Angeles 2, Minnesota 0. Bases on balls—Off Koufax 3, off Kaat 1, off Worthington 1, off Klippstein 1, off Perry 1. Struck out—By Koufax 10, by Kaat 2, by Klippstein 2, by Merritt 1, by Perry 1. Pitching records—Off Kaat 5 hits and 2 runs in 3 innings (pitched to three batters in fourth), off Worthington 0 hits and 0 runs in 2 innings; off Klippstein 2 hits and 0 runs in 1⅔ innings; off Merritt 0 hits and 0 runs in 1⅓ innings; off Perry 0 hits and 0 runs in 1 inning. Hit by pitcher—By Klippstein (W. Davis). Losing pitcher—Kaat.

WORLD SERIES COMPOSITE BOX SCORE: 1965

PITCHING SUMMARY

Los Angeles Dodgers PITCHER	G	IP	H	R	ER	SO	BB	W	L	ERA	Minnesota Twins PITCHER	G	IP	H	R	ER	SO	BB	W	L	ERA
Miller	2	1⅓	0	0	0	0	0	0	0	0.00	Worthington	2	4	2	1	0	2	2	0	0	0.00
Koufax	3	24	13	2	1	29	5	2	1	0.38	Klippstein	2	2⅔	2	0	0	3	2	0	0	0.00
Osteen	2	14	9	2	1	4	5	1	1	0.64	Merritt	2	3⅓	2	1	1	1	0	0	0	2.70
Drysdale	2	11⅔	12	9	5	15	3	1	1	3.86	Grant	3	23	22	8	7	12	2	2	1	2.74
Brewer	1	2	3	1	1	1	0	0	0	4.50	Boswell	1	2⅔	3	1	1	3	2	0	0	3.38
Perranoski	2	3⅔	3	3	3	1	4	0	0	7.36	Kaat	3	14⅓	18	7	6	6	2	1	2	3.77
Reed	2	3⅓	2	3	3	4	2	0	0	8.10	Perry	2	4	5	2	2	4	2	0	0	4.50
											Pascual	1	5	8	3	3	0	1	0	1	5.40
											Pleis	1	1	2	1	1	0	0	0	0	9.00
Totals	7	60	42	20	14	54	19	4	3	2.10	Totals	7	60	64	24	21	31	13	3	4	3.15

BATTING SUMMARY

Los Angeles Dodgers PLAYER-POS.	G	AB	R	H	2B	3B	HR	RBI	BA	Minnesota Twins PLAYER-POS.	G	AB	R	H	2B	3B	HR	RBI	BA
Lefebvre, 2b	3	10	2	4	0	0	0	0	.400	Killebrew, 3b	7	21	2	6	0	0	1	2	.286
Fairly, rf	7	29	7	11	3	0	2	6	.379	Versalles, ss	7	28	3	8	1	1	1	4	.286
Wills, ss	7	30	3	11	3	0	0	3	.367	Valdespino, lf-ph	5	11	1	3	1	0	0	0	.273
Osteen, p	2	3	0	1	0	0	0	0	.333	Grant, p	3	8	3	2	1	0	1	3	.250
Parker, 1b	7	23	3	7	0	1	1	2	.304	Nossek, cf-ph	6	20	0	4	0	0	0	0	.200
Johnson, lf	7	27	3	8	2	0	2	4	.296	Quilici, 2b	7	20	2	4	2	0	0	1	.200
Roseboro, c	7	21	1	6	1	0	0	3	.286	Oliva, rf	7	26	2	5	1	0	1	2	.192
W. Davis, cf	7	26	3	6	0	0	0	0	.231	Kaat, p	3	6	0	1	0	0	0	2	.167
Gilliam, 3b	7	28	2	6	1	0	0	2	.214	Hall, cf	2	7	1	1	0	0	0	0	.143
Tracewski, ph-2b	6	17	0	2	0	0	0	0	.118	Mincher, 1b	7	23	3	3	0	0	1	1	.130
Koufax, p	3	9	0	1	0	0	0	1	.111	Allison, lf	5	16	3	2	1	0	1	2	.125
Kennedy, 3b-pr	4	1	0	0	0	0	0	0	.000	Battey, c	7	25	1	3	0	1	0	2	.120
Reed, p	2	0	0	0	0	0	0	0	.000	Zimmerman, c	2	1	0	0	0	0	0	0	.000
Brewer, p	1	0	0	0	0	0	0	0	.000	Pascual, p	1	1	0	0	0	0	0	0	.000
Perranoski, p	2	0	0	0	0	0	0	0	.000	Merritt, p	2	0	0	0	0	0	0	0	.000
Miller, p	2	0	0	0	0	0	0	0	.000	Klippstein, p	2	0	0	0	0	0	0	0	.000
Drysdale, p-ph	3	5	0	0	0	0	0	0	.000	Worthington, p	2	0	0	0	0	0	0	0	.000
Crawford, ph	2	2	0	1	0	0	0	0	.500	Pleis, p	1	0	0	0	0	0	0	0	.000

BATTING SUMMARY (continued)

Los Angeles Dodgers

PLAYER-POS.	G	AB	R	H	2B	3B	HR	RBI	BA
Moon, ph	2	2	0	0	0	0	0	0	.000
LeJohn, ph	1	1	0	0	0	0	0	0	.000
Totals	7	234	24	64	10	1	5	21	.274

Minnesota Twins

PLAYER-POS.	G	AB	R	H	2B	3B	HR	RBI	BA
Boswell, p	1	0	0	0	0	0	0	0	.000
Perry, p	2	0	0	0	0	0	0	0	.000
Rollins, ph	3	2	0	0	0	0	0	0	.000
Totals	7	215	20	42	7	2	6	19	.195

WORLD SERIES HIGHLIGHTS: 1966

BALTIMORE (AL) DEFEATS LOS ANGELES (NL), 4 GAMES TO 0

FIRST GAME (Oct. 5, at Los Angeles)
BALTIMORE 310 100 000   5 9 0
LOS ANGELES 011 000 000   2 3 0
McNally, Drabowsky (3d)
Drysdale, Moeller (3d), R. Miller (5th), Perranoski (8th)

Don Drysdale was hit hard in the first inning when the Robinson boys, Frank and Brooks, hit successive home runs and the Orioles jumped out to a 3–0 lead. But the Dodgers kept chipping away at McNally, scoring a run in the second inning and another in the third. Then Moe Drabowsky came in to relieve McNally and handcuffed the Dodgers for 6⅔ innings. Drabowsky struck out 11 while allowing the Dodgers just one hit the rest of the way.

SECOND GAME (Oct. 6, at Los Angeles)
BALTIMORE 000 031 020   6 8 0
LOS ANGELES 000 000 000   0 4 6
Palmer
Koufax, Perranoski (7th), Regan (8th), Brewer (9th)

Jim Palmer outpitched Sandy Koufax, who was not up to his usual form, as a result, the Orioles reached Sandy for six hits and four runs and a 6–0 win. Palmer set down the Dodgers with four base hits while striking out six.

THIRD GAME (Oct. 8, at Baltimore)
LOS ANGELES 000 000 000   0 6 0
BALTIMORE 000 010 00x   1 3 0
Osteen, Regan (8th)
Bunker

The Orioles only managed three hits off Dodger pitcher Claude Osteen, but one of them was a home run by Paul Blair that was enough to insure an Oriole victory by a 1–0 score.

FOURTH GAME (Oct. 9, at Baltimore)
LOS ANGELES 000 000 000   0 4 0
BALTIMORE 000 100 00x   1 4 0
Drysdale
McNally

Don Drysdale and the Orioles' Dave McNally hooked up in one of the most exciting pitching duels in World Series history. Both pitchers allowed only four hits; the big difference was a dramatic 400-foot home run by Frank Robinson in the fourth inning that gave the Orioles a 1–0 victory and the World's championship in a four-game sweep over the Dodgers.

WORLD SERIES BOX SCORES: 1966 (FOUR GAMES)

GAME 1

BALTIMORE (A.L.)	AB	R	H	O	A	E	LOS ANGELES (N.L.)	AB	R	H	O	A	E
Aparicio, ss	5	0	0	4	1	0	Wills, ss	3	0	0	6	5	0
Snyder, cf-lf	3	1	1	2	0	0	W. Davis, cf	4	0	1	1	0	0

GAME 1 (continued)

BALTIMORE (A.L.)	AB	R	H	O	A	E	LOS ANGELES (N.L.)	AB	R	H	O	A	E
F. Robinson, rf	5	1	2	1	0	0	L. Johnson, rf	3	1	0	3	0	0
B. Robinson, 3b	5	1	1	2	1	0	T. Davis, lf	3	0	0	1	0	0
Powell, 1b	5	0	1	3	0	0	Lefebvre, 2b	3	1	1	3	5	0
Blefary, lf	3	0	1	2	0	0	Parker, 1b	4	0	1	9	0	0
Blair, cf	0	0	0	0	0	0	Gilliam, 3b	2	0	0	1	1	0
D. Johnson, 2b	4	1	2	0	2	0	Roseboro, c	4	0	0	3	0	0
Etchebarren, c	3	1	1	13	0	0	Drysdale, p	0	0	0	0	1	0
McNally, p	0	0	0	0	0	0	*Stuart	1	0	0	0	0	0
Drabowsky, p	2	0	0	0	0	0	Moeller, p	0	0	0	0	0	0
Totals	35	5	9	27	4	0	†Barbieri	1	0	0	0	0	0
							R. Miller, p	0	0	0	0	1	0
							‡Covington	1	0	0	0	0	0
							Perranoski, p	0	0	0	0	1	0
							§Fairly	1	0	0	0	0	0
							Totals	30	2	3	27	14	0

Baltimore   3 1 0 1 0 0 0 0 0—5
Los Angeles   0 1 1 0 0 0 0 0 0—2

*Flied out for Drysdale in second.
†Struck out for Moeller in fourth.
‡Struck out for R. Miller in seventh.
§Struck out for Perranoski in ninth.
Runs batted in—Aparicio, Snyder, F. Robinson 2, B. Robinson, Lefebvre, Gilliam. Two-base hits—Parker, D. Johnson, Powell. Home runs—F. Robinson, B. Robinson, Lefebvre. Stolen base—Wills. Sacrifice hit—McNally. Left on bases—Baltimore 9, Los Angeles 8. Earned runs—Baltimore 5, Los Angeles 2. Bases on balls—Off McNally 5, off Drabowsky 2, off Drysdale 2, off Moeller 1, off R. Miller 2. Struck out—By McNally 1, by Drabowsky 11, by Drysdale 1, by R. Miller 1, by Perranoski 1. Pitching records—Off McNally 2 hits and 2 runs in 2⅓ innings; off Drabowsky 1 hit and 0 runs in 6⅔ innings; off Drysdays 4 hits and 4 runs in 2 innings; off Moeller 1 hit and 1 run in 2 innings; off R. Miller 2 hits and 0 runs in 3 innings; off Perranoski 2 hits and 0 runs in 2 innings. Winning pitcher—Drabowsky. Losing pitcher—Drysdale.

GAME 2

BALTIMORE (A.L.)	AB	R	H	O	A	E	LOS ANGELES (N.L.)	AB	R	H	O	A	E
Aparicio, ss	5	0	2	4	1	0	Wills, ss	4	0	0	3	1	0
Blefary, lf	5	0	0	1	0	0	Gilliam, 3b	4	0	0	2	3	1
F. Robinson, rf	3	2	1	1	0	0	W. Davis, cf	4	0	0	2	0	3
B. Robinson, 3b	4	1	1	1	1	0	Fairly, rf	3	0	0	3	0	1
Powell, 1b	3	1	2	8	0	0	Lefebvre, 2b	3	0	0	3	0	0
D. Johnson, 2b	4	0	2	2	4	0	L. Johnson, lf	4	0	1	1	0	0
Blair, cf	3	1	0	4	0	0	Roseboro, c	4	0	1	8	1	0
Etchebarren, c	3	1	0	6	0	0	Parker, 1b	2	0	1	5	1	0
Palmer, p	4	0	0	0	2	0	Koufax, p	2	0	0	0	1	0
Totals	34	6	8	27	8	0	Perranoski, p	0	0	0	0	1	1
							Regan, p	0	0	0	0	0	0
							*T. Davis	1	0	1	0	0	0
							Brewer, p	0	0	0	0	0	0
							Totals	31	0	4	27	8	6

Baltimore   0 0 0 0 3 1 0 2 0—6
Los Angeles   0 0 0 0 0 0 0 0 0—0

*Singled for Regan for eighth.
Runs batted in—Aparicio, Powell, D. Johnson. Two-base hits—L. Johnson, Aparicio. Three-base hits—F. Robinson. Sacrifice hit—Powell. Double play—Gilliam, Roseboro and Parker. Left on bases—Baltimore 6, Los Angeles 7. Earned runs—Baltimore 3. Bases on balls—Off Palmer 3, off Koufax 2, off Perranoski 1, off Regan 1. Struck out—By Palmer 6, by Koufax 2, by Perranoski 1, by Regan 1, by Brewer 1. Pitching records—Off Koufax 6 hits and 4 runs in 6 innings; off Perranoski 2 hits and 2 runs in 1⅓ innings; off Regan 0 hits and 0 runs in ⅔ innings; off Brewer 0 hits and 0 runs in 1 inning. Wild pitches—Regan, Palmer. Winning pitcher—Palmer. Losing pitcher—Koufax.

GAME 3

LOS ANGELES (N.L.)	AB	R	H	O	A	E	BALTIMORE (A.L.)	AB	R	H	O	A	E
Wills, ss	3	0	1	1	6	0	Aparicio, ss	3	0	1	1	3	0
Parker, 1b	4	0	1	10	1	0	Blefary, lf	3	0	0	3	0	0
Regan, p	0	0	0	0	1	0	Snyder, lf	0	0	0	0	0	0

GAME 3 (continued)

LOS ANGELES (N.L.)	AB	R	H	O	A	E
W. Davis, cf	4	0	0	2	0	0
Fairly, rf-1b	3	0	1	2	0	0
Lefebvre, 2b	4	0	0	3	4	0
L. Johnson, lf-rf	4	0	2	1	0	0
Roseboro, c	3	0	0	4	0	0
Kennedy, 3b	3	0	0	0	2	0
Osteen, p	2	0	0	1	0	0
*T. Davis, lf	1	0	1	0	0	0
Totals	31	0	6	24	14	0

BALTIMORE (A.L.)	AB	R	H	O	A	E
F. Robinson, rf	3	0	0	1	0	0
B. Robinson, 3b	2	0	0	1	1	0
Powell, 1b	3	0	1	9	1	0
D. Johnson, 2b	3	0	0	3	3	0
Blair, cf	3	1	1	3	0	0
Etchebarren, c	3	0	0	6	0	0
Bunker, p	2	0	0	0	3	0
Totals	25	1	3	27	11	0

```
Los Angeles    0 0 0   0 0 0   0 0 0—0
Baltimore      0 0 0   0 1 0   0 0 x—1
```

*Singled for Osteen in eighth.
Run batted in—Blair. Two-base hit—Parker. Home run—Blair. Sacrifice hit—Wills. Double plays—Aparicio, D. Johnson and Powell; Wills, Lefebvre and Parker; Lefebvre, Wills and Parker. Left on bases—Los Angeles 6, Baltimore 1. Earned run—Baltimore 1. Bases on balls—Off Osteen 1, off Bunker 1. Struck out by Osteen 3, By Regan 1, by Bunker 6. Pitching records—Off Osteen 3 hits and 1 run in 7 innings; off Regan 0 hits and 0 runs in 1 inning. Winning pitcher—Bunker. Losing pitcher—Osteen.

GAME 4

LOS ANGELES (N.L.)	AB	R	H	O	A	E
Wills, ss	3	0	0	2	3	0
W. Davis, cf	4	0	0	1	0	0
L. Johnson, rf	4	0	1	4	0	0
T. Davis, lf	3	0	0	2	0	0
Lefebvre, 2b	2	0	1	1	1	0
Parker, 1b	3	0	0	7	0	0
Roseboro, c	3	0	0	7	1	0
Kennedy, 3b	2	0	1	0	1	0
*Stuart	1	0	0	0	0	0
Drysdale, p	2	0	0	0	2	0
†Ferrara	1	0	1	0	0	0
‡Oliver	0	0	0	0	0	0
Totals	28	0	4	24	8	0

BALTIMORE (A.L.)	AB	R	H	O	A	E
Aparicio, ss	3	0	1	0	3	0
Snyder, cf-lf	3	0	0	0	0	0
F. Robinson, rf	3	1	1	3	0	0
B. Robinson, 3b	3	0	1	0	3	0
Powell, 1b	3	0	1	7	0	0
Blefary, lf	2	0	0	1	0	0
Blair, cf	0	0	0	2	0	0
D. Johnson, 2b	3	0	0	7	3	0
Etchebarren, c	3	0	0	7	1	0
McNally, p	3	0	0	0	0	0
Totals	26	1	4	27	10	0

```
Los Angeles    0 0 0   0 0 0   0 0 0—0
Baltimore      0 0 0   1 0 0   0 0 x—1
```

*Struck out for Kennedy in ninth.
†Singled for Drysdale in ninth.
‡Ran for Ferrara in ninth.
Run batted in—F. Robinson. Home run—F. Robinson. Double plays—Lefebvre, Wills and Parker; Aparicio, D. Johnson and Powell; B. Robinson, D. Johnson and Powell; Etchebarren and D. Johnson. Left on bases—Los Angeles 3, Baltimore 2. Earned run—Baltimore 1. Bases on balls—Off Drysdale 1, off McNally 2. Struck out—By Drysdale 5, by McNally 4. Winning pitcher—McNally. Losing pitcher—Drysdale.

WORLD SERIES COMPOSITE BOX SCORE: 1966

PITCHING SUMMARY

Baltimore Orioles

PITCHER	G	IP	H	R	ER	SO	BB	W	L	ERA
Palmer	1	9	4	0	0	6	3	1	0	0.00
Bunker	1	9	6	0	0	6	1	1	0	0.00
Drabowsky	1	6⅔	1	0	0	11	2	1	0	0.00
McNally	2	11⅓	6	2	2	5	7	1	0	1.59
Totals	4	36	17	2	2	28	13	4	0	0.50

Los Angeles Dodgers

PITCHER	G	IP	H	R	ER	SO	BB	W	L	ERA
R. Miller	1	3	2	0	0	1	2	0	0	0.00
Regan	2	1⅔	0	0	0	2	1	0	0	0.00
Brewer	1	1	0	0	0	1	0	0	0	0.00
Osteen	1	7	3	1	1	3	1	0	1	1.29
Koufax	1	6	6	4	1	2	2	0	1	1.50
Drysdale	2	10	8	5	5	6	3	0	2	4.50
Moeller	1	2	1	1	1	0	1	0	0	4.50
Perranoski	2	3⅓	4	2	2	2	1	0	0	5.40
Totals	4	34	24	13	10	17	11	0	4	2.65

BATTING SUMMARY

Baltimore Orioles

PLAYER-POS.	G	AB	R	H	2B	3B	HR	RBI	BA
Powell, 1b	4	14	1	5	1	0	0	1	.357
F. Robinson, rf	4	14	4	4	0	1	2	3	.286
D. Johnson, 2b	4	14	1	4	1	0	0	1	.286
Aparicio, ss	4	16	0	4	1	0	0	2	.250
B. Robinson, 3b	4	14	2	3	0	0	1	1	.214
Snyder, cf-lf	3	6	1	1	0	0	0	1	.167
Blair, cf	4	6	2	1	0	0	1	1	.167
Etchebarren, c	4	12	2	1	0	0	0	0	.083
Blefary, lf	4	13	0	1	0	0	0	0	.077
McNally, p	2	3	0	0	0	0	0	0	.000
Drabowsky, p	1	2	0	0	0	0	0	0	.000
Palmer, p	1	4	0	0	0	0	0	0	.000
Bunker, p	1	2	0	0	0	0	0	0	.000
Total	4	120	13	24	3	1	4	10	.200

Los Angeles Dodgers

PLAYER-POS.	G	AB	R	H	2B	3B	HR	RBI	BA
Ferrara, ph	1	1	0	1	0	0	0	0	1.000
L. Johnson, rf-lf	4	15	1	4	1	0	0	0	.267
T. Davis, lf-ph	4	8	0	2	0	0	0	0	.250
Parker, 1b	4	13	0	3	2	0	0	0	.231
Kennedy, 3b	2	5	0	1	0	0	0	0	.200
Lefebvre, 2b	4	12	1	2	0	0	1	1	.167
Fairly, ph-rf-1b	3	7	0	1	0	0	0	0	.143
Wills, ss	4	13	0	1	0	0	0	0	.077
Roseboro, c	4	14	0	1	0	0	0	0	.071
W. Davis, cf	4	16	0	1	0	0	0	0	.063
Gilliam, 3b	2	6	0	0	0	0	0	1	.000
Drysdale, p	2	2	0	0	0	0	0	0	.000
Moeller, p	1	0	0	0	0	0	0	0	.000
R. Miller, p	1	0	0	0	0	0	0	0	.000
Perranoski, p	2	0	0	0	0	0	0	0	.000
Koufax, p	1	2	0	0	0	0	0	0	.000
Regan, p	2	0	0	0	0	0	0	0	.000
Brewer, p.	1	0	0	0	0	0	0	0	.000
Osteen, p	1	2	0	0	0	0	0	0	.000
Covington, ph	1	1	0	0	0	0	0	0	.000
Barbieri, ph	1	1	0	0	0	0	0	0	.000
Stuart, ph	2	2	0	0	0	0	0	0	.000
Oliver, pr	1	0	0	0	0	0	0	0	.000
Totals	4	120	2	17	3	0	1	2	.142

WORLD SERIES HIGHLIGHTS: 1974

OAKLAND (AL) DEFEATS LOS ANGELES (NL), 4 GAMES TO 1

```
FIRST GAME (Oct. 12, at Los Angeles)
OAKLAND . . . . . . . . . . . . . . . . . . . . . . .010 010 010   3  6  2
LOS ANGELES . . . . . . . . . . . . . . . . . .000 010 001   2 11  1
Holtzman (5), Fingers (5), Hunter (9)
Messersmith (8), Marshall (9)
```

Reggie Jackson homered in the second inning of a game marked by outstanding pitching by Ken Holtzman, the Oakland hurler, and Andy Messersmith of the Dodgers. After Jackson's home run Oakland never relinquished the lead in a close game they finally won, 3 to 2.

```
SECOND GAME (Oct. 13, at Los Angeles)
OAKLAND . . . . . . . . . . . . . . . . . . . . . . .000 000 002   2  6  0
LOS ANGELES . . . . . . . . . . . . . . . . . .010 002 00x   3  6  1
Blue (7), Odom (8)
Sutton (8), Marshall (9)
```

Don Sutton limited the Oakland A's to only five hits and struck out nine as he outpitched Vida Blue to give the Dodgers a 3–2 victory in the second game of the Series. Joe Ferguson homered in the sixth inning to provide the Dodgers with the margin of victory.

```
THIRD GAME (Oct. 15, at Oakland)
OAKLAND . . . . . . . . . . . . . . . . . . . . . . .002 100   00x–3  5  2
LOS ANGELES . . . . . . . . . . . . . . . . . .000 000   001  2  7  2
Hunter (7), Fingers (8)
Downing (4), Brewer (4), Hough (5), Marshall (7)
```

Catfish Hunter, Oakland's premier pitcher, scattered seven hits and held the hard-hitting Dodgers scoreless for seven innings to give the A's their second 3 to 2 victory of the Series. Rollie Fingers relieved Hunter for the save.

FOURTH GAME (Oct. 16, at Oakland)
LOS ANGELES 000 200 000   2 7 1
OAKLAND 001 004 00x   5 7 0
Messersmith (6), Marshall (7)
Holtzman (8), Fingers (8)

Pinch hitter Jim Holt of the Athletics drove in two runs as the A's hammered Dodger pitcher Andy Messersmith in a four-run sixth inning. Oakland pitcher Ken Holtzman also homered to give the Athletics a 5 to 2 victory.

FIFTH GAME (Oct. 17, at Oakland)
LOS ANGELES 000 002 000   2 5 1
OAKLAND 110 000 10x   3 6 1
Sutton (5), Marshall (6)
Blue (7), Odom (7), Fingers (8)

Joe Rudi, the Athletics first baseman, homered off relief pitcher Mike Marshall to give the Athletics a 3 to 2 lead in the seventh inning. The Athletics held on to their slim margin as relief pitcher Rollie Fingers held the Dodgers in check over the last two innings to wrap up the World Series for Oakland.

WORLD SERIES BOX SCORES: 1974 (FIVE GAMES)

GAME 1

OAKLAND (A.L.)	AB	R	H	O	A	E	LOS ANGELES (N.L.)	AB	R	H	O	A	E
Campaneris, ss	2	1	1	0	5	1	Lopes, 2b	5	1	0	5	0	0
North, cf	2	0	0	4	0	0	Buckner, lf	5	0	2	2	0	0
Bando, 3b	4	0	0	1	1	0	Wynn, cf	4	1	1	1	0	0
Jackson, rf	3	1	1	0	0	1	Garvey, 1b	5	0	2	6	1	0
C. Washington, rf	0	0	0	0	0	0	dPaciorek	0	0	0	0	0	0
Rudi, lf	4	0	2	6	0	0	Ferguson, rf-c	3	0	0	2	1	0
Tenace, 1b	3	0	1	6	1	0	Cey, 3b	3	0	1	0	5	1
Fosse, c	3	0	0	7	0	0	Russell, ss	4	0	1	2	0	0
Green, 2b	3	0	0	3	2	0	Yeager, c	3	0	1	9	1	0
cHolt	1	0	0	0	0	0	aCrawford, rf	1	0	1	0	0	0
Maxvill, 2b	0	0	0	0	0	0	Messersmith, p	3	0	2	0	4	0
Holtzman, p	1	1	1	0	1	0	bJoshua	1	0	0	0	0	0
Fingers, p	2	0	0	0	0	0	Marshall, p	0	0	0	0	0	0
Hunter, p	0	0	0	0	0	0	Totals	37	2	11	27	12	1
Totals	28	3	6	27	10	2							

Oakland   0 1 0 0 1 0 0 1 0—3
Los Angeles   0 0 0 0 1 0 0 0 1—2

Bases on balls—Off Holtzman 2 (Ferguson, Wynn), off Fingers 1 (Cey), off Messersmith 3 (Holtzman, Jackson, North), off Marshall 1 (Fosse).
Strikeouts—By Holtzman 3 (Lopes, Ferguson, Messersmith), by Fingers 3 (Garvey, Yeager, Russell), by Hunter 1 (Ferguson), by Messersmith 8 (Tenace, Green, North, Bando 2, Rudi, Fosse 2), by Marshall 1 (Fingers).
aSingled for Yeager in eighth.
bGrounded out for Messersmith in eighth.
cPopped out for Green in ninth.
dRan for Garvey in ninth.
Runs batted-in—Jackson, Campaneris, Wynn. Two-base hit—Holtzman. Home runs—Jackson, Wynn. Sacrifice hits—Campaneris 2, North, Tenace. Caught stealing—Buckner, North. Double plays—Campaneris, Green and Tenace; Ferguson and Yeager. Wild pitch—Messersmith. Hit by pitcher—By Fingers (Ferguson). Left on bases—Oakland 6, Los Angeles 12.

GAME 2

OAKLAND (A.L.)	AB	R	H	O	A	E	LOS ANGELES (N.L.)	AB	R	H	O	A	E
Campaneris, ss	4	0	1	0	1	0	Lopes, 2b	4	0	0	3	2	0
North, cf	4	0	0	3	0	0	Buckner, lf	4	0	0	3	0	0
Haney, c	0	0	0	2	0	0	Wynn, cf	3	0	0	0	0	0

GAME 2 (continued)

OAKLAND (A.L.)	AB	R	H	O	A	E		LOS ANGELES (N.L.)	AB	R	H	O	A	E
Bando, 3b	3	1	0	0	1	0		Garvey, 1b	4	1	2	7	0	0
Jackson, rf	3	1	2	2	0	0		Ferguson, rf	3	1	1	0	0	0
Rudi, lf	4	0	1	3	0	0		Cey, 3b	3	1	0	2	1	0
fH. Washington	0	0	0	0	0	0		Russell, ss	3	0	1	2	3	1
Tenace, 1b	3	0	0	8	0	0		Yeager, c	3	0	2	10	1	0
Fosse, c	2	0	0	5	0	0		Sutton, p	2	0	0	0	1	0
aAlou	1	0	0	0	0	0		Marshall, p	0	0	0	0	1	0
Odom, p	0	0	0	0	0	0		Totals	29	3	6	27	9	1
eMangual	1	0	0	0	0	0								
Green, 2b	2	0	0	1	2	0								
bHolt	1	0	1	0	0	0								
cMaxvill, 2b	0	0	0	0	0	0								
Blue, p	2	0	0	0	1	0								
dC. Washington, cf	1	0	1	0	0	0								
Totals	31	2	6	24	5	0								

```
Oakland         0 0 0  0 0 0  0 0 2—2
Los Angeles     0 1 0  0 0 2  0 0 x—3
```

*Pitched to two batters in ninth.
Bases on balls—Off Blue 2 (Wynn, Cey), off Odom 1 (Ferguson), off Sutton 2 (Tenace, Jackson).
Strikeouts—By Blue 5 (Buckner, Sutton, Lopes, Wynn 2), by Odom 2 (Wynn, Garvey), by Sutton 9 (Campaneris 2, North, Rudi, Fosse, Blue 2, Green, Alou), by Marshall 2 (Tenace, Mangual).
aStruck out for Fosse in eighth.
bSingled for Green in eighth.
cRan for Holt in eighth.
dSingled for Blue in eighth.
eStruck out for Odom in ninth.
fRan for Rudi in ninth.
Runs batted in—Yeager, Ferguson 2, Rudi 2. Two-base hits—Campaneris, Jackson. Home run—Ferguson. Stolen base—Ferguson. Sacrifice hit—Sutton. Double plays—Sutton, Lopes and Garvey; Russell and Garvey. Wild pitch—Sutton. Hit by pitcher—By Sutton (Bando). Left on bases—Oakland 5, Los Angeles 6.

GAME 3

LOS ANGELES (N.L.)	AB	R	H	O	A	E		OAKLAND (A.L.)	AB	R	H	O	A	E
Lopes, 2b	3	0	2	1	0	0		North, cf	4	1	1	5	0	0
Buckner, lf	4	1	1	2	0	0		Campaneris, ss	4	0	2	3	2	1
Wynn, cf	4	0	1	0	0	0		Bando, 3b	3	1	0	0	1	0
Garvey, 1b	4	0	1	10	0	0		Jackson, rf	3	0	0	2	0	0
Crawford, rf	4	1	1	1	0	0		C. Washington, rf	0	0	0	0	0	0
Ferguson, c	3	0	0	9	0	2		Rudi, lf	4	0	1	2	0	0
dAuerbach	0	0	0	0	0	0		Tenace, 1b	2	0	1	4	0	0
Cey, 3b	4	0	0	1	3	0		cH. Washington	0	0	0	0	0	0
Russell, ss	4	0	1	0	3	0		Holt, 1b	0	0	0	1	0	0
Downing, p	1	0	0	0	3	0		Fosse, c	4	0	0	5	0	0
Brewer, p	0	0	0	0	0	0		Green, 2b	3	1	0	4	4	1
aLacy	1	0	0	0	0	0		Hunter, p	2	0	0	1	1	0
Hough, p	0	0	0	0	0	0		Fingers, p	0	0	0	0	0	0
bJoshua	1	0	0	0	0	0		Totals	29	3	5	27	8	2
Marshall, p	0	0	0	0	1	0								
Totals	33	2	7	24	10	2								

```
Los Angeles     0 0 0  0 0 0  0 1 1—2
Oakland         0 0 2  1 0 0  0 0 x—3
```

Bases on balls—Off Downing 4 (Tenace 2, Bando, Green), off Hough 1 (Jackson), off Hunter 1 (Lopes, Ferguson).
Strikeouts—By Downing 3 (North, Green, Hunter), by Brewer 1 (Bando), by Hough 4 (Rudi, Tenace, Hunter, North), by Marshall 1 (Jackson), by Hunter 4 (Ferguson 2, Cey, Lacy), by Fingers 1 (Cey).
aStruck out for Brewer in fifth.
bFlied out for Hough in seventh.
cRan for Tenace in eighth.
dRan for Ferguson in ninth.
Runs batted in—Rudi, Campaneris, Buckner, Crawford. Two-base hit—Campaneris. Home runs—Buckner, Crawford. Stolen bases—Lopes 2, Jackson. Sacrifice hit—Hunter. Double plays—Green and Campaneris; Green and Tenace; Green, Campaneris and Holt. Wild pitch—Hough. Left on bases—Los Angeles 6, Oakland 8.

GAME 4

LOS ANGELES (N.L.)	AB	R	H	O	A	E	OAKLAND (A.L.)	AB	R	H	O	A	E
Lopes, 2b	4	0	0	8	5	0	Campaneris, ss	3	0	0	1	4	0
Buckner, lf	4	0	1	1	0	0	North, cf	3	1	0	3	0	0
Wynn, cf	3	0	1	1	0	0	Bando, 3b	3	1	1	0	4	0
Garvey, 1b	4	1	2	7	2	0	Jackson, rf	3	1	1	0	0	0
Ferguson, rf	3	1	0	0	0	0	Rudi, 1b-lf	3	0	0	10	0	0
Cey, 3b	4	0	1	0	0	0	C. Washington, lf	3	1	2	0	0	0
Russell, ss	4	0	1	0	4	0	Tenace, 1b	0	0	0	1	0	0
Yeager, c	3	0	1	6	1	0	Fosse, c	2	0	1	6	0	0
dJoshua	1	0	0	0	0	0	aHolt	1	0	1	0	0	0
Messersmith, p	1	0	0	1	0	1	bH. Washington	0	0	0	0	0	0
cPaciorek	1	0	0	0	0	0	Haney, c	0	0	0	4	0	0
Marshall, p	0	0	0	0	1	0	Green, 2b	2	0	0	2	4	0
Totals	32	2	7	24	13	1	Holtzman, p	3	1	1	0	2	0
							Fingers, p	0	0	0	0	0	0
							Totals	26	5	7	27	14	0

```
Los Angeles    0 0 0   2 0 0   0 0 0—2
Oakland        0 0 1   0 0 4   0 0 x—5
```

Bases on balls—Off Messersmith 4 (Bando, North, Jackson, C. Washington), off Holtzman 2 (Ferguson, Wynn).
Strikeouts—By Messersmith 4 (Bando, Fosse, Jackson, Holtzman), by Marshall 2 (North, C. Washington), by Holtzman 7 (Wynn, Garvey, Lopes 2, Cey, Messersmith, Yeager), by Fingers 2 (Ferguson, Russell).
a Singled for Fosse in sixth.
bRan for Holt in sixth.
cGrounded out for Messersmith in seventh.
dGrounded into double play for Yeager in ninth.
Runs batted in—Holtzman, Russell 2, Bando, Holt 2, Green. Two-base hits—Buckner, Yeager, Wynn. Three-base hit—Russell. Home run—Holtzman. Caught stealing—Campaneris. Sacrifice hits—Messersmith, Green, Rudi. Double plays—Lopes and Garvey; Russell. Lopes and Garvey; Green, Campaneris and Tenace. Wild pitch—Holtzman. Hit by pitcher—By Messersmith (Campaneris). Left on bases—Los Angeles 6, Oakland 4.

GAME 5

LOS ANGELES (N.L.)	AB	R	H	O	A	E	OAKLAND (A.L.)	AB	R	H	O	A	E
Lopes, 2b	2	1	0	2	2	0	Campaneris, ss	4	0	2	2	4	0
Buckner, lf	3	0	1	3	0	0	North, cf	4	1	0	2	0	1
Wynn, cf	2	0	0	3	0	0	Bando, 3b	3	0	0	1	3	0
Garvey, 1b	4	0	1	4	0	0	Jackson, rf	2	0	0	2	1	0
Ferguson, rf	4	0	1	3	0	0	Rudi, 1b-lf	3	1	2	7	0	0
Cey, 3b	3	0	1	2	0	0	C. Washington, lf	3	0	1	3	0	0
Russell, ss	3	0	0	0	1	0	Fingers, p	0	0	0	1	1	0
bCrawford	1	0	0	0	0	0	Fosse, c	3	1	1	4	1	0
Yeager, c	2	0	0	7	1	1	Green, 2b	3	0	0	5	2	0
cJoshua	1	0	0	0	0	0	Blue, p	2	0	0	0	2	0
Sutton, p	1	0	0	0	1	0	Odom, p	0	0	0	0	0	0
aPaciorek	1	1	1	0	0	0	Tenace, 1b	1	0	0	1	0	0
Marshall, p	0	0	0	0	1	0	Totals	28	3	6	27	14	1
Totals	27	2	5	24	6	1							

```
Los Angeles    0 0 0   0 0 2   0 0 0—2
Oakland        1 1 0   0 0 0   1 0 x—3
```

Bases on balls—Off Sutton 1 (Jackson), off Blue 5 (Lopes 2, Cey, Yeager, Marshall), off Fingers 1 (Wynn).
Strikeouts—By Sutton 3 (Blue 2, Jackson), by Marshall 4 (Bando, Fosse, Green, Tenace), by Blue 4 (Yeager 2, Sutton, Ferguson).
aDoubled for Sutton in sixth.
bPopped out for Russell in ninth.
cGrounded out for Yeager in ninth.
Runs batted in—Bando, Fosse, Wynn, Garvey, Rudi. Two-base hit—Paciorek. Home runs—Fosse, Rudi. Stolen bases—North, Campaneris. Caught stealing—Lopes, C. Washington. Sacrifice hit—Buckner. Sacrifice flies—Bando, Wynn. Double play—Campaneris, Green and Rudi. Left on bases—Los Angeles 6, Oakland 3.

WORLD SERIES COMPOSITE BOX SCORE: 1974

PITCHING SUMMARY

Oakland Athletics PITCHER	G	IP	H	R	ER	SO	BB	W	L	ERA
Odom	2	1⅓	0	0	0	2	1	1	0	0.00
Hunter	2	7⅔	5	1	1	5	2	1	0	1.17
Holtzman	2	12	13	3	2	10	4	1	0	1.50
Fingers	4	9⅓	8	2	2	6	2	1	0	1.93
Blue	2	13⅔	10	5	5	9	7	0	1	3.29
Totals	5	44	36	11	10	32	16	4	1	2.05

Los Angeles Dodgers PITCHER	G	IP	H	R	ER	SO	BB	W	L	ERA
Hough	1	2	0	0	0	4	1	0	0	0.00
Brewer	1	⅓	0	0	0	1	0	0	0	0.00
Marshall	5	9	6	1	1	10	1	0	1	1.00
Downing	1	3⅔	4	3	1	3	4	0	1	2.45
Sutton	2	13	9	4	4	12	3	1	0	2.77
Messersmith	2	14	11	8	7	12	7	0	2	4.50
Totals	5	42	30	16	13	42	16	1	4	2.79

BATTING SUMMARY

Oakland Athletics PLAYER-POS.	G	AB	R	H	2B	3B	HR	RBI	BA
Holt, ph-1b	4	3	0	2	0	0	0	2	.667
C. W'ton, rf-ph-cf-lf	5	7	1	4	0	0	0	0	.571
Holtzman, p	2	4	2	2	1	0	1	1	.500
Campaneris, ss	5	17	1	6	2	0	0	2	.353
Rudi, lf-1b	5	18	1	6	0	0	1	4	.333
Jackson, rf	5	14	3	4	1	0	1	1	.286
Tenace, 1b	5	9	2	2	0	0	0	0	.222
Fosse, c	5	14	1	2	0	0	1	1	.143
Bando, 3b	5	16	3	1	0	0	0	2	.063
North, cf	5	17	3	1	0	0	0	0	.059
Alou, ph	1	1	0	0	0	0	0	0	.000
Mangual, ph	1	1	0	0	0	0	0	0	.000
Fingers, p	4	2	0	0	0	0	0	0	.000
Hunter, p	2	2	0	0	0	0	0	0	.000
Blue, p	2	4	0	0	0	0	0	0	.000
Green, 2b	5	13	1	0	0	0	0	1	.000
H. Washington, pr	3	0	0	0	0	0	0	0	.000
Haney, c	2	0	0	0	0	0	0	0	.000
Maxvill, 2b-pr	2	0	0	0	0	0	0	0	.000
Odom, p	2	0	0	0	0	0	0	0	.000
Totals	5	142	16	30	4	0	4	14	.211

Los Angeles Dodgers PLAYER-POS.	G	AB	R	H	2B	3B	HR	RBI	BA
Messersmith, p	2	4	0	2	0	0	0	0	.500
Paciorek, pr-ph	3	2	1	1	1	0	0	0	.500
Garvey, 1b	5	21	2	8	0	0	1	.381
Yeager, c	4	11	0	4	1	0	0	1	.364
Crawford, ph-rf	3	6	1	2	0	0	1	1	.333
Buckner, lf	5	20	1	5	1	0	1	1	.250
Russell, ss	5	18	0	4	0	1	0	2	.222
Wynn, cf	5	16	1	3	1	0	1	2	.188
Cey, 3b	5	17	1	3	0	0	0	0	.176
Ferguson, rf-c	5	16	2	2	0	0	1	2	.125
Lopes, 2b	5	18	2	2	0	0	0	0	.111
Downing, p	1	1	0	0	0	0	0	0	.000
Lacy, ph	1	1	0	0	0	0	0	0	.000
Sutton, p	2	3	0	0	0	0	0	0	.000
Joshua, ph	4	4	0	0	0	0	0	0	.000
Marshall, p	5	0	0	0	0	0	0	0	.000
Auerbach, pr	1	0	0	0	0	0	0	0	.000
Brewer, p	1	0	0	0	0	0	0	0	.000
Hough, p	1	0	0	0	0	0	0	0	.000
Totals	5	158	11	36	4	1	4	10	.228

WORLD SERIES HIGHLIGHTS: 1977

NEW YORK (AL) DEFEATS LOS ANGELES (NL), 4 GAMES TO 2

FIRST GAME (Oct. 11, at New York)
LOS ANGELES 200 000 001 000   3 6 0
NEW YORK................ 100 001 010 001   4 11 0
Sutton (7), Rautzhan (8), Sosa (8), Garman (12), Rhoden (12)
Gullett (9), Lyle (9)

Paul Blair, playing as a defensive replacement for Reggie Jackson, slammed a single in the 12th inning off Dodger relief pitcher Rick Rhoden to score Willie Randolph with the winning run in a slam-bang 4 to 3 game.

SECOND GAME (Oct. 12, at New York)
LOS ANGELES 212 000 001   6 9 0
NEW YORK.................... 000 100 000   1 5 0
Hooton
Hunter (3), Tidrow (3), Clay (7), Lyle (9)

The Dodgers exploded for five runs in the first three innings on home runs by Steve Garvey, Ron Cey, Reggie Smith, and Steve Yeager to romp over the Yankees, 6 to 1. Burt Hooton went the distance, holding the Yanks to five hits.

THIRD GAME (Oct. 14, at Los Angeles)
NEW YORK.....................300 110 000   5 10 0
LOS ANGELES 003 000 000   3 7 1
Torrez
John (6), Hough (7)

Yankee center fielder Mickey Rivers led the Yankee offensive with three hits, including two doubles, as the Yanks pounded starter Tommy John for 10 hits in a 5 to 3 win.

FOURTH GAME (Oct. 15 at Los Angeles)
NEW YORK.....................030 001 000   4 7 0
LOS ANGELES 002 000 000   2 4 0
Guidry
Rau (2), Rhoden (2), Garman (9)

Ron Guidry limited the Dodgers to four hits, while striking out seven Dodgers in an overpowering performance. Reggie Jackson homered and doubled as the Yankees defeated the Dodgers, 4 to 2.

FIFTH GAME (Oct. 16, at Los Angeles)
NEW YORK.....................000 000 220   4 9 2
LOS ANGELES 100 432 00x   10 13 0
Gullett (5), Clay (5), Tidrow (6), Hunnter (7)
Sutton

Catcher Steve Yeager slammed a home run with the bases full to drive in four runs as the Dodgers romped to a 10–4 win, clobbering four Yankee pitchers for 13 hits.

SIXTH GAME (Oct. 18, at New York)
LOS ANGELES 201 000 001   4 9 0
NEW YORK.....................020 320 01x   8 8 1
Hooton (4), Sosa (4), Rau (5), Hough (7)
Torrez

Reggie Jackson was the hitting star of the final game of the Series, exploding for three successive home runs as the Yankees outslugged the Dodgers for an 8 to 4 victory.

WORLD SERIES BOX SCORES: 1977 (SIX GAMES)

GAME 1

LOS ANGELES (N.L.)	AB	R	H	O	A	E	NEW YORK (A.L.)	AB	R	H	O	A	E
Lopes, 2b	5	1	0	4	2	0	Rivers, cf	6	0	0	8	1	0
Russell, ss	6	1	1	4	3	0	Randolph, 2b	5	3	2	2	4	0
Smith, rf	4	0	1	2	1	0	Munson, c	4	1	2	9	1	0
Cey, 3b	3	0	0	3	2	0	Jackson, rf	2	0	1	1	0	0
Garvey, 1b	4	0	1	8	3	0	Blair, rf	2	0	1	1	0	0
Baker, lf	4	1	1	2	0	0	Chambliss, 1b	5	0	1	11	1	0
Burke, cf	3	0	1	2	0	0	Nettles, 3b	4	0	0	0	4	0
aMota	1	0	0	0	0	0	Piniella, lf	5	0	2	3	0	0
Monday, cf	1	0	0	0	0	0	Dent, ss	5	0	2	0	3	0
Yeager, c	3	0	0	4	1	0	Gullett, p	1	0	0	1	1	0
cLandestoy	0	0	0	0	0	0	Lyle, p	2	0	0	0	0	0
Grote, c	1	0	0	3	3	0	Totals	41	4	11	36	15	0
Sutton, p	2	0	0	1	1	0							
Rautzhan, p	0	0	0	0	1	0							
Sosa, p	0	0	0	0	0	0							
bLacy	1	0	1	0	0	0							
Garman, p	0	0	0	0	0	0							
dDavalillo	1	0	0	0	0	0							
Rhoden, p	0	0	0	0	0	0							
Totals	39	3	6	33	17	0							

Bases on balls—Off Gullett 6 (Lopes, Smith, Garvey, Cey, Sutton, Yeager), off Sutton 1 (Randolph), off Rautzhan 2 (Jackson, Nettles), off Garman 1 (Munson), off Rhoden 1 (Munson).

Strikeouts—By Gullett 6 (Burke, Sutton, Lopes 2, Smith, Cey), by Lyle 2 (Garvey, Monday), by Sutton 4 (Gullett, Randolph, Munson, Piniella), by Sosa 1 (Piniella), by Garman 3 (Lyle 2, Rivers).
aFlied out for Burke in ninth.
bSingled for Sosa in ninth.
cRan for Yeager in ninth.
dGrounded out for Garman in twelfth.
Runs batted in—Russell, Cey, Lacy, Chambliss, Randolph, Munson, Blair. Two-base hits—Munson, Randolph. Three-base hit—Russell. Home run—Randolph. Caught stealing—Smith. Sacrifice hits—Gullett 2. Sacrifice fly—Cey. Hit by pitcher—By Gullett (Baker), by Sutton (Jackson). Left on bases—Los Angeles 8, New York 12.

GAME 2

LOS ANGELES (N.L.)	AB	R	H	O	A	E	NEW YORK (A.L.)	AB	R	H	O	A	E
Lopes, 2b	4	0	0	2	1	0	Rivers, cf	4	0	0	4	0	0
Russell, ss	4	1	1	0	4	0	Randolph, 2b	4	1	1	2	2	0
Smith, rf	3	2	2	2	0	0	Munson, c	4	0	1	3	3	0
Cey, 3b	4	1	1	1	1	0	Jackson, rf	4	0	0	0	0	0
Garvey, 1b	4	1	2	6	1	0	Chambliss, 1b	4	0	0	11	2	0
Baker, lf	4	0	0	2	0	0	Nettles, 3b	2	0	1	0	6	0
Monday, cf	3	0	1	0	0	0	Piniella, lf	3	0	1	4	0	0
Burke, cf	1	0	0	5	0	0	Dent, ss	2	0	1	0	1	0
Yeager, c	4	1	2	9	0	0	bJohnson	1	0	0	0	0	0
Hooton, p	3	0	0	0	0	0	Stanley, ss	0	0	0	1	0	0
Totals	34	6	9	27	7	0	Hunter, p	0	0	0	1	0	0
							Tidrow, p	1	0	0	0	0	0
							aZeber	1	0	0	0	0	0
							Clay, p	0	0	0	1	1	0
							cWhite	1	0	0	0	0	0
							Lyle, p	0	0	0	0	0	0
							Totals	31	1	5	27	15	0

Bases on balls—Off Clay 1 (Smith), off Hooton 1 (Nettles).
Strikeouts—By Tidrow 1 (Hooton), by Hooton 8 (Randolph, Munson, Jackson 2, Chambliss, Dent, Tidrow, Zeber).
aStruck out for Tidrow in fifth.
bFlied out for Dent in seventh.
cFlied out for Clay in eighth.
Runs batted in—Cey 2, Yeager, Smith 2, Garvey. Two-base hit—Smith. Home runs—Cey, Yeager, Smith, Garvey. Caught stealing—Garvey, Monday. Double play—Garvey, Russell and Garvey. Left on bases—Los Angeles 2, New York 4.

GAME 3

NEW YORK (A.L.)	AB	R	H	O	A	E	LOS ANGELES (N.L.)	AB	R	H	O	A	E
Rivers, cf	5	1	3	4	0	0	Lopes, 2b	4	0	0	1	4	0
Randolph, 2b	4	0	0	1	2	0	Russell, ss	4	0	0	2	4	0
Munson, c	5	1	1	9	0	0	Smith, rf	3	1	1	2	0	0
Jackson, rf	3	2	1	0	0	0	Cey, 3b	3	0	0	1	1	0
Blair, rf	1	0	0	0	0	0	Garvey, 1b	4	1	2	9	1	0
Piniella, lf	3	0	2	2	0	0	Baker, lf	4	1	2	1	0	1
Chambliss, 1b	4	0	1	8	1	0	Monday, cf	4	0	0	2	0	0
Nettles, 3b	4	1	1	1	4	0	Yeager, c	4	0	2	9	1	0
Dent, ss	3	0	1	1	2	0	John, p	2	0	0	0	0	0
Torrez, p	3	0	0	1	1	0	aDavalillo	1	0	0	0	0	0
Totals	35	5	10	27	10	0	Hough, p	0	0	0	0	0	0
							bMota	1	0	0	0	0	0
							Totals	34	3	7	27	11	1

Strikeouts—By John 7 (Chambliss, Torrez 2, Munson 2, Jackson, Nettles), by Hough 2 (Jackson, Munson), by Torrez 9 (Russell, Monday 2, John 2, Smith, Baker, Mota, Lopes).
aHit into force play for John in sixth.
bStruck out for Hough in ninth.
Runs batted in—Munson, Jackson, Piniella, Rivers, Chambliss, Baker 3. Two-base hits—Rivers 2, Munson, Yeager. Home run—Baker. Stolen bases—Lopes, Rivers. Sacrifice hit—Torrez. Double play—Garvey, Russell and Garvey. Hti by pitcher—By John (Piniella). Left on bases—New York 8, Los Angeles 7.

GAME 4

NEW YORK (A.L.)	AB	R	H	O	A	E	LOS ANGELES (N.L.)	AB	R	H	O	A	E
Rivers, cf	4	0	1	3	0	0	Lopes, 2b	2	1	1	3	6	0
Randolph, 2b	4	0	0	3	2	0	Russell, ss	4	0	0	1	5	0
Munson, c	4	0	1	8	1	0	Smith, cf	4	0	0	1	0	0
Jackson, rf	4	2	2	2	0	0	Cey, 3b	4	0	2	0	0	0
Blair, rf	0	0	0	0	0	0	Garvey, 1b	4	0	0	14	1	0
Piniella, lf	4	1	1	2	0	0	Baker, lf	4	0	0	2	0	0
Chanbliss, 1b	3	1	1	8	0	0	Lacy, rf	2	0	0	1	0	0
Nettles, 3b	3	0	0	1	3	0	Yeager, c	3	0	0	4	2	0
Dent, ss	3	0	1	0	2	0	Rau, p	0	0	0	0	0	0
Guidry, p	2	0	0	0	0	0	Rhoden, p	2	1	1	1	1	0
Totals	31	4	7	27	8	0	aMota	1	0	0	0	0	0
							Garman, p	0	0	0	0	0	0
							Totals	30	2	4	27	15	0

Bases on balls—Off Guidry 3 (Lopes 2, Lacy).
Strikeouts—By Rhoden 5 (Rivers, Munson 2, Piniella, Guidry), by Guidry 7 (Russell 2, Cey, Lacy, Smith, Garvey 2).
aFlied out for Rhoden in eighth.
Runs batted in—Piniella, Nettles, Dent, Jackson, Lopes 2. Two-base hits—Jackson, Chambliss, Rhoden, Cey. Home runs—Lopes, Jackson. Stolen base—Lopes. Caught stealing—Lopes. Sacrifice hit—Guidry. Double plays—Russell, Lopes and Garvey; Lopes, Russell and Garvey. Left on bases—New York 1, Los Angeles 4.

GAME 5

NEW YORK (A.L.)	AB	R	H	O	A	E	LOS ANGELES (N.L.)	AB	R	H	O	A	E
Rivers, cf	4	0	0	4	0	0	Lopes, 2b	5	1	2	2	5	0
Randolph, 2b	4	0	1	3	1	0	Russell, ss	5	1	2	1	1	0
Munson, c	4	1	2	5	0	0	Smith, cf-rf	4	2	1	6	0	0
Johnson, c	0	0	0	0	0	0	Cey, 3b	4	0	0	0	2	0
Jackson, rf	4	2	2	1	0	0	Garvey, 1b	4	2	2	9	0	0
Chambliss, 1b	4	1	2	8	0	0	Baker, lf	4	3	3	2	0	0
Nettles, 3b	4	0	2	0	3	1	Lacy, rf	3	1	2	1	0	0
Piniella, lf	4	0	0	3	0	1	Burke, cf	1	0	0	3	0	0
Dent, ss	4	0	0	0	3	0	Yeager, c	2	1	1	2	0	0
Gullett, p	1	0	0	0	1	0	cOates, c	1	0	0	1	0	0
Clay, p	0	0	0	0	0	0	Sutton, p	4	0	0	0	0	0
aZeber	1	0	0	0	0	0	Totals	37	10	13	27	8	0
Tidrow, p	0	0	0	0	1	0							
bWhite	1	0	0	0	0	0							
Hunter, p	0	0	0	0	0	0							
dBlair	1	0	0	0	0	0							
Totals	36	4	9	24	9	2							

```
New York      0 0 0  0 0 0  2 2 0— 4
Los Angeles   1 0 0  4 3 2  0 0 x—10
```

Bases on balls—Off Gullett 1 (Smith).
Strikeouts—By Sutton 2 (Gullett, Zeber), by Gullett 4 (Cey, Garvey, Sutton 2), by Hunter 1 (Sutton).
aStruck out for Clay in sixth.
bPopped out for Tidrow in seventh.
cFlied out for Yeager in seventh.
dFlied out for Hunter in ninth.
Runs batted in—Nettles, Dent, Munson, Jackson, Russell, Baker 2, Yeager 4, Lacy, Smith 2. Two-base hits—Garvey, Randolph, Nettles. Three-base hit—Lopes. Home runs—Yeager, Smith, Munson, Jackson. Sacrifice fly—Yeager. Left on bases—New York 5, Los Angeles 5.

GAME 6

LOS ANGELES (N.L.)	AB	R	H	O	A	E	NEW YORK (A.L.)	AB	R	H	O	A	E
Lopes, 2b	4	0	1	0	4	0	Rivers, cf	4	0	2	1	0	0
Russell, ss	3	0	0	1	4	0	Randolph, 2b	4	1	0	2	3	0
Smith, rf	4	2	1	1	0	0	Munson, c	4	1	1	6	0	0
Cey, 3b	3	1	1	0	1	0	Jackson, rf	3	4	3	5	0	0
Garvey, 1b	4	1	2	13	0	0	Chambliss, 1b	4	2	2	9	1	0

GAME 6 (continued)

LOS ANGELES (N.L.)	AB	R	H	O	A	E
Baker, lf	4	0	1	2	0	0
Monday, cf	4	0	1	3	0	0
Yeager, c	3	0	1	4	2	0
bDavalillo	1	0	1	0	0	0
Hooton, p	2	0	0	0	0	0
Sosa, p	0	0	0	0	0	0
Rau, p	0	0	0	0	0	0
aGoodson	1	0	0	0	0	0
Hough, p	0	0	0	0	0	0
cLacy	1	0	0	0	0	0
Totals	34	4	9	24	11	0

NEW YORK (A.L.)	AB	R	H	O	A	E
Nettles, 3b	4	0	0	0	0	0
Piniella, lf	3	0	0	2	1	0
Dent, ss	2	0	0	1	4	1
Torrez, p	3	0	0	1	2	0
Totals	31	8	8	27	11	1

```
Los Angeles    2 0 1  0 0 0  0 0 1—4
New York       0 2 0  3 2 0  0 1 x—8
```

Bases on balls—Off Torrez 2 (Cey, Russell), off Hooton 1 (Jackson), off Sosa 1 (Dent). Strikeouts—By Torrez 6 (Baker, Yeager, Hooton, Cey 2, Goodson), by Hooton 1 (Torrez), by Rau 1 (Nettles), by Hough 3 (Torrez, Munson, Nettles).
aStruck out for Rau in seventh.
bBunted safely for Yeager in ninth.
cPopped out for Hough in ninth.
Runs batted in—Garvey 2, Smith, Davalillo, Chambliss 2, Jackson 5, Piniella. Two-base hit—Chambliss. Three-base hit—Garvey. Home runs—Chambliss, Smith, Jackson 3. Sacrifice fly—Piniella. Double plays—Dent, Randolph and Chambliss; Chambliss, Dent and Chambliss. Passed ball—Munson. Left on bases—Los Angeles 5, New York 2.

WORLD SERIES COMPOSITE BOX SCORE: 1977

PITCHING SUMMARY

New York Yankees

PITCHER	G	IP	H	R	ER	SO	BB	W	L	ERA
Lyle	2	4⅔	2	1	1	0	2	1	0	1.93
Guidry	1	9	4	2	2	3	7	1	0	2.00
Clay	2	3⅔	2	1	1	1	0	0	0	2.45
Torrez	2	18	16	7	5	5	15	2	0	2.50
Tidrow	2	3⅔	5	2	2	0	1	0	0	4.91
Gullett	2	12⅔	13	10	9	7	10	0	1	6.39
Hunter	2	4⅓	6	5	5	0	1	0	1	10.38
Totals	6	56	48	28	25	16	36	4	2	4.02

Los Angeles Dodgers

PITCHER	G	IP	H	R	ER	SO	BB	W	L	ERA
Garman	2	4	2	0	0	1	3	0	0	0.00
Rautzhan	1	⅓	0	0	0	2	0	0	0	0.00
Hough	2	5	3	1	1	0	5	0	0	1.80
Rhoden	2	7	4	2	2	1	5	0	1	2.57
Hooton	2	12	8	5	5	2	9	1	1	3.75
Sutton	2	16	17	7	7	1	6	1	0	3.94
John	1	6	9	5	4	3	7	0	1	6.00
Rau	2	2⅓	4	3	3	0	1	0	1	11.57
Sosa	2	2⅓	3	3	3	1	1	0	0	11.57
Totals	6	55	50	26	25	11	37	2	4	4.09

BATTING SUMMARY

New York Yankees

PLAYER-POS.	G	AB	R	H	2B	3B	HR	RBI	BA
Jackson, rf	6	20	10	9	1	0	5	8	.450
Munson, c	6	25	4	8	2	0	1	3	.320
Chambliss, 1b	6	24	4	7	2	0	1	4	.292
Piniella, lf	6	22	1	6	0	0	0	3	.273
Dent, ss	6	19	0	5	0	0	0	2	.263
Blair, rf-ph	4	4	0	1	0	0	0	1	.250
Rivers, cf	6	27	1	6	2	0	0	1	.222
Nettles, 3b	6	21	1	4	1	0	0	2	.190
Randolph, 2b	6	25	5	4	2	0	1	1	.160
Johnson, ph-c	2	1	0	0	0	0	0	0	.000
Tidrow, p	2	1	0	0	0	0	0	0	.000
Guidry, p	1	2	0	0	0	0	0	0	.000
Gullett, p	2	2	0	0	0	0	0	0	.000
Lyle, p	2	2	0	0	0	0	0	0	.000
White, ph	2	2	0	0	0	0	0	0	.000
Zeber, ph	2	2	0	0	0	0	0	0	.000
Torrez, p	2	6	0	0	0	0	0	0	.000

Los Angeles Dodgers

PLAYER-POS.	G	AB	R	H	2B	3B	HR	RBI	BA
Rhoden, p	2	2	1	1	1	0	0	0	.500
Lacy, ph-rf	4	7	1	3	0	0	0	2	.429
Garvey, 1b	6	24	5	9	1	1	1	3	.375
Davalillo, ph	3	3	0	1	0	0	0	1	.333
Yeager, c	6	19	2	6	1	0	2	5	.316
Baker, lf	6	24	4	7	0	0	1	5	.292
Smith, rf-cf	6	22	7	6	1	0	3	5	.273
Burke, cf	3	5	0	1	0	0	0	0	.200
Cey, 3b	6	21	2	4	1	0	1	3	.190
Lopes, 2b	6	24	3	4	0	1	1	2	.167
Monday, cf	4	12	0	2	0	0	0	0	.167
Russell, ss	6	26	3	4	0	1	0	2	.154
Goodson, ph	1	1	0	0	0	0	0	0	.000
Grote, c	1	1	0	0	0	0	0	0	.000
Oates, ph-c	1	1	0	0	0	0	0	0	.000
John, p	1	2	0	0	0	0	0	0	.000
Mota, ph	3	3	0	0	0	0	0	0	.000

BATTING SUMMARY (continued)

New York Yankees

PLAYER-POS.	G	AB	R	H	2B	3B	HR	RBI	BA
Clay, p	2	0	0	0	0	0	0	0	.000
Hunter, p	2	0	0	0	0	0	0	0	.000
Stanley, ss	1	0	0	0	0	0	0	0	.000
Totals	6	205	26	50	10	0	8	25	.244

Los Angeles Dodgers

PLAYER-POS.	G	AB	R	H	2B	3B	HR	RBI	BA
Hooton, p	2	5	0	0	0	0	0	0	.000
Sutton, p	2	6	0	0	0	0	0	0	.000
Garman, p	2	0	0	0	0	0	0	0	.000
Hough, p	2	0	0	0	0	0	0	0	.000
Rau, p	2	0	0	0	0	0	0	0	.000
Sosa, p	2	0	0	0	0	0	0	0	.000
Landestoy, pr	1	0	0	0	0	0	0	0	.000
Rautzhan, p	1	0	0	0	0	0	0	0	.000
Totals	6	208	28	48	5	3	9	28	.231

WORLD SERIES HIGHLIGHTS: 1978

NEW YORK (AL) DEFEATS LOS ANGELES (NL), 4 GAMES TO 2

FIRST GAME (Oct. 10, at Los Angeles)
```
NEW YORK.................000 000 320    5  9 1
LOS ANGELES..............030 310 31x   11 15 2
```
Figueroa (2), Clay (2), Lindblad (3), Tidrow (4)
John (8), Forster (8)

Davey Lopes was the star of the opening game of the Series, hitting two home runs and batting in five runs as the Dodgers collected 14 hits in a decisive 11 to 5 triumph. Bill Russell and Dusty Baker contributed three hits each in a free-swinging game.

SECOND GAME (Oct. 11, at Los Angeles)
```
NEW YORK.................002 000 100    3 11 0
LOS ANGELES..............000 103 00x    4  7 0
```
Hunter (7), Gossage (7)
Hooton (7), Forster (7), Welch (7)

Third baseman Ron Cey batted in all four of the Dodger runs with a single and a three-run homer. And Bob Welch got the save, dramatically striking out Reggie Jackson in the ninth inning to end a Yankee threat and nail down a 4 to 3 win.

THIRD GAME (Oct. 13, at New York)
```
LOS ANGELES..............001 000 000    1  8 0
NEW YORK.................110 000 30x    5 10 1
```
Sutton (7), Rautzhan (7), Hough (8)
Guidry

Mickey Rivers cracked out three hits and veteran outfielder Roy White slammed a two-run homer in a 5–1 Yankee victory. Ron Guidry limited the Dodgers to eight hits, going the distance.

FOURTH GAME (Oct. 14, at New York)
```
LOS ANGELES..............000 030 000 0  3  6 1
NEW YORK.................000 002 010 1  4  9 0
```
John (8), Forster (8), Welch (8)
Figueroa (5), Tidrow (6), Gossage (9)

Reggie Smith homered in the fifth inning with two men on base to give the Dodgers a 3 to 0 lead over the Yankees. In the eighth inning the Yanks finally tied the score at 3–3, and then won the game in the tenth inning as Lou Piniella singled to score Roy White.

FIFTH GAME (Oct. 15, at New York)
```
LOS ANGELES..............101 000 000    2  9 3
NEW YORK.................004 300 41x   12 18 0
```
Hooton (3), Rautzhan (3), Hough (4)
Beattie

Jim Beattie, starting in his first World Series game, went the distance, holding the Dodgers to nine scattered hits. The Yankees drove four Dodger pitchers to cover with an 18-hit attack in a 12 to 2 easy win. It was also the first complete game of Beattie's major league career.

SIXTH GAME (Oct. 17, at Los Angeles)
NEW YORK..................030 002 200 7 11 0
LOS ANGELES 101 000 000 2 7 1
Hunter (7), Gossage (8)
Sutton (6), Welch (6), Rau (8)

Catfish Hunter pitched seven-hit ball, and Bucky Dent and Brian Doyle had three hits each as the Yankees went on to clinch their 22nd World Series, 7–2. Davey Lopes hit a home run and single in the losing Dodger effort.

WORLD SERIES BOX SCORES: 1978 (SIX GAMES)

GAME 1

NEW YORK (A.L.)	AB	R	H	O	A	E	LOS ANGELES (N.L.)	AB	R	H	O	A	E
Rivers, cf	4	0	0	4	0	0	Lopes, 2b	5	2	2	1	2	1
Blair, cf	1	0	0	1	0	0	Russell, ss	5	1	3	3	5	1
White, lf	4	0	1	2	0	0	Smith, rf	5	0	1	1	0	0
Munson, c	4	1	0	4	1	0	Garvey, 1b	5	1	2	14	0	0
Jackson, dh	4	1	3	0	0	0	Cey, 3b	4	1	1	0	4	0
Piniella, rf	4	2	1	2	0	0	Baker, lf	4	2	3	1	0	0
Nettles, 3b	4	0	1	0	2	0	Monday, cf	2	2	1	0	0	0
Chambliss, 1b	4	1	1	5	0	0	aNorth, cf	1	1	1	0	0	0
Stanley, 2b	2	0	1	4	1	0	Lacy, dh	3	0	1	0	0	0
bJohnson	1	0	0	0	0	0	Yeager, c	4	1	0	7	0	0
Doyle, 2b	0	0	0	1	0	0	John, p	0	0	0	0	4	0
Dent, ss	4	0	1	1	3	1	Forster, p	0	0	0	0	0	0
Figueroa, p	0	0	0	0	0	0	Totals	38	11	15	27	15	2
Clay, p	0	0	0	0	0	0							
Lindblad, p	0	0	0	0	0	0							
Tidrow, p	0	0	0	0	0	0							
Totals	36	5	9	24	7	1							

New York   0 0 0 0 0 0 3 2 0— 5
Los Angeles   0 3 0 3 1 0 3 1 x—11

Bases on balls—Off John 2 (White, Stanley), off Figueroa 1 (Lacy), off Clay 2 (Cey, Monday).
Strikeouts—By John 4 (White 2, Munson, Nettles), by Forster 3 (Johnson, Blair, White), by Clay 2 (Smith, Garvey), by Lindblad 1 (Monday), by Tidrow 1 (Garvey).
aDoubled for Monday in seventh.
bStruck out for Stanley in eighth.
Runs batted in—Jackson, Piniella, Nettles, Dent 2, Lopes 5, Smith, Baker, North 2, Lacy. Two-base hits—Monday, Stanley, North, Russell. Home runs—Baker, Lopes 2, Jackson. Caught stealing—Smith. Wild pitch—Clay. Double plays—Lopes, Russell and Garvey; Dent, Stanley and Chambliss; Munson and Doyle. Left on bases—New York 6, Los Angeles 6.

GAME 2

NEW YORK (A.L.)	AB	R	H	O	A	E	LOS ANGELES (N.L.)	AB	R	H	O	A	E
White, lf	5	2	2	1	0	0	Lopes, 2b	4	1	1	3	4	0
Thomasson, cf	3	0	1	2	0	0	Russell, ss	4	0	1	2	1	0
aBlair, cf	1	0	1	2	0	0	Smith, rf	4	2	1	3	0	0
Munson, c	4	1	1	3	1	0	Garvey, 1b	3	0	1	6	1	0
Jackson, dh	4	0	1	0	0	0	Cey, 3b	3	1	2	1	1	0
Nettles, 3b	4	0	0	3	3	0	Baker, lf	3	0	0	2	0	0
Piniella, rf	4	0	2	2	0	0	Monday, cf	3	0	0	1	0	0
Spencer, 1b	4	0	1	8	1	0	North, cf	0	0	0	0	0	0
Doyle, 2b	3	0	1	2	1	0	Lacy, dh	3	0	0	0	0	0
bJohnson	1	0	0	0	0	0	Yeager, c	3	0	1	8	1	0
Stanley, 2b	0	0	0	0	0	0	Hooton, p	0	0	0	1	0	0

GAME 2 (continued)

LOS ANGELES (N.L.)	AB	R	H	O	A	E	NEW YORK (A.L.)	AB	R	H	O	A	E
Dent, ss	4	0	1	0	1	0	Forster, p	0	0	0	0	1	0
Hunter, p	0	0	0	1	0	0	Welch, p	0	0	0	0	0	0
Gossage, p	0	0	0	0	0	0	Totals	30	4	7	27	9	0
Totals	37	3	11	24	7	0							

```
New York      0 0 2  0 0 0  1 0 0—3
Los Angeles   0 0 0  1 0 3  0 0 x—4
```

†Pitched to one batter in seventh.
Bases on balls—Off Hooton 1 (Munson), off Forster 1 (Blair).
Strikeouts—By Hooton 5 (Jackson, Nettles 2, Munson, Dent), by Forster 3 (Munson, Nettles, Spencer), by Welch 1 (Jackson), by Hunter 2 (Monday, Yeager).
aDoubled for Thomasson in seventh.
bHit into double play for Doyle in eighth.
Runs batted in—Jackson 3, Cey 4. Two-base hits—Munson, Jackson, Blair. Home run—Cey. Stolen base—White. Caught stealing—Thomasson. Hit by pitcher—By Hooton (Jackson). Wild pitch—Hooton. Double plays—Nettles and Spencer; Cey, Lopes and Garvey. Left on bases—New York 10, Los Angeles 2.

GAME 3

LOS ANGELES (N.L.)	AB	R	H	O	A	E	NEW YORK (A.L.)	AB	R	H	O	A	E
Lopes, 2b	5	0	1	3	2	0	Rivers, cf	4	0	3	2	0	0
Russell, ss	4	0	2	2	3	0	bBlair, cf	0	0	0	0	0	0
Smith, rf	4	0	1	2	0	0	White, lf	3	2	1	2	0	0
Garvey, 1b	4	0	1	4	2	0	Munson, c	4	1	1	4	1	0
Cey, 3b	3	0	0	0	1	0	Jackson, dh	3	0	1	0	0	0
Baker, lf	3	0	2	5	0	0	Piniella, rf	4	0	1	1	0	0
Lacy, dh	4	0	1	0	0	0	Nettles, 3b	4	1	1	2	5	0
North, cf	3	1	0	5	0	0	Chambliss, 1b	3	0	1	8	0	0
Yeager, c	1	0	0	2	1	0	Doyle, 2b	4	0	0	7	2	0
aMota	0	0	0	0	0	0	Dent, ss	4	1	1	0	5	1
Grote, c	0	0	0	0	0	0	Guidry, p	0	0	0	1	1	0
Ferguson, c	1	0	0	0	0	0	Totals	33	5	10	27	14	1
Sutton, p	0	0	0	0	0	0							
Rautzhan, p	0	0	0	0	0	0							
Hough, p	0	0	0	1	0	0							
Totals	32	1	8	24	9	0							

```
Los Angeles   0 0 1  0 0 0  0 0 0—1
New York      1 1 0  0 0 0  3 0 x—5
```

Bases on balls—Off Guidry 7 (Smith, Baker, North, Cey, Yeager, Mota, Russell), off Sutton 3 (Jackson, Chambliss, White).
Strikeouts—By Guidry 4 (Cey, Lacy, Ferguson, Smith), by Sutton 2 (Munson 2).
aWalked for Yeager in sixth.
bRan for Rivers in seventh.
Runs batted in—Russell, White, Munson, Jackson, Piniella, Dent. Two-base hit—Garvey. Home run—White. Stolen bases—North, Piniella. Caught stealing—Russell, Rivers. Double plays—Nettles, Doyle and Chambliss; Dent, Doyle and Chambliss. Left on bases—Los Angeles 11, New York 7.

GAME 4

LOS ANGELES (N.L.)	AB	R	H	O	A	E	NEW YORK (A.L.)	AB	R	H	O	A	E
Lopes, 2b	4	1	0	0	4	0	Blair, cf	4	1	2	2	0	0
Russell, ss	5	0	2	3	4	1	cRivers	1	0	0	0	0	0
Smith, rf	4	1	1	1	1	0	White, lf	3	2	1	4	0	0
Garvey, 1b	4	0	0	15	0	0	Munson, c	3	1	2	8	0	0
Cey, 3b	4	0	1	0	4	0	Jackson, dh	4	0	2	0	0	0
Baker, lf	4	0	0	0	0	0	Piniella, rf	5	0	1	5	1	0
Monday, dh	2	0	1	0	0	0	Nettles, 3b	4	0	0	2	1	0
North, cf	4	0	0	2	0	0	Chambliss, 1b	4	0	0	4	1	0
Yeager, c	3	1	1	5	0	0	Stanley, 2b	3	0	0	1	1	0
aDavalillo	1	0	0	0	0	0	bSpencer	1	0	0	0	0	0

GAME 4 (continued)

LOS ANGELES (N.L.)	AB	R	H	O	A	E	NEW YORK (A.L.)	AB	R	H	O	A	E
Grote, c	0	0	0	3	0	0	Doyle, 2b	0	0	0	0	0	0
John, p	0	0	0	0	0	0	Dent, ss	4	0	1	4	2	0
Forster, p	0	0	0	0	0	0	Figueroa, p	0	0	0	0	0	0
Welch, p	0	0	0	0	0	0	Tidrow, p	0	0	0	0	0	0
							Gossage, p	0	0	0	0	0	0
Totals	35	3	6	29	13	1	Totals	36	4	9	30	6	0

```
Los Angeles    0 0 0   0 3 0   0 0 0   0—3
New York       0 0 0   0 0 2   0 1 0   1—4
```

Bases on balls—Off Figueroa 4 (Smith, Monday, Garvey, Lopes), off Gossage 1 (Monday), off John 2 (Munson 2), off Welch 1 (White). Strikeouts—By Figueroa 2 (Smith, Russell), by Tidrow 4 (Cey, Baker 2, Yeager), by Gossage 2 (Smith, Garvey), by John 2 (Jackson, Blair), by Welch 3 (Nettles, Chambliss, Spencer).
aFlied out for Yeager in ninth.
bStruck out for Stanley in ninth.
cFouled out for Blair in tenth.
Runs batted in—Smith 3, Munson, Jackson, Piniella. Two-base hits—Yeager, Munson. Home run—Smith. Stolen bases—Garvey, Munson. Sacrifice hit—White. Hit by pitcher—By Forster (Jackson). Double play—Piniella, Chambliss and Dent. Left on bases—Los Angeles 7, New York 8.

GAME 5

LOS ANGELES (N.L.)	AB	R	H	O	A	E	NEW YORK (A.L.)	AB	R	H	O	A	E
Lopes, 2b	4	2	2	3	5	0	Rivers, cf	5	2	3	0	0	0
Russell, ss	5	0	2	1	4	1	bBlair, cf	1	1	0	0	0	0
Smith, rf	4	0	1	2	0	1	White, lf	5	2	2	2	0	0
Garvey, 1b	4	0	1	10	0	1	Johnstone, rf	0	0	0	1	0	0
Cey, 3b	3	0	1	0	0	0	Munson, c	5	1	3	8	1	0
Baker, lf	4	0	0	2	0	0	Heath, c	0	0	0	0	0	0
Monday, cf	3	0	0	2	0	0	Jackson, dh	3	0	1	0	0	0
Lacy, dh	4	0	0	0	0	0	Piniella, rf	4	0	1	4	0	0
Yeager, c	2	0	1	1	0	0	Thomasson, lf	1	0	0	0	0	0
aOates, c	1	0	1	3	1	0	Nettles, 3b	5	0	1	1	2	0
Hooton, p	0	0	0	0	0	0	Spencer, 1b	4	2	1	6	0	0
Rautzhan, p	0	0	0	0	0	0	Doyle, 2b	5	2	3	5	1	0
Hough, p	0	0	0	0	0	0	Dent, ss	4	2	3	0	2	0
							Beattie, p	0	0	0	0	1	0
Totals	34	2	9	24	10	3	Totals	42	12	18	27	7	0

```
Los Angeles    1 0 1   0 0 0   0 0 0— 2
New York       0 0 4   3 0 0   4 1 x—12
```

Bases on balls—Off Beattie 4 (Monday, Cey, Oates, Lopes), off Hootn 2 (Jackson, Dent), off Hough 2 (Jackson, Spencer). Strikeouts—By Beattie 8 (Cey, Lacy 2, Smith, Garvey 2, Russell, Baker), by Hooton 1 (Jackson), by Hough 5 (Dent, Rivers, Thomasson, Nettles, Blair).
aWalked for Yeager in seventh.
bRan for Rivers in seventh.
Runs batted in—Russell, Smith, Rivers, White 3, Munson 5, Piniella, Dent. Two-base hits—Russell, Munson, Dent. Stolen bases—Lopes, Rivers, White, Russell. Caught stealing—Monday. Wild pitch—Hough. Passed ball—Yeager, Oates. Double plays—Russell, Lopes and Garvey; Lopes, Russell and Garvey; Nettles, Doyle and Spencer. Left on bases—Los Angeles 9, New York 10.

GAME 6

NEW YORK (A.L.)	AB	R	H	O	A	E	LOS ANGELES (N.L.)	AB	R	H	O	A	E
Rivers, cf	4	0	0	1	0	0	Lopes, 2b	4	1	2	0	2	0
Blair, cf	1	0	0	0	0	0	Russell, ss	3	0	1	0	3	0
White, lf	4	1	1	4	0	0	Smith, rf	4	0	0	2	0	0
Thomasson, lf	0	0	0	1	0	0	Garvey, 1b	4	0	0	9	0	0
Munson, c	5	0	1	6	1	0	Cey, 3b	4	0	1	1	2	0
Jackson, dh	5	1	1	0	0	0	Baker, lf	3	0	0	2	0	0
Piniella, rf	4	1	1	0	0	0	Monday, cf	3	0	0	2	0	0
Johnstone, rf	0	0	0	0	0	0	Ferguson, c	3	1	2	11	0	1
Nettles, 3b	4	1	1	0	5	0	Davalillo, dh	2	0	1	0	0	0
Spencer, 1b	3	1	0	9	1	0	Sutton, p	0	0	0	0	0	0

GAME 6 (continued)

NEW YORK (A.L.)	AB	R	H	O	A	E
Doyle, 2b	4	2	3	2	3	0
Dent, ss	4	0	3	3	3	0
Hunter, p	0	0	0	1	0	0
Gossage, p	0	0	0	0	0	0
Totals	38	7	11	27	13	0

LOS ANGELES (N.L.)	AB	R	H	O	A	E
Welch, p	0	0	0	0	0	0
Rau, p	0	0	0	0	1	0
Totals	30	2	7	27	8	1

```
New York      0 3 0  0 0 2  2 0 0—7
Los Angeles   1 0 1  0 0 0  0 0 0—2
```

Bases on balls—Off Sutton 1 (Spencer), off Welch 1 (White), off Hunter 1 (Russell). Strikeouts—By Sutton 6 (Munson, Jackson 2, Spencer 2, White), by Welch 2 (Rivers, Munson), by Rau 3 (Blair, White, Jackson), by Hunter 3 (Smith, Garvey, Monday), by Gossage 2 (Lopes, Garvey). Runs batted in—Jackson 2, Doyle 2, Dent 3, Lopes 2. Two-base hits—Doyle, Ferguson 2. Home runs—Lopes, Jackson. Stolen base—Lopes. Caught stealing—Russell. Sacrifice hit—Davalillo. Wild pitch—Sutton. Double plays—Doyle, Dent and Spencer; Nettles, Doyle and Spencer. Left on bases—New York 6, Los Angeles 3.

WORLD SERIES COMPOSITE BOX SCORE: 1978

PITCHING SUMMARY

New York Yankees

PITCHER	G	IP	H	R	ER	SO	BB	W	L	ERA
Gossage	3	6	1	0	0	1	4	1	0	0.00
Guidry	1	9	8	1	1	7	4	1	0	1.00
Tidrow	2	4⅔	4	1	1	0	5	0	0	1.93
Beattie	1	9	9	2	2	4	8	1	0	2.00
Hunter	2	13	13	6	6	1	5	1	1	4.15
Figueroa	2	6⅔	9	6	6	5	2	0	1	8.10
Clay	1	2⅓	4	4	3	2	2	0	0	11.57
Lindblad	1	2⅓	4	3	3	0	1	0	0	11.57
Totals	6	53	52	23	22	20	31	4	2	3.74

Los Angeles Dodgers

PITCHER	G	IP	H	R	ER	SO	BB	W	L	ERA
Forster	3	4	5	0	0	1	6	0	0	0.00
Rau	1	2	1	0	0	0	3	0	0	0.00
John	2	14⅔	14	8	5	4	6	1	0	3.07
Welch	3	4⅓	4	3	3	2	6	0	1	6.23
Hooton	2	8⅓	13	7	6	3	6	1	1	6.48
Sutton	2	12	17	10	10	4	8	0	2	7.50
Hough	2	5⅓	10	5	5	2	5	0	0	8.44
Rautzhan	2	2	4	3	3	0	0	0	0	13.50
Totals	6	52⅔	68	36	32	16	40	2	4	5.46

BATTING SUMMARY

New York Yankees

PLAYER-POS.	G	AB	R	H	2B	3B	HR	RBI	BA
Doyle, 2b	6	16	4	7	1	0	0	2	.438
Dent, ss	6	24	3	10	1	0	0	7	.417
Jackson, dh	6	23	2	9	1	0	2	8	.391
Blair, cf-ph-pr	6	8	2	3	1	0	0	0	.375
White, lf	6	24	9	8	0	0	1	4	.333
Rivers, cf-ph	5	18	2	6	0	0	0	1	.333
Munson, c	6	25	5	8	3	0	0	7	.320
Piniella, rf	6	25	3	7	0	0	0	4	.280
Thomasson, cf-lf	3	4	0	1	0	0	0	0	.250
Stanley, 2b	3	5	0	1	1	0	0	0	.200
Chambliss, 1b	3	11	1	2	0	0	0	0	.182
Spencer, 1b-ph	4	12	3	2	0	0	0	0	.167
Nettles, 3b	6	25	2	4	0	0	0	1	.160
Johnson, ph	2	2	0	0	0	0	0	0	.000
Beattie, p	1	0	0	0	0	0	0	0	.000
Clay, p	1	0	0	0	0	0	0	0	.000
Figueroa, p	2	0	0	0	0	0	0	0	.000
Gossage, p	3	0	0	0	0	0	0	0	.000
Guidry, p	1	0	0	0	0	0	0	0	.000
Heath, c	1	0	0	0	0	0	0	0	.000
Hunter, p	2	0	0	0	0	0	0	0	.000
Johnstone, rf	2	0	0	0	0	0	0	0	.000
Lindblad, p	1	0	0	0	0	0	0	0	.000
Tidrow, p	2	0	0	0	0	0	0	0	.000
Totals	6	222	36	68	8	0	3	34	.306

Los Angeles Dodgers

PLAYER-POS.	G	AB	R	H	2B	3B	HR	RBI	BA
Oates, ph-c	1	1	0	1	0	0	0	0	1.000
Ferguson, c	2	4	1	2	2	0	0	0	.500
Russell, ss	6	26	1	11	2	0	0	2	.423
Davalillo, ph-dh	2	3	0	1	0	0	0	0	.333
Lopes, 2b	6	26	7	8	0	0	3	7	.308
Cey, 3b	6	21	2	6	0	0	1	4	.286
Baker, lf	6	21	2	5	0	0	1	1	.238
Yeager, c	5	13	2	3	1	0	0	0	.231
Garvey, 1b	6	24	1	5	1	0	0	0	.208
Smith, rf	6	25	3	5	0	0	1	5	.200
Monday, cf-dh	5	13	2	2	1	0	0	0	.154
Lacy, dh	4	14	0	2	0	0	0	1	.143
North, ph-cf	4	8	2	1	1	0	0	2	.125
Forster, p	3	0	0	0	0	0	0	0	.000
Grote, c	2	0	0	0	0	0	0	0	.000
Hooton, p	2	0	0	0	0	0	0	0	.000
Hough, p	2	0	0	0	0	0	0	0	.000
John, p	2	0	0	0	0	0	0	0	.000
Mota, ph	1	0	0	0	0	0	0	0	.000
Rau, p	1	0	0	0	0	0	0	0	.000
Rautzhan, p	2	0	0	0	0	0	0	0	.000
Sutton, p	2	0	0	0	0	0	0	0	.000
Welch, p	3	0	0	0	0	0	0	0	.000
Totals	6	199	23	52	8	0	6	22	.261

WORLD SERIES HIGHLIGHTS: 1981

LOS ANGELES (NL) DEFEATS NEW YORK (AL), 4 GAMES TO 2

FIRST GAME (Oct. 20, at New York)
Los Angeles 000 010 020 3 5 0
New York 301 100 00x 5 6 0
Reuss (3), Castillo (3), Goltz (4), Niedenfuer (5), Stewart (8)
Guidry (8), Davis (8), Gossage (8)

Bob Watson's first inning three-run homer was the deciding margin of victory for the Yankees as they took the first game, 5 to 3. Graig Nettles' spectacular back-handed stab of Steve Garvey's drive down the third-base line in the eighth inning with two men on saved the game for Guidry and the Yanks. Goose Gossage pitched two innings to get the save.

SECOND GAME (Oct. 21, at New York)
Los Angeles 000 000 000 0 4 2
New York 000 010 02x 3 6 1
Hooton (6), Forster (7) Howe (8), Stewart (8)
John (7), Gossage (8)

Pitchers Tommy John and Goose Gossage combined to shut out the Dodgers on only four hits as the Yankees made it two straight by a 3–0 margin.

THIRD GAME (Oct. 23, at Los Angeles)
New York 022 000 000 4 9 0
Los Angeles 300 020 00x 5 11 1
Righetti (2), Frazier (3), May (5), Davis (8)
Valenzuela

The Dodgers' sensational freshman pitcher, Fernando Valenzuela, gave up nine hits and seven walks, but he also struck out nine and was in command after the third inning. Ron Cey homered for the Dodgers, while Cerone and Watson homered for the Yankees as the Dodgers eked out a 5 to 4 win.

FOURTH GAME (Oct. 24, at Los Angeles)
New York 211 002 010 7 13 1
Los Angeles 002 013 20x 8 14 2
Reuschel (4), May (4), Davis (5), Frazier (6), John (7)
Welch (1), Goltz (1), Forster (4), Niedenfuer (5), Howe (6)

Jay Johnstone, an ex-Yankee, pinch hit for pitcher Tom Niedenfuer in the sixth inning and belted a two-run home run, as the Dodgers squeezed out another one-run victory over the Yanks, 8–7, evening the Series at two games each.

FIFTH GAME (Oct. 25, at Los Angeles)
New York 010 000 000 1 5 0
Los Angeles 000 000 20x 2 4 3
Guidry (7), Gossage (8)
Reuss

Jerry Reuss and Ron Guidry were hooked up in a 1–0 pitchers' duel through the first six innings. But in the seventh, Guerrero and Steve Yeager hit back-to-back home runs and the Dodgers held on to win their third straight game, 2 to 1.

SIXTH GAME (Oct. 28, at New York)
Los Angeles 000 134 010 9 13 1
New York 001 001 000 2 7 2
Hooton (6), Howe (6)
John (5), Frazier (5), Davis (6), Reuschel (6), May (7), La-
  Roche (9)

Pedro Guerrero drove in five runs with a home run, triple, and single as the Dodgers took their fourth straight game from the Yankees and the Series. While the Dodgers were pounding out 13 hits against five Yankee pitchers, Hooton and Steve Howe were holding the Yankees to just seven hits. For the Dodgers it was their fifth World Series championship in the team's history.

WORLD SERIES BOX SCORES: 1981 (SIX GAMES)

GAME 1

LOS ANGELES (N.L.)	AB	R	H	O	A	E	NEW YORK (A.L.)	AB	R	H	O	A	E
Lopes, 2b	3	1	0	3	1	0	Randolph, 2b	3	0	0	3	3	0
Russell, ss	3	0	0	2	1	0	Mumphrey, cf	3	2	2	3	0	0
cJohnstone	1	0	1	0	0	0	Winfield, lf	3	0	0	0	1	0
Stewart, p	0	0	0	0	0	0	Piniella, rf	4	1	2	4	0	0
Baker, lf	2	0	1	3	0	0	Watson, 1b	3	1	2	8	0	0
Garvey, 1b	4	0	1	5	0	0	Nettles, 3b	3	0	0	1	3	0
Cey, 3b	4	0	1	0	1	0	Cerone, c	3	0	0	8	0	0
Guerrero, cf	3	0	0	3	0	0	Milbourne, ss	4	1	0	0	2	0
Monday, rf	4	0	0	4	0	0	Guidry, p	2	0	0	0	0	0
Yeager, c	3	1	1	3	0	0	Davis, p	0	0	0	0	0	0
dLandreaux	1	0	0	0	0	0	Gossage, p	0	0	0	0	0	0
Reuss, p	1	0	0	0	1	0	Totals	28	5	6	27	9	0
Castillo, p	0	0	0	0	2	0							
Goltz, p	0	0	0	0	0	0							
aSax, ph	1	0	0	0	0	0							
Niedenfuer, p	0	0	0	0	0	0							
bThomas, ss	0	1	0	1	1	0							
Totals	30	3	5	24	7	0							

```
Los Angeles    0 0 0   0 1 0   0 2 0—3
New York       3 0 1   1 0 0   0 0 x—5
```

Bases on balls—Off Castillo 5 (Watson, Cerone, Randolph, Mumphrey, Winfield), off Stewart 1 (Nettles), off Guidry 2 (Baker, Guerrero), off Davis 2 (Thomas, Lopes).
Strikeouts—By Reuss 2 (Winfield, Guidry), by Guidry 6 (Monday 2, Guerrero, Yeager, Reuss, Garvey), by Gossage 2 (Guerrero, Monday). Game-winning RBI—Watson.
aFlied out for Goltz in fifth.
bWalked for Niedenfuer in eighth.
cSingled in one run for Russell in eighth.
dGrounded out for Yeager in ninth.
Runs batted in—Johnstone, Baker, Yeager, Winfield, Piniella, Watson 3. Two-base hit—Piniella. Home runs—Yeager, Watson. Stolen bases—Mumphrey, Piniella. Sacrifice hit—Guidry. Sacrifice fly—Baker. Passed ball—Cerone. Double play—Thomas and Garvey. Left on bases—Los Angeles 5, New York 6.

GAME 2

LOS ANGELES (N.L.)	AB	R	H	O	A	E	NEW YORK (A.L.)	AB	R	H	O	A	E
Lopes, 2b	3	0	0	7	3	1	Mumphrey, cf	2	0	0	1	0	0
eMonday	1	0	0	0	0	0	Milbourne, ss	4	0	1	1	3	1
Howe, p	0	0	0	0	0	0	Winfield, lf	4	0	0	1	0	0
Stewart, p	0	0	0	0	0	1	Gamble, rf	2	0	0	2	0	0
Russell, ss	4	0	1	0	5	0	fPiniella	1	0	1	0	0	0
Baker, lf	4	0	0	0	0	0	gBrown, rf	0	1	0	0	0	0
Garvey, 1b	3	0	2	6	0	0	Nettles, 3b	4	1	2	1	5	0
Cey, 3b	4	0	0	0	3	0	Watson, 1b	4	0	2	13	0	0
Guerrero, rf	4	0	0	4	0	0	Cerone, c	2	0	0	7	0	0
Landreaux, cf	3	0	0	4	0	0	Randolph, 2b	2	1	0	1	3	0
Yeager, c	2	0	0	1	0	0	John, p	1	0	0	0	2	0
bJohnstone	1	0	0	0	0	0	aMurcer	0	0	0	0	0	0
Scioscia, c	0	0	0	1	0	0	Gossage, p	1	0	0	0	0	0
Hooton, p	2	0	1	0	0	0	Totals	27	3	6	27	13	1
Forster, p	0	0	0	0	1	0							
cSmith	1	0	1	0	0	0							
dSax, 2b	0	0	0	0	0	0							
Totals	32	0	4	24	12	2							

Bases on balls—Off Hooton 4 (Mumphrey, Gamble, Cerone, Randolph), off Forster 1 (Mumphrey), off Stewart 1 (Cerone), off Gossage 1 (Garvey).
Strikeouts—By Hooton 1 (Nettles), by Stewart 1 (Gossage), by John 4 (Hooton 2, Baker, Landreaux), by Gossage 3 (Monday, Cey, Guerrero).

Game-winning RBI—Milbourne.
aSacrificed for John in seventh.
bFlied out for Yeager in eighth.
cSingled for Forster in eighth.
dRan for Smith in eighth.
eStruck out for Lopes in eighth.
fSingled for Gamble in eighth.
gRan for Piniella in eighth and scored.
Runs batted in—Milbourne, Watson, Randolph. Two-base hit—Milbourne. Sacrifice hits—John, Murcer. Sacrifice fly—Randolph. Double play—Russell, Lopes and Garvey. Left on bases—Los Angeles 6, New York 9.

GAME 3

NEW YORK (A.L.)	AB	R	H	O	A	E	LOS ANGELES (N.L.)	AB	R	H	O	A	E
Randolph, 2b	2	0	0	5	3	0	Lopes, 2b	4	1	2	7	3	1
Mumphrey, cf	5	0	0	0	0	0	Russell, ss	5	1	2	0	3	0
Winfield, lf	3	0	0	2	0	0	Baker, lf	4	0	0	2	0	0
Piniella, rf	5	1	1	0	0	0	Garvey, 1b	4	1	2	7	1	0
Watson, 1b	4	1	2	9	0	0	Cey, 3b	2	2	2	2	3	0
Cerone, c	4	2	2	5	1	0	Guerrero, cf-rf	3	0	1	1	0	0
Rodriguez, 3b	4	0	2	1	3	0	Monday, rf	2	0	1	2	0	0
Milbourne, ss	2	0	2	2	4	0	bThomas, cf	1	0	0	0	0	0
Righetti, p	1	0	0	0	0	0	Yeager, c	1	0	0	2	0	0
Frazier, p	1	0	0	0	0	0	aScioscia, c	3	0	1	4	1	0
May, p	0	0	0	0	0	0	Valenzuela, p	3	0	0	0	1	0
cMurcer	1	0	0	0	0	0	Totals	32	5	11	27	12	1
Davis, p	0	0	0	0	0	0							
Totals	32	4	9	24	11	0							

Bases on balls—Off Righetti 2 (Valenzuela, Cey), off Frazier 2 (Cey, Monday), off Valenzuela 7 (Randolph 3, Winfield 2, Milbourne 2). Strikeouts—By Righetti 1 (Garvey), by Frazier 1 (Guerrero), by May 2 (Baker, Guerrero), by Davis 1 (Lopes), by Valenzuela 6 (Winfield, Righetti, Cerone, Frazier, Mumphrey, Piniella).
Game-winning RBI—None.
aGrounded out for Yeager in third.
bHit into double play for Monday in seventh.
cBunted into double play for May in eighth.
Runs batted in—Watson, Cerone, Milbourne, Cey 3, Guerrero. Two-base hits—Lopes, Cerone, Watson, Guerrero. Home runs—Cey, Watson, Cerone. Caught stealing—Randolph. Sacrifice hits—Righetti, Lopes. Hit by pitcher—By Righetti (Guerrero). Double plays—Randolph and Watson; Milbourne, Randolph and Watson; Russell, Lopes and Garvey; Cey and Lopes. Left on bases—New York 9, Los Angeles 9.

GAME 4

NEW YORK (A.L.)	AB	R	H	O	A	E	LOS ANGELES (N.L.)	AB	R	H	O	A	E
Randolph, 2b	5	3	2	2	0	0	Lopes, 2b	5	2	2	5	2	0
Milbourne, ss	4	1	1	1	3	0	Russell, ss	5	0	1	2	5	1
Winfield, cf-lf-cf	4	0	0	4	0	0	Garvey, 1b	5	1	3	5	1	0
Jackson, rf	3	2	3	2	0	1	Cey, 3b	5	0	2	1	1	0
Gamble, lf	4	1	2	2	0	0	Baker, lf	5	1	1	4	0	0
cBrown, cf	0	0	0	1	0	0	Monday, rf	3	1	1	2	0	0
fPiniella, lf	1	0	0	0	0	0	Thomas, cf	1	0	0	3	0	0
Watson, 1b	3	0	1	5	0	0	Guerrero, cf-rf	3	0	2	2	1	0
Cerone, c	5	0	2	7	0	0	Scioscia, c	1	1	0	2	0	0
hRobertson	0	0	0	0	0	0	eYeager, c	0	0	0	1	0	0
Rodriguez, 3b	4	0	2	0	3	0	Welch, p	0	0	0	0	0	0
gFoote	1	0	0	0	0	0	Goltz, p	0	0	0	0	0	0
Reuschel, p	2	0	0	0	0	0	aLandreaux	1	1	1	0	0	0
May, p	1	0	0	0	1	0	Forster, p	0	0	0	0	0	0
Davis, p	0	0	0	0	0	0	bSmith	1	0	0	0	0	0
Frazier, p	1	0	0	0	0	0	Niedenfuer, p	0	0	0	0	0	0
John, p	0	0	0	0	0	0	dJohnstone	1	1	1	0	0	0
iMurcer	1	0	0	0	0	0	Howe, p	0	0	0	0	1	1
Totals	39	7	13	24	7	1	Totals	36	8	14	27	11	2

```
New York      2 1 1  0 0 2  0 1 0—7
Los Angeles   0 0 2  0 1 3  2 0 x—8
```

Bases on balls—Off Reuschel 1 (Monday), off Davis 1 (Scioscia), off Frazier 1 (Guerrero), off Welch 1 (Winfield), off Goltz 1 (Watson), off Forster 2 (Randolph, Jackson), off Niedenfuer 1 (Jackson).
Strikeouts—By Reuschel 2 (Russell, Baker), by May 1 (Smith), by Davis 2 (Baker, Monday), by John 2 (Garvey, Thomas), by Goltz 2 (Rodriguez, Reuschel), by Howe 1 (Foote).
Game-winning RBI—Yeager.
aDoubled for Goltz in third.
bStruck out for Forster in fourth.
cRan for Gamble in sixth.
dHit two-run homer for Niedenfuer in sixth.
eHit sacrifice fly for Scioscia in seventh.
fGrounded out for Brown in eighth.
gStruck out for Rodriguez in ninth.
hRan for Cerone in ninth.
iReached first base safely on error in ninth.
Runs batted in—Randolph, Milbourne, Jackson, Gamble, Watson 2, Cerone, Lopes 2, Russell, Cey 2, Yeager, Johnstone 2. Two-base hits—Milbourne, Landreaux, Garvey, Monday. Three-base hit—Randolph. Home runs—Randolph, Johnstone, Jackson. Stolen bases—Lopes 2, Winfield. Sacrifice hits—Milbourne, Scioscia. Howe. Sacrifice fly—Watson, Yeager. Double plays—None. Left on bases—New York 12, Los Angeles 10.

GAME 5

NEW YORK (A.L.)	AB	R	H	O	A	E	LOS ANGELES (N.L.)	AB	R	H	O	A	E
Randolph, 2b	3	0	0	0	0	0	Lopes, 2b	3	0	0	3	3	3
Milbourne, ss	4	0	1	1	1	0	Russell, ss	4	0	0	0	7	0
Winfield, cf-lf	4	0	1	4	0	0	Garvey, 1b	4	0	1	12	1	0
Jackson, rf	4	1	1	0	0	0	Cey, 3b	2	0	0	0	2	0
Gossage, p	0	0	0	0	0	0	aLandreaux, cf	0	0	0	1	0	0
Watson, 1b	3	0	0	6	0	0	Baker, lf	4	0	0	2	0	0
Piniella, lf-rf	4	0	2	3	0	0	Guerrero, rf	3	1	1	1	0	0
bBrown	0	0	0	0	0	0	Yeager, c	3	1	2	7	0	0
Cerone, c	4	0	0	8	1	0	Thomas, cf-3b	3	0	0	0	0	0
Rodriguez, 3b	3	0	0	2	3	0	Reuss, p	2	0	0	1	2	0
Guidry, p	3	0	0	0	0	0	Totals	28	2	4	27	15	3
Mumphrey, cf	0	0	0	0	0	0							
Totals	32	1	5	24	5	0							

```
New York       0 1 0   0 0 0   0 0 0—1
Los Angeles    0 0 0   0 0 0   2 0 x—2
```

Bases on balls—Off Guidry 2 (Cey, Reuss), off Gossage 1 (Lopes), off Reuss 3 (Randolph, Watson, Rodriguez).
Strikeouts—By Guidry 9 (Lopes, Reuss, Garvey 2, Cey, Baker 2, Guerrero, Thomas), by Reuss 6 (Winfield 2, Guidry 2, Jackson, Rodriguez).
Game-winning RBI—Yeager.
aRan for Cey in eighth.
bRan for Piniella in ninth.
Runs batted in—Piniella, Guerrero, Yeager. Two-base hits—Jackson, Yeager. Home runs—Guerrero, Yeager. Stolen bases—Lopes, Landreaux. Hit by pitcher—By Gossage (Cey). Double plays—Russell, Lopes and Garvey; Lopes and Garvey. Left on bases—New York 7, Los Angeles 6.

GAME 6

LOS ANGELES (N.L.)	AB	R	H	O	A	E	NEW YORK (A.L.)	AB	R	H	O	A	E
Lopes, 2b	4	2	1	1	2	1	Randolph, 2b	3	1	2	2	2	0
Russell, ss	4	0	2	0	5	0	Mumphrey, cf	5	0	1	2	0	0
Garvey, 1b	4	1	1	9	0	0	Winfield, lf	4	0	0	2	0	0
Cey, 3b	3	1	2	1	1	0	Jackson, rf	5	0	0	3	0	0
bThomas, 3b	2	1	0	0	0	0	Watson, 1b	5	0	0	10	0	0
Baker, lf	5	2	2	2	0	0	Nettles, 3b	3	0	2	1	2	1
Guerrero, cf-rf	5	1	3	6	0	0	cRodriguez, 3b	1	1	1	0	0	0
Monday, rf	3	0	1	1	0	0	Cerone, c	3	0	0	7	2	0
Landreaux, cf	1	0	0	1	0	0	Milbourne, ss	2	0	0	0	3	1
Yeager, c	5	0	1	6	0	0	John, p	1	0	0	0	1	0
Hooton, p	2	1	0	0	0	0	aMurcer	1	0	0	0	0	0
Howe, p	2	0	0	0	0	0	Frazier, p	0	0	0	0	0	0
Totals	40	9	13	27	8	1	Davis, p	0	0	0	0	0	0
							Reuschel, p	0	0	0	0	0	0
							dGamble	0	0	0	0	0	0
							ePiniella	1	0	1	0	0	0

GAME 6 (continued)

LOS ANGELES (N.L.)	AB	R	H	O	A	E	NEW YORK (A.L.)	AB	R	H	O	A	E
							May, p	0	0	0	0	0	0
							fBrown	1	0	0	0	0	0
							LaRoche, p	0	0	0	0	0	0
							Totals	35	2	7	27	10	2

```
Los Angeles    0 0 0  1 3 4  0 1 0 — 9
New York       0 0 1  0 0 1  0 0 0 — 2
```

Bases on balls—Off Hooton 5 (Randolph, Winfield, Milbourne 2, Cerone), off Howe 1 (Randolph), off Davis 2 (Hooton, Lopes), off Reuschel 2 (Garvey, Monday), off May 1 (Lopes).
Strikeouts—By Hooton 2 (Jackson, Cerone), by Howe 3 (Jackson, Brown, Mumphrey), by John 2 (Cey, Hooton), by Frazier 1 (Monday), by Davis 1 (Yeager), by May 2 (Howe, Landreaux), by LaRoche 2 (Howe, Lopes).
Game-winning RBI—Cey.
aFlied out for John in fourth.
bDrove in one run on forceout for Cey in sixth.
cRan for Nettles in sixth and scored.
dAnnounced for Reuschel in sixth.
eSingled in one run for Gamble in sixth.
fStruck out for May in eighth.
Runs batted in—Russell, Thomas, Cey, Guerrero 5, Yeager, Randolph, Piniella. Two-base hits—Nettles, Randolph. Three-base hit—Guerrero. Home runs—Randolph, Guerrero. Stolen bases—Randolph, Lopes, Russell. Caught stealing—Russell. Sacrifice hit—Russell. Double plays—None. Left on bases—Los Angeles 10, New York 12. Umpires—Stello (N.L.) plate, Barnett (A.L.) first, Colosi (N.L.) second, Cooney (A.L.) third, Harvey (N.L.) left, Garcia (A.L.) right. Time—3:09.

WORLD SERIES COMPOSITE BOX SCORE: 1981

PITCHING SUMMARY

Los Angeles Dodgers PITCHER	G	IP	H	R	ER	SO	BB	W	L	ERA	New York Yankees PITCHER	G	IP	H	R	ER	SO	BB	W	L	ERA
Niedenfuer	2	5	3	2	0	1	0	0	0	0.00	Gossage	3	5	2	0	0	2	5	0	0	0.00
Forster	2	2	1	0	0	3	0	0	0	0.00	LaRoche	1	1	1	0	0	2	0	0	0	0.00
Stewart	2	1⅔	1	0	0	2	1	0	0	0.00	John	3	13	11	1	1	0	8	1	0	0.69
Hooton	2	11⅓	8	2	2	9	3	1	1	1.59	Guidry	2	14	8	3	3	4	15	1	1	1.93
Reuss	2	11⅔	10	5	5	3	8	1	1	3.86	May	3	6⅓	5	2	2	1	5	0	0	2.84
Howe	3	7	7	3	3	1	4	1	0	3.86	Reuschel	2	3⅔	7	3	2	3	2	0	0	4.91
Valenzuela	1	9	9	4	4	7	6	1	0	4.00	Righetti	1	2	5	3	3	2	1	0	0	13.50
Goltz	2	3⅓	4	2	2	1	2	0	0	5.40	Frazier	3	3⅔	9	7	7	3	2	0	3	17.18
Castillo	1	1	0	1	1	5	0	0	0	9.00	Davis	4	2⅓	4	8	6	5	4	0	0	23.14
Welch	1	0*	3	2	2	1	0	0	0	—	Totals	6	51	51	27	24	20	44	2	4	4.24
Totals	6	52	46	22	19	33	24	4	2	3.29											

BATTING SUMMARY

Los Angeles Dodgers PLAYER-POS.	G	AB	R	H	2B	3B	HR	RBI	BA	New York Yankees PLAYER-POS.	G	AB	R	H	2B	3B	HR	RBI	BA
Johnstone, ph	3	3	1	2	0	0	1	3	.667	Piniella, rf-ph-lf	6	16	2	7	1	0	0	3	.438
Smith, ph	2	2	0	1	0	0	0	0	.500	Rodriguez, 3b-pr	4	12	1	5	0	0	0	0	.417
Garvey, 1b	6	24	3	10	1	0	0	0	.417	Nettles, 3b	3	10	1	4	1	0	0	0	.400
Cey, 3b	6	20	3	7	0	0	1	6	.350	Jackson, rf	3	12	3	4	1	0	1	1	.333
Guerrero, cf-rf	6	21	2	7	1	1	2	7	.333	Gamble, rf-lf-ph	3	6	1	2	0	0	0	1	.333
Yeager, ph-c	6	14	2	4	1	0	2	4	.286	Watson, 1b	6	22	2	7	1	0	2	7	.318
Scioscia, c-ph	3	4	1	1	0	0	0	0	.250	Milbourne, ss	6	20	5	5	2	0	0	3	.250
Russell, ss	6	25	1	6	0	0	0	0	.240	Randolph, 2b	6	18	5	4	1	1	2	3	.222
Monday, rf-ph	5	13	1	3	1	0	0	0	.231	Mumphrey, cf	5	15	2	3	0	0	0	0	.200
Lopes, 2b	6	22	6	5	1	0	0	2	.227	Cerone, c	6	21	2	4	1	0	1	3	.190
L'ndreaux, ph-cf-pr	5	6	1	1	1	0	0	0	.167	Winfield, lf-cf	6	22	0	1	0	0	0	1	.045
Baker, lf	6	24	3	4	0	0	0	1	.167	Davis, p	4	0	0	0	0	0	0	0	.000
Forster, p	2	0	0	0	0	0	0	0	.000	LaRoche, p	1	0	0	0	0	0	0	0	.000
Goltz, p	2	0	0	0	0	0	0	0	.000	Robertson, pr	1	0	0	0	0	0	0	0	.000
Niedenfuer, p	2	0	0	0	0	0	0	0	.000	Brown, pr-rf-cf-ph	4	1	1	0	0	0	0	0	.000
Stewart, p	2	0	0	0	0	0	0	0	.000	Foote, ph	1	1	0	0	0	0	0	0	.000
Castillo, p	1	0	0	0	0	0	0	0	.000	Gossage, p	3	1	0	0	0	0	0	0	.000
Welch, p	1	0	0	0	0	0	0	0	.000	May, p	3	1	0	0	0	0	0	0	.000

BATTING SUMMARY (continued)

Los Angeles Dodgers

PLAYER-POS.	G	AB	R	H	2B	3B	HR	RBI	BA
Sax, ph-pr-2b	2	1	0	0	0	0	0	0	.000
Howe, p	3	2	0	0	0	0	0	0	.000
Reuss, p	2	3	0	0	0	0	0	0	.000
Valenzuela, p	1	3	0	0	0	0	0	0	.000
Hooton, p	2	4	1	0	0	0	0	0	.000
Th'mas, ph-ss-cf-3b	5	7	2	0	0	0	0	1	.000
Totals	6	198	27	51	6	1	6	26	.258

New York Yankees

PLAYER-POS.	G	AB	R	H	2B	3B	HR	RBI	BA
Righetti, p	1	1	0	0	0	0	0	0	.000
Frazier, p	3	2	0	0	0	0	0	0	.000
John, p	3	2	0	0	0	0	0	0	.000
Reuschel, p	2	2	0	0	0	0	0	0	.000
Murcer, ph	4	3	0	0	0	0	0	0	.000
Guidry, p	2	5	0	0	0	0	0	0	.000
Totals	6	193	22	46	8	1	6	22	.238

DODGER BATTING LEADERS

DODGER LIFETIME BATTING LEADERS

HOME RUNS

Duke Snider	389	Babe Herman	112
Gil Hodges	361	Davey Lopes	99
Roy Campanella	242	Reggie Smith	97
Ron Cey	228	Steve Yeager	94
Steve Garvey	211	John Roseboro	92
Carl Furillo	192	Ron Fairly	92
Willie Davis	154	Tommy Davis	86
Dusty Baker	144	John Frederick	85
Dolf Camilli	139	Jack Fournier	82
Jackie Robinson	137	Joe Ferguson	82
Zack Wheat	131	Jim Lefebvre	74
Pee Wee Reese	126	Willie Crawford	74
Frank Howard	123		

MOST GAMES PLAYED

Zack Wheat	2322	Wes Parker	1288
Pee Wee Reese	2166	Jim Johnston	1266
Gil Hodges	2006	John Roseboro	1254
Jim Gilliam	1956	Roy Campanella	1215
Willie Davis	1952	Jake Daubert	1213
Duke Snider	1923	Dixie Walker	1207
Bill Russell	1911	Davey Lopes	1207
Carl Furillo	1806	Hy Myers	1166
Steve Garvey	1727	John Hummel	1139
Maury Wills	1593	Tom Daly	1094
Ron Cey	1481	Ivy Olson	1053
Jackie Robinson	1382	Cookie Lavagetto	1043
Ron Fairly	1306		

MOST DOUBLES

Zack Wheat	464	Mike Griffin	210
Duke Snider	343	Johnny Frederick	200
Steve Garvey	333	Ron Cey	200
Pee Wee Reese	330	Wes Parker	194
Carl Furillo	324	Tom Daly	190
Willie Davis	321	Jimmy Johnston	181
Jim Gilliam	304	Roy Campanella	178
Gil Hodges	294	Ron Fairly	168
Dixie Walker	274	Davey Lopes	165
Jackie Robinson	273	Jim Sheckard	162
Bill Russell	244	John Roseboro	162
Babe Herman	232	Hy Myers	155

MOST TRIPLES

Zack Wheat	171	Tom Daly	76
Willie Davis	110	Jim Johnston	73
Hy Myers	97	Jim Gilliam	71
Jake Daubert	87	Harry Lumley	66
John Hummel	82	Babe Herman	66
Duke Snider	82	Tom Burns	65
Pee Wee Reese	80	Mike Griffin	64
Jim Sheckard	76	Dixie Walker	56

MOST TRIPLES (continued)

Maury Wills	56	Candy LaChance	52
Dolf Camilli	55	Ivy Olson	51
Jackie Robinson	54	Del Bissonette	50
Bill Russell	53	Casey Stengel	50
Willie Keeler	53		

MOST AT BATS

Zack Wheat	8859	Davey Lopes	4590
Pee Wee Reese	8058	Jake Daubert	4552
Willie Davis	7495	Dixie Walker	4492
Jim Gilliam	7119	Hy Myers	4448
Gil Hodges	6881	Roy Campanella	4205
Bill Russell	6671	Jim Gilliam	4158
Duke Snider	6640	Wes Parker	4157
Steve Garvey	6543	Tom Daly	4113
Carl Furillo	6378	Ivy Olson	4112
Maury Wills	6156	John Roseboro	4020
Jackie Robinson	4877	Ron Fairly	3880
Jim Johnston	4841	John Hummel	3845
Ron Cey	4660		

MOST RUNS BATTED IN

Duke Snider	1271	Dusty Baker	587
Gil Hodges	1254	Dolf Camilli	572
Zack Wheat	1223	Jim Gilliam	558
Carl Furillo	1058	Mike Griffith	544
Steve Garvey	994	Ron Fairly	541
Pee Wee Reese	885	Bill Russell	531
Roy Campanella	856	Hy Myers	496
Willie Davis	849	Tom Burns	476
Ron Cey	842	John Roseboro	471
Jackie Robinson	734	Wes Parker	470
Dixie Walker	725	Tommy Davis	465
Tom Daly	614	Jim Sheckard	420
Babe Herman	594		

MOST HITS

Zack Wheat	2804	Dixie Walker	1395
Pee Wee Reese	2170	Jake Daubert	1387
Willie Davis	2090	Ron Cey	1378
Steve Garvey	1968	Hy Myers	1253
Duke Snider	1955	Davey Lopes	1204
Carl Furillo	1910	Mike Griffin	1166
Jim Gilliam	1889	Roy Campanella	1161
Gil Hodges	1884	Wes Parker	1110
Bill Russell	1758	Ivy Olson	1100
Maury Wills	1732	Babe Herman	1093
Jackie Robinson	1518	Jim Gilliam	1084
Jim Johnston	1440	Ron Fairly	1010

MOST RUNS SCORED

Pee Wee Reese	1338	Duke Snider	1199
Zack Wheat	1255	Jim Gilliam	1163

MOST RUNS SCORED (continued)

Gil Hodges	1088	Ron Cey	715
Willie Davis	1004	Dixie Walker	666
Jackie Robinson	947	Jake Daubert	648
Carl Furillo	895	Roy Campanella	627
Mike Griffin	881	Jim Sheckard	564
Maury Wills	876	Wes Parker	548
Steve Garvey	852	Babe Herman	540
Tom Daly	787	Dolf Camilli	540
Davey Lopes	759	Wally Gilbert	534
Bill Russell	731	Hy Meyers	512
Jim Johnston	727		

DODGER BATTING RECORDS, ONE SEASON

RECORD	NUMBER	PLAYER	YEAR
Highest Batting Average	.393	Babe Herman	1930
Highest Slugging Percentage	.678	Babe Herman	1930
Most Games	165	Maury Wills	1960
Most at Bats	695	Maury Wills	1962
Most Runs	143	Babe Herman	1930
Most Hits	241	Babe Herman	1930
Most Singles	179	Willie Keeler	1900
	179	Maury Wills	1962
Most Doubles	52	Johnny Fredericks	1929
Most Triples	22	Hy Myers	1920
Most Home Runs (Left handed)	43	Duke Snider	1956
Most Home Runs (Right handed)	42	Gil Hodges	1954
Most Home Runs at Home	25	Gil Hodges	1954
	25	Duke Snider	1956
Most Home Runs (Road)	24	Gil Hodges	1951
Most Home Runs (One Month)	15	Duke Snider	1953 (Aug.)
Most Extra Base Hits	94	Babe Herman	1930
Most Total Bases	416	Babe Herman	1930
Most Runs Batted In	153	Tommy Davis	1962
Most Bases on Balls	148	Eddie Stanky	1945
Most Strikeouts	149	Bill Grabarkewitz	1970
Fewest Strikeouts (150 Games)	15	Jim Johnston	1923
Most Hit by Pitch	16	Lou Johnson	1965
Most Sacrifice Hits	32	Jim Casey	1907
Most Stolen Bases	104	Maury Wills	1962
Longest Batting Streak (Games)	31	Willie Davis	1969
Most Pinch Hits	15	Manny Mota	1974
Most Grounded into Double Plays	27	Carl Furillo	1956

DODGERS WITH 100 OR MORE RBI'S IN A SEASON

YEAR	PLAYER	RBI's	YEAR	PLAYER	RBI'S
1922	Zack Wheat	112	1930	Glenn Wright	126
1923	Jake Fournier	102	1930	Babe Herman	130
1924	Jake Fournier	116	1932	Hack Wilson	123
1925	Zack Wheat	103	1934	Sam Leslie	102
1925	Jake Fournier	130	1938	Dolf Camilli	100
1928	Del Bissonette	106	1939	Dolf Camilli	104
1929	Babe Herman	113	1941	Dolf Camilli	120
1930	Del Bissonette	113	1942	Dolf Camilli	109

DODGERS WITH 100 OR MORE RBI'S IN A SEASON (continued)

YEAR	PLAYER	RBI's	YEAR	PLAYER	RBI'S
1943	Babe Herman	100	1954	Gil Hodges	130
1945	Luis Olmo	110	1955	Gil Hodges	102
1945	Dixie Walker	124	1955	Roy Campanella	107
1946	Dixie Walker	116	1955	Duke Snider	136
1949	Carl Furillo	106	1956	Duke Snider	101
1949	Gil Hodges	115	1962	Frank Howard	119
1949	Jackie Robinson	124	1962	Tommy Davis	153
1950	Carl Furillo	106	1970	Wes Parker	111
1950	Duke Snider	107	1974	Jimmy Wynn	108
1950	Gil Hodges	113	1974	Steve Garvey	111
1951	Duke Snider	101	1975	Ron Cey	110
1951	Gil Hodges	103	1977	Ron Cey	101
1951	Roy Campanella	108	1977	Steve Garvey	115
1952	Gil Hodges	102	1978	Steve Garvey	113
1953	Gil Hodges	122	1979	Steve Garvey	110
1953	Duke Snider	126	1980	Steve Garvey	106
1953	Roy Campanella	142	1982	Pedro Guererro	100
1954	Duke Snider	130	1983	Pedro Guererro	103

DODGER SINGLE GAME RECORDS (FROM 1900)

BATTING

RECORD	NUMBER	PLAYER	DATE
Most Hits	6	Casey Stengel	Sept. 12, 1912
		Willie Davis	May 24, 1973 (19 innings)
		Cookie Lavagetto	Sept. 23, 1939
		Walter Gilbert	May 30, 1931
		John DeBery	June 23, 1929
		Jack Fournier	June 29, 1923
		George Cutshaw	Aug. 9, 1915
Most Runs	5	Steve Garvey (last Player)	Aug. 28, 1977
Most Hits, First Game in Major Leagues	6	Casey Stengel	Sept. 17, 1912
Most Consecutive Hits	10	Ed Konetchy	June 28–July 1, 1919
Most Singles	6	Willie Davis	May 24, 1973
Most Doubles	3	Many Players	
Most Triples	3	Jim Sheckard	April 18, 1901
Most Home Runs	4	Gil Hodges	Aug. 31, 1950
Most Home Runs (Extra Innings)	3	Don Demeter	April 21, 1959 (11 innings)
Most Consecutive Home Runs	3	Gene Hermanski	Aug. 5, 1948
		Duke Snider	May 30, 1950
		Roy Campanella	Aug. 26, 1950
		Tom Brown	Sept. 18, 1950
Two Home Run Games, One Right Handed, One Left Handed	2	Wes Parker	June 5, 1966
		Jim Lefebvre	May 7, 1966
		Maury Wills	May 30, 1962
		Jim Russell	July 26, 1950
Most Extra-Base Hits	5	Steve Garvey	Aug. 28, 1977
Most Total Bases	17	Gil Hodges	Aug. 31, 1950
Most RBI's	9	Gil Hodges	Aug. 31, 1950
Most RBI's, One Inning	5	Dusty Baker	Sept. 13, 1977

MOST EXTRA-BASE HITS IN A GAME

PLAYER	DATE	2B	3B	HR	TOTAL
Steve Garvey	August 28, 1977	3		2	5
Monte Ward	August 22, 1892	2	1	1	4
George Treadway	August 20, 1894	2	1	1	4
Jim Sheckard	May 13, 1899	4	0	0	4
Tom Daly	June 26, 1901	3	1	0	4
Babe Herman	June 5, 1929	2	2	0	4
Lefty O'Doul	August 4, 1932	1	0	3	4
Sam Leslie	August 4, 1935	3	0	1	4
John Cooney	August 21, 1937	3	1	0	4
Pete Reiser	June 2, 1942	3	1	0	4
Gil Hodges	June 25, 1949	1	1	2	4
Gil Hodges	August 31, 1950	0	0	4	4
Duke Snider	June 1, 1954	1	0	3	4
Jack Robinson	June 17, 1954	2	0	2	4
Dave Lopes	August 20, 1974	1	0	3	4

DODGER NATIONAL LEAGUE LEADERS

MOST HOME RUNS, ONE SEASON

1903	Jim Sheckard	9	1924	Jack Fournier	27
1904	Harry Lumley	9	1941	Dolf Camilli	34
1906	Tim Jordan	12	1956	Duke Snider	43
1908	Tim Jordan	12			

MOST RUNS SCORED, ONE SEASON

1941	Pete Reiser	117	1953	Duke Snider	132
1943	Arky Vaughan	112	1954	Duke Snider	120
1945	Eddie Stanky	128	1955	Duke Snider	126
1949	Pee Wee Reese	132			

MOST BASE HITS, ONE SEASON

1900	Willie Keeler	208	1962	Tommy Davis	230
1919	Ivy Olson	164	1978	Steve Garvey	202
1950	Duke Snider	199	1980	Steve Garvey	200

MOST DOUBLES, ONE SEASON

1913	Carlisle Smith	40	1941	Pete Reiser	39
1929	Johnny Frederick	52	1970	Wes Parker	47

MOST TRIPLES, ONE SEASON

1901	Jim Sheckard	21	1945	Luis Olmo	13
1904	Harry Lumley	18	1953	Jim Gilliam	17
1907	Whitey Alperman	16	1959	Wally Moon	11
1918	Jake Daubert	15	1959	Charlie Neal	11
1919	Hy Myers	14	1962	Willie Davis	10
1920	Hy Myers	22	1962	Maury Wills	10
1941	Pete Reiser	17	1970	Willie Davis	16

MOST TOTAL BASES, ONE SEASON

1916	Zack Wheat	262	1950	Duke Snider	343
1919	Hy Myers	223	1953	Duke Snider	370
1941	Pete Reiser	299	1954	Duke Snider	378

BEST SLUGGING PERCENTAGE, ONE SEASON

1901	Jim Sheckard	.536	1941	Pete Reiser	.558
1906	Harry Lumley	.477	1953	Duke Snider	.627
1916	Zack Wheat	.461	1957	Duke Snider	.598
1919	Hy Myers	.436			

BATTING CHAMPIONS

1892	Dan Brouthers	.335	1944	Dixie Walker	.357
1913	Jake Daubert	.350	1949	Jackie Robinson	.342
1914	Jake Daubert	.329	1953	Carl Furillo	.344
1918	Zack Wheat	.335	1962	Tommy Davis	.346
1932	Lefty O'Doul	.368	1963	Tommy Davis	.326
1941	Pete Reiser	.343			

GRAND SLAM HOME RUNS IN CHRONOLOGICAL ORDER

Fielder Jones	April 28, 1900	Cookie Lavagetto	September 26, 1939
Tom Daly	June 19, 1900	Cookie Lavagetto	April 26, 1940
Joe Kelley	September 23, 1901	Dixie Walker	June 29, 1940
Jim Sheckard	September 23, 1901	Pee Wee Reese	July 3, 1940
	September 24, 1901	Joe Medwick	September 6, 1940
Jim Sheckard	August 17, 1903	Babe Phelps	September 18, 1940
Tim Jordan	August 15, 1906	Dixie Walker	May 6, 1940
Harry Lumley	June 25, 1907	Pete Reiser	May 25, 1941
Tex Erwin	July 28, 1911	Dixie Walker	May 31, 1942
George Cutshaw	September 28, 1914	Dolf Camilli	August 3, 1942
Zack Wheat	September 16, 1916	Dolf Camilli	August 23, 1942
Tommy Griffith	June 24, 1919	Augie Galan	July 5, 1943
Eddie Brown	May 13, 1925	Arky Vaughan	July 26, 1943
Zack Taylor	June 4, 1925	Howie Schultz	May 17, 1944
Zack Wheat	August 24, 1925	Luis Olmo	May 18, 1945
Max Carey	September 14, 1927	Dixie Walker	July 18, 1945
Del Bissonette	June 16, 1928	Pee Wee Reese	June 4, 1947
Babe Herman	July 13, 1929	Carl Furillo	June 22, 1947
Billy Rhiel	July 23, 1929	Bruce Edwards	August 18, 1947
Babe Herman	September 17, 1929	Preston Ward	April 29, 1948
Del Bissonette	July 9, 1930	Pee Wee Reese	May 9, 1948
Gordon Slade	May 30, 1931	Jackie Robinson	June 24, 1948
Johnny Frederick	June 29, 1931	Gil Hodges	May 14, 1949
Hack Wilson	June 8, 1932	Gil Hodges	June 12, 1949
Danny Taylor	June 11, 1932	Gene Hermanski	July 2, 1949
Joe Stripp	September 25, 1932	Gene Hermanski	July 28, 1949
Hack Wilson	May 14, 1933	Bruce Edwards	August 7, 1949
Tony Cuccinello	June 23, 1933	Carl Furillo	September 11, 1949
Sam Leslie	July 6, 1934	Roy Campanella	April 21, 1950
Danny Taylor	July 24, 1935	Roy Campanella	June 11, 1950
Jim Bucher	September 3, 1937	Gil Hodges	June 20, 1950
Eddie Wilson	September 12, 1937	Gil Hodges	September 20, 1950
Dolf Camilli	June 12, 1938	Erv Palica	September 24, 1950
Cookie Lavagetto	May 28, 1939	Pee Wee Reese	May 6, 1951

GRAND SLAM HOME RUNS IN CHRONOLOGICAL ORDER

Duke Snider	May 15, 1951	Tommy Davis	June 2, 1961
Gil Hodges	May 22, 1951	Norm Larker	July 26, 1961
Billy Cox	May 23, 1951	Don Drysdale	August 9, 1961
Roy Campanella	August 5, 1951	Willie Davis	July 2, 1962
Roy Campanella	September 3, 1951	Tommy Davis	September 10, 1962
Gil Hodges	September 5, 1951	Ken McMullen	July 4, 1963
Carl Furillo	April 19, 1952	Ron Fairly	July 21, 1963
Roy Campanella	May 23, 1952	John Roseboro	September 12, 1963
Carl Furillo	June 8, 1952	Nate Oliver	August 30, 1964
Pee Wee Reese	July 19, 1952	Willie Davis	September 9, 1964
Gil Hodges	August 5, 1952	Ron Fairly	July 16, 1968
Roy Campanella	August 7, 1952	Bill Sudakis	September 9, 1968
Gil Hodges	August 31, 1952	Andy Kosco	April 15, 1969
Andy Pafko	September 11, 1952	Maury Wills	August 16, 1969
Gil Hodges	July 16, 1953	Tom Haller	July 22, 1970
Billy Cox	July 17, 1953	Willie Davis	August 5, 1970
Wayne Belardi	July 18, 1953	Bill Buckner	July 27, 1971
Duke Snider	August 9, 1953	Willie Crawford	May 25, 1973
Duke Snider	August 11, 1953	Steve Yeager	August 5, 1974
Pee Wee Reese	September 9, 1953	Jimmy Wynn	September 15, 1974
Gil Hodges	May 16, 1954	Ken McMullen	April 25, 1975
Don Hoak	August 8, 1954	Ron Cey	June 18, 1975
Carl Furillo	August 14, 1954	Ron Cey	June 7, 1976
Duke Snider	May 8, 1955	Ron Cey	April 24, 1977
Carl Furillo	May 14, 1955	Ron Cey	May 5, 1977
Gil Hodges	August 3, 1955	Steve Garvey	June 22, 1977
Don Zimmer	September 9, 1955	Steve Yeager	August 22, 1977
Duke Snider	May 13, 1956	Steve Garvey	August 28, 1977
Carl Furillo	July 15, 1956	Dusty Baker	September 12, 1977
Chico Fernandez	August 4, 1956	Dusty Baker	June 12, 1978
Gil Hodges	July 18, 1957	Davey Lopes	July 6, 1978
Carl Furillo	July 28, 1957	Steve Garvey	July 26, 1978
Gil Hodges	August 23, 1958	Reggie Smith	August 16, 1978
John Roseboro	April 29, 1960	Joe Ferguson	April 6, 1979
Frank Howard	May 17, 1960	Dusty Baker	July 24, 1979
Norm Sherry	May 31, 1960	Derrel Thomas	August 10, 1979
Wally Moon	June 4, 1960	Dave Lopes	September 2, 1979
Frank Howard	July 28, 1960	Ron Cey	September 25, 1979
Tommy Davis	July 30, 1960	Steve Garvey	September 28, 1979
Frank Howard	April 29, 1961		

6

DODGER PITCHING LEADERS

DODGER LIFETIME PITCHING LEADERS

MOST WINS

NAME	WON	LOST	YEARS WITH DODGERS
Don Sutton	230	175	1966–1980
Don Drysdale	209	166	1958–1969
Dazzy Vance	190	131	1922–1932
Brickyard Kennedy	176	149	1892–1901
Sandy Koufax	165	87	1955–1966
Burleigh Grimes	158	121	1918–1926
Claude Osteen	147	126	1965–1973
Johnny Podres	136	104	1953–1966
Nap Rucker	135	136	1907–1916
Don Newcombe	123	66	1949–1958
Carl Erskine	122	78	1948–1959
Jeff Pfeffer	113	80	1913–1921
Watson Clark	106	88	1927–1933 1934–1937**
Van Lingle Mungo	102	99	1931–1941
Burt Hooton	99	68	1975–1983
Preacher Roe	93	37	1948–1954
Ed Stein	91	66	1892–1898
Tommy John	87	42	1972–1978
Whitlow Wyatt	80	45	1939–1944
Ralph Branca	80	58	1944–1954, 1956
Doug Rau	80	58	1972–1980
Kirby Higbe	70	38	1941–1947
Hugh Casey	70	41	1939–1948
Clem Labine	70	52	1950–1960
Sherry Smith	69	70	1915–1922

**Clark traded to Giants in 1933, traded back to Dodgers in 1934.

PERCENTAGE LEADERS

PITCHER	WON	LOST	PERCENTAGE
Preacher Roe	93	37	.715
Tommy John	87	42	.674
Sandy Koufax	165	87	.655
Don Newcombe	123	66	.651
Kirby Higbe	70	38	.648
Whitlow Wyatt	80	45	.640
Hugh Casey	70	41	.631
Carl Erskine	122	78	.610
Dazzy Vance	190	131	.598
Burt Hooton	99	68	.593
Jeff Pfeffer	113	80	.586
Ed Stein	91	66	.580
Ralph Branca	80	58	.580
Clem Labine	70	52	.574
Don Sutton	230	175	.568
John Podres	136	104	.567
Burleigh Grimes	158	121	.566
Don Drysdale	209	166	.557
Stan Williams	57	46	.553
Curt Davis	66	54	.550
Jim Brewer	61	51	.550
Watson Clark	106	88	.546

PERCENTAGE LEADERS (continued)

PITCHER	WON	LOST	PERCENTAGE
Jack Dunn	56	47	.544
Brickyard Kennedy	176	149	.542

LOWEST EARNED RUN AVERAGE

PITCHER	EARNED RUN AVERAGE (ERA)	PITCHER	EARNED RUN AVERAGE (ERA)
Jeff Pfeffer	2.31	Don Drysdale	2.95
Nap Rucker	2.42	Doc Scanlon	2.96
Ron Perranoski	2.55	Tommy John	2.98
Rube Marquard	2.58	Bill Singer	3.03
Jim Brewer	2.62	Don Sutton	3.07
Andy Messersmith	2.67	Claude Osteen	3.09
Sandy Koufax	2.76	Harry McIntire	3.11
Elmer Stricklett	2.85	Leon Cadore	3.11
George Bell	2.85	Hugh Casey	3.11
Whitlow Wyatt	2.86	Al Downing	3.16
Sherry Smith	2.91	Dazzy Vance	3.17
Burt Hooton	2.91	Oscar Jones	3.20
Jay Hughes	2.93		

MOST SAVES

PITCHER	GAMES SAVED	PITCHER	GAMES SAVED
Jim Brewer	125	Joe Black	20
Ron Perranoski	101	Pete Mikkelsen	20
Clem Labine	83	Ralph Branca	18
Charlie Hough	60	Bob Castillo	18
Hugh Casey	50	Sherry Smith	16
Ed Roebuck	43	Watson Clark	16
Mike Marshall	42	Nap Rucker	14
Jim Hughes	39	Van Lingle Mungo	14
Larry Sherry	39	Dutch Leonard	14
Phil Regan	27	Les Webber	14
Steve Howe	25	Curt Davis	13
Bob Miller	24	Pete Richert	13
Terry Forster	24	Carl Erskine	13
Jack Quinn	23		

MOST GAMES PLAYED

PITCHER	NUMBER OF GAMES	PITCHER	NUMBER OF GAMES
Don Sutton	534	Claude Osteen	339
Don Drysdale	518	Nap Rucker	336
Jim Brewer	474	Carl Erskine	335
Ron Perranoski	457	Watson Clark	322
Clem Labine	425	Ed Roebuck	322
Charlie Hough	401	Burleigh Grimes	317
Sandy Koufax	397	Hugh Casey	293
Brickyard Kennedy	381	Van Lingle Mungo	284
Dazzy Vance	378	Ralph Branca	283
John Podres	366	Bob Miller	275

MOST GAMES PLAYED (continued)

PITCHER	NUMBER OF GAMES	PITCHER	NUMBER OF GAMES
Don Newcombe	258	Sherry Smith	229
Burt Hooton	247	Jeff Pfeffer	226
Larry Sherry	232		

MOST COMPLETE GAMES

PITCHER	COMPLETE GAMES PITCHED	PITCHER	COMPLETE GAMES PITCHED
Brickyard Kennedy	279	Jeff Pfeffer	157
Dazzy Vance	212	Don Sutton	156
Burleigh Grimes	205	Sandy Koufax	137
Nap Rucker	186	Ed Stein	136
Don Drysdale	167	Harry McIntire	119

MOST STRIKEOUTS

PITCHER	NO. OF STRIKEOUTS	PITCHER	NO. OF STRIKEOUTS
Don Sutton	2,652	Ralph Branca	757
Don Drysdale	2,486	Brickyard Kennedy	749
Sandy Koufax	2,396	Doug Rau	694
Dazzy Vance	1,918	Jim Brewer	672
Johnny Podres	1,331	Stan Williams	657
Nap Rucker	1,217	Jeff Pfeffer	656
Claude Osteen	1,162	Tommy John	649
Van Lingle Mungo	1,031	Preacher Roe	632
Bill Singer	989	Watson Clark	620
Carl Erskine	981	Andy Messersmith	611
Burleigh Grimes	952	Doc Scanlon	584
Burt Hooton	929	Whitlow Wyatt	540
Don Newcombe	913		

MOST SHUTOUTS

PITCHER	NO. OF SHUTOUTS	PITCHER	NO. OF SHUTOUTS
Don Sutton	52	George Bell	17
Don Drysdale	49	Whitlow Wyatt	17
Sandy Koufax	40	Van Lingle Mungo	16
Nap Rucker	38	Doc Scanlon	15
Claude Osteen	34	Harry McIntire	14
Dazzy Vance	30	Watson Clark	14
Jeff Pfeffer	25	Carl Erskine	14
Johnny Podres	23	Curt Davis	13
Don Newcombe	22	Andy Messersmith	13
Burleigh Grimes	20	Al Downing	12
Burt Hooton	20	Ralph Branca	12
Bill Singer	18	Preacher Roe	12

MOST INNINGS PITCHED

PITCHER	INNINGS PITCHED	PITCHER	INNINGS PITCHED
Don Sutton	3,728	Watson Clark	1,659
Don Drysdale	3,432	Burt Hooton	1,631
Brickyard Kennedy	2,857	Ed Stein	1,402
Dazzy Vance	2,758	Ralph Branca	1,325
Burleigh Grimes	2,426	Harry McIntire	1,301
Claude Osteen	2,397	Preacher Roe	1,279
Nap Rucker	2,375	Bill Singer	1,273
Sandy Koufax	2,324	Leon Cadore	1,251
Johnny Podres	2,030	Doc Scanlon	1,221
Jeff Pfeffer	1,748	Tommy John	1,198
Van Lingle Mungo	1,738	Sherry Smith	1,197
Carl Erskine	1,719	Doug Rau	1,086
Don Newcombe	1,662		

DODGER PITCHING RECORDS, ONE SEASON

PERFORMANCE	RECORD	YEAR	PITCHER
Most Victories (Right Hander)	29	1900	Joe McGinnity
Most Victories (Left Hander)	27	1966	Sandy Koufax
Highest Percentage (Los Angeles)	(14–1) .933	1966	Phil Regan
Highest Percentage (Brooklyn)	(16–2) .889	1940	Fred Fitzsimmons
Highest Percentage (20-Game Winner)	(22–3) .880	1951	Preacher Roe
Lowest E.R.A.	1.58	1916	Rube Marquard
Most Games Lost	27	1910	George Bell
Most Games (Los Angeles)	106	1974	Mike Marshall
Most Games (Brooklyn)	62	1956	Clem Labine
Most Games Started (Los Angeles)	42	1965	Don Drysdale
Most Games Started (Brooklyn)	41	1904	Oscar Jones
Most Complete Games	38	1904	Oscar Jones
Most Games Finished (Los Angeles)	83	1974	Mike Marshall
Most Games Finished (Brooklyn)	47	1956	Clem Labine
Most Innings Pitched	378	1904	Oscar Jones
Most Strikeouts (Los Angeles)	382	1965	Sandy Koufax
Most Strikeouts (Brooklyn)	262	1924	Dazzy Vance
Most Bases on Balls	151	1901	Bill Donovan
Most Hit Batsmen	41	1900	Joe McGinnity
Most Wild Pitches (Los Angeles)	17	1958	Sandy Koufax
Most Wild Pitches (Brooklyn)	15	1916	Lawrence Cheney
Most Runs	188	1905	Harry McIntire
Most Earned Runs	138	1925	Burleigh Grimes
Most Hits	364	1900	Joe McGinnity
Most Home Runs (Los Angeles)	38	1970	Don Sutton
Most Home Runs (Brooklyn)	35	1955	Don Newcombe
Most Shutouts (Left hander)	11	1963	Sandy Koufax
Most Shutouts (Right hander)	9	1972	Don Sutton
Most Shutouts (Brooklyn)	7	1918	Burleigh Grimes
	7	1941	Whitlow Wyatt
Most Strikeouts, One Game (Los Angeles, 9 Innings)	18	1959	Sandy Koufax (Aug. 31)
	18	1962	Sandy Koufax (Apr. 24)
Most Strikeouts, One Game (Brooklyn, 9 Innings)	16	1909	Nap Rucker
Most Victories, Lifetime	230	1966–1980	Don Sutton
Most Innings Pitched, Lifetime	3,728	1966–1980	Don Sutton

DODGER PITCHING RECORDS, ONE SEASON (continued)

PERFORMANCE	RECORD	YEAR	PITCHER
Most Strikeouts, Lifetime	2,652	1966–1980	Don Sutton
Most Shutouts, Lifetime	52	1966–1980	Don Sutton
Most Consecutive Games Won	15	1924	Dazzy Vance
Most Consecutive Games Lost	14	1908	James Pastorius

MOST CONSECUTIVE WINS IN A SEASON

PITCHER	CONSECUTIVE WINS	YEAR	PITCHER	CONSECUTIVE WINS	YEAR
Phil Regan	13	1966	Bill Doak	10	1924
Burt Hooton	12	1975	Larry French	10	1942
Sandy Koufax	11	1965	Whit Wyatt	10	1943
Sandy Koufax	11	1964	Preacher Roe	10	1951
Tom Lovett	11	1890	*Preacher Roe	10	1951
Joe McGinnity	10	1900	Preacher Roe	10	1953
Burleigh Grimes	10	1918	Don Newcombe	10	1953
Dazzy Vance	10	1923			

*Roe reeled off two streaks of 10-consecutive wins in 1951.

DODGER TWENTY-GAME WINNERS

PITCHER	YEAR	WON	LOST	PITCHER	YEAR	WON	LOST
Bill Donovan	1901	25	15	Ralph Branca	1947	21	12
Henry Schmidt	1903	22	13	Preacher Roe	1951	22	3
Joe McGinnity	1906	27	12	Don Newcombe	1951	20	5
Nap Rucker	1911	22	18	Carl Erskine	1953	20	6
Ed Pfeffer	1914	23	12	Don Newcombe	1955	20	5
Ed Pfeffer	1916	25	11	Don Newcombe	1956	27	7
Burleigh Grimes	1920	23	11	Don Drysdale	1962	25	9
Burleigh Grimes	1921	22	13	Sandy Koufax	1963	25	5
Burleigh Grimes	1923	21	18	Sandy Koufax	1965	26	8
Dutch Ruether	1922	21	12	Don Drysdale	1965	23	12
Dazzy Vance	1924	28	6	Sandy Koufax	1966	27	9
Burleigh Grimes	1924	22	13	Bill Singer	1969	20	12
Dazzy Vance	1925	22	9	Claude Osteen	1969	20	15
Dazzy Vance	1928	22	10	Al Downing	1971	20	9
Watson Clark	1932	20	12	Claude Osteen	1972	20	11
Luke Hamlin	1939	20	13	Andy Messersmith	1974	20	6
Whitlow Wyatt	1941	22	10	Don Sutton	1976	21	10
Kirby Higbe	1941	22	9	Tommy John	1977	20	7

DODGER NO-HIT GAMES

PITCHER	DATE	OPPONENT	SCORE
Samuel Kimber	Oct. 4, 1884	Toledo	0–0 (11-inning tie)
Bill Terry	July 24, 1886	St. Louis	1–0
Bill Terry	May 27, 1888	Louisville	4–0
Tom Lovett	July 31, 1891	New York	6–0

DODGER NO-HIT GAMES (continued)

PITCHER	DATE	OPPONENT	SCORE
Edward Stein	July 20, 1894	Chicago	1–0 (6 innings)
Mal Eason	July 20, 1906	St. Louis	2–0
Nap Rucker	Sept. 5, 1908	Boston	6–0
Dazzy Vance	Sept. 13, 1925	Philadelphia	10–1
Fred Frankhouse	Aug. 27, 1937	Cincinnati	5–0 (7 innings)
Tex Carleton	April 30, 1940	Cincinnati	3–0
Ed Head	April 23, 1946	Boston	5–0
Rex Barney	Sept. 9, 1948	New York	2–0
Carl Erskine	June 19, 1952	Chicago	5–0
Carl Erskine	May 12, 1956	New York	3–0
Sal Maglie	Sept. 25, 1956	Philadelphia	5–0
Harry McIntire	*Aug. 1, 1906	Pittsburgh	0–1
Sandy Koufax	June 30, 1962	New York	5–0
Sandy Koufax	May 11, 1963	San Francisco	8–0
Sandy Koufax	June 4, 1964	Philadelphia	3–0
Sandy Koufax	**Sept. 9, 1965	Chicago	1–0
Bill Singer	July 20, 1970	Philadelphia	5–0
Jerry Reuss	June 27, 1980	San Francisco	8–0

*McIntire lost the game.
**Perfect game.

LOS ANGELES DODGER ONE-HIT GAMES

PITCHER	DATE	OPPONENT	SCORE
Sandy Koufax	May 23, 1960	Pirates	1–0
John Podres, Larry Sherry	Aug. 4, 1963	Astros	4–0
Don Drysdale	May 25, 1965	Cardinals	2–0
Claude Osteen	June 17, 1965	Giants	3–0
Sandy Koufax	June 20, 1965	Mets	2–1
Mike Kekich	Aug. 4, 1968	Mets	2–0
Don Sutton	May 1, 1969	Giants	5–0
Don Sutton	June 19, 1971	Astros	4–0
Don Sutton	May 9, 1974	Padres	6–0
Don Sutton	May 15, 1975	Reds	3–1
Don Sutton	Aug. 18, 1977	Giants	7–0
Doug Rau	May 11, 1979	Expos	7–0
Bob Welch	May 29, 1980	Braves	3–0

MOST STRIKEOUTS IN 9-INNING GAME

PITCHER	DATE	STRIKEOUTS	OPPONENT
Nap Rucker	July 24, 1909	16	Pittsburgh
Dazzy Vance	May 2, 1922	15	New York
Dazzy Vance	August 1, 1924	15	St. Louis
Dazzy Vance	Sept. 26, 1926	15	Chicago
Dazzy Vance	June 17, 1927	15	Chicago
Karl Spooner	Sept. 26, 1953	15	New York
Sandy Koufax	May 6, 1958	15	Philadelphia
Sandy Koufax	May 6, 1960	15	Philadelphia

DODGER NATIONAL LEAGUE LEADERS

DODGER CY YOUNG AWARD WINNERS

PITCHER	YEAR	WON	LOST	PERCENTAGE
Don Newcombe	1956	27	7	.794
Don Drysdale	1962	25	9	.735
Sandy Koufax	1963	25	7	.833
Sandy Koufax	1965	26	8	.765
Sandy Koufax	1966	27	9	.750
*Mike Marshall	1974	15	12	.556
Fernando Valenzuela	1981	13	7	.650

*Marshall was also credited with 21 games saved.

MOST COMPLETE GAMES, ONE SEASON

PITCHER	YEAR	COMPLETE GAMES	PITCHER	YEAR	COMPLETE GAMES
Joe McGinnity	1900	45	Ned Garvin	1903	30
Oscar Jones	1904	38	Nap Rucker	1908	30
Kaiser Wilhelm	1908	33	Jeff Pfeffer	1916	30
Burleigh Grimes	1923	33	Burleigh Grimes	1921	30
Oscar Jones	1903	31	Burleigh Grimes	1924	30
Bill Donovan	1902	30			

WON AND LOST PERCENTAGE, ONE SEASON
(15 OR MORE DECISIONS, ONE SEASON)

PITCHER	YEAR	WON	LOST	PERCENTAGE
Burleigh Grimes	1920	23	11	.676
Freddy Fitzsimmons	1940	16	2	.889
Whit Wyatt	1943	14	5	.737
Ralph Branca	1949	13	5	.722
Preacher Roe	1951	22	3	.880
Carl Erskine	1953	20	6	.769
Don Newcombe	1955	20	5	.800
Don Newcombe	1956	27	7	.794
John Podres	1961	18	5	.783
Ron Perranoski	1963	16	3	.842
Sandy Koufax	1964	19	5	.792
Sandy Koufax	1965	26	8	.765
Phil Regan	1966	14	1	.933
Tommy John	1974	13	3	.813
Rick Rhoden	1976	12	3	.800

MOST SHUTOUTS, ONE SEASON

PITCHER	YEAR	NO. OF SHUTOUTS	PITCHER	YEAR	NO. OF SHUTOUTS
Nap Rucker	1912	6	Van Lingle Mungo	1935	4
Clarence Mitchell	1921	3	Whit Wyatt	1940	5
Dazzy Vance	1922	6	Whit Wyatt	1941	7
Dazzy Vance	1925	6	Don Newcombe	1949	5
Dazzy Vance	1928	4	John Podres	1957	6
Doug McWeeney	1928	4	Roger Craig	1959	4
Dazzy Vance	1930	4	Don Drysdale	1959	4

MOST SHUTOUTS, ONE SEASON (continued)

PITCHER	YEAR	NO. OF SHUTOUTS	PITCHER	YEAR	NO. OF SHUTOUTS
Sandy Koufax	1963	11	Andy Messersmith	1975	7
Sandy Koufax	1964	7	Jerry Reuss	1980	6
Sandy Koufax	1966	5	Fernando Valenzuela	1981	8
Al Downing	1971	5			

AWARDS AND HIGHLIGHTS

DODGERS IN BASEBALL'S HALL OF FAME

PLAYER	POSITION	YEARS WITH DODGERS	G	AB	R	H	2B	3B	HR	PCT
Dave Bancroft	SS	1928–29	1913	7182	1048	2004	320	77	32	.279
Dan Brouthers	1B	1892–93	1658	6725	1507	2349	446	212	103	.349
George Kelly	1B	1932	1622	5993	819	1778	337	76	148	.297
Billy Herman	2B	1941–46	1922	7707	1163	2345	486	82	47	.304
Hugh Jennings	SS, 1B	1899–1900, 1903	1264	4840	989	1520	227	88	19	.314
Rabbit Maranville	SS	1926	2670	10078	1255	2605	380	177	28	.258
Monte Ward	SS	1890–92	1810	7579	1403	2151	232	95	26	.283
Heinie Manush	OF	1937–38	2009	7653	1287	2524	491	160	110	.330
Joe Medwick	OF	1940–43, 1946	1984	7635	1198	2471	540	113	205	.324
Zack Wheat	OF	1909–26	2406	9106	1289	2884	476	172	132	.317
Max Carey	OF	1926–29	2466	9363	1545	2665	419	159	69	.285
Kiki Cuyler	OF	1938	1879	7161	1305	2299	394	158	157	.321
Duke Snider	OF	1947–62	2143	7161	1259	2116	358	85	407	.295
Lloyd Waner	OF	1944	1993	7772	1201	2459	281	118	28	.316
Willie Keeler	OF	1893, 1899–1902	2124	8564	1720	2955	234	155	32	.345
Tom McCarthy	OF	1896	1258	5055	1050	1485	194	58	43	.294
Paul Waner	OF	1943–44	2549	9459	1626	3152	603	190	112	.333
Roy Campanella	C	1948–57	1215	4205	627	1161	178	18	242	.276
Jackie Robinson	2B	1947–56	1382	4877	947	1518	273	54	137	.311
Joe Kelley	OF	1899–1901	1827	6982	1424	2244	353	189	66	.321
Frank Robinson	OF	1972	2787	10006	1829	2943	528	72	586	.294

DODGER PITCHERS IN BASEBALL'S HALL OF FAME

PITCHER	YEARS WITH DODGERS	G	IP	W	L	PCT	H	SO	BB	ERA
Burleigh Grimes	1918–26	615	4178	270	212	.560	4406	1512	1295	3.52
Waite Hoyt	1932, 1937–38	674	3762	237	182	.566	4037	1206	1003	3.59
Sandy Koufax	1955–66	397	2325	165	87	.655	1754	817	2396	2.76
Rube Marquard	1915–20	536	3307	201	177	.532	3233	1593	858	3.08
Joe McGinnity	1900	467	3455	247	145	.630	3236	1058	803	2.66
Dazzy Vance	1922–32, 1935	442	2967	197	140	.585	2809	2045	840	3.24

DODGER MANAGERS IN BASEBALL'S HALL OF FAME

	BIRTH DATE	YEARS MANAGED
Wilbert Robinson	6/2/1863	1914–1930
Casey Stengel	7/30/1890	1912–17, 1934–36

NATIONAL LEAGUE MOST VALUABLE PLAYER AWARD WINNERS

YEAR	NAME	YEAR	NAME
1941	Dolf Camilli	1956	Don Newcombe
1949	Jackie Robinson	1962	Maury Wills
1951	Roy Campanella	1963	Sandy Koufax
1955	Roy Campanella	1974	Steve Garvey

NATIONAL LEAGUE ROOKIES OF THE YEAR

YEAR	PLAYER	YEAR	PLAYER
1947	Jackie Robinson	1969	Ted Sizemore
1949	Don Newcombe	1979	Rick Sutcliffe
1952	Joe Black	1980	Steve Howe
1953	Junior Gilliam	1981	Fernando Valenzuela
1960	Frank Howard	1982	Steve Sax
1965	Jim Lefebvre		

DODGERS ALL-TIME STOLEN BASE LEADERS

PLAYER	NUMBER OF BASES STOLEN	PLAYER	NUMBER OF BASES STOLEN
Maury Wills	490	Willie Keeler	128
Davey Lopes	418	John Hummel	114
Willie Davis	335	Tom Daly	107
Pee Wee Reese	232	Hy Myers	100
Jim Sheckard	209	Duke Snider	99
Zack Wheat	203	Bill Buckner	93
Jim Gilliam	203	Ivy Olson	88
Jackie Robinson	197	Fielder Jones	87
Jake Daubert	187	Pete Reiser	78
George Cutshaw	166	Joe Kelly	77
Jim Johnston	164	Bill Maloney	77
Bill Russell	157	Casey Stengel	77
Bill Dahlen	146		

DODGER STOLEN BASE NATIONAL LEAGUE CHAMPIONS

PLAYER	YEAR	STOLEN BASES	PLAYER	YEAR	STOLEN BASES
Jim Sheckard	1903	67	Maury Wills	1960	50
Pete Reiser	1942	20	Maury Wills	1961	35
Arky Vaughan	1943	20	Maury Wills	1962	104
Pete Reiser	1946	34	Maury Wills	1963	40
Jackie Robinson	1947	29	Maury Wills	1964	53
Jackie Robinson	1949	37	Davey Lopes	1975	77
Pee Wee Reese	1952	30	Davey Lopes	1976	63

DODGERS SELECTED FOR ALL-STAR GAMES

PLAYER	YEAR	POSITION	PLAYER	YEAR	POSITION
Tony Cuccinello	1933	2B	Leo Durocher		SS
Al Lopez	1934	C	Cookie Lavagetto		3B
Van Mungo		P	Joe Medwick		LF
Van Mungo	1936	P	Babe Phelps		C
Van Mungo	1937	P	Whit Wyatt		P
Leo Durocher	1938	SS	Billy Herman	1941	2B
Cookie Lavagetto		3B	Cookie Lavagetto		3B
Babe Phelps		C	Joe Medwick		LF
Dolf Camilli	1939	1B	Mickey Owen		C
Cookie Lavagetto		3B	Pete Reiser		CF
Babe Phelps		C	Whit Wyatt		P
Whit Wyatt		P	Leo Durocher	1942	MGR
Pete Coscarart	1940	2B	Billy Herman		2B

DODGERS SELECTED FOR ALL-STAR GAMES (continued)

PLAYER	YEAR	POSITION	PLAYER	YEAR	POSITION
Joe Medwick		LF	Jackie Robinson		3B
Mickey Owen		C	Duke Snider		OF
Pee Wee Reese		SS	Walter Alston	1954	MGR
Pete Reiser		CF	Roy Campanella		C
Arky Vaughan		3B	Carl Erskine		P
Whit Wyatt		P	Gil Hodges		1B
Augie Galan	1943	OF	Pee Wee Reese		SS
Billy Herman		2B	Jackie Robinson		OF
Mickey Owen		C	Duke Snider		OF
Dixie Walker		OF	Gil Hodges	1955	1B
Augie Galan	1944	OF	Don Newcombe		P
Mickey Owen		C	Duke Snider		OF
Dixie Walker		OF	Walter Alston	1956	MGR
Kirby Higbe	1946	P	Roy Campanella		C
Pete Reiser		OF	Jim Gilliam		2B
Dixie Walker		OF	Clem Labine		P
Ralph Branca	1947	P	Duke Snider		OF
Bruce Edwards		C	Walter Alston	1957	MGR
Pee Wee Reese		SS	Gino Cimoli		OF
Eddie Stanky		2B	Gil Hodges		1B
Dixie Walker		OF	Clem Labine		P
Leo Durocher	1948	MGR	John Podres	1958	P
Ralph Branca		P	John Roseboro		C
Pee Wee Reese		SS		1959	
Ralph Branca	1949	P	First game:	(Two Games)	
Roy Campanella		C	Don Drysdale		P
Gil Hodges		1B	Wally Moon		OF
Don Newcombe		P	Second game:		
Pee Wee Reese		SS	Don Drysdale		P
Jackie Robinson		2B	Jim Gilliam		3B
Preacher Roe		P	Charlie Neal		2B
Burt Shotton	1950	MGR	Wally Moon		OF
Roy Campanella		C		1960	
Gil Hodges		1B		(Both Games)	
Don Newcombe		P	Walter Alston		MGR
Pee Wee Reese		SS	Norm Larker		1B
Jackie Robinson		2B	Charlie Neal		2B
Preacher Roe		P	John Podres		P
Duke Snider		OF	Stan Williams		P
Roy Campanella	1951	C	First game:	1961	
Gil Hodges		1B	Sandy Koufax		P
Don Newcombe		P	John Roseboro		C
Pee Wee Reese		SS	Maury Wills		SS
Jackie Robinson		2B	Second game:		
Preacher Roe		P	Don Drysdale		P
Duke Snider		OF	Sandy Koufax		P
Roy Campanella	1952	C	John Roseboro		C
Carl Furillo		OF	Maury Wills		SS
Gil Hodges		1B	Tommy Davis	1962	OF
Pee Wee Reese		SS	Maury Wills		SS
Jackie Robinson		2B	John Roseboro		C
Preacher Roe		P	Don Drysdale		P
Duke Snider		OF	Sandy Koufax		P
Charlie Dressen	1953	MGR	Tommy Davis		OF
Roy Campanella		C	Maury Wills		SS
Carl Furillo		OF	John Roseboro		C
Gil Hodges		1B	Don Drysdale		P
Pee Wee Reese		SS	John Podres		P

DODGERS SELECTED FOR ALL-STAR GAMES (continued)

PLAYER	YEAR	POSITION	PLAYER	YEAR	POSITION
Maury Wills	1963	SS	Andy Messersmith		P
Tommy Davis		OF	Don Sutton		P
Sandy Koufax		P	Jim Wynn		OF
Don Drysdale		P	Ron Cey	1976	3B
Walter Alston	1964	MGR	Steve Garvey		1B
Don Drysdale		P	Bill Russell		SS
Sandy Koufax		P	Rick Rhoden		P
Maury Wills	1965	SS	Ron Cey	1977	3B
Don Drysdale		P	Steve Garvey		1B
Sandy Koufax		P	Don Sutton		P
Walter Alston	1966	MGR	Reggie Smith		OF
Sandy Koufax		P	Tommy Lasorda	1978	MGR
Jim Lefebvre		2B	Ron Cey		3B
Phil Regan		P	Steve Garvey		1B
Maury Wills		SS	Davey Lopes		2B
Walter Alston	1967	MGR	Reggie Smith		OF
Claude Osteen		P	Rick Monday		OF
Don Drysdale		P	Tommy John		P
Don Drysdale	1968	P	Tommy Lasorda	1979	MGR
Tom Haller		C	Steve Garvey		1B
Bill Singer	1969	P	Davey Lopes		2B
Claude Osteen	1970	P	Ron Cey		3B
Bill Grabarkewitz		3B	Steve Garvey	1980	1B
Willie Davis	1971	OF	Davey Lopes		2B
Don Sutton	1972	P	Jerry Reuss		P
Jim Brewer	1973	P	Bill Russell		SS
Willie Davis		OF	Reggie Smith		OF
Manny Mota		OF	Bob Welch		P
Bill Russell		SS	Dusty Baker	1981	OF
Claude Osteen		P	Steve Garvey		1B
Don Sutton		P	Pedro Guerrero		OF
Ron Cey	1974	3B	Burt Hooton		P
Steve Garvey		1B	Davey Lopes		2B
Mike Marshall		P	Fernando Valenzuela		P
Andy Messersmith		P	Fernando Valenzuela	1982	P
Don Sutton		P	Steve Howe		P
Jim Wynn		OF	Dusty Baker		OF
Walter Alston	1975	MGR	Dusty Baker	1983	OF
Ron Cey		3B	Pedro Guerrero		OF
Steve Garvey		1B	Steve Sax		2B
Mike Marshall		P			

DODGERS ALL-TIME ROSTER AT A GLANCE

Dodgers All-Time Roster at a Glance

PLAYER/POSITION

A
Abbey, Bert, P
Abrams, Calvin, OF
Aderholt, Morris, OF
Aguirre, Hank, P
Ainsmith, Eddie, C
Aitchison, Raleigh, P
Albosta, Ed, P
Alcaraz, Luis, IF
Alexander, Doyle, P
Allen, Frank, P
Allen, Horace, OF
Allen, Johnny, P
Allen, Richie, 1B-3B-OF
Almada, Mel, OF
Alperman, Whitey, 2B
Alvarez, Orlando, OF
Amoros, Sandy, OF
Anderson, Ferrell, C
Anderson, John, OF-1B
Andrews, Stan, C
Ankenman, Pat, SS
Antonello, Bill, OF
Appleton, Ed, P
Archer, Jimmy, C
Aspromonte, Bob, IF
Auerbach, Rick

B
Babb, Charley, SS
Babich, John, P
Bailey, Abe, P
Bailey, Gene, OF
Bailey, Bob, IF-OF
Baird, Doug, 3B
Barbieri, Jim, OF
Baker, Dusty, OF
Baker, Tom, P
Baldwin, Lady, P
Ballou, Win, P
Bancroft, Dave, P
Bankhead, Dan, P
Banta, Jack, P
Barber, Turner, OF
Barger, Cy, P
Barkley, Red, SS
Barnes, Jesse, P
Barney, Rex, P
Barr, Robert, P
Barrett, Bobby, 3B
Bartley, Boyd, SS
Bashang, Al, OF
Basinski, Ed, 2B-SS
Batch, Heinie, 3B-OF
Baxes, Jim, 3B
Beck, Dutch, SS
Beck, Walter, P
Becknith, Joe, P
Behrman, Hank, P
Belardi, Wayne, OF
Bell, George, P
Benge, Ray, P
Berg, Moe, 2B-SS
Bergen, Bill, C
Berres, Ray, C
Bessent, Don, P
Bilko, Steve, 1B

PLAYER/POSITION

Birkofer, Ralph, P
Birrer, Babe, P
Bissonette, Del, 1B
Black, Joe, P
Blethen, Climax, P
Boehler, George, P
Bohne, Sammy, SS-3B
Bolling, Jack, 1B
Bonner, Frank, 2B
Boone, Ike, OF
Bordagaray, Frency, 3B-OF
Borkowski, Bob, OF
Boyer, Ken, IF
Boyle, Ralph, OF
Brack, Gibby, OF
Bradley, Mark, SS-2B
Bradshaw, Joe, P
Bragan, Bob, C-IF
Branca, Ralph, P
Brandt, Ed, P
Bressler, Rube, OF
Brett, Ken, P
Brewer, Jim, P
Brewer, Tony, OF
Bridges, Rocky, IF
Brock, Greg, 1B
Broderick, Matt, 2B
Brouthers, Dan, 1B
Brown, Eddie, OF
Brown, Elmer, P
Brown, Lloyd, P
Brown, Mace, P
Brown, Tommy, IF-OF
Browne, George, OF
Browning, Pete, OF
Brubaker, Bruce, P
Brumley, Mike, C
Bucher, Jimmy, IF-OF
Buckner, Bill, IF-OF
Buker, Cyril, P
Bunning, Jim, P
Burch, Bill, OF
Burdock, Jack, 2B
Burk, Sandy, P
Burke, Glenn, OF
Burns, Tom, OF
Burright, Larry, IF
Burrill, Frank, C
Bushong, Doc, C
Butcher, Max, P
Butler, John A., C
Butler, John S., SS-3B

C
Cadore, Leon, P
Caldwell, Bruce, 1B
Callahan, Leo, OF
Calmus, Dick, P
Camilli, Dolph, 1B
Camilli, Doug, C
Campanella, Roy, C-OF
Campanis, Alex, 2B
Campanis, Jim, C
Campbell, Gil, C
Canavan, Jim, 2B
Cannizzaro, Chris, C
Cantrell, Guy, P
Cantwell, Ben, P

Carey, Andy, IF
Carey, Max, OF
Carleton, Tex, P
Carroll, Owen, P
Carsey, Kid, P
Caruthers, Bob, P
Casey, Hugh, P
Casey, Doc, 3B
Castillo, Robert, P
Cassidy, Pete, IF
Catterson, Tom, OF
Cey, Ron, IF
Chandler, Ed, P
Chapman, Ben, P
Chapman, Glenn, 2B-OF
Cheney, Larry, P
Chervinko, Paul, C
Chipman, Bob, P
Churn, Clarence, P
Cimoli, Gino, OF
Cisar, George, OF
Clabaugh, Moose, OF
Clancy, Bud, 1B
Clark, Bob, C
Clark, Watson, P
Clement, Wallace, OF
Cohen, Alta, OF
Colavito, Rocky, OF
Collins, Hubert, 2B-OF
Collins, William, OF
Collum, Jackie, P
Connors, Chuck, 1B
Coombs, Jack, P
Cooney, Johnny, 1B-OF
Corbitt, Claude, 3B
Corcoran, Tom, SS
Corgan, Chuck, IF
Corkhill, Pop, OF
Corriden, Johnny, OF
Coscarart, Pete, 2B
Coulson, Robert, OF
Covington, Wes, OF
Cox, Dick, OF
Cox, Billy, IF
Crable, George, P
Craig, Roger, P
Crane, Ed, P
Crane, Sam, SS
Crawford, Willie, OF
Crocker, Claude, P
Cronin, John, P
Cross, Lafayette, 3B
Crouch, Bill, P
Cruz, Henry, OF
Cuccinello, Tony, 2B
Cullenbine, Roy, OF
Cullop, Nick, OF
Culver, George, P
Curtis, Clifton, P
Cutshaw, George, 2B
Cuyler, Hazen, OF

D

Dahlen, Bill, SS
Dahlgren, Babe, 1B
Daily, Con, C
Daley, Jud, OF

Dalton, Jack, OF
Daly, Tom, 2B
Daniel, Jake, 1B
Dantonio, John, C
Dapper, Cliff, C
Darnell, Bob, P
Daub, Dan, P
Daubert, Jake, 1B
Davalillo, Vic, OF
Davidson, Bill, OF
Davis, Alfonzo, P
Davis, Curt, P
Davis, Otis, OF
Davis, Tommy, IF-OF
Davis, Willie, OF
Day, Pea Ridge, P
Deal, Lindsay, OF
Dean, Tommy, SS
DeBerry, Hank, C
Decatur, Art, P
Dede, Art, C
Dedeaux, Raoul, SS
Deisel, Pat, C
DeJesus, Ivan, SS
Dell, Wheezer, P
Delmas, Bert, 2B
Demeter, Don, OF
DeMontreville, Gene, 2B
Dent, Elliott, P
Dessau, Frank, P
Dickerman, Leo, P
Dietz, Dick, C
Dillon, Frank, 1B
Dobbs, Johnny, OF
Dockins, George, P
Dolan, Pat, OF
Donovan, Patsy, OF
Doolan, Mickey, 2B
Douglas, Phil, P
Dowd, Snooks, 2B
Downey, Red, OF
Downing, Al, P
Downs, Red, 2B
Doyle, Carl, P
Doyle, Jack, 1B
Drake, Tom, P
Dresser, Ed, SS
Drysdale, Don, P
Dudley, Clise, P
Duffie, John, P
Dunn, Jack, P
Durham, Lou, P
Durning, Dick, P
Durocher, Leo, SS
Durrett, Elmer, OF

E

Earle, William, C-2B
Earnshaw, George, P
Eason, Mal, P
Eayrs, Edwin, P
Eckhardt, Oscar, OF
Edwards, Bruce, C
Edwards, Hank, OF
Egan, Dick, IF
Ehrhardt, Rube, P
Eisenstat, Harry, P

PLAYER/POSITION

Elberfeld, Kid, SS
Elliott, Jumbo, P
Elliott, Rowdy, C
Elston, Don, P
Ely, Fred, SS
English, Woody, IF
English, Gil, IF
Enzmann, John, P
Epperly, Al, P
Erskine, Carl, P
Erwin, Ross, C
Espey, Cecil, OF
Essegian, Chuck, OF
Esterbrook, Dude, 2B
Evans, LeRoy, P
Evans, Russell, P

F
Fabrique, Bunny, SS
Fairey, Jim, OF
Fairly, Ron, 1B-OF
Fallon, George, 2B
Farmer, Al, C
Farrell, Dick, P
Farrell, Duke, C-1B
Faulkner, Jim, P
Felix, Gus, OF
Ferguson, Alex, P
Ferguson, Joe, C
Fernandez, Chico, SS
Ferrara, Al, OF
Ferrell, Wesley, P
Fette, Lou, P
Fewster, Chick, 2B
Finlayson, Pembroke, P
Finn, Mickey, 2B-3B
Fischer, Bill, C
Fisher, Chauncey, P
Fisher, Bob, SS
Fitzsimmons, Fred, P
Fitzsimmons, Tom, 3B
Fletcher, Sam, P
Flood, Tim, 2B
Flowers, Jake, IF
Ford, Horace, SS
Forster, Terry, P
Foster, Alan, P
Fournier, Jack, 1B
Foutz, Dave, P-OF
Fowler, Art, P
Frankhouse, Fred, P
Franklin, Jim, P
Franks, Herman, C
Frederick, Johnny, OF
Freigau, Howard, IF
French, Larry, P
French, Ray, SS
Frey, Linus, SS-2B
Fuchs, Charles, P
Fuller, Charles, C
Furillo, Carl, OF

G
Gabrielson, Len, OF
Gaddy, John, P
Galan, Augie, IF-OF

PLAYER/POSITION

Gallagher, Joe, OF
Gallivan, Phil, P
Garman, Mike, P
Garvey, Steve, IF-OF
Garvin, Virgil, P
Gastright, Henry, P
Gatins, Frank, 3B
Gautreaux, Sid, C
Gentile, Jim, 1B
George, Greek, C
Geraghty, Ben, SS
Gessler, Harry, 1B-OF
Getz, Gus, 3B
Giallombardo, Bob, P
Gilbert, Charley, OF
Gilbert, Wally, 3B
Gillenwater, Carden, OF
Gilliam, Jim, IF-OF
Gionfriddo, Al, OF
Giuliani, Angelo, C
Gleason, Roy, OF
Glossop, Alben, IF
Gochnaur, John, SS
Golden, Jim, P
Gooch, Johnny, C
Goodson, Ed, 3B
Gordonier, Ray, P
Grabarkewitz, Bill, IF
Graham, Jack, 1B
Grant, Mudcat, P
Gray, Dick, IF
Greene, Nelson, P
Greenfield, Kent, P
Gregg, Hal, P
Griffin, Mike, OF
Griffith, Bert, OF
Griffith, Darrell, IF-OF
Griffith, Tommy, OF
Grim, John, C
Grimes, Burleigh, P
Griner, Dan, P
Grissom, Lee, P
Grote, Jerry, C
Guerrero, Pedro, 3B
Gulden, Brad, C
Gumbert, Addison, P

H
Haas, Bert, 1B
Haddock, George, P
Hale, John, OF
Hall, John, P
Hall, Robert, OF
Haller, Tom, C
Hallman, Bill, 2B
Hamlin, Luke, P
Hamrick, Odbert, OF
Hannahs, Gerald, P
Hansford, F. C., P
Hargreaves, Charley, C
Harkness, Tim, 1B
Harper, George, P
Harper, Harry, P
Harris, Bill, P
Harris, Joe, OF
Hart, William F., P
Hart, William W., SS-3B

PLAYER/POSITION

Hartse, Chris, C
Hassett, Buddy, 1B-OF
Hatcher, Mickey, OF
Hatfield, Gil, 3B
Hatten, Joe, P
Haughey, Chris, P
Haugstad, Phil, P
Hayworth, Ray, C
Head, Ed, P
Hearne, Hugh, C
Heckinger, Mike, C
Hehl, Jake, P
Heimach, Fred, P
Heitman, Harry, P
Hemming, George, P
Hendrick, Harvey, 1B-3B-OF
Henion, Lafayette, P
Henley, Weldon, P
Henline, Butch, C
Henry, Dutch, P
Henshaw, Roy, P
Herman, Floyd ("Babe"), 1B-OF
Herman, Billy, 2B
Hermanski, Gene, OF
Hernandez, Enzo, SS
Herring, Art, P
Hershiser, Orel, P
Heydeman, Greg, P
Hickman, David, OF
Hickman, Jim, OF
Higby, Kirby, P
Higgins, Robert, C
High, Andy, IF
Hildebrand, George, OF
Hill, Bill, P
Hines, Henry, OF
Hoak, Don, 3B
Hockett, Orris, OF
Hodges, Gil, 1B-C-OF
Hollingsworth, Al, P
Hollingsworth, John, P
Holmes, Jim, P
Holmes, Tommy, OF
Holton, Brian, P
Hood, Wallace, OF
Hooton, Burt, P
Hopp, Johnny, 1B-OF
Horton, Elmer, P
Hough, Charles, P
Householder, Ed, OF
Howard, Frank, 1B-OF
Howe, Steve, P
Howell, Harry, P
Howell, Dixie, C
Hoyt, Waite, P
Hobbell, Wilbur, P
Hudson, Johnny, IF
Hudson, Rex, P
Hug, Ed, C
Hughes, James J., P
Hughes, James R., P
Hughes, Mike, P
Hummel, John, IF-OF
Humphrey, Al, OF
Hungling, Bernie, C
Hunt, Ron, IF
Hunter, George, P-OF
Hurley, Pat, C

PLAYER/POSITION

Hutcheson, Joe, OF
Hutchinson, Ira, P
Hutson, Roy, OF
Hutton, Tom, 1B

I
Inks, Bert, P
Irwin, Charley, 3B

J
Jacklitsch, Fred, C
Jackson, Ransom, 3B
Jacobson, Merwin, OF
Janvrin, Hal, IF
Jarvis, LeRoy, C
Jeffcoat, George, P
Jennings, Hugh, IF
John, Tommy, P
Johnson, Lou, OF
Johnston, Jimmy, IF-OF
Johnston, Ivy, 2B
Johnstone, Jay, OF
Jones, Arthur, P
Jones, Fielder, OF
Jones, Johnny, SS
Jones, Oscar, P
Jones, Ross, 3B
Jordan, Dutch, IF
Jordan, Jimmy, IF
Jordan, Tim, 1B
Jorgensen, Johnny, 3B
Joshua, Von, OF
Joyce, Scrappy, 3B
Judge, Joe, 1B

K
Kampouris, Alex, 2B
Karst, John, 3B
Keeler, Willie, OF
Kehn, Chet, P
Kekich, Mike, P
Kellert, Frank, OF
Kelley, Joe, 1B-OF
Kelly, George, 1B
Kennedy, Bill, P
Kennedy, John, IF
Kent, Maurice, P
Kilduff, Pete, 2B
Kimball, Newel, P
King, Clyde, P
Kinslow, Tom, C
Kipp, Fred, P
Kirkpatrick, Enos, IF
Kitson, Frank, P
Klippstein, Johnny, P
Klugman, Joe, 2B
Klumpp, Elmer, C
Knetzer, Elmer, P
Knolls, Oscar, P
Koch, Barney, IF
Koenecke, Len, OF
Konetchy, Ed, 1B
Korwan, Jim, P
Kosco, Andy, OF
Koufax, Sandy, P

PLAYER/POSITION

Koukalik, Joe, P
Koupal, Lou, P
Koy, Ernie, OF
Krueger, Ernie, C

L

Labine, Clem, P
LaChance, Cancy, 1B
Lacy, Lee, IF
Lagrow, Lerrin, P
Lamanske, Frank, P
Lamar, Bill, OF
Lamb, Ray, P
Landestoy, Rafel, 2B
Landreaux, Ken, OF
Landrum, Joe, P
Larker, Norm, 1B-OF
Lary, Lyn, SS-3B
Lasorda, Tom, P
Latimer, Tacks, C
Lavagetto, Harry ("Cookie"), 3B
Law, Rudy, P
Lazzeri, Tony, 2B-3B
Leard, Bill, 2B
Lee, Hal, OF
Lee, Leron, OF
Lefebvre, Jim, IF
Lehman, Ken, P
LeJeune, Sheldon, OF
Lembo, Steve, C
Lennox, Eddie, 3B
Leonard, Emil, P
Leslie, Sam, 1B
Lewellyn, Dennis, P
Lewis, Phil, SS
Lillis, Bob, IF
Lindsey, Jim, P
Lindstrom, Fred, OF
Livingston, Mickey, C
Loes, Billy, P
Loftus, Dick, OF
Logan, Bob, P
Lohrman, Bill, P
Lombardi, Ernie, C
Lombardi, Vic, P
Long, Tom, P
Lopes, Dave, IF
Lopez, Al, C
Loudenslager, Charles, 2B
Lovett, Tom, P
Lucas, Ray, P
Lucid, Con, P
Lumley, Harry, OF
Lund, Don, OF
Luque, Adolfo, P

M

Macon, Max, P
Maglie, Sal, P
Magoon, Topsy, SS
Mails, Duster, P
Malay, Charles, 2B-OF
Maldonado, Candy, OF
Malinosky, Tony, SS
Mallette, Malcolm, P
Maloney, Bill, OF

PLAYER/POSITION

Mamaux, Al, P
Mancuso, Gus, C
Manuel, Charlie, OF
Manush, Heinie, OF
Maranville, Rabbit, SS-2B
Marichal, Juan, P
Marquard, Rube, P
Marriott, Bill, 3B
Marrow, Buck, P
Marshall, Bill, C
Marshall, Mike, P
Marshall, Mike, OF
Martin, Morris, P
Martinez, Teddy, 3B
Mattingly, Earl, P
Mauch, Gene, IF
Mauriello, Ralph, P
Mauro, Carmen, OF
McBean, Alvin, P
McCabe, Bill, OF
McCarren, Bill, 3B-OF
McCarthy, John A., OF
McCarty, Lew, C
McCormick, Mike, 3B
McCormick, Myron, OF
McCreedie, Walter, OF
McCreery, Tom, OF
McDermott, Terry, IF
McDermott, Terry, 1B
McDevitt, Danny, P
McDougal, John, P
McElveen, Pryor, IF
McFarlan, Dan, P
McFarland, Chappie, P
McFamwell, Ed, 1B
McGann, Dan, 1B
McGinnity, Joe, P
McGlothin, Pat, P
McGraw, Bob, P
McGuire, Deacon, C
McIntyre, Harry, P
McJames, James, P
McKenna, Kit, P
McLish, Cal, P
McMagkin, John, P
McMahon, John ("Sadie"), P
McManus, Francis, C
McMillan, Tommy, SS
McMullen, Ken, 3B
McWeeney, Doug, P
Medwick, Joe, OF
Melton, Rube, P
Merkle, Fred, 1B
Messersmith, Andy, P
Meusel, Emil ("Irish"), OF
Meyer, Benny, OF
Meyer, Lee, SS
Meyer, Russ, P
Meyers, Chief, C
Michael, Gene, SS
Mickens, Glenn, P
Mikkelsen, Pete, P
Miksis, Eddie, IF
Miles, Don, OF
Miljus, John, P
Miller, Fred, P
Miller, Hack, OF
Miller, Larry, P

PLAYER/POSITION

Miller, Otto, C
Miller, Ralph, P
Miller, Robert, P
Miler, Rodney, IF
Miller, Walter, P
Millies, Walter, C
Milliken, Bob, P
Mills, Buster, OF
Minner, Paul, P
Mitchell, Bob
Mitchell, Clarence, P
Mitchell, Dale, OF
Mitchell, Fred, P
Mitchell, Johnny, SS
Moeller, Joe, P
Mohart, George, P
Monday, Rick, OF
Moon, Wally, OF
Moore, Austin, P
Moore, Dee, C-3B
Moore, Eddie, IF
Moore, Gene, OF
Moore, Randy, OF-C
Moore, Ray, P
Morales, Jose, C
Moran, Herbie, OF
Morgan, Bobby, IF
Morgan, Eddie, OF
Morrison, Johnny, P
Moryn, Walt, OF
Moss, Ray, P
Mota, Manny, OF
Moulder, Glen, P
Mowrey, Mike, 3B
Mullen, Bill, 3B
Mulvey, Joe, 3B
Mungo, Van Lingle, P
Munn, Leslie, P
Murch, Simeon, 1B
Myers, Hi, OF

N
Nahem, Sam, P
Naylor, Earl, OF
Neal, Charley, IF
Negray, Ron, P
Neis, Bernie, OF
Nelson, Rocky, 1B
Nen, Dick, 1B
Newcombe, Don, P
Newsom, Bobo, P
Newton, Eustace, P
Niedenfuer, Tom, P
Nixon, Al, OF
Nops, Jeremiah, P
Norman, Fred, P
North, Bill, OF
Northen, Hub, OF

O
O'Brien, John, 2B
O'Brien, Robert, P
O'Brien, William ("Darby"), OF
Ock, Harold, C
O'Doul, Frank ("Lefty"), OF
Oeschger, Joe, P

PLAYER/POSITION

Oliver, Nate, IF
Olmo, Luis, IF-OF
Olson, Ivan, SS
O'Mara, Oliver, SS
O'Neil, Mickey, C
Onis, Manuel, C
Orengo, Joe, 3B
Ortega, Phil, P
Osborne, Tiny, P
Osgood, Charles, P
Ostermueller, Fritz, P
Owen, Mickey, C
Owens, Tom, 2B

P
Paciorek, Tom, IF-OF
Padgett, Don, C
Pafko, Andy, OF-3B
Page, Phil, P
Palica, Irv, P
Palmquist, Ed, P
Parker, Wes, IF-OF
Parks, Art, OF
Partridge, Jay, 2B
Pascual, Camilo, P
Pasley, Kevin, C
Pastorius, Jim, P
Pattee, Harry, 2B
Patterson, Dave, P
Pattison, Jim, P
Payne, Harley, P
Peck, Hal, OF
Peña, Alejandro, P
Pena, Jose, P
Perconte, Jack, P
Perkins, Charley, P
Perranoski, Ron, P
Peterson, Jim, P
Petty, Jesse, P
Pfeffer, Jeff, P
Pfister, George, C
Pfund, LeRoy, P
Phelps, Ed, C
Phelps, Gordon, C
Phelps, Ray, P
Picinich, Val, C
Pignatano, Joe, C
Plitt, Norman, P
Podbielan, Clarence, P
Podres, Johnny, P
Poffenberger, Cletus, P
Polly, Nick, 3B
Poole, Ed, P
Popovich, Paul, IF
Posedel, Bill, P
Post, Sam, 1B
Potter, Dykes, P
Pounds, William, P
Powell, John, 1B
Powell, Paul, OF
Pressnell, Forest, P
Purdin, John, P

Q
Quinn, Jack, P

PLAYER/POSITION

R

Rachunok, Steve, P
Rackley, Marv, OF
Radtke, Jack, 2B
Ragan, Pat, P
Rarow, Ed, P
Ramazzotti, Bob, IF
Ramsdell, Willard, P
Rau, Doug, P
Rautzen, Lance, P
Reardon, Phil, OF
Redmond, Harry, 2B
Reed, Howard, P
Reese, Harold ("Pee Wee"), SS
Regan, Phil, P
Reidy, Bill, P
Reis, Bobby, P-IF
Reiser, Harold ("Pete"), IF-OF
Reisler, Frank, P
Repulski, Rip, OF
Reulbach, Ed, P
Reuss, Jerry, P
Reyes, Gilberto, C
Rhiel, Billy, 2B
Rhoden, Rick, P
Richards, Paul, C
Richardson, Denny, 2B
Richert, Pete, P
Riconda, Harry, IF
Riggert, Joe, OF
Riggs, Lew, 3B
Ripple, Jimmy, OF
Ritter, Lou, C
Rizzo, Johnny, OF
Roberts, Jim, P
Robinson, Earl, IF
Robinson, Frank, OF
Robinson, Jackie, IF-OF
Robles, Sergio, C
Rochelli, Lou, 2B
Rodas, Rich, P
Rodriguez, Ellie, C
Roe, Preacher, P
Roebuck, Ed, P
Roenicke, Ron, OF
Roettger, Oscar, OF
Rogers, Lee, P
Rogers, Packey, IF
Rojek, Stan, IF
Romano, Jim, P
Roseboro, John, C
Rosen, Goodwin, OF
Rosenfeld, Max, OF
Ross, Don, 3B
Rowe, Ken, P
Rowe, Lynwood ("Schoolboy"), P
Roy, Jean Pierre, P
Roy, Luther, P
Royster, Jerry, IF
Rucker, George ("Nap"), P
Rudolph, Ernest, P
Ruether, Walter ("Dutch"), P
Rush, Andy, P
Russell, Bill, IF-OF
Russell, Jack, P
Russell, Jim, OF
Rutherford, John, P
Ryan, Jack, P

PLAYER/POSITION

Ryan, John, C
Ryan, Wilfred ("Rosy"), P

S

Sandlock, Mike, C-IF
Savage, Ted, OF
Sax, Dave, C
Sax, Steve, 2B
Sayles, Bill, P
Scanlan, William ("Doc"), P
Schardt, Wilbur, P
Scheer, Allen, OF
Schliebner, Fred, 1B
Schmandt, Ray, IF
Schmidt, Henry, P
Schmitz, Johnny, P
Schumutz, Charles, P
Scheiberg, Frank, P
Schofield, Dick, IF
Schott, Gene, P
Schreiber, Paul, P
Schultz, Howard, 1B
Schultz, Joe, 3B
Schupp, Ferdie, P
Scioscia, Mike, C
Seabring, Jim, OF
Seats, Tom, P
Sells, Dave, P
Sexauer, Elmer, P
Shanahan, Greg, P
Sharrott, George, P
Shaute, Joe, P
Shea, Mervyn, C
Sheckard, Jimmy, OF
Sheehan, John, 3B
Sheehan, Tom, 3B
Sheridan, Gene, IF
Sherlock, Vince, 1B
Sherry, Larry, P
Sherry, Norman, C
Shindle, Bill, 3B
Shirley, Bart, IF
Shoch, George, IF-OF
Shriver, Harry, P
Shuba, George, OF
Siebert, Dick, 1B
Simpson, Joe, OF
Sims, Duke, C
Singer, Bill, P
Sington, Fred, OF
Sizemore, Ted, IF
Skaff, Frank, 3B
Skowron, Bill, 1B
Slade, Gordon, SS
Sloat, Dwain, P
Smith, Alex, C-3B-OF
Smith, Anthony, SS
Smith, Charley, IF
Smith, George, P
Smith, George ("Germany"), SS
Smith, Happy, OF
Smith, J. Carlisle, 3B
Smith, Jack, P
Smith, Reggie, OF
Smith, Sherrod, P
Smyres, Clarence, OF
Smyth, Jim, OF

PLAYER/POSITION

Smythe, Harry, P
Snider, Edwin ("Duke"), OF
Snyder, John, C
Solomon, Eddie, P
Sommerville, Andy, P
Sosa, Elias, P
Sothern, Dennis, OF
Spencer, Daryl, IF
Spencer, Roy, C
Spooner, Karl, P
Stainback, Tuck, OF
Stallings, George, C
Standaert, Jerry, IF
Stanhouse, Don, P
Stanky, Eddie, 2B
Stark, Monroe, SS
Statz, Arnold ("Jigger"), OF
Steele, Jim, P
Steelman, Morris, P
Stein, Ed, P
Stengel, Casey, OF
Stephenson, Jerry, P
Stevens, Ed, 1B
Stewart, Dave, P
Stewart, John, 2B
Stimson, Bob, C
Stock, Milt, IF
Stovey, Harry, OF
Strahler, Mike, P
Strang, Sammy, IF
Stricklett, Elmer, P
Stripp, Joe, 3B
Stryker, Sterling, P
Stuart, Dick, 1B-OF
Sudakis, Bill, C-IF
Sukeforth, Clyde, C
Sullivan, Bill, C
Sunkel, Tom, P
Sutcliffe, Rick, P
Sutton, Don, P
Swift, Bill, P

T
Tamulis, Vito, P
Tatum, Tom, OF
Taylor, Danny, OF
Taylor, Harry, P
Taylor, Zack, C
Templeton, Chock, P
Tepsic, Joe, OF
Terry, William ("Adonis"), P
Terwilliger, Wayne, IF
Thatcher, Ulysses, P
Thielman, Henry, P
Thomas, Derrel, 3B
Thomas, Fay, P
Thomas, Ray, C
Thomasson, Gary, OF
Thompson, Charles, C
Thompson, Don, OF
Thompson, Fresco, 2B
Thormahlen, Herb, P
Thurston, Hollis ("Sloppy"), P
Tierney, James ("Cotton"), IF
Todd, Al, C
Tooley, Bert, SS
Torborg, Jeff, C

PLAYER/POSITION

Tracewski, Dick, IF
Treadway, George, OF
Tremark, Nick, OF
Tremper, Overton, OF
Tucker, Tommy, 1B
Tyson, Al, OF

U
Underwood, Fred, P

V
Valdes, Rene, P
Valentine, Bob, IF
Valenzuela, Fernando, P
Valle, Hector, C
Valo, Elmer, OF
Vance, Clarence ("Dazzy"), P
Vance, Sandy, P
Van Cuyk, Chris, P
Van Cuyk, John, P
Vaughan, Floyd ("Arny"), IF
Versalles, Zoilo, IF
Vickers, Harry, P-OF
Voight, Paul, P
Vosmik, Joe, OF

W
Wachtel, Paul, P
Wade, Ben, P
Wagner, Bert, 3B
Wagner, Bill, P
Walker, Al ("Rube"), C
Walker, Fred ("Dixie"), OF
Walker, Fred M., P
Wall, Joe, C
Wall, Stan, P
Walls, Lee, OF
Waner, Lloyd, OF
Waner, Paul, OF
Ward, Chuck, SS
Ward, John Montgomery, IF
Ward, Preston, 1B
Warner, Jackie, IF
Warren, Tom, P
Warwick, Carl, OF
Wasdell, Jim, 1B-OF
Washington, Ron, OF-SS
Watkins, George, OF
Webb, Hank, P
Webber, Les, P
Weiss, Gary, SS
Welch, Bob, P
Wells, John, P
Werhas, John, IF
West, Max, OF
Weyhing, Gus, P
Wheat, Zack, OF
Wheeler, Ed, IF
White, Bill, IF
White, Larry, P
White, Myron, OF
Whiting, Jesse, P
Whitman, Dick, OF
Whitted, George, OF
Wicker, Kemp, P

Dodgers All-Time Roster at a Glance

PLAYER/POSITION

Wilhelm, Hoyt, P
Wilhelm, Irving, P
Willhite, Nick, P
Williams, Dick, IF-OF
Williams, Leon, P
Williams, Stan, P
Williams, Woody, SS
Wills, Maury, SS
Wilson, Ed, OF
Wilson, Gormer, P
Wilson, Lewis ("Hack"), OF-2B
Windhorn, Gordon, OF
Winford, Jim, P
Winham, Lafayette, P
Winsett, Tom, OF
Winston, Henry, P
Wise, Brett, P
Witt, Whitey, OF
Wojey, Pete, P
Wright, Clarence, P
Wright, Glenn, SS
Wright, Ricky, P

PLAYER/POSITION

Wrigley, Zeke, SS
Wurm, Frank, P
Wyatt, Whitlow, P
Wynn, Jimmy, OF

Y

Yale, William, 1B
Yarrison, Byron, P
Yeager, Joe, P
Yeager, Steve, C
Yingling, Earl, P

Z

Zachary, Al, P
Zachary, Tom, P
Zachry, Pat, P
Zahn, Geoff, P
Zimmer, Don, IF
Zimmerman, Ed, 3B
Zimmerman, William, OF